A History of
Civilization
1300 to 1815

A History of Civilization

1300 to 1815

Fifth Edition

Crane Brinton

John B. Christopher
University of Rochester

Robert Lee Wolff
Archibald Cary Coolidge Professor of History
Harvard University

Prentice-Hall, Inc., Englewood Cliffs, New Jersey

Library of Congress Cataloging in Publication Data

Brinton, Clarence Crane, 1898–1968.
   A history of civilization.

   Contents: v.1. Prehistory to 1300 v.2. 1300 to
1815 v.3. 1815 to the present.
   Includes bibliographies and index.
   1. Civilization—History. I. Christopher, John B.,
joint author. II. Wolff, Robert Lee, joint author.
III. Title
CB69.B74 1976   909   75-21293
ISBN 0-13-389791-5 (vol. 1) pbk.
0-13-389817-2 (vol. 2)
0-13-389825-3 (vol. 3)

Printed in the United States of America

10 9 8 7 6 5 4 3 2

Design by A Good Thing, Inc.

Art research by Roberta Guerrette and Olivia Beuhl

Maps by Vincent Kotschar

Prentice-Hall International, Inc., London
Prentice-Hall of Australia, Pty. Ltd., Sydney
Prentice-Hall of Canada, Ltd., Toronto
Prentice-Hall of India Private Limited, New Delhi
Prentice-Hall of Japan, Inc., Tokyo
Prentice-Hall of Southeast Asia (Pte.) Ltd., Singapore

Contents

Preface

With this fifth edition *A History of Civilization* is available for the first time in a choice of paperback formats—two volumes, with the break at 1715, and three volumes, breaking at about 1300 and 1815. Readers familiar with earlier hard-cover editions will find that their generous allotment of maps, the end-of-chapter reading suggestions, and most of their other features have weathered the paperback revolution; the illustrations have been selected with particular care to tie in closely with the text. Throughout the book we have endeavored to take account of new historical evidence and interpretations that have appeared since the fourth edition as well as of increasing student interest in social and cultural history. We have reorganized some chapters to attain greater clarity and coherence, and sharpened the introductory sections of many chapters to provide a simplified chart of a particular historical terrain before elaborating on its detailed topography.

To summarize the most significant changes: We have revised Chapter 1 in the light of recent archaeological finds and of advances in deciphering languages. Chapter 4 includes a new section on the immediate background of Christianity as well as added material on Augustine, the most celebrated of the early Church fathers. We have completely revamped the chapters on the medieval West to aid the reader's understanding of a complex and often bewildering period. Chapter 7 discusses the Church and ecclesiastical culture together with the great confrontation between the papacy and the Holy Roman Empire, and Chapter 8 the English and French monarchies plus secular literature. To enlarge the treatment of the forces that made possible the birth of modern western civilization, discussion of the burgeoning money economy has been shifted to chapter 11 (The Renaissance) from Chapter 10 (War and Politics in the Late Middle Ages). The much-debated crises of the fourteenth and seventeenth centuries receive augmented treatment in Chapters 10 and 15, respectively, and many sections on the arts are enriched, in Chapter 6 (Islam), 11 (Renaissance), 15 (Baroque) and 23 (19th century). We have added an entirely new chapter (32) on the major political developments since 1970 and have incorporated substantial new material in the final chapter (33) recapitulating the intellectual and cultural history of the twentieth century.

The successful completion of a complicated project requires help from many people. We wish to acknowledge our debt to our senior co-author, the late Crane Brinton, whose gift for catching the essential style of a civilization still informs this history; to readers who have taken the trouble to write down their specific suggestions for improving the text; and to the men and women of Prentice-Hall, Inc., for their patience and expertise in the lengthy process of converting manuscript into book form.

John B. Christopher
Robert Lee Wolff

A Note on the Reading Suggestions

A list of suggestions for additional reading is appended to each chapter of these volumes (except that the bibliographies for Chapters 30, 31, and 32 are consolidated into a single list). Since such brief bibliographies must be highly selective, we therefore stress four different categories of works: (1) standard authorities, both older and recent, and both concise and detailed; (2) diverse interpretations representing a spectrum of views, enabling the reader to realize that the past often provokes as much controversy as the present; (3) collections of source materials—texts of laws and decrees, memoirs, letters, chronicles and other items to help a student formulate his own interpretation of events; (4) historical novels and dramas that reflect with reasonable faithfulness the externals of the past and, what is even more difficult, its internal features as well, the motivations, values, and lifestyles of bygone generations.

Our lists star with an asterisk all titles available in paperbacks. New titles are constantly appearing in paperback, and old ones vanishing, so that an indispensable tool is the latest volume of *Paperbound Books in Print* (R. R. Bowker Co.), which lists tens of thousands of items by title, author and subject and is usually to be found in most libraries and bookstores. For a fuller list of works on a given topic, particularly scholarly books published only in hard covers, the handiest tool is the subject cards in a library catalog. In addition, useful up-to-date bibliographies may be found in the two volumes of P. Gay and R. Webb, *Modern Europe* (*Harper & Row), and in the revised *Harvard Guide to American History* (Harvard University Press, 1974).

New scholarly books are often reviewed in the Sunday book section of *The New York Times, The New York Review of Books,* and the London weekly, *The Times Literary Supplement.* Almost all scholarly titles are eventually reviewed in at least one of the major professional journals, such as *The American Historical Review* and *The Journal of Modern History,* or one of the more specialized ones, such as *The Middle East Journal* or *Speculum* (for medieval studies). Three periodicals consist entirely of critiques—*History: Reviews of New Books, Reviews in American History,* and *Reviews in European History.* Journals occasionally publish review articles evaluating at length a book of especial significance or assessing all the major recent publications in a given field, the French Revolution, for instance. Finally, the latest discoveries of historical evidence and innovations in interpretation appear frequently in journal articles months or even years before they do in books. A complete list of the journals concerned with history would itself require an article; a few useful titles, in addition to those already cited, include *History and Theory, The Journal of Interdisciplinary History, The Journal of the History of Childhood* (for psychohistory), *The Journal of the History of Ideas, The Journal of Medieval and Renaissance Studies, The Renaissance Quarterly, The Journal of British Studies, French Historical Studies,* and two British publications, *Past and Present* and *History Today.*

Maps

A History of
Civilization
1300 to 1815

1300 to 1715

The Renaissance

Introduction

Renaissance—"rebirth"—is the name traditionally bestowed upon the remarkable outpouring of intellectual and artistic energy and talent that accompanied the passage of Europe from the Middle Ages to the modern epoch. The term is often extended to politics and economics. The preceding chapter has described the acceleration of political change, especially toward the close of the last medieval century, the fifteenth. The present chapter examines first the emergence of capitalism and banking and the sometimes revolutionary impact of these powerful new forces on agriculture, industry, and trade. It turns next to the rise of vernacular literatures and of humanistic philosophy, to the contemporaneous quickening of science and religion, and then to the fine arts, the highest expression of Renaissance genius. The chapter concludes with an attempt to identify some of the distinctive features of Renaissance life.

Throughout the chapter we confront the basic problems that the Renaissance raises for the historian. Relatively little difficulty arises in ascertaining when and where the Renaissance began, how far it spread, and for how long it continued. It started in Italy around 1300 and continued for three centuries, in the course of which the economic, intellectual, and cultural currents flowing from its homeland eventually reached France, the Low Countries, Germany, and England and also, though with diminished force, Spain and Portugal. By 1600, with Europe increasingly preoccupied by the great Protestant-Catholic antagonism issuing from the Reformation, it had virtually come to an end, giving way to the culture called baroque.

What has been much more difficult to establish and has aroused lively controversy among scholars is the degree to which the term *Renaissance* should be interpreted literally. Were the classical values of ancient Greece and Rome in fact reborn at the close of the Middle Ages? Could such a rebirth alone possibly account for the extraordinarily productive careers of Renaissance writers, sculptors, painters, architects, musicians, and scientists? Until the middle of the nineteenth century most educated people would have given a simple affirmative response to both questions. The chief reason for the classical revival appeared to be the capture of Constantinople by the Turks in 1453 and the subsequent flight of Greek scholars to Italy and other countries of western Europe. The manner in which the eighteenth-century historian Edward Gibbon saluted the event is indicative:

> Before the revival of classical literature, the barbarians in Europe were immersed in ignorance; and their vulgar tongues were marked with the rudeness and poverty of their manners. The students of the more perfect idioms of Rome and Greece were introduced to a new world of light and science: to the society of the free and polished nations of antiquity; and to a familiar converse with those immortal men who spoke the sublime language of eloquence and reason. . . . As soon as it had been deeply saturated with the celestial dews, the soil was quickened into vegetation and life; the modern idioms were refined; the classics of Athens and Rome inspired a pure taste and a generous emulation; and in Italy, as afterwards in France and England, the pleasing reign of poetry and fiction was succeeded by the light of speculative and experimental philosophy.[*]

Today, these simple answers no longer suffice. We know that long before 1453 knowledge of Greek writings was filtering into the West from Muslim Spain, from Sicily, and from Byzantium itself. Moreover, Greek influence was by no means the only catalyst of the Renaissance. In an influential study first published in 1860, Professor Jacob Burckhardt of the University of Basel in Switzerland insisted that much of the credit for Renaissance productivity must go also to the genius

*E. Gibbon, *The Decline and Fall of the Roman Empire*, chap. 66.

and individualism of Italians. Burckhardt, however, accepted the traditional contrast between medieval darkness and Renaissance light that had first been drawn by the men of the Renaissance themselves and that Gibbon expressed so extravagantly. Today, of course, it is almost universally agreed that a great Christian civilization had in fact come to maturity during the Middle Ages, and that the cultural heritage from classical antiquity had never actually disappeared from the medieval West. Some historians have contended that the cultural rebirth had occurred much earlier than the fourteenth or fifteenth century, in the "Carolingian Renaissance" or the "Renaissance of the twelfth century" centered at the court of Eleanor of Aquitaine.

But to find that the germ of the Renaissance had been planted and had sprouted long before 1300—to deny any originality to the Renaissance, as a few historians do—is to swing the pendulum of reinterpretation too far. The intellectuals and artists of the Renaissance owed a substantial debt to their medieval predecessors, and they were often as religious, as credulous, as caste-conscious and "feudal" as their forebears. Yet they were also materialistic, skeptical, and individualistic to a degree almost unknown in the Middle Ages. The distinguished Italian historian Federico Chabod has observed that the new secular credo could be summed up as "art for art's sake, politics for politics' sake, science for science's sake."* Men were attempting to create things, to do things, and to study things as ends in themselves rather than as the means to the glorification of God and to salvation, much as Machiavelli divorced political thought from theology or as Machiavellian rulers cultivated power politics.

II A Money Economy
Trade

During the Renaissance the more developed areas of Europe that are loosely termed the West—that is, the areas to the west of the Adriatic Sea and the Elbe River—were taking giant steps along the road from the subsistence economy of the early Middle Ages to a money economy. But it was also a long and uneven road from an economy based on home-grown produce paid for in kind to one relying heavily on imports paid for in money. By the fifteenth century the West had long been importing salt, from the salt mines of Germany or the sea-salt pans of the Atlantic coast, in order to preserve food. To make food tasty if it had begun to spoil, the West had long sought the spices of the East; and to wash it down western Europeans had already developed a taste for the wines of the Rhine, of Burgundy, and of Bordeaux. The furs of eastern Europe, the wool of England and Spain, and the woolen cloth of Flanders and Italy all commanded good markets

*F. Chabod, *Machiavelli and the Renaissance* (London, 1958), p. 184.

among the residents of chilly medieval buildings. At the close of the Middle Ages, supplies of palatable food and warm clothing were steadily increasing. Salt fish, for example, was cheap and did not spoil. In the fourteenth century, such a boom occurred in the herring fisheries along the narrow Baltic waters between Denmark and Sweden that, according to the inflated report of one traveler, the Baltic fisheries employed three hundred thousand people in catching fish, salting them down, and making the barrels to pack them in.

Trade slumped during the serious economic depression of the early 1300s and the prolonged aftermath of the Black Death and the Hundred Years' War. Recovery came in the fifteenth century, and by the later 1400s the trade of the West could for the first time be compared in volume and variety with that of Rome in the days of the empire, of Byzantium at its tenth-century peak, and of Norman and Hohenstaufen Sicily. Meantime, Western merchants developed more elaborate commercial procedures and organizations, of which the Hanseatic towns of the Baltic and the trading cities of Italy provide the most telling illustrations.

In the fourteenth and fifteenth centuries the membership of the Hanse (the German word means "league") included almost a hundred towns, among which Lübeck, Hamburg, Bremen, and Danzig were the leaders. The weakness of the Holy Roman Empire and the fact that many of the Hanseatic towns began as autonomous frontier outposts east of the Elbe in the course of the *Drang nach Osten* ("the push to the East") enabled the Hanse to play an independent political and military role in addition to exercising widespread economic power. Its policies were determined by meetings of representatives from the member towns, held usually at Lübeck.

The Hanse was not the first important confederation of commercial towns in Europe, nor was it the first to resist control by a higher political authority. Alliances of communes in Lombardy and in Flanders had blocked the ambitions, respectively, of Hohenstaufen emperors and French kings. The Hanse, however, operated on a grander scale. Its ships carried Baltic fish, timber, grain, furs, metals, and amber to western European markets and brought back cloth, wine, and spices; for a time, Hanseatic vessels controlled the lucrative transport of wool from England to Flanders. Hanseatic merchants, traveling overland with carts and pack trains, took their Baltic wares to Italy. The Hanse maintained especially large depots at Venice, Bruges, London, Novgorod (in northwestern Russia), and Bergen, on the Norwegian coast, where the Hanseatic colony was said to number three thousand. These foreign establishments enjoyed so many special rights of maintaining their own German officials and laws that they were colonial outposts of a Hanseatic empire. The Hanse itself had its own legal code (the Law of Lübeck), its own diplomats, and its own flag. It made treaties, declared war, and sometimes resorted to undeclared war; in 1406, to teach a forceful lesson to

English vessels poaching on fishing grounds off Norway, Hanseatic captains seized ninety-six English seamen, bound them hand and foot, and cast them overboard.

After 1500 the fortunes of the Hanse declined rapidly. The shifting of trade routes from the Baltic to the Atlantic ended the prosperity of many Hanseatic towns to the advantage of Holland and England. The loosely organized Hanse was no match for the stronger monarchical governments growing up along the rim of its Baltic preserve in Sweden, Russia, and some of the German princely states. Internally, the Hanse was weakened by the mounting conservatism and restrictiveness of its merchants and by rivalries among member towns and competing merchant families. Only a minority of the member towns usually sent representatives to the deliberations in Lübeck, and very few of them could be counted on for men and arms in an emergency. Moreover, Hanseatic trading activities were carried on in a relatively primitive fashion by a multitude of individual merchants who entered temporary partnerships for a single venture rather than establishing permanent firms.

The truly big business of the last medieval centuries was to be found not along the Baltic but in the cities of the Mediterranean, many of which were already thriving veterans of trade, enriched and toughened by the Crusades—in Italy, Venice, Genoa, Pisa, Lucca, Florence, Milan, and a dozen others; in France, Marseilles, Montpellier, and Narbonne; and in Spain, Barcelona. Venice furnishes an excellent case study. It was the East-West trade that brought wealth to Venetian merchants—from the East, spices, silk, cotton, sugar, dyestuffs, and the alum needed to set colors, and from the West, wool and cloth. The area of Venetian business was enormous, from England and Flanders to the heart of Asia, which the thirteenth-century Venetian Marco Polo traversed to reach China.

The main carrier of Venetian trade was the galley. By 1300, the designers of the arsenal, the government-operated shipyard, had improved the traditional long, narrow, oar-propelled galley of the Mediterranean into a swifter and more capacious merchant vessel, relying mainly on sails and employing oarsmen chiefly for getting in and out of port. In the fifteenth century, these merchant galleys had space for 250 tons of cargo—a capacity that seems ridiculously small by present-day standards but commodious enough for lucrative shipments of spices and other items small in bulk and large in value. Records from the early fifteenth century show approximately forty-five galleys sailing annually, among them four to Flanders, two to southern France, three to the Black Sea, three to Alexandria, four to Beirut, and two or three transporting pilgrims to Jaffa in the Holy Land. The Flanders fleet, which touched also at London and Southampton, was a very important economic institution because from its initiation in 1317 it provided a service between Italy and northwestern Europe that was cheaper and more secure than the older overland route.

Fifteenth-century Hanseatic merchants.

The state supervised the activities of these galleys from the cradle to the grave. Since the average life of galleys was ten years, government experts tested their seaworthiness periodically, and the arsenal made needed replacements. The government provided for the defense of the galleys and their cargoes by requiring that at least twenty of the crew be bowmen. The captains of the Flanders galleys were directed to protect the health of the crew by enlisting a physician and a surgeon, and to maintain the prestige of the city with two fifers and two trumpeters. For the Flanders fleet the government also laid down the policies of the captains (get to Bruges before the Genoese, and avoid "affrays and mischiefs" in English ports, even if the crew have to be denied shore leave). The republic also maintained an ambassador in England to smooth the way for its merchants.

Industry

The expansion of trade stimulated the industries that furnished the textiles, metals, and ships required by merchants. The towns of Flanders and Italy developed the weaving of woolen cloth into a big business, with many workmen and high profits for a relatively few entrepreneurs. In the early fourteenth century, it is estimated, two hundred masters controlled the wool guild of Florence, which produced nearly one hundred thousand pieces of cloth annually and employed thirty thousand men. By and large, only the two hundred had the capital—the saved-up funds—to finance the importation of raw wool from England and put it through the long process that ended with the finished cloth. The earlier practice of grouping in a single guild all artisans engaged in making a single product was giving way to the modern division—and tension—between capital and labor, and, within the ranks of labor, between the highly skilled and the less skilled. The preceding chapter noted the strife in late fourteenth-century Florence among the seven great guilds, the fourteen lesser guilds, and the Ciompi, the workers excluded from guild membership.

Despite the growth of capitalism, Europe had not yet experienced a true industrial revolution, and manufacturing continued to be what the Latin roots of the word suggest that it was—making by hand—though many hand tools were ingenious and efficient. The modern aspects of late medieval industry, confined largely to a few advanced crafts, were the increase in output, the mass production of standardized articles, and the specialization of the labor force. In Lübeck, Hanseatic capitalists promoted the mass output of rosaries by hiring beadmakers and supplying them with materials. In the Hapsburg lands of central Europe, the silver mines inaugurated round-the-clock operation by dividing their labor force into three parts, each working an eight-hour daily shift. In Florence, twenty or more different specialized crafts participated in woolen production—washing, combing, carding, spinning, weaving, dyeing, and so forth. But the actual work was subcontracted, in effect, to small domestic shops according to the "put-out system": instead of the worker's going to a mill or a factory, the work went to the worker in his home.

The largest industrial establishment in Europe was probably the Venetian arsenal, which normally employed a thousand men and during emergencies many more. These workmen, called arsenalotti, formed a pyramid of skills, with stevedores and other unskilled laborers at the bottom; at the next level, the sawyers, who cut the timbers for the galleys, and the caulkers, who made the wooden hulls seaworthy; then the pulleymakers and mastmakers; and at the top, the highly skilled carpenters, who shaped the lines of the hull. Supervisors, like modern foremen, disciplined the arsenalotti, checking on their presence at their posts during the working day; anyone who reported late, after the arsenal bell had ceased tolling its summons to work, forfeited a day's pay. By the sixteenth century, the process of adding a superstructure to the hull and outfitting the vessel was so efficient that it took the arsenalotti only two months to complete and equip a hundred galleys for a campaign against the Turks.

Banking

The expansion of industry and trade promoted the rise of banking, as merchants invested their accumulated capital in trading enterprises. In addition, kings, popes, and other rulers borrowed money to meet the expenses of war and administration. The risks of lending were great—rulers, in particular, were likely to repudiate their debts—but so too were the potential profits. Florentine bankers were known to charge 266 percent annual interest on an especially risky loan, and in 1420 the Florentine government vainly tried to put a ceiling of 20 percent on interest rates. Bankers were moneychangers as well as moneylenders, for only experts could establish the relative value of the hundreds upon hundreds of coins in circulation, varying enormously in reliability and precious metallic content and minted by every kind of governmental unit from the national monarchy down to the small city and the tiny feudal principality.

Bankers also facilitated the transfer of money over long distances. Suppose an English exporter, A, sold wool to an Italian importer, Z; it would be slow and dangerous for Z to pay A by shipping coins to him. Now suppose that two others entered the transaction: Y, an Italian woolen manufacturer who sold cloth to B, an English importer. It was safer and speedier if Z paid Y in Italy what he really owed to A in England, and if B paid A what he really owed Y. This sort of transaction was facilitated by bills of exchange, which bankers bought and sold.

The great European bankers were Italians, the "Lombard" bankers, though many of them came not from Lombardy but from Florence, Siena, and other towns in Tuscany. By the late 1200s, Italian bankers had become the fiscal agents of the pope, charged with the transfer of papal revenues from distant countries to Rome. The beautiful florins minted by Florence were the first gold coins made outside Byzantium to gain international currency because of their reliability. The great Florentine banking families of the Bardi and the Peruzzi financed imports of English wool and the export of finished cloth. Both firms advanced large sums to the kings of England and France at the outbreak of the Hundred Years' War, and both failed in the 1340s when Edward III defaulted on his debts. The repercussions of the failure, felt for more than a generation, included new attempts to democratize the Florentine government and the revolt of the Ciompi in 1378. Florentine banking rallied in the fifteenth century under the dynamic Cosimo de' Medici, whose activities involved companies for woolen and silk manufacture as well as the Medici bank and branch firms in Venice, Milan, Rome, Avignon, Geneva, Bruges, and London. However, the inefficiency of branch managers together with the extravagance of Lorenzo the Magnificent caused the failure of the Medici bank before the century was out.

The house of Jacques Coeur in Bourges, France (fifteenth century).

Meanwhile, money and banking were thriving elsewhere. The golden ducats of Venice joined the florins of Florence in international popularity, and the Bank of Saint George, founded at Genoa in 1407, eventually took over much of the Mediterranean business done by Spanish Jews before their persecution in the late 1400s. In London, the celebrated merchant and moneylender Sir Richard (Dick) Whittington served as lord mayor for three terms around 1400. In France, Jacques Coeur of Bourges (1395–1456) used private wealth to secure public office, and public office to augment his private wealth.

Coeur made a fortune by trading with the Muslim Near East and transporting pilgrims to the Holy Land. King Charles VII of France sent him on diplomatic missions, made him the chief royal fiscal agent, and placed him in charge of the royal mint; Coeur financed the final campaigns of the Hundred Years' War. Aided by the royal favor, Coeur acquired a string of textile workshops and mines, bought landed estates from impoverished nobles, lent money to half the dignitaries of France, and obtained noble husbands and high church offices for his own middle-class relatives. At Bourges he met the cost of embellishing the cathedral and built himself an elegant palace. While Coeur thus demonstrated the eminence that a bourgeois could reach, too many highly placed people owed him too much money. He was disgraced by Charles VII, who trumped up a charge against him to avoid repaying loans.

In Germany, powerful banking families flourished in the small Bavarian cities of Augsburg and Nuremberg; the most famous was the Fugger family of Augsburg. The founder of Fugger prosperity was a linen weaver and trader in the late fourteenth century. His sons and grandsons imported textiles and luxuries from Venice and began buying up silver and lead mines. In the late 1400s, the Fuggers became bankers to the Hapsburgs and, after the failure of the Medici bank, to the papacy as well. With the Fuggers, as with Jacques Coeur, wealth bred more wealth, power, and eventual ruin. Through Hapsburg favor they secured silver, iron, and copper mines in Hungary and the Tyrol, and in the 1540s the family fortune is estimated to have exceeded a quarter of a billion of our present-day dollars. Thereafter it dwindled as the flood of gold and silver from America ended the central European mining boom, and as the Fuggers themselves made extensive loans to the Hapsburg Philip II of Spain who went through repeated bankruptcies. In 1607, the family firm went bankrupt.

Two quotations convey something of the personality of these German bankers. Here is the epitaph that Jacob Fugger, a grandson of the founder, composed for his own tomb in the early sixteenth century:

To the best, greatest God! Jacob Fugger of Augsburg, the ornament of his class and people, imperial councillor under Maximilian I and Charles V, who was behind no one in the attainment of extraordinary wealth, in generosity, purity of morals, and greatness of soul, is, as he was not comparable with anyone in his lifetime, even after death not to be counted among the mortals.*

But the haughty Fuggers were not just "robber barons"; here is the inscription at the entrance to the Fuggerei, a garden village that they built for the poor of Augsburg:

Ulrich, George, and Jacob Fugger of Augsburg, blood brothers, being firmly convinced that they were born for the good of the city, and that for their great prosperity they have to thank chiefly an all-powerful and benevolent God, have out of piety, and as an example of special generosity founded, given, and dedicated 106 dwellings, both buildings and furnishings, to those of their fellow citizens who live righteously, but are beset by poverty.†

Town and Countryside

While Augsburg, with its special housing development for low-income families, may appear to have resembled a modern metropolis, its total population at the zenith of Fugger power probably never exceeded twenty thousand. In fact, none of the centers of international economic life five or six hundred years ago was really a big city at all. One set of estimates for the fourteenth century puts the population of Venice, Florence, and Paris in the vicinity of one hundred thousand each; that

*M. Beard, *A History of the Business Man* (New York, 1938), pp. 239–240.
†J. Strieder, *Jacob Fugger the Rich* (New York, 1931), p. 176.

of Genoa, Milan, Barcelona, and London at about fifty thousand; and that of the biggest Hanseatic and Flemish towns between twenty and forty thousand. Most Europeans still lived in the countryside.

The urban minority, however, was beginning to bring important changes to the life of the rural majority. Ties between town and countryside were especially close in areas where towns were numerous—Lombardy, Tuscany, Flanders, the Rhine Valley, and northern Germany. Merchants often invested their wealth in farm properties, nobles who acquired interests in towns usually retained their country estates, and peasants often moved to town as workmen or became artisans on the farm itself under the put-out system. Rural laborers made prayer beads for the capitalists of Lübeck and spun woolen yarn for the guild masters of Florence. Town governments sometimes improved adjacent farmland on the pattern established by the medieval communes of Milan and Siena, which had drained nearby marshes to increase the amount of cultivable land.

The development of a money economy greatly altered the agrarian institutions of the West. Many manors now specialized in a single crop, like grain or wool, olives or grapes, and therefore purchased items that they themselves no longer produced. The lords of these one-crop manors, depending increasingly on a monetary income, became capitalists on a modest scale. The more enterprising wanted to sweep away what seemed to them inefficient medieval survivals, demanding that their peasants pay rent in money rather than in commodities or in work on the demesne land. The sheep-raising capitalists of sixteenth-century England got the right of enclosure, of fencing off for their own flocks common lands where peasants had traditionally pastured their own livestock. In Spain, the great guild of sheep-raisers, the Mesta, secured comparable exclusive rights to vast tracts of pasture. Urban businessmen wanted property in a form that they might readily buy and sell, free from the restrictions of feudal tenure; they wanted laborers whom they could hire and fire, free from the restrictions of serfdom. All these forces, together with the labor shortage and peasant unrest created by the Black Death, precipitated the end of serfdom, which virtually disappeared in most areas of western Europe by 1500.

Thus, at the heart of economic and social relationships, the cash nexus of the capitalist was beginning to replace the medieval complex of caste and service. These new developments blurred the old lines between classes. The ordinary individual very probably made a gain in real income by becoming a wage-earning worker or rent-paying tenant farmer instead of a serf. Yet he also lost something—the security, the inherited job, the right to certain lands—which he had possessed in the days of manorialism. Despair and discontent came to the surface in the Jacquerie and the English peasant uprising of 1381 and continued as undercurrents in the more prosperous Europe of the fifteenth century. In towns and cities, too, pressures mounted, as the guilds became more exclusive and the separation between the wealthy master and the ordinary workman widened. In Venice, pressures were kept under control, but elsewhere they sometimes exploded, as in the Flemish towns on the eve of the Hundred Years' War and in the revolt of the Florentine Ciompi.

A very important political result of the economic changes we have been surveying was the expanded role of the business class, the bourgeoisie. Sometimes the bourgeois themselves ruled, as did the Medici in Florence and the merchants of Venice and the Hanse. Sometimes they provided monarchs with the money or the professional skills to further dynastic and national interests. Archbishop Morton helped Henry VII to bring law and order back to England; Fugger money supported the Hapsburgs; Charles VII could not have brought France successfully out of the Hundred Years' War without the support of Jacques Coeur. Yet Coeur's disgrace underscored the fact that, while holders of political power were beholden to the wielders of economic power, the reverse was also true.

The economic leaders made their mark not only on politics but on the whole style of the age. No medieval man, apart from such a rare specimen as the emperor Frederick II, would have manifested the presumptuousness, the lack of humility, found in the epitaph of Jacob Fugger. The bourgeois were beginning to invade the Church's near-monopoly of the support of culture. The Medici, the Fuggers, Coeur, and the well-to-do generally supported the patronage of art and learning and the financing of public monuments. The palace or the library of the rich man challenged the monastery or the church-dominated university as a center of scholarship. In the late fifteenth century, we shall shortly see, the intellectual life of Florence revolved around the Platonic Academy subsidized by Lorenzo the Magnificent. Finally, there was little to distinguish the rich and cultivated prelate from the rich and cultivated layman. Such Renaissance popes as Sixtus IV, Alexander VI, and Julius II, like their contemporaries in the business world, were great admirers and amassers of material wealth and great connoisseurs of art.

III Literature and Thought

The burgeoning capitalism and secularism of the Renaissance centuries did not mean that all medieval values were rejected or all medieval customs supplanted. A good case in point is linguistic: the new vernaculars, the "native" or "local" languages, became important media of literary expression without seriously undermining the traditional preeminence of Latin in the realm of learning. Linguistically, the Renaissance had a kind of split personality or dyarchy (dual rule), with the vernaculars dominating the world of popular culture and Latin that of "serious" thought.

The Vernaculars

The vernaculars of the western European countries emerged gradually, arising deep in the Middle Ages as the spoken languages of the people, then becoming vehicles for popular writing, and finally achieving official recognition. Many vernaculars—Spanish, Portuguese, Italian, and French—developed from Latin; these were the Romance (Roman) languages. Castilian, the core of modern literary Spanish, attained official status in the thirteenth century when the king of Castile ordered that it be used for government records. In Italy, the vernacular scarcely existed as a literary language until the eve of the Renaissance when Dante employed the dialect of his native Tuscany in the *Divine Comedy,* and it was not until the early sixteenth century that Tuscan Italian won out over the rival dialect of Rome as the standard medium for vernacular expression.

In medieval France, two families of vernaculars appeared. Southern Frenchmen spoke the *langue d'oc,* so called from their use of *oc* (the Latin *hoc*) for "yes"; their northern cousins spoke the *langue d'oïl,* in which "yes" was *oïl,* (the modern *oui*). The epic verses of the *Song of Roland,* the rowdy *fabliaux,* and the chronicles of Villehardouin and Joinville were all composed in the *langue d'oïl,* while the troubadours at the court of Eleanor of Aquitaine sang in Provençal, a variety of the *langue d'oc.* By 1400, the *langue d'oïl* of the Paris region was well on its way to replacing Latin as the official language of the whole kingdom, though a century later champions of this French tongue were complaining that it was used only for frivolous writing. Provençal eventually died out; however, another offshot of the *langue d'oc* survives in Catalan, used in both Spain and France at the Mediterranean end of the Pyrenees, and the name *Languedoc* is still applied to southern France west of the Rhone.

In Germany and in England, the vernaculars were derived ultimately not from Latin but from an ancient Germanic language. The minnesingers of thirteenth century Germany composed their poetry in Middle High German, the predecessor of modern literary German. The Anglo-Saxons of England had spoken a dialect of Low German which incorporated some words of Scandinavian or Celtic origin and later added many borrowings from Norman French and Latin to form the English vernacular. As we have already noted, English achieved official recognition in the fourteenth century; meantime, it was also coming into its own as a literary language with such popular works as *Piers Plowman* and Chaucer's *Canterbury Tales.*

Use of a common language undoubtedly heightened among Englishmen a common sense of national purpose and a common mistrust of foreigners who did not speak the King's English. The vernaculars also accelerated the emergence of distinctive national styles in France and in Spain. Yet the triumph of particularism in fifteenth-century Germany and Italy demonstrated that the vernaculars could not by themselves create national political units. Nor did the vernaculars divide Western culture into watertight national compartments. Translations kept ideas flowing across national frontiers, and some of the vernaculars themselves became international languages. In the Near East, the Italian that had been introduced by the Crusaders was the *lingua franca*, the Western tongue most widely understood.

Humanism

Meantime, Latin remained the international language of the Church and of the academic world. Scholars worked diligently to perfect their Latin and, in the later Renaissance, to learn at least the rudiments of Greek and sometimes of Hebrew too. They called themselves humanists, that is, devotees of what Cicero had termed *studia humanitatis,* or humane studies. While these were more restricted than the "humanities" or "liberal arts" of modern higher education, they usually included rhetoric, grammar, history, poetry, and ethics. Humanism was far more than a linguistic term, and the humanist was usually much more than a philologist. His studies of the great men and great ideas of the classical past led him to cherish the values of antiquity, pagan though they might be. Machiavelli, as the preceding chapter noted, found greater virtue in pre-Christian Greece and Rome than he did in the nominally Christian society of his own day. Other humanists, we shall

Portrait of Dante, attributed to the school of Giotto.

find, sought a kind of highest moral denominator in the best ancient doctrines and in the loftiest Christian aspiration.

Altogether, humanism revolutionized men's attitudes toward the classical heritage. The medieval schoolmen had not disdained this heritage; they admired and copied its forms but transformed or adapted its ideas to fortify their own Christian views. They found in Vergil's *Aeneid,* for instance, not only the splendor of epic poetry but also an allegory of man's sojourn on earth. The humanists of the Renaissance, in turn, transformed their medieval heritage in the more secular spirit of their own age and in the light of their own more extensive knowledge of the classics. They revered both the style and the content of the classics and began to study them for their own sake, not to strengthen or enrich their faith. Reverence for the classics did not prevent some humanists from becoming enthusiastic advocates of the vernacular; the reverse was also true, as vernacular writers acquired the habit of studying Cicero and other classical masters to improve their own style (the passage from Gibbon quoted in the introduction to this chapter is a good specimen of Ciceronian English).

Writers of the Early Italian Renaissance

Dante Alighieri (1265–1321) was the first major Italian writer to embody some of the qualities that were to characterize Renaissance literature. As an earlier chapter has already noted, much of Dante's writing and outlook bore the stamp of the Middle Ages. The grand theme of the *Divine Comedy* was medieval, and the chivalric concept of disembodied love inspired his devotion to Beatrice, whom he seldom saw. His hostility to the political ambitions of Boniface VIII did not express a Machiavellian anticlericalism but the reaction of a good Christian who wanted the pope to keep out of politics. Yet Dante not only chose the vernacular for the *Divine Comedy* but also wrote a treatise in Latin urging others to follow his example. He modeled the style of the *Comedy* on the popular poetry of the Provençal troubadours rather than on the epic verse of the ancients. He gave the classics their due by including among the characters of the *Comedy* a host of figures from antiquity, both real and mythological. The Trojan Hector, Homer, Vergil's Aeneas. Vergil himself, Euclid, Plato, Socrates, Caesar, and other virtuous pagans dwell forever in Limbo on the edge of Hell, suffering only the hopelessness of the unbaptized who can never reach God's presence. Significantly, Dante also placed in Limbo the Muslims Saladin and Averroës.

The concerns of this world are constantly with Dante in the other world. The lost souls in Hell are real people, from Judas through corrupt medieval clerics down to Dante's own fellow Florentines. Dante was not one of the medieval intellectuals who withdrew from society to the sanctuary of holy orders. Deeply involved in Florentine politics, he became a refugee from Guelf factionalism, and adopted the good Renaissance expedient of obtaining the patronage of the despot ruling Verona. As a man of letters, he achieved a remarkable popular success during his own lifetime. Half a century after his death, a group of Florentine citizens honored the memory of their exiled compatriot by founding a public lectureship for a person "well trained in the book of Dante."

Popular fame and classical enthusiasm obsessed the next important Italian literary figure, Petrarch (Francesco Petrarca, 1304–1374). Since his father was a political exile from Florence, the young Petrarch lived for a time at the worldly papal court in Avignon and attended the law school at the University of Bologna. As a professional man of letters, he collected and copied the manuscripts of ancient authors, produced the first accurate edition of the Roman historian Livy, and found in an Italian cathedral some forgotten letters by Cicero that threw new light on Cicero's political activities. Petrarch so admired the past that he addressed a series of affectionate letters to Cicero and other Roman worthies; he also composed a Latin epic in the style of the *Aeneid* to celebrate Scipio Africanus, the hero of the Second Punic War. He tried to learn Greek and failed, but at least he could gaze reverently at his manuscripts of Homer and Plato.

Petrarch's attainments led the Senate of Rome (then a kind of municipal council) to revive the Greco-Roman recognition of excellence and crown him with a wreath of laurel in an elaborate ceremony. The new laureate reveled in the honor, for he longed to be ranked with the ancient Romans to whom he addressed his letters. Ironically, the writings of Petrarch most admired in modern times are not those in his cherished Latin but those he esteemed the least, the vernacular love poems he addressed to his adored Laura, whom he courted in vain until she died during the Black Death. In these lyrics, Petrarch perfected the verse form known as the Italian sonnet, fourteen lines long, divided into one set of eight lines and another of six, each with its own rhyme scheme. The word "sonnet" means "little song," and Petrarch developed his sonnets from vernacular folk songs. Almost despite himself, therefore, he proved to be one of the founders of modern vernacular literature.

Petrarch is an excellent instance of the intermixture of old and new in the Renaissance. He exemplified emerging humanism by his devotion to the classics and his deep feeling for the beauties of this world; for him Laura was a real woman, not a disembodied chivalric heroine. He criticized medieval Schoolmen because of their rationalism, their dependence on Aristotle as an infallible authority, and their preoccupation with detail, all of which led them, in his judgment, to miss the true spirit of Christianity in their concern with its letter. But he admired Augustine almost as much as he admired Cicero, believing that the religious teachings of the one and the Stoic morality of the other could counter the materialism he observed around him. "I am filled with bitter indignation against the mores of today," he wrote in a letter to Livy, "when men value nothing except gold and silver and desire nothing except sensual pleasures." * We shall encounter other humanists who shared Petrarch's low estimate of existing society and his belief that classical learning and Christian precepts could both contribute to ennoble the human spirit.

Petrarch's friend and pupil, Giovanni Boccaccio (1313–1375), shared his master's estimate of mankind but not his confidence in the possibility of human improvement. Boccaccio, who was the son of a Florentine banker, spent part of his youth at the frivolous court of the Angevin kings of Naples, and turned to letters after his apprenticeship in banking left him disillusioned by the sharp business practices of wealthy Florentines. He became a humanist scholar and eventually held the Dante memorial lectureship at Florence; meantime, he went Petrarch one better by learning Greek, and aided his master in tracking down old manuscripts, once finding a copy of Tacitus in the Benedictine abbey on Monte Cassino. His distress at the negligence of the clergy in conserving manuscripts together with his observation of clerical corruption made him strongly anticlerical.

Anticlericalism is a recurrent theme in his *Decameron*, the first major prose work in the Italian vernacular, which recounts the stories told by a group of young Florentines who have moved to a country villa during the Black Death. Most of the plots in the *Decameron* were not original with Boccaccio, who borrowed freely from classical and Eastern sources and from the bawdy *fabliaux* of medieval France, particularly those exposing clerical peccadilloes. He retold these earthy tales in a graceful and entertaining way, and with a lighthearted disenchantment based on his own worldly experience. Here is the gist of one of the stories:

> You must know, then, that there was once in our city a very rich merchant called Arriguccio Berlinghieri, who . . . took to wife a young gentle woman ill sorting with himself, by name Madam Sismonda, who, for that he, merchant-like, was much abroad and sojourned little with her, fell in love with a young man called Ruberto.†

Arriguccio discovers his wife's infidelity and gives her the beating of her life—or so he thinks. The beating occurs in a darkened room, Sismonda has directed her maid to take her place, and it is actually the maid whom Arriguccio had thrashed. Unaware of the deception, he summons Sismonda's brothers to witness her disgrace. "The brothers,—seeing her seated sewing with no sign of beating on her face, whereas Arriguccio avouched that he had beaten her to a mummy,—began to marvel." Sismonda immediately accuses her hapless husband of "fuddling himself about the taverns, fore-

---

*M. P. Gilmore, *Humanists and Jurists* (Cambridge, Mass., 1963), p. 6.
†This and the following quotations are from the eighth story of the seventh day, as translated in the Modern Library edition of the *Decameron*.

gathering now with this lewd woman and now with that and keeping me waiting for him . . . half the night." The result: the brothers give Arriguccio a thorough beating. And Boccaccio's moral:

> Thus the lady, by her ready wit, not only escaped the imminent peril but opened herself a way to do her every pleasure in time to come, without evermore having any fear of her husband.

Classical Scholarship

The men of letters who followed Petrarch and Boccaccio may be divided into three groups. First, there were the conservers of classical culture, the bookworms, scholars, cultivated despots and businessmen, all the heirs of Petrarch's great humanistic enthusiasm for classical antiquity. Second were the vernacular writers—many of them not Italians—who took the path marked out by the *Decameron*, from Chaucer at the close of the fourteenth century down to Rabelais and to Cervantes in the sixteenth. And third there were the synthesizers, headed by Pico della Mirandola and Erasmus, who endeavored to fuse Christianity, classicism, and other elements into a universal philosophy of man.

The devoted antiquarians of the fifteenth century uncovered a really remarkable number of ancient manuscripts. They ransacked monasteries and other likely places, in Italy and Germany, in France and Spain. They pieced together the works of Cicero, Tacitus, Lucretius, and other Latin authors. Collecting Greek manuscripts became a regular business, transacted for Italian scholars and patrons by agents in Constantinople both before and after 1453. They did their work so thoroughly that almost all the Greek classics we now possess reached the West before 1500. To preserve, catalog, and study these literary treasures, the first modern libraries were created. Cosimo de' Medici supported three separate libraries in and near Florence and employed forty-five copyists. Humanist popes founded the library of the Vatican, today one of the most important collections in the world, and even the minor duchy of Urbino in northern Italy had a major library, assembled by its cultivated duke.

Greek scholars as well as Greek manuscripts made the journey from Byzantium to Italy. One of the earliest of them, Manuel Chrysoloras (1368–1415) came to Italy to seek help for the beleaguered Byzantines against the Turks and remained to teach at Florence and Milan. He did literature a great service by insisting that translations into Latin from the Greek should not be literal, as they had been in the past, but should convey the message and spirit of the original. The revival of Greek studies reached maturity in the 1460s with the emergence of the informal circle of Florentine humanists known as the Platonic Academy. The Greek language, however, never equaled Latin in popularity because of its difficulty, a fact that discouraged interest in the Greek drama and led most humanists to study Plato in Latin translation.

The classicists of the fifteenth century made a fetish of pure and polished Latin. The learned composed elaborate letters designed less for private reading than for the instruction of their colleagues. Papal secretaries began to make ecclesiastical correspondence conform to what we should call a manual of correct style. At their worst, these men were pedants, exalting manner over matter, draining vitality from the Latin language. But at their best, they were keen and erudite scholars who sifted out the inaccuracies and forgeries in defective manuscripts to establish definitive texts of ancient writings.

Lorenzo Valla (1407–1457) represented classical scholarship at its best. One of the few important figures of the Italian Renaissance not identified with Florence, Valla was reared in Rome and passed much of his adult life there and at Naples. Petty and quarrelsome, fond of exchanging insults with rival humanists, he also commanded both immense learning and the courage to use it against the most sacred targets. He even criticized the supposedly flawless prose of Cicero and took Thomas Aquinas to task for his failure to know Greek. His own expert knowledge of the language led him to point out errors and misinterpretations in the Vulgate, as compared to the Greek New Testament, and thereby to lay the foundation for humanist biblical scholarship.

Valla's fame rests above all on his demonstration that the Donation of Constantine, long a basis for justifying papal claims to temporal dominion, was actually a forgery. He proved his case by showing that both the Latin in which the Donation was written and the events to which it referred dated from an era several centuries after Constantine, who had been emperor in the early fourth century. When Valla published this exposé in 1440, he was secretary to Alfonso the Magnanimous, king of Aragon, whose claim to Naples was being challenged by the papacy on the basis of the Donation itself. The pope might well have been expected to condemn Valla as a heretic. Nothing of the kind occurred, and Valla soon accepted a commission to translate Thucydides under papal auspices.

Chaucer and Rabelais

The second group of literary men, the vernacular writers, illustrate once again the broad range of the Renaissance. Geoffrey Chaucer, like Dante, belongs both to the Middle Ages and to the Renaissance. As an earlier chapter has noted, his *Canterbury Tales* have a medieval setting; they are told by pilgrims on their way to the shrine of the martyred Becket, not by the secular young people of the *Decameron*. Yet Chaucer's tales are not unlike Boccaccio's; he, too, used the vernacular and borrowed stories from the *fabliaux*. Although Chaucer apparently had not actually read the *Decameron*, he was familiar enough with other writings of Boccaccio to use the plot of one for his Knight's Tale and of another for *Troilus and Criseyde*, the long narrative poem about two lovers in the Trojan War. The Clerk's

Tale, he reveals, "I Lerned at Padowe of a worthy clerk . . ., Fraunceys Petrark, the laureat poete," and the Wife of Bath mentions "the wyse poete of Florence That Highte Dant."

Chaucer came to know Italian literature in the course of several trips to Italy on official business for the English king. He led a busy and prosperous life in the thick of politics, domestic and international. Coming from a family of well-to-do London merchants, he was a justice of the peace in Kent, represented the county in the House of Commons, and filled important royal posts. Chaucer showed that the English vernacular was coming of age and that in England, as in Italy, the profession of letters was no longer a clerical monopoly.

The medieval values still evident in the writings of Chaucer had largely vanished a century and a half later in the works of the Frenchman François Rabelais (ca. 1494–1553). Rabelais contributed far more to literature than the salacious wit for which he is famous. He studied the classics, particularly Plato and the ancient physicians; practiced and taught medicine; and created two of the great comic figures of letters, Gargantua and his son Pantagruel. The two are giants, and everything they do is of heroic dimensions. The abbey of Theleme (the Greek word for "will"), which Gargantua helps to found, permits its residents a wildly unmonastic existence:

All their life was spent not in lawes, statutes or rules, but according to their own free will and pleasure. They rose out of their beds, when they thought good: they did eat, drink, labour, sleep, when they had a minde to it and were disposed for it. . . . In all their rule, and strictest tie of their order, there was but this one clause to be observed,

DO WHAT THOU WILT.*

To Rabelais free will meant self-improvement on a grand scale. Gargantua exhorts Pantagruel to learn everything: he is to master Arabic in addition to Latin, read the New Testament in Greek and the Old in Hebrew, and study history, geometry, architecture, music, and civil law. He must also know "the fishes, all the fowles of the aire, all the several kinds of shrubs and trees," "all the sorts of herbs and flowers that grow upon the ground: all the various metals that are hid within the bowels of the earth." "In brief," Gargantua concludes, "let me see thee an Abysse, and bottomless pit of knowledge."† Both his insatiable appetite for knowledge and the exuberance with which Rabelais wrote about it represent important aspects of the Renaissance style.

The Philosophical Humanists

Another facet of the Renaissance style was highlighted by the third group of writers, the philosophical human-

*F. Rabelais, *Gargantua and Pantagruel*, Urquhart trans. (New York, 1883), book I, chap. 57.
†Ibid., book I, chap. 8.

ists, who aspired not only to universal knowledge but also to a universal truth and faith. They were centered first at Florence, attracted by the Platonic Academy founded in 1462 by Cosimo de' Medici, two years before his death, when he decided to underwrite the translation of Plato's works into Latin. He entrusted the commission to Marsilio Ficino (1433–1499), a medical student turned classicist, who translated not only the whole body of Plato's writings but some of the Neoplatonists' works as well. These followers of Plato, who flourished in the third century A.D. and later, long after the master, cultivated the search for God through mystical experiences. The opportunity for stressing the compatibility of Neoplatonism with Christianity exerted a strong attraction on Ficino and his circle.

Ficino, who was also a priest, argued that religious feeling and expression were as natural to man as barking was to dogs or neighing to horses. Man, he wrote, has the unique faculty called intellect, which he described as an "eye turned toward the intelligible light" or God. He coined the term "platonic love" to describe the love that transcends the senses and may also lead man to mystical communion with God. He supported his arguments with appeals to a wide range of authorities—the wise men of the ancient Near East, the prophets of the Old Testament, the apostles of the New, and the Greek philosophers, including Pythagoras and Aristotle in addition to Plato. Ficino seemed to be attempting a synthesis of all philosophy and religion.

The attempt was pressed further by Ficino's pupil, Pico della Mirandola (1463–1494). Pico crowded much into his thirty-one years and would have delighted Rabelais's Gargantua, for he knew Arabic and Hebrew in addition to Greek and Latin and studied Jewish allegory, Arab philosophy, and medieval Scholasticism, which, almost alone among humanists, he respected. Pico's tolerance was as broad as his learning. In his short *Oration on the Dignity of Man*, he cited approvingly Chaldean and Persian theologians, the priests of Apollo, Socrates, Pythagoras, Cicero, Moses, Paul, Augustine, Muhammad, Saint Francis, Thomas Aquinas, and many others.

In all the varied beliefs of this galaxy, Pico hoped to find the common denominator of a universal faith. This process of syncretism, of borrowing and assimilating from many sources, he was unable to complete, but, together with Ficino, he helped to found the great humane studies of comparative religion and comparative philosophy. And he reaffirmed and strengthened Ficino's idea that man was unique, the link between the mortal physical world and the immortal spirtual one, the hinge of the universe, so to speak. This concept of the uniqueness of man and his central position in the universe lay at the core of the Renaissance style. Yet among the Platonic humanists, the medieval element also remained strong; Pico, in his final years, gave away his worldly possessions and became an ardent supporter of the fanatical preacher Savonarola.

The "Prince of Humanists," the man who gave the

Hans Holbein's portrait of Erasmus.

those who claim to be wise. Erasmus mocked any group inflated by a sense of its own importance—merchants, churchmen, scientists, philosophers, courtiers, and kings. In *The Praise of Folly* he also punctured the pretensions of nations:

> And now I see that it is not only in individual men that nature has implanted self-love. She implants a kind of it as a common possession in the various races, and even cities. By this token the English claim . . . good looks, music, and the best eating as their special properties. The Scots flatter themselves on the score of high birth and royal blood, not to mention their dialectical skill. Frenchmen have taken all politeness for their province. . . . The Italians usurp *belles lettres* and eloquence; and they all flatter themselves upon the fact that they alone, of all mortal men, are not barbarians. . . . The Greeks, as well as being the founders of the learned disciplines, vaunt themselves upon their titles to the famous heroes of old.*

In appraising human nature, in general, Erasmus tempered criticism with geniality. In what proportions, asks an ironic passage in *The Praise of Folly,* did Jupiter supply men with emotion and reason?

> Well, the proportions run about one pound to half an ounce. Besides, he imprisoned reason in a cramped corner of the head, and turned over all the rest of the body to the emotions. After that he instated two most violent tyrants, as it were, in opposition to reason: anger, which holds the citadel of the breast, and consequently the very spring of life, the heart; and lust, which rules a broad empire lower down. . . .†

So, Erasmus concludes, we must cherish particularly the few outstanding individuals who have led great and good lives. Christ heads his list of great men; Cicero and Socrates rank very high. Plato's account of the death of Socrates moved Erasmus so deeply that he wanted to cry out, "Pray for us, Saint Socrates."

Erasmus possessed most of the main attributes of Renaissance humanism. He coupled a detached view of human nature with faith in the dignity of man or at least of a few individuals. He joined love of the classics with respect for Christian values. While he was both testy and vain, he had little use for the fine-spun arguments of Scholasticism and was a tireless advocate of what he called his "philosophy of Christ," the application of the doctrines of charity and love taught by Jesus. Yet, although Erasmus always considered himself a loyal son of the Church, he nevertheless helped to destroy the universality of Catholicism. His edition of the Greek New Testament raised disquieting doubts about the accuracy of the Latin translation in the Vulgate and therefore of Catholic biblical interpretations. His repeated insistence on elevating the spirit of piety above the letter of formal religious acts seemed to diminish the importance of the clergy, and his attacks on clerical laxity implied that the wide gap

most mature expression of the impulse to draw on all wisdom, was not Italian but Dutch—Desiderius Erasmus (1466–1536). He might also be called the foremost citizen of the Republic of Letters, for he studied, taught, and lived at Oxford and Cambridge, at Paris, and in Italy, and he particularly relished the free atmosphere of "mini" city-states like Louvain in the Low Countries, Basel in Switzerland, and Freiburg in the Rhineland. Building on Valla's scholarship, Erasmus published a scholarly edition of the Greek New Testament. He carried on a prodigious correspondence in Latin and compiled a series of *Adages* and *Colloquies* to give students examples of good Latin composition. Because Erasmus never regarded elegance of style as an end in itself, he assailed the "knowledge factories" of the grammarians:

> As for those stilted, insipid verses they display on all occasions . . ., obviously the writer believes that the soul of Virgil has transmigrated into his own breast. But the funniest sight of all is to see them admiring and praising each other, trading compliment for compliment, thus mutually scratching each other's itch.*

This passage is from the satirical *Praise of Folly,* in which Erasmus employed the female Folly, as many of his contemporaries used the jester or fool, to contrast the spontaneous natural reactions of the supposedly foolish with the studied and self-serving artificiality of

*Desiderius Erasmus, *The Praise of Folly,* trans. Hoyt Hopewell Hudson (copyright 1941, © 1969 by Princeton University Press, Princeton Paperback, 1970), p. 71. Reprinted by permission of Princeton University Press.

*Ibid., p. 61.
†Ibid., p. 23.

between the lofty ideals and the corrupt practices of the Church could not long endure. A famous sixteenth-century epigram states: "Where Erasmus merely nodded, Luther rushed in; where Erasmus laid the eggs, Luther hatched the chicks; where Erasmus merely doubted, Luther laid down the law." When Luther did lay down the law in the Protestant revolt, however, the growing dogmatism and belligerence of the rebels soon alienated Erasmus. Both his fidelity to the Christian tradition, as he understood it, and his humanist convictions committed Erasmus to the position that the only weapons worthy of man were reason and discussion.

IV Science and Religion
An Age of Preparation

Humanism both aided and impeded the advance of science, so that the Renaissance centuries did not witness a dramatic rebirth of this discipline but rather constituted an age of preparation for the scientific revolution that was to come in the seventeenth century of Galileo and Newton. To this preparation the major contribution of the humanists was increased availability of ancient scientific authorities, as works by Galen, Ptolemy, Archimedes, and others were for the first time translated from Greek into the more accessible Latin. But an important contribution also came from the Scholastic tradition, which survived robustly throughout the Renaissance centuries, notably at the universities of Paris and Padua, despite the scorn the humanists heaped upon it. The Scholastics' insistence on systematic work habits and their enthusiasm for Aristotle promoted scientific studies.

Where humanism thwarted the advancement of science was its disposition to put old authorities high on a pedestal, beyond the reach of criticism. Few men of the Renaissance believed it possible to improve on the astronomy taught by Ptolemy during the second century A.D., or on the medicine taught by Galen in the same century. Galen, for example, had advanced the erroneous theory that the blood moved from one side of the heart to the other by passing through invisible pores in the thick wall of tissue separating the two sides of the organ. Actually, as Harvey was to discover in the seventeenth century, the blood gets from the one side to the other by circulating through the body and lungs. Galen's theory of invisible pores kept Leonardo da Vinci from anticipating Harvey; when the great artist's anatomical investigations led him to the brink of discovery, he backed away because he could not believe that Galen might have erred.

Da Vinci (1452–1519) exemplifies both the shortcomings and the achievements of Renaissance science. Taking notes in a hit-or-miss fashion, and in a secretive left-handed writing that must be held up to a mirror to be read, he did not have the modern scientist's concern for the systematic cataloging of observations and the frequent publication of findings and speculations. Yet Leonardo also showed remarkable inventiveness, drawing plans for lathes, pumps, war machines, flying machines, and many other contraptions, not all of them workable, but all highly imaginative. He had a passionate curiosity for anatomy and proportions, and for almost everything about man and nature. His accurate drawings of human embryos differed radically from the older notion of the fetus as a perfectly formed miniature human being. Moreover, Leonardo did not always bow before established authority, as he did before Galen. His geological studies convinced him that the earth was far older than the men of his time thought it to be. The Po River, he estimated, must have been flowing for two hundred thousand years to wash down the sediments forming its alluvial plain in northern Italy.

Invention and Technology

The best-known invention of the Renaissance—the printed book—furnishes an instructive case history of the way in which many technological advances contributed to the end result. The revolution in book production began in the twelfth century when Muslims in Spain introduced a technique first developed by the Chinese and began to make paper by shredding old rags, processing them with water, and then pressing the liquid out of the finished sheets. The cost of the new product was only a fraction of that of the sheepskin parchment or calfskin vellum theretofore employed for manuscripts. The next step came when engravers, adapting another Chinese technique, made a mirror image of a drawing on a woodblock or copper plate that could make many identical woodcuts or engravings. Sentences were then added to the plates or blocks to explain the drawings. Finally, movable type was devised, each piece representing a single letter on a minute bit of engraving that could be combined with other pieces to form words, sentences, a whole page, and then salvaged to be used over and over again. This crucial invention was perfected during the 1440s, almost certainly in the German Rhineland; Johann Gutenberg, who used to receive the credit for it, has been the focus of a scholarly controversy that has deflated his old heroic reputation.

The new invention gained wide popularity because printed books were not only much cheaper than manuscripts but also less prone to copyists' errors, which pyramided over the years because a copyist often failed to correct the mistakes in the manuscript he was following and made fresh ones of his own. By 1500 the total number of volumes in print had reached the millions, and Italy alone had some seventy-three presses employing movable type. The most famous of them, the Aldine Press in Venice (named for its founder, Aldus Manutius, 1450–1515), sold inexpensive, scholarly editions of the classics printed in a beautiful typeface that was said to be modeled on the handwriting of Petrarch and is the source of modern italics. Without the perfection of printing, Erasmus might not have become the acknowledged arbiter of European letters. Without it, Luther could not have secured the rapid distribution of his antipapal tracts, and the Protestant Reformation might not have rent Christian Europe asunder.

Although no other single invention can be compared with printing on the score of quick and decisive effects, many innovations ultimately had comparable influence. Gunpowder, for example, brought from China to medieval Europe, was used in the later campaigns of the Hundred Years' War. Improved firearms and artillery were to doom both the feudal knight and the feudal castle, for both were vulnerable to the new weapons. In navigation, as we have seen, the Venetians made galleys swifter, more capacious, and more seaworthy. At the same time, important marine aids came into general use, particularly the magnetic compass and the sailing charts, which, at least for the Mediterranean, established a high level of accuracy. By the close of the fifteenth century, Europeans possessed the equipment needed for the oncoming age of world discovery.

On land, the mining industry scored impressive technological advances. The engineers of the late medieval centuries solved some of the problems of extracting and smelting silver, iron, and other ores. Then, in 1556, a German physician and mining expert published a comprehensive treatise on the practices of the industry—*De re metallica* (All about Metals), which was translated from Latin into English in 1912 by an American mining engineer and his wife, the future President Hoover. Following the sixteenth-century custom, the author called himself Agricola, a Latinized version of his German name, Bauer ("peasant"). Agricola's treatise was an early specimen of those handbooks that are indispensable to the engineer, and its detailed observations on soil structures made it a pioneer study in geology as well.

Medicine

The wide dissemination of printed books with clear anatomical illustrations advanced medical skills, which were also improved by the partial lifting of the old ban against dissection of human cadavers. Pharmacology also progressed, thanks to experiments with the chemistry of drugs made by the eccentric Swiss physician Paracelsus (Theophrastus Bombastus von Hohenheim, 1493–1541). Despite his classical name, Paracelsus delighted in iconoclastic gestures, such as insisting on lecturing in German and burning the works of Galen to show his contempt for classical authority. The French surgeon Ambroise Paré (1517–1590), who also had little reverence for antiquity, laid the foundations for modern surgery by developing new techniques, notably that of sewing up blood vessels with stitches rather than cauterizing them with a hot iron. Yet many so-called physicians were quacks, and many teachers of medicine merely repeated the demonstrations that

Galen had made more than a thousand years earlier without attemtping to confirm the validity of his findings.

A striking exception to this rule was furnished by the physicians and scholars of the University of Padua. Protected against possible ecclesiastical censorship by the overlordship of Venice, which controlled the city, they maintained a lively tradition of scientific inquiry that presaged the seventeenth-century triumphs of the experimental method. In 1537, a young Belgian named Vesalius (1514–1564), trained at Paris, took a teaching post at Padua. Vesalius repeated the dissections of Galen, but watched for possible errors; thus he rejected Galen's notion of invisible pores in the wall of tissue within the heart because he could not find such pores. In 1543, Vesalius published *De humanis corporis fabrica* (Concerning the Structure of the Human Body), prepared with admirable concern for anatomical accuracy and detail, and illustrated with elaborate woodcuts.

Astronomy

The year 1543 marked not only the appearance of Vesalius' treatise but also the launching of modern astronomical studies with the publication of Copernicus' *De revolutionibus orbium coelestium* (Concerning the Revolutions of Heavenly Bodies). Born in Poland, of German extraction, Nicolaus Copernicus (1473–1543) studied law and medicine at Padua and other Italian universities, and spent thirty years as canon of a cathedral near Danzig. His work in mathematics and astronomy led him to attack the hypothesis of the geocentric (earth-centered) universe derived from Ptolemy and other astronomers of antiquity. In its place, he advanced the revolutionary new hypothesis of the heliocentric (sun-centered) universe.

The concept of the geocentric universe generally accepted in the sixteenth century included an elaborate system of spheres. Around the stationary earth there revolved some eighty spheres, each, as it were, a separate sky containing some of the heavenly bodies, each moving on an invisible circular path, each transparent so that we mortals could see the spheres beyond it. This imaginative and symmetrical picture of the universe had already come under attack before Copernicus, for observers could not make it tally with the actual behavior of heavenly bodies. Copernicus used these earlier criticisms and his own computations to arrive at the heliocentric concept, which required that the earth move around the sun rather than remain stationary.

The Copernican hypothesis had quite radical implications. It destroyed the idea of the earth's uniqueness by suggesting that it acted like other heavenly bodies, and thus opened the way to attacks on the uniqueness of the earth's human inhabitants. Nevertheless, once Copernicus had reversed the roles of the sun and the earth, his universe retained many Ptolemaic characteristics. Its heavens were still filled with spheres revolving along invisible orbits; only they now moved about a stationary sun, instead of the stationary earth, and Copernican astronomy required thirty-four of them, not eighty. The revolution in astronomy begun by Copernicus did not reach its culmination for a hundred and fifty years. The circular orbits of Copernicus had to yield to elliptical orbits; the scheme of thirty-four spheres had to be modified; and a theory explaining the forces that kept the universe together had to be put forward. And all these developments had to await the genius of Galileo and Newton and the observations made possible by the invention of the telescope.

Music

In the medieval curriculum music was part of the quadrivium, the fourfold way to knowledge, along with astronomy, arithmetic, and geometry. The bracketing of music with the sciences is not too surprising, since a great deal of mathematics underlies musical theory and notation. The mainstay of medieval sacred music was the Gregorian chant or plainsong, which relied on a single voice and thus did not involve the harmonizing of two or more voices. At the close of the Middle Ages more intricate innovations appeared. Musicians in the Burgundian domains of the Low Countries and northern France developed the technique of polyphony (from the Greek, "many voices"), which combined several voices in complicated harmony. When French and Flemish musicians journeyed to Italy in the fifteenth century, they introduced polyphonic music and borrowed in return the simple tunes of the dances and folksongs they encountered in southern Europe. Flemish composers even based masses on rowdy popular tunes. The end products of the interaction were the sacred and secular polyphonic compositions of the internationally renowned Fleming Josquin des Pres (ca. 1450–1521) and the hundred-odd masses of the Italian Palestrina (ca. 1526–1594). In spite of the popular borrowings much of this music sounds quite otherworldly today, since it lacks the dissonances and the strong rhythms and climaxes to which we are accustomed.

The secularism and individualism of the Renaissance and its taste for experimentation also affected music. New instruments were developed or imported—the violin, doublebass, and harpsichord; the organ, with its complement of keyboards, pedals, and stops; the kettledrum, which was adopted from the Polish army; and the lute, which originated in medieval Persia and reached Italy by way of Spain. Composers and performers began to lose the anonymity associated with the Middle Ages, although the era of prima donnas and other "stars" had not quite arrived. Paid professional singers staffed the famous choirs of Antwerp cathedral and of the Vatican. Josquin des Pres found patrons at the courts of Milan, Rome, and Paris, and both the pope and various cardinals commissioned Palestrina to write masses. A retinue of musicians became a fixture of court life, with the dukes of Burgundy, Philip the Good, and Charles the Bold, leading the way. Lower down the social scale, German artisans, calling themselves mastersingers, organized choral groups; the most famous of them, Hans Sachs, a cobbler in Nuremberg in the 1500s, was later immortalized in Wagner's opera *Die Meistersinger*.

The Renaissance and the Church

While the relations between musicians and the Church were generally harmonious, Renaissance science as a whole sometimes aroused discord. Even though Copernicus dedicated his great book to the pope, Christendom did not welcome a theory that questioned the belief in an earth-centered and man-centered universe. By 1543, however, Western Christendom was preoccupied by its division into the warring factions of Catholic and Protestant. To what extent was the Renaissance responsible for the shattering religious crisis of the Reformation? A more detailed examination of the causes of the Reformation will be found in the next chapter; here a few generalizations about the relationship between the Renaissance and the church may be suggested.

First, the Renaissance did not make the Reformation inevitable. It is an oversimplification to suppose that the religious individualism of Luther arose directly out of the more general individualism of the Renaissance. Looking back over the checkered culture of the age, one can find many elements—materialism, self-indulgence, power politics—that are hard to reconcile with traditional Christian values. If pushed to extremes, these elements could indeed become anti-Christian—but they were seldom pushed to extremes. Even the most ruthless condottieri of politics and business, men like Cesare Borgia and Jacob Fugger, remained nominal Christians. Also, a pronounced anticlerical like Machiavelli reserved his most stinging criticism for the pope's claim to temporal authority, not his claim to ecclesiastical supremacy.

Second, the most characteristic intellectual movement of the Renaissance—humanism—did not propose the abandonment of traditional Christian values. Men such as Pico and Erasmus proposed to enrich or purify Christianity; they did not intend to subvert it. As a matter of fact, the Neoplatonic doctrines cherished by Pico and the Platonic Academy had long been identified with the mystical aspects of the Catholic faith. Erasmus, perhaps the most representative thinker of humanism, was too strongly attached to Catholicism and too moderate in temperament to be a revolutionary.

Finally, a religious crisis was indeed gathering during the Renaissance, but it was more internal than external. That is, the Church was only to a limited extent the victim of outside forces operating beyond its control, like the challenge presented to its old international dominion by the new national monarchies. If the Church of the 1400s had been strong and healthy, it might have met such external challenges successfully. Except in Spain, however, the Church set a flabby and unedifying example by and large, although many honorable exceptions to the prevailing laxity and backwardness could be found. Priests were often illiterate, untrained, underpaid, and immoral; many bishops— following good medieval precedent, it must be admitted—behaved as politicians, not as churchmen.

Perhaps the worst shortcomings existed at the top, in the papacy itself. In the fourteenth and early fifteenth centuries, the papacy experienced the crises of Babylonian Captivity, the Great Schism, and the Conciliar Movement. It emerged from the ordeal with its power reinvigorated, notably by its victory over the reformers who sought to make church councils a check against unlimited papal absolutism. But the triple crisis gravely damaged the spiritual prestige of the office, since such Renaissance popes as Sixtus IV, Alexander VI, and Julius II did little to repair the damage. For three-quarters of a century after 1450 the see of Peter was occupied by men who scored political and military successes and lavished money on learning and on the arts. They bequeathed to posterity, among other treasures, the Vatican Library, the Sistine Chapel, and the early parts of the Basilica of Saint Peter. But this munificence increased the burden of ecclesiastical taxation and other fiscal demands, and increased also the resentment that higher levies usually arouse. Papal indifference to spiritual functions enfeebled the Church at a time when it needed firm and dedicated control. The Church was ruled by connoisseurs and condottieri when it needed reformers.

Intellectually, too, the clergy were losing the vitality they had possessed in the age of Abelard and Aquinas. Some of the monks and friars on university faculties hardly qualified as teachers; they blindly defended a decadent Scholasticism against the new humanist studies and provoked a blistering satire, *The Letters of Obscure Men*. The story began when Johann Reuchlin (1455–1522), a German humanist working with Pico at Florence, learned Hebrew in order to read the great books of Judaism. On returning to Germany, he aroused the wrath of theological faculties by suggesting that a knowledge of the sacred Jewish writings might enable a man to be a better-informed Christian. Arraigned in an ecclesiastical court, Reuchlin, who was a layman, assembled in his defense testimonials from leading humanists, *The Letters of Eminent Men*. Then, in 1516 and 1517, a couple of his friends published *The Letters of Obscure Men*, supposedly exchanged between Reuchlin's clerical opponents but actually a hoax designed to laugh the opposition out of court by mocking the futility of theological hair-splitting. One of the "obscure men" related an experience in a Roman tavern:

> For you must know that we were lately sitting in an inn, having our supper, and were eating eggs, when on opening one, I saw that there was a young chicken within.
>
> This I showed to a comrade; whereupon quoth he to me, "Eat it up speedily, before the taverner sees it, for if he mark it, you will have to pay for a fowl."
>
> In a trice I gulped down the egg, chicken and all.

> And then I remembered that it was Friday!
>
> Whereupon I said to my crony, "You have made me commit a mortal sin, in eating flesh on the sixth day of the week!"
>
> But he averred that it was not a mortal sin—nor even a venial one, seeing that such a chickling is accounted merely as an egg, until it is born.
>
> Then I departed, and thought the matter over.
>
> And by the Lord, I am in a mighty quandary, and know not what to do.
>
> It seemeth to me that these young fowls in eggs are flesh, because their substance is formed and fashioned into the limbs and body of an animal, and possesseth a vital principle.
>
> It is different in the case of grubs in cheese, and such-like, because grubs are accounted fish, as I learnt from a physician who is also skilled in Natural Philosophy.
>
> Most earnestly do I entreat you to resolve the question that I have propounded. For if you hold that the sin is mortal, then, I would fain get shrift here, ere I return to Germany.*

Although Reuchlin lost his case and was sentenced to pay the costs of the trial, he managed to avoid making any payment.

Attempts at Renewal and Reform

Dedicated Christians, both lay and clerical, were aware that the Church needed a thorough cleansing. Papal opposition, however, blocked fresh attempts within the ecclesiastical hierarchy to increase the powers of representative church councils. And the great renovation fostered by Queen Isabella and Cardinal Jiménez was restricted to Spanish lands. Meantime, a quiet Catholic renewal had been advanced by the activities of the Brothers and Sisters of the Common Life. Founded in the Low Countries in the 1370s, they consisted of lay people who pooled their resources in communal living and followed the spiritual discipline of a monastic order without, however, taking religious vows. They also emphasized service to one's fellow man as a way of practicing the ideals of Christianity. Opposed to Scholasticism, the Brethren of the Common Life started schools of their own, which had a high reputation in fifteenth-century Europe. Erasmus, who was educated in one of them, complained that the curriculum was too orthodox and rigid, yet he adopted the goals of the Brethren in his own "philosophy of Christ," with its belief that the example of Jesus should guide men in their daily lives. A similar theme, expressed in more mystical terms, ran through the enormously popular *Imitation of Christ*, written by Thomas à Kempis, one of the Brethren. Its message, like that of the Common Life movement, was addressed to the inner life of the individual rather than to the reform of the Christian community or its institutions.

A more radical and sweeping reform movement

---

*Adapted from F. G. Stokes, ed., *Epistolae obscurorum virorum* (New Haven, 1925), pp. 445–447.

was launched by the Dominican friar Savonarola (1452–1498), who won the favor of the Medici through the influence of Pico. His eloquent sermons and reputed gift of predicting the future soon made him the most popular preacher in Florence. Sparing no one in his denunciations of un-Christian conduct he delivered this typical tirade:

> You Christians should always have the Gospel with you, I do not mean the book, but the spirit, for if you do not possess the spirit of grace and yet carry with you the whole book, of what advantage is it to you? And again, all the more foolish are they who carry round their necks Breviaries, notes, tracts and writings, until they look like pedlars going to a fair. Charity does not consist in the writing of papers. The true books of Christ are the Apostles and saints, and true reading consists in imitating their lives. But in these days men are like books made by the Devil. They speak against pride and ambition and yet they are immersed in them up to their eyes. They preach chastity and maintain concubines. They enjoin fasting and partake of splendid feasts. . . . Only look to-day at the prelates. They are tied to earthly vanities. They love them. The cure of souls is no longer their chief concern. . . . In the Primitive Church the chalices were made of wood and the prelates of gold—today—chalices of gold, prelates of wood!*

He particularly abominated Pope Alexander VI, whom he cursed for "a devil" and "a monster" presiding over a "ribald" and "harlot" church.

In the political confusion following the death of Lorenzo the Magnificent (1492), Savonarola gained power and prestige in Florence, attracting many enthusiastic supporters, including Pico and the artists Botticelli and Michelangelo. By 1497, he was virtual dictator of the Florentine republic and organized troops of boys and girls to tour the city, collect all "vanities," from cosmetics to pagan books and paintings, and burn them on public bonfires. This hysterical pitch of zeal could not be sustained for long, and when Alexander VI placed Florence under an interdict and excommunicated Savonarola, his popular following began to disperse, especially after he had failed in his promise to bring a miracle to pass. Savonarola was condemned for heresy; on May 23, 1498, he was hanged and his body was burned. Savonarola perished not only at the hands of his political and ecclesiastical enemies but also through his own fanaticism. Like most extreme puritans, he did not realize that morals could not be transformed overnight; he was in a sense too unworldly to survive. But the church that he sought to purge was too worldly to survive without undergoing the major crisis of the Reformation.

V   The Fine Arts

Even more than the writers and preachers of the Renaissance its artists displayed an extraordinary range of interests and talents. They found patrons both among the princes of the church and among merchant princes, condottieri, and secular rulers. They took for subjects their own patrons and the pagan gods and heroes of antiquity as well as Christ, the Virgin, and saints. Although their income was often meager, they enjoyed increasing status both as technicians and as creative personalities; they boasted of their skills and attainments, for in the arts, too, the anonymous or community stamp of medieval culture was yielding to the ego-trip of the individual.

The artists liberated painting and sculpture from subordination to architecture, which had been the "queen of the arts" during the Middle Ages. The statues, carvings, altarpieces, and stained glass contributing so much to Romanesque and Gothic churches had seldom been entities in themselves but only parts of a larger whole. In the Renaissance the number of freestanding pictures and sculptures—each one an independent aesthetic object—steadily increased.

In painting important advances came with the development of *chiaroscuro* (Italian, "bright-dark"), stressing contrasts of light and shade, and with the growing use of perspective, both of which enhanced the three-dimensional quality of a picture. In the early Renaissance, painters worked in fresco or tempera: fresco involved the application of pigments to the wet plaster of a wall, and painters had to work swiftly before the plaster dried; in tempera they mixed pigments with a sizing, often of eggs, which allowed them to work after the plaster had dried but gave the end-product a muddy look. Oil paints, developed first in Flanders and brought to Italy in the last half of the fifteenth century, overcame the deficiencies of fresco and tempera by permitting leisurely, delicate work and ensuring clearer and more permanent colors.

The Flemish origin of oil paints serves as a reminder that modern scholarship has exploded the old idea that the artistic Renaissance was exclusively an Italian phenomenon existing in splendid isolation and impervious to influences from other quarters of Europe or from the preceding medieval centuries. An older Gothic strain persisted even in Italy, evident in Milan where throughout the Renaissance centuries much money and energy went into building the cathedral, a celebrated specimen of the Gothic "wedding-cake" style. Late Gothic artists, especially those in the Low Countries during the Burgundian ascendancy of the fourteenth and fifteenth centuries, contributed to the Renaissance not only by introducing oil paints but also by stressing decorative richness and an almost photographic realism in depicting the details of nature. Botanists can identify dozens of flowers and plants in the famous Ghent altarpiece (*The Adoration of the Lamb*) of the Van Eyck brothers, who worked in the early fifteenth century. The commercial links between Flemish and Italian cities promoted cultural interchange, and Italians were eager to buy paintings by the Van Eycks and other Flemish masters and also admired the tapes-

*P. Misciatelli, *Savonarola* (New York, 1930), pp. 60–61.

tries, the music, and the fashions of the opulent Burgundian court.

Yet, in spite of these qualifications diluting the unique Italian quality of Renaissance art, it is evident that without Giotto, Masaccio, Leonardo, Michelangelo and other Italian men of genius the Renaissance could never have become one of the very great ages in the history of art. In sculpture it rivaled the golden centuries of Greece, and in painting it was more than a rebirth, for it transformed a rather limited medium into a dazzling new aesthetic instrument. It is no wonder that historians in general often adopt the Italian custom of calling these centuries trecento, quattrocento, and cinquecento (literally, "300s," "400s," and "500s," in abbreviated reference to the 1300s, 1400s and 1500s).

Painting in Italy

Prior to the trecento, Italian artists were much influenced by the Byzantine tradition and produced two-dimensional paintings lacking in depth or movement. Giotto (1276–1337), the father, or perhaps grandfather, of Renaissance painting, though often following Byzantine models, sought to make his paintings less stiff and austere and more lifelike and emotional. He learned much from the realistic statues of Italian sculptors who had studied the striking sculptures on the portals of Gothic cathedrals such as Chartres. Perhaps the best place to view Giotto's achievement is the Arena Chapel at Padua, near Venice, where he executed a series of frescoes creating the illusion of three dimensions by his use of foreshortening and perspective. *Joachim and the Shepherds* shows the pious Joachim returning to his sheepfold after being excluded from the temple because his failure to beget children was taken as a sign that he was accursed by God. His entry from the left of the fresco heightens its drama as the viewer's eyes, in the left-to-right movement of reading, go from Joachim to his dog, with right paw raised in greeting, and then to the lively-looking sheep. Joachim seems downcast by his unjust exclusion, while the *chiaroscuro* on the folds of his cloak suggests the substantial body underneath. In the *Lamentation*, also in the Arena Chapel, the emotional intensity surrounding the burial of Christ is conveyed by the angels who seem to be beating their wings in anguish as they fly above the mourners.

As a person, Giotto exemplified the versatile Renaissance individual, hungry for fame and success. He was no anonymous craftsman, content to work in obscurity, and added to his income from lucrative art commissions by lending money, running a debt-collection service, and renting looms at high fees to weavers in the woolen trade. The richest man in Padua, Enrico Scrovegni, commissioned Giotto to decorate the Arena Chapel on behalf of the soul of his father, whom Dante's *Divine Comedy* placed in hell because he had been a notorious usurer. In Florence, the great banking families of Bardi and Peruzzi employed Giotto to execute frescoes in the Church of Santa Croce.

The example of the Bardi and Peruzzi was followed by many later rich Florentines whose patronage made their city the artistic capital of the Renaissance. Lorenzo the Magnificent, for example, subsidized the painter Botticelli (1445–1510) as well as the humanists of the Platonic Academy. Court painters were commonplace in other states, both in Italy and elsewhere. In Milan the Sforza usurper, Il Moro, made Leonardo da Vinci in effect his minister of fine arts and director of public works; after Il Moro's fortunes collapsed, Leonardo found new patrons in Cesare Borgia, the pope, and the French kings Louis XII and Francis I. The Renaissance popes, who also employed Botticelli, Raphael, Michelangelo, and other luminaries, had a keen aesthetic appreciation coupled with a determination to have Rome surpass Florence in artistic eminence.

The mixture of worldly and religious motives among patrons also characterized the works they commissioned. Artists applied equal skill to scenes from classical mythology, to portraits of their secular contemporaries, and to such Christian subjects as the Madonna, the Nativity, and the Crucifixion. Often the sacred and the secular could be found in the same picture. In the *Last Judgment,* in the Arena Chapel, Giotto portrayed Scrovegni, the donor, on the same scale as the saints, and in the Peruzzi Chapel he framed religious frescoes with medallions depicting the members of the endowing family. Giotto's successors sometimes brought the whole family of the donor into the picture, as in Botticelli's *Adoration of the Magi,* which shows Cosimo and Lorenzo de' Medici as well as the artist himself.

Renaissance artists at first made classical and pagan subjects like Jupiter or Venus just another lord and lady of the chivalric class. Later they restored the sense of historical appropriateness by using classical settings and painting the figures in the nude; at the same time, however, they also created an otherworldly quality. When Botticelli was commissioned by the Medici to do *The Birth of Venus,* he made the goddess, emerging full-grown from a seashell, more ethereal than sensual, and he placed the figures in the arrangement usual for the baptism of Christ. In *Primavera,* Botticelli's allegory of spring, the chief figures—Mercury, Venus, The Three Graces, Flora (bedecked with blossoms), and Spring herself (wafted in by the West Wind)—are all youthful, delicate, and serene, as if this were the Platonic idea of springtime. Botticelli seems to have moved in the circle of Pico della Mirandola and the Florentine Neoplatonists, and his paintings often suggest an aspiration to some mystic Platonic realm.

Botticelli used line and color to achieve artistic effects; in contrast, Masaccio (1401–1428), a talented Florentine of an earlier generation, relied on mass and perspective. In painting the *Expulsion from Eden* for a

Florentine chapel, Masaccio intensified the sense of tragedy by bold *chiaroscuro* treatment of the bodies of Adam and Eve, who appear to be overwhelmed by shame and sorrow. Masaccio, who was called "Giotto reborn," anticipated some of the achievements of the Italian "High Renaissance," the last decades of the quattrocento and the first five or six of the cinquecento. The High Renaissance is studded with so many important names—Raphael, Giorgione, Carpaccio, Tintoretto, Veronese—that we can only sample its brilliance by examining three of its leading masters, Leonardo, Michelangelo, and Titian.

Leonardo da Vinci (1452–1519) completed relatively few pictures, since his scientific activities and innumerable odd jobs for his patrons consumed much of his energy. In addition, his celebrated fresco, *The Last Supper,* began to deteriorate during his own lifetime because the mold on the damp monastery wall in Milan destroyed the clarity of the oil pigments he used. Luckily, Leonardo's talent and his extraordinary range of interests may also be studied in his drawings and notebooks. The drawings include preliminary sketches of paintings, fanciful war machines, and mere doodles along with remarkably realistic portrayals of human embryos and of deformed or suffering individuals. Leonardo combined a zeal for scientific precision with a taste for the grotesque that recalls the gargoyles of a Gothic cathedral.

From his intensive study of human anatomy Leonardo drew up rules for indicating the action of human muscles and for the proportions among the various parts of the human body. When he applied his own rules with the brush, he sought not only to render nature faithfully but also to show people in motion rather than in static repose. In *The Madonna of the Rocks,* the Virgin extends her left hand over the Christ child, who raises the fingers of his right hand in a gesture of blessing; the angel supports the child and points a finger toward the infant Saint John, whose hands are clasped in prayer. The arrangement of the four figures in a pyramid, the foreshortening of the arms, the careful painting of hair and clothing, and the details of plants and flowers in the background all reveal Leonardo's sense of geometry and passion for accuracy.

In composing the *Last Supper* Leonardo departed dramatically from previous interpretations, which depicted the solemn moment of the final communion, with the treachery of Judas suggested only by placing him in isolation from the others, who often looked, it has been observed, as though they were sitting for a group portrait. Leonardo divided the apostles into four groups of three men each around the central figure of Christ—an innovation that was most effective psychologically, even though it would have been physically impossible for the thirteen men to have eaten together at the small table depicted. Leonardo's second departure was to choose the tense moment when Jesus announced the coming betrayal and to place Judas

Self-portrait of Leonardo da Vinci.

among the apostles, relying on facial expression and bodily posture to convey the guilt of the one and the consternation of the others.

Michelangelo Buonarotti (1475–1564), though best known as a sculptor, ranks among the immortals of painting as a result of one prodigious achievement—the frescoes he executed for the Sistine Chapel in the Vatican. Pope Sixtus IV had built the chapel and his nephew, Pope Julius II (1503–1513), entrusted the commission of decorating its walls and ceiling to Michelangelo. He covered a huge area (54 by 134 feet) with 343 separate figures and spent four years working almost single-handed, assisted only by a plasterer and a color mixer, painting on his back atop a scaffold, sometimes not even descending for his night's rest and arguing with the impatient pope from his lofty perch. Michelangelo depicted the grandest scenes from the

Titian's portrait of his friend, Pietro Aretino (1492–1556), author of ribald satirical comedies.

in a mantle, an ever-changing patriarch: hovering over the waters, he is benign; giving life to the motionless Adam or directing Eve to arise, he is gently commanding; creating the sun and the moon, he is the formidable all-powerful deity. In this vast gallery of figures, nude and draped, Michelangelo summed up all that the Renaissance had learned about perspective, anatomy, and motion.

Both Michelangelo and Leonardo had received their artistic training in Florence; Titian (1477–1576) was identified with Venice, and the rich reds and purples that are his hallmark exemplify the flamboyance and pageantry of the city. Titian's longevity, productivity, and success were extraordinary. At the start, he was engaged to do frescoes for the Venetian headquarters of German merchants, and he went on to do portraits of rich merchants, provide *Madonna*s and altarpieces for churches and monasteries, and execute a battle scene for the palace of the doge. In the middle decades of the sixteenth century he was offered commissions by half the despots of Italy and crowned heads of Europe. A gallery of Titian's portraits makes a fine introduction to the high politics of the cinquecento—a condottiere, shrewd, cultivated and worn from the della Rovere family that had produced Sixtus IV and Julius II; Paul III, one of the last of the Renaissance popes, crafty, bent with age, and flanked by his grandsons, one watchful, the other buttering up the old man; and, finally, the emperor Charles V, burdened with all the problems of the vast Hapsburg domains.

Book of Genesis, which he placed in a sequence that reflected a Neoplatonic belief in the ascent from the fleshly to the sublime. He began over the chapel entrance with *The Drunkenness of Noah* and ended over the altar with *The Creation.* God appears repeatedly, draped

Dürer's self-portrait of 1500.

Painting in Northern Europe

In northern Europe the masters of the cinquecento were influenced by their native Gothic traditions as well as by Titian and other Italians. The ranking northern painters included two Germans, Dürer (1471–1528) and Holbein (1497–1543), and two from the Low Countries, Bosch (1462–1516) and Pieter Brueghel (1520–1569). Dürer received commissions from the emperor Maximilian (the grandfather of Charles V), and Brueghel from wealthy businessmen of Antwerp and Brussels. Holbein, who was armed with an introduction from Erasmus when he went to England, executed portraits of Henry VIII and his courtiers as well as a likeness of Erasmus that catches the humanist's wit and intelligence.

Dürer, who became identified with Lutheranism in his later years, created what has been termed the first great Protestant art, in which he simplified traditional Christian themes by pruning them of what Lutherans regarded as superfluous Catholic trimmings. But this was only one facet of Dürer's many-sided talent. His fascination with nature led him to include rather docile wild creatures in many pictures, notably the Virgin in the unusual pose of *The Madonna with Many Animals.* His realistic and compassionate portrait of his aged mother might almost have been taken from

Leonardo's notebooks. And his improvements in the techniques of woodcuts and engravings enabled him to mass-produce his own drawings as illustrations for printed books. Dürer was the first artist in history to become a bestseller.

Northern art retained the medieval fascination with the monstrous and supernatural. Dürer showed this Gothic strain in a series of woodcuts depicting the Four Horsemen and other grim marvels of the Apocalypse. Bosch, who reflected the piety and reforming spirit of the Brethren of the Common Life, made his paintings graphic sermons filled with nightmarish apparitions illustrating the omnipresence of sin and evil and foreshadowing the techniques and effects of the surrealists of our own century. Brueghel's works contain coats-of-arms that actually fight, shellfish that fly, and monstrous hybrids that have insect wings, artichoke bodies, and flower heads. Other paintings of Brueghel are realistic and sensitive comments on human misery, such as *The Blind Leading the Blind* with its file of wretches falling down. Brueghel also favored two types of painting otherwise neglected in the cinquecento. One was the landscape: his series illustrating farming activities through the year was somewhat in the tradition of late medieval books of hours but with new attention to the changing light and atmosphere of the seasons. The other was the densely populated scene of everyday life—children's games and peasant weddings, dances and festivals, depicted with Rabelaisian gusto yet suggesting that people are doomed to repeat endlessly the same simple pleasures and obvious follies. On the whole, northern art was more didactic, more concerned with moralizing, than its Italian counterpart.

Sculpture

In the Renaissance, sculpture and painting enjoyed a close organic relationship, and Italian pictures owed some of their three-dimensional quality to the artists' study of the sister discipline. Leading painters like Michelangelo and Leonardo were accomplished sculptors, the latter, for example, producing miniature anatomical horses stripped of their hides to show the bones and muscles. The first major Renaissance sculptor was Donatello (1386–1466), whose statue of the condottiere Gattamelata in Padua is a landmark in the history of art. The subject is secular, the treatment classical (Gattamelata looks like the commander of a Roman legion), and the medium bronze, not the stone of medieval sculpture. Donatello created the first statue of a nude male since antiquity, a bronze David who, however, looks more like a handsome youth than the inspired slayer of Goliath. Yet Donatello's wooden statue of Mary Magdalen, all lank hair and skin and bones, though criticized as "an emaciated monster," is a saint who really looks the part.

Still another gifted Florentine, Verrocchio (1435–1488), extended the concern for social and political realism. His *David* looks like a plebeian lad, and his statue of the condottiere Colleoni in Venice, mounted on a muscular horse, is tougher and rougher than Donatello's Gattamelata. Painter, goldsmith, teacher of Leonardo, and student of architecture, geometry, music, and philosophy, Verrocchio ranked among the universal men of the Renaissance. So did Cellini (1500–1571), goldsmith, engraver, devotee of high living, and author of a famous egotistical autobiography. Cellini boasted as patrons two popes as well as King

Pieter Brueghel the Elder's "The Blind Leading the Blind," 1563.

Brunelleschi's dome for the Cathedral in Florence.

Francis I of France and the Medici grand duke of Tuscany, the last of whom commissioned his elegant statue of Perseus holding aloft the head of Medusa, which today commands a place of honor overlooking a central square in Florence.

On the same piazza is a replica of Michelangelo's colossal statue of David, a ham-handed muscular nude more than sixteen feet high, fashioned from an enormous block of marble abandoned by another sculptor. Michelangelo went on to carry sculpture to a summit it had not attained since the age of Pericles, perhaps to the highest peak in its whole history. Michelangelo showed his ingenuity in solving technical problems with the world-famous *Pietà*, now in Saint Peter's, which shows the Virgin mourning the dead Christ. It was exceedingly difficult to pose a seated woman with a limp adult body across her lap, yet Michelangelo succeeded triumphantly. The face of Mary is sorrowful yet composed and younger than that of Christ, for Michelangelo explained that she is the eternal Virgin, always youthful, and would not grieve as an earthly mother would. In a statue of Moses, commissioned by Julius II for his tomb, Michelangelo made one side of the prophet's face show compassion and the other reveal the stern lawgiver, somewhat as he depicted the varying aspects of God on the Sistine ceiling.

Architecture

In 1546, at the age of seventy, Michelangelo agreed to become the chief architect of Saint Peter's in Rome.

Though he died long before the great basilica was completed in 1626, and though his successors altered many details of his plan, the huge dome, which was the key feature of the whole structure, followed his basic design. Saint Peter's exemplifies many of the features that distinguish Renaissance architecture from Gothic. Gothic cathedrals are topped by great spires and towers; Saint Peter's is crowned by Michelangelo's massive dome, which rises 435 feet above the floor below yet is almost dwarfed by the massive structure underneath. Gothic buildings, with their great windows, pointed arches, and high-flung vaults, create an impression of strain and instability; Saint Peter's appears indestructible because of its heavier walls, stout columns, and round arches.

Michelangelo modelled the dome on the one completed a century earlier by Brunelleschi (1377–1446) for the cathedral in Florence, itself a monumental achievement. Covering a space 350 feet wide by 300 high, beautifully proportioned, shaped more like a cup than a bowl and with greater stress on the vertical than the domes of antiquity, Brunelleschi's dome required 25,000 tons of stone, which were hoisted into place without immense scaffolding in a tour de force of engineering. It earned its designer a place as an architectural innovator comparable to that of Giotto in painting.

Renaissance architects shared the humanists' enthusiasm for Platonic and Pythagorean concepts of perfect ideas and perfect geometrical forms. Palladio (1518–1580), the leading architectural theorist of the *cinquecento,* stressed the symbolic value of designing churches on the plan of the Greek cross, which had four arms of equal length in contrast to the Latin cross used in Gothic churches, which had one long arm forming the nave. If the ends of the arms of the Greek cross were rounded and the spaces between the arms filled with rounded chapels, then the structure became a circle. Some scholars have interpreted the new popularity of the Greek-cross design as a shift from the medieval emphasis on the sacrifice of Christ to the Renaissance celebration of the perfection of God. Palladio himself designed many elegant structures—the much-photographed Church of San Giorgio Maggiore on an island at the mouth of the Grand Canal in Venice, and palaces, public buildings, villas, and a theater in the area of Vicenza, his home town, in the hinterland of Venice.

In Renaissance Europe private individuals had the wherewithal for lavish residences, and the increasing prevalence of law and order meant that a man's home no longer needed to be a fortress. Elaborately symmetrical villas dotted the Italian countryside, and in the cities the characteristic structure was the *palazzo,* not necessarily a ruler's palace but an imposing townhouse combining business offices and residential apartments; many examples survive today in Rome, Florence, Venice, and other Italian cities. The palazzo was generally three-storied and rectangular, with windows arranged in symmetrical rows and the monotony of regularity relieved by such devices as pillars, pilasters and cornices and by the use of different finishes of stone, rough or smooth, for different stories. The fame of Italian builders spread far afield, and in Moscow Italian experts supervised the remodeling of the Kremlin for Ivan III. Often the Italian style was combined with older native architecture to produce striking hybrid designs, such as the great châteaux built in the Loire valley of France during the sixteenth century, which combined elements from the feudal castle, the Gothic church, and the Italian palazzo.

VI The Art of Daily Living

Indoors, Renaissance buildings reflected the improving standard of life among the well-to-do. The small classical rooms were easier to heat than the vast drafty halls of the Middle Ages, and items of furniture began to multiply beyond the spartan medieval complement of built-in beds, benches, cupboards, and tables. Although chairs were still largely reserved for the master of the house and important guests, the variety of chests, benches, or stools on which people could perch was increasing. Chests, which were used not only for storage and sitting but also as trunks on a journey, were usually elaborately painted or carved, sometimes on the model of ancient sarcophagi—one more instance of the Renaissance passion for the classical. New articles of furniture served more specialized purposes: the bookcase to house the new printed books (medieval manuscripts had been kept in chests); the writing desk or bureau (a name derived from *burrus,* the red color of the felt used to protect its surface from the counters used in calculations); and the jewel cabinet, a miniature chest on high legs often encrusted with ivory or inlaid work.

The popularity of brooches, pendants, and other forms of jewelry with intricate gold settings attested both to the affluence and to the discriminating taste of Renaissance men and women. The fact that silversmiths made elaborately etched helmets, shields, and suits of armor better fitted for show than for military use was a sign of the vanishing medieval preoccupation with security. Along with gold and silver work fine glass was highly esteemed, particularly the elaborate and delicate work of Venetian craftsmen. Families in moderate circumstances as well as the rich had embroidered household linens and handsome brass and pewter utensils. One real luxury, however, was a mirror, small and made of polished metal, for mirror glass had not yet been perfected.

What the Italian man of the Renaissance saw when he looked into the mirror was a basic gown or tunic surmounted by a cape or cloak, the whole made of increasingly colorful and elegant material. Personal cleanliness advanced with the custom of the weekly bath and change of body linen; bodily wastes were disposed of in the outside privy or in a "close-stool"

Michelangelo's marble statue of David, 1501–1504.

Detail of Donatello's statue of Mary Magdalen, ca. 1454.

Palladio's Palazzo Chiericati, Vicenza.

(commode) indoors. In Italy table manners made a real breakthrough with the substitution of the fork for the fingers, the fading of the old habit of tossing bones and other debris from a meal onto the floor beneath the table, and the use of easily cleaned tiles or mosaics for flooring. Elsewhere progress was slower: in England the fork was not in common use until the seventeenth century (witness Henry VIII tackling a chicken with his bare hands), and the floor of the great hall in many a house was still covered with rushes, "sweetening the rushes" being the putting of a fresh layer of rushes on top and sprinkling fragrant herbs to counter the stench from the lower layers.

Castiglione's *Courtier*

The changing values and ideals of Renaissance men and women, living as they did in a world no longer medieval but not yet fully modern, may be studied in *The Courtier,* a dialogue on manners published by the Italian Castiglione in 1528. Castiglione knew his subject: himself an elegant aristocrat, he had spent years on diplomatic missions and at the highly civilized court of Urbino. He begins his delineation of the ideal courtier with a group of traits differing very little from those commended in the paladins of medieval chivalry:

> I will have this our Courtier to be a gentleman born and of a good house. For it is a great deal less dispraise for him that is not born a gentleman to fail in the acts of virtue than for a gentleman.
>
> I will have him by nature to have not only a wit and a comely shape of person and countenance, but also a certain grace . . . that shall make him at the first sight acceptable and loving unto who so beholdeth him.
>
> I judge the principal and true profession of a Courtier ought to be in feats of arms, the which above all I will have him to practise lively.*

The chivalry of Castiglione has all the patronizing attitude of the patrician toward the plebeian, yet it never gets out of hand; it is restrained by the sense of balance and grasp of reality that we have already found in some of the humanists. In love, the perfect gentleman should adore in his lady "no less the beauty of the mind than of the body." In duels and private quarrels, he

*Adapted from B. Castiglione, *The Courtier,* trans. T. Hoby, modernized (1907), pp. 21, 23, 26.

should be far more moderate than the medieval knight thought to be honorable. He should excel in sport, like the knight of old, should hunt, wrestle, swim, "play at tennis." He should also receive a good education

> . . . in those studies which they call Humanity, and . . . have not only the understanding of the Latin tongue, but also of the Greek, because of the many and sundry things that with great excellency are written in it. Let him much exercise himself in poets, and no less in orators and historiographers, and also in writing both rhyme and prose, and especially in this our vulgar tongue.*

Here in *The Courtier* we encounter once again the celebrated Renaissance concept of the universal man that we have already met in the writings of Pico and Rabelais.

Finally, when Castiglione praises the beauty of the universe (which is, of course, Ptolemaic, not Copernican), he puts into words more eloquently than any of his contemporaries the style of the Renaissance:

> Behold the state of this great engine of the world, which God created for the health and preservation of everything that was made: The heaven round beset with so many heavenly lights; and in the middle the Earth environed with the elements and upheld with the very weight of itself. . . . These things among themselves have such force by the

*Ibid., p. 70.

knitting together of an order so necessarily framed that, with altering them any one jot, they should all be loosed and the world would decay. They have also such beauty and comeliness that all the wits men have can not imagine a more beautiful matter.

> Think now of the shape of man, which may be called a little world, in whom every parcel of his body is seen to be necessarily framed by art and not by hap, and then the form altogether most beautiful. . . . Leave Nature, and come to art. . . . Pillars and great beams uphold high buildings and palaces, and yet are they no less pleasureful unto the eyes of the beholders than profitable to the buildings. . . . Besides other things, therefore, it giveth a great praise to the world in saying that it is beautiful. It is praised in saying the beautiful heaven, beautiful earth, beautiful sea, beautiful rivers, beautiful woods, trees, gardens, beautiful cities, beautiful churches, houses, armies. In conclusion, this comely and holy beauty is a wondrous setting out of everything. And it may be said that good and beautiful be after a sort one self thing. . . .*

A medieval man might also have coupled the good and the beautiful, but he would have stressed the good, the mysterious ways in which God led man to righteousness. Medieval man had a vision of God's world. The age of humanism, which Castiglione interpreted so faithfully, had a vision not only of God's world but also of nature's world and man's world.

*Ibid., pp. 348–349.

Reading Suggestions on the Renaissance
General Accounts
E. P. Cheyney, *The Dawn of a New Era, 1250–1453,* and M. P. Gilmore, *The World of Humanism, 1453–1517* (*Torchbooks). The first two volumes in an important series, The Rise of Modern Europe. Gilmore's is particularly informative on the topics considered in this chapter.

The New Cambridge Modern History. Vol. 1: *The Renaissance* (Cambridge Univ., 1957). Chapters by experts in many fields; uneven but useful for reference.

J. R. Major, *The Age of the Renaissance and Reformation* (*Lippincott), and E. F. Rice, Jr., *The Foundations of Early Modern Europe, 1460–1559* (*Norton). Up-to-date general introductions.

J. H. Plumb, *The Italian Renaissance* (*Torchbooks). Concise historical and cultural survey.

D. Hay, *The Renaissance in Its Historical Background* (*Cambridge Univ.). Valuable treatment of the topic by a British scholar.

G. Mattingly et al., *Renaissance Profiles* (*Torchbooks). Lively sketches of nine representative Italians, including Petrarch, Machiavelli, Leonardo, and Michelangelo.

Interpretations
J. Burckhardt, *The Civilization of the Renaissance in Italy,* 2 vols. (*Torchbooks). The classic statement of the view that the Renaissance was unique and revolutionary.

W. K. Ferguson, *The Renaissance in Historical Thought: Five Centuries of Interpretation* (Houghton, 1948). Valuable and stimulating

monograph. Ferguson has edited two useful collections of essays: *Renaissance Studies* (Univ. of Western Ontario, 1963) and *Facets of the Renaissance* (*Torchbooks).

D. Hay, ed., *The Renaissance Debate* (*Holt). Excerpts illustrating contrasting points of view.

F. Chabod, *Machiavelli and the Renaissance* (*Torchbooks). The chapter "The Concept of the Renaissance" is most suggestive.

L. Olschki, *The Genius of Italy* (Cornell Univ., 1954). Scholarly essays on many aspects of the Renaissance.

The Economy
The Cambridge Economic History of Europe. Vol. 2: *Trade and Industry in the Middle Ages;* Vol. 3: *Economic Organization and Policies in the Middle Ages* (Cambridge Univ., 1954, 1965). Advanced scholarly work and a mine of information.

F. C. Lane, *Venetian Ships and Shipping of the Renaissance* (Johns Hopkins Univ., 1934). Unusually interesting monograph.

A. W. O. von Martin, *Sociology of the Renaissance* (*Torchbooks). Instructive study of Italian society in the fourteenth and fifteenth centuries.

M. Beard, *A History of Business,* 2 vols. (*Ann Arbor). With thumbnail sketches of Renaissance millionaires (formerly entitled *A History of the Businessman*).

R. de Roover, *Rise and Decline of the Medici Bank, 1397–1494* (*Norton). Case history of the profits and pitfalls of Renaissance finance.

R. Ehrenberg, *Capital and Finance in the Renaissance: A Study of the Fuggers and Their Connections* (Harcourt, 1928). Another instructive case history.

Literature and Thought

P. O. Kristeller, *Renaissance Thought,* 2 vols. (*Torchbooks). Valuable study, stressing its diversity, by a ranking scholar.

E. Garin, *Italian Humanism* (Blackwell, 1965). Good scholarly survey.

R. Weiss, *The Spread of Italian Humanism* (Hutchinson's University Library, 1964). Lucid, brief introduction.

R. R. Bolgar, *The Classical Heritage and Its Beneficiaries from the Carolingian Age to the End of the Renaissance* (*Torchbooks). The last third of this scholarly study treats the Renaissance.

G. Highet, *The Classical Tradition: Greek and Roman Influences on Western Literature* (*Galaxy). Lively general survey.

M. P. Gilmore, *Humanists and Jurists* (Belknap-Harvard Univ., 1963). Six essays; especially instructive on Erasmus.

G. Holmes, *The Florentine Enlightenment, 1400–1450* (*Pegasus). Informative monograph on humanists obsessed with classicism.

N. A. Robb, *Neoplatonism of the Italian Renaissance* (Allen & Unwin, 1953). Good solid treatment of an intellectual common denominator of the age.

J. Huizinga, *Erasmus and the Age of the Reformation* (*Torchbooks). Excellent analysis by a distinguished Dutch scholar.

W. Kaiser, *Praisers of Folly* (Harvard Univ., 1963). Folly and fools in the writings of Erasmus, Rabelais, and Shakespeare.

Science

M. Boas, *The Scientific Renaissance, 1450–1630* (*Torchbooks). Helpful detailed account.

H. Butterfield, *The Origins of Modern Science, 1300–1800,* rev. ed. (*Free Press). A controversial interpretation, minimizing the scientific contribution of the Renaissance.

A. C. Crombie, *Medieval and Early Modern Science,* 2nd ed. (Harvard Univ., 1963). Volume 2 of this standard survey treats the Renaissance.

G. Sarton, *Six Wings: Men of Science in the Renaissance* (Indiana Univ., 1956), *The Appreciation of Ancient and Medieval Science during the Renaissance* (*A. S. Barnes), and *The History of Science and the New Humanism* (*Indiana Univ.). Clear studies by a pioneering historian of science.

L. Thorndike, *Science and Thought in the Fifteenth Century* (Columbia Univ., 1929). By a specialist on medieval science.

C. Singer et al., *A History of Technology* (Clarendon, 1954–1958). Volumes 2 and 3 relate to the Renaissance. Singer has also written *A Short History of Anatomy and Physiology* (*Dover).

A. Castiglioni, *A History of Medicine,* 2nd ed., rev. (Knopf, 1958). An excellent manual.

E. Garin, *Science and Civic Life in the Italian Renaissance* (*Anchor). A helpful scholarly survey.

Music

E. J. Dent, *Music of the Renaissance in Italy* (British Academy, 1954). Meaty lecture by a great authority.

G. Reese, *Music in the Renaissance* (Norton, 1954). Detailed study.

Religion

A. Hyma, *The Christian Renaissance* (Shoe String, 1965). Reprint of an older work stressing an aspect of the Renaissance often neglected.

R. Ridolfi, *Savonarola* (Knopf, 1959). Biography of the famous Florentine preacher-dictator.

Fine Arts

C. Gilbert, *History of Renaissance Art throughout Europe* (Abrams, 1973). Comprehensive and profusely illustrated introduction.

More detailed scholarly accounts may be found in various volumes of the "Pelican History of Art" (Penguin): J. White, *Art and Architecture in Italy, 1250–1400* (1966); L. Heydenreich and W. Lotz, *Architecture in Italy, 1400–1600* (1974); C. Seymour, *Sculpture in Italy, 1400–1500* (1966); S. J. Freedberg, *Painting in Italy, 1500–1600* (1971); and A. Blunt, *Art and Architecture in France, 1500–1700* (1953).

M. Levey, *The Early Renaissance* (*Penguin). Stressing the interrelations of art and civilization in general.

H. Wölfflin, *Classic Art: An Introduction to the Italian Renaissance,* 3rd ed. (*Phaidon). An older and still very useful interpretation.

F. Antal, *Florentine Painting and Its Social Background* (Kegan, Paul, 1948). Suggestive attempt to relate art to social and economic currents.

E. Panofsky, *Renaissance and Renascences in Western Art* (*Torchbooks); *Studies in Iconology: Humanistic Themes in the Renaissance* (*Torchbooks); *The Life and Art of Albrecht Dürer* (*Princeton Univ. Press). Stimulating studies by an eminent scholar.

K. M. Clark, *Leonardo da Vinci* (*Penguin). Lively and perceptive assessment of his art.

O. Benesch, *The Art of the Renaissance in Northern Europe* (Harvard Univ., 1945). Examines the interrelations of art, religion, and intellectual developments.

R. Wittkower, *Architectural Principles in the Age of Humanism* (*Norton). Important study of the links between humanism and design.

B. Lowry, *Renaissance Architecture* (*Braziller). Brief introduction.

Detroit Institute of Arts, *Decorative Arts of the Italian Renaissance* (Detroit, 1958). Informative illustrated catalogue of a comprehensive exhibition.

Sources and Fiction

J. B. Ross and M. M. McLaughlin, *The Portable Renaissance Reader* (*Viking).

W. L. Gundesheimer, ed., *The Italian Renaissance* (*Prentice-Hall). Selections from eleven representative writers, including Valla, Pico, Leonardo, and Castiglione.

E. Cassirer et al., *The Renaissance Philosophy of Man* (*Phoenix). Excerpts from Petrarch, Pico, Valla, and other humanists, with helpful commentary.

Erasmus, *The Praise of Folly* (*Princeton Univ.).

S. Putnam, ed., *The Portable Rabelais: Most of Gargantua and Pantagruel* (*Viking).

T. B. Costain, *The Moneyman* (Doubleday, 1947). Good novel about Jacques Coeur.

The Protestant Reformation

I Introduction

In October 1517, at Wittenberg in the German electorate of Saxony, the Augustinian monk Martin Luther drew up ninety-five theses for theological disputation, and thereby touched off the sequence of events that produced the Protestant Reformation. The long-accepted fact that Luther inscribed his theses on a large placard that he affixed to the door of the court church at Wittenberg on October 31 has recently been challenged as inaccurate.* The challenge has provoked a debate among scholars, the majority of whom apparently continue to regard the traditional account of the posting of the theses as authentic. Whatever the actual details may have been, they are in a sense unimportant, for the central historical fact remains that Luther's provocative theses were soon translated from Latin into German and were read and debated far beyond the local academic and religious community for which they had originally been intended.

The term "Protestant" dates from 1529, when a meeting of the Diet of the Holy Roman Empire at Speyer rescinded a grant of toleration to Lutherans it had made three years earlier. A minority of delegates—six Lutheran princes and fourteen Lutheran city delegates—thereupon lodged a formal "protest" with the Diet. In Europe the term "Reformed" is often used synonymously with "Protestant," and "Reformation" is the accepted word for the Protestant movement everywhere except in Catholic tradition, which refers to the Protestant "revolt." The difference is significant, because early Protestant leaders like Luther and Calvin did not conceive of themselves as rebels or initiators, beginning new churches, but as returning to the true old Church.

In fact, however, the Protestant leaders did prove to be revolutionaries. The Reformation not only created a major schism in the Church but also constituted a

*E. Iserloh, *The Theses Were Not Posted* (New York, 1968).

major social, economic, and intellectual revolution. In the Middle Ages the Catholic church had faced many reform movements—the Cluniac, the Cistercian, the Franciscan, and, in the century or so before Luther, movements like those of Wycliffe and Hus that anticipated Protestant doctrines and had almost ended by setting up separate or schismatic religious bodies. The Reformation came in a time when the authority of the pope was no longer automatically accepted but had been brought under open discussion by the Conciliar Movement, though the movement itself had failed to set general church councils above the pope.

More important, the Reformation came in a time when men were still groping to replace the old values and institutions being dissolved by the Renaissance. It came in a time of great religious ferment, of economic change, of violence, uncertainty, even a sense of doom—in a time well described by the phrase of the Dutch historian Huizinga as "the autumn of the Middle Ages." Men everywhere were seeking something, not usually specific political or economic reforms, but something less definite—spiritual salvation, renewal, the better world of Christian promise. Luther, notably, appealed from what he held to be existing evil to a good already in men's souls or at least potentially present in them. Hence the Lutheran appeal from *works*, the established conventions of religion, to *faith*, to something not evident to the outward eye but inside us all, if we could but see it.

Although Luther, when he drew up his theses, had no clear intention of setting up a separate religious body, he soon participated in organizing a church outside the Catholic communion. The Lutheran Church proved to be the first of many Protestant churches—Anglican, Calvinist, Anabaptist, and dozens more. By the middle of the sixteenth century the medieval unity of Catholic Christendom had given way to the multiplicity of "denominations" we know so well.

II Protestant Founders: Martin Luther

Luther's Spiritual Crisis

Martin Luther (1483–1546) was a professor of theology at the University of Wittenberg. In 1517, he was undergoing a great religious awakening, in effect a conversion, after a long period of spiritual despair. Luther's parents were of peasant stock; his father, authoritarian in discipline as medieval fathers seem to have been, became a miner and in time a prosperous investor in a mining enterprise. Very ambitious for his son, he was able to send him to the University of Erfurt, then the most prestigious in Germany, for the study of law as preparation for a professional career. The young man, however, yearned instead to enter the religious life and took the decisive step in 1505 as a result of a traumatic experience. On his way back to Erfurt he was terrified by a severe thunderstorm and prayed to the patron saint of miners—"Help, Saint Anne, I will become a monk!" ("I want to become a monk" is another translation.) Against his father's opposition, Luther joined the

Martin Luther, by Lucas Cranach the Elder.

Augustinian friars (or canons), an elite order both socially and intellectually.

While Luther's lifelong enthusiasm for music found satisfaction in the Augustinian devotion to psalm-singing, he underwent a prolonged and intense personal crisis. Luther was convinced that he was lost—literally lost, for as the psychoanalyst Erik Erikson points out in his *Young Man Luther,* modern depth psychology calls his predicament an identity crisis. None of Luther's good works, neither the monastic discipline of his order nor his pilgrimage in 1510 to Christian shrines in Rome, could free him of the gnawing feeling that he could not attain God's grace and was destined for the hell of lost souls. Finally, a wise confessor advised the desperate young man to study the Bible and to become a teacher of Scripture. Through his reading in the Epistles of Paul and the writings of Augustine, Luther gradually found a positive answer to his anxiety. The answer was that man should have faith in God, faith in the possibility of his own salvation. This answer had indeed long been the answer of the Roman church; what later separated Luther doctrinally from this church was his emphasis on faith alone, to the exclusion of works.

The Attack on Indulgences

Fortified by his intense conviction of the great importance of faith, Luther questioned Catholic practices that in his view were abuses and tended to corrupt or weaken faith. He cast his questions in the form of ninety-five theses, written in the manner of medieval Scholasticism as a challenge to academic debate. The specific abuse that the Ninety-five Theses sought to prove un-Christian was what Luther called the "sale" of indulgences, and in particular the activities of a talented ecclesiastical fundraiser, a Dominican named Tetzel. Tetzel was conducting a "drive" for voluntary contributions to help fill the treasury of a great institution that could not extend its taxing powers sufficiently to keep up with the rising costs of an era of inflation and luxurious living. Tetzel was raising money to rebuild Saint Peter's in Rome, and he had papal authorization for his campaign. One of the great German ecclesiastical princes also had a stake in the indulgences. This was Albert, brother of the elector of Brandenburg, who held two major sees, the archbishopric of Mainz and that of Magdeburg, and had paid a very large sum to the papacy for a dispensation permitting him to do so. In order to get the money, he had borrowed heavily from the Fuggers, and to repay them, he would use his share in the proceeds of the indulgences.

Indulgences made possible remission of the punishment for sins. Only God can forgive a sin, but the repentant sinner also has to undergo punishment on earth in the form of penance and after death in purgatory, where he atones by painful but temporary punishment for his sins and is prepared for heaven. Indulgences could not assure the forgiveness of sins, according to the theory advanced by the medieval Schoolmen, but they could remit penance and part or all of the punishment in purgatory. The Church claimed authority to grant such remission by drawing on the Treasury of Merit, a storehouse of surplus good works accumulated by the holy activities of Christ, the Virgin, and the saints. Only the priest could secure for a layman a draft, as it were, on this heavenly treasury. The use of the word *sale* in connection with indulgences became a form of Protestant propaganda; the Catholics insisted that an indulgence was not sold, that it was "granted" by the priest and any monetary contribution made by the recipient was a freewill offering.

The doctrine of indulgences was too complex for the ordinary layman to grasp completely. To the man in the street it must have looked as though a sinner could obtain forgiveness of sin as well as remission of punishment if only he secured enough indulgences. A man such as Tetzel, by making extravagant claims for the power of his indulgences, strengthened the popular feeling summed up in the saying, "The moment the money tinkles in the collection box, a soul flies out of purgatory." * In the Ninety-five Theses Luther vehemently objected to the whole procedure and the doctrine behind it:

23. If any remission of all penalties whatsoever can be granted to anyone, it can only be to those who are most perfect, in other words to very few.

24. It must therefore follow that the greater part of the people are deceived by that indiscriminate and high-sounding promise of freedom from penalty.†

At the theological level Luther's quarrel with his ecclesiastical superiors was over one of the oldest and most abiding tensions of Christian thought, the tension between faith and good works. Faith is inward and emotional belief, and good works are the outward demonstration of that belief expressed by the individual's good deeds, his partaking of the sacraments, and his submitting to the discipline of penance. Indulgences held out the promise that men might secure extra good works by drawing on those stored up in the Treasury of Merit. While Christian practice usually insists on the need for both faith and works, in times of crisis men tend to pursue one extreme or the other. In response to the Ninety-five Theses, the challenged papal party stiffened into a resistance that in turn drove the Lutherans into further resistance. Moreover, Luther's own increasing hostility to things-as-they-were in Germany drove him to emphasize things-as-they-ought-to-be. He was driven to minimize the use of works and, at his most excited moments, to deny their validity altogether. In the Ninety-five Theses he attacked not all works but only those, like indulgences, that he felt to be wrong. Yet in his theses he also made some very harsh state-

*O. Chadwick, *The Reformation* (Grand Rapids, Mich., 1965), p. 42.
†E. G. Rupp and B. Drewery, eds., *Martin Luther* (New York, 1970), p. 20.

The sixteenth century German Dominican monk Johann Tetzel riding on an ass selling indulgences.

ments about the pope, and soon thereafter, under pressure of combat, Luther rejected works entirely and declared that men are saved by faith alone. He went on to deny that priests are necessary intercessors and to affirm the priesthood of all true believers, "every man his own priest."

The Defiance of Papacy and the Empire

The Roman church was quickly alerted to the high importance of the issues that Luther had raised. Tetzel had aroused such indignation that he dared not appear in public, and the archbishop of Mainz complained to the pope of the disastrous financial implications. Pope Leo X (1513–1521), a Medici and the son of Lorenzo the Magnificent but possessing little of the family's intelligence or decisiveness, soon had to give up the pretense that the storm over the Ninety-five Theses was a tempest in a teapot. Accordingly, in 1518, at Augsburg, Luther was summoned before the papal legate, and general of the Dominican order, Cardinal Cajetan, and was directed to recant some of his propositions on indulgences; Luther quietly defied Cajetan. In 1519, at Leipzig, a learned theologian, John Eck, taxed Luther in debate with disobeying the authoritative findings of popes and church councils. Luther denied that popes and councils were necessarily authoritative and, carrying his revolt further, explicitly declared adherence to some of Hus's teachings that had been declared heretical by the Council of Constance a century earlier. In 1520, Luther brought his defiance to its highest pitch by publishing a pamphlet, *To the Christian Nobility of the German Nation on the Improvement of the Christian Estate,* which stated in part:

> It has been devised that the Pope, bishops, priests and monks are called the spiritual estate; princes, lords, artificers and peasants are the temporal estate. This is an artful lie and hypocritical device, but let no one be made afraid by it, and that for this reason: that all Christians are truly of the spiritual estate, and there is no difference among them, save of office alone. As St. Paul says (*I Corinthians* XII), we are all one body, though each member does its own work, to serve the others. This is because we have one baptism, one Gospel, one faith, and are all Christians alike. . . .*

Luther's adherence to justification by faith alone had led him to reject the central Catholic doctrine of works, that only the priest had the God-given power to secure for the layman remission of punishment for sin. In his appeal, *To the Christian Nobility,* he declared the priesthood of all believers by sweeping aside the distinction between clergy and laity. The complete break between the rebel and the Church was now at hand. Late in 1520, a papal bull condemned Luther's teachings, and Luther burned the bull; in January 1521, he was excommunicated; and in April 1521, after a most dramatic session of the imperial Diet at Worms, the emperor Charles V placed him under the ban of the empire, which made him an outlaw and was the civil consequence of excommunication. Shortly before the ban was imposed, Luther was asked in front of the Diet if he would recant. He replied:

> Since your serene Majesty and your lordships request a simple answer, I shall give it, with no strings and no catches. Unless I am convicted by the testimony of scripture or plain reason (for I believe neither in Pope nor councils alone, since . . . they have often erred and contradicted themselves), I am bound by the scriptures I have quoted, and my conscience is captive to the Word of God. I neither can nor will revoke anything, for it is neither safe nor honest to act against one's conscience. Amen†

The famous words credited to Luther at the very close of his statement—"Here I stand. I can do no other. God help me."—are not included in the earliest known document containing Luther's statement at Worms, but

they are entirely in harmony with what we are sure he actually said.

The empire and the papacy took their drastic actions in vain. Luther was already gathering a substantial following and becoming a national hero. He had the protection of the ruler of his own German state, the elector Frederick the Wise of Saxony (1463–1525), and was soon to secure the backing of other princes. Frederick arranged to "kidnap" the outlaw on his way back from Worms, and Luther vanished into seclusion at the castle of the Wartburg, where he began work on his celebrated translation of the Bible into vigorous and effective German. In the next year, Luther returned to Wittenberg and remodeled the church in Saxony.

The Reasons for Luther's Success

More than theology was at issue in Luther's revolt and its success. The Church that he attacked was, especially in Rome, under the influence of the half-pagan Renaissance, with its new wealth and new fashion of good living. The papacy, triumphant over the councils, had become embroiled in Italian politics. The Rome Luther visited as a young man, when the warlike Julius II was pope, presented a shocking spectacle of intrigue, ostentation, and corruption. One part of Luther's success was his attack on practices abhorrent to decent men; another part was his particular attack on the exploitation of Germans by Italians and by Tetzel and other Italianate Germans. In *To the Christian Nobility* he claimed:

> For Rome is the greatest thief and robber that has ever appeared on earth, or ever will. . . . Poor Germans that we are—we have been deceived! We were born to be masters, and we have been compelled to bow the head beneath the yoke of tyrants. . . . It is time the glorious Teutonic people should cease to be the puppet of the Roman pontiff.*

While the nationalistic and economic factors present in the Lutheran movement help explain its success, they do not wholly account for it. As always in human affairs, ideas and ideals worked together with material interests and powerful emotions such as patriotism to move the men of the Reformation. The princes who supported Luther stood to gain financially, not only by the cessation of the flow of German money to Italy, but by the confiscation of Catholic property, especially monastic lands, which was not needed for the new Lutheran cult. Luther gave them a new weapon in their eternal struggle against their feudal overlord, the emperor. The princes were also moved by Luther's German patriotism, and some, like Frederick the Wise of Saxony, sympathized with many of his ideas. Philip of Hesse, who had both an amorous disposition and a sensitive conscience, found Luther obliging enough to condone bigamy when he took a second wife without divorcing the first.

---

*Ibid., p. 43.
†Ibid., p. 60.

*H. S. Bettenson, ed., *Documents of the Christian Church* (New York, 1947), pp. 278–279.

It is true that what Luther started was soon taken out of his hands by princes who joined the reform movement to strengthen their political power and fill their treasuries. Yet Lutheranism without Luther is inconceivable. He wrote the pamphlets that did for this revolution what Tom Paine and the Declaration of Independence did for the American Revolution. Earlier, Luther had been dismayed when his Ninety-five Theses were translated into German without his authorization; now he deliberately wrote *To the Christian Nobility* in the vernacular to reach the largest possible number of readers. That his expectations were fulfilled is one more demonstration of the combined power of the vernacular and the printing press. Luther's defiance of the papal legate Cajetan, of the papal champion Eck, and of the pope himself were well known among Germans, deepening their nationalistic emotions. His marriage to a former nun and their rearing of a large family dramatized the break with Rome. His translation of the Scriptures and the hymns he composed—"Ein Feste Burg" (A Mighty Fortress), above all—became a part of German life and made Luther's language one of the bases of modern literary German. The power and intensity of his language may still be sensed over the centuries—as Erik Erikson relates in his *Young Man Luther:*

In my youth, as a wandering artist I stayed one night with a friend in a small village by the Upper Rhine. His father was a Protestant pastor; and in the morning, as the family sat down to breakfast, the old man said the Lord's Prayer in Luther's German. Never having "knowingly" heard it, I had the experience, as seldom before or after, of poetry fusing the esthetic and the moral: those who have once suddenly "heard" the Gettysburg Address will know what I mean.*

And back of all this was Luther's conviction that he was doing what he had to do.

Moreover, Luther's doctrine of justification by faith alone has been attractive to many religious dispositions, responding in a more general way to the same needs that the Brethren of the Common Life had tried to meet. Saint Paul at the very beginnings of Christianity set up the contrast between the Spirit—invisible, in a sense private to the believer—and the Letter—only too visible, only too public. Established churches have always tended to balance spirit and letter, invisible and visible, internal and external, faith and works. But to the ardent, crusading Christian even a successful balance of this sort seems a surrender to materialism: he will have none of this compromise, but will imperiously assert the primacy of the spirit. In Luther's day, the established Roman church had lost its medieval balance; the world was too much with it. The Lutheran felt the new church offered him something he could not get in the old.

A final reason for Luther's success applies to many other revolutionary movements as well: the relative

*E. H. Erikson, *Young Man Luther* (London, 1958), p. 10.

weakness of the forces opposing him. Religious opposition centered in the top levels of the Catholic bureaucracy; Pope Leo X did not so much head it as prove its willing instrument. But there were many moderate Catholics, anxious to compromise and avert a schism, both within the Church and on its margin among the humanist scholars, notably Erasmus. The great liberal Catholic historian, Lord Acton, later claimed that if the Catholic church had been headed by a pope willing to reform in order to conserve even Luther might have been reconciled. Luther's ablest associate, Melancthon, was a moderate and a humanist (his great uncle was John Reuchlin, the "hero" of *The Letters of Obscure Men*). Yet, once Luther had been excommunicated and outlawed and had gained powerful political backing, the way to compromise was probably blocked, for Luther's associates could have been won away from him only by concessions too great for a Catholic to make.

Politically, the opposition was centered in the youthful Charles V, who became the Holy Roman emperor in 1519. The combined inheritance of his Austrian Hapsburg father and his Spanish mother made Charles ruler not only of the German empire but also of Hungary, the Low Countries, Spain, Spanish America, and parts of Italy. On the map this looked like the nearest thing to a European superstate since the days of Charlemagne, and Charles wanted very much to make it such a state in reality. The activity of Luther's princely supporters in Germany threatened Charles' power there and might of itself have sufficed to turn him against Luther. But he was also a cautious, conventional Catholic and not ready to exert his great influence on the side of the moderate Catholics. Instead of seeking a compromise, he decided to fight the Lutherans.

But he did not lead the fight personally. Though Charles bore the Hapsburg name, there was little of the German about him: he spoke French, not German, and felt most at home in Ghent and Brussels in the Belgian lands of his Burgundian grandmother. In 1521 he entrusted the government of Germany to his younger brother, Ferdinand, who formed alliances with Bavaria and other Catholic German states to oppose the Lutheran states. Thus began a long series of alliances, the fruits of which were the religious wars of the next few generations, and the division of Germany into, roughly, a Protestant north and east and a Catholic south and west, which has endured to this day. In addition, Charles had too many other fights on his hands to concentrate on Germany. Spanish cities rose in revolt early in his reign, the Low Countries were chronically restless, and the Ottoman Turks, who annexed most of Hungary in the 1520s and then besieged Vienna, continued to threaten Charles' frontiers in central Europe and his lines of communication on the Mediterranean. Above all, Charles' huge inheritance encircled the only remaining great power on the Continent, France, which was already engaged with the Hapsburgs in a struggle for control of Italy. The struggle broadened into an

The emperor Charles V, by Titian.

intermittent general war between Charles V and the French king, Francis I (1515-1547), which outlasted both monarchs and prevented any sustained pressure on the German Protestants by imperial Hapsburg power.

The military arm of the Protestants was the League of Schmalkalden (named for the town where it was founded in 1531), linking cities and princes, with Philip of Hesse in the van. When Charles finally crushed the league with Spanish troops in 1547, his victory was short-lived because it threatened to upset the balance of power and alarmed both the papacy and the German princes, Catholic as well as Protestant. In 1555, in the twilight of his reign, Charles felt obliged to accept the Peace of Augsburg, a religious settlement negotiated by the German Diet.

The peace formally recognized the Lutherans as established in the German states where they held power at the time. Its guiding principle was expressed in the Latin "cuius regio eius religio" (he who rules establishes the religion), which meant in practice that, since the elector of Saxony was Lutheran, all his subjects should be too, whereas, since the ruler of Bavaria was Catholic, all Bavarians should be Catholic. No provision was made for Catholic minorities in Lutheran states, or Lutheran minorities in Catholic. The settlement also fell short of full toleration by failing to recognize any Protestants except Lutherans; the growing numbers of Calvinists and still more radical Protestants were bound to press for equal treatment in the future. More trouble was also bound to arise from the failure to deal with the question of "ecclesiastical reservation," that is, what disposition should be made of Church property in a German state headed by a prelate who had turned Protestant. Yet with all these deficiencies the Peace of Augsburg did make possible the permanent establishment of Protestantism on a peaceful basis in Germany.

A Conservative Revolutionary

While Luther was a great revolutionary, he was also in some respects a staunch conservative. For example, he did not push his doctrines of justification by faith and the priesthood of all believers to their logical extreme of anarchy. If religion is wholly a matter between man and his maker, an organized church is unnecessary. When radical reformers inspired by Luther attempted to apply these anarchical concepts to the churches of Saxony in the early 1520s, they created immense confusion and popular unrest, which resulted in riots and vandalism. Luther, who had no sympathy with such experiments, left his sanctuary in the Wartburg and returned to Wittenberg to drive out the radicals. He and his followers then organized a Saxon church that permitted its clergy to marry and put increased stress on sermons but that also possessed ordained clergymen, ritual, dogmas, even some sacraments—a whole apparatus of good works.

The Lutherans did not found their church as an alternative to the Roman Catholic but as the one true church. Where a Lutheran church was founded, a Catholic church ceased to be; the Lutherans commonly just took over the church building. Stimulated by Luther and his clerical and academic disciples, this process at first went on among the people of Germany without the intervention of political leaders. But very soon the lay rulers of certain states took a hand. In Saxony, Hesse, Brandenburg, Brunswick, and elsewhere in northern Germany, princes and their administrators superintended and hastened the process of converting the willing to Lutheranism and evicting the unwilling. Much excitement was caused in 1525 when the head of the Teutonic Knights, the crusading order controlling Prussia at the eastern corner of the Baltic, turned Lutheran, dissolved the order, and became the first duke of Prussia. Meantime, many of the free cities also opted for Lutheranism, usually not on the initiative of the municipal government but as a result of pressure from the guilds.

Still other social groups took the occasion of the Lutheran revolt to assert themselves. Just beneath the princes, lay and ecclesiastical, in the German social pyramid and like them a legacy of the Middle Ages were the knights, the lesser nobility. Some of them held a castle and a few square miles direct from the emperor, and were in theory as sovereign as the elector of a substantial state such as Saxony or Brandenburg; others were simply minor feudal lords. Many knights were younger sons, without land but nevertheless gentlemen, whose only career could be that of arms. The knightly class as a whole was losing power to the princes and was caught in the squeeze of rising prices and the need to maintain an aristocratic life style. Luther's challenge to the established order, and the opportunity it gave to take over ecclesiastical holdings, was too good a chance to be missed. The knights rose in 1522 and were eventually put down by the bigger lords, but only after a struggle.

The really bitter social conflict of the early German Reformation, however, was not this Knights' War but the Peasants' Rebellion of 1524-1525. In many ways it resembled the peasant revolts of the fourteenth century in England and France. It resisted attempts by money-hungry lords, lay and ecclesiastical, to increase manorial dues; it lacked coordination and effective military organization; it was cruelly put down by the possessing classes; and it was a rising, not of the most oppressed peasants, but of those who were beginning to enjoy some prosperity and who wanted more. In Germany the Peasants' Rebellion centered not in the east, where serfdom was most complete and the status of the peasant the lowest, but in the south and southwest, where the peasantry were beginning to emerge as free, landowning farmers. Yet in one very important respect this sixteenth-century German uprising looks more modern, more democratic, than its medieval counterparts in western Europe. Even more clearly than the English Peasants' Revolt, which had been influenced by Wycliffe and his followers, it was led by educated men who were not themselves peasants and who had a program, a set of revolutionary ideas of what the new social structure should be. Their leaders drew up a series of demands known as the Twelve Articles, which were couched in biblical language (thus showing their relation to the Reformation) and demanded that each parish have the right to choose its own priest, that the tithes paid to the clergy and the dues paid to the lord be reduced, and that the peasants be allowed to take wood and game from the forests.

Although the Twelve Articles were relatively moderate, Luther was horrified at what the peasants' leaders had found in the Bible he had translated into German so that they might read it. He burst into impassioned abuse that sounds even stronger than his abuse of the Catholics, writing a tract entitled *Against the Murdering Thieving Hordes of Peasants.* From this time on, Luther turned definitely to the princes, and the church he founded became itself an established church, respectful toward civil authority. He is quoted as saying: "The princes of the world are gods, the common people are Satan." In fairness to Luther, it may be pointed out that his conservatism in social, economic, and political matters was by no means inconsistent with his fundamental spiritual position. For if the visible, external world is really wholly subordinate to the invisible, spiritual world, the most one can hope for in the world of politics is that it be kept in as good order as possible,

so that the spiritual may thrive. Authority, custom, law, existing institutions combine to provide this orderliness. Kings and princes are better for this wretched world than democratically chosen representatives of the people; obedience is better than discussion.

Luther's conservative views brought him increasing support from kings and princes. By the mid-sixteenth century, Lutheranism had become the state religion in most of the principalities of northern Germany and in the kingdoms of Sweden and Denmark, together with the Danish dependencies of Norway and Iceland, and the Swedish province of Finland. The Scandinavian monarchs, in particular, appear to have been attracted to the Reformation for secular reasons, for the opportunity to curb unruly bishops and to confiscate monastic wealth. Because of this as well as Luther's increasing conservatism it is hardly surprising that the initiative in the Reformation was soon transferred from the Lutherans to other Protestant founders.

III Zwingli, Calvin, and Other Founders

Zwingli

Among the other founders of Protestantism the first in importance is Calvin, but the first in time was Ulrich Zwingli (1484–1531). Almost contemporaneously with Luther's spectacular revolt, Zwingli, a German, began in the Swiss city of Zurich a quieter reform that soon spread to Bern and Basel in Switzerland and to Augsburg and other south German cities. His movement produced no great single organized church, and when it was only a decade old its founder died in battle against the staunchly Catholic forest cantons of Switzerland. Zwingli's reform proved significant because it extended and deepened some of the fundamental theological and moral concepts of Protestantism, and had a wide influence on some of its less conservative and more austere forms. Zwingli was a scholarly humanist trained in the tradition of Erasmus. Like Luther, he sought to combat what seemed to him the perversion of primitive Christianity that endowed the consecrated priest with a miraculous power not shared by the laity. But, where the doctrine of the priesthood of the true believer drove the emotional Luther to the edge of anarchism, the humanistic Zwingli preached that individuals might achieve a community discipline that would promote righteous living. This discipline would arise from the social conscience of enlightened and emancipated people led by their pastors.

Zwingli believed in a personal God, powerful and real yet transcendental in the sense of being far above the petty world of sense experience. Because his God was not to be approached by mere sacraments, Zwingli was more hostile to sacraments than Luther was. He distrusted what many Protestants feel is the continuous Catholic appeal to "superstition," to belief in saints, and to the use of images, incense, and candles. In the

Ulrich Zwingli: a contemporary painting.

early 1520s, Zwingli began the process of abolishing the Catholic liturgy, making the sermon and a responsive reading the core of the service, and simplifying the church building into an undecorated hall, in which a simple communion table in the midst of the congregation replaced the elevated altar of the Catholics. He thus started on the way toward the puritanical simplicity of the later Calvinists.

A good example of Zwingli's attitude is his view of communion. The Catholic doctrine of transubstantiation holds that by the miraculous power of the priest the elements in the Eucharist, the bread and the wine, become in substance the body and blood of Christ, although their "accidents," their chemical makeup, remain those of bread and wine. Luther refused to eliminate the miraculous completely and, in an acrimonious meeting with Zwingli, insisted that Christ had meant himself to be taken literally when he offered bread to his disciples and said, "This is my body." In rejecting transubstantiation, Luther put forward a difficult doctrine called consubstantiation, which states that in communion the body and blood are mysteriously present in the bread and wine. Zwingli, however, went all the way to what is now the usual Protestant position, that partaking of the elements in communion commemorates Christ's last supper in a purely symbolic way. It is not sharing in a sacrament through a miracle, but simply sharing anew the memory of Christ's stay on earth.

John Calvin in 1534.

Calvin

In addition to German-speaking Zurich, Bern, and Basel, another Swiss city ripe for Protestant domination was French-speaking Geneva, where the citizens in 1536 won a ten-year struggle with their Catholic bishop, who was also their political ruler. A new religious and political regime developed there under the leadership of the French-born Jean Cauvin—John Calvin (1509–1564). Calvin shaped the Protestant movement as a faith and a way of life in a manner that gave it a European and not merely a German and Scandinavian basis. Particularly in early Protestant history, *Reformed* meant Calvinist as opposed to the more conservative Lutheran.

Calvin's career had many parallels with Luther's. Both men had ambitious fathers who had made their way up the economic and social ladder; the senior Calvin had risen from an artisan to perform clerical and legal services for the municipal and ecclesiastical authorities in a French town and had eventually gained the considerable distinction of admission to citizenship in the town. Both fathers gave their sons superior education; the young Calvin studied theology and, in deference to his father, law. Both young men experienced spiritual crises, Calvin's resulting in his conversion to Protestantism in his early twenties, though apparently with little of the storm and stress experienced by Luther. Both men took wives (as Zwingli did, too). In temperament, however, the two men differed markedly:

in contrast to the emotional, outgoing Luther, Calvin was a very private person, an intellectual, a humanist scholar much interested in Roman Stoic philosophy with its puritanical morality, an austere man, earnest, high-minded, very certain of his convictions and of his vocation in persuading others to accept them.

In 1536 Calvin published his *Institutes of the Christian Religion,* which laid the doctrinal foundation for a Protestantism that, like Zwingli's, broke completely with Catholic church organization and Catholic ritual. The very title, *Institutes,* suggested Justinian's code; and Calvin's system, reflecting his legal training, had a logical rigor and completeness that gave it great conviction. (Fuller discussion of Calvin's moral and theological ideas may be found in the next section of this chapter.) Also in 1536, while on a journey, Calvin happened to pass through Geneva and was invited to remain. There he organized his City of God and made Geneva a Protestant Rome, a magnet for Protestant refugees from many parts of Europe who received indoctrination in Calvin's faith and then returned, sometimes at the risk of their lives, to spread the word in their own countries. Within a generation or two, Calvinism had spread to Scotland, where it was led by a great preacher and organizer, John Knox; to England, whence it was brought to Plymouth in New England; to parts of the Rhineland; to the Low Countries, where it was to play a major role in the Dutch revolt against Spanish rule; and even to Bohemia, Hungary, and Poland.

In France, where concern over the worldliness of the Catholic church was very great, Calvin's ideas found ready acceptance. Soon there were organized Calvinist churches, especially in the southwest, called Huguenot (probably from the German *Eidgenossen*, "covenanted"). But France was a centralized monarchy, and King Francis I was not eager, as so many of the German princes were, to stir up trouble with Rome. In 1516, he had signed with the pope the Concordat of Bologna, which increased the royal authority over the Gallican church. In the mid-sixteenth century only a few intellectuals could conceive of the possibility of subjects of the same ruler professing and practicing differing religious faiths. In France, therefore, Protestantism had to fight not for toleration but to succeed Catholicism as the established faith. The attempt failed, but only after wars of religion lasting for a generation in the later 1500s, as the next chapter will show, and after Calvinism had left its mark on the French conscience.

Henry VIII

In England, by contrast, the established church became Protestant. The signal for the English Reformation was the desire of King Henry VIII (1509–1547) to put aside his wife, Catherine of Aragon, because she had not given him the male heir he felt that the recently arrived Tudor dynasty required. In 1529 Henry decided to rest his case on the grounds that Catherine had been married first to his deceased brother Arthur, and that marriage with the widow of a brother was against canon law. But Henry's case was hardly strengthened by the circumstance that he had taken twenty years to discover the existence of this impediment. Moreover, Catherine was the aunt of the emperor Charles V, whom the pope could scarcely risk offending by granting an annulment, the more so since Charles' troops had staged the terrible sack of Rome in 1527. Nevertheless, Henry pressed his case hard through his minister, Cardinal Wolsey, whom he finally dismissed in disgrace for his failure. In 1533 Henry married Anne Boleyn, whom he had made pregnant; Cranmer, the obliging archbishop of Canterbury recently appointed by Henry, pronounced the annulment of the marriage with Catherine. When the pope excommunicated Henry and declared the annulment invalid, Henry's answer was the Act of Supremacy (1534), which made the king supreme head of the church in England.

Much more than the private life of Henry VIII was involved in the English Reformation. Henry could not have secured the Act of Supremacy and other Protestant legislation from Parliament if there had not

Henry VIII and Catherine of Aragon.

been a considerable body of opinion favorable to the breach with Rome, particularly among the prosperous middle classes. Many English scholars were in touch with reformers on the Continent, and one of them, Tyndale, studied with Luther and published an English translation of the New Testament (1526). Antipapal sentiment, which was an aspect of English nationalism, had long existed; it had motivated the fourteenth-century statutes of Provisors and Praemunire, which limited the right of the pope to intervene in the affairs of the English church. Anticlericalism went back to the days of Wycliffe; in the days of Henry VIII it was aimed particularly at the monasteries, which were still wealthy landowners but had degenerated since their great medieval days. In the eyes of many Englishmen, the monasteries had outlived their purpose and needed to be reformed or abolished. Between 1535 and 1540 Henry VIII closed the monasteries and confiscated their property; the larger establishments were not directly suppressed but persuaded to "dissolve" voluntarily. During the 1540s the Crown sold much of the land, usually at a price twenty times its yearly income. The principal purchasers, aside from short-term speculators, were members of the rising merchant class, of the nobility, and, above all, of the country gentry or "squire-archy." The dissolution of the monasteries, by increasing the wealth of the landed gentry, amounted to a social and economic revolution; it contributed to the high rate of economic growth in Tudor England and also to the social dislocations accompanying that growth. It is another illustration of how closely the religious and the secular threads were interwoven in the Reformation.

Yet Henry VIII, though he must be numbered among the founders of Protestantism, did not really consider himself a Protestant. The Church of England set up by the Act of Supremacy was in his eyes—and remains today in the eyes of some of its communicants, the High Church Anglicans—a Catholic body. Henry hoped to retain Catholic doctrines and ritual, doing no more than abolish monasteries and deny the pope's position as head of the church in England. Inevitably, his policies aroused opposition, in part from Roman Catholic Englishmen who greatly resented the break with Rome, but still more from militant Protestants. Henry had hardly given the signal for the break with Rome when Low Church Anglicans began to introduce within the Church of England such Protestant practices as marriage of the clergy, use of English instead of Latin in the ritual, and abolition of auricular confession and the invocation of saints.

Henry used force against the Catholic opposition and executed some of its leaders, notably John Fisher, a cardinal and bishop of Rochester who had stoutly defended Catherine of Aragon, and Sir Thomas More, author of *Utopia,* who had succeeded Wolsey as chancellor. Henry tried to stem the Protestant tide by appealing to a willing Parliament, many members of which had already been enriched by the spoliation of the Catholic church. In 1539, Parliament passed the statute of the Six Articles, reaffirming transubstantiation, celibacy of the priesthood, confession, and other Catholic doctrines and ritual, and making their denial heresy. By this definition, there were far too many heretics to be repressed, for the patriotic Englishman was against Rome and all its works. England from now on was to be a great center of religious variation and experimentation, and the Anglican church, substantially more Protestant than Henry had intended, became a kind of central national core of precarious orthodoxy.

Anabaptists and Other Radicals

One major item is left to consider in this survey of Protestant origins. Socially and intellectually less "respectable" than the soon-established Lutheran and Anglican churches, or the sober Calvinists, was a whole group of radical sects, the left wing of the Protestant revolution. In the sixteenth century, most of them were known as Anabaptists, from the Greek for "baptizing again." Some of Zwingli's followers had come to hold that the Catholic sacrament of baptism of infants had no validity, since the infant was too young to "believe" or "understand." Here again Luther's doctrine of faith as a direct relation between the believer and God is involved—only for the Anabaptist it is a relation of rational understanding by the believer. Here also is a characteristic Protestant appeal to individual understanding or conscience, closer to the "right reason" of the Schoolmen than to the scientific or commonsensible reason that was to prevail in the eighteenth-century Enlightenment.

The Anabaptists at first baptized again when the believer could hold that he was voluntarily joining the company of the elect. Later generations were never baptized until they came of age, so the prefix *ana-* was dropped, and we have the Baptists of our time. The assumption that the beneficiaries of adult baptism were in effect "saved" could lead to exclusiveness and smugness, a kind of spiritual snobbery that brought accusations of self-righteousness against radical congregations.

Baptism, however, was but one of many issues separating the radicals from other Protestants. A modern scholar defines Anabaptists as those "who gathered and disciplined a 'true church' upon the apostolic pattern as they understood it." * The issue of what the primitive church had been like in the days of the apostles had been joined as early as 1521 when the extremists tried to impose their convictions on the church at Wittenberg during Luther's absence in the Wartburg. Anabaptist preaching of the need to reform both Church and society contributed to the demands put forward by the rebellious German peasants in 1524–1525 and also to the violence sometimes employed by the rebels and always used by those suppressing them.

*F. H. Littell, *The Anabaptist View of the Church* (Boston, 1958), p. xvii.

The Anabaptists split under the pressure of persecution and with the spread of private reading and interpretation of the Bible. For some Catholic observers, the proliferation of Protestant sects seems due inevitably to the Protestant practice of seeking in the Bible for an authority they refused to find in the established dogmas of Catholic authority. The Bible contains an extraordinary variety of religious experience from rigorous ritual to intense emotional commitment and mystical surrender. Especially the apocalyptic books of the Old Testament and the Revelation of Saint John the Divine of the New can be made to yield almost anything a lively imagination wants to find. Many of the leaders of these new sects were uneducated men with a sense of grievance against the established order, who were seeking to bring heaven to earth, quickly. They were in large part landowning farmers, miners, artisans yet felt themselves to be "have nots," almost proletarians, because they were pinched by inflation.

The most spectacular manifestation of extreme Anabaptism gave the conservatives and moderates as great a shock as had the German Peasants' Rebellion. In the mid-1530s, a group of Anabaptists led by John of Leiden, a Dutch tailor, got control of the city of Münster in northwest Germany, expelled its prince-bishop, and set up a biblical utopia. We know about them chiefly from their opponents, who surely exaggerated their doctrines and practices. Still, even allowing for the distortions of propaganda, it seems clear that the Anabaptists of Münster were behaving in ways contrary to Western traditions. For one thing, they preached, and apparently practiced, polygamy; John of Leiden was reported to have taken sixteen wives, one of whom he later decapitated in public when she displeased him. They pushed the Lutheran doctrine of justification by faith to its logical extreme in anarchism, or, in theological language, antinomianism, from the Greek "against law." Each man was to be his own law, or rather, to find God's universal law in his own conscience, not in written law and tradition. They did not believe in class distinctions or in the customary forms of private property. They were disturbers of an established order that was strong enough to put them down by force; their leaders were executed and the rank and file either slain or dispersed.

The great majority of Anabaptists were very far removed from the men of Münster. Many sought to bring the Christian life to earth in quieter and more constructive ways. They established communities where they lived as they thought the primitive Christians had lived, in brotherhood, working, sharing, and praying together. These communities bore many resemblances to monasteries, though their members had taken no vows and did not observe celibacy. This sober majority of Anabaptists, too, met violent persecution in the sixteenth century but survived thanks to the discipline and to the repeated Christian turning of the other cheek insisted upon by their gifted leader, Menno Simons, a Dutch ex-priest. Something of their spirit lives on today in such diverse groups as the Baptists, the Friends, the Hutterites of Canada, and the Mennonites and Amish among the "Pennsylvania Dutch."

Two other radical strains in Protestantism were the mystical and the Unitarian. The former was exemplified by one of the few aristocratic reformers, Caspar von Schwenkfeld, a former Teutonic Knight and a convert to Lutheranism, who believed that the true church was to be found not in any outward observances but solely in the inner spirit of the individual. His stress on the spiritual and the mystical and his antagonism toward formalistic religion contributed later to the development of German pietism in reaction to the established Lutheran church. Some of his eighteenth-century followers settled in eastern Pennsylvania, where there are still Schwenkfelder churches.

Unitarianism today is usually identified with rejection of the Trinity as an irrational concept and the view that Christ was simply an inspired human being. But this version of Unitarianism derives largely from the rationalistic Enlightenment of the eighteenth century; sixteenth-century Unitarianism was a very different matter and much more mystical in outlook. Its most famous advocate, the Spanish physician Servetus (1511–1553), believed that Christ was the Son of God yet at the same time denied the existence of the Trinity and its doctrine that Father and Son were coeternal. Thereby Servetus hoped to make it easier for humanity to acquire a mystic identification with Christ; he also hoped that it would be possible to reconcile the Jewish and Muslim traditions of Spain with the Christian. His teachings, and the uncompromising way he presented them, greatly alarmed many Protestants as well as Catholics; he was prosecuted for heresy at Geneva by Calvin himself and burned at the stake in 1553. Other Unitarian victims of persecution were the Socinians, named for the Italian theologian Fausto Sozzini (*Socinus* in Latin, 1539–1604), who preached in eastern Europe. The Socinians were mainly in Poland, Hungary, and Transylvania, areas where the weakness of central government and the power of local landlords had permitted Protestantism to make great inroads before the Catholic Counter-Reformation was launched.

IV Protestant Beliefs and Practices
Common Denominators

The most obvious characteristic of the Protestant churches, especially in their formative period, was the wide gap that separated one from another, Anglican from Calvinist, Lutheran from Anabaptist. Yet there were certain common beliefs and practices that linked all the Protestant sects and set them apart from Catholicism. The first of these common denominators was the Protestant repudiation of Rome's claim to be the one true faith. The difficulty here was that each Protestant sect initially considered itself to be the one true faith, the legitimate successor to Christ and his apostles. Some early Protestants were confident that their particular belief would eventually prevail through the slow process of education and conversion. Others, however, could not wait and, though they had once been persecuted themselves, did not hesitate to persecute in their turn when they rose to power; witness Calvin's condemnation of Servetus. The humanist Castellio (or Châteillon) attacked Calvin's action in a book on "whether heretics are to be persecuted" (1554), which asserted that coercion should not be used to change man's religious ideas. While many other humanists shared Castellio's opposition to enforced conformity with an established church, they expressed a minority opinion. In the sixteenth and seventeenth centuries relatively few Europeans accepted what we take for granted today: the separation of church and state and the peaceful coexistence of many creeds all tolerated by an impartial government. The doctrine of religious toleration would emerge into full prominence only with the eighteenth-century Enlightenment.

A second common denominator of Protestantism was the fact that all its churches, even the conservative Anglican and Lutheran, made certain reductions in organization, ritual, and other religious externals. All the sects relaxed the requirement of clerical celibacy and either banned or sharply curtailed monasticism. All reduced somewhat the seven sacraments; a general Protestant minimum was to retain baptism and communion. But theological justifications of these sacraments ranged widely, from Lutheran consubstantiation to the view of the Eucharist as purely symbolic. Veneration of saints, pilgrimages, and the use of rosaries and amulets disappeared among all Protestants; the more radical also banished musical instruments (if not singing), sculptures, paintings, and stained glass, indeed all the arts except the oratorical.

Beneath these outward signs Protestants were linked by the fact that they were all rebels in origin. They had almost always protested in the name of a purer, primitive church, maintaining that Rome was the wicked innovator. (This appeal of the rebel to the past in order to legitimatize his revolt often recurs in Western history.) The Protestants turned from a corrupt established order to seek refuge in a higher law; all of them had at least a tinge of Luther's recourse to individual judgment. This individualism is an important legacy of Protestantism to the modern world.

The Conservative Churches

The divergent beliefs and practices that separate the Protestant churches one from another may be arranged most conveniently in order of their theological distance from Catholicism, beginning with those nearest to it. The Church of England has managed to contain elements from almost the whole Protestant range, from High Churchmen all the way to extreme Low Church-

men who come close to being Unitarians. It permits its clergy to marry and, although it does have some religious orders today, it does not put anything like the Catholic emphasis on the regular clergy. Yet the Church of England does keep a modified form of the Catholic hierarchy, with archbishops and bishops, though without acknowledging the authority of the pope. Perhaps the central core of Anglicanism has been a tempered belief in hierarchy and authority from above, a tempered ritualism, and a tempered acceptance of this imperfect world—a moderate attitude not far from the outlook of Thomas Aquinas. Indeed, Richard Hooker, who wrote a great defense of the Anglican church in the 1590s (*The Laws of Ecclesiastical Polity*), relied heavily on Aquinas; he is usually called "the judicious Hooker" because of his efforts to reconcile divergent points of view.

But there has also been a strong puritanical current in the broad stream of Anglicanism and its American counterpart, Episcopalianism. Puritanism, which may be defined as a combination of plain living and high thinking with earnest evangelical piety, was an important variant of the Low Church attitude. While some Puritans reluctantly left the Anglican communion in the late sixteenth and early seventeenth century, many others remained within it.

The Church of England assumed its definitive form during the reign of Elizabeth I (1558–1603), daughter of Henry VIII and Anne Boleyn. The Thirty-nine Articles enacted by Parliament in 1563 were a kind of constitution for the church. The articles rejected the more obvious forms of Romanism—the use of Latin, auricular confession, clerical celibacy, the allegiance to the pope. They also affirmed the Protestant stand on one of the great symbolic issues of the day—the Eucharist—by giving both the bread and the wine to communicants, as the reformers had long demanded, in contrast to the Catholic custom of giving only the wafer. In interpreting the Lord's Supper the articles rejected both Catholic transubstantiation and Zwinglian symbolism and attempted to find a compromise somewhere in between. Finally, the Thirty-nine Articles sought very emphatically to void the anarchistic dangers implicit in the doctrines of justification by faith and the priesthood of the believer.

The Church of England has always seemed to its enemies, and even to some of its friends, a bit too acquiescent in the face of civil authority. In what was once a word of abuse, the Church of England has seemed Erastian, so called after Erastus, a sixteenth-century Swiss theologian and a disciple of Zwingli who objected to the theocratic practices of the Calvinists. To check abuses by the religious authorities Erastus wanted to increase the power of the political authorities. The term *Erastianism*, however, has come to imply that the state is all-powerful against the church and that the clergy should be simply a moral police force. While Anglicanism seldom went this far in practice, a touch of subservience to the political powers that be, a modified Erastianism, does remain in the Church of England, and we shall encounter it in the English civil and religious strife of the seventeenth century.

To outsiders the Lutheran church has appeared even more Erastian than the Anglican. As the state church in much of northern Germany and in Scandinavia, it was often a docile instrument of its political masters. And in its close association with the rise of Prussia, though Prussia's Hohenzollern rulers later became Calvinist, it was brought under the rule of the strongly bureaucratic Prussian state.

Luther, like so many others upon whom character and fate have thrust rebellion, was at heart a conservative about things of this world, as we have seen. He wanted the forms of Lutheran worship to recall the forms he was used to. Once it had become established, Lutheranism preserved many practices that seem Catholic in origin but that to Luther represented a return to early Christianity before the corruption by Rome. Lutheranism preserved the Eucharist, now interpreted by the doctrine of consubstantiation, and it also preserved bishops, gowns, and something of the plastic arts. The tradition of good music in the church was not only preserved but greatly fortified. The Lutheran church, however, had a strong evangelical party, the germ of the later pietist movement, as well as a conservative High Church party.

Calvinism

For Calvinists the main theological concern is not so much Luther's problem of faith against good works as the related problem of predestination against free will. The problem is an old one in Christianity, already evident in the fifth-century struggle over the heresy of Pelagius, who believed in human goodness and in complete free will, whereas his opponents stressed man's sinfulness and God's goodness. To the logical mind, the problem arises from the concept that God is all-powerful, all-good, all-knowing. If this is so, he must determine everything that happens, even willing that the sinner must sin. For if he did not so will, the individual would be doing something God did not want him to do, and God would not be all-powerful. There is a grave difficulty here: if God wills that the sinner sin, the sinner cannot help himself or be blamed for his sin. We seem to be at a dead end, where the individual can always claim, no matter what he does, that he is doing what God makes him do. We seem to have cut the ground from under individual moral responsibility, just as John of Leiden and his Antinomians did when they took several wives at once and argued that God must want them to, since they wanted to. The dilemma is clear. If the individual has free will to choose for himself between good and evil acts, to do what God does not want him to do, then it looks as though God is not all-powerful. If he has no such choice because his acts are subject to predestination, then it looks as though the individual were morally irresponsible.

At least to an outsider, it may seem that Christians solved the dilemma most frequently by embracing both horns at once—by holding that God determines every human act, and yet that human beings may do things God does not want them to do. Theologians do not of course put the matter this way. Most of their basic solutions preserve the moral responsibility of the individual by asserting the profound distance between God and man, a distance that the miracle—the grace—of faith alone can bridge. This means that for the individual to claim that whatever he does is what God wants him to do is to make the incredibly presumptuous claim that he knows God's will, that his petty human understanding is on a par with God's. The individual can never be certain that what he wants to do is what God wants him to do. Therefore he should look about him and see what signs he can, limited though his vision be, of God's intentions. These he will find in Christian tradition and Christian history. To be concrete: if the individual is tempted to commit adultery, he will not follow the Antinomian and say that God wants him to do so; he will follow Christian tradition and recognize the adulterous desire as an indication that he is being tempted to do wrong and that if he does it he will not be saved, but damned.

Calvin himself, though he would certainly not have put it this way, would have reached the same conclusion. But he was, as we have noted, a logician. Both his temperament and his environment led him to reject what he believed to be the Catholic emphasis on easy salvation by indulgences and the like. He put his own emphasis on the hard path of true salvation, on the majesty of God and the littleness of man. He evolved therefore an extreme form of the doctrine of predestination.

In Calvin's system, Adam's original sin was unforgivable. God, however, in his incomprehensible mercy, sent Jesus Christ to this earth and let him die on the cross to make salvation possible for some—but emphatically not all, nor by any means a majority—of Adam's progeny, stained though they were by original sin. Very few—in fact, only the elect—could attain this salvation, and that through no merit of their own, and certainly not on the wholesale scale the Roman Catholic church of the sixteenth century was claiming. The elect were saved only through God's free and infinite grace, by means of which they were given the strength to gain salvation. Grace is not like anything else that touches human life on earth. It is not of a piece with law, morals, philosophy, and other human ways of relating man to his environment—to hold that it is was to Calvin one of the errors of the Catholic church. But it is not wholly divorced from these earthly relations—to hold that it is the error of the Antinomian. The elect actually tend to behave in a certain way, an identifiable way, a way not wholly misrepresented if it is called puritanical.

Our modern world has exaggerated the gloom of Calvinist puritanism, and the spiritual pride and exclusiveness of its adherents. Yet where the Calvinists were in complete control of an area (as in sixteenth-century Geneva) or in partial control of larger areas (as in England, Scotland, the Netherlands, or puritan Massachusetts), they censored, forbade, banished, and punished. Particularly in Geneva, where all trace of the Roman hierarchy had vanished along with the prince-bishop, the local Catholic tradition of scrutinizing the morals of the populace continued on an intensive scale. Every week a consistory composed of pastors and of lay elders appointed by the city council met and passed judgment on all accused of improper behavior. Though the consistory sometimes failed to get its decisions enforced, its activities were tantamount to a Protestant inquisition. In their own minds the members of the Geneva consistory and other representatives of the puritan spiritual police were God's agents, doing God's work. These firm believers in the inability of human efforts to change anything were among the most ardent of workers toward getting men to change their behavior. To an amazing extent, they succeeded, and they helped make the Industrial Revolution and the modern world.

The note of Christianity the Calvinists most clearly emphasized is not so much asceticism or otherworldliness as austerity. The Calvinist did not seek to annihilate the senses but sought rather to select among worldly desires those that would further man's salvation, and to curb or suppress those that would not. This world is for most of us, the Calvinist believed, an antechamber to hell and eternal suffering; if you really feel this, you are not likely to be much amused. The Calvinist thought that human pleasures—music, dancing, gambling, fine clothes, drinking, playgoing, and fortune-telling, among others—were the kind of thing Satan liked. Although the Calvinist did not hold that all sexual intercourse is sinful, he believed firmly that the purpose God had in mind in providing sex was the continuation of the race, and not the sensuous pleasures of the participants. Those pleasures are all the more dangerous since they may lead to extramarital indulgence, which is a very great sin.

Calvinism also sounded very loudly the ethical note of Christianity. The Calvinist had a high moral code; he was always trying to live up to his code, and to see that other people did so too. Both inward and outward directions of this effort are important. The Calvinist certainly felt the "civil war in the breast," the struggle between what has become famous as the puritan conscience and the temptations of this world. This notion of a higher part of human consciousness that can and should censor and suppress the promptings of a lower part has left a firm imprint on the West. In its outgoing direction, this Calvinist ethical concern has taken many forms other than that of the total, police-enforced prohibition. The Calvinist also believed in persuasion; he made the sermon a central part of his worship. He believed in hellfire and in the moral uses of fear of hellfire, he believed in emotional conversion, and he was a good missionary, though not at his best among primitive peoples.

Calvinism appears in pure or diluted form in many sects, Presbyterian and Congregational in Britain, Reformed on the Continent; it influenced even the Anglicans and the Lutherans. Theologically, its main opponent is a system of ideas called Arminianism, from Jacob Arminius, a late-sixteenth-century Dutch divine. Arminianism may be classified among the freewill theologies, for Arminius held that election (and of course damnation) were conditional in God's mind—not absolute as Calvin had maintained—and that therefore what a man did on earth could change his ultimate fate. Generally, Arminianism was more tolerant of the easy ways of this world than Calvinism, less "puritanical," more Erastian. Though at first condemned by the Dutch Reformed Church, it later exerted a strong influence on other Protestant churches, notably the Baptist and the Methodist.

Calvinism can hardly be accused of being Erastian. Where it did become the established state church—in Geneva, in the England of the 1650s, in Massachusetts, for instance—the Calvinist church ran or tried to run the state. This theocracy was never fully realized, even in Geneva, where the city council refused to surrender all its prerogatives. Where Calvinism had to fight to exist, it preached and practiced an ardent denial of the omnipotence of the state over the individual. Later generations turned these affirmations of popular rights to the uses of their own struggles against kings—and churchmen. In this sense, Calvinism helped create modern democracy. Its basic original concepts are not, however, democratic, if democracy is based, as we think it is, on equalitarian principles and on a generally compassionate and hopeful view of human beings, a minimizing of the legacy of original sin. But Calvin might not recognize his twentieth-century children, for Calvinism today is no longer the vigorous, fundamentalist, fighting creed it was in the sixteenth century. Its churches almost everywhere take a kindlier view of human nature and human potential and have moderated their reforming zeal.

The Radicals

The radical Protestant sects were usually greatly influenced by Calvinist theology and Calvinist example. Their practices, however, varied widely: sometimes the congregation shouted and danced and sang hymns with great fervor; yet the Mennonites put great stress on silent prayer and meditation. Among the radicals, preaching was even more important than in other forms of Protestantism, and more emotionally charged with hopes of heaven and fears of hell. Many sects were vigorously chiliastic—that is, they expected an immediate Second Coming of Christ and the end of this world. Many were in aim, and among themselves in practice, economic equalitarians, communists of a sort. They did not share wealth, however, so much as the poverty that seemed to them, as it had seemed to Francis of Assisi, an essential part of the Christian way.

Almost all of them had some beliefs, some goals, that alarmed conventional men and women. Many refused to take oaths on grounds of conscience. Most distrusted the state, regarding it as a necessary instrument operated by sinners to punish other sinners, an institution from which true Christians should hold aloof. What is most striking about these sects is the extraordinary range of their ideals and behavior. Some of them really behaved as badly as their conservative enemies have charged. John of Leiden, crowned at Münster as "King David" with two golden jeweled crowns, one royal, one imperial, with his "Queen Diavara" and a whole harem in attendance, seems a mad parody of the Protestant appeal to the Bible. Yet most Anabaptists were shocked by what went on at Münster and were for the most part pious and earnest pacifist Christians, living simply and productively as do their modern successors, Baptists, Mennonites, and Quakers.

These left-wing sects often displayed a remarkable combination of pacifist principles and ardent combativeness (so long as the weapons were not ones to inflict bodily injury). These men were fighting to end fighting. Here is Jacob Hutter, who founded the Hutterite sect of Moravian Anabaptists, addressing the governor-general of Moravia, Ferdinand of Hapsburg, a good Catholic who was ruling the Germanies for his brother Charles V:

> Woe, woe! unto you, O ye Moravian rulers, who have sworn to that cruel tyrant and enemy of God's truth, Ferdinand, to drive away his pious and faithful servants. Woe! we say unto you, who fear that frail and mortal man more than the living, omnipotent, and eternal God, and chase from you, suddenly and inhumanly, the children of God, the afflicted widow, the desolate orphan, and scatter them abroad. . . . God, by the mouth of the prophet, proclaims that He will fearfully and terribly avenge the shedding of innocent blood, and will not pass by such as fear not to pollute and contaminate their hands therewith. Therefore, great slaughter, much misery and anguish, sorrow and adversity, yea, everlasting groaning, pain and torment are daily appointed you.*

Such men too were martyrs, and they were persecuted by more moderate reformers with a violence as firm and principled as that which Protestant tradition attributes to the Catholic Inquisition.

Not all sectarians of the left were as violently nonviolent as Hutter. An even stronger and more lasting note is that sounded by the English John Bunyan (1628–1688), whose *Pilgrim's Progress* has long been read far beyond the circles of the Baptist sect in which he was a lay preacher. This book is an allegory of life seen as a pilgrimage, which, while full of trials, is by no

*J. T. van Braght, *Martyrology*, 1:151–153, quoted in R. J. Smithson, *The Anabaptists* (London, 1935), pp. 69–71.

means a series of horrors and leads toward a happy end and the joys of Beulahland.

V The Catholic Reformation

The first Catholic response to the Protestant challenge was to stand pat and try to suppress the rebels; such was the papal policy toward Luther. Yet the religious ferment from which Protestantism emerged was originally a ferment within the Catholic church, to which many who remained Catholics had contributed. Erasmus and other Christian humanists greatly influenced the early stages of what has come to be called the Catholic Reformation. Particularly in Spain, as the next chapter will show, but spreading throughout the Catholic world, there was a revival of mysticism and of popular participation in religion.

The Catholic church rallied its spiritual and material forces and achieved a large measure of reform from within. By winning back areas in Germany, Bohemia, Hungary, and Poland, it established the territorial limits of Protestantism in the West substantially where they now are. This Catholic Reformation, which Protestants usually call the Counter-Reformation, was no mere negative defense but a positive spiritual renewal. Although it did not restore the medieval unity of Christendom, it did reinvigorate fundamental Catholic beliefs and practices.

They could not have been preserved, however, without the aid of the secular arm. Both the Catholic and the Protestant reformations were inseparably tied up with domestic and international politics, as the next chapter relates in detail. The powerful house of Hapsburg, both in its Spanish and its German branches, was the active head of political Catholicism in the next few generations. The French monarchs, though their support was often more political than religious, nonetheless helped to keep France in the Catholic ranks, and in the seventeenth century the French participated in a many-sided Catholic revival. In southern Germany and in Italy, the reigning princes were powerful influences behind the old religion.

In addition, following the precedent set by the Cluniacs, Cistercians, and mendicant orders of the Middle Ages, new orders of the regular clergy greatly aided the Catholic renewal. This reforming current was already gathering strength when the papacy was still in the lax hands of Leo X, Luther's opponent. During Leo's pontificate an earnest group formed at Rome the Oratory of Divine Love, dedicated to the deepening of spiritual experience through special services and religious exercises. In the 1520s, the Oratory inspired the foundation of the Theatines, an order aimed particularly at the education of the secular clergy. In the 1520s also a new branch of the Franciscans appeared, the Capuchins, to lead the order back to Francis' own ideals of poverty and preaching to the poor. During the next decade or so, half a dozen other new orders were established, among them the Ursuline nuns, pioneers in the education of girls.

The Jesuits and the Inquisition

The greatest of these clerical orders by far was the Society of Jesus, founded in 1540 by the Spaniard Ignatius Loyola (1491–1556). Loyola, who had been a soldier, turned to religion after receiving a painful wound in battle. From the first, the Jesuits were the soldiery of the Catholic church. Their leader bore the title of general, and a military discipline was laid down in Loyola's *Spiritual Exercises,* which set the rules for the order. The following extracts from the *Exercises* bring out the Jesuit emphasis on total obedience—*corpselike* was Loyola's adjective—together with the realistic Jesuit estimate of what can be expected of ordinary human beings. Note also the moderate Jesuit position on predestination, free will, and good works:

> 1. Always be ready to obey with mind and heart, setting aside all judgment of one's own, the true spouse of Jesus Christ, our holy mother, our infallible and orthodox mistress, the Catholic Church, whose authority is exercised over us by the hierarchy.

> 13. That we may be altogether of the same mind and in conformity with the Church herself, if she shall have defined anything to be black which to our eyes appears to be white, we ought in like manner to pronounce it to be black. For we must undoubtedly believe, that the Spirit of our Lord Jesus Christ, and the Spirit of the Orthodox Church His Spouse, by which Spirit we are governed and directed to Salvation, is the same. . . .

> 14. It must also be borne in mind, that although it be most true, that no one is saved but he that is predestinated, yet we must speak with circumspection concerning this matter, lest perchance, stressing too much the grace or predestination of God, we should seem to wish to shut out the force of free will and the merits of good works; or on the other hand, attributing to these latter more than belongs to them, we derogate meanwhile from the power of grace.*

Born in controversy, the Jesuits have always been a center of controversy. To their hostile critics, who have been numerous both within and without the Catholic church, the Jesuits have seemed unscrupulous soldiers of the pope, indulging in dirty fighting, and not just on the battlefield, if such tactics seemed likely to bring victory. They have been accused of preaching and practicing the doctrine that the end justifies the means and also of pursuing worldly power and success. Yet Jesuit devotion to Catholic tradition was too deep for them to make Machiavelli's mistake of underestimating the hold the moral decencies have on human beings. And the historical record leaves no doubt of Jesuit success in bolstering the spiritual as well as the material credit of Catholicism in the critical days of the sixteenth and seventeenth centuries. Jesuits were everywhere, in Hungary, in Poland, in England, in Holland, trying to win back lands and peoples from the Protestants. They were winning new lands and peoples on the expanding frontiers of the West, in India, in China, in Japan, in North America. They were martyrs,

*Bettenson, *Documents,* pp. 363, 364–365.

Ignatius Loyola: the only authentic portrait of the saint, by Coello.

preachers, teachers, social workers, counselors of statesmen, always disciplined, never lapsing into the kind of fleshly worldliness that had been the fate of other monastic orders. As realists, they particularly sought to influence the politically powerful and to mold the young men who would later become leaders. Their schools rapidly acquired great fame not only for the soundness of their Catholic doctrines but also for their humanistic classical teaching and their insistence on good manners and adequate food and exercise.

While the Society of Jesus was the chief new instrument of the Catholic Reformation, an old instrument of the Church was also employed—the Inquisition. This special ecclesiastical court in its papal form was started in the thirteenth century to put down the Albigensian heresy, and in its Spanish form was started in the fifteenth century to bolster the efforts of the new Spanish monarchy to force religious uniformity on its subjects. Both papal and Spanish inquisitions were medieval courts, which used medieval methods of torture, and both were employed against the Protestants in the sixteenth century.

Protestant tradition sometimes makes both the Inquisition and the Jesuits appear as the promoters of a widespread reign of terror. Certainly the Jesuits and their allies made full use of the many pressures and persuasions any highly organized society can bring to bear on nonconformists. And the Inquisition did perpetrate horrors against former Muslims in Spain and against Catholics-turned-Protestants in the Low Countries. But the Inquisition does not appear to have been a really major force in stemming the Protestant tide. It was most active in countries of southern Europe—Italy, Spain, Portugal—where Protestantism was never a real threat. And in the regions where the Catholic Reformation was most successful in winning back large numbers to the Roman faith—the Germanies, the Slavic and Magyar marches of the East—sheer persecution was not a decisive factor.

The Council of Trent

The Catholic Reformation was not a change of dogma, not a change of spiritual direction. If anything, revulsion against the Protestant tendency toward some form of the "priesthood of the believer" hardened Catholic doctrines into a firmer insistence on the miraculous power of the priesthood. Protestant variation promoted Catholic uniformity. Not even on indulgences did the Church yield; interpreted as a spiritual rather than a monetary transaction, indulgences were reaffirmed by the Council of Trent. The work of this council ties together the various measures of reform and illustrates clearly the fact that what the Catholic Reformation reformed was not doctrine but practice.

The council met in Trent, a small city in the Alpine borderlands of Austria and Italy, in 1545 at the call of Paul III (1534–1549), the first of a line of reforming popes. A member of the ambitious Farnese family, Paul

was in many respects a secular Renaissance figure, but he also realized that reform of the Church was overdue and made it imperative to run the risk of convoking another general council. To liberals—including liberal Catholics—the Council of Trent has seemed no true general council, but an instrument in the hands of the popes and the Jesuits, a mere rubber stamp. Certainly in conception it was meant to provide at least a chance for reconciliation with the Protestants. Leading figures in the more conservative Protestant groups were invited but did not attend. The French clergy, with the Gallican suspicion of papal power, did not cooperate freely, and part of the work of the Council of Trent was not accepted in France for some fifty years. The council was caught in the web of the religious wars and intrigues of high politics, and its work was several times interrupted. Nevertheless it continued to meet off and on for twenty years until it completed its work of reaffirming and codifying doctrine in 1564.

On matters of doctrine, the Council of Trent took a stand that ruled out all possibility of a compromise with the Protestants on the major issues separating them from Catholics. It reaffirmed the essential role of the priesthood, reaffirmed all seven sacraments, reaffirmed the great importance of both faith and works, reaffirmed that both the Scriptures and the spokesmen of the Church were authorities on theology. The uncompromisingly traditional stand taken by the council

A session of the Council of Trent, 1555.

is evident in the *Professio fidei Tridentina* (the Trent Profession of Faith), which for long was subscribed to by converts to Catholicism. It runs in part:

> I most firmly acknowledge and embrace the Apostolical and ecclesiastical traditions and other observances and constitutions of the same Church. I acknowledge the sacred Scripture according to that sense which Holy Mother Church has held and holds, to whom it belongs to decide upon the true sense and interpretation of the holy Scriptures, nor will I ever receive and interpret the Scriptures except according to the unanimous consent of the Fathers. . . .
>
> I profess likewise that true God is offered in the Mass, a proper and propiatory sacrifice for the living and the dead, and that in the most Holy Eucharist there are truly, really and substantially the body and the blood, together with the soul and divinity of our Lord Jesus Christ, and that a conversion is made of the whole substance of bread into his body and of the whole substance of wine into his blood, which conversion the Catholic Church calls transubstantiation.*

The Council of Trent and the reforming popes of the later sixteenth century effected in Catholic practice the kind of change that had been achieved under Cluniac auspices five hundred years earlier. The council insisted on the strict observance of clerical vows and on the ending of such abuses as the sale of church offices and the nonresidence of prelates. It called for the establishment of seminaries to give priests better training. To promote discipline among the laity, it imposed censorship on a large scale, issuing the *Index,* a list of books that Catholics were not to read because of the peril to their faith, including the works of such anticlericals as Machiavelli and Boccaccio in addition to the writings of heretics and Protestants.

Under Pius V, pope from 1566 to 1572, a standard catechism, breviary, and missal were drawn up to embody for purposes of instruction the codifying work of the Council of Trent. In short, the whole structure of the Church, both for the training of the priesthood and for the training of the layman, was tightened and given a new spirit. The papal court was no longer just another Italian Renaissance court. It is true that, especially among the upper clergy and in the monasteries, laxity had again crept in by the eighteenth century. That same century witnessed the spread of excessive rationalism, especially among the teaching clergy in France, Italy, and in the Hapsburg domains. But the widespread corruption against which Luther and his fellows inveighed never again prevailed in the West.

The strength of the Catholic Reformation is shown by the fact that, once it was well launched, the Protestants made few further territorial inroads. Within a century of Luther's revolt, the broad lines of the territorial division in the West between areas dominantly

Catholic and areas dominantly Protestant were established much as they are today. England, Scotland, Holland, northern and eastern Germany (with a southward projection in Württemberg and Switzerland), and Scandinavia were predominantly Protestant. Ireland, Belgium, France, southern Germany (with a northern projection in the valley of the Rhine), the Hapsburg lands, Poland, Italy, and the Iberian peninsula were predominantly Catholic. But except for the last two, only predominantly. There were Catholic minorities in England, Scotland, and Holland, and the two faiths interpenetrated most confusedly in a greatly divided Germany; there were Protestant minorities in Ireland, France, and even in some of the Hapsburg lands, notably Hungary, the Jesuits had won back.

VI Conclusion: Protestantism and Progress
How Modern Was Protestantism?

The Reformation has often been interpreted, especially by Protestants, as something peculiarly modern, forward-looking, and democratic, as distinguished from the stagnant and class-conscious Middle Ages. This view seems to gain support from the fact that those parts of the West that in the last three centuries have been most prosperous, that have worked out democratic government most successfully, and that have made the most striking contributions to science, technology, and culture were predominantly Protestant. Moreover, the states that, since the decline of Spain after 1600, have risen to a preponderance of power and prestige in the West—France, the British Empire, Germany, and the United States—have been with one exception predominantly Protestant. And the exception, France, has had since the eighteenth century a strong element that, though not in the main Protestant, is strongly anticlerical. It looks as if the nations that went Protestant also went modern and progressive.

The contention that Protestantism is a cause or at least an accompaniment of political and cultural leadership in the modern West needs to be examined carefully. It has what modern philosophers have called "the truth of the myth," that is, many Protestants and secularists in these prosperous countries have long believed that Protestantism was a major part of what made them thrive. To the average Victorian Englishman, for instance, at the height of British power and wealth, the fact that his country had gone Protestant in the sixteenth century was at least as important as Magna Carta—and the existence of good deposits of coal and iron—in producing the prosperous England of which he was so proud. The historian must record the acceptance of the myth; he must also attempt to go back to the events that were used to construct the myth.

We find that Protestantism in the sixteenth century looks in many ways quite different from Protestantism seen from the nineteenth and twentieth centuries, just

*Ibid., pp. 374–375.

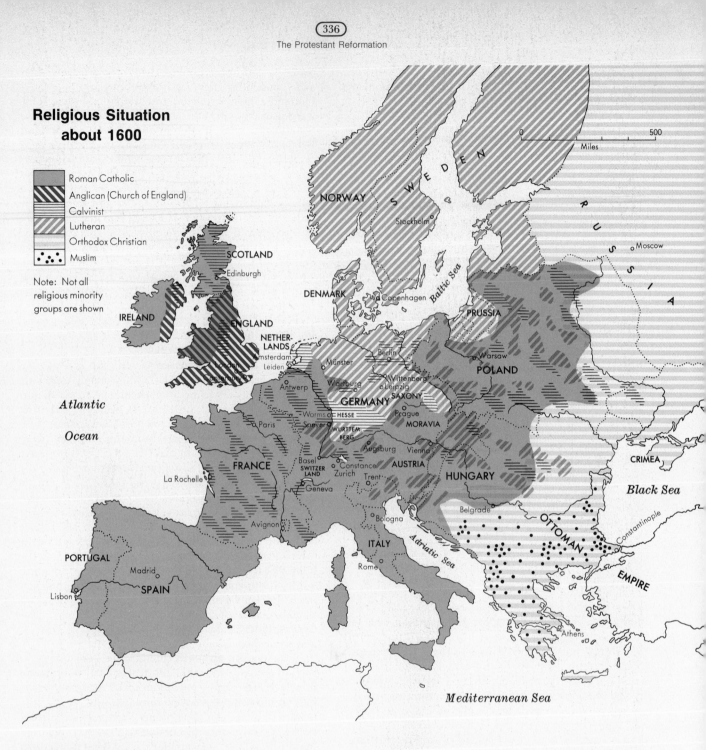

Religious Situation about 1600

Roman Catholic
Anglican (Church of England)
Calvinist
Lutheran
Orthodox Christian
Muslim

Note: Not all religious minority groups are shown

as Magna Carta in the thirteenth century looks quite different from Magna Carta viewed from the twentieth. First, sixteenth-century Protestants were not rationalists; they were almost as "superstitious" as the Catholics. Luther threw his ink bottle at the devil, or so they tell the tourists at the castle of the Wartburg where they point out the dark patch on the wall where the bottle struck; the Calvinists burned witches, or at any rate hanged them. To put the matter more positively, the Protestants for the most part shared with their Catholic opponents very fundamental Christian conceptions of

original sin, the direct divine governance of the universe, the reality of heaven and hell, and—most important—they did not have, any more than the Catholics did, a general conception of life on this earth as capable of progressing toward a better life for future generations.

Second, the early Protestants were by no means tolerant, by no means believers in the separation of church and state. When they were in a position to do so, they used governmental power to prevent public worship in any form other than their own. Many of

The Renaissance

Donatello's statue and the four following color plates may suggest the extraordinary range and innovativeness of Renaissance art. Although three of the works illustrate traditional religious subjects, all three break with medieval artistic conventions in their treatment. Donatello's John the Baptist can function as a freestanding work rather than as a small part of a larger architectural ensemble, which had been characteristic of medieval sculpture. Giotto's *Lamentation* and Michelangelo's *David and Goliath,* while they are units in a whole series of paintings, show how Renaissance artists applied new techniques to heighten dramatic effect—*chiaroscuro* in the case of Giotto, and oil paints in that of Michelangelo.

Leonardo's portrait of Ginevra de' Benci marks a still greater departure from earlier artistic norms: the subject is secular, and both the lady's hair and the foliage of the background are painted with the meticulous care of a great scientist. Finally, the hardworking peasants in Brueghel's *Harvesters* show that the commissions of Renaissance artists were not limited to grand biblical themes or to the glorification of well-to-do patrons.

Saint John the Baptist, by Donatello.
European Art Color, Peter Adelberg, N.Y.C.

The Lamentation, by Giotto: detail.
Scrovegni Chapel, Padua. Scala.

Ginevra de' Benci, by Leonardo da Vinci.
National Gallery of Art, Washington. The Granger Collection.

Pendentive, west wall, the Sistine Chapel: David and Goliath, by Michelangelo.

The Harvesters, by Pieter Brueghel the Elder: detail.
The Metropolitan Museum of Art, Rogers Fund, 1919.

The Seventeenth Century

In contrast to Donatello's John the Baptist, whose saintly quality is emphasized by his emaciated body and crude garments, Bernini's St. Sebastian is a martyr in his physical prime. Fashioned when the sculptor was still in his teens and influenced by Michelangelo, it is a rather mild example of the melodramatic qualities that earned seventeenth-century art the label of *baroque,* a word derived from the term for a large irregular pearl. The exaggerations of baroque art have led some critics to compare it unfavorably with the classical restraint of Renaissance art, citing particularly some of Bernini's later sculptures and the two extravagant constructions—the baldachin and "St. Peter's chair"—that he designed for the interior of St. Peter's in Rome.

Yet Bernini himself continued the Renaissance tradition of versatility in a distinguished career as sculptor, architect, and urban planner. And, as the paintings in the two succeeding plates show, baroque masters could be as subtle as their Renaissance predecessors. Velásquez, the court painter of the Spanish Hapsburgs, made the princess Maria Theresa (the future queen of Louis XIV) look reasonably regal without concealing her ugly thick Hapsburg lips. The Dutch Rembrandt, who shared his countrymen's fascination with light, imparted a golden glow to many of his paintings including the portrait of his son.

Saint Sebastian, by Gianlorenzo Bernini.
European Art Color, Peter Adelberg, N.Y.C.

The Infanta Maria Theresa, by Diego Velásquez.
The Metropolitan Museum of Art, the Jules S. Bache Collection, 1949.

The Artist's Son, Titus, by Rembrandt.
The Metropolitan Museum of Art, bequest of Benjamin Altman, 1913.

them persecuted those who disagreed with them, both Protestants of other sects and Catholics—that is, they banished them or imprisoned them or even killed them.

Third, the early Protestants were hardly democratic, at least in the sense that the word has for twentieth-century Americans. Logically, the Protestant appeal from the authority of the pope backed by Catholic tradition to the conscience of the individual believer fits in with such notions as "individualism," "rights of man," and "liberty." Some historians have even found a correlation between the Protestant appeal to the authority of the Bible and the later American appeal to the authority of a written constitution. But most of the early Protestant reformers certainly did not hold that all men are created equal; rather, they believed in an order of rank, in a society of status. Lutheranism and Anglicanism were clearly conservative in their political and social doctrines. Calvinism can be made to look very undemocratic indeed if we concentrate on its conception of an elect few chosen by God for salvation and an unregenerate majority condemned to eternal damnation. And in its early years in Geneva and in New England, Calvinism came close to being a theocracy, an authoritarian rule of the "saints."

In the long run, however, Calvinism favored the domination of a fairly numerous and prosperous middle class. As we shall see shortly, the most persuasive argument for a causal relation between Protestantism and modern Western democratic life does not proceed directly from the ideas of the early Protestants about men in society, but from the way Protestant moral ideals fitted in with the strengthening of a commercial and industrial middle class. Finally, among the Anabaptists and other radical sects, we do find even in the sixteenth century demands for political, social, and economic equality. But where these demands are made, they are cast in biblical language and rest on concepts of direct divine intervention quite strange to us. Moreover, many of these sects tended not so much toward active social revolt to improve earthly standards of living as toward a peculiarly Protestant form of withdrawal from things of this earth, toward pacifism, mysticism, and a spiritual exclusiveness quite compatible with leaving the unregenerate majority in possession of this unworthy physical world.

The Protestant Reformation, then, did not create modern society single-handedly. But it did challenge those in authority in many parts of Europe and did start all sorts of men, some of them in humble circumstances, thinking about fundamental problems of life in this world as well as in the next. Its educators and propagandists, using the new weapon of the printing press, began the drive toward universal literacy. It was one of the great destroyers of the medieval synthesis. Its most important positive action can best be traced through its part in forming the way of life of the middle classes who were to lay the foundations of modern Western democracy.

The Weber Thesis

The German sociologist Max Weber explored this question in *The Protestant Ethic and the Spirit of Capitalism*, first published in 1904. The thesis that he advanced has aroused a storm of controversy, in part because he touched on the sensitive area of religion and in part because a mere sociologist dared to invade the sensitive province of the historian. Though many historians nowadays reject his conclusions, the Weber thesis remains a stimulating and suggestive contribution to the ventilation of an issue that can never be fully resolved.

What started Weber's exploration was evidence suggesting that in his own day German Protestants had a proportionately greater interest in the world of business, and German Catholics a proportionately smaller interest, than their ratio in the German population would lead one to expect. Why was this so? Weber's answer—his celebrated thesis—may be summarized as follows. The accumulation of capital requires some abstention from immediate consumption; the entrepreneur, if he is a true capitalist, must plow some of his profits back into his enterprise so that he produces still more and makes higher profits, with a higher potential for future capital. To achieve this a businessman must not only curb his expenditures but also work very hard; he must spend the bulk of his time making money.

Weber argued that Protestantism, especially in its Calvinist form, encouraged this sort of life. It encouraged hard work because, as the maxim put it, "The devil lies in wait for idle hands." Work keeps a man from temptation to run after women, or play silly games, or drink, or do many other things unpleasing to the Calvinist God. More, work is positively a good thing, a kind of tribute we pay to the Lord. Luther, too, glorified work of all kinds and preached the doctrine of the dignity of the vocation a man is called to, be it ever so humble. In almost all forms of Protestantism we find this feeling, so contrary to the contempt for work of the field and countinghouse evident in the tradition of chivalry.

So much for work, the positive side of the equation. But on the negative side, Protestantism, and in particular Calvinism, discouraged many kinds of consumption that took energies away from the large-scale production that is the essence of the modern economic system. The Calvinist, to put it mildly, discouraged the fine arts, the theater, the dance, expensive clothes, what the American economist Veblen called "conspicuous consumption" generally. But he did not discourage—in fact he encouraged by his own way of living—the satisfaction of the simple needs of solid, substantial food and adequate shelter and clothing and the like, all needs most readily supplied by large-scale industry serving a mass demand. The Calvinist represents a new development of the perennial Christian ascetic tradition.

A society with many Calvinists tended to produce

much, to consume solidly but without waste or ostentation. Therefore, under competitive conditions, its business leaders accumulated capital, which they could invest in the methods of production that have so enriched the West. All work and no play—well, not much—made the Calvinist society an economically prosperous one.

The Scots, the Dutch, the Swiss, the Yankees of New England—all of them markedly Calvinistic peoples—have long had a popular reputation for thrift, diligence, and driving a hard bargain. And it is surprising how many concrete bits of evidence reinforce the Weber thesis. The Protestant societies at once cut down the number of holy days—holidays without work. They kept Sunday very rigorously as a day without work, but the other six were all work days. The Calvinists even eliminated Christmas, and, since there were as yet no national lay equivalents of the old religious festivals, no Fourth of July or Labor Day, the early modern period in most Protestant countries had a maximum of work days per year. This is a marginal matter, but it is in part by such margins that economic growth is won. Many Protestant theologians rejected the medieval Catholic doctrine that regarded interest on investments beyond a low, "just" rate as usury, and they also rejected most of the medieval attitudes suggested by the term "just price" in favor of something much closer to modern ideas of free competition in the market. In the market, God would certainly take care of his own!

Finally, the firm Calvinist retention of the other world as the supreme, but for the individual never certain, goal helped shield the newly rich from the temptation to adopt the standards of a loose-living, free-spending upper class. Prosperity might be a token that a man was predestined to election, but so, too, was the cautious way he husbanded his profits. Among Calvinists, family fortunes founded by hard work and inconspicuous consumption tended to hold together for several generations at least.

Weber's thesis must not be taken as the sole explanation of capitalism in early modern times, for it is but one of many variables in a complex situation. The stirrings of modern economic life far antedated Luther and Calvin and were first evident in regions that were never won over to Protestantism—Italy, southern Germany, Belgium. Banking began in Florence and other northern Italian cities under Catholic rulers in an era when usury was still prohibited, at least in theory. Almost certainly rules against usury would have been relaxed with the sanction of the Catholic church even if there had been no Protestant Reformation. Moreover, there is no perfect coordination between Protestantism and industrial development on the one hand and Catholicism and industrial backwardness, or notably slower development, on the other. Belgium, the German Rhineland, Piedmont, and Lombardy are striking examples of Catholic regions that have kept well up to the fore in general productiveness and prosperity. Finally, no sensible explanation of the rise of a modern industrial economy can neglect the simple facts of geography and natural resources. Even if Italy had turned Calvinist, it still would not have enjoyed the coal and iron deposits that contributed to Protestant Britain's headstart in industrialism.

Yet the Protestant ethic did perhaps provide the extra fillip that started the West on its modern path—along with the expansion of Europe, which helped the Atlantic nations over the Mediterranean nations; along with the natural resources of northern and western Europe; along with the damp, temperate climate that made hard work easier than in the Mediterranean; along with free enterprise, freedom for science and invention, relatively orderly and law-abiding societies, and whatever else goes to produce that still not fully understood phenomenon, economic growth.

The Reformation and Nationalism

One final generalization about the Reformation is much less disputable than attempts to tie Protestantism in with modern individualism, democracy, and industrialism. After the great break of the sixteenth century, both Protestantism and Catholicism became important elements in the formation of modern nationalism. Here again the trap of one-way causation must be avoided. Neither Protestants nor Catholics were always patriots: French Huguenots sought help from the English enemy, and French Catholics from the Spanish enemy. But where a specific form of religion became identified with a given political unit, religious feeling and patriotic feeling each reinforced the other. This is most evident where a political unit had to struggle for its independence. Protestantism heightened Dutch resistance to the Spaniard; Catholicism heightened Irish resistance to the Englishman. But even in states already independent in the sixteenth century, religion strengthened patriotism. England from Elizabeth I on has, despite the existence of a Catholic minority, proudly held itself up as a Protestant nation; Spain has with equal pride identified itself as a Catholic nation. In the great wars to which we now turn, religion and politics were inextricably combined.

Reading Suggestions on the Protestant Reformation

General Accounts

O. Chadwick, *The Reformation* (*Penguin). A comprehensive survey addressed to the general reader.

R. H. Bainton, *The Reformation of the Sixteenth Century* (*Beacon). Excellent introduction by a Protestant scholar, who has written several more specialized works on the period.

E. H. Harbison, *The Age of Reformation* (*Cornell Univ.). A brief, perceptive introduction.

G. R. Elton, *Reformation Europe, 1517–1559* (*Torchbooks). A lively survey summarizing many of the findings in the more ponderous *New Cambridge Modern History*, Vol. 2: *The Reformation* (Cambridge Univ., 1958), which Elton edited.

A. G. Dickens, *Reformation and Society in Sixteenth-Century Europe* (*Holt). Informative, broad survey, with many illustrations.

H. G. Koenigsberger and G. L. Mosse, *Europe in the Sixteenth Century* (*Holt). Up-to-date, scholarly survey, with excellent bibliographies.

E. F. Rice, Jr., *The Foundations of Early Modern Europe, 1460–1559* (*Norton). Recent brief introduction.

J. Huizinga, *Erasmus and the Age of Reformation* (*Torchbooks). By a celebrated Dutch historian.

Luther

R. H. Bainton, *Here I Stand: A Life of Martin Luther* (*Mentor). Sympathetic, scholarly, readable.

E. H. Erikson, *Young Man Luther* (*Norton). Luther's "identity crisis" persuasively presented.

H. Grisar, *Martin Luther: His Life and Works* (Herder, 1930). From the Catholic point of view.

E. G. Schwiebert, *Luther and His Times* (Concordia, 1952). From the Lutheran point of view; particularly useful for the setting and the effects of Luther's revolt.

K. Brandi, *The Emperor Charles V* (*Humanities). Comprehensive study of Luther's antagonist.

H. Holborn, *A History of Modern Germany*, Vol. 1: *The Reformation* (Knopf, 1959). Scholarly and readable.

The Other Founders

J. Courvoisier, *Zwingli: A Reformed Theologian* (*John Knox). Good study of an important and often neglected figure.

F. Wendel, *Calvin: The Origins and Development of His Religious Thought* (Harper, 1963). Translation of a solid study by a French scholar.

G. Harkness, *John Calvin: The Man and His Ethics* (*Apex). A good short introduction.

J. Mackinnon, *Calvin and the Reformation* (Longmans, 1936). Substantial longer study.

J. J. Scarisbrick, *Henry VIII* (*Univ. of California). The first major scholarly assessment since A. F. Pollard, *Henry VIII* (*Torchbooks), which appeared early in this century.

A. G. Dickens, *The English Reformation* (*Schocken). Detailed study down to 1559, with useful bibliography.

T. M. Parker, *The English Reformation to 1558,* 2nd ed. (*Oxford). Excellent short account.

G. H. Williams, *The Radical Reformation* (Westminster, 1962). Encyclopedic and indispensable study of the Anabaptists and other left-wing reformers.

F. H. Littell, *The Anabaptist View of the Church,* 2nd ed. (Starr King, 1958). Perceptive, brief introduction.

The Catholic Reformation

H. Daniel-Rops, *The Catholic Reformation* (Dutton, 1962). Admirable study by a French Catholic scholar.

A. G. Dickens, *The Counter-Reformation* (*Holt). Comprehensive survey by an English Protestant scholar.

B. J. Kidd, *The Counter-Reformation* (S. P. C. K., 1933). Scholarly account by an Anglican.

P. Janelle, *The Catholic Reformation* (Bruce, 1951). Scholarly account by a Catholic.

R. Fülop-Miller, *Jesuits: History of the Society of Jesus* (*Capricorn), and H. Boehmer, *The Jesuits* (Castle, 1928). Respectively, by a Catholic and a Protestant.

Protestantism and Progress

M. Weber, *The Protestant Ethic and the Spirit of Capitalism* (*Scribner's). Advances the famous thesis on the interrelationship of religion and economics.

R. H. Tawney, *Religion and the Rise of Capitalism* (*Mentor). Turns the Weber thesis around to emphasize economic motivation.

L. W. Spitz, ed., *The Reformation: Basic Interpretations* (*Heath). Useful introduction to divergent scholarly views.

E. Troeltsch, *Protestantism and Progress* (*Beacon). By a leading modern religious philosopher.

P. Tillich, *The Protestant Era* (*Phoenix). Abridged from a longer study by a ranking modern theologian.

Sources

H. S. Bettenson, ed., *Documents of the Christian Church,* 2nd ed. (*Oxford). Admirable compilation, particularly valuable for the Reformation.

E. G. Rupp and B. Drewery, eds., *Martin Luther* (St. Martin's, 1970). An anthology of his significant writings, with helpful editorial comment.

H. J. Hillerbrand, *The Reformation in Its Own Words* (*Torchbooks). Another useful compilation of primary material.

Châteillon, *Concerning Heretics,* ed. R. H. Bainton (Columbia Univ., 1935). One of the earliest arguments for religious freedom, not merely toleration.

Dynastic Politics and Warfare
1494-1648

I The Balance of Power

Historians have chosen a number of different dates to mark the watershed between medieval and modern. Protestants pick 1517 and the Ninety-Five Theses, while Americans often think of 1492 as the great year. For the kingdoms of western Europe, historians single out the appearance of strong, ambitious monarchs—1461, Louis XI in France; 1469, the marriage of Ferdinand of Aragon and Isabella of Castile; 1485, Henry VII and the advent of the Tudors in England. For international relations they are likely to choose a more obscure date—1494, when Charles VIII of France began what has been called the first modern war by leading his army over the Alps toward the conquest of Italy.

All such dates are arbitrary, for, as our discussion of the Renaissance has shown, the dividing line between medieval and modern culture cannot be placed in a single country or a single year. Moreover, it can be argued that what really makes the modern world "modern" is the combination of rationalism, natural science, technology, and economic organization that has given men a new power over natural resources. By this standard, the great change came in the eighteenth century, and the sixteenth and seventeenth were but preparation. Still, for the historian of international relations, a difference between the medieval and modern organization of the European state system is noticeable as early as the late 1400s.

The Competitive State System

Western society, in early modern times, was a group of states, big, middle-sized, and small, each striving to grow, usually by annexing other states or at least bringing them under some sort of control. At any given moment some states were on the offensive, trying to gain land, power, and wealth; others were on the defen-

sive, trying to preserve what they had. Even states we now think of as peaceful small democracies, like Sweden and Denmark, took the offensive in quest of territorial empire three centuries ago, and Sweden almost became a great power.

The constituent units in this competitive system are usually termed sovereign states, which means in practice that their rulers had armed forces to implement their policies. After the height of feudal disintegration, perhaps in the tenth century, a continuous though irregular process of reducing the number of sovereign states got under way and lasted down to World War I. If a feudal lord with armed retainers can be called sovereign because he could make war on his own initiative, then the tenth-century West had thousands of sovereign units. By the end of the Middle Ages, however, the little feudal units had been absorbed into much bigger states over much of the West, with the partial exception of much-fragmented Germany. When local wars occurred, they were seldom wars between states but rather civil wars, risings of dissident nobles against their sovereigns. The shadowy unity of Western Christendom was destroyed at the end of the Middle Ages, but so too was the real disunity of numerous local units capable of organizing war among themselves.

As the modern state system began to take shape in the fifteenth and sixteenth centuries, the three well-organized monarchies of Spain, France, and England dominated western Europe; the smaller states of Scotland, Portugal, and Scandinavia generally played a subordinate role. In central Europe, the Holy Roman Empire, with its many quasi-sovereign member states, did not have the kind of internal unity enjoyed by the Atlantic powers. Yet under the leadership of the Austrian Hapsburgs, the empire took a leading part in international competition. Between France and the empire lay the zone of fragmentation where the fifteenth-century dukes of Burgundy had tried to weld many small units into a revived middle kingdom. Out of this zone have come the states of Holland, Belgium, Luxembourg, Switzerland, and Italy. Renaissance Italy, as we have already seen, was divided into several sovereign states that comprised a junior state system with wars, diplomacy, and balance of power. As early as the fourteenth century, Italy anticipated on a small scale the international politics of Europe in later centuries. To the southeast was the new and expanding Ottoman Empire, with European lands reaching to the central Danube valley. To the east, Muscovite Russia was beginning to become a great state, and Poland-Lithuania was already great in size if not in power.

Over the last five hundred years certain states have attempted to disrupt this state system: sixteenth-century Spain; the France of Louis XIV in the seventeenth century and of the Revolution and Napoleon a century later; the Germany of the Kaiser and Hitler and, to a lesser degree, the Russia of Stalin in the twentieth century. They have tried to reduce or obliterate the sovereignty of other states. Each time this has happened, the threatened units sooner or later joined together in a coalition against the aggressive power to maintain the system and, in the time-honored phrase, to restore or redress the balance of power. The phrase is a descriptive one, not a moral principle, and it is a convenient thread through the intricacies of international politics in the modern West. We take up this thread in 1494.

Dynastic State and Nation State

First, however, we must examine briefly the nature of the political units that made up the competitive state system. It is the custom to call them dynastic states up to about the end of the eighteenth century and nation states thereafter. What this distinction implies may be found in the change of title imposed on Louis XVI by the Revolution in 1791—from king of France, which suggests that the kingdom was real estate belonging to the Bourbon dynasty, to king of the French, which suggests that he was the leader accepted by the French nation. In the early modern period some states were loose agglomerations of formerly independent units that might be separated from each other by foreign territory, that sometimes spoke different languages, and that were tied together almost solely by the ruling dynasty. The widely scattered Hapsburg realm is a good example. In war and diplomacy the dynastic ruler and his circle of nobles and bureaucrats acted as a team with a certain team spirit, but the various peoples in such a dynastic state had relatively little sense of patriotism, of common national effort and ambitions. Early modern wars were not total wars, and, except in their disastrous effects on government finances, and on taxes, they scarcely touched the lives of the common people who were not actually in the way of contending armies

Sixteenth-century woodcut: an army besieging a city.

trying to live off the land. In the peace settlements, no one talked about "national self-determination of peoples" or worried greatly about transferring areas and populations from one dynasty to another.

On the other hand, the distinction between dynastic states and nation states must not be overdrawn. Especially in the great Atlantic monarchies a degree of national patriotism existed in the sixteenth century and, in England and France, it had already been evident during the Hundred Years' War when the English referred scornfully to the French as frogs, and Frenchmen retaliated by calling the English *les godons*, the French mispronunciation of *goddams*. At the time of the great Spanish Armada (1588) Englishmen showed intense patriotic emotion, hating and fearing Spaniards both as foreigners and as militantly anti-Protestant Catholics. Even in divided Germany, Luther could count on Germans to dislike Italians. Hatred of the foreigner bound men together at least as effectively as love of one another.

The differences between the present-day state and the early modern state are generally exaggerated today. They are real, and they make the dynastic wars of the sixteenth, seventeenth, and even eighteenth centuries seem petty and bewildering, but they are not in the main differences in kind. They are differences in the degree of efficiency, of centralization, of the ability to command vast numbers of men and great resources, and of the rapidity of movement.

The Instruments of Foreign Policy

By 1500, almost all the European sovereign states possessed in at least rudimentary form most of the social and political organs of a modern state, lacking only a large literate population brought up in the ritual and faith of national patriotism. Notably they had two essential instruments: a professional diplomatic service and a professional army. The fifteenth and sixteenth centuries saw the steady development of modern diplomatic agencies and methods. Governments established central foreign offices or ministries, sent diplomats and regular missions to foreign courts, and organized espionage under the cover of open diplomacy. Formal peace conferences were held and formal treaties were signed, with all the ceremony and protocol we associate with such occasions. Finally, to govern these formal relations a set of rules began to take shape that is rather too grandly termed "international law," for it often proved impossible to enforce.

The apparatus of international politics developed most fully in Renaissance Italy and found its classic expression in the admirably organized diplomatic service of the Republic of Venice. The detailed reports Venetian ambassadors sent back to the Senate from abroad are among the first documents of intelligence work we have. They are careful political and social studies of the personalities and lands involved rather than mere gossipy cloak-and-dagger reports. In those days, the diplomat was a most important maker of policy in his own right. With rapid travel impossible, his government could not communicate with him in time to prescribe his acts minutely, and he often had to make important decisions on his own. Good or bad diplomacy, good or bad intelligence about foreign lands, made a vital difference in a state's success or failure in the struggle for power.

The armed forces made still more difference. The early modern centuries were the great days of the professional soldier, freed from the limitations of feudal warfare and not yet tied to the immense economic requirements and inhuman scale of modern warfare. The officer class in particular could plan, drill, and campaign on a fairly large but quite manageable scale; they could, in effect, handle warfare as a skill, even as an art or a pleasure. The common soldiers, too, for the most part were mercenaries; the word "soldier" in fact comes from *solidus,* the Latin for "piece of money." Some of these mercenaries were recruited at home, usually among the poor and dispossessed, sometimes by impressment. Others were foreigners who made a career of soldiering, particularly Swiss and Germans; thousands of them served in the armies of Francis I of France together with Englishmen, Scots, Poles, Italians, Albanians, and Greeks.

These professional forces were often trained to parade, to dress ranks, and to keep discipline, and they were whipped if they broke discipline, though threats of punishment did not always prevent desertions when pay was late or rations inadequate. Each regiment or unit commonly wore the same uniforms, but whole armies usually displayed such an extraordinary variety of garb that in battle recognition of friend and foe was not easy. Tactics and strategy in the field were under the control of an officer hierarchy that culminated in a commanding general, who in turn was subject to some control by the central government. In short, though these armies would look anarchic to a modern professional of the spit-and-polish school, they were far better organized and disciplined than feudal levies had been.

Yet the early modern armies also show many feudal survivals, many forms of entrenched privilege, many ways of twisting away from centralized control. The officer class continued to preserve many of its old habits of chivalry, such as the duel, which often seriously menaced internal discipline. If the feudal lord no longer brought his own knights for the forty days of allotted time, his descendant as regimental colonel often raised his own regiment and financed it himself. Weapons were of an extraordinary variety. Reminders of the old hand-to-hand fighting survived in the sword and in the pike, the long shaft used by foot soldiers against the armored knight and his mount. Hand firearms—arquebus, musket, pistol, and many others—were slow-loading and slow-firing, and usually not even capable of being aimed with any accuracy. The cannon, quite unstandardized as to parts and caliber, and heavy and hard to move, fired solid balls, rather than exploding shells.

Armies on the march lived mostly off the land, even when they were in home territory. But they were beginning to develop the elaborate modern organization of supply and the modern service of engineers. Both the growth of military technology and differences of national temperament were reflected in the shift of military predominance from Spain to France about 1600. Spain, the great fighting nation of the sixteenth century on land, excelled in infantry, where the pike was a major weapon. France, the great fighting nation of the seventeenth and early eighteenth centuries on land, excelled in artillery, engineering, and fortification, all services that were more plebeian, less suited to the former feudal nobility than infantry and cavalry.

Meanwhile, the first modern navies were also growing up. In the later Middle Ages, Venice, Genoa, and Pisa had all begun to assemble fleets of galleys disciplined both as individual ships and in fleet maneuvers. In the Renaissance, Venice took the lead with its arsenal and its detailed code of maritime regulations. Naval organization, naval supply, the dispatch and handling of ships, all required more orderly centralized methods than an army; they could not tolerate the survival of feudal individualism, indiscipline, and lack of planning. The officer class, as in the armies, was predominantly aristocratic, but it came usually from the more adventurous, the less custom-ridden part of that class. During the sixteenth century, naval supremacy passed out of the Mediterranean to the Atlantic, where it rested briefly with Spain, and thence passed in the seventeenth century to the northern maritime powers of England, Holland, and France.

II Hapsburg and Valois, Tudor, and Orange

The Italian Wars of Charles VIII and Louis XII

Charles VIII of France (1483–1498) inherited from his parsimonious father Louis XI a well-filled treasury and a good army. He continued Louis' policy of extending the royal domain by marrying the heiress of the duchy of Brittany, hitherto largely independent of the French crown. Apparently secure on the home front, Charles decided to expand abroad. As the remote heir of the Angevins who had seized the throne of Naples in the thirteenth century, Charles disputed the right of the Aragonese Ferrante to hold that throne. He chose to invade Italy, however, not only because he had this tenuous genealogical claim but also because Renaissance Italy was rich, and was divided into small rival political units—it looked, in short, to be easy picking. So it was at first, for in the winter of 1494–1495 Charles paraded his army through to Naples in triumph. But his acquisition of Brittany had already disturbed his neighbors, and his possession of Naples threatened the balance of power in Italy. The French intrusion provoked the first of the great modern coalitions, the so-called Holy League composed of the papacy (which, remember, was also an Italian territorial state), the empire, Spain, Venice, Milan, and soon England. This coalition forced the French armies out of Italy without much trouble in 1495.

Charles was followed on the French throne by his cousin of the Orléans branch of the Valois family, Louis XII (1498–1515). Louis married Charles' widow to make sure of Brittany, and then tried again in Italy, reinforced by still another genealogical claim, this time to Milan. Since his grandmother came from the Visconti family, Louis regarded the Sforza dukes as simple usurpers; he proceeded to drive Il Moro from Milan in 1499. In this second French invasion, the play of alliances was much subtler and more complicated, quite worthy of the age of Machiavelli. Louis tried to insure himself from the isolation that had ruined Charles by allying in 1500 with Ferdinand of Aragon, with whom he agreed to partition Naples. Then, in 1508, Louis helped form one of those cynical coalitions that look on paper as though they could break the balance-of-power principle, because they are the union of the strong against a much weaker victim. This was the League of Cambray, in which Louis, Ferdinand, Pope Julius II, and the emperor Maximilian joined to divide up the lands held in the lower Po Valley by the rich but—on land—militarily weak Republic of Venice.

The practical trouble with such combinations is that the combiners do not really trust one another, and usually fall to quarreling over the pickings. All went well for the despoilers until Ferdinand, having taken the Neapolitan towns he wanted, decided to desert Louis. The pope, frightened at the prospect that France and the empire might squeeze him out entirely, in 1511 formed another "Holy League" against France with Venice and Ferdinand, later joined by Henry VIII of England and the emperor Maximilian. Despite some early successes in the field, the French could not hold out against such a coalition, for they now had a war on two fronts. Henry VIII attacked the north of France and won at Guinegate (1513) the "battle of the spurs," so called from the speed with which the French cavalry spurred their flight from the battlefield. In Italy too the French were defeated, and Louis XII, like Charles VIII, was checkmated.

Charles V versus Francis I

These two French efforts were, however, merely preliminaries. The important phase of this first great modern test of the balance of power was to follow immediately, and to take a basically different form. For there were now really two aggressors: the French house of Valois, still bent on expansion, and the house of Hapsburg. When the Hapsburg Charles V succeeded his grandfather Maximilian as emperor in 1519, he was a disturber by the mere fact of his existence rather than by temperament or intent. He had inherited Spain, the Low Countries, the Hapsburg lands in central Europe as well as the headship of the Holy Roman Empire, and the preponderance in Italy. He apparently had France squeezed in a perfect vise.

The vise almost closed. Louis XII's successor, Francis I (1515–1547), was badly defeated by the largely Spanish Hapsburg forces at Pavia in 1525 and was himself taken prisoner and held in Madrid until he signed a treaty giving up all the Valois Italian claims and ceding the duchy of Burgundy. This treaty he repudiated the moment he was safely back in France. It is probable that Charles V would not have destroyed France entirely even had he been able to; in these early modern wars there were accepted limits to what might decently be done to the defeated. The belligerents convey the impression of engaging in a kind of professional athleticism that was often bloody and unscrupulous yet subject to certain rules of the game. The players sometimes changed sides; one of the imperial commanders at the battle of Pavia in which the French were so severely beaten was the Constable de Bourbon, a great French noble at odds with his king.

The same Bourbon commanded the Spanish and German mercenaries of the emperor at the time of the horrible sack of Rome in 1527. Pope Clement VII (1523–1534), a Medici and a good Italian at heart, had first supported Charles V but turned against him after his victory at Pavia. In the League of Cognac, 1526, he allied himself with the other main Italian powers

Francis I of France: portrait by Joos van Cleve.

and with Francis. In reply, Charles besieged Rome, but he did not plan the sack, which took place when his mercenaries became infuriated by delays in pay and supplies. By the end of the decade, Charles had made peace with the pope and with Francis, and in 1530 he was crowned by the pope as emperor and as king of Italy, the last ruler to receive this double crown, this inheritance of Charlemagne. But the world over which Charles symbolically ruled was very different from that of Charlemagne, and Charles was in fact no emperor but a new dynast in a new conflict of power.

France was still in the vise between the Spanish and the German and Netherlandish holdings of Charles, and Francis I, a proud, consciously virile Renaissance prince, was not one to accept for long so precarious a position—above all, a position in which he lost face. He used the death of the Sforza ruler of Milan in 1535 to reopen the old claim to Milan and to begin the struggle once more. Neither Francis nor Charles lived to see the end of this particular phase of the Hapsburg-Valois rivalry. Neither side secured decisive military victory. In 1559 the important Treaty of Cateau-Cambrésis confirmed Hapsburg control of Milan and Naples. It marked the failure of France to acquire a real foothold in Italy, but it also marked the failure of the Hapsburgs to reduce the real strength of France, which retained the important bishoprics of Metz, Toul, and Verdun on her northeastern frontier, first occupied during the 1550s. The Hapsburg vise had not closed largely because France proved militarily, economically, and politically strong enough to resist the pressure. But the vise itself was a most imperfect instrument; Charles' German arm was paralyzed by the political consequences of the Reformation and the stubborn resistance of Protestant princes.

The last phase of the personal duel between the aging rivals, Charles and Francis, shows how many variables entered the play of the balance of power. To gain allies, Francis did not hesitate to turn to Charles' rebellious German subjects. Although head of a Catholic country, whose king had long been called "the eldest son of the Church," he allied himself with the Protestant duke of Cleves and even concluded an alliance with the Muslim Ottoman emperor, Suleiman the Magnificent, who attacked Charles from the rear in Hungary.

One other participant in the complex struggles of the first half of the sixteenth century was England, which, though not yet a great power, was already a major element in international politics. The men who set English policy were probably not guided by a consciously held theory of the balance of power, but they often behaved as though they had arrived intuitively at the conclusion that they should intervene on behalf of the group that was being defeated. In addition, England had on her northern border an independent Scotland, which tended to side with France, the great hereditary English enemy. Yet the English were quite capable of supporting the hereditary enemy if they thought Charles V was too strong. After Charles had won at Pavia and taken Rome, the English minister Wolsey worked out an alliance with France in 1527. The English were also capable of reversing themselves. In 1543, when Charles was beset by Protestants and Turks, Henry VIII came to his aid against France, but not too vigorously. In the campaign of 1544, when a German army was actually marching on Paris down the Marne valley, the English had landed on the Channel coast and, had they really pressed matters, Paris might have fallen. But the English rather deliberately besieged the Channel port of Boulogne, and Francis escaped with his capital city intact.

The Wars of Philip II

The first great Hapsburg effort to dominate Europe ended with the Peace of Augsburg and the Treaty of Cateau-Cambrésis four years later. The second effort at domination was less Hapsburg than Spanish. In 1556, Charles V abdicated both his Spanish and imperial crowns and retired to a monastery, where he died two years later. His brother, who became Emperor Ferdinand I (1556–1564), secured the Austrian Haps-

Marble bust of Philip II of Spain, from the workshop of Leone Leoni.

burg territories. His son, King Philip II of Spain (1556–1598), got also the Spanish lands overseas, the Burgundian inheritance of the Netherlands, and Milan and Naples in Italy. Even without Germany, Philip's realm was a supranational state, drawing much gold and silver from the New World and threatening France, England, and the whole balance of power. Like his father, Philip II found Protestantism intolerable, a divisive force that must be wiped out by force if necessary. His attempt to invade England and restore Catholicism has made him one of the villains of Anglo-Saxon and Protestant tradition, the cold-blooded "devil of the south." In fact, he was no lover of war for its own sake but a serious hard-working administrator and a devout and dutiful Catholic.

Philip had five major points of involvement. (1) So long as Italy remained divided into the five major units of Milan, Venice, Tuscany, Papal States, and Naples, it was to be a stake in the balance of power, a source of lands to be annexed by expansionist states. (2) In France Philip was bound to appear as the Catholic champion in the civil and religious strife that prevailed during the second half of the century. (3) In the Mediterranean, which Ottoman naval power was threatening to turn into a Muslim lake, the Spanish fleet, under Philip's illegitimate half-brother Don John of Austria, participated in a Christian victory over the Ottoman fleet off the west coast of Greece in 1571. This

Europe in 1555

Possessions of the House of Hapsburg
- Austrian
- Spanish

Boundary of the Empire
■ Battle sites

NORWAY

Stockh

SCOTLAND

North Sea

o Edinburgh

DENMARK

Copenhagen o

Baltic

IRELAND

ENGLAND

Dublin o

Bosworth
Field ■

BRANDENBURG

Bremen o

Elbe R.

Münster o

Berlin o

Oder R.

London o

Wittenberg o

SILESIA

Canterbury o

Amsterdam o
Leiden o

Cleves o

Wartburg o

HESSE

Torgau o

SAXONY

Leipzig o

Calais o

NETHERLANDS

Antwerp o

Rhine R.

THE EMPIRE

Prague o

BOHEMIA

Atlantic Ocean

BRITTANY

Ivry ■

Vervins o

LUXEMBOURG

o Metz

Speyer o

WÜRTTEM-
BERG

MORAVIA

Paris o

Verdun o

Danube R.

Augsburg o

AUSTRIA

Nantes o

FRANCHE
COMTÉ

Toul o

Vienna o

Loire R.

FRANCE

BURGUNDY

Basel o

Constance o

BAVARIA

STYRIA

La Rochelle o

Zurich o

TYROL

CARINTHIA

HU

Cognac o

SWITZERLAND

Trent o

AUVERGNE

Geneva o

SAVOY

MILAN
Pavia ■

CARNIOLA

M

Valladolid o

NAVARRE

BASQUE
PROV.

Avignon
(to the Papacy)

Rhône R.

Po R.

Padua o

Venice o

VENETIAN REPUBLIC

Tordesillas o

PROVENCE

Genoa o

Bologna o

Adriatic Sea

PORTUGAL

SPAIN

Ebro R.

ARAGON

TUSCANY

PAPAL
STATES

NAPLES

Lisbon o

Madrid o

Tagus R.

Toledo o

CORSICA
(to Genoa)

Rome o

Naples o

CASTILE

Guadalquivir R.

Palos o

Seville o

BALEARIC IS.

SARDINIA

Cadiz o

Mediterranean Sea

SICILY

10

(Tributary to Ottoman Empire)

B A R B A R Y   S T A T E S

MALTA

TEUTONIC
ORDER

Moscow

Volga R.

R U S S I A

PRUSSIA

L I T H U A N I A

W. Dvina R.

Oka R.

Ural R.

saw

POLAND

Kiev

UKRAINE

Dnieper R.

Don R.

KHANATE

OF THE

Volga R.

Caspian Sea

stula R.

TRANSYLVANIA

MOLDAVIA

Dniester R.

CRIMEA

Y

Belgrade

WALLACHIA

Black Sea

Danube R.

MONTE-
NEGRO

O T T O M A N   E M P I R E

Constantinople

PERSIA

Salonika

Aegean Sea

Tigris R.

ANIANS

Lepanto

Athens

Euphrates R.

PELOPONNESUS

(to Venice)

RHODES

0   500

CRETE

CYPRUS
(to Venice)

Miles

20   25   30   35   40   45

Inset map

0   100
Miles

Amsterdam

London

Leiden

Utrecht

60

Armada sea fight

Bruges

Antwerp

Calais

FLANDERS

Scheldt R.

Boulogne

Guinegate

ARTOIS

NETHERLANDS

Cambray

Cateau-
Cambrésis

55

FRANCE

50

25   30   35   40   45

55

45

40

50

35

battle of Lepanto checked but did not immediately roll back Ottoman expansion. (4) In the New World and on the wide seas connecting it with the Old World, England and France were beginning to challenge the monopoly Spain and Portugal had tried to set up, as the next chapter will relate. (5) In the Netherlands, the revolt of Philip's Dutch Protestant subjects soon involved him also in a struggle with their champion, Tudor England.

The Dutch revolt was the dramatic focus of Philip's wars. Charles V had come to count heavily on the wealth of the Netherlands, estimated to be the highest per capita in Europe, to finance his constant wars. But he made no attempt to integrate into a unified superstate the seventeen provinces of the Netherlands, which were very jealous of their traditional autonomy. There were few effective institutions to bind the seventeen together; each province had its own medieval Estates or Assembly, dominated by the nobility and wealthy merchants, which raised taxes and armies. In the mid-sixteenth century the area was still overwhelmingly Catholic, with small minorities of Anabaptists and Lutherans; Calvinism was just starting to move northward across the French border.

Whereas Charles V had liked the Netherlands and made Brussels his favorite place of residence, Philip II was thoroughly Spanish in outlook and never visited the area after the early years of his reign. Not only Philip's temperament and nature antagonized his subjects in the Low Countries but also his up-to-date ideas about centralized efficient rule, which led him to curtail their political and economic liberties. The inhabitants cherished their traditional autonomy and, as a commercial and seafaring people, they were intent on conducting business without the restrictions imposed on trade and industry by Spanish regulations. Those who were Protestant resented and feared Philip's use of the Inquisition in the Netherlands.

This explosive mixture of religion, politics, and economic interests produced the revolt. Philip sent Spanish garrisons to the Netherlands and attempted to enforce edicts against heretics. Opposition, which centered at first in the privileged classes who had been most affected by Philip's political restrictions, soon spread to the common people. In 1566, when a group of two hundred nobles petitioned Philip's regent to adopt a more moderate policy, an official sneeringly referred to "these beggars." The name stuck, proudly adopted by the rebels. The political restlessness, combined with an economic slump and the growing success of the Calvinists in winning converts, touched off riots in August 1566, which resulted in heavy destruction of Catholic churches in such major centers as Ghent, Antwerp, and Amsterdam. Philip responded to this "Calvinist fury" in 1567 by dispatching to the Netherlands an army of twenty thousand Spaniards headed by the unyielding, politically stupid duke of Alba.

In those days the Spanish infantry was the best in Europe, and the rebels were ill armed and ill prepared. Their eventual success was a heroic achievement against great odds; it was, however, no extraordinary victory of weakness over strength, but rather a victory fully consonant with a fact of Western political life—that no thoroughly disaffected population can be long held down by force alone. Alba had the force, and he set up a Council of Troubles—later dubbed the Council of Blood—which resorted to executions, confiscations, and severe taxation on a large scale. The number of victims executed under the Council of Blood totaled about a thousand, yet all the repression accomplished was to heighten the opposition to Spanish policy. In 1573 Alba gave up in despair.

Meantime, the rebel "Beggars" turned to a kind of naval guerrilla warfare, gained control of the ports of the populous northern province of Holland, and then ended effective Spanish authority in Holland and adjacent areas. Large numbers of Protestant refugees, especially Calvinists, from other provinces resettled themselves in Holland as a result. The historical split was appearing between the largely Catholic southern Netherlands and the mainly Protestant north—to use popular terminology, between Belgium and Holland (the name of the province is often, though inaccurately, applied to all seven northern provinces). It was to be a religious, not a linguistic split, for Dutch was the language both of the north and of Flanders in the south; French was spoken only in the Walloon country of the southeast. North and south had much to unite them, and union of all seventeen provinces was the goal of the rebel leader, William of Orange, the Silent, prince in the 1570s. William, who got his nickname because his silences could be discreet or deceptive by turn, was a convivial nobleman with firm political convictions but few religious ones (he was, at different periods, a Lutheran, a Catholic, and a Calvinist).

William's goal of unity seemed almost assured in the wake of widespread revulsion at the "Spanish Fury" of 1576, when Spanish troops, desperate because their pay was two years in arrears, sacked the great Belgian port of Antwerp and massacred several thousand of its inhabitants. But in 1578, when the duke of Parma arrived to govern the Netherlands, Phillip's policies at last showed signs of a willingness to compromise in the face of facts. By political concessions to old privileges of self-rule, Parma won back the ten southern provinces, which remained largely Catholic after the exodus of many Calvinists to the north. It was too late to win back the northern provinces, except perhaps by radical religious concessions, which Philip could not make.

In 1581 the Dutch took the decisive step of declaring themselves independent of the Spanish Crown. They made good that declaration by their courageous use of their now much better-organized land forces and by the fact that Philip faced grave internal economic problems just when he had been drawn into fighting on other fronts. He had to cope with the Turks, the French Protestants, and the anti-Spanish moderate wing of French Catholics. In 1584 the Dutch were deprived of their first great national leader when William the Silent was assassinated. But his death did not profit the Spanish cause since it created a hero-martyr not only to the Dutch but to all Protestants.

In 1585 the English queen, Elizabeth I, after long hesitancy, finally came out on the side of the Dutch and sent an army to their aid. The English had been sympathetic with the Dutch all along, but Elizabeth had feared that, with France in the midst of civil war, a Franco-Spanish alliance against English and Dutch was quite possible. But here too Philip showed himself incapable of diplomacy: he permitted France to maneuver into neutrality, and he provoked England by fomenting Catholic plots against Elizabeth. The English in turn provoked Spain: for years they had been preying on Spanish commerce on the high seas, and Hawkins, Drake, and other sailors had been raiding Spanish possessions in the new world.

The great armada of unwieldy men-of-war that Philip sent out to invade England was defeated in the Channel, in July 1588, by a skillfully deployed lighter English fleet, and was utterly destroyed afterward by a great storm. The battle was the beginning of the end of Spanish preponderance, the beginning of English greatness in international politics, and the decisive step in the achievement of Dutch independence. These por-tentous results were not so evident in 1588 as they are now; but even at the time the defeat of the Spanish Armada was viewed as a great event, and the storm that finished its destruction was christened the "Protestant wind."

In 1598 Philip II died in the great, severe palace of the Escorial he had built near Madrid. He had ordered an open coffin put beside his sick bed, and a skull with a crown of gold. Save for the seven northern provinces of the Netherlands—and even these had never officially given up—the great possessions that had been his when he began his reign were intact. In 1580 he had added Portugal by conquest and brought the whole Iberian peninsula under a single rule. Yet he left his kingdom worn out, drained of men and money. And whatever his goals in international politics had been, whether a Spanish hegemony, a revived Western empire, or merely the extinction of the Protestant heresy, he had realized none of them.

III The Catholic Monarchies: Spain and France

The states that took part in these dynastic and religious wars experienced an uneven working out of the new

The Escorial, the combined palace, monastery, and mausoleum built by Philip II near Madrid.

businesslike aims and methods characterizing the passage of domestic politics from the medieval to the modern world. They all had paid professional armies and paid professional civilian bureaucrats. They had a central financial system, a central legal system that made some attempt to apply the law uniformly to all subjects, and a central authority—king, king and council, king and parliament, estates, cortes, or other assembly—that could make new laws. Such labels as Age of Absolutism and Divine Right Monarchy are frequently pinned on the early modern centuries, and not without reason. Over most of Europe the ultimate control of administration usually rested with a hereditary monarch who claimed the God-given right to make final decisions. But, while the greater nobles were losing power and influence to the monarchy, the lesser nobles continued to dominate the countryside, where medieval local privileges survived vigorously almost everywhere, together with local ways of life quite different from those of the court and the capital.

Spanish Absolutism

Sixteenth-century Spain offers a case study of the clash between the ideal of absolutism and the recalcitrance of the varied groups on which the monarchy sought to impose its centralized, standardized rules. The reigns of two hard-working monarchs, the emperor Charles V (as king of Spain he was Charles I, 1516–1556) and Philip II, span almost the whole century. Charles, who was more a medieval survival than a modern king, did little to remodel the instruments of government he had inherited from his grandparents, Ferdinand and Isabella. Brought up in the Low Countries, he came to Spain a stranger, with a Flemish entourage that already had the modern northern European contempt for the "backward" south. Charles' election to the imperial throne in 1519 made him further suspect in Spain; the aristocrats were restless in the face of the new monarchical dignity, and the municipalities disliked the growth of central fiscal controls. In 1520 a league of Spanish cities, led by Toledo, rose up in the revolt of the comuneros (the name applied to the rebels). The comuneros were put down in 1521, but Charles had been frightened out of what reforming zeal he may have had and in the future did his best not to offend his Spanish subjects.

Philip II, unlike his father, grew up as a Spaniard first of all, and was much more willing and able to build a more professional centralized regime in Spain. He devised a system of councils, topped by a council of state, which were manned by great nobles but had only advisory powers. Final decisions rested with Philip, and the details were worked out by a series of private secretaries and local organs of government, not staffed by nobles. Philip also reduced the Cortes, the representative assemblies, to practical impotence. In Castile, nobles and priests, because they did not pay direct taxes, no longer attended the session of the Cortes, and the delegates of the cities were left as a powerless rump. The Cortes of Aragon, while retaining more power, was seldom convoked by Philip. Above all, Philip had assured sources of income—his tax of a fifth of the value of the precious cargoes from America, direct taxes from the constituent states of his realm, revenues from the royal estates and from the sale of offices and patents of nobility, revenues from the authorized sale, at royal profit, of dispensations allowed by the pope (permission to eat meat on Fridays and during Lent, and even something very close to the very indulgences that had raised Germany against the pope). Philip, like most continental monarchs of his time, had no need to worry over representative bodies with control of the purse. Yet he was always heavily in debt and on three occasions suspended payments on his obligations; his bankruptcies triggered that of the famous Fugger firm in Augsburg.

Even in this matter of revenue, where Philip's power at first sight looks so complete, the limitations of the absolute monarch of early modern times are clear. Except by borrowing and hand-to-mouth expedients like the sale of offices, he could not notably increase his income. He could not summon any representative group together and get them to vote new monies. In the first place, the constituent parts of his realm, Castile, Aragon, Navarre and the Basque provinces (both at the western end of the Pyrenees, adjoining France), the Italian lands, the Low Countries, the Americas, and the newest Spanish lands, named after the monarch himself, the Philippine Islands, had no common organs of consultation. Each had to be dealt with as a separate problem, and the slowness of communication with his far-flung domains further delayed the always deliberate process of decision making. For the most part the nobility and clergy were tax exempt, and could not be called upon for unusual financial sacrifices. Add to all this the difficulty of collection, the opportunities for graft, and the lack of a long-accumulated administrative and financial experience, and one can see why Philip could not have introduced a more systematic general taxation.

Outside the financial sphere, the obstacles to really effective centralization were even more serious. The union of the crowns of Aragon and Castile, achieved by the marriage of Ferdinand and Isabella, had by no means made a unified Spain. To this day regionalism—to give it a mild name—is probably more intense in Spain than in any other large European state. In those days, some of the provinces did not even accept extradition arrangements for the surrender of criminals within the peninsula. Many of them could and did levy customs dues on goods from the others. The northern regions, which had never been totally conquered by the Muslims, preserved all sorts of privileges known as *fueros*. Aragon still kept the office of *justicia mayor*, a judge nominated by the Crown but for life and entrusted with an authority somewhat remotely like that of the United States Supreme Court.

What the house of Austria, as the Hapsburg dynasty was termed in Spain, might have accomplished had they been able to expend their full energies on uniting and developing their Spanish lands can never be known. What they did do was exhaust the peninsula and weaken their lands overseas in the effort to secure hegemony over Europe and subdue the Protestant heresy. This was indeed the great age of Spain, when both on land and on sea the Spanish were admired as the best fighters, when Spain seemed to be the richest of states and destined to be the mistress of both the Americas. It was also the age of Loyola and Cervantes, the golden age of Spanish religion, literature, and art, but it was a brief flowering, and Spanish greatness largely vanished in the seventeenth century.

The Spanish Economy

Spain is a classical instance of a great state's failure to maintain a sound economic underpinning for its greatness. The Iberian peninsula is mountainous, and its central tableland is subject to droughts, but its agricultural potential is considerable, more than that of Italy for example; and it has mineral resources, notably iron. Spain was the first of the major European states to secure lands overseas and to develop the navy and merchant marine to integrate the vast resources of the New World with a base in the Old World. Yet all this wealth slipped through Spain's fingers in a few generations. An important factor here was the immense cost of the wars of Charles V and Philip II; in particular, the Low Countries, which had brought much revenue to Charles, became a pure drain on Philip's overburdened finances.

Governmental expenditure on armed forces, though in itself unproductive, is not fatal to a national economy if it stimulates greater productivity in the nation and its dependencies. But this was not true of sixteenth-century Spain. She drew from the New World immense amounts of silver and many commodities—sugar, indigo, tobacco, cocoa, hides—without which she could hardly have fought her European wars. But all this was not enough to pay for world dominion. The bullion passed through Spanish hands into those of bankers and merchants in other European countries, partly to pay for the Spanish armies and navies, and partly to pay for the manufactured goods sent to the New World. These goods, which the colonies were forbidden to make for themselves, Spain could not supply from her own meager industrial production. Although a royal decree gave Spanish merchants a monopoly on trade with the Indies, as the century wore on they were reduced to the role of middlemen, sending to the Indies items imported from the rest of Europe. In addition, the English, Dutch, and other competitors invaded their theoretical monopoly by large-scale smuggling of goods into Spain's colonies. Thus, while Spain's governmental expenditures did prime the economic pumps, the pumps were foreign, not Spanish, and by 1600 Spain's home industry was on the decline.

The free-trade economists of the nineteenth century attributed Spain's failure to exploit her economic opportunities to the prevalence of monopoly under governmental supervision. Sixteenth-century Spain was certainly moving toward the economic policy called mercantilism (the reference is not to individual merchants but to the mercantile or commercial system), which was to reach its fullest development in seventeenth-century France. Although Spain lacked the true mercantilist passion for building national wealth under government auspices, she used many mercantilist techniques, the endless regulation in general and the narrow channeling of colonial trade in particular. In Castile, a single institution, the Casa de Contratación (House of Trade) in Seville, controlled every transaction with the Indies and licensed every export and import. The amount of paperwork, in an age unblessed by typewriters and copiers, to say nothing of computers, was staggering.

Beyond all this, the whole direction of Spanish civilization diverted creative energies away from industrial channels. Warfare, politics, religion, art, farming, or simply living like a hidalgo (hijo de algo, "son of somebody," hence "nobleman," "gentleman") were all respectable activities. But what Americans call business was not an activity on which Spanish society put a premium. Not that Spaniards were lazy: the epitome of so much we think of as Spanish, Don Quixote, was hardly a lazy man, but his activity was not exactly productive of material wealth. If we take into consideration the numerous holidays, the habit of the siesta, the large numbers of beggars, soldiers, priests, monks, and hidalgos, as well as the lack of encouragement to new enterprises and techniques, and the heavy hand of an inefficient bureaucracy, then it becomes clear that the total Spanish effort was bound to be inadequate in competition with nations better organized for modern economic life. Spain, in short, presents almost the antithesis of the picture of what goes into the "capitalist spirit" drawn by Weber in his hypothesis on the Protestant ethic.

The Spanish Style

Yet the Spanish supremacy, though shortlived, was real enough, and it helped make our present-day world. Half the Americas speak Spanish (or a rather similar tongue, Portuguese) and carry, however altered, a cultural inheritance from the Iberian peninsula. French, Dutch, and English national unity and national spirit were hardened in resistance to Spanish aggression. The Spanish character, the Spanish "style," was set—some may say hardened—in this Golden Age, which has left to the West some magnificent paintings and one of the few really universal books, *Don Quixote* by Miguel de Cervantes (1547–1616). This Spanish style is not at all like those of France and Italy, so often tied with Spain as "Latin"—a term that is very misleading if the "Latin" peoples are grouped together as "sunny." For the Spanish spirit is among the most serious, most darkly passionate, most unsmiling in the West; it is a striving spirit, carrying to the extreme the chivalric point of honor.

In art this spirit stands out in the paintings of a master who was Spanish only by adoption, El Greco (1541–1614). "The Greek," born on Crete, was schooled in the late Byzantine manner of painting and later studied with Titian in Venice. In his thirties he settled at Toledo, the religious capital of Castile, which in medieval days had been the intellectual center of Muslim Spain. El Greco's Byzantine and High Renaissance training served as foundations for a highly personal way of dealing with religious themes best illustrated in his masterpiece, *The Burial of the Count of Orgaz*, in the church of Santo Tomé at Toledo. This fourteenth-century nobleman had made generous endowments in honor of Saint Augustine and Saint Stephen, both of whom, according to legend, miraculously appeared after his death to bury his body. The painting shows both the earthly and heavenly realms, as the saints gently lift the corpse in the presence of aristo-

cratic mourners, who gaze upward toward the angel bearing the count's soul to heaven. There the Virgin and St. John are waiting to intercede for him with Christ and St. Peter.

The lower scene might almost have been painted by Titian or another great portraitist of the Renaissance, even though the mourners have the grave, prominent eyes of the Byzantine school. The upper scene could only have been the work of El Greco. The billowing clouds are pearly gray with a cold, luminous quality (one critic has called it "ectoplasmic"); the elongated, slender figures have tapering fingers, narrow heads, and unnaturally large Byzantine eyes; even the cherubs are slim, with none of the pink chubbiness usually associated with them. Stretching toward heaven like a Gothic pinnacle, *The Burial of the Count of Orgaz* is an extraordinary effort to record the mystic's unrecordable experience.

Two other paintings by El Greco provide additional insights into the Spanish spirit during the Catholic Reformation. One is his portrait of Cardinal Niño de Guevara, the Archbishop of Toledo and the Grand Inquisitor of Spain, which one historian has labeled "terrifying" because it conveys so vividly the sitter's combination of tension, asceticism and bigotry. The other is *A View of Toledo*, the first Spanish landscape painting, depicting the city's majestic hilltop site above the gorge of the Tagus River. To make the composition more dramatic El Greco rearranged the location of the city's landmarks and filled the nighttime sky with "ectoplasmic" clouds and reflected lightning, communicating a sense of eeriness and foreboding.

In religion, during the generations following Ignatius Loyola, the Spanish style was expressed most strikingly in the careers of Saint Teresa of Avila (1515–1582) and Saint John of the Cross (1542–1591), who brought back the tortured ecstasies of the early Christian ascetics and added a dark, rebellious note of their own. Theirs was no attempt to withdraw into monastic isolation but a heroic effort to combat this world of the senses and thus transcend it. They worked vigorously together to reform Spanish monasticism, and John, in particular, was harshly persecuted by established religious interests. They were both familiar figures to the Spanish common people, who in their own way identified themselves with these saints in their struggle. Here is part of an account of what followed the death of John of the Cross:

Hardly had breath ceased than . . . crowds assembled in the street and poured into the convent. Pressing into the room where he lay, they knelt to kiss his feet and hands. They cut off pieces from his clothes and bandages and even pulled out the swabs that had been placed on his sores. Others took snippings from his hair and tore off his nails, and would have cut pieces from his flesh had it not been forbidden. At his funeral these scenes were repeated. Forcing their way past the friars who guarded his body, the

El Greco's portrait of Cardinal Don Fernando Niño de Guevara.

mob tore off his habit and even took parts of his ulcered flesh.*

The creations of Cervantes, in their very different way, likewise carry the mark of the Spanish style. Spain is Don Quixote tilting with the windmills, aflame for the Dulcinea he has invented, quite mad. But it is also the knight's servant, Sancho Panza, conventional, earthy, unheroic, and sane enough, though his sanity protects him not at all from sharing his master's misadventures. Cervantes almost certainly meant no more than an amusing satire of popular tales of chivalry. But his story has got caught up in the web of symbolism we live by, and the Don and his reluctant follower are for us Spain forever racked between fantasy and common sense. This tension runs all through *Don Quixote.* Chivalry is indeed silly, and worth satire—gentle satire:

"I would inform you, Sancho, that it is a point of honor with knights-errant to go for a month at a time without eating, and when they do eat, it is whatever may be at hand. You would certainly know that if you had read the histories as I have. There are many of them, and in none have I found any mention of knights eating unless it was by chance or at some sumptuous banquet that was tendered them; on other days they fasted. And even though it is well understood that, being men like us, they could not go without food entirely, any more than they could fail to satisfy the other necessities of nature, nevertheless, since they spent the greater part of their lives in forests and desert places without any cook to prepare their meals. . ."

"Pardon me, your Grace," said Sancho, "but seeing that, as I have told you, I do not know how to read or write, I am consequently not familiar with the rules of the knightly calling. Hereafter, I will stuff my saddlebags with all manner of dried fruit for your Grace, but inasmuch as I am not a knight, I shall lay in for myself a stock of fowls and other more substantial fare."†

The extreme of pride—pride of status, of faith, of nation—has seemed to the outside world the mark of Spain. Perhaps there is little to choose among the triumphant prides of nations in triumph. Yet as the "shot heard round the world" sounds very American, so the Cid, the legendary hero of the reconquest from the Muslims, is very Spanish in these verses as he goes off to his Crusade:

Por necesidad batallo
Y una vez puesto en la silla
Se va ensanchando Castilla
Delante de mi caballo.   [*I fight by necessity:*
                            But once I am in the saddle,
                            Castile goes widening out
                            Ahead of my horse.]

*G. Brenan, "A Short Life of St. John of the Cross," in *The Golden Horizon*, ed. C. Connolly (London, 1953), pp. 475–476.

†*Don Quixote*, trans. Samuel Putnam (New York, 1949), 1:78–79.

France: The Last Valois Kings

North of the Pyrenees the long-established French monarchy began to move toward a more efficient absolutism after the Hundred Years' War, particularly under Louis XI. In this development France had certain advantages. None of its provinces—not even Brittany with its Celtic language and autonomous traditions, nor Provence with its language of the troubadours, its ties with Italy, its earlier history as a separate unit—shows quite the intense regionalism that may be found in Catalonia or the Spanish Basque provinces. Moreover, unlike the Iberian peninsula, Italy, or Greece, most of France is not cut up by mountain ranges into isolated compartments. Yet despite these assets France was still imperfectly tied together under Francis I (1515–1547). Many provinces, especially Brittany and others that had come under direct Valois rule fairly recently, retained their own local representative bodies (Estates), their own local courts (parlements), and many other privileges. The national bureaucracy was as yet only a patchwork, and the nobility, though it had lost most of its old governmental functions to royal appointees, held on to feudal memories and attitudes.

As we have seen, however, the kingdom of Francis I was strong enough to counter the threat of encirclement by Charles V. The king himself was not another Louis XI, however. Self-indulgence weakened his health and distracted him from the business of government; his extravagant court and, far more, his frequent wars drained the finances of the state. Yet in many respects Francis was a good Renaissance despot, thoroughly at home in the age of Machiavelli. At the beginning of his reign he extended the royal gains made at papal expense in the Pragmatic Sanction of Bourges (1438). In the Concordat of Bologna (1516), the pope allowed the king a very great increase in control over the Gallican church, including the important right to choose bishops and abbots. In the face of treason, Francis responded by confiscating the estates of the Constable de Bourbon when he defected to the Hapsburgs. In adversity he had courage: witness his successful recovery after the disaster at Pavia in 1525. In diplomacy he was unscrupulous and flexible: witness his alliances with the Turks and with the German Protestants. Good-looking (until his health broke down), amorous, lavish, courtly, Francis did things in the grand manner. It is reported that it took eighteen thousand horses and pack animals to move the king and his court on their frequent journeys. He built the famous châteaux of Chambord and Fontainebleau, and in Paris he remodeled the great palace of the Louvre and founded the Collège de France, second only to the old Sorbonne as an educational center. He patronized Leonardo, Cellini, and other artists and men of letters.

Francis was the last strong monarch of the house of Valois. After his death in 1547, his son Henry II and his grandsons were barely able to maintain the prestige of the Crown in the face of crippling disorders. The second half of the sixteenth century was the age of French civil and religious wars, a crisis that almost undid the centralizing work of Louis XI and his successors.

The religious map of France in the 1550s showed a division by class as well as by territory. While Protestantism scarcely touched the French peasantry, except in parts of the south, the Huguenots were strong among the nobility and among the rising classes of capitalists and artisans. The region of Paris, Brittany, most of Normandy, and the northern areas bordering on the Low Countries remained ardently Catholic. Protestantism was gaining in the southwest and in south-central France, especially in the lands of the old Albigensian heresy. Even in these regions, however, the employer class was more likely to be Protestant, the workers to be Catholic. The French nobility took up Protestantism partly in response to a missionary campaign directed toward them from Geneva and partly for political reasons. The old tradition of local feudal independence among the nobles encouraged resistance to the centralized Catholic monarchy and its agents. The German princes in revolt had everything to gain in a worldly way by confiscation of church property and establishment of an Erastian Lutheran church. But, after the Concordat of 1516, the French kings had everything to lose by a Protestant movement that strengthened their restive nobility and that in its Calvinist form was the very opposite of Erastian.

Sporadic warfare began soon after the death of Henry II in 1559 (ironically, he was fatally wounded in a tournament celebrating the Treaty of Cateau-Cambrésis). For the next generation the crown passed in succession to Henry's three sons—Francis II (1559–1560), Charles IX (1560–1574), and Henry III (1574–1589)—and France was torn by civil and religious strife. Since Charles IX was a boy of ten at his accession, authority was exercised by his mother, Catherine de' Medici, who shared the humanistic and artistic tastes of her famous Florentine family and, contrary to Protestant prejudice, had no particular religious convictions. But Catherine was determined to preserve intact the magnificent royal inheritance of her sons, which seemed to be threatened by the rapid growth of the Huguenots, by their increasing pressure for official recognition, and by Catholic counterpressure against concessions. What especially worried Catherine was the apparent polarization of the high nobility by the religious issue—the great family of Guise was zealously dedicated to the Catholic cause, and the powerful families of Bourbon and Montmorency to the Huguenot.

Success in scattered fighting during the 1560s netted the Huguenots some gains. Their ambitious leader, Coligny, who was linked to the Montmorencys, gained great influence over the unstable Charles IX and apparently seriously hoped to take over control of the government. Panicky at the danger to the prospects for her sons and to her own position, Catherine threw in her lot with the Guises and persuaded Charles to follow suit. The result was the massacre of Huguenots on Saint Bartholomew's Day (August 24, 1572). Three thousand victims fell in Paris, including Coligny, many of them dragged from their beds in the first hours of the morning according to a prearranged plan; thousands more perished in the provinces. In spite of Saint Bartholomew's Day and subsequent reverses in the field, the Huguenots remained strong. As the warfare continued, the Catholic nobles organized a threatening league headed by the Guises, and both sides negotiated with foreigners for help, the Catholics with Spain and the Protestants with England. Thus the French crown found itself pushed into opposition to both groups.

The French civil and religious strife culminated in the War of the Three Henrys (1585–1589)—named for Henry III, the Valois king and the last surviving grandson of Francis I; Henry, duke of Guise, head of the Catholic League; and the Bourbon Henry of Navarre, the Protestant cousin and heir-apparent of the childless king (his grandmother had been the sister of Francis I). The threat that a Protestant might succeed pushed the Catholic League to propose violating the rules of succession by making an uncle of Henry of Navarre king, the Catholic cardinal of Bourbon. But this attempt to alter the succession alienated moderate French opinion, already disturbed by the extremes of both Catholics and Protestants.

Paris, on the other hand, was fanatically Catholic, and a popular insurrection there (May 1588), frightened Henry III out of his capital, which triumphantly acclaimed Guise as king. Henry III responded by conniving at the assassination of the two great men of the Catholic League, Henry of Guise and his brother Louis. Infuriated, the league rose in full revolt, and Henry III took refuge in the camp of Henry of Navarre, where he in turn was assassinated by a monk.

The First Bourbon: Henry IV

Henry of Navarre was now by law Henry IV (1589–1610), the first king of the house of Bourbon. In the decisive battle of Ivry (March 1590) he defeated the Catholics, who had set up the aged cardinal of Bourbon as "King Charles X." But Henry's subsequent efforts to besiege Paris were repeatedly frustrated by Spanish troops sent down from Flanders by Philip II. Philip planned to have the French Estates General put Henry aside and bestow the crown on the Spanish infanta, Isabella, daughter of Philip II and his third wife, Elizabeth of Valois, who was the child of Henry II and Catherine de' Medici. In the face of this new threat, Henry was persuaded that if he would abjure his own Protestant faith he could rally the moderate Catholics and secure at least tolerated status for the Protestants. He turned Catholic in 1593 and Paris surrendered, giving rise to the perhaps apocryphal tale that he had remarked, "Paris is well worth a Mass." Henry now declared war against Spain and brought it to a successful conclusion with the Treaty of Vervins, 1598, which essentially confirmed the Cateau-Cambrésis settlement of 1559.

Within France the Edict of Nantes, also in 1598, endeavored to achieve a lasting religious settlement. While it did not bring complete religious freedom, it did provide for a large measure of toleration. The Huguenots were granted substantial civil liberties and were allowed the exercise of their religion in certain towns and in the households of great Huguenot nobles. Public worship by Huguenots was forbidden in episcopal and archiepiscopal cities, and most particularly in Paris. Of the two hundred towns where Huguenots could worship, they were to fortify and garrison one hundred at government expense as symbols of safeguard.

The intellectual preparation for the Edict of Nantes and for the revival of the French monarchy under Henry IV had been in large part the work of a group of men known as *politiques,* a term that comes closer to meaning "political moralist" than "politician." The greatest of them, Jean Bodin, who died in 1596, held that the sole possibility of peace and quiet in a divided France lay in obedience to a king above petty civil strife. Bodin and his colleagues stressed the need for political unity to maintain law and order, yet they were not absolutists but moderates who by no means preached that the king must be obeyed no matter what he did. The politiques were convinced that under the supremacy of the French state Frenchmen should be allowed to practice different forms of the Christian religion. They believed that the basic aim of the belligerents in the religious wars—to put down by force those who disagreed on matters of faith—was un-Christian. Here is how one of them, Michel de l'Hospital, who was also a practicing Catholic, stated their position:

> If they are Christians, those who try to spread Christianity with arms, swords, and pistols do indeed go contrary to their professed faith, which is to suffer force, not to inflict it. . . . Nor is their argument, that they take arms in the cause of God, a valid one, for the cause of God is not one that can be so defended with such arms. . . . Our religion did not take its beginnings from force of arms, and is not to be kept and strengthened by force of arms. . . .
>
> Let us pray God for the heretics, and do all we can to reduce and convert them; gentleness will do more than harshness. Let us get rid of those devilish names of seditious factions, Lutherans, Huguenots, Papists: let us not change the name of Christian.*

Henry IV was particularly fortunate in arriving on the French scene when the passions of civil war were nearing exhaustion and the nation was ready for pacification. The high degree of success he achieved also depended greatly on his own personal qualities. A realist rather than a cynic, as the remark about Paris being

Portrait of Henry IV (Henry of Navarre).

worth a Mass might suggest, Henry balanced concessions to the Huguenots with generous subsidies to the Catholic League for disbanding its troops, and he declined to summon the Estates General because of its potential for proving troublesome. Other kings in other days, like Louis XI of France and Henry VII of England, had accomplished the restoration of law and order, but only Henry of Navarre became a genuinely popular hero. Witty, dashing, with a pronounced taste for pretty women and bawdy stories, he was the most human king the French had had for a long time, and the best-liked monarch in their whole history. His court casually included his wife, his mistresses, and his children, legitimate and otherwise. He made jokes about his financial difficulties. And, most of all, he convinced his subjects that he was truly concerned for their welfare; Henry IV is still remembered as the king who remarked that every peasant should have a chicken in his pot on Sunday.

Henry's economic experts reclaimed marshes for farm land, encouraged the luxury crafts in Paris, and

*P. J. S. Dufey, ed., *Oeuvres complètes de Michel de l'Hospital* (Paris, 1824), 1:395–402. Our translation.

planted thousands of mulberry trees to foster the culture and manufacture of silk. They extended canals and launched a program of building roads and bridges that eventually won France the reputation of maintaining the best highways in Europe. Faced with a heavy deficit when he took office, Henry's chief minister, the Huguenot Sully (1559–1641), systematically lowered it until he brought government income and expenditure into balance. His search for new revenues had some unhappy consequences, however. He not only continued the old custom of selling government offices but permitted the beneficiary to transmit the office to his heir on payment of an annual fee—a lucrative new source of royal income but an even greater source of future difficulty, since more and more officeholders were more concerned with enjoying and protecting their vested interests than with the faithful execution of their duties. For the rest, the incidence of taxation remained lopsided, with some provinces much more heavily burdened than others, and with the poor paying much more than their fair share. Collection remained in the hands of contractors called "farmers," and the treasury suffered loss of revenue from entrusting this public function to often unscrupulous private entrepreneurs. Fiscal weakness was to remain the Achilles' heel of the French monarchy for the next two centuries.

IV The Protestant States: Tudor England and the Dutch Republic

Henry VIII, 1509–1547

In England Henry VII had already established the new Tudor monarchy on a firm footing. That Henry VIII did not run through his heritage and leave an exhausted treasury and discredited monarchy was not because he lacked the will to spend lavishly. As Martin Luther wrote of him, "Junker Heintz will be God and does whatever he lusts."* Henry loved display, elaborate palaces (Hampton Court, near London, is the best known), and all the trappings of Renaissance monarchy. His "summit conference" with Francis I, a kindred luxurious spirit, near Calais in 1520 has gone down in tradition as the Field of the Cloth of Gold. Democratic critics have often accused European royalty of ruinous expenditures on palaces, retinues, pensions, mistresses, and high living in general; yet such expenditures were usually a relatively small part of government outlays. War was the really major cause of disastrous financial difficulties for modern governments. Henry's six wives, his court, his frequent royal journeys did not beggar England; the wars of Charles V and Philip II did beggar Spain.

Henry VIII made war in a gingerly manner, never really risking big English armies on the Continent, and contenting himself with playing a rather cautious game of balance of power. He made full use of the opportunities afforded him by the English Reformation to add to royal revenues by confiscation of monastic property, and, even more important, by rewarding his loyal followers with lands so confiscated. Henry thus followed in the footsteps of his father in helping create a new upper class, which soon became a titled or noble class. In contrast to France, the new class was on the whole loyal to the Crown and yet, in contrast to some of the German states, by no means subservient to the Crown, by no means a mere ennobled bureaucracy. Under Henry VIII and his successors the newly rich continued to thrive, and many other Englishmen prospered. But Tudor England also had a class of the newly poor as a result of the great enclosures of land for sheepfarming; small farmers, who lost their right to pasture animals on former common lands now enclosed in private estates, lost the margin that had permitted them to make ends meet.

Lacking the patience to attend to administrative details, Henry relied heavily on members of the new Tudor nobility as his chief assistants—Wolsey in the early part of his reign, then Cranmer who as archbishop of Canterbury enabled Henry to marry Anne Boleyn, and, above all, Thomas Cromwell, later made earl of Essex, who superintended the precarious ramifications of the break with Rome. Cromwell exploited the printing press to disseminate propaganda favoring the royal point of view. He was a master administrator, who endeavored to make the royal administration more loyal, professional, and efficient, less tied to the king's household and to special interests, in short, more modern in character. He achieved a great deal, but he antagonized other ambitious royal servants. Discredited with the king by the action of his enemies, Cromwell was executed in 1540. Wolsey, too, had been disgraced and died awaiting execution.

Henry could be ruthless, yet he could be tactful and diplomatic, as in his handling of Parliament to get everything he wanted, including statutes that separated the English church from Rome, and grants for his wars and conferences. Henry's Parliaments were very far from being elected legislatures based on wide suffrage. The House of Lords had a safe majority of men—titled nobles and, after 1534, bishops of the Anglican church—who were in fact of Tudor creation or allegiance. The House of Commons was composed of the knights of the shire, chosen by the freeholders of the shires, and of the burgesses, representatives of incorporated towns or boroughs (not by any means all towns). In most boroughs, a very narrow electorate chose these members of Parliament. Since the majority of the people of the shires were agricultural workers or tenants, rather than freeholders of land, the county franchise, too, was limited. The knights of the shire were chosen from among, and largely by, the squires and the lesser country gentlemen. Royal favor and royal patronage, as well as the patronage of the great lords, could pretty well mold the shape of a House of Commons.

Still, even the Tudor Parliaments were nearer a

*Quoted in J. J. Scarisbrick, *Henry VIII* (Berkeley, 1968), p. 526.

modern legislative assembly than the parallel assemblies of the Continent. The great point of difference lay in the composition of the House of Commons, which had emerged from the Middle Ages not as a body representing an urban bourgeoisie but as a composite of the rural landed gentry and the ruling groups in the towns. On the Continent, the assemblies corresponding to the English Parliament usually sat in three distinct houses—one representing the clergy, another all the nobles, great and small, and a third the lay commoners. Some countries, as for instance Sweden, had four estates—clergy, nobles, townsmen, and peasants.

Historians today emphasize the fact that the political differences between England and the Continent reflected differences in social structure. England certainly had a nobility or aristocracy ranging from barons through viscounts, earls, and marquesses to dukes at the top. These nobles, plus Anglican bishops, composed the House of Lords. In England, younger sons of nobles were not themselves titled nobles, as they were on the Continent, but were members, usually top members, of a complex group. In addition to the younger sons and descendants of nobles this group included the squires and rich bankers and merchants, who almost always acquired landed estates and became squires. It also included leading lawyers and civil servants, the Anglican clergy, dons at Oxford and Cambridge (who at first were usually in Anglican orders), officers in the army and navy, and a scattering of others in the liberal professions. This large and diverse group was never a closed caste and remained open to socially mobile men from the lower classes. The imprecise terms "gentry" and "gentlemen" are sometimes applied to this group, although the former is too exclusively rural in connotation and the latter is not always accurate in its implication that gentlemen invariably own enough property or capital so that they do not have to work for a living. Perhaps "ruling elite" or "establishment" would be as good names as any for this uniquely English class.

By the beginning of the Tudor era Parliament had already obtained much more than the purely advisory powers that were all that the French Estates General, for instance, really had. Parliament emerged from the Middle Ages with the power to make laws or statutes, which did, however, require royal consent. In terms of constitutional structure, the Tudor parliaments could have quarreled as violently with the Crown as the Stuart parliaments did in the next century. Yet, although the Tudor monarchs had their difficulties with Parliament, they usually got what they wanted without serious constitutional crises. This was particularly true of Henry VIII and Elizabeth I, who succeeded in part, as we have noted, because their parliaments, if not precisely packed, were generally recruited from men indebted to the Crown for their good fortune. But the Tudors also succeeded because they were skillful rulers, willing to use their prestige and gifts of persuasion to win the consent of Parliament, careful to observe the constitutional and human decencies. Both Henry and Elizabeth were good, hearty persons, sure of themselves and their dignity, immensely popular with all classes of their subjects. Both were fortunate enough to be able to incorporate in their persons strong national feelings of patriotic resistance to the two most hated foreign foes, the Roman church and the Spanish monarchy.

Edward VI and Mary

The course of Tudor domestic history, however, did not run with perfect smoothness. Henry VII had faced two pretenders; Henry VIII met opposition to his religious policy. A Catholic minority, strong in the north, continued throughout the sixteenth century to oppose the Protestant majority, sometimes in arms, sometimes in intrigues. The death of Henry VIII in 1547 marked the beginning of a period of extraordinary religious oscillation.

Henry was succeeded by his only son, the ten-year-old Edward VI, borne by his third wife, Jane Seymour. Led by the young king's uncle, the Duke of Somerset, Edward's government pushed on into Protestant ways. The Six Articles, by which Henry had sought to preserve the essentials of Roman Catholic theology, worship, and even church organization, were repealed in 1547. The legal title of the statute commonly called the Six Articles had been "An Act for Abolishing Diversity in Opinion." The goal was still uniformity, and in the brief reign of Edward VI an effort was made to prescribe uniformity of religious worship through a prayerbook and articles of faith duly imposed by Parliament. Cranmer, archbishop of Canterbury, was much influenced by the ideas of Zwingli, and had committed himself by his marriage—as did Luther—to a clear, symbolic break with Roman Catholicism. Under his supervision, the patient majority of the English people was pushed into Protestant worship.

Then, in 1553, the young king, Edward VI, always a frail boy, died. Protestant intriguers vainly attempted to secure the crown for a Protestant, Lady Jane Grey, a great-granddaughter of Henry VII and a quiet, scholarly young woman with no ambitions. But Edward VI was followed by his older sister Mary, daughter of Catherine of Aragon, whom Henry VIII had put aside. Mary had been brought up a Catholic, and at once began to restore the old ways. Of course there was a rebellion, which flared into the open when Mary announced a marriage treaty by which she was to wed Philip II of Spain. Yet Mary prevailed against the rebels, and Lady Jane Grey was executed for a plot in which she had never really participated. A Catholic cardinal was made archbishop of Canterbury under Rome, and Cranmer was burned at the stake. Catholic forms of worship came back to the parishes, but significantly the church land settlement of Henry VIII remained undisturbed. The vigorous persecution of Protestants—most of the nearly three hundred people burnt were from the lower classes, and many were women—gave Mary her lasting epithet of Bloody and laid the foundations of the English Protestant hatred and suspicion of Catholicism, traces of which still survive today.

Elizabeth I

When Mary died after a short reign, in 1558, the last of Henry's children left was Elizabeth, daughter of Anne Boleyn. She had been declared illegitimate by Parliament in 1536 at her father's request. Henry's last will, however, rehabilitated her, and she now succeeded as Elizabeth I (1558–1603). She had been brought up a Protestant, and once more the English churchgoer was required to switch religion. This time the Anglican church was firmly established; the prayer book and Thirty-nine Articles of 1563 issued under Elizabeth (and noted in the preceding chapter) have remained

Portrait of Queen Elizabeth I by an unknown artist. The map of England is at her feet.

to this day the essential documents of the Anglican faith.

The Elizabethan settlement, moderate and permanent though it was, did not fully solve the religious problem. England still had a Catholic party, Catholic Spain was a serious enemy, and independent Scotland could always be counted on to take the anti-English side. The new queen of Scotland was Mary Stuart, granddaughter of Henry VIII's sister Margaret, and therefore the heiress to the English throne should Elizabeth die without issue. Mary, who was Catholic and whose mother was a member of the fanatically Catholic Guise family of France, did not wait for Elizabeth's death to press her claim. On the ground that Elizabeth was illegitimate, she assumed the title of queen of England and Scotland.

Meantime, numerous Protestant groups not satisfied with the Thirty-nine Articles were coming to the fore. Collectively, these people were called Puritans, since they wished to purify the Anglican church of what they considered papist survivals in belief, ritual, and church government. In practice, their proposals ranged from moderate to radical. The moderates would have settled for a simpler ritual and retained the office of bishop. The Presbyterians would have replaced bishops with councils (synods) of elders, or presbyters, and adopted the full Calvinist theology. The Brownists, named for their leader Robert Browne, would have gone still further and made each congregation an independent body.

Thus Elizabeth faced a decidedly grim prospect during the early years of her reign. The troubles of Edward and Mary had undone some of the work of the two Henrys; dissension seemed all around her; yet she was to reign for nearly fifty years. Her personality was hardly heartwarming. She was vain (or simply proud), not altogether immune to flattery, but too intelligent to be led astray by it in great matters. She was a good Renaissance realist (a better one than Machiavelli himself), somewhat too overpowering and impressive for a woman, but very effective in the pageantry and posing of public life. She was loved by her people if not by her intimates. She never married, but in the early years of her reign she played off foreign and domestic suitors one against another with excellent results for her foreign policy, in which she was always trying to avoid the expenses and dangers of war, trying to get something for nothing. One may believe that her spinsterhood settled on her at first as no more than a policy of state, and later as a convenient habit. She had male favorites, but probably not lovers.

Mistrusting the great aristocrats, Elizabeth picked her ministers from the ranks just below the nobility, talented men like Burleigh and Walsingham who put her government in splendid order. Thanks to skillful diplomacy, which made full use of the French and Dutch opposition to Spain, the showdown with Philip was postponed until 1588, when the kingdom was ready for it. Mary, Queen of Scots, proved no match at all for her gifted cousin, not merely because she was not a good politician, but even more because she had no sure Scottish base to work from. Mary was Catholic, and Scotland under the leadership of John Knox was on its way to becoming one of the great centers of Calvinism. Mary managed everything wrong, including, and perhaps most important in a puritanical land, her love affairs. Her subjects revolted against her, and she was forced in 1568 to take refuge in England, where Elizabeth had her put in confinement. Mary alive was at the very least a constant temptation to all who wanted to overthrow Elizabeth. Letters, which Mary declared were forged, and over which historians still debate, involved her in what was certainly a real conspiracy against Elizabeth, and she was tried, convicted, and executed in 1587, to become a romantic legend.

The dramatic crisis of Elizabeth's reign was the war with Spain, resolved in the defeat of the great Spanish Armada in 1588. But her old age was not to be altogether serene. Forced to turn frequently to Parliament for approval of financial measures, she met mounting criticism of her religious policy from Puritan members of the House of Commons. She got her money not by making concessions to the Puritans but by grudgingly conceding more rights to the Commons. The Commons responded not with expressions of gratitude but with bolder criticism of the queen's policy, and at what proved to be the last meeting of Parliament Elizabeth attended, failed to salute her appearance with the usual salvo of applause. The stage was being set for the great seventeenth-century confrontation between the Crown and Parliament.

During Elizabeth's final years the stage was also being set for a drama that was to have an even longer run—the Irish question. The ruling Anglo-Irish landed class was out of touch with the native peasants. In 1542 the country had been made a kingdom, but hardly an independent one, since the crowns of England and Ireland were to be held by the same person. Earlier, in 1495, a statute had put the Irish Parliament firmly under English control and had made laws enacted by the English Parliament applicable to Ireland as well. Attempts to enforce Protestant legislation passed by the English Parliament outraged the native Irish, who had remained faithful Catholics. In 1597 the Irish rose in revolt; the rebellion was put down bloodily in 1601, but the basic Irish problem remained unsolved. The favorite of Elizabeth's old age, the Earl of Essex, lost influence by his failure to cope with the Irish rebels; he then became involved in a plot against the queen and was executed.

The English Renaissance

The Age of Elizabeth, then, was marked by intrigue, war, rebellion, and personal and party strife. Yet there were solid foundations under the state and society that produced the wealth and victories of the Elizabethan Age and its attainments in literature, music, architecture, and science. The economy prospered in an era of unbridled individual enterprise that was often unscrupulous and, in raids on the commerce of foreigners like the Spaniards, piratical. The solid administrative system was based on a substantial degree of national unity made possible by the absence of the extreme local differences and conflicts encountered on the Continent. A common sentiment kept Englishmen together and traced for most of them limits beyond which they would not carry disagreement. Elizabeth herself played a large part in holding her subjects together. Her religious policy, for example, was directed at stretching the already broad principles and practices of the Church of England so that they would cover near-Catholicism at one extreme and near-Congregationalism at the other. There was a limit to this stretching, and Elizabeth did not grant either Catholics or Brownists the right to practice their religion publicly. But, in contrast to Mary's severity, Elizabeth's persecution was largely a matter of fining offenders.

The Age of Elizabeth was marked by a great flowering of culture that extended beyond the chronological limits of her reign, 1558 to 1603, back to the reign of Henry VIII and forward to that of her successor, James I. This was the English Renaissance, when ladies and gentlemen cultivated all the muses, played the lute, sang madrigals, admired contemporary painting, and dressed as did their counterparts in the pacesetter of European style, Italy. The glory of the English Renaissance resided in its literature, for England was not a land of great original creations in music and the plastic arts. The greatness of Elizabethan England, when it is not in the deeds of Drake, Hawkins, Thomas Cromwell, Burleigh, and the Tudors themselves, lies in the words of Thomas More, William Shakespeare, Francis Bacon, Edmund Spenser, Ben Jonson, and many others who are part of the formal higher education of English-speaking people all over the world.

Their writings have suffered popular admiration and neglect as well as the thorough academic working-over that goes with the status of established classics. They belong to a culture now four hundred years past, and their authors wrote English before its structure and its word order were tamed, partly by the influence of French prose, into their present straightforward simplicity. For most of us, they are much easier to read about than to read. Yet on the whole they have survived intact as classics, and Shakespeare, notably, continues even outside the English-speaking world to be a kind of George Washington of letters, above reproach. He is the necessary great writer of a great people, as is Dante for the Italians, Goethe for the Germans, Pascal or Molière or Racine for the French, Cervantes for the Spanish, Tolstoy or Dostoevsky for the Russians.

These Elizabethans are overwhelmingly exuberant; they are exuberant even in refinement, full-blooded even in erudition. To a later generation, the polite, orderly admirers of measure and sense in the late seventeenth and eighteenth centuries, these Elizabethans were uncouth, undisciplined. To the nineteenth-century romantics, they were brothers in romance. The love of the excessive is obvious in much Elizabethan writing, in the interminable, allusion-packed, allegory-mad stanzas of Spenser's *Faerie Queene*, in the piling up of quotations from the ancient Greeks and Romans, in Shakespeare's fondness for puns and all kinds of rhetorical devices, in the extraordinarily bloody tragedies—remember, for example, the stage littered with corpses at the end of *Hamlet*.

The Elizabethans were also exuberant patriots, lovers of their country in the first flush of its worldly success. Here is one of the most famous speeches in Shakespeare, that of the dying John of Gaunt in *Richard II*, in itself an admirable sample of the English Renaissance, right down to the inevitable allusion to Greco-Roman mythology:

> *This royal throne of kings, this scepter'd isle,*
> *This earth of majesty, this seat of Mars,*
> *This other Eden, demi-paradise,*
> *This fortress built by Nature for herself*
> *Against infection and the hand of war,*
> *This happy breed of men, this little world,*
> *This precious stone set in the silver sea,*
> *Which serves it in the office of a wall*
> *Or as a moat defensive to a house,*
> *Against the envy of less happier lands,*
> *This blessed plot, this earth, this realm, this England.*

The Dutch Republic

Almost contemporaneous with the Elizabethan Age was the great age of the Dutch, which extended from the late sixteenth century through the first three quarters of the seventeenth. The United Provinces of the Northern Netherlands, as we have seen, gained effective independence from Spain before the death of Philip II, though formal international recognition of their status was delayed until 1648. The Dutch state was a republic in the midst of monarchies, but it was an aristocratic merchant society, far from being a popular democracy. Despite its small size (approximately that of the state of Maryland), it was a great power, colonizing in Asia, Africa, and the Americas, trading everywhere, supporting an active and efficient navy.

In economic life, the Dutch were the pacesetters of seventeenth-century Europe, and Amsterdam succeeded Antwerp (as Antwerp had earlier succeeded Bruges) as the major trading center of northwestern Europe. Dutch ships played a predominant role in the international carrying trade: in the mid-seventeenth century it is estimated that the Dutch operated between half and three-quarters of the world's merchant vessels. The Dutch also controlled the very lucrative North Sea herring fisheries. Their East India Company, founded in 1602, assembled and exploited a commercial empire. It paid large regular dividends and was a pioneer instance of the joint-stock company, sponsored by the state and pooling the resources of many businessmen who would scarcely have risked such a formidable undertaking on an individual basis. The Bank of Amsterdam, founded in 1609, was also a model, minting its own florins and so innovative in services to depositors that it made Amsterdam the financial capital of Europe. The Dutch invented life insurance and perfected the actuarial calculations on which it is based. Specialized industries flourished in particular cities and towns: diamond cutting, printing, and bookbinding at Amsterdam; shipbuilding at Zaandam; gin distilling at Schiedam; woolens at Leiden and linens at Haarlem. The Dutch, together with their Catholic cousins under Spanish rule in Flanders, were in the van of European agricultural progress; they created new farm plots called polders by diking and draining lands formerly under the sea, and they experimented with new techniques of scientific farming and with new crops. Among the latter were tulips, imported from the Ottoman Empire; the growing of tulip bulbs in the fields around Haarlem set off a wild financial speculation, the "Tulipomania" of the 1630s.

In government, the Dutch republic was no model of up-to-date efficiency, for the United Provinces were united in name only, fragmented by Dutch deference to traditional local home rule. The seven provinces sent delegates (*Hooge Moogende*, "high mightinesses") to the Estates General, which functioned like a diplomatic congress rather than a central legislature. Each province did have a chief executive, the stadholder, originally the local lieutenant of the Spanish king in the days of Hapsburg rule, and the fact that most of the provinces chose as stadholder the incumbent prince of the house of Orange made him a symbol of national unity. Twice in the seventeenth century, however, the preponderance of the Orange stadholder was challenged by the ranking local official of the most important province, the grand pensionary of Holland. In the first quarter of the century the grand pensionary, Jan van Olden Barneveldt, who was also the organizer of the East India Company, dominated Dutch politics until he was executed because of his support for Arminian doctrines of free will against Calvinist predestination. In the third quarter, the grand pensionary, Jan De Witt, an actuarial expert, ran the republic until he was lynched by a mob when the soldiers of Louis XIV overran an ill-prepared Holland in the 1670s.

In religion, Dutch practicality brought wide toleration. The beneficiaries were the substantial minority of Catholics, Protestant dissidents from Calvinist orthodoxy—Lutherans, Anabaptists, and eventually even Arminians—and Jewish refugees from Spain, Portugal, Poland, and Lithuania. The Jews made a considerable contribution to Dutch prosperity, and a still larger one was made by Calvinist refugees from the southern

Vermeer's "View of Delft," painted ca. 1658.

Netherlands. Dutch freedom made Holland a major publishing center of works in French and English and carried Dutch universities, especially that at Leiden, to the top of the European learned world. Individual Dutchmen made distinguished contributions to European culture, and the name of one of them—Rembrandt—has become a synonym for artistic genius. (Further particulars of Dutch artistic and intellectual achievements will be found in Chapter 15.)

The style of Dutch civilization in its great age was solid, reasonable, sober, but far from colorless, by no means puritanical in any ascetic sense. It is also a persuasive exhibit in support of Weber's thesis on the Protestant ethic. This little nation, through intelligence, hard work, hard trading, and adventurous exploration—and exploitation—overseas, won a high place in the world. But by 1700 the great days of the Dutch republic were coming to an end, as it was eclipsed by its larger and more powerful neighbors, Britain, France, and Prussia. Like the Swedes, who won a brief preponderance at about the same time, the Dutch did not have the resources at home to support the status of a great power.

V Germany and the Thirty Years' War

Like the great wars of the sixteenth century, the Thirty Years' War, 1618–1648, was in part a conflict over religion, and like them it had a Hapsburg focus. This time, however, the focus was more on the Austrian than the Spanish Hapsburgs, and so the bulk of the fighting took place in Germany. While the Hapsburg emperor, Ferdinand II (1619–1637), did not aspire to universal rule, he did make the last serious political and military effort to unify Germany under Catholic rule. The Thirty Years' War began as a conflict between Catholics and Protestants; it ended as an almost purely political struggle to reduce the power of the Hapsburgs in favor of France and a newcomer to high international politics, Sweden.

The Peace of Augsburg in 1555 did not bring complete religious peace to Germany. It did not recognize Calvinism, to say nothing of the more radical Protestant sects, and it left unsettled the problem of ecclesiastical reservation. On this latter issue, an imperial decree provided that if a Catholic prelate were converted to Protestantism the property formerly under his control should remain in Catholic hands. But this

The hanging of thieves during the Thirty Years' War: a contemporary engraving.

was a one-sided proclamation; it had not been formally negotiated with the Protestants, who greatly resented it.

By the opening of the seventeenth century, the religious situation in Germany was becoming increasingly unsettled. In spite of the Augsburg peace, Calvinism had spread rapidly since 1555. Calvinist princes, ignoring the provision in the settlement against proselytizing, sponsored active missions in both Lutheran and Catholic regions. They also banded together in the Protestant Union (1608), which led Catholic German states to form the rival Catholic League (1609). It is important to note that more than religion was involved and that both the Union and the League had political ambitions as well. Both represented the interests of German particularism—that is, of the individual states—against those of the Holy Roman Empire, even though the Catholic League and its leader, Maximilian of Bavaria, were to ally with the emperor Ferdinand.

The German religious situation concerned the Spanish Hapsburgs as well as their Austrian cousins. After the Dutch revolt, the Spaniards wanted to stabilize a line of communications between their Belgian and Italian lands traversing the Rhine valley and the Alps. The Dutch and the French both wanted to thwart Spanish plans of securing this overland route, and the Bourbon monarchs of France did not relish the idea of being encircled by Hapsburg territory any more than their Valois predecessors had. A major physical obstacle blocking Spanish communications was the Palatinate, a rich vineyard area in the Rhineland ruled by a Calvinist elector.

The Struggle over Bohemia and the Palatinate, 1618–1625

In 1618 the Elector Palatine was Frederick, who also headed the Protestant Union and was married to the daughter of James I of England. Frederick hoped to break the Catholic hold on the office of emperor upon the death of the emperor Matthias, who was old and childless and had already chosen as his heir the strongly Catholic Hapsburg prince, Ferdinand. The electors of Saxony, Brandenburg, and the Palatinate were Protestants; if there could be four Protestant electors instead of three when Matthias died, the majority could then install a Protestant emperor. Because three electors were Catholic archbishops the only way to elect an additional Protestant was to oust the one lay Catholic elector, the king of Bohemia, a position filled in name by the emperor Matthias and in practice by his heir, Ferdinand, who was styled "king-elect."

Bohemia, today a part of Czechoslovakia, was then a Hapsburg crown land; its Czech inhabitants wanted local independence from the rule of Germans and of Vienna. Some Czechs expressed their national defiance of the Germans by following the faith that John Hus had taught them two centuries before, and that was called Utraquism (from the Latin for "both") because it gave the laity communion in both wine and bread. While Utraquists, Lutherans, and Calvinists were all tolerated in Bohemia, the state religion was Catholic, and the prospect of Ferdinand's becoming king of Bohemia and then emperor alarmed Czech Protestants. When Protestant leaders opposing invasion of Czech religious liberties were arrested, a revolt broke out, beginning with the famous defenestration of Prague (May 23, 1618), in which two Catholic imperial governors were thrown out of a window into a courtyard seventy feet below. They landed on a pile of dung, and escaped with their lives.

The Czech rebels set up their own government and offered the crown of Bohemia to Frederick of the Palatinate. Frederick went off to Prague but without making adequate provision for defense of his home territories in the Rhineland, which the Spaniards occupied in 1620. Meantime, Catholics in Bohemia, Spain, and Flanders rallied against the Czech rebels with money and men. On the death of the emperor Matthias in 1619, the imperial electors chose the Hapsburg Ferdinand as his successor (Emperor Ferdinand II, 1619–1637). Maximilian of Bavaria, head of the Catholic League, supported Ferdinand's cause in Bohemia in return for a promise of receiving Frederick's electoral post; even the Lutheran elector of Saxony also supported Ferdinand. The Protestant Union remained neutral, as did England, although the Protestant Frederick was very popular in his father-in-law's kingdom. In Bohemia, Maximilian and the Catholic forces won the battle of the White Mountain (1620), derisively nicknamed the "winter king" because of his brief tenure, Frederick fled, and Ferdinand made the Bohemian throne hereditary in his own family. He also abolished toleration of Czech Utraquists and Calvinists, but granted it temporarily to Lutherans because of his obligations to the elector of Saxony. He executed the leaders of the rebellion, confiscated their lands, and sanctioned terrible destruction in Bohemia.

The continued presence of Spanish forces in the Palatinate upset the balance of power. The Lutheran king of Denmark, Christian IV (1588–1648), feared the Hapsburgs would move north toward the Baltic; the French faced a new Hapsburg encirclement; and the Dutch were threatened by an immediate Spanish attack. The Dutch made an alliance with Christian IV, and another with the fugitive Frederick, agreeing to subsidize his attempt to reconquer the Palatinate. When fighting resumed, Frederick was defeated again, whereupon the emperor Ferdinand transferred the Palatine electorate to Maximilian of Bavaria (1625).

In France, meantime, Cardinal Richelieu, chief minister of Louis XIII (1610–1643), recognized the Hapsburg danger and took steps to counter it. He was ready to arrange a dynastic marriage between the future Charles I of England and Louis XIII's sister, Henrietta Maria, and to make an alliance with other Protestants: Frederick, the Dutch, Christian IV, and Gustavus Adolphus, the Lutheran king of Sweden. By the summer of 1624 the new coalition was taking shape, but was shattered by Spanish victories in Holland (1625) and the unwillingness of Gustavus to serve under the Danes, traditional enemies of the Swedes. Christian IV had to defend the Protestants alone.

Intervention by Denmark and Sweden, 1625–1635

A vigorous and ambitious monarch, King Christian IV had taken full advantage of the increased authority that Lutheranism gave to royalty. When he intervened in the war, he sought not only to defend his coreligionists but also to extend Danish political and economic hegemony over northern Germany. To check the Danish invasion, the German Catholics enlisted the help of the private army of Wallenstein (1583–1634), a general who, though born of a German Protestant family in Bohemia, was reared a Catholic and fought on the imperial side. He recruited and paid an army that lived off the land by requisition and plunder,

sometimes at the expense of Catholic and imperial sympathizers. Wallenstein, who had bought huge tracts of Bohemian real estate confiscated from Czech rebels, was in fact a German condottiere, a private citizen seeking to becoming a ruling prince, perhaps even emperor of a rejuvenated Germany. He never came close to success, but his army was a major factor in the war at its most critical period. Together with the forces of the Catholic League under Count Tilly, Wallenstein's army defeated the Danes and moved northward into Danish territory.

Then, at the height of the imperial and Catholic success, the emperor Ferdinand and his advisers overreached themselves. In the Edict of Restitution (1629) they attempted a one-sided resolution of the long-vexing question of ecclesiastical reservation by demanding the restoration of all clerical estates that had passed from Catholic to Lutheran hands since 1551, three generations earlier. The edict also affirmed the Augsburg exclusion of the Calvinists and the radical Protestants from toleration. The Treaty of Lübeck, also in 1629, allowed Christian IV to recover his Danish lands but exacted from him a promise not to intervene again in Germany. This seemed to the outside world a sign that Hapsburg power was actually spreading to the Baltic, a region thoroughly Protestant and hitherto only on the margin of imperial control. The old pattern was then repeated: the Hapsburgs were trespassing beyond their customary spheres of influence; those upon whom they encroached resisted the trespass; and the trespasser was finally forced to withdraw.

More and more the emperor Ferdinand became indebted to the ambitious Wallenstein, and less and less could he control him. Wallenstein planned to found a new Baltic trading company with the remnants of the Hanseatic organization, and by opening the Baltic to the Spaniards make possible a complete victory over the Dutch. When Ferdinand asked him for troops to use in Italy against the French, Wallenstein, intent on his northern plans, refused. Soon Ferdinand dismissed Wallenstein, leaving the imperial forces under the command of Tilly and of Maximilian of Bavaria, who had been alarmed by Wallenstein's activities and was placated by his departure. If Ferdinand had also placated the Protestants by revoking the Edict of Restitution, peace might have been possible. But he failed to do so, and the war resumed with Gustavus Adolphus as the Protestant champion.

Called the Lion of the North, Gustavus Adolphus (reigned 1611–1632) was a much stronger champion than Christian had been. Like Christian, he had ambitions for political control over northern Germany, and he hoped that Sweden might assume the old Hanseatic economic leadership. He had tamed the unruly Swedish nobility, given his country an efficient government and a sound economy, taken lessons from the Dutch in military tactics, and proved himself and his armies against Russia and Poland by establishing a Swedish foothold on the eastern shores of the Baltic, notably

The siege of Magdeburg, 1631.

by taking the great Hanseatic city of Riga. A Lutheran but tolerant of Calvinists, Gustavus brought a large, well-disciplined army equipped with hymnbooks, and added to it all the recruits, even prisoners, that he could induce to join him. Sharing the hardships of his troops, he usually restrained them from plunder. Richelieu agreed to subsidize his forces, and Gustavus agreed not to fight against Maximilian and to guarantee freedom of worship for Catholics. The Protestant electors of Brandenburg and Saxony denounced the Edict of Restitution and mobilized, in part to revive the Protestant cause, but also to protect the Germans against the Swedes.

German Protestant hesitation ended after a Catholic victory that probably did more to harm the Catholic cause than a defeat—the fall and sack of Magdeburg, the "Maiden City" of the Protestants and a great symbol of their cause. Stormed by the imperialists in May 1631, it was almost wholly destroyed by fire and pillage. The imperial general Pappenheim, who commanded at the storming of the walls, estimated that twenty thousand people were killed. Each side sought to blame the sack on the other and to enlist in its cause public opinion all over Europe. A volume issued in 1931 on the three-hundredth anniversary of the sack takes forty-six pages to list contemporary accounts in European newspapers (then in their infancy), pamphlets, broadsides, popular songs, and cartoons. The Protestants accused the imperial commander-in-chief, Tilly, of planning the destruction of the city and its inhabitants, an accusation from which most historians absolve him, for the

imperial troops clearly got out of hand. The Catholics countered by accusing the Protestants of setting the fires themselves as a "scorched-earth" tactic. But in the long run, as the outpourings of the press took effect, the Protestant cause was strengthened.

The Protestant electors of Brandenburg and Saxony now allied themselves with Gustavus. At Breitenfeld in September 1631, Gustavus defeated Tilly; combined with a defeat of the Spaniards off the Dutch coast, this turned the tide against the Hapsburgs. The Saxons invaded Bohemia and recaptured Prague in the name of Frederick of the Palatinate, while Gustavus invaded the Catholic lands of south-central Germany, taking Frankfurt and Mainz, and obtaining the alliance of many princes and free cities. In the crisis, Ferdinand turned back to Wallenstein, who consented to return to his command.

Gustavus had been more successful than Richelieu, his sponsor, had expected; indeed, too successful, since not only the Hapsburgs but Maximilian and the Catholic League, still friends of France, were suffering from the Swedes. Gustavus was planning to reorganize all Germany, to unite Lutheran and Calvinist churches, and even to become emperor—aims opposed by all the German princes, Catholic and Protestant alike. But the strength of Gustavus' position declined: his allies were untrustworthy and his enemies, Maximilian and Wallenstein, drew together. In November 1632 the Swedes won the battle of Lützen, defeating Wallenstein; Gustavus Adolphus, however, was killed.

Once more a moment had arrived when peace

might have been possible, yet the fighting, and the plague, famine, and death accompanying it, continued. The pope, suspect among the cardinals as hostile to the Catholic cause, wanted peace. Richelieu preferred war, in order to further French aims in the Rhineland; the Swedes needed to protect their heavy investment and come out of the fighting with some territory; the Spaniards hoped that Gustavus' death meant that the Hapsburg cause could be saved and the Dutch defeated. Gustavus' chancellor, Oxenstierna, an able diplomat, was recognized by the German Protestants in 1633 as chief of the Protestant cause.

Wallenstein negotiated with the enemies of the empire (he wanted the French to recognize him as king of Bohemia); his army began to dribble away and he was again dismissed by the emperor Ferdinand. On February 24, 1634, an English mercenary in the imperial service murdered Wallenstein and won an imperial reward. At Nordlingen, in September 1634, the forces of Ferdinand defeated the Protestants, thereby lessening the influence of Sweden and making Cardinal Richelieu the chief strategist for the Protestant cause, which now became the Bourbon cause.

The Hapsburg-Bourbon Conflict, 1635-1648

The remainder of the Thirty Years' War was a Hapsburg-Bourbon conflict, a sequel to the Hapsburg-Valois wars. The Protestant commander had to promise future toleration for Catholicism in Germany, and undertake to keep on fighting indefinitely in exchange for French men and money. More and more the original religious character of the war became transformed into a purely dynastic and political struggle. The armies themselves on both sides were made up of a mixture of men from just about every nationality in Europe; they fought as professional soldiers, changing sides frequently, and taking their women and children with them everywhere. On the imperial side camp followers were kept in some kind of order by officials known informally as "provosts of the harlots."

In 1635 the emperor Ferdinand at last relinquished the Edict of Restitution and made a compromise peace with the elector of Saxony. Most of the other Lutheran princes signed also. Alarmed by the imperial gains and by the renewed activity of the Spaniards in the Low Countries, Richelieu made new arrangements with Oxenstierna in Germany and a new alliance with the Dutch. No longer confining himself to the role of subsidizer, he declared war on Spain. The war would go on, though the only German allies the French and Swedes still had were a few Calvinist princes.

A great Dutch naval victory over Spain (1639) put an end to the power of the Spanish navy, which had been declining for some years. The power of Spain was further sapped by unrest in Catalonia and by the revolt (1640) of Portugal, which reestablished its independence. The death of Richelieu (1642) and of Louis XIII (1643) did not alter French policy. A few days after the death of Louis, the French defeated the Spaniards so thoroughly that Spain was temporarily knocked out of the war and permanently removed from effective competition for European hegemony. Another factor making for a negotiated settlement of the war was the accession of the peace-loving Christina, daughter of Gustavus Adolphus, as Swedish queen in 1644.

By then, peace conferences were already under way in the northwestern area of Germany called Westphalia—between Hapsburgs and Swedes at Osnabrück, and between Hapsburgs and French nearby at Münster. The problems to be settled were many and delicate, and differences between the allies that had been unimportant during open warfare proved critical when it came to negotiating a religious settlement. The conferences dragged on for several years while the fighting and destruction continued. The Dutch made a separate peace with the Spaniards, and pulled out of the French alliance after they learned of secret French negotiations with Spain hostile to their interests. French victories forced the wavering emperor Ferdinand III (reigned 1637-1657) to agree to the terms that had been so painstakingly hammered out, and on October 24, 1648, the Peace of Westphalia put an end to the Thirty Years' War.

The Peace of Westphalia

In religion the terms of the peace extended the *cuius regio eius religio* principle of the Augsburg settlement to Calvinists as well as to Lutherans and Catholics. Princes could still "determine" the faith of their territories, but the right of dissidents to emigrate was recognized. In most of Protestant Germany multiplicity of sects was in fact accepted. On the question of ecclesiastical reservation the year 1624 was designated by compromise as the normal year for establishing the status of Church property; for the Protestants this was a great advance over the Edict of Restitution. States forcibly converted to Catholicism during the war won the right to revert to Protestantism; for Protestants in Hapsburg territories, however, there was no toleration.

Territorially, though some of the separate German states came out well, Germany herself was a victim. France secured part of Alsace and sovereignty over the long-occupied bishoprics of Metz, Toul, and Verdun—all on the western margins of the Holy Roman Empire. Sweden received most of Pomerania, along the Baltic shore of Germany, three votes in the German Diet, and a large cash indemnity to pay the one hundred thousand troops (chiefly non-Swedish mercenaries) still under her flag. As recompense for the loss of Pomerania, Brandenburg received the archbishopric of Magdeburg and several other bishoprics. The family of Maximilian of Bavaria kept the electorate of the Palatinate and a part of its territory; the rest was returned to the son of Frederick who was restored as an elector, thus raising the total number of electors to eight. German particularism gained, as the individual

Europe in 1648

Legend:
- Brandenburg-Prussia
- Austrian Hapsburg Lands
- Spanish Hapsburg Lands
- Swedish possessions
- Venetian possessions
- Ottoman Empire
- Boundary of the Holy Roman Empire
- ■ Battle sites

Approximate division line between Puritans and Cavaliers in England, May, 1643

NORWAY

Oslo

SCOTLAND

Edinburgh
Dunbar ■ Berwick

North Sea

DENMARK

Copenhagen

Stockholm

Baltic

ULSTER

Drogheda ■

IRELAND

Dublin

Wexford

Preston ■ ■ Marston Moor

ENGLAND

Nottingham

Worcester

Naseby ■

London

Lübeck

Hamburg

POMERANIA

Bremen

Elbe R.

BRANDENBURG

Berlin

Oder R.

Texel

UNITED NETHERLANDS

Osnabrück

Münster

THE

WEST-PHALIA

Magdeburg

Lützen

SAXONY

SILES

Atlantic Ocean

SPANISH NETHERLANDS

Rocroy ■

Rhine R.

EMPIRE

Prague

BOHEMIA

MORAVI

Seine R.

Paris

Verdun

PALATINATE

Heidelberg

Metz

Nantes

Orléans

Toul

Strasbourg

Loire R.

ALSACE

BAVARIA

Danube R.

AUSTRIA

Vienna

FRANCE

FRANCHE COMTÉ

SWITZERLAND

VALTELLINE

STYRIA

CARINTHIA

Geneva

TYROL

CARNIOLA

HU

Bordeaux

Rhône R.

SAVOY

PIEDMONT

MILAN

Po R.

Venice

Avignon (to the Papacy)

Genoa

VENETIAN REPUBLIC

Marseilles

Florence

PAPAL STATES

Rag

PORTUGAL

Burgos

Ebro R.

CORSICA (to Genoa)

Rome

NAPLES

Lisbon

Tagus R.

Madrid

SPAIN

Barcelona

SARDINIA

Naples

Valencia

BALEARIC IS.

Guadalquivir R.

Seville

Granada

Mediterranean Sea

SICILY

Palermo

ALGIERS
(Tributary to Ottoman Empire)

TUNIS

MALTA

0   500

Miles

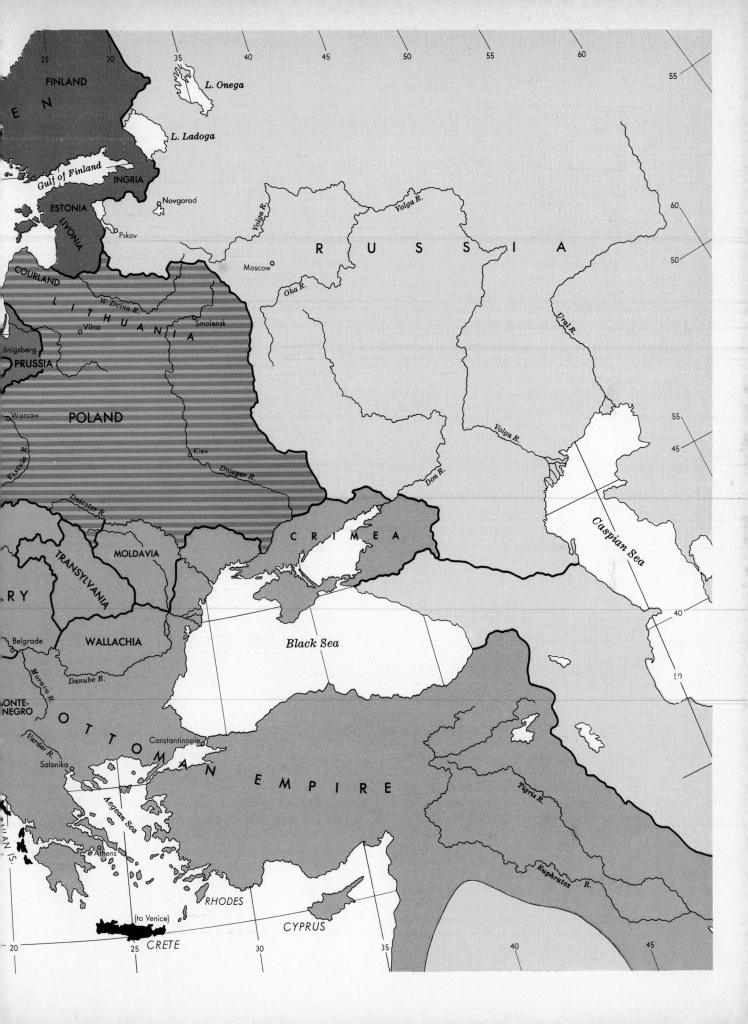

German states secured the right to conduct their own foreign affairs, making treaties among themselves and with foreign powers if these were not directed against the emperor. This last was a face-saving for the Hapsburgs, for the fact that the constituent states now had their own foreign services, their own armies, their own finances—three earmarks of independent sovereignty—showed that the Holy Roman Empire of the German nation was no longer a viable political entity. The Westphalian settlement also recognized formally the independence of the Dutch republic, already independent in fact for over half a century, and of the Swiss confederation, the nucleus of which had first broken away from Hapsburg control during the later Middle Ages.

For more than two centuries after 1648, the Thirty Years' War was blamed for everything that later went wrong in Germany. We know now that the economic decline of Germany had begun well before the war opened in 1618 and that the figures of deaths and destruction recorded in contemporary chronicles were inflated and are highly unreliable. Yet, even when allowance is made for exaggerations, scholars estimate that the overall diminution in the German population was from about twenty-one million in 1618 to less than thirteen and a half million in 1648. Some historians also trace to this destructive war aspects of modern Germany that have made her a disturbing influence in the modern world. They point to a national sense of inferiority heightened by her delayed achievement of national unity, a lack of the slow ripening in self-government that a more orderly growth in early modern times might have encouraged, a too strong need for authority and obedience brought out in response to the anarchic conditions of the seventeenth century. These are dangerously big generalizations that are at most suggestive; they can by no means be proved.

On the other hand, it is evident that the final outcome of the war raised almost as many problems as it solved. It did not end hostilities between two of the chief belligerents, France and Spain, who continued to fight for another eleven years. The Peace of Westphalia satisfied neither the pope, who denounced it, nor many Protestants, who felt betrayed by it. Politically, the fresh successes of German particularism limited the Hapsburgs' direct power in Germany to their family lands and enabled such states as Bavaria, Saxony and, above all, Brandenburg-Prussia to move to the fore in German affairs. In addition, non-Austrian Germans harbored bitter resentment against the Hapsburgs for having fought this most terrible of dynastic and religious wars to protect family interests. And it was a most terrible war, not just because of its length but because of its savage character and the large armies involved. The Swedish force alone numbered two hundred thousand at its peak and was the largest to be put in the field since Roman days. Despite the enormous loss of life, however, the war made little change in the social hierarchy of Germany; once the fighting was over, the nobility often succeeded in forcing the peasants back onto the lands by denying them the right to leave their village or engage in home industry. One can appreciate why some recent historians have pronounced the Thirty Years' War a crucial event in the development of a crisis in seventeenth-century Europe, which Chapter 15 examines in more detail.

Reading Suggestions on Dynastic Politics and Warfare

General Accounts

The New Cambridge Modern History (Cambridge Univ.). The first four volumes of this lengthy collaborative project contain much information on the topics covered in this chapter.

H. G. Koenigsberger and G. L. Mosse, *Europe in the Sixteenth Century* (*Holt). An excellent survey with useful bibliographical footnotes.

E. F. Rice, Jr., *The Foundations of Early Modern Europe, 1460–1559* and R. S. Dunn, *The Age of Religious Wars, 1559–1689* (*Norton). Enlightening brief surveys; part of a series published recently.

J. H. Elliott, *Europe Divided, 1559–1598* (*Torchbooks). Useful introduction to the Age of Philip II.

M. R. O'Connell, *The Counter Reformation, 1559–1610,* and C. J. Friedrich, *The Age of the Baroque, 1610–1660* (*Torchbooks). Comprehensive volumes, with full bibliographies, in the Rise of Modern Europe series. Friedrich's is particularly stimulating.

H. Trevor-Roper, ed., *The Age of Expansion* (McGraw-Hill, 1968). Sumptuously illustrated collaborative volume touching on many topics in European and world history from the mid-sixteenth to mid-seventeenth century.

The Cambridge Economic History of Europe, Vol. 4: *The Economy of Expanding Europe in the Sixteenth and Seventeenth Centuries* (Cambridge Univ., 1967). Scholarly chapters by experts on selected aspects of the economy rather than a general survey.

War and Diplomacy, 1494–1598

L. Dehio, *The Precarious Balance: Four Centuries of the European Power Struggle* (*Vintage). A German historian interprets the shifting balance of power, beginning with the sixteenth century.

G. Mattingly, *Renaissance Diplomacy* (*Sentry). A stimulating and indispensable introduction.

C. Petrie, *Earlier Diplomatic History, 1492–1713* (Macmillan, 1949). A useful manual.

C. H. Carter, *The Secret Diplomacy of the Habsburgs, 1598–1625* (Columbia Univ., 1964.) An instructive case study in diplomatic history.

C. W. C. Oman, *A History of the Art of War in the Sixteenth Century* (Dutton, 1973). Highly interesting study of a neglected aspect of history.

J. F. C. Fuller, *A Military History of the Western World,* 3 vols. (*Funk & Wagnalls). By an informative, somewhat unorthodox general; volumes I and II contain material relevant to this chapter.

Spain

J. Lynch, *Spain under the Habsburgs,* 2 vols. (Oxford Univ., 1964, 1969). A thorough and up-to-date scholarly study; the first volume treats the sixteenth century, and the second the seventeenth.

J. H. Elliott, *Imperial Spain, 1469–1716* (E. Arnold, 1963). Another good scholarly introduction. Elliott is the author of an important monograph: *The River of Catalans: A Study in the Decline of Spain, 1598–1640* (Cambridge Univ., 1963).

R. T. Davies, *The Golden Century of Spain* (*Torchbooks) and *Spain in Decline, 1621–1700* (St. Martin's, 1957). Popular accounts addressed to the general reader.

K. Brandi, *The Emperor Charles V* (*Humanities). Thorough study of the ruler of a troubled dynastic conglomerate.

C. Petrie, *Philip II of Spain* (Norton, 1963). An interesting and impartial biography.

F. Braudel, *The Mediterranean and the Mediterranean World in the Age of Philip II,* 2 vols. (Harper, 1972). An important geographical and socio-economic study of Spain's involvement with Italy and the Ottoman Empire.

France

A. Guérard, *France in the Classical Age: The Life and Death of an Ideal* (Braziller, 1956). Lively, provocative, and highly personal interpretation of French history from the Renaissance to Napoleon.

J. E. Neale, *The Age of Catherine de' Medici* (*Torchbooks). Excellent short introduction to the French civil and religious wars.

J. W. Thompson, *The Wars of Religion in France, 1559–1576* (Univ. of Chicago, 1909). A detailed narrative; still very useful.

J. Héritier, *Catherine de Medici* (St. Martin's, 1963). A sound biography.

A. J. Grant, *The Huguenots* (Butterworth, 1934). A brief and reasonably dispassionate study.

W. J. Stankiewicz, *Politics and Religion in Seventeenth Century France* (Univ. of California, 1960). Goes back to the politiques of the late sixteenth century.

Q. Hurst, *Henry of Navarre* (Appleton, 1938). Standard biography.

England

C. Read, *The Tudors* (*Norton). Excellent introduction to the interrelations of personalities and politics. Read also published *The Government of England under Elizabeth* (*Univ. of Virginia) and scholarly studies of her chief ministers.

J. D. Mackie, *The Earlier Tudors, 1485–1558,* and J. B. Black, *The Reign of Elizabeth, 1558–1603* (Clarendon, 1952, 1960). Comprehensive, scholarly volumes in the Oxford History of England.

S. T. Bindoff, *Tudor England* (*Penguin). Sound, scholarly introduction.

G. R. Elton, *The Tudor Revolution in Government* (*Cambridge Univ.). Important study of the shift to a bureaucratic state.

J. J. Scarisbrick, *Henry VIII* (*Univ. of California). The first new scholarly biography in more than half a century; may be supplemented by the still more recent psychological study by L. B. Smith, *Henry VIII: The Mask of Royalty* (*Sentry).

J. E. Neale, *Queen Elizabeth I: A Biography* (*Anchor). By a great scholar, author also of *The Elizabethan House of Commons* (*Penguin) and *Elizabeth I and Her Parliaments,* 2 vols. (Cape, 1953, 1957).

E. Jenkins, *Elizabeth the Great* (*Capricorn). Sound biography focused more on the person than the queen.

W. MacCaffrey, *The Shaping of the Elizabethan Regime* (*Princeton Univ.). Able study of her early years in power.

W. P. Haugaard, *Elizabeth and the English Reformation* (Cambridge Univ., 1968). Excellent scholarly assessment.

G. Mattingly, *The Armada* (*Sentry). A truly great work of history.

A. Fraser, *Mary, Queen of Scots* (*Dell). Recent biography of Elizabeth's impulsive antagonist.

The Dutch Republic

C. J. Cadoux, *Philip of Spain and the Netherlands* (Butterworth, 1947). Moderate restatement of the liberal Protestant view of the question.

P. Geyl, *The Revolt of the Netherlands, 1555–1609* (*Barnes & Noble) and *The Netherlands in the Seventeenth Century,* 2 vols. (Barnes & Noble, 1961, 1964). Detailed studies by a distinguished Dutch historian who regrets the disruption of the unity of the Low Countries. A briefer statement may be found in his *History of the Low Countries* (St. Martin's, 1964).

J. Huizinga, *Dutch Civilization in the Seventeenth Century and Other Essays* (*Torchbooks). The title essay is a thoughtful evaluation by another distinguished Dutch historian.

C. V. Wedgwood, *William the Silent* (*Norton). Sound biography of the Dutch national hero.

V. Barbour, *Capitalism in Amsterdam in the Seventeenth Century* (*Ann Arbor). Illuminating study of an important factor in Dutch success.

Germany and the Thirty Years' War

H. Holborn, *A History of Modern Germany.* Vol. 2: *The Reformation* (Knopf, 1959). This authoritative study goes down to 1648.

C. V. Wedgwood, *The Thirty Years' War* (*Anchor). Full and generally well-balanced narrative.

S. H. Steinberg, *The "Thirty Years' War" and the Conflict for European Hegemony, 1600–1660* (*Norton). Briefer, more recent account.

G. Pagès, *The Thirty Years' War* (*Torchbooks). Translation of an older French study, stressing the diplomatic side of the war.

T. K. Rabb, ed., *The Thirty Years' War: Problems of Motive, Extent, and Effect* (*Heath). Sampler of differing views of these controversial questions.

M. Roberts, *Gustavus Adolphus: A History of Sweden, 1611–1632,* 2 vols. (Longmans, 1953, 1958). Sympathetic detailed biography.

Sources and Fiction

N. Roelker, ed., *The Paris of Henry of Navarre* (Harvard Univ., 1958). Selections from the informative *Mémoires-journaux* of Pierre de l'Estoile, a rich source of social history.

H. Haydn, ed., *The Portable Elizabethan Reader* (*Viking). A good anthology.

S. Putnam, ed., *The Portable Cervantes* (*Viking). Selections from the editor's admirable translation of *Don Quixote.*

H. J. C. von Grimmelshausen, *Simplicius Simplicissimus* (*Bobbs-Merrill). Picaresque but realistic novel written in the seventeenth century and set against the background of war-ravaged Germany.

W. Scott, *Kenilworth* (*Airmont). By the famous Scottish novelist of the romantic era; the setting is Elizabethan England.

The Expansion of Europe in Early Modern Times

I Exploration and Expansion, Old and New

During the early modern centuries, when Europeans were experiencing the Renaissance and the Reformation, with its long aftermath of traumatic conflict, some of them took part in a remarkable expansion that carried European sailors, merchants, missionaries, settlers, and adventurers to almost every quarter of the globe. What Westerners confidently call "the known world" moved outward at a breathtaking pace, although relatively few Westerners, then or now, realized that non-Western peoples—the Chinese or American Indians, for example—had their own different concept of the "known world." In the age of Homer, the known world of the West had encompassed little more than the eastern Mediterranean and its fringes. Under Alexander the Great and the Romans, it was still centered on the Mediterranean and the western fringes of Asia, with much of the interior of Europe and Africa hazy or blank, and with the Americas still unsuspected. Then the explorations of the late Middle Ages launched a continuous process that culminated in the full fruition of geographical knowledge.

Westerners were not the first people to move and migrate over vast reaches of water. Even earlier than the Viking voyages in the Atlantic, the Polynesians, for example, who came from southern China, had accomplished the daring feat of settling remote Pacific islands. But the Polynesians and other early migrants kept no written records and no significant ties with their places of origin. They were not societies in expansion, but groups of individuals on the move. The expansion of the West was very different. From the very start in ancient Greece and Rome, records were kept, maps were made, and the nucleus always remained in touch with its offshoots. Western society has expanded *as a society*, often as a group of states.

The modern Western expansion, which began in the mid-fifteenth century, differed also in important ways from the expansion that had carried the cultures of the ancient Near East as far as western and northern Europe. In the first place, this modern expansion was much faster and covered more ground. Although some secrets of the Arctic and the Antarctic, some details of the wilder interiors of the world, were not known to us until the twentieth century, it is broadly true that the whole world was revealed to Europeans within two and a half or three centuries after 1450—within four long lifetimes. In the second place, this modern expansion was the first time our Western society crossed great oceans. Ancient and medieval Western navigation had clung to the narrow seas and the shorelines. The ancients had even commonly drawn up their boats on land to spend the night. Now Westerners crossed the Atlantic and the Pacific, far from the protecting land. In the third place, this expansion carried Westerners well outside the orbit of relations with Byzantines and Muslims, who were also successors to the cultures of Socrates and Christ, into relations with a bewildering variety of races, creeds, and cultures, from naked savages to cultivated Chinese. Not since the Germanic peoples had been tamed and converted in the early Middle Ages had Westerners come into close contact with primitive peoples. Finally, and of very great importance, expanding Europe possessed a margin of superior material and technological strength that enabled Western society to do what no society had ever done before—extend its influence around the world.

An important element of that margin was the possession of firearms; yet firearms could be legally or illegally acquired by non-Europeans, and very soon were. The strength by which Europeans overcame the world was a compound of technological and economic superiority and of superior political and social organization, which in turn permitted superior military organization. This superiority was not applied from a common Western center, but rather by half a dozen competing Western nations, each anxious to cut the others' throats, and quite willing to arm and organize natives against its Western competitors. Frenchmen in North America armed the Indians against the British and the British armed them against the French. Yet not even the Iroquois were able to maintain themselves against white society. French, British, Portuguese, Dutch, Spanish, and later German and American peoples intrigued against one another in the Far East, and yet not until the mid-twentieth century did any Asian nation (save only Japan, and Japan not until about 1900) really compete successfully in war and politics with a Western land. So great was the Western advantage that the rivalries of competing powers did not delay the process of expansion but probably stimulated and hastened it.

How far this physical superiority in the expansion of the West throughout the world was also a spiritual and moral superiority is a problem we in the West today cannot answer as confidently as did our fathers. But you will not understand the successful expansion of Europe if you do not realize that those who carried out the expansion, though moved often by greed, by sheer despair over their lot at home, by the Renaissance enthusiasm for new things, and by many other motives, were also moved by the conviction that they were doing God's work, the work of civilization, that they were carrying with them a better way of life. They were self-reliant and energetic people, capable of great endurance and courage, and they made over the face of the globe.

Why did men living on the Atlantic coasts of Europe in the second half of the fifteenth century venture out on an ocean that ancient and medieval mariners had not seriously tried to explore? While we cannot answer the question with finality, so small a thing as the magnetic compass helped make ocean voyages possible. Without the compass, earlier mariners had been helpless, except when clear weather gave them sun or stars as guides. The actual origins of the compass are obscure, but we know that the Chinese were aware of magnetic polarity nearly two thousand years ago and that the compass itself was used in Mediterranean navigation by the close of the Middle Ages. Not only were better instruments and better methods of determining a ship's position at sea available but shipbuilders were constructing vessels that were longer and narrower than the traditional Mediterranean ships and better able to withstand the long swells of the ocean. Technologically, the way was ready for the great explorations. In addition, the rising political and economic power of the Atlantic states—Portugal, Spain, France, and England—led their merchants to search for new routes to India, since the old Near Eastern route was controlled by the Ottoman Turks and by the Italians, especially the Venetians and the Genoese. To those who interpret everything in terms of economics, Renaissance men discovered new worlds because the aggressive drives natural to nascent capitalism sent them on their way.

Yet technology and the politics of the trade routes had to be taken advantage of by men, men in the state of mind that sent Columbus out across the unknown ocean—to see with his own eyes what was there, to test his theory that because the earth is round one can travel from Europe westward and reach Asia. The explorations of Europeans were guided in part by the new spirit of empirical science that impelled men if, for instance, they heard about unicorns to go out and try to find some. Their medieval predecessors did not need to see a unicorn to believe in its existence. The new scientific spirit, however, did not immediately banish unicorns, mermaids, and sea serpents from men's minds. The first reports of newly discovered worlds resulted in a whole new set of wonders, some real or merely exaggerated, which the publishing of accounts of travel brought to all Europe.

Nothing makes more clear the consecutive, planned, deliberately scientific nature of these early modern explorations and settlements than the contrast with the sporadic, unplanned, and perhaps wholly mythical earlier oceanic navigation. Tradition is full of these early voyages, and of Atlantis, a lost continent now sunk beneath the waves but once inhabited, which Plato and later commentators tell about. Phoenicians, Irishmen, Norsemen, and Breton fishermen have all been credited with the "discovery" of America, a discovery that was never widely reported in the medieval West. Of all these tales of pre-Columbian discovery, that of the Vikings' reaching the North American continent about the end of the tenth century is most likely. There is not the slightest doubt that Norsemen reached Iceland and settled it, and that they had outposts in Greenland. Their heroic sagas credit Leif Ericson with reaching a Wineland (or Vinland), which may have been somewhere along the New England or Canadian coast, although a famous map showing Vinland has been proved a forgery. It is quite possible that all during the Middle Ages, more probably toward their close, fishermen from northwest Europe fished the Grand Banks off the coast of Newfoundland. Yet even if hundreds of Europeans reached the New World before Columbus, they did not establish a permanent link between the two worlds; they were not explorers of the kind we are about to discuss, and they were, above all, not supported by an organized social purpose.

II East by Sea to the Indies
Prince Henry and the Portuguese

The first of the great names in modern expansion is not that of a bold explorer or conquistador, but of an organizing genius who directed the work of others. Prince Henry of Portugal (1394–1460), known as "the Navigator," was a deeply religious man who may well have been moved above all by a desire to convert the populations of India and the Far East, whose existence had been well known to Westerners since the travels of Marco Polo in the thirteenth century. Indeed, there was a widespread conviction in the West that these distant peoples were in fact already Christian and for true salvation needed only to be brought in direct contact with the Roman Catholic church. One of the great medieval legends was that of Prester (that is, Priest) John, a powerful Christian ruler somewhere out in the East. Prester John was never found, and the Portuguese in India were soon disabused of their first notion that the Hindus—since they were not Muslims—must be Christians.

Prince Henry and his associates presumably also wanted to promote Portuguese commerce and national power as well as the Christian faith. They hoped to break the monopoly over the trade in gold from sub-Saharan Africa held by Arab merchants from North Africa. They went about their work carefully, sending out frequent, well-equipped expeditions. In the Atlantic, their vessels discovered Madeira and the Azores, uninhabited islands where the Portuguese and other Europeans then began to settle. The main thrust southward gradually crept along the harsh desert coast of Africa where the Sahara meets the Atlantic, until in 1445 the Portuguese moved eastward past Cape Verde, where the land began to grow greener, thus arousing false hopes that the southernmost point of the continent was near. Whether Henry himself believed that Africa could be circumnavigated is not absolutely certain, but according to legend the Phoenicians had done it, and Greco-Roman geographers had believed that Africa was surrounded by the ocean.

By 1472, after Prince Henry's death, the Portuguese reached the end of the bulge of West Africa at the Cameroons and faced the disheartening fact that the coast was once more trending southward, not eastward. But they kept on, stimulated by royal patronage, and in the next generation two great explorers finished the job. In 1488, Bartholomeu Dias, blown far south by a great storm, turned northeast and found that he had rounded the great cape later called Good Hope. He was followed by Vasco da Gama, who set out in 1497 with four ships to reach India and worked northward along the east coast of Africa, coming soon to an area of Arab trading where the route to India was well known. Despite Arab jealousy of the intruder, da Gama secured a pilot and reached the Malabar coast of India at Calicut ten months and fourteen days out from Lisbon. The Portuguese now had an ocean route to the East.

On the next great voyage toward India, the Portuguese made a lucky strike that was to break the Spanish monopoly in South America and ensure that one of the great Latin American states would be Portuguese in language and culture. Pedro Cabral, in 1500, started out to repeat da Gama's voyage to India. But by now the Portuguese were used to long voyages on the open ocean, far from sight of land, and they no longer needed to creep around the coast of Africa. Cabral kept boldly southward from the bulge of Africa and was apparently blown somewhat westward of his course so that he made a landfall on the bulge of the South American continent in what is now Brazil. He at once detached a ship and sent it home to announce his discovery. Since the voyages of Columbus were well known to navigators by this time, some geographers think that Cabral set out deliberately to see what he could find south of the westward route Columbus had taken. Six years previously, by the Treaty of Tordesillas (1494), Spain and Portugal had agreed to partition their newly discovered lands along a north-south line three hundred and seventy leagues (about a thousand miles) west of the Azores, so that eastern Brazil fell within the Portuguese sphere.

The main Portuguese push, however, was toward India and the Far East. The explorer was succeeded by that other characteristic agent of European expansion, the trader, who by no means worked alone. He was aided and protected by the power of his state, which aimed to set up for its nationals a monopoly of commerce with the newly discovered lands. The great figure of early Portuguese imperialism is Affonso de Albuquerque, governor of the Indies from 1509 to 1515, under whom the Portuguese founded their capital at Goa in India, whence they organized regular trade routes toward southeast Asia and China. By 1557 they had established a base at Macao on the Chinese coast near Canton, and begun trade with the Japanese.

Africa

The two new worlds thus opened to Europeans were very different both from Europe and from each other. Africa—excluding North Africa, from Morocco to Egypt, which had long been part of the Mediterranean world—was hot, relatively thinly populated, poor by current European standards. India, China, and much of southeast Asia were even then thickly populated, with great wealth accumulated in a few hands, with much that Europeans wanted in the way of spices, silks, and other luxuries. Africa was in a sense bypassed, though the many coastal stations that the Europeans founded soon carried on a flourishing trade in slaves. The African tribes on the great westward bulge of the continent had already left a mark on history, for they had set up two empires whose names have been revived by present-day African states after gaining their independence. Medieval Ghana controlled a much larger area than its modern namesake until it was overthrown by Muslim invaders from North Africa in the eleventh century. At the time when the Portuguese reached West Africa parts of the interior were controlled by the black empire of Mali, centered at Timbuktu, on the upper Niger River. Caravans organized by North African traders came to Timbuktu to buy gold and slaves and to sell some of the wares of civilization.

In central and southern Africa, by contrast, the tribes were not far from the Stone Age, without cities

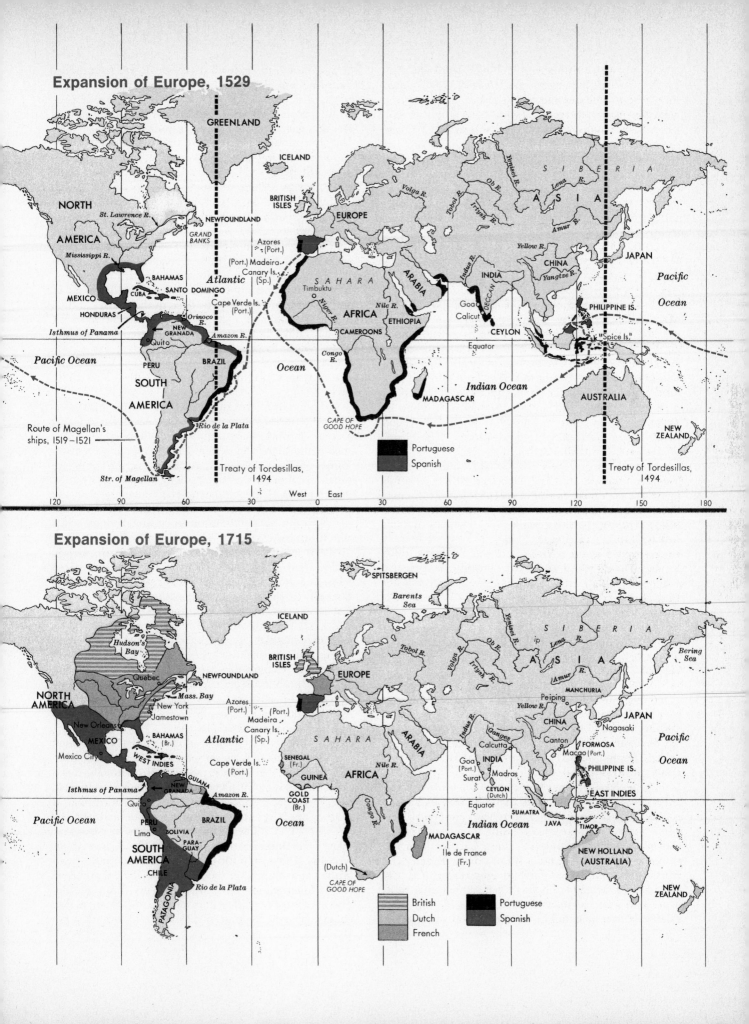

Expansion of Europe, 1529

GREENLAND
ICELAND
BRITISH ISLES
EUROPE
S I B E R I A
A S I A
JAPAN
CHINA
Pacific Ocean

NORTH AMERICA
St. Lawrence R.
NEWFOUNDLAND
GRAND BANKS
Mississippi R.
Azores (Port.)
Atlantic
BAHAMAS
MEXICO
CUBA
SANTO DOMINGO
HONDURAS
Isthmus of Panama
Quito
PERU
NEW GRANADA
Orinoco R.
Amazon R.
BRAZIL
SOUTH AMERICA
Rio de la Plata
Route of Magellan's ships, 1519–1521
Str. of Magellan
Pacific Ocean

(Port.) Madeira
Canary Is. (Sp.)
Cape Verde Is. (Port.)
SAHARA
Timbuktu
Niger R.
AFRICA
CAMEROONS
Congo R.
Ocean
CAPE OF GOOD HOPE

Volga R.
Tobol R.
Irtysh R.
Ob R.
Yenisei R.
Lena R.
Amur R.
Yellow R.
Yangtze R.
ARABIA
Nile R.
ETHIOPIA
Indus R.
INDIA
Goa
Calicut
DECCAN
CEYLON
Equator
Indian Ocean
MADAGASCAR
PHILIPPINE IS.
"Spice Is."
AUSTRALIA
NEW ZEALAND

Treaty of Tordesillas, 1494
West   East
Treaty of Tordesillas, 1494

■ Portuguese
■ Spanish

120   90   60   30   0   30   60   90   120   150   180

Expansion of Europe, 1715

SPITSBERGEN
Barents Sea
ICELAND
BRITISH ISLES
EUROPE
S I B E R I A
A S I A
Bering Sea
Pacific Ocean

NORTH AMERICA
Hudson's Bay
Quebec
Mass. Bay
New York
Jamestown
NEWFOUNDLAND
New Orleans
MEXICO
Mexico City
BAHAMAS (Br.)
Atlantic
WEST INDIES
Isthmus of Panama
Quito
NEW GRANADA
GUIANA
Amazon R.
PERU
Lima
BOLIVIA
PARAGUAY
BRAZIL
CHILE
SOUTH AMERICA
PATAGONIA
Rio de la Plata
Pacific Ocean

Azores (Port.)
(Port.) Madeira
Canary Is. (Sp.)
Cape Verde Is. (Port.)
SENEGAL (Fr.)
GUINEA
GOLD COAST (Br.)
SAHARA
AFRICA
Nile R.
Congo R.
Ocean
(Dutch)
CAPE OF GOOD HOPE

Volga R.
Tobol R.
Irtysh R.
Ob R.
Yenisei R.
Lena R.
ip
Amur R.
MANCHURIA
Peiping
Yellow R.
CHINA
Canton
Macao
FORMOSA (Port.)
JAPAN
Nagasaki
Pacific Ocean
ARABIA
Ganges
Calcutta
Goa (Port.)
Surat
INDIA
Madras
CEYLON (Dutch)
Equator
SUMATRA
JAVA
TIMOR
PHILIPPINE IS.
EAST INDIES
Indian Ocean
MADAGASCAR
Ile de France (Fr.)
NEW HOLLAND (AUSTRALIA)
NEW ZEALAND

▤ British
▤ Dutch
▤ French
■ Portuguese
■ Spanish

and states, with cultures so different from those of Europe that few Europeans made any effort to understand them. Nor did the Europeans, at least in these centuries, do much to undermine these primitive cultures. Save for the enforced mass migration of blacks as slaves, most of them to the Americas, save for some trade in ivory and other tropical goods, Africa had for years little effect on Europe, and Europe little on Africa. Except for South Africa, where the Dutch began settlement in the seventeenth century, Africa was not to be subject to colonialism until the partitions of the nineteenth century.

India

The India that Europeans reached around Africa had been marginally in touch with Europe for several thousand years. Alexander the Great had campaigned in northern India, and throughout the Middle Ages the Arabs had served as a link in trade and in the transmission of such Indian inventions as "Arabic numerals," which are actually Hindu in origin. Now a direct link was forged between the West and India, never to be loosened. The link did not take the form of union or assimilation, for West and East hardly communicated at the higher levels of cultural interchange. The Portuguese were contemptuous of the Indians once they discovered that they were not the Christians of Prester John. Among the Dutch, French, and British who followed the Portuguese to India, this attitude of contempt became set in the conventional idea of white superiority. While this feeling of European superiority has probably been exaggerated both in Western literary tradition and in the minds of educated Indians quick to take offense, still it was always present, most clearly reflected centuries later in Kipling's famous "Ballad of East and West":

Oh, East is East, and West is West, and never the twain shall meet,
Till Earth and Sky stand presently at God's great Judgment Seat. . . .

Western superiority was at bottom a superiority on the battlefield. Long after the initial European monopoly of firearms had ended, a European army or navy, or a native one trained and commanded by Europeans, could always prevail over a purely native force. In India, at least, European domination was greatly helped by the political and military disunity of the subcontinent. When the Portuguese reached India, Muslim invaders were consolidating foreign rule of the sort that for thousands of years had periodically brought comparative order to northern India. The Muslim empire was misleadingly called Mogul (Mughal or Mongol), for its rulers were Turks from central Asia and its founder was a descendant of Tamerlane. It had little hold over the regions of southern India where Europeans established their footholds. Local Indian rulers, whether they were Muslim or Hindu in faith, were in intense rivalry and were a ready prey to European promises of aid. All the European powers found it easy, not merely to win Indian princes to their side, but to raise and train on their own responsibility native armies to fight under Portuguese, French, Dutch, or British flags.

Perhaps the lack of political and social integration in India is the basic reason why a few handfuls of Europeans were able to dominate the country until 1945. China, too, saw her armed forces beaten whenever they came into formal military conflict with European or European-trained armies or fleets; China, too, was forced to make all sorts of concessions to Europeans—treaty ports, and above all extraterritoriality, that is, the right of Europeans to be tried in their own national courts for offenses committed on Chinese soil. Yet China, unlike India, was never "annexed" by a European power, never lost its "sovereignty." For China preserved a fairly strong central government and had many strands of ethical and political unity that India lacked.

The variety and range of Indian life are extraordinary. Some of the more isolated parts of India in the Deccan or southern peninsula were inhabited by tribesmen of no higher level than many African tribesmen. Some, on the northern edges, were warrior tribesmen much like those of the highlands of Central Asia. In the great valleys of the Indus and the Ganges, and in the richer parts of the Deccan, there was a wealthy, populous society basically Hindu in culture, though when the Europeans arrived, it was dominated in many areas by invaders of Muslim faith and culture. Hindu society itself was the result of an amalgamation between earlier native stocks and invaders from the north who certainly spoke a language closely related to Greek, Latin, and indeed our own, and who probably were white "Indo-Europeans" or "Aryans." The early history of India, however, is most confusing, and we cannot tell how many these invaders were, or just where they came from, though the invasion apparently had taken place between 2000 and 1200 B.C. It seems almost certain that the white invaders' consciousness of differing from the natives is responsible basically for the characteristic Indian institution of caste.

According to the laws of caste, men and women were by the fact of birth settled for life in a closed group that pursued a given occupation and occupied a fixed position in society. When the Europeans reached India, there were apparently something over a thousand castes, plus a group at the bottom without caste, the "untouchables." The ruling groups were of two main castes, the Brahmins or priests, and the Kshatriya or warriors. The great multiplicity of castes lay in the third group, the Vaisya or commonalty, and was based largely on vocation or trade. In theory, marriage between members of different castes was forbidden, as was change of caste through social mobility. In fact, in the centuries since the invasion by the "Indo-Europeans" considerable human intermixture had undoubtedly occurred. Yet even today the upper classes in most of India are lighter in color than the lower.

The most striking thing about Indian culture was the high place occupied by the priestly caste, the Brahmins. The Brahmin faith has strains of a most otherworldly belief in the evils of the life of the flesh and the attainment of salvation by a mystic transcendence of the flesh in ascetic denial. With this is a doctrine of the transmigration of souls, in which sinful life leads to reincarnation in lower animal life, and virtuous life leads, at least in some forms of Hindu belief, to ultimate freedom from flesh of any sort and reunion with the perfect, the ineffable. But official Brahminism became a series of rigid and complicated rituals, and the religion of the common people retained from earlier times an elaborate polytheism lush with gods and goddesses who were by no means ethereal, but fleshly indeed. Against all this worldliness there rose in the sixth century B.C. a great religious leader, Gautama Buddha, himself of noble stock. Buddhism accepts the basic Brahminical concept of the evil of this world of the flesh, but it finds salvation, the nirvana of peaceful release from the chain of earthly birth and rebirth, in a life ascetic but not withdrawn, a life of charity and good works. Although Buddhism died out in the land of its birth, it spread to China, Japan, and southeastern Asia.

In these lands it took two forms, still existing. In the northern lands of Tibet, China, Japan, the Mahayana (Great Vehicle) continued in theology to emphasize Buddha's strong ethical desire to make nirvana available to all. In southeastern Asia and Ceylon, the Hinayana (Lesser Vehicle) prevailed. In theory, the Hinayana relies more on ritual, and its monks are wholly detached from the world. Buddhism remains one of the world's great higher religions. It has made some converts among Western intellectuals, especially in an altered form known as Zen Buddhism, originally a kind of Japanese stoicism.

The religious thought of India has left a residue of greater otherworldliness, of greater emphasis on a mystical subduing of the flesh, of a revulsion from the struggle for wealth, satisfaction of the common human appetites, worldly place and power, than has Christianity or Islam. In practice, Indian life, even before the Europeans came, displayed plenty of violence, plenty of greed, cruelty, and self-indulgence. Except as superstition and taboo and ritual, little of the higher religions had seeped down to the masses. To some Western minds, the educated classes of India have seemed to take refuge in otherworldly doctrines as a psychological defense against the worldly superiority of the West and the poverty and superstition of their own masses. But the fact remains that for three hundred years educated Indians have insisted that they feel differently about the universe and man's place in it than do we, that theirs is a higher spirituality.

China

China, too, resisted the West, and in many ways more successfully than did India. A very old civilization that goes back several thousand years before Christ was established in the valleys of the Yangtze and the Yellow rivers. Like the other civilizations bordering the great nomadic Eurasian heartland—the Mesopotamian, the Indian, the European—it was subject to periodic incursions of tribesmen. It was against such incursions that the famous Great Wall of China was built in the third century B.C. On the whole, the Chinese protected their basic institutions against the victorious nomads, whom they absorbed after a few generations. At just about the time when the first Europeans were setting up permanent trade relations with China, the last of these "barbarian" conquests occurred. Early in the seventeenth century, Mongolian tribes established a state of their own in eastern Manchuria, to the north of China proper. In 1644, they seized the Chinese capital of Peking and established a dynasty that lasted until 1911. But the Manchus, like other outsiders before them, left Chinese institutions almost untouched.

Chinese history is by no means the uneventful record of a "frozen" and unchanging society that some Westerners have thought. It is filled with the rise and fall of dynasties; with periods of effective governmental centralization and periods of "feudal" disintegration; with wars, plagues, and famines; and with the gradual spread of Chinese culture southward and eastward to the region of Canton, to Vietnam, to Korea, and to Japan. Under the flux many elements of continuity existed. At the base of Chinese social life was a communal village organization, held together by very strong family ties, a cult of ancestor worship, and a tradition of hard work on the farm. The Chinese village, basically unchanged until the Communist reform of our own day, was one of the oldest socio-economic organizations in the civilized world. At the top of this society was an emperor, the Son of Heaven, whose subjects were conditioned to at least formal imperial unity in somewhat the same manner as early medieval Westerners were conditioned to the unity of Roman Catholic Christendom.

The business of running this vast empire was entrusted to one of the most remarkable ruling classes history has recorded, the mandarins, a bureaucracy of intellectuals, or at least of men who could pass examinations in literary and philosophical classics requiring a rigorously trained memory. The mandarin class, though it was susceptible to graft and to nepotism and proved not very resilient in the face of new European ideas, had served the state for thousands of years, and its existence is one of the reasons for the extraordinary stability of Chinese society. Although in theory the class was one open to talents, the necessary education was too expensive and too difficult for any but a few gifted, lucky, and persistent poor boys. Just as in India, then, China had a small upper class that enjoyed a style of living hardly available to aristocracy in the medieval

A mandarin: engraving from John Ogilby's "Atlas Chinensis," 1671.

West, and an immense population at the very margin of existence.

It has often been remarked that China never had a religion, in the sense that Buddhism, Christianity, and Islam are religions with a firm doctrine of salvation. The Chinese millions had their superstitions, their demons, their otherworld. But the upper class took little interest in mysticism and otherworldliness; they demonstrated a realistic acceptance of the world as it is, and a concern with human relations, with politeness and decorum. Their conventional Confucianism was a code of manners and morals, not a sacramental religion. Confucius, a sage who flourished in the fifth century B.C., was no prophet but a moralist who taught an ethical system of temperance, decorum, obedience to those who were wise and good. This lack of commitment to an otherworldly religion, however, has by no means made the Chinese more receptive to Western ideas. Down to the establishment of the Communist regime at any rate, China resisted westernization more effectively than any other great culture.

The Portuguese Empire

The empire that the Portuguese founded in Asia and Africa was a trading empire, not an empire of settlement. They established along the coasts of Africa, India, and China a series of posts over which they hoisted the Portuguese flag as a sign that these bits of territory had been annexed to the Portuguese crown. Such posts were often called factories after the factors or commercial agents who were stationed there to trade with the natives. As all the European colonial powers were to do later on, the Portuguese offered guns, knives, cheap cloth, and gadgets of all sorts. In return they got gold and silver (when they could), pepper and other spices, still essential for making meat palatable in pre-refrigeration days, silks and other luxuries, and, finally, raw materials such as cotton and, in Brazil, tobacco and sugar.

Two guiding principles of this trade were accepted by almost all contemporaries, whether in the mother country or in the colonies, as simple facts of life. First, in this trade the mother country was the determining element, and would naturally provide manufactured goods and services while the colony produced raw materials. Second, foreigners, nationals of other European lands, were excluded from this trade; they could not deal directly with the colony or take part in the commerce between mother country and colony. The Portuguese, in sum, followed a policy of mercantilism, symbolized by the virtual monopoly Lisbon exercised over European imports of pepper and cinnamon during the sixteenth century.

Armed forces were essential to the establishment and maintenance of this colonial system. Relatively small land forces proved sufficient both to keep the natives under control and to ward off rival European powers from the trading posts. A large and efficient navy was also necessary, for the easiest way to raid a rival's trade was to wait until its fruits were neatly concentrated in the hold of a merchant vessel, and then take it at sea as a prize. Pirates were often openly an unofficial adjunct of a given navy, called privateers and operating only against enemies or neutrals, never against their own nationals. A navy was, then, essential to protect the sea routes of a colonial power. The Portu-

guese fleet was not only a merchant fleet; under the command of governors like Albuquerque, it was a great military fleet that brushed aside Arab opposition and for a few decades ruled the oceans of the Old World.

The Portuguese made no serious attempt to settle large numbers of their own people either in the hot coastlands of Africa or in the already densely populated lands of India and the Far East. Nor, with the one exception we are about to encounter, did they attempt to make over these natives into pseudo-Portuguese. Many natives were enlisted in the armed forces or used as domestic help and in subordinate posts such as clerks, and they inevitably picked up, however imperfectly, the language and culture of the colonial power. But neither among the primitive tribes of Africa nor among the Indian and Chinese masses did this process of europeanization go very fast or far. The Portuguese left the old ruling chiefs and old ruling classes pretty much as they had found them. The native upper classes monopolized most of the limited European wares, and Europe could not yet flood non-European markets with cheap manufactured goods made by power-driven machinery. Nothing Western touched the masses of natives in the

A view of Macao, the Portuguese outpost in China, in 1598, by Theodore de Bry.

AMACAO.

sixteenth century, nothing tempted them away from their millennial ways of life, in anything like the degree our twentieth-century West attracts and tempts the East.

There is one exception. The Portuguese and the Spanish, and even their relatively secular-minded rivals, the English, Dutch, and French, did attempt to Christianize the natives. Some of these attempts were coercive, as at Goa where the Portuguese pulled down all the native temples and made it impossible to practice traditional religion. From the first, however, much sincerity, devotion, and hard work also went into the missionary movement. The earliest missionaries underestimated the obstacles they were to encounter. Many of them were in a sense partly converted themselves; that is, they came to be very fond of their charges and convinced that these were in fact almost Christians already. Some of the Jesuits in China, the first European intellectuals to live in this very civilized country, seriously believed that with just a bit more effort the full reconciliation between Christianity and Confucianism could be achieved.

From the start, difficulties arose between the missionaries, anxious to protect their charges, and the traders and colonial officials, driven by their very place in the system to try to exploit the natives. Local chiefs and monarchs regarded converts as potential traitors, more loyal to their Western faith than to their Eastern rulers. Finances and manpower were always serious problems, with so many to convert and tend, and with so few men and so little money to do the work. Measured in statistical terms, the effort to convert India and the Far East to Christianity did not make a serious impression on the masses—something under a million converts by 1600. The greatest missionary successes tended to occur in areas of Buddhism, then in a state of decay comparable to that of Catholicism on the eve of the Reformation, and the greatest failures in areas of Islam, for Muslims have very seldom abandoned their faith for any other. Yet the influence of Christianity cannot be measured in terms of actual church memberships in the East; it has been far greater on the upper and intellectual classes than on the masses and is an important part of the whole Western impact on the East.

The Portuguese, though first in the field in the East, very soon had to yield to newer rivals. Like the Spaniards, they suffered from an inadequate home industry; their banking, their business methods, their initiative—if not their scruples—were not up to competition with the aggressive expanding powers of northwest Europe. Though monopolizing the import of pepper from the East, they sought the assistance of the more knowledgeable merchant community of Antwerp in distributing the pepper to European markets. The cloth and other wares they traded in the East they often had to import from countries with more developed industries. After the sixteenth century, they ceased to add to their empire and their wealth, and sank back to a secondary place in international politics. A great epic poem, the *Lusiads* (1572) of Luis de Camoëns (Camões), is their monument.

The sixty years of union between the Spanish and Portuguese monarchies, 1580–1640, accelerated the decline of Portugal's imperial fortunes by involving her in prolonged worldwide warfare with Spain's great adversary, the Dutch republic. Better-equipped and better-disciplined Dutch forces drove the Portuguese from most of their posts in Indonesia and from Ceylon and parts of the Indian coast. Yet a Portuguese empire did survive along the old route around Africa to Goa, on the island of Timor in Indonesia, and in Macao in China. And it survived all the way down to 1974, when the overthrow of the right-wing dictatorship in Lisbon ended the stubborn Portuguese effort to resist the increasingly determined attempts by natives to expel the Portuguese from their major African colonies —Portuguese Guinea and Angola on the west coast, and Mozambique on the east. Thus the first colonial empire in Africa became the last. It endured so long because until 1974 the Portuguese never voluntarily relinquished any territories; the Republic of India had to seize Goa by force in 1961. Another reason for the longevity of the empire in the face of such active and hungry competitors as the French, Dutch, and British lay in the fact that, while Portugal's most successful rivals took away her leadership, they left her a partner in the competition. Finally, the survival of the Portuguese empire was greatly aided by the fact that the greatest of the European imperial powers, England, remained through modern times in alliance with Portugal. The complete victory of France or the Netherlands in the colonial scramble might possibly have brought an end to the Portuguese empire.

III West by Sea to the Indies
Columbus and Later Explorers

In the earliest days of concerted effort to explore the oceans, the rulers of Spain had been too busy disposing of the last Muslim state in the peninsula, Granada, and uniting the disparate parts of Spain to patronize scientific exploration as the Portuguese had done. But individual Spanish traders were active, and Spain was growing in prosperity. When Portuguese mariners found the three groups of Atlantic islands—Azores, Madeira, and Canaries—a papal decree assigned the Canaries to the crown of Castile and the others to Portugal. Once the marriage of Ferdinand and Isabella had united Aragon and Castile, Queen Isabella wanted to catch up with the Portuguese. So in 1491, when the fall of Granada seemed imminent, she commissioned Columbus to try out his plan to reach India by going west.

Columbus (1451–1506) was an Italian, born in Genoa. He was essentially self-educated and, at least in navigation and geography, had educated himself very well. His central conception, that it would be possible to reach the Far East—"the Indies"—by sailing westward from Spain, was not uniquely his. That the earth is a globe was a notion entertained by ancient Greek geographers and revived with the renaissance of the classics. Toscanelli at Florence in 1474, Behaim at Nuremberg in the very year of Columbus' voyage, published maps that showed the earth as a globe—but without the Americas, and with the combined Atlantic and Pacific much narrower than they are in fact. The growth of oceanic navigation had made it possible to act on this notion by deliberately sailing west on the Atlantic. But it was still a strikingly novel idea, and a persistent, innovating personality was needed to win support for such an expedition.

With the sole aim of reaching the Indies Columbus might not have been able to set out. But, as his commission from Queen Isabella shows, he was also charged to discover and secure for the Spanish crown new islands and territories, a mission that probably reflects the importance of ancient and medieval legends about Atlantis, Saint Brendan's isle, and other lands beyond the Azores. Even if he did not reach the Indies, there seemed a chance that he would reach something new.

He reached a New World. Setting out from Palos near Cadiz on August 3, 1492, in three very small ships, he made a landfall on an island of the Bahama group on October 12 of the same year, and eventually went on to discover the large islands we know as Cuba and Santo Domingo (Haiti). On a second voyage, in 1493, he went out with seventeen ships and some fifteen hundred colonists, explored further in the Caribbean, and laid the foundations of the Spanish Empire in America. On his third voyage in 1498–1500, he reached the mouth of the Orinoco in South America but encountered difficulties among his colonists and was sent home in irons by the royal governor Bobadilla, who took over the administration of the Indies for the Crown. He was released on his return to Spain, and in 1502–1504 made a fourth and final voyage, in which he reached the mainland at Honduras. He died in comparative obscurity in Spain (1506), totally unaware that he had reached, not Asia, but a new continent.

That continent was, by a caprice of history, not destined to bear his name, though it is now liberally sprinkled with other place names in his honor. News of Columbus' voyage soon spread by word of mouth in Europe, for printing was still in its infancy. There were no newspapers or geographical institutes; the international learned class—the humanists—were more interested in Greek manuscripts than in strange lands; and, from early Portuguese days on, governments had done their best to keep their discoveries as secret as possible. The most effective spreading of the word in print about the New World was done by another Italian in the Spanish service, Amerigo Vespucci, who wrote copiously about his alleged explorations in the immediate footsteps of Columbus. Scholars doubt that Vespucci really made all the discoveries, from the southeastern United States to the tip of South America, that

he claimed to have made. But his letters came to the attention of a German theoretical geographer, Martin Waldseemüller, who in 1507 published a map blocking out a landmass in the southern part of the New World that he labeled, from the latinized form of Vespucci's first name, America.

After Columbus, the roster of discovery grew rapidly. Ponce de León reached Florida in 1512, and Balboa in 1513 crossed the Isthmus of Panama and saw a limitless ocean, on the other side of which the Indies did indeed lie, for it was the Pacific. Many other Spaniards and Portuguese in these first two decades of the sixteenth century explored in detail the coasts of what was to be Latin America. It was now quite clear that an immense landmass lay athwart the westward route from Europe to Asia, and that even the narrow Isthmus of Panama was an obstacle not readily to be overcome by a canal. Maritime exploration then turned to the problem of getting around the Americas by sea and into the Pacific. North America proved an obstacle indeed, for none of the great estuaries—Chesapeake, Delaware, Hudson—promising though they looked to the first explorers, did more than dent the great continent, the breadth of which was totally unknown. The St. Lawrence looked even better, for to its first French explorers it seemed like the sought-for strait. But even the St. Lawrence gave out, and the rapids near Montreal, which showed it was only another river after all, received the ironic name of Lachine (China), for this was not the way to China. Not until the mid-nineteenth century was the usually ice-choked "Northwest Passage" in the Arctic discovered by the Englishman Sir John Franklin.

The "Southwest Passage" was found only a generation after Columbus in the course of an expedition that is the most extraordinary of all the great voyages of discovery. Ferdinand Magellan, a Portuguese in the Spanish service, set out in 1519 with a royal commission bidding him to find a way westward to the Spice Islands of Asia. Skirting the coast of South America, he found and guided his ships through the difficult fogbound passage that bears his name, the Straits of Magellan, reached the Pacific, and crossed it in a voyage of incredible hardship. Scurvy alone, a disease we now know to be caused by lack of vitamin C, meant that he and his men had to surmount torturing illness. After he had reached the islands now known as the Philippines, Magellan was killed in a skirmish with the natives. One of his captains, however, kept on along the known route by the Indian Ocean and the coast of Africa. On September 8, 1522, the *Victoria* and her crew of 18 men—out of 5 ships and 243 men that had sailed in 1519—landed at Cadiz. For the first time, men had circumnavigated the earth and had proved empirically that the world is round.

What these explorations cost in terms of human suffering, what courage and resolution were needed to carry them through, is very hard for our easy-traveling generation to imagine. Here, from the bare report the sailor Pigafetta gives of Magellan's expedition, is a firsthand account of one of the crises:

> Wednesday, the twenty-eighth of November, 1520, we came forth out of the said strait, and entered into the Pacific sea, where we remained three months and twenty days without taking in provisions or other refreshments, and we only ate old biscuit reduced to powder, and full of grubs, and stinking from the dirt which the rats had made on it when eating the good biscuit, and we drank water that was yellow and stinking. We also ate the ox hides which were under the mainyard. . . . Besides the above-named evils, this misfortune which I will mention was the worst, it was that the upper and lower gums of most of our men grew so much that they could not eat, and in this way so many suffered, that nineteen died.*

Foundation of the Spanish Empire

As a by-product of Magellan's voyage, the Spaniards who had sponsored him got a foothold in the Far East, which they had reached by sailing west. As we have seen, by the Treaty of Tordesillas in 1494 Spain and Portugal had divided the world—the world open to trade and empire—along a line that cut through the Atlantic in such a way that Brazil became Portuguese. This same line, extended round the world, cut the Pacific so that some of the islands Magellan discovered came into the Spanish half. Spain conveniently treated the Philippines as if they also came in the Spanish half of the globe, though they are just outside it, and colonized them from Mexico.

Up to now, we have concerned ourselves mostly with maritime explorations and the founding of coastal trading stations. The Spaniards in the New World, however, very soon explored by land, and acquired thousands of square miles of territory. To the explorer by sea there succeeded the conquistador, often of the impoverished, noble hidalgo class, half explorer, half soldier and administrator, and all adventurer. Of the conquistadores, two, Hernando Cortés and Francisco Pizarro, have come down in history with a special aura of tough romance. With a handful of men they conquered the only two civilized regions of the New World: the Aztec empire of Mexico, taken by Cortés with 600 soldiers in 1519, and the Inca empire of Peru, taken by Pizarro with 180 soldiers in 1531–1533. The narrative of these conquests, whether in the classic nineteenth-century histories of the American William Prescott or in the narratives of actual participants, remains among the most fascinating if not among the most edifying chapters of Western history. A book of this scope cannot do justice to the drama of the conquerors of Mexico and Peru, nor to the many other Spaniards who in search of glory, salvation, gold, and excitement toiled up and down these strange new lands—Quesada in New Granada (later Colombia); Coronado, de Soto,

and Cabeza de Vaca in the southwest of what became the United States; Mendoza in La Plata (the lands around the river Plate—today Uruguay and Argentina); Valdivia in Chile; Alvarado in Guatemala; and many others, not least Ponce de León hunting for the fountain of eternal youth in Florida.

Unlike the great cultures of India and the Far East, the pre-Columbian cultures of the Americas crumbled under the impact of the Europeans. From Mexico to Bolivia, Paraguay, and Patagonia (in southern Argentina), millions of people survive who are of American Indian stock, and any understanding of Latin America requires some knowledge of their folkways and traditions. Mexican artists and intellectuals in our day proudly hold up their Indian heritage against the Yankees, and against their own europeanized nineteenth-century rulers. But the structure of the Aztec and the Inca empires has simply not survived. The sun god in whose name the Inca ruled, the bloody Aztec god of war, Huitzilopochtli, are no longer a part of the lives of men, as are Confucius and Buddha. Yet the fact that the civilizations of Peru and Central America once existed as large territorial states, and made high achievements in art and science, is further evidence against naive Western notions of white superiority.

Well before the end of the sixteenth century, the work of the conquistadores had been done, and in Latin America the first of the true European colonial empires—in contrast to the trading empires in Africa and Asia—had been founded. Nowhere, save in the region of La Plata and in central Chile, was the native Indian stock eliminated and replaced by a population almost entirely of Old World stock—something that has happened in the United States and Canada save for a tiny Indian minority. Over vast reaches of Mexico and Central and South America, a crust of Spanish or Portuguese formed at the top of society and made Spanish or Portuguese the language of culture; a class of mixed blood, the *mestizos,* was gradually formed from the union, formal or informal, of Europeans and natives; and in many regions the Indians continued to maintain their stock and their old ways of life almost untouched. Finally, wherever, as in the Caribbean, the Indians were exterminated under the pressure of civilization, or, as in Brazil, they proved inadequate as a labor force, the importation of slaves from Africa added another ingredient to the racial mixture.

Moreover, geography and the circumstances of settlement by separate groups of adventurers in each region combined to create a number of separate units of settlement tied together only by their dependence on the Crown and destined to become the independent nation-states of Latin America today. Geography alone was perhaps a fatal obstacle to any subsequent union of the colonies, such as was achieved by the English colonies that became the United States of America. Between such apparently close neighbors as the present Argentine and Chile, for instance, lay the great chain of the Andes, crossed only with great difficulty by high

*Lord Stanley of Alderly, *The First Voyage Round the World by Magellan, translated from the accounts of Pigafetta, and other contemporary writers* (London, 1874), pp. 64–65.

Machu Picchu, ancient Inca city in the Andes of Peru. Corn and potatoes were grown on the terraces.

mountain passes. Also between the colonies of La Plata and the colonies of Peru and New Granada lay the Andes and the vast tropical rain forests of the Amazon basin, still almost unconquered today. The highlands of Mexico and Central America are as much invitations to local independence as were the mountains of Hellas to the ancient Greeks. Cuba and the other Caribbean islands have the natural independence of islands.

Latin American Empires Evaluated

The Spaniards transported to the New World the centralized administrative institutions of Castile. At the top of the hierarchy were two viceroyalties, that of Peru with its capital at Lima and that of New Spain with its capital at Mexico City. From Lima the viceroy ruled for the Crown over the Spanish part of South America, except Venezuela. From Mexico City the viceroy ruled over the mainland north of Panama, the West Indies, Venezuela, and the Philippines, Each capital had an *audiencia,* a powerful body staffed by professional law-

yers and operating both as a court of law and as an advisory council. During the sixteenth century additional audiencias were established in Santo Domingo, Guatemala, Panama, New Granada, Quito, Manila, and other major centers. In Madrid, a special Council of the Indies formulated colonial policy and supervised its execution.

This was certainly a centralized, paternalistic system of government, which has rightly enough been contrasted with the "salutary neglect" in which the North American colonies were generally left by the home government until the crisis that led to the American Revolution. But it was not—given the vast areas and the varied peoples under its control, it could not be—as rigid in practice as it was in theory. The rudiments of popular consultation of the Spanish colonists existed in the *cabildos abiertos* or assemblies of citizens in the towns. Moreover, as time went on the bureaucracy itself came to be filled largely with colonials, men who had never been in the home country, and who developed a sense of local patriotism and independence.

Early sixteenth-century stone carving of the Aztec god Zipe Totec.

Castrovirrena: a Peruvian mining town in 1613. Llamas are being led toward the town from the works.

Madrid and Seville were simply too far away to enforce all their decisions. Notably in the matter of trade, it proved impossible to maintain the rigid monopolies of mercantilistic theory, which sought to confine trade wholly to the mother country, and to prohibit, or severely limit, domestic industry in the colonies. Local officials connived at a smuggling trade with the English, Dutch, French, and North Americans, which in the eighteenth century reached large proportions.

The hand of Spain was heaviest in the initial period of exploitation, when the rich and easily mined deposits of the precious metals in Mexico and Peru were skimmed off for the benefit both of the Spanish crown, which always got its *quinto,* or fifth, and of the conquistadores and their successors, Spaniards all. This gold and silver did the natives no good, but in the long run it did no good to Spain, since it went to finance a vain bid for European supremacy and to pay for wares needed by the colonies that the mother country did not produce. By the early seventeenth century, when the output of precious metals began a long decline, the economy and society of Spanish America had stabilized. The economy was not progressive, but neither was it hopelessly backward. Colonial wares—sugar, tobacco, chocolate, cotton, hides, and much else— flowed out of Latin America in exchange for manufactured goods and for services. Creoles (American-born of pure European stock) and mestizos were the chief beneficiaries of this trade. Above the African slaves in the social pyramid, but well below the mestizos, were the native Indians. This, then, was a system of social caste based on color, one that never became so rigid as that in North America but that still damaged native pride and self-respect.

Especially in the Caribbean, but to a degree everywhere, the whites tried to use native labor on farms, in the mines, and in transport. The results were disastrous, for epidemics of smallpox and other new diseases introduced by the Europeans decimated the ranks of the native population. In the West Indies the Carib Indians were wiped out, and in central Mexico, scholars have estimated, the total population fell from about nineteen million when Cortés arrived to only some two and a half million eighty years later. Here, as with the gold and silver, some ironic spirit of history seems to have taken revenge on the whites: though the question of the origin of syphilis is still disputed, many historians of medicine believe that it was brought from the West Indies, where it was mild, to Western civilization, where it became virulent. The attempt to regiment native labor in a plantation system or to put it on a semi-manorial system of forced labor, known as the *encomienda,* proved almost as disastrous. The encomiendas, which had been developed in Spain itself for lands reconquered from the Muslims, grouped farming villages whose inhabitants were "commended" to the protection of a conquistador or colonist. The "protector" thereby acquired both a source of income without engaging in demeaning labor and an economic base for a potential defiance of central authority. The shortage of native labor made recourse to black slaves inevitable. A final element in the social and racial situation was the character of the colonial whites, who tended to be aggressive and insensitive; by and large, except for some clerics, the gentler souls stayed home.

Yet against all these forces making for harshness and cruelty, there were counteracting forces. Spanish imperial policy toward the natives was in aim by no means ungenerous, and even in execution holds up well in the long and harsh record of intercourse between whites and nonwhites all over the globe. The New Laws of 1542 forbade the transmission of encomiendas by inheritance, thereby striking a blow against feudal decentralization. The New Laws also forbade the enslavement of native Indians, who were regarded as wards of the Crown. The central government in Spain passed many laws to protect the Indians, and though these were often flouted in the colonies—a phenomenon not unknown in the English colonies—they put a limit to wholesale exploitation of the natives. Their cause was championed by men of great distinction, and notably by Bartolomé de las Casas (1474–1566), "Father of the Indians," bishop of Chiapas in Mexico.

Unlike their counterparts in Africa and Asia, the Indian masses were converted to Christianity. More than Spanish pride was involved in the grandiose religious edifices constructed by the colonists and in their elaborate services. Many priests seemed to realize the need to fill the void left in the lives of the Indians by the destruction of old temples and the suppression of complex pagan rituals. Church and state in the Spanish and Portuguese colonies in the New World worked hand in hand, undisturbed for generations by the troubles roused in Europe by the Protestant Reformation and the rise of a secular anti-Christian movement. The Jesuits in Paraguay set up among the Guarani Indians a remarkable society, a benevolent despotism, a utopia of good order, good habits, and eternal childhood for the Guarani. On the northern fringes of the Spanish world, where it was to meet the Anglo-Saxons, a long line of missions in California and the Southwest held the frontier. Everywhere save in wildest Amazonia and other untamed areas, the Christianity of the Roman Catholic church brought to the natives a veneer of Western tradition, and made them in some sense part of this strange new society of the white men.

In their close union of church and state, in their very close ties with the home country, in their mercantilist economics, and in still other respects, the Portuguese settlements in Brazil resembled those of the Spaniards elsewhere in Latin America. Yet there were significant differences. The Portuguese settlements were almost entirely rural: Brazil had nothing to compare with the urban splendor of Mexico City or Lima. A large number of black slaves were imported into the tropical areas of Brazil, and, because the white males drew no sexual color line, the races became more thoroughly mixed in colonial times than they did in most Spanish colonies except Cuba. Finally, perhaps because of the relative proximity of Brazil to European waters, the Portuguese had more troubles with rival nations than the Spaniards did. The existence on relatively recent maps of those fragments of imperial hopes—French Guiana, Surinam (Netherlands Guiana, partially autonomous in 1975 and scheduled for independence by the end of the year), and Guyana (independent since 1966, but a British colony before then)—bears witness to the fact that the northern maritime nations made a serious effort to settle on the northern fringes of Brazil.

IV The North Atlantic Powers and Russia

Spain and Portugal enjoyed a generation's head start in exploration and one of nearly a century in founding empires of settlement. Without this head start, which they owed in part to their position as heirs of the Mediterranean trade, Spain and Portugal could scarcely have made the great mark in the world that they did. For the northern Atlantic states soon made up for their late start. As early as 1497 the Cabots, father and son, Italians in the English service, saw something of the North American coast, and gave the English territorial claims based on their explorations. In the first half of the sixteenth century the explorations of another Italian, Verrazzano, and the Frenchman Jacques Cartier gave France competing claims, which were reinforced in the early seventeenth century by the detailed explorations of Champlain. Dutch claims began with the voyages of Henry Hudson, an Englishman who entered their service in 1609.

English, Dutch, and Swedes in North America

The English did not immediately follow up the work of the Cabots. Instead, they put their energies into the profitable business of interloping, that is, of breaking into the Spanish trading monopoly. John Hawkins, in 1562, started the English slave trade, and his nephew, Francis Drake, penetrated to the Pacific, reached California, which he claimed for England under the name of New Albion, and returned to England by the Pacific and Indian oceans, completing the first English circumnavigation of the globe (1577–1580). Under Sir Humphrey Gilbert in 1583 the English staked out a claim to Newfoundland, which gave them a share in the great fishing grounds off northeastern North America.

In 1584, Sir Walter Raleigh unsuccessfully attempted to found a settlement on Roanoke Island (in present-day North Carolina) in a land the English named Virginia, after their Virgin Queen, Elizabeth. Early in the next century the English established two permanent footholds at Jamestown in Virginia (1607) and at Plymouth on Massachusetts Bay (1620). Both were to become colonies of settlement, in which the sparse Indian population was exterminated and replaced by men and women for the most part of British stock. But in their inception both were nearer the pattern of trading posts set by the Spanish and Portuguese. Both were established by chartered trading companies with headquarters in England; both, and especially the Virginian, cherished at first high hopes that they would find, as the Spaniards had, great stores of precious metals. Both were disappointed in these hopes and only just managed to survive the first terrible years of hardship. Tobacco, first cultivated in 1612, and the almost legendary Captain John Smith, explorer and man of resourcefulness, saved the Virginia colony; and furs (notably beaver), codfish, and Calvinist toughness saved Plymouth. Both colonies gradually built up an agricultural economy, supplemented by trade with the mother country and interloping trade with the West Indies. Neither received more than a few tens of thousands of immigrants from abroad. Yet both these and the later colonies expanded by natural increase in a country of abundant land for the taking. The thirteen colonies by 1776 were a substantial series of settlements with almost three million inhabitants.

Before these English colonies were completed one important and one very minor foreign group had to be pushed out. The Dutch, following up the explorations of Hudson, had founded the colony of New Amsterdam (1626) at the mouth of the river that bears his name and had begun to push into the fur trade. This made them rivals of the English and of the French, farther north in Canada. In a war with England in the 1660s, however, the Dutch lost New Amsterdam, which was annexed by the English in 1664 and renamed New York. The Dutch, though very few in number, left descendants prominent in the future United States, as such names as *Stuyvesant, Schuyler,* and *Roosevelt* suggest.

The minor competitors were the Swedes, who founded Fort Christiana (1638) on the Delaware near present-day Wilmington. But New Sweden was never a great enterprise, and in 1655 Fort Christiana was taken over by the Dutch, who in turn were ousted by the English. Pennsylvania, chartered to the wealthy English Quaker William Penn in 1681, filled the vacuum left by the expulsion of Swedes and Dutch from the Delaware. It was to become the keystone colony before it became the keystone state.

The arch of colonies, in which Pennsylvania formed the keystone, reached from Maine to Georgia and numbered thirteen, each founded separately and each with its own charter. American tradition perhaps exaggerates the differences between the southern and northern groups of colonies. Massachusetts was not wholly settled by democratic plain people, "Roundheads," nor was Virginia settled wholly by great English landowners, gentlemen or "Cavaliers," and their retainers. All the colonies were settled by a varied human lot, which ranged from the gentry at the top down to members of the poorest classes, who immigrated either as indentured servants or as impressed seamen who deserted ship.

Still, it is true that New England was for the most part settled by Calvinist Independents (Congregationalists), already committed to wide local self-government and to a distrust of a land-owning aristocracy; and it is true that the southern colonies, especially tidewater Virginia, were settled for the most part by Anglicans used to the existence of social distinctions and to large landholdings. In Virginia, the Church of England became the established church; in Massachusetts, the Puritan Congregationalists, nonconformists in the homeland, almost automatically became conformists in their new home, and set up their own variety of state church. Geography, climate, and a complex of social and economic factors drove the South to plantation monoculture of tobacco, rice, indigo, or cotton even in colonial days and drove New England and the Middle Colonies to small farming by independent farmerowners and to small-scale industry and commerce. Yet the small farmers in the Piedmont sections of Virginia and the Carolinas represented a very northern mixture of Presbyterians, Scotch-Irish, and Germans from Pennsylvania. Some historians hold that the natural environment, and not any original difference of social structure and religious belief, accounts for the diverging cultures of North and South and their eventual armed conflict.

To us who are their heirs, it has seemed that these English colonists brought with them the religious freedom, the government by discussion, and the democratic society of which we are so proud. So they did, though they brought the seeds, the potentialities, rather than the fully developed institutions. These colonists came from an England where the concept of freedom of religion was only beginning to emerge; it was quite natural for the Virginians and the New Englanders to set up state churches. Yet these immigrants represented too many conflicting religious groups to enforce anything like the religious uniformity that prevailed in the Spanish colonies or in Canada. Even in Calvinist New England "heresy" appeared from the start, with the presence of Baptists, Quakers, and even Anglicans. Moreover, some of the colonies were founded by groups that from the first practiced religious freedom and separated church and state. In Pennsylvania, founded by Quakers who believed firmly in such separation; in Maryland, founded in part to give refuge to the most distrusted of groups at home, the Catholics; in Rhode Island, founded by Roger Williams and others unwilling to conform to the orthodoxy of Massachusetts Bay—in all these colonies there was something like the complete religious freedom that was later embodied in the Constitution of the United States.

The seeds of democracy, too, existed, although the early settlers, not only in Virginia but even in the North, readily accepted class distinctions. No formal colonial nobility ever arose, however, and the early tendency to develop a privileged gentry or squirearchy in the coastal regions was balanced by the equalitarianism of the frontier and by careers open to talent in the towns. Government by discussion was firmly planted in the colonies from the start. All of them, even the proprietary colonies, which were granted to a single proprietor (Pennsylvania) or to a group of proprietors (the Carolinas and Georgia), had some kind of colonial legislative body.

Here we come to the critical difference between the English colonies in the New World and the Spanish and French colonies. In Spain and France the governments were already centralized bureaucratic monarchies; their representative assemblies were no more than consultative and had no power over taxation. Royal governors in Latin America and in New France could really run their provinces, leaning on men they appointed and recalled, and raising funds by their own authority. England, while also a monarchy, was a parliamentary monarchy, torn by two revolutions in the seventeenth century. Though the Crown was represented in most colonies by a royal governor, the English government had no such bureaucracy as the Spanish and French had. Royal governors in the English colonies had hardly even a clerical staff and met with great difficulty in raising money from their legislative assemblies. The history of the colonies is full of bickerings in which the governor, with little local support and only sporadic backing from the home government, was often stalemated. Furthermore, in all the colonies the established landowners, merchants and professional men, though not necessarily all adult males, participated not only in colonial assemblies but also in local units of government—towns in New England, counties elsewhere. Finally, the settlers brought with them the common law of England, with its trial by jury and its absence of bureaucratic administrative law.

New France

To the north of the thirteen colonies, in the region of the Bay of Fundy and in the St. Lawrence basin, the French built on the work of Cartier and Champlain. New France was to be for a century and a half a serious threat to its southern neighbors. The St. Lawrence and the Great Lakes gave the French easy access to the heart of the continent, in contrast to the Appalachian ranges that stood between the English and the Mississippi. The French were also impelled westward by their search for furs, which are goods of great value and comparatively little bulk, easily carried in canoes and small boats. Moreover, led by the Jesuits, the Catholic French gave proof of a far greater missionary zeal than did the Protestant English. The priest, as well as the *coureur des bois* (trapper), led the push westward. Finally, the French in North America were guided by a conscious imperial policy directed from the France of the Bourbon monarchs, *la grande nation* at the height of its prestige and power.

Accordingly, it was the French, not the English, who explored the interior of the continent. By 1712 they had built up a line of isolated trading posts, with miles of empty space between, thinly populated by Indians, which completely encircled the English colonies on the Atlantic coast. The story of these French explorers, missionaries, and traders, admirably told by the American historian Francis Parkman, is one of the most fascinating pages of history. The names of many of them—La Salle, Père Marquette, Joliet, Frontenac, Cadillac, Iberville—are a part of our American heritage. Lines of outposts led westward from Quebec to the Great Lakes, and other lines moved northward up the Mississippi to meet them from Mobile and New Orleans, where a colony named Louisiana, after Louis XIV, had been founded at the beginning of the eighteenth century.

Yet, impressive though this French imperial thrust looks on the map, it was far too lightly held to be equal to the task of pushing the English into the sea. It was a trading empire with military ambitions, and except in Quebec it never became a true colony of settlement. And even there it never grew in the critical eighteenth century beyond a few thousand inhabitants. Frenchmen simply did not come over in sufficient numbers, and those who did come spread themselves out over vast distances as traders and simple adventurers. Frenchmen who might have come, the Huguenots who might have settled down as did the Yankee Puritans, were excluded by a royal policy bent on maintaining the Catholic faith in New France.

The Indies, West and East

The northwestern European maritime powers intruded upon the pioneer Spanish and Portuguese both in the New World and in the Old. The French, Dutch, and English all sought to gain footholds in South America, but had to settle for the unimportant Guianas. They broke up thoroughly the Spanish hold on the Caribbean, however, and ultimately made that sea of many islands a kaleidoscope of colonial jurisdictions and a center of constant naval wars and piracy. Today, these West Indian islands are a depressed area, with the tourist industry their main hope; in early modern times, however, they were one of the great prizes of imperialism. The cheap slave labor that had replaced the exterminated Carib Indians raised for their masters on the plantations the great staple crops: tobacco, fruits, coffee, and, most basic of all, cane sugar (there was then no threat of competition from the beet sugar that northern countries began to produce around 1800).

By 1715 the French, Dutch, and English had also laid the bases of trading and colonial empires in Asia and Africa. India proved to be the richest prize, and the most ardently fought for. The Mogul Empire was not strong enough in southern India to keep the Europeans out, but it did prove strong enough to confine them on the whole to the coastal fringes. Gradually, in the course of the seventeenth century both the French and the English established themselves in India on the heels of decaying Portuguese power and wealth. The English defeated a Portuguese fleet in 1612 and immediately thereafter got trading rights at Surat on the western coast. Although the able and active Mogul emperor Aurangzeb tried to revoke their rights in 1685, he soon found their naval and mercantile power too much to withstand. In 1690, the English founded in Bengal in eastern India the city they were to make famous, Calcutta. Meanwhile, the French had got a foothold on the south coast near Madras, at Pondi-chéry, and soon had established other stations. By the beginning of the eighteenth century, the stage was set in India as in North America for the decisive struggle for overseas empire between France and Britain.

Both countries operated in India, as they had ini-tially in North America, by means of chartered trading companies, the English East India Company and the French Compagnie des Indes Orientales. In their trad-ing activities the companies were backed up by their governments when it was evident that the whole rela-tion with India could not be purely commercial and that some territories around the trading posts had to be held. Although both countries became involved in Indian politics and warfare to support their trading companies, neither attempted to found a New England or New France in the East.

The Dutch entered even more vigorously into the competition, founding their own East India (1602) and West India (1621) companies. In sharp contrast to the close government supervision exerted by Spain and Portugal over colonial activities every step of the way, the Dutch granted these private business ventures full sovereign powers. They had the right to maintain their own fighting fleets and armies, declare war and wage it, negotiate peace, and govern dependent territories. The Netherlands East India Company succeeded in pushing the Portuguese out of Ceylon and then, by-passing India proper, concentrated on southeastern Asia, especially the East Indies. Here again they pushed the Portuguese out, save for part of the island of Timor, and they also discouraged English interlopers. And through it all the company paid an annual dividend averaging 18 percent. In spite of their rapid decline as a great power in the eighteenth century, the Dutch got so firm a hold in Java and Sumatra that their empire in Indonesia was to last until the mid-twentieth cen-tury.

Africa and the Far East

To reach the East all three of the northern maritime powers used the ocean route around Africa that the Portuguese had pioneered in the fifteenth century. All three got African posts, with the Dutch occupying the strategic Cape of Good Hope at the southern tip of the continent in 1652. While the cape was at first a fitting station for Dutch ships on the long voyage to Indonesia and the Far East, it was empty except for primitive tribes and had a temperate climate. Though immigra-tion was never heavy, a colony of settlement grew up peopled by Dutch and by French Huguenots, the an-cestors of the Afrikaners of South Africa today. In West Africa the Dutch took from the Portuguese posts on the Gold and Guinea coasts and won a share of the increasingly lucrative slave trade.

The French also worked down the Atlantic coast, taking Senegal (1626) at the westernmost point of the African bulge, and later acquiring in the Indian Ocean the large island of Madagascar and the smaller one of Mauritius, taken from the Dutch. The British secured a foothold at the mouth of the Gambia River near Senegal (1662) and later made acquisitions at the ex-pense of the French and the Dutch. Thus by the eight-eenth century a map of Africa and adjacent waters shows a series of coastal stations controlled by various European powers. But the interior remained for the most part unexplored, untouched except by slavers and native traders. Only in the nineteenth century was "the Dark Continent" opened to European expansion.

The Far East, too, was not truly opened to Western imperialism until the nineteenth century. In China, the Portuguese did cling to Macao, and the Dutch, on their heels as always, obtained a station on Taiwan (1624), an island that the Portuguese had christened Formosa ("beautiful"). The Jesuits, bringing with them Euro-pean instruments and learning that interested the Chi-nese, were tolerated in the seventeenth century, but they made little headway in missionary activity. At bottom the Chinese, convinced that their empire was the Mid-dle Kingdom, central in a spiritual and cultural sense, regarded most Europeans as barbarians who should be paying them tribute.

In Japan, the reaction against European penetra-tion was even stronger than in China. The Portuguese won trading privileges in the sixteenth century, fol-lowed by the Dutch in 1609; meantime, the great Jesuit missionary, Francis Xavier, began work in 1549. Though Christianity did not make wholesale conver-sions, it did make considerable headway. The Toku-gawa family, the feudal military rulers of Japan from 1600 to 1868, feared Christianity not only as a threat to national traditions but also as a threat to their own rule, because of the opportunities it might give Euro-pean powers to intervene in Japanese politics and in-trigue with their enemies. They therefore decided to close their land entirely to foreign dangers. In the early seventeenth century, they suppressed Christianity by force and sealed off Japan. Foreigners were refused entry, and Japanese were refused exit; even the building of large ships capable of sailing the ocean was for-bidden. The Dutch, who had persuaded the Japanese that Protestants were less subversive than the Catholic Portuguese, were allowed, under strict supervision, to retain an island in Nagasaki harbor, where after 1715 they were limited to two ships a year. Not until the American Commodore Perry came to Japan in 1853 was this amazing self-blockade really broken.

East by Land to the Pacific

The expansion of Europe in the early modern centuries was not restricted to the Atlantic maritime powers. The

The Great Wall of China, built in the third century B.C. to guarantee an isolation that proved elusive.

Russian exploration and conquest of Siberia offer all sorts of parallels with European expansion in the New World, from the chronological (the Russians crossed the Urals from Europe into Asia in 1483) to the political, for the expanding Muscovite state of Russia was a "new" monarchy, newer in some ways than the Spain of Charles V and Philip II or the England of Elizabeth I. This Russian movement has also been likened to the American expansion from the Atlantic seaboard to the Pacific. Compared with the Russian advance to the Pacific, the American westward movement was relatively slow: the Russians covered some five thousand miles in about forty years; we took longer to go a shorter distance. But the Russian advance left vast areas "behind the lines" unsettled and unabsorbed, whereas our own more gradual movement was more thorough. In contrast to the American, who faced formidable mountains and deserts, the Russian had easier going on the enormous flatlands of the Siberian river basins. For the Americans too, the Indians often posed serious military and political problems, whereas the Siberian tribesmen, widely scattered across the area, seem on the whole to have helped the Russians. Though enormous

in extent, Siberia continued to be very sparsely inhabited.

The victories of Ivan the Terrible over the Volga Tatars led to the first major advances, with private enterprise in the van. By the end of the sixteenth century the Stroganov family had obtained huge concessions in the Ural area, where they made a great fortune in the fur trade and discovered and exploited Russia's first iron mines. The Stroganovs hired bands of Cossack explorers, who led the eastward movement; their Daniel Boone was the famous Yermak, whose exploits took on legendary proportions. At a suitable point on a river basin, the spearhead of the advance party would build a wooden palisade and begin to collect furs from the surrounding area. Almost before the defense of each new position had been consolidated, the restless advance guard would have moved hundreds of miles farther eastward to repeat the process until Okhotsk on the Pacific was reached in the 1640s.

The government followed at some distance behind with administrators and tax collectors, soldiers and priests, as each new district was opened up. A Siberian bureau in Moscow had nominal responsibility for the

The Dutch outpost in Nagasaki harbor, 1689.

government of the huge area, but decisions had to be made on the spot because of the communications problem, although the Russians had an efficient postal service working quite early. Thus the Siberians always tended to have the independence traditionally associated with men of the wide open spaces, and reinforced by the Cossack and outlaw traditions from which many of them sprang. Because Ohkotsk and its neighborhood along the Pacific were intensely cold, and the ocean frozen for many months in the year, the Russians were soon looking enviously southward toward the valley of the Amur River, which flowed into the Pacific at a point where the harbors were open all the year round.

Explorations in this area brought the Russians into contact with the Chinese, whose lands they were now casually invading. But the Chinese government of the period did not care very much about these regions, which, from its own point of view, were far-northerly outposts. In 1689 the Chinese signed with Moscow the Treaty of Nerchinsk, the first they had concluded with any European state. The treaty stabilized the frontier, demilitarized the Amur valley, and kept the Russians out of Manchuria, the home territory of the ruling Chinese dynasty, though it recognized the Russian ad-

vances farther north. It also provided the two powers with a buffer zone of Mongolian territory, which acknowledged Chinese overlordship. Thus, with almost incredible speed the Russians had acquired an empire whose riches are still incompletely exploited today and had staked out a future as an Asian power with interests in the Pacific at just about the time the English took New Amsterdam from the Dutch.

North by Sea to the Arctic

By 1715, the expansion of Europe was beginning to affect almost every part of the globe. European explorers, missionaries, traders, proconsuls of empire, had spread out in all directions. Even Arctic exploration, stimulated by the hope of finding a Northwest or a Northeast Passage that would shorten the route to the Far East, had already gone a long way by the beginning of the eighteenth century. Henry Hudson had found not only the Hudson River but also Hudson's Bay in the far north of Canada. In the late seventeenth century, English adventurers and investors formed an enterprise that still flourishes in Canada today—the Hudson's Bay Company, originally set up for fur trading along the great bay to the northwest of the French settlement in Quebec. In the late sixteenth century, the Dutch had penetrated far into the European Arctic, had discovered the island of Spitsbergen to the north of Norway, and had ranged eastward across the Barents Sea named after their leader. Early in the eighteenth century the Russians also explored most of the long Arctic coasts of their empire, and the Dane Bering, in Russian service, discovered the Aleutian Islands and the sea and strait bearing his name separating northeastern Siberia from Alaska.

V The Impact of Expansion

The Human and Economic Record

The record of European expansion contains pages as grim as any in history. The African slave trade, begun by the Portuguese and entered by other peoples for its financial gains, is a series of horrors, from the rounding up of the slaves by native chieftains in Africa through their transportation across the Atlantic to their sale in the Indies. What strikes a modern most of all is the matter-of-fact acceptance of this trade, as if the blacks were so much livestock. The Dutch slave ship *St. Jan* (note the irony of the saint's name) started off for Curaçao in the West Indies in 1659. Her log recorded every day or so deaths of slaves aboard, until between June 30 and October 29 a total of 59 men, 47 women, and 4 children had died. There were still 95 slaves aboard when disaster struck, thus matter-of-factly recorded:

Nov. 1. Lost our ship on the Reef of Rocus, and all hands immediately took to the boat, as there was no prospect of saving the slaves, for we must abandon the ship in consequence of the heavy surf.

Nov. 4. Arrived with the boat at the island of Curaçao; the Hon'ble Governor Beck ordered two sloops to take the slaves off the wreck, one of which sloops with eighty four slaves on board was captured by a privateer.*

And here is the Hon'ble Governor Beck's report to his Board of Directors in Holland:

What causes us most grief here is, that your honors have thereby lost such a fine lot of negroes and such a fast sailing bark which has been our right arm here.

Although I have strained every nerve to overtake the robbers of the negroes and bark, as stated in my last, yet have I not been as successful as I wished. . . .

We regret exceedingly that such rovers should have been the cause of the ill success of the zeal we feel to attract the Spanish traders hither for your honors' benefit, . . . for the augmentation of commerce and the sale of the negroes which are to come here more and more in your honors' ships and for your account. . . .

I have witnessed with pleasure your honors' diligence in providing us here from time to time with negroes. That will

*E. Donnan, ed., *Documents Illustrative of the History of the Slave Trade to America,* (Washington, D.C., 1930), 1:143.

be the only bait to allure hither the Spanish nation, as well from the Main as from other parts, to carry on trade of any importance. But the more subtly and quietly the trade to and on this island can be carried on, the better will it be for this place and yours.*

Americans need hardly be reminded of the fact that we virtually exterminated the native Indian population east of the Mississippi and that, if they massacred us when they could, we replied in kind often enough, and with superior means. There were, of course, exceptions to this bloody rule. In New England, missionaries like John Eliot did set up little bands of "praying Indians," and in Pennsylvania, the record of the relations between the Quakers and the Indians was excellent. The white man's diseases, which in those days could hardly have been controlled, and the white man's alcoholic drinks, which were quite as hard to control, did more to exterminate the red men than did fire and sword.

Seen in terms of economics, however, the expansion of Europe in early modern times was by no means the pure "exploitation" and "plundering" it sometimes appears to be in the rhetoric of antiimperialists. There was robbery, just as there was murder or enslavement. There was, in dealing with the natives, even more giving of slight or nominal value in exchange for land and goods of great value. Just as all Americans are familiar with the slogan "The only good Indian is a dead Indian," so they know for how little the Indians sold the island of Manhattan. Finally, the almost universally applied mercantilist policy kept money and manufacturing in the hands of the home country. It relegated the colonies to the production of raw materials, a role that tended to keep even colonies of settlement in a relatively primitive and economically dependent condition.

While Europeans took the lion's share of colonial wealth in the early modern centuries, some of the silver from America financed European imports of spices and luxuries from Asia. Not many European mercantilist monopolies were watertight in practice so that enterprising natives shared in the new trade and its profits. Although few Europeans settled in India or in Africa, their wares, and especially their weapons, began gradually the modernizing process that would ultimately produce the worldwide "revolution of rising expectations" of our own day. By the eighteenth century this process was only beginning, and in particular few of the improvements in public health and sanitation that Europeans would bring to the East later on had yet come about; nor had greater public order come to India or Africa as it eventually would.

Effects of Expansion on the West

The West has in its turn been greatly affected by its relations with other peoples. The list of items that have

*Ibid., 1:150–151.

come into Western life since Marco Polo and Columbus is long. It includes foodstuffs above all; utensils and gadgets, pipes for smoking, hammocks and pajamas; styles of architecture and painting, bungalows and Japanese prints; and much else. Some of the novelties caught on more quickly than others. Tobacco, brought into Spain in the mid-sixteenth century as a soothing drug, had established itself by the seventeenth century as essential to the peace of mind of many European males. Maize or Indian corn (in Europe, "corn" refers to cereal grains in general) was imported from the New World and widely cultivated in well-watered areas of Spain and Italy. Potatoes, on the other hand, though their calorie content is high and though they are cheaper to grow in most climates than the staple bread-stuffs, did not immediately catch on in Europe. In France, they had to be popularized in a regular campaign that took generations to be effective. Tomatoes, the "love-apples" of our great-grandfathers, were long believed to be poisonous and were cultivated only for their looks. Tea and coffee, which Europeans and North Americans now take for granted as imports everyone uses, were just beginning to become available in large quantities by 1700.

Among Westerners, knowledge of non-European beliefs and institutions eventually penetrated to the level of popular culture, where it is marked by a host of words—"powwow," "kowtow," "taboo," "totem," for instance. At the highest level of cultural interchange, that of religion and ethical ideas, however, the West took little from the new worlds opened after Columbus. The first impression of Westerners, not only when they met the relatively primitive cultures of the New World, but even when they met the old cultures of the East, was that they had nothing to learn from them. Once the process of interchange had gone far enough, some individuals were impressed with the mysticism and otherworldliness of Hindu philosophy and religion, and with the high but quite this-worldly ethics of Chinese Confucianism. Others came to admire the dignity and simplicity of the lives of many primitive peoples. But for the most part what struck the Europeans—when they bothered at all to think about anything more than money making and empire building—was the poverty, dirt, and superstition they found among the masses in India and China, the low material standards of primitive peoples everywhere, the heathenness of the heathens.

Yet exposure to these very different cultures also stimulated Western minds and broadened intellectual horizons. The first effect was perhaps no more than to increase the fund of the marvelous and incredible. Early accounts of the New World are full of giants and pygmies, El Dorados where the streets are paved with gold, fountains of eternal youth, wonderful plants and animals. Soon, however, serious science was encouraged. A dip into any of the early accounts of voyages, say the famous collection edited in English by Richard Hakluyt in 1582, gives an impression more of the realis-

tic sense and careful observation of these travelers than of their credulity and exaggerations. Here is modern geography already well on its way to maturity, and here too are the foundations of the modern social sciences of anthropology, comparative government, even of economics. A good example is the report by an early seventeenth-century Italian traveler on the puzzling Hindu institution of caste:

The whole Gentile-people of *India* is divided into many sects or parties of men, known and distinguisht by descent or pedigree, as the Tribes of the Jews sometimes were; yet they inhabit the Country promiscuously mingled together, in every City and Land several Races one with another. 'Tis reckon'd that they are in all eighty four; some say more, making a more exact and subtle division. Every one of these hath a particular name, and also a special office and Employment in the Commonwealth, from which none of the descendants of that Race ever swerve; they never rise nor fall, nor change condition: whence some are Husbandmen, others Mechanicks, as Taylers, Shoemakers and the like; others Factors or Merchants, such as they whom we call *Banians,* but they in their Language more correctly *Vania;* others, Souldiers, as the *Ragiaputi;* . . . so many Races which they reckon are reduc'd to four principal, which, if I mistake not, are the Brachmans, the Souldiers, the Merchants and the Artificers; from whom by more minute sub-division all the rest are deriv'd, in such number as in the whole people there are various professions of men.*

It may well be that the intellectual effects of the great discoveries were on the whole unsettling, disturbing. They helped, along with the new astronomy, the new mechanics, the Protestant Reformation, and much else, to break the medieval "cake of custom." They helped, literally, to make a New World of ideas and ideals. Such changes are always hard on ordinary human beings, for they demand that men change their minds, something that most of us find very hard to do.

The great discoveries also helped to revolutionize the economy and society of Europe; we already have seen some instances of how this came about. By the middle of the seventeenth century, Spain is estimated to have imported eighteen thousand tons of bullion from the Americas—enough to increase the gold supply of Europe by 20 percent and the silver supply by 300 percent. Everywhere new coins were circulated, and everywhere prices rose—by some 400 percent in Spain during the sixteenth century, by less dramatic but substantial amounts elsewhere. This rise in prices accompanied and helped to cause a general economic expansion that ultimately produced the Industrial Revolution.

In the long process of inflation and expansion, which has continued with ups and downs to the present, some groups gained and others lost. In general, merchants, financiers, and businessmen in general enjoyed a rising standard of living. Those on relatively fixed incomes suffered, including landed proprietors, unless

*E. Grey, ed., *The Travels of Pietro della Valle in India* (London, 1892), 1:78–79.

they turned to large-scale capitalist farming, and also governments, unless they were able to find new sources of income. Wage earners, artisans, peasants, and the general majority of people usually did not find their incomes keeping pace with the rise in prices. In short, here as elsewhere, the effects of expansion were unsettling, even harsh, as well as stimulating.

The American historian Walter P. Webb, in *The Great Frontier,* made a still more sweeping generalization about the effects of expansion. The vast lands of the "frontier" in the New World, he maintained, were a bonanza or windfall, and supplied the real force behind the great increase in man's power to get more out of his natural environment with less sacrifice—and this unprecedented wealth and power, in turn, constitute the great innovation of modern Western civilization. As a sympathetic British historian recently observed, Webb's frontier thesis "deserves two cheers for gallantry, although not—regrettably—three cheers for success." * Once again we find that the attempt to make a single explanation of the great movements of history is dangerous. The opportunities for expansion that the discoveries gave to Europeans were obviously one factor in the rapid growth of productivity, population, and technical skills. By the late sixteenth century the easily acquired supplies of silver from the New World were priming the pumps of developing capitalism in northwest Europe.

But, by the mid-seventeenth century, the effects of this particular pump-priming were fading, as silver became scarcer and more costly, and as the colonial manufactures began to increase, and the colonial market for European goods to diminish, in defiance of the strictures of mercantilism. The frontier theory of modern Western capitalist society is no more convincing as a sole explanation than, say, the Marxist theory of economic determinism or the Weber thesis about the Protestant ethic. The roots of the great discoveries themselves, like the roots of capitalism, Protestantism and modern science, lie deep in the Middle Ages. Before

*J. H. Elliott, *The Old World and the New* (Cambridge, 1970), p. 59.

new worlds could be accessible to European enterprise trade, navigation and government organization all had to arrive at the point where Henry the Navigator, Columbus, da Gama, and the others could proceed methodically to the explorations and the conquests that had been there, after all, for the Greeks, the Phoenicians, the Romans, or the Vikings to make, had they been able and willing.

Toward One World

"There is only one world, and although we speak of the Old World and the New, this is because the latter was lately discovered by us, and not because there are two." * These words were written by a Spaniard in sixteenth-century Peru. By the beginning of the eighteenth century—although there were still blank spots on the map, especially in the African interior and the Pacific northwest of America, and although Japan and China still tried to exclude European influence—it was already clear that only one system of international politics existed in the world. All general European wars now tended to be world wars, fought, if only by privateers, on the seven seas and, if only by savages and frontiersmen, on distant continents. Sooner or later, any considerable transfer of territory overseas and any great accession of strength or wealth in any quarter of the globe affected the international balance of power.

The One World of the eighteenth century was not one world of the spirit; the great mass of Europeans were ignorant of what really went on in the hearts and minds of men elsewhere. But already Western goods penetrated almost everywhere, led by firearms and liquor, but followed by a great many other commodities, not all of them "cheap and nasty," as later critics of imperialism would complain. Already an educated minority was appearing, from professional geographers to journalists, diplomats, and businessmen, who dealt with what were now quite literally the affairs of the world.

*Ibid., p. 102.

Reading Suggestions on the Expansion of Europe
Background and General Accounts

J. H. Parry, *The Age of Reconnaissance* (*Mentor) and *The Establishment of the European Hegemony, 1415–1715: Trade and Exploration in the Age of the Renaissance* (*Torchbooks). Excellent introductions by a ranking expert in the field.

C. E. Nowell, *The Great Discoveries and the First Colonial Empires* (*Cornell Univ.). Handy brief introduction.

B. Penrose, *Travel and Discovery in the Renaissance, 1420–1620* (*Atheneum). Very informative survey with accounts of voyages not easily available elsewhere.

J. N. L. Baker, *A History of Geographical Discovery and Exploration,* rev. ed. (Barnes & Noble, 1963). A standard work.

P. Sykes, *A History of Exploration from the Earliest Times to the Present* (Routledge, 1934). A comprehensive treatment of the subject.

C. R. Beazley, *The Dawn of Modern Geography,* 3 vols. (John Murray, 1897–1906). An authoritative account; stops in 1420 but useful for the background of this chapter.

G. Jones, *The Norse Atlantic Saga* (Oxford Univ., 1964). A reliable summary of Viking exploration.

H. Trevor-Roper, ed., *The Age of Expansion: Europe and the World, 1559–1660* (McGraw-Hill, 1968). Less comprehensive in treatment than the title suggests, but with enlightening chapters on the Spaniards, the Dutch, and the Far East.

The Portuguese

C. R. Boxer, *The Portuguese Seaborne Empire, 1415–1825* (Knopf, 1969). Admirable study in the History of Human Society series. Boxer has also written a succinct survey covering the same period: *Four Centuries of Portuguese Expansion* (*Univ. of California).

E. Sanceau, *Henry the Navigator* (Norton, 1947). A good biography of the Portuguese sponsor of exploration.

H. H. Hart, *Sea Road to the Indies* (Macmillan, 1950). Deals with da Gama and other Portuguese explorers.

C. McK. Parr, *So Noble a Captain* (Crowell, 1953). A very scholarly treatment of Magellan and his circumnavigation.

The Spaniards

J. H. Parry, *The Spanish Seaborne Empire* (Knopf, 1966). Excellent account in the useful History of Human Society series.

S. E. Morison, *Admiral of the Ocean Sea,* 2 vols. (Little, Brown, 1942). The best book on Columbus; by a historian who retraced Columbus' route in a small ship. He has also published the briefer *Christopher Columbus, Mariner* (*Mentor).

C. H. Haring, *The Spanish Empire in America* (*Harcourt). A standard treatment of the subject.

W. H. Prescott, *The Conquest of Mexico* and *The Conquest of Peru* (many editions). Celebrated narratives written more than a century ago; may be sampled in various abridgments, among them *The Portable Prescott* (*Viking).

L. B. Hanke, *The Spanish Struggle for Justice in the Conquest of America* (*Little, Brown). Study of an important and often neglected side of the Spanish record.

The Dutch

C. R. Boxer, *The Dutch Seaborne Empire, 1600–1800* (Hutchinson, 1965). Full, up-to-date survey by a capable scholar: another volume in the History of Human Society series.

A. Hyma, *The Dutch in the Far East* (Wahr, 1942). Stressing social and economic developments.

B. H. M. Vlekke, *Nusantara: A History of Indonesia,* rev. ed. (Lorenz, 1959). Introduction to the most important region of Dutch imperial activity.

The French and the British

J. B. Brebner, *The Explorers of North America, 1492–1806* (*Meridian). Good brief survey.

G. Lanctot, *History of Canada,* 2 vols. (Harvard Univ., 1963–1964). Detailed study to 1713; by a French-Canadian scholar.

G. M. Wrong, *The Rise and Fall of New France,* 2 vols. (Macmillan, 1928). Sound study by an English-Canadian scholar.

S. E. Morison, ed., *The Parkman Reader* (Little, Brown, 1955). Selections from the celebrated multivolumed *France and England in North America* by the nineteenth-century historian Francis Parkman.

J. H. Rose, ed., *The Cambridge History of the British Empire,* Vol. 1 (Cambridge Univ., 1929). Detailed survey to 1783.

Africa, Asia, and the Pacific

H. Labouret, *Africa before the White Man* (Walker, 1963); B. David-son, *Africa in History* (Macmillan, 1969); R. Oliver and J. D. Fage, *A Short History of Africa* (*Penguin). Three helpful introductions. Fage has also written *A History of West Africa* (*Cambridge Univ.) and other useful books on the continent.

B. Davidson, *The African Slave Trade* (*Atlantic Monthly). By a prolific writer on African history.

A. L. Basham, *The Wonder That Was India* (*Evergreen). A more careful survey of Indian history up to the Muslim invasions than the title might suggest.

E. O. Reischauer and J. K. Fairbank, *East Asia: The Great Tradition* (Houghton, 1960). An expert survey of China, Japan, and Korea from the beginnings. Reischauer has also written *Japan: The Story of a Nation* (*Knopf).

R. Grousset, *The Rise and Splendor of the Chinese Empire* (*Univ. of California). An enlightening study of Chinese culture.

K. S. Latourette, *China* (*Spectrum). Excellent introduction.

G. B. Sansom, *A History of Japan, 1334–1615* and *A History of Japan, 1615–1867* (*Knopf). Perceptive accounts by a leading British expert.

C. Lloyd, *Pacific Horizons* (Allen & Unwin, 1946), and *Captain Cook* (Faber & Faber, 1952). Readable modern reviews of early Pacific exploration.

The Americas

J. Soustelle, *Daily Life of the Aztecs on the Eve of the Spanish Conquest* (*Stanford Univ.). Instructive study by an anthropologist.

S. J. and B. Stein, *Colonial Heritage of Latin America* (*Oxford Univ.). Essays stressing its economic dependence on the mother countries.

A. P. Newton, *The European Nations in the West Indies, 1493–1688* (Black, 1933). Excellent study of a great arena of colonial rivalry.

C. M. Andrews, *The Colonial Period of American History,* Vols. 1, 2, 3 (*Yale Univ.). Detailed study of the European settlements.

D. J. Boorstin, *Americans: The Colonial Experience* (*Vintage). A provocative briefer treatment.

L. B. Wright, *Cultural Life of the American Colonies, 1607–1763* (*Torchbooks). An especially good volume in the New American Nation series.

The Impact of Expansion

J. H. Elliott, *The Old World and the New, 1492–1650* (*Cambridge Univ.). Stimulating lectures on the impact of the New World upon the Old.

The Cambridge Economic History, Vol. 4 (Cambridge Univ., 1967). Scholarly essays on expanding Europe in the sixteenth and seventeenth centuries.

W. P. Webb, *The Great Frontier: An Interpretation of World History* (Houghton, 1952). Assigns the New World a crucial role in the developing wealth and power of the Old.

E. J. Hamilton, *American Treasure and the Price Revolution in Spain, 1501–1650* (Harvard Univ., 1934). Long a standard study, but its stress on the central role of bullion has been challenged by more recent scholarship.

Sources and Historical Fiction

I. R. Blacker, ed., *The Portable Hakluyt's Voyages* (*Viking). Excerpts from the famous late sixteenth-century collection.

J. R. Levenson, *European Expansion and the Counter-Example of*

Asia (*Prentice-Hall). Materials on technology, religion, social structure, and "spirit."

E. D. Genovese and R. Foner, *Slavery in the New World* (*Prentice-Hall). Materials on the comparative slave policies of the imperial powers.

L. Wallace, *The Fair God* (*Popular Library). A real thriller, a century old, on the Aztecs of Mexico; by the author of *Ben Hur.*

C. S. Forester, *To the Indies* (Little, Brown, 1940). Fine novel on Columbus.

R. Sabatini, *The Sea Hawk* (Houghton, 1923). A good melodramatic novel of adventures on the sea in the late sixteenth century.

W. Cather, *Shadows on the Rock* (*Random House). Sensitive re-creation of life in New France by a twentieth-century American novelist.

15

Divine-Right Monarchy— and Revolution

I Introduction

The Peace of Westphalia in 1648 brought to a close not only the Thirty Years' War but also a whole epoch in European history. It ended the age of the Reformation and Counter-Reformation, when wars were both religious and dynastic in motivation and the chief threats to a stable international balance came from the Catholic Hapsburgs and from the militant Protestants of Germany, the Netherlands, and Scandinavia. After 1648 religion, though continuing to be a major source of friction in France and the British Isles, ceased to be a significant international issue. The main force jeopardizing the European balance was the entirely secular ambition of Bourbon France, for seventy-two years— 1643 to 1715—under a single monarch, Louis XIV, who inherited the throne at the age of four and a half. Louis was the embodiment of the characteristic early modern form of royal absolutism, monarchy by divine right, and he was the very personification of royal pride, elegance, and luxury. To the French, Louis XIV was *le grand monarque,* and his long, long reign marked the culmination of their *grand siècle,* the great century that had begun under Cardinal Richelieu in the twenty years before Louis' accession and that was marked by the international triumph of French arms and French diplomacy and, still more, of French ways of writing, building, dressing, and eating, the whole style of life of the upper classes in *la grande nation.*

While the culture of *la grande nation* went from one triumph to another, Louis XIV's bid for political hegemony was ultimately checked. His most resolute opponent was England, still in the throes of the greatest political upheaval in her history. The upheaval resulted from the collision between the forces of the Stuart monarchy and High Church Anglicanism, on the one hand, and those of Parliament and the Puritans, on the other. The final settlement was a compromise weighted in favor of the parliamentary side, but still a compromise

and therefore compatible with the modern image of England as the country of gradual, orderly change. This was not the image prevailing in the seventeenth century, after decades of violence and flux, with one English king executed and another obliged to go into exile. In those days England was synonymous with revolution.

The English political turmoil was not the only seventeenth-century revolution. Alfred North Whitehead, the eminent English mathematician and philosopher of the early twentieth century, called the 1600s "the century of genius." It was the century of Galileo and Francis Bacon, of Descartes and Pascal, of Newton and Locke, and of many others who helped to lay the foundations of modern science, to provide it with indispensable tools, and to establish the patterns of thought and procedure that we call rational, empirical, and inductive. This intellectual and scientific revolution had repercussions more far-reaching than those emanating from the court or the culture of Louis XIV's France or even from the England of revolution and civil war. The "century of genius" was the prelude to what has been termed "the great modern revolution," the practical applications of the new science and technology to the production of raw materials and finished goods—the agricultural and industrial revolutions.

Some historians of the mid-twentieth century have found the mid-seventeenth century an age of crisis comparable in its disturbing effects to the famines and Black Death of the fourteenth century. Demographers note the decline in population not only in war-ravaged Germany but in Spain and some other countries as well. Economic historians point to the severely depressing effects of the Thirty Years' War and also to the social upheavals accompanying the struggle between the capitalism of the rising middle class and the agrarianism of the traditional landed classes. Political historians stress the multiplicity of revolutions, successful and abortive, against extravagant, corrupt, and inefficient monarchies not just in England but in Portugal, Spain, France, and elsewhere. Still other historians, however, while admitting that the seventeenth century experienced more than its share of troubles, reject these attempts to find a single dominant pattern, whether demographic, economic, or political. To them it was an age of crises (in the plural, not the singular) whose interrelations have not yet been convincingly demonstrated.

II Bourbon France
Louis XIII and Richelieu

France's *grand siècle* was almost blighted in the bud when, in 1610, in the prime of his career, the capable and popular Henry IV was assassinated by a madman. The new king, Louis XIII (1610–1643), was only nine years old; the queen mother, Marie de' Medici, served as regent but showed little of her famous family's political skill. Her Italian favorites and French nobles, Cath-

olic and Huguenot alike, carried on a hectic competition that threatened to undo all that Henry IV had accomplished. During these troubles the French representative body, the Estates General, met in 1614 for what was destined to be its last session until 1789 on the eve of the great French Revolution. Significantly, the meeting was paralyzed by tensions between the noble deputies of the second estate and the bourgeois of the third. Meanwhile, Louis XIII, though barely in his teens, attempted to assert his personal authority and reduce the role of his mother. Poorly educated, sickly, nervous, and subject to spells of depression, Louis needed expert help.

He was fortunate in securing the assistance of the remarkably talented Richelieu (1585–1642), who proved to be an efficient administrator and a sincere but not an ardent Catholic as bishop of a remote diocese in western France. Tiring of provincial life, Richelieu moved to Paris and showed great skill and considerable unscrupulousness in political maneuvering during the confused days of Marie de' Medici's regency. He emerged as the conciliator between the king and

An illustration from Abraham Bosse's ''Le Palais Royal'' (1640) gives a good picture of French fashions and tastes.

his mother, and was rewarded with election to the College of Cardinals and then, in 1624, with selection by Louis as his chief minister. While the king maintained a lively interest in affairs of state, Richelieu was the virtual ruler of France for the next eighteen years. He proved to be a good Machiavellian and a good politique, subordinating religion and every nonpolitical consideration to *raison d'état* (reason of state), a phrase that he probably coined himself.

When Richelieu entered the king's service, he claimed to have promised Louis that he would "ruin the Huguenot party, humble the pride of the great nobles, recall all his subjects to their duty, and raise his name among foreign nations to the level where it ought to be." * The promise proved to be a largely accurate forecast of Richelieu's program and accomplishments. *Raison d'état* made the "ruin" of the Huguenots his first priority, for the political privileges they had received by the Edict of Nantes made them a major obstacle to the creation of a centralized state. The hundred fortified towns they governed, chiefly in southwestern France, constituted a state within the state, a hundred centers of potential rebellion that Richelieu was determined to bring under control. Alarmed, the Huguenots did in fact rebel. It took the royal forces fourteen months to besiege and take their chief stronghold, the Atlantic port of La Rochelle, which finally fell in 1628 after the besiegers constructed a great jetty to seal off the access of its harbor to the sea. (Louis XIII, incidentally, was so excited by the project that he wanted to lend the masons a hand in the work.) Thereupon Richelieu canceled the political and military clauses of the Edict of Nantes but left intact its grant of partial religious toleration to the Huguenots.

The siege of La Rochelle lasted so long because France had no navy worthy of the name. In the next ten years Richelieu created a fleet of thirty-eight warships for the Atlantic and, for the Mediterranean, a dozen galleys manned by slaves (an exception to the rule that whites were never enslaved in the modern West). Meanwhile, he guided France expertly through the Thirty Years' War, committing French resources only when concrete gains seemed possible, and ensuring favorable publicity by supplying exaggerated accounts of French victories to the *Gazette de France*. In every way Richelieu was a great practitioner of realistic power politics.

Raison d'état, indeed, motivated all his policies. He lived in elaborate style, accompanied on his travels by his private choir and corps of musicians, not just because he was fond of music but because he believed such a retinue befitted the chief minister of a splendid kingdom. In 1635, he founded the famous French Academy, to compile a dictionary of the French language and to set the standards and style of the national culture. He tried to humble the factious nobles, though

with only partial success, by ordering the destruction of some of their châteaux and forbidding the favorite aristocratic indulgence of private duels. More effective was his transfer of supervision over the local administration from nobles and from officeholders of dubious loyalty who had purchased their posts to the more reliable *intendants*. These royal officials had existed earlier but performed only minor functions; now they were given greatly increased powers over justice and the police and especially over apportioning and collecting taxes.

Richelieu made possible *la grande nation* of Louis XIV by building an efficient, centralized state. But in a sense he built too well, making the French governments so centralized, so professionally bureaucratic, that it had no place for the give-and-take of politics. Except for attempting to equalize the incidence of taxes among the provinces of France, Richelieu did little to remedy the chronic fiscal weakness of the government, particularly corruption in tax collection and the piling up of deficits. His concentration on *raison d'état* led him to take an extraordinarily callous view of the subjects on whose loyal performance of their duties the welfare of the state depended. He once wrote: "All politicians agree that when the people are too comfortable it is impossible to keep them within the bounds of their duty . . . they must be compared to mules which, being used to burdens, are spoiled more by rest than by labour." *

Mazarin and the Fronde

The deaths of Richelieu and Louis XIII in successive years (1642, 1643), the accession of a child king, and the regency of the hated Hapsburg queen mother, Anne of Austria (she was a Hapsburg from Spain, where the dynasty was called the house of Austria)—all seemed to threaten a repetition of the crisis following the death of Henry IV. The crisis was averted, or at any rate delayed, by the new chief minister, Mazarin (1602–1661). Picked and schooled by Richelieu himself, Mazarin, too, was a cardinal (though not a priest as his predecessor had been) and a past master of *raison d'état*. He, too, was careless about the finances of the French state, but, unlike Richelieu, he amassed an immense personal fortune during his public career, bestowing lavish gifts on his five Italian nieces, who married into the high French nobility, and collecting a magnificent library, which he willed to the French state. He antagonized both branches of the French aristocracy—the nobles of the sword, descendants of feudal magnates, and the nobles of the robe (the reference is to the gowns worn by judges and other officials), descendants of commoners who had bought their way into government office. The former resented being excluded from the regency by a foreigner; the latter, who had invested heavily in government securities, particu-

*Quoted in C. J. Friedrich, *The Age of the Baroque, 1610–1660* (New York, 1952), p. 198 n. Our translation.

*Quoted in C. V. Wedgwood, *Richelieu and the French Monarchy* (New York, 1950), p. 137.

Triple portrait of Richelieu, by Champaigne.

larly disliked Mazarin's casual way of borrowing money to meet war expenses and then letting the interest payments on government loans fall into arrears.

The discontent boiled over in the Fronde, 1648–1653, named for the slingshot used by Parisian children to hurl pellets at passersby, and one of the several midcentury uprisings in Europe. Some of the rioting involved participation by the peasantry and the common people of Paris, both impoverished by the economic depression accompanying the final campaigns of the Thirty Years' War. But the Fronde was essentially a noble revolt, led first by the judges of the Parlement of Paris, a high court and a stronghold of the nobles of the robe, and then, after the Peace of Westphalia, by aristocratic officers returned from the Thirty Years' War. Various "princes of the blood," relatives of the royal family, intervened with their private armies. Though Mazarin twice had to flee France and go into exile, the upshot of the Fronde was to confirm him in power and to pave the way for the personal rule of Louis XIV. The youthful king got a bad fright when

the frondeurs actually broke into his bedroom, and he resolved to hold firmly to the reins of state. The Fronde failed essentially because it had no real roots in the country, not even in the rising middle classes. It was a struggle for power between Mazarin and his new bureaucracy and two privileged groups of nobles. Each noble group distrusted the other, and the nobles of the sword were also split by personal feuds; all Mazarin had to do was apply the old Roman maxim "Divide and rule."

Le Grand Monarque

When Mazarin died in 1661, Louis XIV began to rule as well as to reign. At the age of twenty-two the king already displayed an impressive royal presence, as reported by Madame de Motteville, a seasoned observer of the French court:

As the single desire for glory and to fulfill all the duties of a great king occupied his whole heart, by applying himself to toil he began to like it; and the eagerness he had to learn all the things that were necessary to him soon made him full of that knowledge. His great good sense and his good intentions now made visible in him the rudiments of general knowledge which had been hidden from all who did not see him in private. . . .

He was agreeable personally, civil and easy of access to every one; but with a lofty and serious air which impressed the public with respect and awe . . . , though he was familiar and gay with ladies.*

Louis continued to be "familiar and gay with ladies" until finally, after the death of his Spanish queen, he settled down in the 1680s to a proper middle-aged marriage with Madame de Maintenon, a Huguenot turned devout Catholic who had been the governess of his illegitimate children.

Louis XIV, the "Sun King," succeeded so well as *le grand monarque* because by education, temperament, and physique he was ideally suited to the role. It has been remarked that he had received from Mazarin just enough education to be guided always by *raison d'état,* though not by reason itself. Endowed with excellent manners—"civil and easy of access to everyone," as Mme de Motteville observed—he also had admirable

*Memoirs of Madame de Motteville, trans. K. P. Wormeley (Boston, 1902), 3:243.

self-discipline, patience, and staying power. He never lost his temper in public and went through long daily hours in council meetings and elaborate ceremonials with unwearied attention and even enjoyment, to which his conspicuous lack of a sense of humor may have contributed. He had an iron physical constitution, which enabled him to withstand a rigorous schedule, made him indifferent to heat and to cold, and allowed him to survive both a lifetime of gross overeating (an autopsy revealed his stomach was twice normal size) and the crude medical treatment of the day.

He was five feet five inches tall—a fairly impressive height for the day—and added to his stature by shoes with high red heels. To provide a suitable setting for the Sun King, to neutralize the high nobility politically by isolating it in the ceaseless ceremonies and petty intrigues of court life, and also to prevent a repetition of the frondeurs' intrusion into his bedroom in Paris, he moved the capital from Paris to Versailles, a dozen miles away. There on sandy wasteland he built his celebrated palace more than a third of a mile long, flanked by elaborate stables and other outbuildings, approached from Paris by a majestic avenue, and set in an immense formal garden with fourteen hundred fountains, the water for which had to be pumped up from the River Seine at staggering expense. Versailles housed, mainly in cramped uncomfortable quarters, a

The Palace of Versailles: an engraving by P. Menant.

court of ten thousand, including dependents and servants of all sorts.

Divine-Right Monarchy

The admired and imitated French state, of which Versailles was the symbol and Louis XIV the embodiment, can also stand as the best historical example of divine-right monarchy. Perhaps Louis never actually said, "L'état c'est moi" (I am the state), but the phrase has stuck, and it certainly summarizes his convictions about his role. In theory, Louis was for his subjects no mere man but the representative of God on earth—or at least in France. He was not elected by his subjects, nor did he acquire his throne by force of arms; rather, he was born to a position God had planned for the legitimate male heir of the tenth-century Hugh Capet. As God's agent, his word was final, for to challenge it would be to challenge the whole structure of God's universe. Disobedience was a religious as well as a political offense.

Though Louis has been dead less than three centuries, the ideas and sentiments centered on this divine-right monarchy seem so utterly alien today that it takes an effort of the historical imagination not to dismiss them as nonsense. Two clues may help us to understand why they were once held so widely and so firmly. The first is the survival of the characteristic medieval view that right decisions in government are not arrived at by experiment and discussion, but by "finding" the authoritative answer provided for in God's scheme of things. In the days of Louis XIV many people still believed that God through his chosen agents directly managed the state. The second clue lies in the deliberate efforts of Henry IV and Richelieu as well as Louis XIV to fuse the sixteen million inhabitants of France into a single national unit. The problem was to make these millions who were used to thinking and behaving as Normans, Bretons, Flemings, Alsatians, Burgundians, Gascons, Basques, and Provençaux to think and behave as Frenchmen. The makers of the Bourbon monarchy could not rely on a common language, for only a minority as yet spoke standard French; and they could not rely on a common educational system, a common national press, or a common participation in political life, for all of these lay in the future. They could, and did, attempt to set up the king as a symbol of common Frenchness. The king collected taxes, raised armies, touched in a hundred ways the lives of his subjects who had to feel that the king had a right to do all this and that he was doing it *for* them rather than *to* them. A king who was the agent of God was the kind of ruler they could accept.

Divine-right monarchy, with its corollary of obedience on the part of subjects, is thus one phase in the growth of the modern centralized nation-state. It was an institution that appealed to old theological ideas, such as the biblical admonition to obey the powers that be, for "the powers that be are ordained of God," but it was also inspired by the newer ideas of binding men together in a productive, efficient state. In practice, naturally, the institution did not wholly correspond to theories about it. Louis XIV was not the French state, and his rule was not absolute in any full sense of that word. He simply did not have the physical means for controlling in detail what his subjects did, a control much more extensive under modern techniques of communication, propaganda, and administration than it ever was in the days of "absolute" monarchy. Medieval survivals made for diversities in laws, customs, weights and measures, as well as language, that all stood in the way of uniformity. Important groups still clung to medieval rights and immunities, which they felt did not depend on the king's will. Many of these groups were corporations—municipal councils, courts like the parlements in Paris and in some provincial capitals, economic groups such as guilds—which usually possessed written charters and traditional privileges difficult for the government to override. Particularly troublesome were the aristocratic and religious forces, both Catholic and Huguenot, that had been involved in the civil strife of the late sixteenth century.

Nobles, Catholics, and Huguenots

In all the important countries of Europe the feudal nobles maintained themselves into early modern times; the degree to which they were integrated into the new machinery of state was of crucial importance in the development of modern Europe. In Hapsburg Spain, as indeed in the Hapsburg lands of central Europe, the old nobility generally accepted the new strength of the Crown, but maintained much of their privilege and all their old pride of status. In Prussia, as a later chapter will show, they were successfully integrated into the new order, becoming on the whole faithful servants or soldiers of the Crown, but with a social status that set them well above mere bourgeois bureaucrats. In England, as we shall shortly see, the nobility achieved a unique compromise with the Crown. In France, the nobles of the sword were in effect shoved aside by the Crown and deprived for the most part of major political functions, but they were allowed to retain social and economic privileges and important roles as officers in the king's army.

This process of reducing the old French nobility to relative powerlessness at least in national political life had begun during the fifteenth century and had been hastened by the religious and civil wars of the next century. An important part of the nobility, perhaps nearly half, had espoused the Protestant cause, in large part from sheer opposition to the Crown. The victory of Henry IV, purchased by his conversion to Catholicism, was a defeat for the nobility. Under Richelieu and Louis XIV the process was completed by the increasing use of commoners in the task of running the government, from the great ministers of state, through the intendants, down to local administrators and judges. These commoners were usually elevated to the nobility of the robe, which did not have at first the social prestige of the nobility of the sword. The Fronde demonstrated that these new nobles could not be counted upon as loyal supporters of the Crown. Among the old nobles they aroused a contemptuous envy, summed up in the famous complaint of the ultra-aristocratic duc de Saint-Simon that only "vile bourgeois" had the confidence of the king; the nobles of the sword knew they were shelved. By the end of Louis' reign, however, the two kinds of nobility had become better amalgamated, giving the whole order a new lease on life.

In medieval times, the clergy had been a separate order, backed by the supranational power and prestige of the papacy and possessing privileges not wholly in the control of the Crown. Even under Louis XIV the French clergy continued to possess important corporate privileges. They were not subject to royal taxation; they contributed of their own free will a gift of money that they voted in their own assembly. In the centralized France that emerged from the Hundred Years' War the Crown had fostered the evolution of a national Gallican church, firmly Catholic but also controlled by the monarchy, and friendly to new political, social, and economic ideas. Under Louis XIV the Gallican union of throne and altar reached a high point in 1682 when a great assembly of French clerics drew up the Declaration of Gallican Liberties, asserting in effect that the "rules and customs admitted by France and the Gallican church" were just as important as the traditional authority of the papacy. "Ocean itself, immense though it is, has its limits," pronounced Bishop Bossuet, a great defender of Louis's monarchy by divine right. In practice, however, the flamboyant new Gallican claims for French royal authority did not prove to be very important.

Louis XIV took as the goal of his religious policy the application of a traditional French motto—*un roi, une loi, une foi* (one king, one law, one faith). Whereas Richelieu had attacked only the political privileges of the Huguenots, Louis attacked their fundamental right of toleration and finally abolished it. He began by pulling down Huguenot churches not specifically authorized by the Edict of Nantes, then put restrictions on Huguenots' education, their admission to the professions, and their right to marry outside their faith. A campaign for converting Protestants to the Roman faith assumed a coercive aspect through the notorious *dragonnades,* the billeting of dragoons in Huguenot households as a persuasive measure. Misled by exaggerated reports of the success achieved, and pressed by the fanatically anti-Huguenot lower Catholic clergy, Louis

revoked the Edict of Nantes in 1685. After the revocation, fifty thousand Huguenot families fled abroad, notably to Prussia, Belgium, Holland and the Dutch colony in South Africa, England (where they were given a chapel in Canterbury cathedral itself), and the colonies of British North America, as the name of New Rochelle, New York, reminds us. The practical skills and the intellectual gifts of the refugees strengthened the lands that received them, and the departure of industrious workmen and of thousands of veteran sailors, soldiers, and officers weakened the mother country. Some Huguenots remained in France, worshiping underground in spite of persecution.

Within the Catholic church itself, Louis had to contend with two important elements that refused to accept his Gallicanism. The Quietists, a group of religious enthusiasts led by Madame Guyon, sought for a more mystical and emotional faith. Their tendency to exhibitionism and self-righteousness combined with their zeal for publicity belied their name of Quietist and offended the king's sense of propriety. The Jansenists, sometimes called the Puritans of the Catholic church, were a high-minded group whose most distinguished spokesman was the scientist and philosopher Pascal. Named for Cornelius Jansen, bishop of Ypres in the early seventeenth century, the Jansenists took an almost Calvinistic stand on the issue of predestination. They stressed the need to obey the authority of God rather than that of man, no matter how exalted the position of the particular man might be. They therefore questioned both the authority of the pope (and of his agents, the Jesuits) and that of the king. On the surface, Louis was successful in repressing both Quietists and Jansenists, but the latter in particular survived to trouble his successors in the eighteenth century.

The Royal Administration

Just as Louis XIV was never wholly master of the religious beliefs and practices of his subjects, he never quite succeeded in building up an administrative machine wholly under royal control. At Versailles he had three long conferences weekly with his ministers, who headed departments essentially like those of any modern state—War, Finance, Foreign Affairs, Interior. The king kept this top administrative level on an intimate scale; he usually had only four ministers at one time, and gave them virtually permanent tenure. Colbert served as controller general for eighteen years, and Le Tellier for thirty-four as secretary of state for the Army, a portfolio later entrusted to his son, who had been ennobled as the marquis de Louvois. All told, only sixteen ministers held office during the fifty-four years of his personal reign.

From Louis XIV and his ministers, who were directly responsible to him, a chain of command proceeded down through the intendants, whose number was fixed at thirty, with each at the head of a *généralité,* a big administrative unit roughly corresponding to the older province. Below the intendants were their subordinates, the *subdélégués,* and at the bottom were the towns and villages of France, which sometimes defied or ignored the royal command. Even the indefatigable Louis could do no more than exercise general supervision over the affairs of his large and complex kingdom. And he probably could not have achieved even partial success without the invention of printing. For the familiar government printed forms to be filled out were already in existence. And they are still there, duly filled out and filed in their hundreds of thousands in the local archives of France.

In practice, the royal administration was full of difficulties and contradictions. There were many conflicting jurisdictions, survivals of feudalism and the medieval struggle to control feudalism. The officials of Louis XIV, by the very fact of being nobles of the robes, possessed a privileged status they could hand down to their heirs. They, too, tended to form a "corporation" and to be more their own masters in their own bailiwicks than the theory of royal absolutism would allow. The key provincial administrators, the intendants, may seem to have been no more than agents of the Crown. Yet anyone who pursues in local history the detailed records of what they actually did finds that many of them exercised considerable initiative on their own. Nor was the old administrative device of moving the intendants about from one généralité to another sufficient to overcome this centrifugal tendency.

A particularly important potential for trouble existed in the parlements, the supreme courts of appeal in the various provinces, of which one, the Parlement of Paris, enjoyed special prestige and power from its place at the capital and from the size of its territorial jurisdiction, almost half of the kingdom. The judges who staffed the courts headed the nobility of the robe, owned their offices, and were not removable at the will of the king. In addition to the usual work of a court of appeals, the parlements claimed through their function of registering royal edicts before they went into force something approaching the right of judicial review. That is, they claimed to be able to refuse registration of an edict if they thought it unconstitutional, not in accord with higher law of the land. Although the claim negated theoretical royal absolutism, Louis got around it in his own lifetime. The Parlement of Paris had already lost a round in its struggle with the royal power by entering the lists against Mazarin in the Fronde. Now Louis successfully utilized another old institution, the *lit de justice* (literally, "bed of justice"), in which he summoned the Parlement of Paris before him in a formal session and ordered the justices to register a royal edict. In this way, for instance, he enforced measures against Jansenism, which was strong among the judges. But the parlements, too, were to plague his eighteenth-century successors.

Mercantilism and Colbert

Just as divine-right monarchy was not peculiarly French, so the mercantilism identified with the France of Louis XIV was common to many other Western states; but, like divine-right rule, it flourished most characteristically under the Sun King. Mercantilism was part and parcel of the early modern effort to construct strong, efficient political units. The mercantilists quite frankly aimed to make their nation as self-sustaining as possible, as independent as possible of the need to import goods from other nations, which were its rivals and its potential enemies. The mercantilists held that production within a nation should provide the necessities of life for a hard-working population, and the necessities of power for the nation to fight and win wars. They believed that these goals required planning and control from above. They were all for sweeping away the remnants of such medieval institutions as the manor and the guild, which, they felt, reduced the energies and abilities needed in an expanding economy. But they did not believe, as the free-trade economists would later believe, that all that was necessary was to leave individuals free to do whatever they thought would enrich themselves. Instead, the mercantilists would channel the national economic effort by protective tariffs, by government subsidies, by grants of monopolies, by industries directly run by the government, and by encouraging scientific and technological research.

The mercantilists viewed overseas possessions as a special part of France that should be run from the homeland by a strong government. Already in the seventeenth century many foodstuffs and raw materials were more easily available overseas than in Europe. Colonies, therefore, should be encouraged to provide necessities so that the mother country need not import them from her competitors. In return, the mother country would supply industrial goods to the colonies and have a monopoly over colonial trade. This mercantilistic attitude toward colonies was held not only by France and Spain but by the less absolutist governments of England and Holland.

The great French practitioner of mercantilism was Colbert (1619–1683), who had served his apprenticeship under Mazarin and advanced rapidly to become controller general early in the personal reign of Louis. He never quite attained the supremacy reached by Richelieu and Mazarin; he was the collaborator, never the master, of Louis XIV. Other great ministers, Louvois for military affairs especially, stood in the way of his supremacy. Yet Colbert was influential in all matters affecting the French economy, most interested in foreign trade and in the colonies, and therefore in the merchant marine and in the navy. His hand was in everything, in invention, in technological education, in designing and building ships, in attracting foreign experts to settle in France.

Among the industries he fostered were the processing of sugar, chocolate, and tobacco from the colonies; the production of military goods by iron foundries and textile mills; and the luxuries for which the French have been famous ever since. The Gobelins tapestry enterprise in Paris was taken over by the state and its output expanded to include elegant furniture, for which the king was a major customer. Glassblowers and lace-makers were lured away from Venice, despite strenuous efforts by the Venetian republic, including the use of poison, to keep their valuable techniques secret. In a blow against French competitors Colbert imposed heavy tariffs on some Dutch and English products. To promote trade with the colonies and also with the Baltic and the Mediterranean he financed a battery of trading companies, of which only the French East India Company eventually succeeded.

At home, Colbert encouraged reforestation, so that iron foundries could have abundant supplies of charcoal (then essential for smelting); he also promoted the planting of mulberry trees to nourish the silkworms vital to textile output. He even attempted—vainly, as it turned out—to impose what we could call quality control by ordering that defective goods should be prominently exhibited in public, along with the name of the offending producer, and that for a third offense the culprit himself was to be exhibited. He also endeavored, again for the most part in vain, to break down the barriers to internal free trade, like provincial and municipal tariffs or local restrictions on the shipment of grain to other parts of France. He did, however, sponsor the construction of important roads and canals; the Canal du Midi (of the south) linking the Atlantic port of Bordeaux and the Mediterranean port of Narbonne reduced transport charges between the two seas by three-fourths and was described as the greatest engineering feat since Roman days.

Whether the great prosperity France achieved in the first thirty years of Louis's reign came about because of, or in spite of, the mercantilist policies of Colbert is a question difficult to answer. Under the mercantilist regime at any rate, France did attain an undoubted leadership in European industry and commerce. That lead she lost, in part because the last two wars of Louis XIV were ruinously expensive, in part because in the eighteenth century France's rival, England, took to the new methods of power machinery and concentrated on large-scale production of inexpensive goods. France remained largely true to the policies set by Colbert— relatively small-scale production of a variety of luxuries and other consumer goods. But the difference between French and English industry was also a difference in

the focus of national energies. France, like Spain before her, spent an undue proportion of her national product in an unfruitful effort to achieve the political domination of both Europe and the overseas world through the force of arms.

The Goals and Instruments of French Expansion

France was the real victor in the Thirty Years' War, acquiring lands on her northeastern frontier. In a postscript to the main conflict, she continued fighting with Spain until at the Peace of the Pyrenees, 1659, Mazarin secured additional territories: Artois, in the north adjoining Flanders, and Roussillon, at the Catalan-speaking Mediterranean end of the Pyrenees. Well recovered from the wounds of her own religious wars and prospering economically, France was ready for further expansion when the young and ambitious monarch began his personal rule in 1661.

What were the goals of that expansion? To complete the gains of 1648 and 1659 and secure the kingdom's "natural frontiers" along the Rhine and the Alps? To wage a mercantilist war against France's major economic competitors, Holland and England? Or to revive the multinational empire that Charlemagne had ruled nine hundred years earlier? Historians today tend to believe that Louis pursued each of these goals in sequence, as he became more and more powerful and more and more convinced that the proper occupation of a king was the aggrandizement of his kingdom. In addition, Louis was keenly aware of the potentials of cultural imperialism, and he wanted the French language, French taste in the arts, and French social ways to spread their influence over Europe.

While French cultural imperialism went from triumph to triumph, Louis' political and military designs won some successes but met ultimate failure. In North America, in India, in Holland, and on the Rhine, and in dozens of other places, the agents of Louis were working to increase their master's power and prestige. Other peoples became convinced that France was threatening things that they held dear—life, property, independence, self-respect. Under this threat, most of the European states allied themselves against the French aggressor and beat him.

Louis XIV and his talented experts fashioned splendid instruments to support an aggressive foreign policy. In 1661 half a dozen men made up the whole Ministry of Foreign Affairs; half a century later, it had a huge staff of clerks, archivists, coders (and decoders) of secret messages, renegade priests and ladies of easy virtue who operated as clandestine agents, great lords and prelates who lent their dignity to important missions, and professional assistants who did most of their work. The growth of the French army was still more impressive, from a peacetime force of twenty thousand

Nicholas Largillière's "Louis XIV and His Heirs."

to a wartime one almost twenty times larger. In size, the armies of Louis XIV were beginning to assume a truly modern look.

In quality, however, French forces were rather less modern. The ranks were filled not with citizen soldiers raised by some kind of universal conscription but with mercenaries and the victims of impressment. Leadership may be described as semiprofessional. Both the basic larger unit, the regiment, and the basic smaller one, the company, were not only led but also recruited and paid by their commanders—colonel and captain, respectively. These men were usually nobles, who purchased their commissions and behaved as though they were a combination of condottieri and of feudal lords bringing their private forces to do battle for their overlord.

Nevertheless, Louis and his lieutenants almost revolutionized the character of France's fighting forces. At the Ministry of War the father-and-son team of Le Tellier and Louvois arranged the grouping of regiments in a brigade under a general to bring them under closer control. They also introduced two new ranks of officer, major and lieutenant colonel, to give more opportunity to talented commoners; these new commissions were awarded only for merit and were not available for purchase, like a colonelcy or captaincy. Supplies were more abundant, pay was more regular, and an effort was made to weed out the "deadbeats" who appeared only on regimental paydays. The inspector general, Martinet, made his name a byword for the enforcement of rigorous drilling and discipline.

In the field, during Louis' early wars, the king had the invaluable help of two senior commanders, Condé and Turenne, both veterans of the Thirty Years' War. French armies showed particular strength in artillery, engineering and siege techniques, all particularly important in those days before wars of rapid movement, when armies moved ponderously and did much fighting in the waterlogged Low Countries. The French boasted an engineer of genius, Vauban, of whom it was said that a town he besieged was indefensible and one he defended was impregnable (two centuries later, the little city of Belfort in Alsace, which he had fortified, withstood a long Prussian siege). While military medical

Hotel des Invalides from the south.

services remained crude and sketchy, a large veteran's hospital was built in Paris, the Hôtel des Invalides, one of the most impressive monuments of *le grande siècle.*

The First Two Wars of Louis XIV
The main thrust of Louis XIV, unlike that of the Valois, which had been toward Italy, was northeast, toward the Low Countries and Germany. He sought also to secure Spain, if not quite as a direct annexation, at least as a French satellite with a French ruler. Finally, French commitments overseas in North America and in India drove him to attempt, against English and Dutch rivals, the establishment of a great French empire outside Europe.

The first actual war of Louis XIV was a minor affair, but it showed how he was going to move. When he married the daughter of Philip IV of Spain, his bride had renounced her rights of inheritance; now Louis claimed that, since her dowry had never been paid, the renunciation was invalid. His lawyers dug up an old family rule, the right of "devolution," on which he

based his claim that lands in Belgium (then the Spanish Netherlands) should have devolved upon his wife. In the ensuing War of Devolution with Spain, 1667–1668, Turenne won victories, but Louis did not press his advantage. The Dutch, just north of Belgium, felt alarmed for their independence and also for their prosperity because of the discriminatory tariff against their goods introduced by Colbert in 1667. They entered into a Triple Alliance with England and Sweden to prevent Louis's upsetting the balance of power. A compromise peace at Aix-la-Chapelle, 1668, awarded Louis only Lille and other towns on the Franco-Belgian border.

Furious at the Dutch because of their economic ascendancy, their Calvinism, and, most of all, their republicanism, Louis resolved to teach them a lesson. He isolated them diplomatically by buying off Sweden and England, their former partners in the Triple Alliance. In 1672 French forces invaded Holland. The terrified Dutch lynched their bourgeois leader, Jan de Witt, whom they blamed for their military unpreparedness, and turned to the youthful stadholder of Holland (and of several other provinces), William III of Orange, the great-grandson of the martyred hero of Dutch independence, William the Silent. The French advance was halted by the desperate expedient of opening the dikes and flooding polders with the sea water from which they had been reclaimed. Even without the strong leadership of William of Orange, Europe would probably have responded to the threat of French domination by forming an anti-French alliance. As it was, Spain, the Holy Roman Empire, and the German state of Brandenburg-Prussia joined against France and her allies. The coalition was not very effective, and French diplomacy separated the allies at the treaties of Nijmegen (Nimwegen) in 1678–1679 (there were six separate peace arrangements, all told). Holland was left intact at the cost of promising neutrality, and the French gave up their tariff on Dutch goods; Spain ceded to France the Franche Comté (county of Burgundy), part of the Hapsburgs' Burgundian inheritance, plus some towns in Belgium; Prussia, which had defeated Louis' ally, Sweden, at Fehrbellin (1675), was obliged by French pressure to return the Swedes' lands in Germany. The power and prestige of France were now at their peak, as rulers all over Europe, and in particular the host of princelets in Germany, copied the standards of Versailles.

The Last Two Wars

Yet in the last three decades of Louis' reign most of his assets were dissipated, especially the concrete ones of wealth and efficient organization. Not content with the prestige he had won in his first two wars, Louis embroiled himself with most of the Western world in what looked like an effort to destroy the independence of Holland and most of western Germany, and to bring the Iberian peninsula under a French ruler. The prelude to new military aggression was the juridical aggression of the "chambers of reunion," special courts set up by the French, in the early 1680s, to tidy up the loose ends of the peace settlements of the past generation. There were loose ends aplenty on the northern and eastern frontiers of France, a zone of political fragmentation and confused feudal remnants, many of which were under the suzerainty of the Holy Roman emperor. After examining the documents in disputed cases the chambers of reunion "reunited" many strategic bits of land to territories acquainted earlier by France. The French did not hesitate to threaten force to back up these awards, as they did in the case of the former free city of Strasbourg, the chief town of Alsace.

Continued French nibbling at lands in western Germany and Louis' assertion of a dynastic claim to most of the lands of the German elector Palatine set off the third of his wars, the War of the League of Augsburg, 1688–1697. The league against him was put together by his old foe, William of Orange, who after 1688 shared the throne of England with his wife Mary,

daughter of James II. From then on England was thoroughly committed to take sides against Louis. The League of Augsburg also included Spain, the Holy Roman Empire, and the Alpine state of Savoy, which was threatened by Louis' tactics of "reunion." The great naval victory of the English over the French at Cape La Hogue in 1692 showed that England, not France, was to be mistress of the seas. But on land the honors were more nearly even. William was beaten in battle in the Low Countries time and again, but he was never decisively crushed. In Ireland, French attempts to intervene on behalf of the deposed English king, James II, were foiled at the battle of the Boyne (July 1690), the anniversary of which is still celebrated by Protestant "Orangemen" in northern Ireland. France and England also exchanged blows in India and in the West Indies and North America, where the colonists called the conflict King William's War.

The Peace of Ryswick (1697) ending the War of the League of Augsburg was a peace without victory,

Mignard's equestrian portrait of Louis XIV.

The peace congress at Utrecht, 1713.

a general agreement to keep things as they were. It lasted barely four years, for in 1701 Louis XIV took a step that led to his last and greatest conflict, the War of the Spanish Succession (1701–1714). Charles II, the Hapsburg king of Spain and Louis' brother-in-law, died in 1700 without a direct heir. For several years the diplomats of Europe had been striving to arrange a succession that would avoid putting on the throne either a French Bourbon or an Austrian Hapsburg. Although they agreed on a Bavarian prince, he died in 1699, and plans were made to partition the Spanish inheritance between Hapsburgs and Bourbons. Then Charles II died after making a new will that bequeathed his lands intact to Philip of Anjou, grandson of Louis XIV. Louis, after much soul searching, accepted on behalf of Philip, even though he had signed the treaty of partition. The threat to the balance of power was neatly summarized in the remark a gloating Frenchman is supposed to have made, "There are no longer any Pyrenees." England, Holland, Savoy, the Holy Roman Empire, and many German states formed the Grand Alliance to preserve the Pyrenees.

In the bloody war that followed, the French were gradually worn down in defeat. In North America they lost Acadia (Nova Scotia) to the English, and in Europe they were beaten by the allies in four major battles, beginning with Blenheim (1704) and concluding with Malplaquet (1709). The allied armies were commanded by two great generals, Prince Eugene of Savoy and the English John Churchill, Duke of Marlborough. But the French were not annihilated, and Malplaquet cost the Allies twenty thousand casualties, at least as many as the French suffered. By scraping the bottom of the barrel for men and money, the French managed even after Malplaquet to keep armies in the field.

Moreover, the Grand Alliance was weakening. The English, now following their famous policy of keeping any single continental power from attaining too strong a position, were almost as anxious to prevent the union of the Austrian and Spanish inheritances under a Hapsburg as to prevent the union of France and Spain under a Bourbon. At home, they faced a possible disputed succession to the throne, and the mercantile classes were sick of a war that was injuring trade and seemed unlikely to bring any compensating gains. In 1710, the Tory party, inclined toward peace, won a parliamentary majority and began negotiations that culminated in a series of treaties at Utrecht in 1713.

Utrecht was a typical balance-of-power peace, which contained France without humiliating her. She lost to England Newfoundland, Nova Scotia, and the Hudson's Bay territories, but she preserved Quebec and Louisiana, as well as her Caribbean islands. Louis gained in a sense what he had gone to war over, for Philip of Anjou was formally recognized as King Philip V of Spain and secured the Spanish lands overseas. The

French and Spanish crowns were however, by specific provision, never to be held by the same person, so the allies, too, had won a point. Furthermore, England took from Spain the Mediterranean island of Minorca, which she handed back later in the century, and the great Rock of Gibraltar guarding the Atlantic entrance to the Mediterranean, which (as of the mid-1970s) the Spanish are still seeking to recover. The English also gained, by an agreement called the Asiento, the right to supply slaves to the Spanish colonies, a right that gave them also opportunities for smuggling.

The Austrian Hapsburgs, denied the main Spanish succession, were compensated with Belgium and the former Spanish possessions in Italy, Milan and Naples. In Belgium, now the Austrian Netherlands, the Dutch were granted the right to garrison certain fortified towns, the "barrier fortresses," for better defense against possible French aggression. For faithfulness to the Grand Alliance Savoy was rewarded with Sicily; although forced to exchange this prize in 1720 for the lesser island of Sardinia, the Duke of Savoy could call himself king of Sardinia and thus began the long process that united Italy under the crown of Savoy in the nineteenth century. The elector of Brandenburg, too, was rewarded with a royal title, king *in* (not *of*) Prussia, which lay outside the Holy Roman Empire at the southeastern corner of the Baltic.

In all the general European settlements of modern times—Westphalia, Utrecht, Vienna, Versailles—historians discern imperfections that would lead to subsequent unsettlement and another general war. Utrecht is no exception, though of all the settlements it is the one in which victors and vanquished seem closest. First of all, the rivalry between France and England for empire overseas was undiminished. In India, as in North America, each nation was to continue after Utrecht as before, the effort to oust the other from land and trade. In Europe, the Dutch were not really protected against the French by the barrier fortresses in the Austrian Netherlands, and the Austrian Hapsburg emperor, Charles VI, never forgot that he wanted to be "Charles III" of Spain and never gave up hope that he might be able to upset the Utrecht decision. The distribution of Italian lands satisfied nobody, Italian or outsider, and the next two decades were filled with acrimonious negotiations over Italy. In short, no one seemed to have quite what he wanted—which is one of the difficulties of arriving at compromise solutions.

French Aggression in Review

Proponents of the view that Europe underwent a severe crisis during the seventeenth century can find much evidence in the horrors resulting from Louis XIV's aggressions. The total cost of his wars in human lives and economic resources was very great, especially in the deliberate French devastation of the German Palatinate during the War of the League of Augsburg. The battle of Malplaquet, which left forty thousand men wounded, dying, or dead in an area of ten square miles, was not surpassed in bloodshed until Borodino in Napoleon's Russian campaign, a century later. Behind the lines there was much suffering, too, notably in the great famine that struck France in 1693–1694. And the year of Malplaquet, 1709, was one of the grimmest in modern French history, when bitter cold, crop failures, famine, and relentless government efforts to stave off bankruptcy by collecting more taxes caused almost universal misery. The Parisians complained bitterly in this parody of the Lord's Prayer: "Our Father which art at Versailles, thy name is hallowed no more, thy Kingdom is great no more, thy will is no longer done on earth or on the waters. Give us this day thy bread which on all sides we lack. . . ." * These wars were not simply struggles among professional armies directed by professional politicians; they were wars among peoples, wars that brought out feelings of patriotism and hatred for the foreigner and the aggressor, though these feelings lacked as yet the intensity of modern nationalism.

Thus, in comparison with the wars of nationalism and revolution that were to follow and the wars of religion that had gone before, the wars of Louis XIV lacked the all-out drives of "total" wars. Louis set himself up as a champion of Catholicism, especially after the revocation of the Edict of Nantes in 1685, and William of Orange was hailed as a Protestant champion. Yet Louis, unlike his predecessor in aggression, Philip II of Spain, did not entertain any real hope of stamping out Protestantism among the Dutch. William's Protestant victory at the Boyne brought new indignities to Irish Catholics, while in England and New England the French were dreaded as Catholics. In the end, however, the Grand Alliance against Louis was a complete mixture of Catholic and Protestant in which religion played a comparatively minor role.

No lay substitute for the crusading religious spirit had emerged. Unlike Napoleon, Louis XIV was not the product of a revolution; unlike Hitler, he was not the product of a humiliating national defeat. He was indeed the Sun King, presiding over a dazzling court, but he was also the legitimate, even conventional, ruler of a land long used to prominence in Europe. The aggression of Louis XIV was, like the culture of his France, a relatively moderate "classical" aggression, lacking the heaven-storming fervor of aggressions born of revolution.

III Stuart England

English-speaking people throughout the world tend to believe that England has always had a representative

*G. R. R. Treasure, *Seventeenth Century France* (London, 1966), p. 413.

and constitutional government and never went through the stage of divine-right monarchy that France and other continental states experienced. This belief is largely correct, but it would be better stated as follows: To the extent that English government utilized the new methods of professional administration developed in the fifteenth and sixteenth centuries, it may be considered potentially just as absolute as any divine-right monarchy. But representative government provided a check on this potential through the concept of a constitution, a set of rules not to be altered by the ordinary processes of government. These rules might be written down, but they might also be unwritten, a consensus about certain traditions. They came to be regarded as limiting the authority not only of the king but even of a government elected by a majority of the people, a guarantee to individuals that they had "civil rights" and might do certain things even though men in posts of authority disapproved. Without these rules and habits of constitutionalism, and without powerful and widespread human convictions backing them up, the machinery of parliamentary government could be as ruthlessly absolute as any totalitarian government.

In seventeenth-century England the development of potentially absolute institutions was checked and modified by the continued growth of representative institutions. In France kings and ministers were able to govern without the Estates General. In England Parliament met in 1629 and quarreled violently with King Charles I, who then governed for eleven years without calling Parliament. But in 1640 he felt obliged to call Parliament and, though he dismissed it at once when it proved recalcitrant, he had to call another in that same year. This was the famous Long Parliament, which sat—with changes of personnel and with interruptions—for twenty years, and which made the revolution that ended the threat of absolute divine-right monarchy in England. If we understand why Charles, unlike his French counterpart, was obliged to call Parliament, we have gone a long way toward understanding why England had a head start in modern representative government.

Two very basic reasons go back to medieval history. First, as we have already seen, in the English Parliament the House of Commons represented two different social groups not brought together in one house on the Continent, the aristocratic "knights of the shire" and the "burgesses" of the towns and cities. The strength of the Commons lay in the practical working together of both groups, which intermarried quite freely and, in spite of some economic and social tensions, tended to form a single ruling class with membership open to talented and energetic men from the lower classes.

Second, local government continued to be run by magistrates who were not directly dependent on the Crown. We must not exaggerate: England, too, had its bureaucrats, its clerks and officials in the royal pay. But whereas in France and in other continental countries the new bureaucracy tended to take over almost all governmental business, especially financial and judicial affairs, in England the gentry and the higher nobility continued to do important local work. The Elizabethan Poor Law of 1601 put the care of the needy not under any national ministry but squarely on the smallest local units, the parishes, where decisions lay ultimately with the amateur, unpaid justices of the peace, recruited from the gentry. In short, the privileged classes were not, as in France, shelved, thrust aside by paid agents of the central government; nor did they, as in Prussia, become themselves mere agents of the Crown. Instead, they preserved a secure base in local government and an equally firm base in the House of Commons. When Charles I tried to govern without the consent of these privileged classes, when he tried to raise from them and their dependents money to run a bureaucratic government without these privileged amateurs, they had a solid institutional basis from which to resist.

But they had to struggle. They had to fight a civil war. No matter how much emphasis the historian may put on the social and institutional side, he cannot ignore what looks like the sheer accident of human personality. The Tudors from Henry VII to Elizabeth I, with some faltering under Edward VI and Mary, had been strong personalities and had been firmly—quite as firmly as any Valois or Hapsburg—convinced that they were called to absolute monarchy. They had slowly built up a very strong personal rule, handling their parliaments skillfully, giving in occasionally in detail, but holding the reins firmly. Henry VIII and his daughter Elizabeth both commanded the kind of devotion from their subjects that can be built in time into formidable personal rule; their successors could not command such emotional loyalty.

Elizabeth I was childless, and in 1603 she was succeeded by the son of her old rival and cousin, Mary, Queen of Scots. James Stuart, already king of Scotland as James VI, became James I of England (1603–1625), thus bringing the two countries, still legally separate, under the same personal rule. James was a pedant by temperament, very sure of himself, and above all sure that he was as much a divine-right monarch as his French cousins. He was a Scot, and as a foreigner an object of distrust to his English subjects. He lacked entirely the Tudor heartiness and tact, the gift of winning people to him. His son Charles I (1625–1649), under whom the divine-right experiment came to an end, had many more of the graces of a monarch than his father, but he was still no man to continue the work of the Tudors. He was quite as sure as his father had been that God had called him to rule England, but he could neither make the happy compromises the Tudors made nor revive their broad popular appeals.

The fundamental fact about the actual break between the first two Stuarts and their parliamentary opponents is that both were in a sense revolutionaries. Both were seeking to bend the line of English constitutional growth away from the Tudor compromise of a strong crown working with and through a late medieval parliament based on the alliance of nobility, gentry, and commercial classes. James and Charles were seeking to bend the line toward divine-right monarchy of the continental type; the parliamentarians were seeking to bend it toward something even newer, the establishment of a legislative body possessing the final authority in both the making and the carrying out of law and policy.

Behind this struggle lay the fact that the business of state was gradually growing in scope and therefore in cost. The money required by Stuarts—and indeed by Bourbons, Hapsburgs, and the rest of the continental monarchs—did not go just for high living by royalty and the support of parasitic nobles; it went to run a government that was beginning to assume many new functions. Foreign relations, for example, were beginning to take on modern forms, with a central foreign office, ambassadors, clerks, travel allowances, and the like, all requiring more money and personnel. James I and Charles I failed to get the money they needed because those from whom they sought it, the ruling classes, succeeded in placing the raising and spending of it in their own hands through parliamentary supremacy. The Parliament that won that supremacy was a kind of committee of the ruling classes; it was not a democratic legislature, since only a small fraction of the population could vote for members of the Commons.

In this struggle between Crown and Parliament religion played a major part in welding both sides into cohesive fighting groups. The struggle for power in England was in part a struggle to impose a uniform worship on Englishmen. The royalist cause was identified with High Church Anglicanism, that is, with an episcopalian church government and a liturgy and theology that made it a sacramental religion relatively free from left-wing Protestant austerities. The parliamentary cause, at first supported by many moderate Low Church Anglicans, also attracted a strong Puritan or Calvinist element. Later, it came under the control of the Presbyterians and then of the extreme Puritans, who were known as Independents of Congregationalists. The term "Puritanism" in seventeenth-century England is a confusing one, for it was used as a blanket to cover a wide range of religious groups, from moderate evangelical Anglicans all the way to the radical splinter sects of the 1640s and 1650s. The core of Puritanism went back to Zwingli and Calvin, to the repudiation of Catholic sacramental religion and the rejection of music and the adornment of churches. It placed a positive emphasis on sermons, on simplicity in church and out, and on "purifying" the tie between the worshiper and

Portrait of James I by Daniel Mytens, 1621.

his God of what the Puritans considered Catholic "superstitions" and "corruptions."

The Reign of James I, 1603–1625

In the troubled reign of James I, three major issues emerged that intensified the struggle in which his son was to go under—money, foreign policy, and religion. In all three issues, the Crown and its opposition each tried to bend the line of constitutional development in its own direction. In raising money, James sought to make the most of revenues that did not require a parliamentary grant. Parliament sought to make the most of its own control over the purse strings by insisting on the principle that any new revenue raising had to be approved by parliament. When James levied an import duty without a parliamentary grant, an importer of dried currants named Bate refused to pay.

Van Dyck's portrait of Charles I hunting, ca. 1635.

in fact a new claim for parliamentary control of foreign affairs. James responded by dissolving Parliament and imprisoning four of its leaders. The Spanish marriage fell through, but the betrothal of Charles in 1624 to the French princess Henrietta Maria, sister of Louis XIII, who was also Catholic, was hardly more popular with the English people.

In religion, Elizabeth, though refusing to permit public services by Catholics and Puritans, had allowed much variety of practice within the Anglican church. James summed up his policy in the phrase "no bishop, no king"—by which he meant that the enforcement of the bishops' monarchical authority in religion was essential to the maintenance of his own monarchical power. James at once took steps against what he held to be Puritan nonconformity. He called a conference of Anglican bishops and leading Puritans at Hampton Court in 1604, at which he presided in person and used the full force of his pedantic scholarship against the Puritans. After the conference dissolved with no real meeting of minds, royal policy continued to favor the High Church, anti-Puritan party. In spite of James' failure to achieve anything like religious agreement among his subjects, his reign is a landmark in the history of Christianity among English-speaking peoples. In 1611, after seven years' labor, a committee of forty-seven ministers authorized by him achieved the English translation of the Bible that is still widely used. The King James Version remains a masterpiece of Elizabethan prose, perhaps the most remarkable literary achievement a committee has ever made.

Bate's case was decided in favor of the Crown by the Court of Exchequer, and the decision attracted much attention because the judges held the king's powers in general to be absolute. Then a royal "benevolence"—a euphemism for a contribution exacted from an individual—was resisted by a certain St. John, and his appeal was sustained by the chief justice, Sir Edward Coke. James summarily dismissed Coke from office and thereby drew attention once again to his broad use of the royal prerogative.

The Tudors had regarded foreign affairs as entirely a matter of royal prerogative. The delicate problem of marriage for Elizabeth I, for instance, had concerned her Parliaments and the public; but Parliament made no attempt to dictate a marriage, and Elizabeth was careful not to offend her subjects in her own tentative negotiations. On the other hand, when James I openly sought a princess of hated Spain as a wife for his son Charles, the Commons in 1621 made public petition against the Spanish marriage. When James rebuked them for meddling, the House drew up the Great Protestation, the first of the great documents of the English Revolution, in which they used what they claimed were the historic privileges of Parliament to assert what was

The Difficulties of Charles I, 1625–1642

Under Charles I, all his father's difficulties came to a head very quickly. England was involved in a minor war against Spain, and though the members of Parliament hated Spain, they were most reluctant to grant Charles funds to support the English forces. Meanwhile, in spite of his French queen, Charles also became involved in a war against France. This he financed in part by a forced loan from his wealthier subjects and by quartering troops in private houses at the householders' expense. Consequently, Parliament in 1628 passed the Petition of Right—"the Stuart Magna Carta"—which first explicitly stated some of the most basic rules of modern constitutional government: No taxation without the consent of Parliament; no billeting of soldiers in private houses; no martial law in time of peace; no one to be imprisoned except on a specific charge and subject to the protection of regular legal procedure. All these principles were limitations on the Crown.

Charles consented to the Petition of Right in order to secure new grants of money from Parliament. But he also collected duties not sanctioned by Parliament, which thereupon protested by resolutions not only against his unauthorized taxes but also against his High Church policy. The king now veered from conciliation to firmness; in 1629 he had Sir John Eliot, mover of the resolutions, arrested together with eight other members, and then dissolved Parliament. Eliot died a prisoner in the Tower of London, the first martyr on the parliamentary side.

For the next eleven years, 1629–1640, Charles governed without a Parliament. He squeezed every penny he could get out of royal revenues that did not require parliamentary authorization, never quite breaking with precedent by imposing a wholly new tax, but stretching precedent beyond what his opponents thought reasonable. Ship money illustrates Charles' methods. It had been levied by the Crown before, but only on coastal towns for naval expenditures in wartime; Charles now imposed ship money on inland areas and in peacetime. When John Hampden, a very rich gentleman from inland Buckinghamshire refused to pay it, he lost his case in court (1637) but gained wide public support for challenging the king's fiscal expedients.

In religious matters, Charles was under the guidance of a very High Church Archbishop of Canterbury, William Laud, who systematically enforced Anglican conformity and deprived even moderate Puritans of their pulpits. Puritans were sometimes brought before the Star Chamber, long a highly respected administrative court but now gaining a reputation for high-handedness because it denied the accused the safeguards of the common law. In civil matters, Charles made use of an opportunist conservative, Thomas Wentworth, earl of Strafford, who had deserted the parliamentary side and went on to become lord lieutenant of Ireland.

England was seething with repressed political and religious passions underneath the outward calm of these years of personal rule. Yet, to judge from the imperfect statistics available, the relative weight of the taxation that offended so many Englishmen was less than on the Continent and far less than taxation in any modern Western state. The Englishmen who resisted the Crown by taking arms against it were not downtrodden, poverty-stricken people revolting from despair, but self-assertive, hopeful people defending their civil rights and their own forms of worship as well as seeking power and wealth.

The attempts of twentieth-century historians to isolate the economic motives of seventeenth-century English revolutionaries have stirred up a great scholarly controversy, which is linked with efforts to find a Europe-wide crisis in the middle 1600s. The debate has centered on the role of the gentry, that large group of landed aristocrats just under the high nobility, who did much of the fighting in the civil wars. R. H. Tawney, a Labor party intellectual, claimed that the more enterprising, more capitalistic gentleman farmers, rather like rural bourgeois, supported the Puritans. His antagonist,

Hugh Trevor-Roper of Oxford, asserted that on the contrary the gentry backing the Puritans were those who were barely holding their own or sinking down the economic scale in the face of inflation, the enclosure of lands for sheep farming, and the competition of the secular owners of former monastic lands. Neutral historians tend to conclude that these are suggestive though overabstract attempts to define the undefinable, the role of an amorphous social class whose economic status varied and whose political decisions were by no means necessarily made on economic grounds.

Charles I could perhaps have weathered his financial difficulties for a long time if he had not had to contend with the Scots. Laud's attempt to enforce the English High Church ritual and organization came up against the three-generations-old Scottish Presbyterian "Kirk." In 1638, a "Solemn League and Covenant" bound the members of the Kirk to resist Charles by force if need be. Charles marched north against the Scots and worked out a compromise with them in 1639. But even this mild campaign was too much for the treasury, and in 1640 Charles had to call Parliament back into session for the first time in eleven years. This Short Parliament denied him any money until the piled-up grievances against Charles and his father were settled; it was dissolved almost at once. Then the Scots went to war again, and Charles, defeated in a skirmish, bought them off by promising the Scottish army £850 a day until peace was made. Since he could not raise £850 a day, he had to call another Parliament, which became the famous Long Parliament of the Revolution.

Since the Scottish army would not be disbanded until it was paid off, the Long Parliament held it as a club over Charles' head and put through a great series of reforms striking at the heart of the royal power. It abolished ship money and other disputed taxes. It disbanded the unpopular royal administrative courts, such as the Star Chamber, which had become symbols of Stuart absolutism. Up to now, Parliament had been called and dismissed at the pleasure of the Crown; the Triennial Act of 1640 made obligatory the summoning of future Parliaments every three years, even if the Crown did not wish to do so. Parliament also attacked the royal favorites, whom Charles reluctantly abandoned. Archbishop Laud was removed, and Strafford, declared guilty of treason, was executed in May 1641.

Meanwhile, Strafford's harsh policy toward the Irish had borne fruit in a rebellion that amounted to an abortive war for national independence by Irish Catholics and that caused the massacre of thirty thousand Protestants in the northern Irish region of Ulster. Parliament, unwilling to trust Charles with an army to put down this rebellion, drew up in 1641 the Grand Remonstrance summarizing all its complaints. Charles now made a final attempt to repeat the tactics that had worked in 1629. Early in 1642, he ordered the arrest of five of his leading opponents in the House of Commons, including Hampden of the ship-money case. The five took refuge in the privileged political sanctuary of the City of London, where the king could not reach them. Charles I left for the north and in the summer of 1642 rallied an army at Nottingham; Parliament simply took over the central government. The Civil War had begun.

During these first years of political jockeying signs were already evident that strong groups in England and in Parliament wanted something more than a return to the Tudor balance between Crown and Parliament, and between religious conservatives and religious radicals. In politics, the Nineteen Propositions that Parliament submitted to the king in June 1642 would have established parliamentary supremacy over the army, the royal administration, the church, and even the rearing of the royal children. Charles turned down the propositions. In religion, the Root and Branch Bill, introduced in 1641 but not enacted into law, would have radically reformed the Church of England, destroying "root and branch," the bishops and much of what had already become traditional in Anglican religious practices. The moderates in politics and religion were plainly going to have trouble defending their middle-of-the-road policies among the extremists of a nation split by civil war.

The Civil War, 1642–1649

England split along lines partly territorial, partly social and economic, and partly religious. The royalist strength lay largely in the north and west, relatively less urban and less prosperous than other parts and largely controlled by country gentlemen loyal to throne

The House of Commons as shown on the Great Seal of England used by the Commonwealth, 1651.

and altar. Parliamentary strength lay largely in the south and east, especially in the great city of London and in East Anglia, where Puritanism commanded wide support among the gentry. The Scots were always in the offing, distrustful of an English Parliament but quite as distrustful of a king who had sought to foist episcopacy on their kirk.

In the field, the struggle was at first indecisive. The royalists, or Cavaliers, recruited from gentlemen used to riding, had the initial advantage of superior cavalry. What swung the balance to the side of Parliament was the development of a special force, recruited from ardent Puritans in the eastern counties, and gradually forged under strict discipline into the famous "Ironsides." Their leader was a Puritan gentleman named Oliver Cromwell (1599–1658), who won a crucial battle at Marston Moor in 1644. The parliamentary army, now reorganized into the New Model Army, staffed by radicals in religion and politics, stood as Roundheads (from their short-cropped hair, something like a crewcut) against the Cavaliers. At the battle of Naseby in 1645, the New Model was completely victorious over the king, and Charles in desperation took refuge with the Scottish army, who turned him over to the English Parliament in return for £400,000 back pay.

Now a situation arose that was to be repeated, with variations for time and place, in the French Revolution in 1792 and the Russian Revolution in 1917. The group of moderates who had begun the revolution and who still controlled the Long Parliament were confronted by the much more radical group who controlled the New Model Army. In religion, the moderates, seeking to retain some ecclesiastical discipline and formality, were Presbyterians or Low Church Anglicans; in politics, they were constitutional monarchists. The radicals, who were opposed to churches disciplined from a central organization, were Independents or Congregationalists, and they already so distrusted Charles that they were able at least to contemplate that extraordinary possibility, an England under a republican form of government. The situation was complicated by the Presbyterian Scots, who regarded the radical Roundheads as religious anarchists.

The years after 1645 were filled with difficult negotiations, during which Charles stalled for time to gain Scottish help. In 1648, Cromwell beat the invading Scots at Preston, and his army seized the king. Parliament, with the moderates still in control, now refused to do what the army wanted, to dethrone Charles. The Roundhead leaders then ordered Colonel Pride to exclude by force from the Commons ninety-six Presbyterian members. This the Colonel did in December 1648, in true military fashion, with no pretense of legality. After "Pride's Purge" only some sixty radicals remained of the more than five hundred members originally composing the Long Parliament; they were known henceforth as the Rump Parliament. The Rump brought Charles to trial before a special high court of trustworthy radicals, who condemned him to death. On January 30, 1649, Charles I was beheaded.

Cromwell and the Interregnum, 1649–1660

The subsequent eleven years are known to historians as the Interregnum, the interval between two monarchical reigns. This bit of English understatement should not disguise the fact that England was now a republic, under the government known as the Commonwealth. Since the radicals did not dare to call a free election, which would almost certainly have gone against them, the Rump Parliament continued to sit. Thus, from the start, the Commonwealth was the dictatorship of a radical minority come to power through the tight organization of the New Model Army. From the start, too, Cromwell was the dominating personality of the new government. In religion an earnest and sincere Independent, but no fanatic, a patriotic Englishman, strong-minded, stubborn, but not power-mad, by no means unwilling to compromise, Cromwell was nevertheless a prisoner of his position.

He faced a divided England, where the majority was no doubt royalist at heart and certainly sick of the fighting, the confiscations, the endless changes of the last decade. He faced a hostile Scotland and an even more hostile Ireland, where the disorders in England had encouraged the Catholic Irish to rebel once more in 1649. In 1650, Charles II, eldest son of the martyred Charles I, landed in Scotland, accepted the Covenant (thereby guaranteeing the Presbyterian faith as the established Scottish kirk), and led a Scottish army once more against the English. Once more, the English army proved unbeatable at the battle of Worcester (1651), and the hope of the Stuarts took refuge on the Continent, after a romantic escape in disguise. Finally, Cromwell faced a war with Holland (1652–1654) brought on by the Navigation Act of 1651, which deliberately struck at the Dutch carrying trade. It was a typically mercantilistic measure, which forbade the importation of goods into England and the colonies except in English ships or in ships of the country producing the imported goods.

By 1654, Cromwell had mastered all his foes. He himself went to Ireland and suppressed the rebellion with bloodshed that is still not forgotten. In the so-called Cromwellian Settlement, he dispossessed native Irish landholders in favor of Protestants; he achieved order in Ireland, but not peace. He brought the naval war with the Dutch to a victorious close in 1654. Later, Cromwell also waged an aggressive war against Spain (1656–1658), from whom the English acquired the rich Caribbean sugar island of Jamaica. Even in this time of troubles, the British Empire kept growing.

Cromwell, however, could not master the Rump Parliament, which brushed aside his suggestions for an increase in its membership and a reform of its procedures. In April 1653 he forced its dissolution by appearing in Parliament with a body of soldiers. In December 1653 he took the decisive step of inaugurating the regime called the Protectorate, with himself as "lord protector" of England, Scotland, and Ireland, and with a written constitution—the only one Britain has ever had—the Instrument of Government. It provided for an elected Parliament with a single house of 460 members, who were in fact chosen by Puritan sympathizers, since no royalist dared vote. Even so, the lord protector had constant troubles with his parliaments and in 1657 yielded to pressure and modified the Instrument of Government to provide for a second parliamentary house and to put limits on the lord protector's power. Meanwhile, to maintain order, Cromwell had divided the country into twelve military districts, each with a major general commanding a military force.

Oliver Cromwell died in 1658 and was succeeded as lord protector by his son Richard, who was a nonentity. The army soon seized control, and some of its leaders regarded the restoration of the Stuarts as the best way to end the chronic political turbulence. To ensure the legality of the move, General Monk, commander of the Protectorate's forces in Scotland, summoned back the Rump and readmitted the surviving members excluded by Pride's Purge. This partially reconstituted Long Parliament enacted the formalities of restoration, and in 1660 Charles Stuart returned from exile to reign as Charles II.

The Revolution in Review

Was there a Reign of Terror in the English Revolution? Perhaps not, since much of the bloodshed occurred in formal battles between organized armies and was not the revolutionary bloodshed of guillotine, lynching, and judicial murder. Nevertheless, Charles I was beheaded; Strafford, Laud, and others suffered the death penalty; royalists had their properties confiscated. Above all, the Puritans at the height of their rule in the early 1650s attempted to enforce on the whole population the difficult, austere life of the Puritan ideal. This enforcement took the familiar form of "blue laws," of prohibitions on horse racing, gambling, cock fighting, bear baiting, dancing on the green, fancy dress, the theater, on a host of ordinary phases of daily living. This English Reign of Terror and Virtue, coming too early for modern techniques of propaganda and regimentation, was not entirely effective. Many an Anglican clergyman, though officially "plundered"—that is, deprived of his living—continued worship in private houses; many a cock fight went on in secluded spots. Nevertheless, the strict code was there, with earnest persons to try to enforce it, and with implacable enemies to oppose it. The remark of the Victorian historian Macaulay—that the Puritans prohibited bear baiting not because it gave pain to the bear but because it gave pleasure to the spectators—is a sample of the deep hostility that still survives in England toward the reign of the Puritan "saints."

Many Englishmen have seemed rather ashamed of their great revolution, preferring to call it the Civil War or the Great Rebellion, and recalling instead as their Glorious Revolution the decorous movement of 1688–1689, to which we shall come in a moment. Yet the events of 1640–1660 are of major importance, not only in the history of England, but in the history of the West. Here for the first time the monarchy was challenged in a major revolt by politically active private citizens; though the Stuarts were ultimately restored, no English king could ever hope to rule again without a Parliament, or revive the Court of Star Chamber, or take ship money, benevolences, and other controversial taxes. Parliament thenceforward retained that critical weapon of the legislative body in a limited monarchy, control of the public purse by periodic grants of taxes.

Another basic freedom owes much to this English experience. Freedom of speech was a fundamental tenet of the Puritans, even though at the height of their power they did not live up to it. It received a classic expression from the poet John Milton, who was the secretary of the Commonwealth, in his *Areopagitica* (the reference is to the Council of the Areopagus in ancient Athens). While Milton defended free speech principally for an intellectual and moral elite, one of his arguments was characteristically English: attempts to curb free expression just won't work. In practice, the voluminous pamphlet literature of the early years of the great turmoil is a lively manifestation of free speech in action. The extraordinary fermentations of radical minorities foreshadowed modern political and social thought. One such group, the Levelers, found many sympathizers in the revolutionary army and advanced a program later carried by emigrants to the American colonies. They called for political democracy, universal suffrage, regularly summoned parliaments, progressive taxation, separation of church and state, and protection of the individual against arbitrary arrest. There were even hints of the collectivist drive toward economic equality, a goal closely tied to biblical ideas in those days. The Diggers, for example, were a small sect that preached the sharing of earthly goods in a kind of communism. They actually dug up public lands in Surrey near London and began planting vegetables; they were driven off, but not before they had got their ideas into circulation. The Fifth Monarchy men, the Millenarians, and a dozen other radical sects preached the Second Coming of Christ and the achievement of some kind of utopia on earth.

Still more important, there emerged from the English Revolution even more clearly than from the religious wars on the Continent, the conception of religious toleration. The Independents, while they were in opposition, stood firmly on the right of religious groups to worship God as they wished. Though in their brief tenure of power they showed a willingness to persecute, they were never firmly enough in the saddle to make England into a seventeenth-century Geneva. At least one sect held to the idea and practice of religious toleration as a positive good. The Quakers, led by George Fox (1624–1691), were Puritans of the Puritans. They themselves eschewed all worldly show, finding even buttons ostentatious. They found the names of days and months indecently pagan, the polite form "you" in the singular a piece of social hypocrisy, and legal oaths or oathtaking most impious. Hence they met for worship on what they called First Day rather than the day of the sun god; they addressed another person as "thee" or "thou"; and they took so seriously the Protestant doctrine of the priesthood of the believer that they did entirely without a formal ordained ministry. In the Religious Society of Friends, as they are properly known, any worshiper who felt the spirit move might testify in what other sects would call a sermon. Friends felt too deeply the impossibility of forcing anyone to see the "inner light" for them to coerce people to accept their faith. They would abstain entirely from force, particularly from war, and would go their own way in Christian peace.

The Restoration, 1660–1688

The Restoration of 1660 kept Parliament essentially supreme but attempted to undo some of the work of the Revolution. Anglicanism was restored in England and Ireland, though not as a state church in Scotland. Against the "dissenters," as Protestants who would not accept the Church of England were then termed, the so-called Clarendon Code set up all sorts of restrictions. For instance, by the Five Mile Act all Protestant ministers who refused to subscribe to Anglican orthodoxy were forbidden to come within five miles of any town where they had previously preached. Yet the dissenters continued to dissent without heroic sufferings. In characteristically English fashion, the Test Act of 1672, which prescribed communion according to the Church of England on all officeholders, local as well as national, was simply got around in various ways, though it was not actually repealed until 1828. One way was "occasional conformity," by which a dissenter of not too strict conscience might worship as a Congregationalist, say, all year, but might once or twice take Anglican communion. Another, developed in the eighteenth century, was to permit dissenters to hold office, and then pass annually a bill of indemnity legalizing their illegal acts. Dissenters remained numerous, especially among the artisans and middle-class merchants, and as time went on they grew powerful, so that the "nonconformist conscience" was a major factor in English public life. Indeed, the three-century progression of names by which these non-Anglican Protestants were called is a neat summary of their rise in status—the hostile term "dissenter" became "nonconformist" in the nineteenth century and "Free Churchman" in the twentieth.

The Restoration was also a revulsion against Puritan ways. The reign of Charles II (1660–1685) was a period of moral looseness, of gay court life, of the Restoration drama with its ribald wit (the Puritans in power had closed the theaters), of the public pursuit of pleasure, at least among the upper classes. But the new Stuarts had not acquired political wisdom. Charles II dissipated some of the fund of good will with which he started by following a foreign policy that seemed to patriotic Englishmen too subservient to the wicked French king Louis XIV. The cynic is tempted to point out that, if Charles's alliance with Louis in 1670 was most un-English, it did result in the final extinction of any Dutch threat to English seapower. And it sealed a very important English acquisition, that of New Amsterdam, now New York, first taken in the Anglo-Dutch War of 1664–1667.

What really undid the later Stuarts and revealed their political ineptitude was the Catholic problem. Charles II had come under Catholic influence through his French mother and very possibly embraced the Roman religion before he died in 1685. Since he left no legitimate children, the crown passed to his brother, James II (1685–1688), who was already a declared Catholic. In the hope of enlisting the support of the dissenters for the toleration of Catholics, James II issued in 1687 a Declaration of Indulgence, granting freedom of worship to *all* denominations, Protestant dissenters as well as Catholics, in England and Scotland. This was in the abstract an admirable step toward full religious liberty; but to the great majority of Englishmen Catholicism still seemed the great menace to the English nation, and it was always possible to stir them to an

Seventeenth-century Dutch engraving: fireworks in London celebrating the coronation of King William III and Queen Mary II.

irrational pitch by an appeal to their fear of "popery." Actually, by the end of the seventeenth century the few remaining Catholics in England were glad to be left in something like the status of the dissenters and were no real danger to a country overwhelmingly Protestant. In Ireland, however, the Catholics remained an unappeasable majority.

The political situation was much like that under Charles I; the Crown wanted one thing, Parliament wanted another. Although James II made no attempt to dissolve Parliament or to arrest members, he simply went over Parliament's head by issuing decrees, like the Declaration of Indulgence granting full religious toleration, in accordance with what he called the "power of dispensation." Early in his reign, he had made a piddling rebellion by the duke of Monmouth, a bastard son of Charles II, the excuse for two ominous policies. First, his judges organized the "bloody assizes," which punished suspected rebel sympathizers with a severity that seemed out of all proportion to the extent of the rebellion. Second, he created a standing army of thirty thousand men, part of whom he stationed near London in what appeared an attempt to intimidate the capital. To contemporaries it looked as though James were plotting to force both Catholicism and divine-right monarchy on an unwilling England. The result was the Glorious Revolution.

The Glorious Revolution and its Aftermath, 1688–1714

The actual revolution was a coup d'etat engineered at first by a group of James' parliamentary opponents who were called Whigs, in contrast to the Tories who tended to support at least some of the policies of the later Stuart monarchs. The Whigs were the direct heirs of the moderates of the Long Parliament, and they represented an alliance of the great lords and the prosperous London merchants.

James II married twice. By his first marriage he had two daughters, both Protestant—Mary, who had married William of Orange, the Dutch opponent of Louis XIV, and Anne. Then in 1688 a son was born to James and his Catholic second wife, thus apparently making the passage of the crown to a Catholic heir inevitable. The Whig leaders responded with a barrage of propaganda, including a whispering campaign to the effect that the queen had not even been pregnant and a new-born babe had been smuggled into her chamber in a warming pan, so that there might be a Catholic heir. Then the Whigs and some Tories negotiated with William of Orange, who could hardly turn down a proposition that would give him the solid assets of English power in his struggle with Louis XIV. He accepted the offer of the English crown, which he was to share with his wife, the couple reigning as William III (1689–1702) and Mary II (1689–1694). On Novem-

ber 5, 1688, William landed at Tor Bay on the Devon coast with some fourteen thousand soldiers. When James heard the news, he tried to rally support, but everywhere the great lords and even the normally conservative country gentlemen were on the side of the Protestant hero. James fled from London to France in December 1688, giving William an almost bloodless victory.

Early in 1689 Parliament formally offered the crown to William on terms that were soon enacted into law as the Bill of Rights. This famous document, summing up the constitutional practices that Parliament had been working for since the Petition of Right in 1628, is in fact almost a succinct form of written constitution. It lays down the essential principles of parliamentary supremacy—control of the purse, prohibition of the royal power of dispensation, and frequent meetings of Parliament. Three major steps were necessary after 1689 to convert Britain into a parliamentary democracy in which the Crown has purely symbolic functions as the focus of patriotic loyalty. These were, first, the concentration of executive direction in a committee of the majority party in the Parliament—that is, the Cabinet headed by a prime minister, the work of the eighteenth and early nineteenth centuries; second, the establishment of universal suffrage and payment of members of the Commons, the work of the nineteenth century, completed in the twentieth; and third, the abolition of the power of the House of Lords to veto legislation passed by the Commons, the work of the early twentieth century. Thus we can see that full democracy was still a long way off in 1689. William III and Mary II were real rulers, who did not think of themselves as purely ornamental monarchs, without power over policy.

Childless, they were succeeded by Mary's younger sister, Anne (1702–1714). Anne and her nonentity of a husband strove hard to leave an heir to the throne, but all their many children were stillborn or died in childhood. The exiled Catholic Stuarts, however, did better. The little boy born to James II in 1688 and brought up at the court of St. Germain near Paris, grew up to be known as the "Old Pretender." But in 1701 Parliament passed the Act of Settlement, which settled the crown, in default of heirs to Anne, the heir apparent to the sick William III, not on the Catholic pretender but on the Protestant Sophia of Hanover or her issue. Sophia was a granddaughter of James I, and the daughter of Frederick of the Palatinate, the "Winter King" of Bohemia in the Thirty Years' War. On Anne's death in 1714, the crown therefore passed to Sophia's son, George, first king of the house of Hanover. This settlement clearly established the fact that Parliament, and not the divinely ordained succession of the eldest male in direct descent, made the king of England.

In order to ensure the Hanoverian succession in both the Stuart kingdoms, Scotland as well as England, the formal union of the two was completed in 1707 as the United Kingdom of Great Britain. Scotland gave up its own parliament and sent sixteen peers to the Lords and forty-five members to Commons of the Parliament of the United Kingdom at Westminster. The Union Jack, with the superimposed crosses of Saint George (for England) and Saint Andrew (for Scotland), became the national flag of Great Britain. Although the union met with some opposition from both English and Scots, on the whole it went through with surprising ease, so great was Protestant fear of a possible return of the Catholic Stuarts. And, in spite of occasional sentimental outbreaks of Scottish nationalism even in our own day, the union has worked very well. With the whole of England and the colonies open to Scottish politicians and businessmen, the nation famed for its thrifty and canny citizens achieved a prosperity it had never known before.

The Glorious Revolution did not, however, settle one other perennial problem—Ireland. The Catholic Irish rose in support of the exiled James II and were put down at the Boyne in 1690. William then attempted to apply moderation in his dealings with Ireland, but the Protestant "garrison" there soon forced him to return to the Cromwellian policy. Although Catholic worship was not actually forbidden, all sorts of galling restrictions were imposed on the Catholic Irish, including the prohibition of Catholic schools. Moreover, economic persecution was added to the religious, as Irish trade came under stringent mercantilist regulation. This was the Ireland whose misery inspired Jonathan Swift in 1729 to make his "modest proposal" that the impoverished Irish sell their babies as articles of food.

IV The Century of Genius

In the seventeenth century the cultural, as well as the political, hegemony of Europe passed from Italy and Spain to France, England, and Holland. Especially in literature, the France of *le grand siècle* set the imprint of its classical style on the West through the writings of Corneille, Racine, Molière, Boileau, Bossuet, and a host of others. Yet the men who exerted the greatest influence on our culture were not exclusively French and were rather philosophers and scientists than men of letters. The Italian Galileo and the Englishman Newton, together with the Frenchmen Descartes and Pascal, launched the modern scientific revolution and prompted Whitehead to claim that ever since their day we "have been living upon the accumulated capital of ideas provided . . . by the genius of the seventeenth century." *

*A. N. Whitehead, *Science and the Modern World* (New York, 1948), p. 58.

Portrait of Descartes by Frans Hals.

The Scientific Revolution

A major role in the cultivation of a new scientific attitude was taken by the English intellectual and politician Francis Bacon (1561–1626). Though not himself a successful practitioner of science, Bacon was the tireless proponent of the need for the observation of phenomena and the patient accumulation of data. In *The Great Instauration* (the word means "restoration") he wrote:

For all those who before me have applied themselves to the invention of arts have but cast a glance or two upon facts and examples and experience, and straightway proceeded, as if invention were nothing more than an exercise of thought, to invoke their own spirits to give them oracles. I, on the contrary, dwelling purely and constantly among the facts of nature, withdraw my intellect from them no further than may suffice to let the images and rays of natural objects meet in a point, as they do in the sense of vision. . . . And by these means I suppose that I have established for ever a true and lawful marriage between the empirical and the rational faculty, the unkind and ill-starred divorce and separation of which has thrown into confusion all the affairs of the human family.*

*M. T. McClure, ed., *Bacon: Selections* (New York, 1928), pp. 14–15.

By relying on the empirical faculty, which learns from experience, Bacon was promoting what he called induction, which proceeds from the particular to the general. Deduction, the medieval mode of reasoning still in fashion in Bacon's day, by contrast, proceeds from the general to the particular. Deduction is not necessarily antiscientific, for it sometimes produces the hunches advancing theoretical science. What Bacon particularly attacked was the inclination of deductive reason to accept general axioms as "settled and immovable." Ranking high among such established axioms were the views of the universe associated with two authorities of antiquity, Aristotle and Ptolemy. Bacon's contemporary, Galileo (1564–1642), ridiculed blind acceptance of ancient authorities and thereby became embroiled with the Church.

Galileo was also one of the scores of individuals—some famous, some unknown or now forgotten—who contributed to the new instruments that permitted the more exact measurements and more detailed observations of inductive science. It is probable, for example, that Dutch glassmakers first put two lenses together and discovered that they could obtain a greater magnification. By 1610 Galileo was using the new device in the form of a telescope to study the heavens, and later in the century two Dutchmen employed it in the form of a microscope—Swammerdam to analyze blood (he probably discovered the red corpuscles), and Van Leeuwenhoek to view and describe protozoa and bacteria. Working from the experiments of Galileo, other technicians developed such instruments of measurement as the thermometer and the barometer. Using the barometer, the Frenchman Pascal (1623–1662) proved that what we term air pressure diminished with altitude. From this he went on to counter the old adage "Nature abhors a vacuum" by showing that a vacuum is possible.

Charles II of England roared with laughter on being told that members of his Royal Society were weighing the air. Yet the Royal Society for Improving Natural Knowledge, founded in 1662, and its French counterpart, the Académie des Sciences (1666), were important promoters of scientific investigation. The one, in characteristic English fashion, was a private undertaking, though with a royal charter; the other, sponsored by Colbert for the greater glory of Louis XIV and *la grande nation,* was a government institution, whose fellows received salaries and also instructions to avoid discussion of religion and politics. Both societies financed experiments and both published scientific articles in their house organs, the *Philosophical Transactions* and *Journal des savants.*

An international scientific community arose through the formal exchanges of the corresponding secretaries of such academies, and also through the private correspondence among members and their acquaintances. Both professional men and aristocrats joined learned societies, and many a gentleman and an occasional lady dabbled in a private laboratory or observatory. Some did more than dabble, among them Robert Boyle (1627–1691), son of an Irish earl, who discovered the law of physics named after him: that under compression the volume of a gas is inversely proportional to the amount of pressure. While many scientists still published in Latin, their discoveries were popularized in books and articles in the vernacular.

Meantime, the basic language of science—mathematics—was taking a great leap forward. In 1585 Stevin, a Fleming, published *The Decimal, Teaching with Unheard-of Ease How to Perform All Calculations Necessary among Men by Whole Numbers without Fractions.* Another great time-saver was devised by the Scot Napier, with his *Marvelous Rule of Logarithms* (1616), which shortened the laborious processes of multiplying, dividing, and finding square roots. Descartes (1596–1650) worked out analytical geometry, which brought geometry and algebra together through the "Cartesian coordinates," as in the plotting of an equation on a graph. The mathematical achievements of the century culminated in a method for dealing with variables and probabilities. Pascal made a beginning with studies of games of chance, and Dutch insurance actuaries devised tables to estimate the life expectancy of their clients. The English Newton and the German Leibniz (1646–1716), apparently quite independently of each other, invented the calculus. The practical value of these innovations is indicated by the fact that without the calculus, and without Cartesian geometry, Newton could never have made the calculations supporting his revolutionary hypotheses in astronomy and physics.

In astronomy the heliocentric theory advanced by Copernicus in the sixteenth century proved to be only a beginning. It raised many difficulties, notably when observation of planetary orbits did not confirm Copernicus' belief that the planets revolved about the sun in circular paths. The German Kepler (1571–1630) opened the way to a resolution by proving mathematically that the orbits were in fact elliptical. Then Galileo's telescope revealed the existence of spots on the sun, rings around Saturn, and moonlike satellites around Jupiter. All this evidence of corruption in high places led Galileo to publish a book in 1632 defending the heliocentric concept and ridiculing supporters of the traditional geocentric theory. But the Church, headed by traditionalists, brought Galileo before the Inquisition, which placed his book on the *Index* of prohibited works and sentenced him to what amounted to perpetual house arrest. Despite the public recantation Galileo was obliged to make, he is reported to have had the last word, "and yet it does move"—the Earth is not stationary, as the Church insists, but a planet behaving like other planets.

An even more celebrated story recounts Galileo's experiment of dropping balls of different weights from the Leaning Tower of Pisa to test Aristotle's theory that objects fall with velocities proportional to their weight.

While the story itself may be apocryphal, Galileo did in fact disprove Aristotle. Galileo's studies of projectiles, pendulums, and falling and rolling bodies helped establish modern ideas of acceleration and inertia, which Newton later formulated mathematically.

In 1687 Newton published the laws of motion, together with other great discoveries, in *Philosophiae Naturalis Principia Mathematica* (Mathematical Principles of Natural Philosophy). Since he had made many of these findings two decades earlier, when he was still an undergraduate at Cambridge, Newton fits the popular concept of physics as the young man's science par excellence. He went on to secure abundant recognition in his later years, gaining a professorship at Cambridge, a knighthood, the presidency of the Royal Society, and the well-paid post of master of the Mint. Even Newton, however, was not fully modern, for he often devoted himself to experiments in alchemy and unsuccessful efforts to determine the accurate dates of biblical events.

Newton's greatest contribution was the law of gravitation. It followed from his laws of motion, which picture bodies moving not in straightforward fashion of themselves but only in response to forces impressed upon them. These forces are at work in the mutual attraction of the sun, the planets, and their satellites, which are thereby held in their orbits. Newton stated the formula that the force of gravitation is proportional to the product of the masses of two bodies attracted one to the other, and inversely proportional to the square of the distance between them. Newton also promoted the development of optics by using a prism to separate sunlight into the colors of the spectrum. He demonstrated that objects only appear to be colored: their color is not intrinsic but the result of reflection and absorption of light.

Meanwhile, the mechanistic views of the physicists were invading geology and physiology. In 1600, the Englishman Gilbert, in a study of magnetism, suggested that the earth itself was a giant magnet. In 1628, Harvey, the physician of Charles I, published his demonstration that the human heart is a pump driving the blood around a single circulatory system. Harvey's theory, confirmed a generation later by the discovery through microscopic observation of the capillary connections between arteries and veins, discredited the hypothesis, handed down from Galen in classical antiquity, that the blood in the arteries moved quite separately from that in the veins. Finally, in 1679, the Italian Borelli showed that the human arm is a lever, and that muscles do mechanical work.

World-Machine and Rationalism

All these investigations in the various sciences tended to undermine the older Aristotelian concept of something "perfect." Instead of perfect circles, post-Copernican astronomy posited ellipses; instead of bodies moving in straightforward fashion of themselves Newton pictured bodies responding only to forces impressed upon them. All these investigations, in short, suggested a new major scientific generalization, a law of uniformity that simplified and explained and that coordinated many separate laws into one general law. Galileo almost made this achievement, but got into trouble with the Church for suggesting that the earth was not stationary, as had always been thought. It was Newton who finally drew everything together in the grand mechanical conception that has been called the Newtonian world-machine.

The Newtonian world-machine, and the new science of which it was the product, had very important theological and philosophical implications. Natural science of itself does not deal with the great problems of theology and philosophy. It does not give men ends or purposes but rather means, and its theories are explanations, not moral justifications. Yet, historically, the rise of modern science was associated with a definite world-view and system of values, for which the best name is probably *rationalism.* This is a broad term. It is possible to be at the same time a rationalist and a believer in a supernatural God, like Thomas Aquinas and other medieval Schoolmen. In the early modern West, however, rationalism tended to banish God entirely from the universe or at least to reduce him to a First Cause that started the world-machine going but then did not interfere with its operation. The new mechanistic interpretation of the universe regarded God not as the incomprehensible Creator and Judge but simply as the architect of a world-machine whose operations man could grasp if only he would apply his reason properly.

The rationalism and materialism engendered by the scientific revolution found a most articulate spokesman in René Descartes. When he was a young man, as his *Discourse on Method* (1637) relates, he resolved to mistrust all authorities, theological or intellectual. His skepticism swept everything aside until he concluded that there was one thing only he could not doubt: his own existence. There must be reality in the self engaged in the processes of thinking and doubting—in the famous formulation, "Cogito ergo sum" (I think, therefore I am). From this one indubitable fact Descartes reconstructed the world until he arrived at God, a deity poles apart from older patriarchal concepts, a supreme geometer whose mathematical orderliness foreshadowed the great engineer of the Newtonian world-machine. But where Newton would proceed inductively, at least in part, by relying on the data of scientific observations and experiments, Descartes proceeded deductively, deriving the universe and God ultimately from "Cogito ergo sum."

The world that Descartes reconstructed proved to be two separate worlds—that of mind and soul, on the one hand, and that of body and matter, on the other. We confront the famous Cartesian dualism, which the twentieth-century philosopher-mathematician White-head claimed so hypnotized succeeding generations of philosophers that modern philosophy was ruined by their futile endeavors to put matter into mind or mind into matter and thus resolve the dualism. Descartes himself claimed competence to deal in detail only with the material world, yet the way in which he dealt with it intimated that it was the only world that counted. Witness his boast that if given matter and space, he could construct the universe himself.

Progress—and Pessimism

Scientist and rationalist helped greatly to establish in the minds of educated men throughout the West two complementary concepts that were to give the Enlightenment of the eighteenth century a pattern of action toward social change, a pattern still of driving force in our world. These were, first, the concept of a regular "natural" order underlying the irregularity and confusion of the universe as it appears to unreflecting man in his daily experience; and, second, the concept of a human faculty, best called reason, obscured in most men by their faulty traditional upbringing, but capable of being brought into effective play by good—that is, rational—upbringing. Both these concepts can be found in some form in our Western tradition at least as far back as the Greeks. What gives them novelty and force at the end of the seventeenth century is their being welded into the doctrine of progress—the belief that all human beings can attain here on earth a state of happiness, of perfection, hitherto in the West thought to be possible only for Christians in a state of grace, and for them only in a heaven after death.

By no means all the great minds of the seventeenth century shared this optimistic belief in progress and the infallibility of reason. The many-sided legacy of this century of genius is evident, for example, in the contrast between the two most important political writings issuing from the English Revolution—Thomas Hobbes' *Leviathan* and John Locke's *Second Treatise of Government.* Published in 1651 and much influenced by the disorders of the English Civil War, *Leviathan* is steeped in Machiavellian pessimism about the inherent sinfulness of man. The state of nature, when men live without government, is a state of war, Hobbes argues, where men prey upon their fellows and human life is "solitary, poor, nasty, brutish, short." Men's only recourse is to agree among themselves to submit absolutely to the Leviathan, an all-powerful state that will force men into peace.

In a sense, Hobbes turned the contract theory of government upside down by having men consent to yield all their liberties. With Locke it is right side up again. Locke, who knew Robert Boyle and was closely linked with the Royal Society, was also a close associate of the Whig leaders who engineered the Glorious Revo-

lution. His *Second Treatise of Government,* published in 1690 as a defense of their actions, accepted neither the divine-right theory of absolutism nor the Hobbesian justification of absolutism out of desperation. Locke paints a generally cheerful picture of the state of nature, which suffers only from the "inconvenience" (note the mild terminology) of lacking an impartial judicial authority. To secure such an authority men contract among themselves to accept a government, not the omnipotent Leviathan, but a government that respects a man's life, liberty, and property. Should the king seize property by imposing unauthorized taxes or should he follow policies like those of James II, then his subjects are justified in overthrowing their monarch. Locke's relative optimism and his enthusiasm for constitutional government nourished the major current of political thought in the next century, culminating in the American and French revolutions. But events after 1789 brought Hobbesian despair and authoritarianism to the surface once more.

Meantime, exponents of the older Christian tradition continued to flourish on the Continent. One example is the energetic Frenchman Vincent de Paul (1581–1660), who served seven years as a slave in a Turkish galley. While insisting on the observance of strict orthodoxy, Vincent also instituted the systematic care of foundlings, sponsored missions to rural areas neglected by the Church, and launched the Daughters of Charity, an organization that would enable well-to-do women to undertake the good works Vincent believed their wealth and status obligated them to perform.

Another example is Blaise Pascal, who also believed in charity, but in the sense of God's incomprehensible love rather than of philanthropy. Pascal, indeed, was a one-man summation of the complexities of the century of genius. He won an important place in the history of mathematics and physics by his work with air pressure and vacuums and, at the practical level, by his invention of a calculating machine and his establishment of the first horse-drawn bus line in Paris. Yet he was profoundly otherworldly as well and became a spokesman for the high-minded puritanical Jansenists, whose doctrines he defended in lively epigrammatic French, with the skill, fervor, and onesidedness of the born pamphleteer. He dismissed as unworthy the concepts of God as mere master geometer or engineer and sought instead for the Lord of Abraham and the Old Testament prophets. He underwent a great mystical experience one night in November 1654 when he felt with absolute certainty the presence of God and of Christ. He spent his final years in religious meditation and left unfinished at his death one of the most remarkable works of Christian apologetics in existence, the *Pensées* (Thoughts). Here he wrote:

> Man is but a being filled with error. This error is natural, and, without grace, ineffaceable. Nothing shows him the

truth: everything deceives him. These two principles of truth, reason and the senses, besides lacking sincerity, reciprocally deceive each other. The senses deceive reason by false appearances: and just as they cheat reason they are cheated by her in turn: she has her revenge. Passions of the soul trouble the senses, and give them false impressions. They emulously lie and deceive each other.*

A final example is Baruch Spinoza (1632–1677), who tried to reconcile the God of Science and the God of Scripture. Spinoza constructed a system of ethical axioms as rigorously Cartesian and logical as a series of mathematical propositions. He also tried to reunite the Cartesian opposites, matter with mind, body with soul, by asserting that God was present everywhere and in everything. His pantheism caused his ostracism in Holland by his fellow Jews and also by the Christians, who considered him an atheist; his rejection of rationalism and materialism offended intellectuals. Spinoza found few admirers until the romantic revolt against the abstractions and oversimplifications of the Enlightenment.

Literature

Just as Henry IV, Richelieu, and Louis XIV brought greater order to French politics after the civil and religious upheavals of the sixteenth century, so the writers of the seventeenth century disciplined French writing after the Renaissance extravagance of a genius like Rabelais. It was the Age of Classicism, which insisted on the observance of elaborate rules, on the authority of models from classical antiquity, and on the employment of a more polite vocabulary. In the early 1600s the example of greater refinement in manners and speech was set by the circle who met in the Paris *salon* (reception room) of an aristocratic hostess, the marquise de Rambouillet. Later, proper behavior was standardized by the court ceremonial at Versailles and proper vocabulary by the famous dictionary of the French language that the experts of the academy founded by Richelieu finished compiling in the 1690s after more than a half century of labor. Boileau (1636–1711), the chief literary critic of the day, set the rules for writing poetry with his pronouncement "Que toujours le bon sens s'accorde avec le rhyme" (Always have good sense agree with the rhyme). Exaggerated notions of propriety outlawed from polite usage the French counterparts of such terms as *spit* and *vomit* and obliged writers to seek euphemisms for dozens of commonplace activities. Already there are indications of the social cleavage that produced the revolution of 1789 in the enormous gap between the classical French of the court and the plainer, coarser language of the average French person.

On the other hand, the linguistic purification of the seventeenth century also brought substantial benefits. Without its discipline, French could never have won its unique reputation for clarity and elegance. The leading tragic dramatists of *le grand siècle* made observance of all the classical do's and don'ts not an end in itself but a means to probe deeply into the endless variety of human personalities. Corneille (1606–1684) and Racine (1639–1699) usually chose plots from Greek mythology and wrote in the rhymed couplets called alexandrines (the iambic hexameter used for a poem about Alexander the Great). They also respected the unities decreed by Aristotle's *Poetics,* which restricted the action of play to a single place, to one twenty-four-hour span of time, and to a single topic. Within this rigid form the genius of Corneille and Racine created moving portraits of people upholding exalted ideals of honor or crushed by overwhelming emotion. The French tragedies of the seventeenth century are worthy successors to the Greek dramas of the fifth century B.C. not merely because of their classical form but also because of their psychological insight and emotional power.

As a writer of comedies Molière (1622–1673), the other great dramatist of the age, was less constrained to employ a dignified vocabulary and to heed the other canons of classicism. The main characters of his satirical comedies were not only sharply etched individuals but social types as well—the overrefined pedantic ladies of the salons in *Les Précieuses Ridicules,* the hypocrite in *Tartuffe,* the miser in *L'Avare,* the ignorant and self-important newly rich in *Le Bourgeois Gentilhomme.* In Molière, as in all good satire, there is more than a touch of moralizing, and didactic overtones are also present in two other characteristic works of the Great Century. The *Fables* of La Fontaine (1621–1695) which reworked in lively fashion tales borrowed from antiquity, vindicated the author's contention that while he imitated the classics he was by no means enslaved to them. The *Maxims* of La Rochefoucauld (1613–1680), cast in epigrammatic prose of classic purity, were less down to earth in language but even more disenchanted in their estimates of human nature: "We all have enough strength to bear the misfortunes of others." "We generally give praise only to gain it for ourselves." "We always find something not altogether displeasing in the misfortunes of our friends." *

Seventeenth-century English literature also had its cynics, notably Wycherley, Congreve, and the other playwrights who wrote the witty, bawdy, and disillusioned Restoration comedies. Under Charles II and his successors the pendulum of public taste and morality

---

*B. Pascal, *Thoughts, Letters, and Opuscules,* trans. O. W. Wright (Boston, 1882), p. 192.

*The Maxims of La Rochefoucauld, trans. F. G. Stevens (London, 1939), pp. 9, 49, 173.

Diego Velásquez "The Maids of Honor," 1656.

made a particularly violent swing in reaction to the midcentury Puritans who had closed down the theaters as dens of sinfulness. One of those Puritans, John Milton (1608–1674), the secretary of Oliver Cromwell, produced a truly major work of literature, *Paradise Lost*, the only English epic in the grand manner that still attracts many readers. Though Milton was a classical scholar of staggering erudition, his often complex style and his profound belief in Christian humanism really made him a belated representative of an earlier literary age, the last great man of the English Renaissance.

What was needed to prepare for the classical age of English letters was the modernization of the English language by pruning the elaborate flourishes, standardizing the chaotic spelling, and eliminating the long flights of rhetoric characteristic of Elizabethan and early seventeenth century prose. Under the influence of John Dryden (1631–1700), English began to model itself on French, adopting its straightforward word order, its comparatively brief sentences, and its polish,

neatness, and clarity. English letters were ready for the Augustan age, which lasted through the first half of the eighteenth century.

V   The Baroque Era

Baroque, the label usually applied to the arts of the seventeenth century, probably comes from the Portuguese *barroco,* an irregular or mishapen pearl. Some critics have seized upon the suggestion of deformity to deprecate the impurity of seventeenth-century art in contrast to the purity of the Renaissance. Especially among Protestants, the reputation of baroque has suffered because it was identified with the Counter-Reformation and many of its leading artists appeared to be propagandists for Rome. In addition, many viewers may be repelled by the flamboyance of such baroque works as the enormous baldachin, the sculptured canopy over the main altar of Saint Peter's in Rome, or the acres of canvases by Rubens in the Louvre that seem to be populated mainly by hefty pink female flesh.

It is true that baroque art was closely associated with the Jesuits, with the successors of Philip II in Spain, and above all with Rome during the century following the Council of Trent. Papal patronage reached a pinnacle in the pontificate of Urban VIII (1623–1644), the head of the free-spending Barberini family. It is also true that Catholic reformers enlisted the arts in propagating the faith and endowing it with greater emotional intensity. Yet it is equally true that not all the baroque masters were Catholic—Rembrandt, for instance, was a Mennonite, and Sir Christopher Wren an Anglican—nor were all their patrons Catholic prelates or grandees. Portraits of the Protestant Charles I of England brought Van Dyck fame and wealth, and in the Dutch Republic, where the Calvinist churches frowned on all ornamentation, painters won support from the business community and sometimes became prosperous businessmen themselves.

The unprecedented financial success of some artists is one of the distinguishing characteristics of baroque: Rubens, Van Dyck, Wren, and Bernini were able to live like lords, in contrast to the relatively austere existence of such Renaissance masters as Leonardo and Michelangelo. A second characteristic is the baroque stress on sheer size exemplified by the vast canvases of Rubens, the immense palace of Versailles, and Bernini's baldachin in Saint Peter's and his grandiose colonnade outside. A third characteristic is the preoccupation with theatricality, as painters intensified the use of *chiaroscuro* to create the illusion of brilliant lighting and placed figures in the immediate foreground of a canvas to draw the spectator into the scene as a participant. A final characteristic is the realistic depiction of a wide range of humanity, clowns, beggars, gypsies, cardsharps, cripples and dwarfs as well as ordinary people praying, laughing, or eating. In France, for example, Georges de La Tour (1593–1653) took everyday subjects—a woman retrieving a flea as she undresses is a famous instance—and executed them in a nighttime setting that permitted dramatic contrasts of light and shadow.

Painting

The most restrained baroque painter was probably Velásquez (1599–1660), who spent thirty-four years at the court of Philip IV of Spain, interrupted only by two trips to Italy where he purchased for his patron masterpieces by Titian and other Renaissance masters now housed in Madrid's Prado. Velásquez was fascinated by the solution of difficult technical problems. He needed all his skill to soften the receding chins and thick lips of the Hapsburgs and yet make his portraits of Philip IV and the royal family instantly recognizable. His greatest feat of technical wizardry is *The*

Maids of Honor, which has a room to itself in the Prado. A little princess, having her portrait painted, is surrounded by a pet dog, dwarfs, and other attendants; it is the moment when the royal parents are looking in on the scene, but only their reflections are seen, in a mirror at the rear of the room. As Velásquez turns to greet them and looks at the viewer, the latter realizes he is standing where the royal couple must have stood. Painted with the adroit use of mirrors, *The Maids of Honor* is a splendid example of baroque attempts to make the spectator an active participant.

Unlike the aristocratic Velásquez, the Flemish Rubens (1577–1640) was the baroque counterpart of the Renaissance universal man. A diplomat and linguist, an ardent student of antiquity and archaeology, he amassed a fortune from his painting and collected impressive honors (knighting by Charles I of England, elevation to the nobility by the King of Spain). Rubens made his studio, with its two hundred students, a veritable factory of art, and he himself is estimated to have contributed at least in part to over two thousand pictures, whose subjects ranged from simple portraits to

Rubens' "Marie de' Medici Landing in Marseilles."

A Rembrandt self-portrait (1640).

ambitious political themes. He painted the ceiling of the Whitehall Banqueting Hall in London saluting James I as the uniter of Scotland and England; he did an allegory of the city of Antwerp as Andromeda, a mythological princess who was chained to a rock until she was liberated, in this instance by a Spanish governor; and he was commissioned by Marie de' Medici, the widow of Henry IV of France, to execute a series of canvases glorifying Henry and herself. As monarchs by divine right, Henry and Marie are portrayed more as mythological figures than as mere mortals; artistically, the pictures are significant for the generous employment of the mother-of-pearl flesh tones, which are Rubens' hallmark.

One of Rubens' pupils was his fellow Fleming, Van Dyck (1599–1641), whose portraits of Charles I captured the casual elegance and confident authority of the Stuart monarch, making him appear the embodiment of Castiglione's ideal courtier. Although courtly values had few followers among the Flemings' northern neighbors in the Netherlands, the officers of Dutch civic guards and the governing boards of guilds and other important organizations of Dutch merchants liked to be portrayed for posterity. Middle-class families favored small cheerful pictures, preferably showing the leisure activities cherished by these hard-working people. The consequence was a veritable explosion of artistic enterprise that coincided with the heyday of Dutch prosperity during the first two-thirds of the century. With the French invasion of the 1670s, both the economic and artistic hegemony of the Dutch began to fade.

Seventeenth-century Dutch painters were admired both for their subtle depiction of light and color in landscapes and for their talented exploitation of the artistic possibilities of the interiors of Dutch houses, with their highly polished or well-scrubbed floors and their strong contrasts of light and shade. The best-known baroque painters in the Netherlands are Frans Hals (1580–1666) and Rembrandt (1609–1669). Hals used bold strokes to paint cheerful contingents of civic guards, laughing musicians, and tavern topers. As he aged, he himself became a chronic toper; yet in his eighties, a penniless inmate in a poorhouse, he painted the most remarkable group portrait of baroque art—*The Women Regents of the Haarlem Hospital,* dour, formidable, and ageing matrons in all their Calvinist severity.

Rembrandt, too, attained fame early, then slipped into obscurity and poverty; he documented his troubles in a series of moving self-portraits. He, too, executed famous group portraits—*The Night Watch* and *The Syndics of the Drapers' Guild* (this last arranged by a friend in the textile business, but all the proceeds went to his creditors). Rembrandt painted an exceptional scientific subject, *The Anatomy Lesson of Dr. Tulp,* with a physician explaining the structure of blood vessels and tendons in the arm of an executed criminal, about the only kind of cadaver available to anatomists in those days. Rembrandt's paintings often show the fascination with *chiaroscuro* and with the gold evening light that is so typical of baroque, and he often strives for direct involvement of the viewer as well. In successive sketches for *Ecce Homo,* when Pilate allows the crowd to choose between Christ and Barabbas, Rembrandt progressively eliminated the crowd, and the beholder of the final version realizes that he is one of an unseen multitude choosing Barabbas over Christ. In his difficult later years, when he lived in the most squalid quarter of Amsterdam, Rembrandt seemed particularly drawn to biblical figures and their tribulations—Saul and David, the prodigal son and his father—and used residents of the Jewish ghetto as models. Consequently, Rembrandt has been called the greatest Protestant religious painter, a rare exception to the rule that Protestant tradition has not welcomed the visual arts.

Architecture and the Art of Living

To obtain a fair sample of baroque painting one should visit the Louvre, the Prado, the National Gallery in London, the Rijksmuseum in Amsterdam, the Metropolitan in New York and perhaps half a dozen other institutions. To sample baroque architecture and urban planning one need visit only Rome, where Urban VIII and other popes sponsored churches, palaces, gardens, fountains, avenues, and piazzas in a determination to make their capital the most spectacular city in Europe. A tour should begin at Saint Peter's, which, apart from Michelangelo's dome, is a legacy of baroque rather than the Renaissance. The proportions of Michelangelo's Greek-cross design were destroyed when a greatly lengthened nave was constructed in the early 1600s. With the vast space of the nave leading into the vast space beneath the dome, it was imperative to find a way of filling the latter.

Urban VIII entrusted the commission to the young architect, Bernini (1598–1680), who hit on the ingenious solution of the baldachin or tabernacle, an enormously magnified and strengthened version of the flimsy little canopy used to cover the sacrament. Four enormous spiral bronze columns, modeled after those supposedly used in Solomon's temple, support an elaborate bronze canopy, topped by an orb and a cross, the papal emblems. The decoration made generous use of the Barberini family symbols, the bees and the laurel. This 85-foot-high structure filled the void without blocking the view from the nave through the apse. To secure the bronze for the columns and canopy the bronze roof of the Pantheon, the best preserved monument of ancient Rome, was melted down—whence the epigram of Urban VIII's physician, *Quod non fecerunt Barbari, fecerunt Barberini* (What the Barbarians didn't do, the Barberini did).

Under a successor of Urban, Alexander VII

Bernini's baldacchino above the main altar at St. Peter's, Rome.

(1655–1667), Bernini undertook to fill the void between the baldachin and the wall of the apse, producing what is known, with astonishing understatement, as Saint Peter's chair. It is an elaborately carved throne borne on the shoulders of four great bronze figures, the front pair representing two Latin fathers (Saint Ambrose and Saint Augustine) and the rear pair two Greek fathers (Saint Athanasius and Saint Chrysostom). Their positions were intended to symbolize the ideal of unity between Latin and Greek churches as well as the preponderance of the Latin. Around and above the throne are clouds leading up to a sunburst of golden rays and heavenly creatures, in the midst of which is a dove, symbol of the Holy Spirit. This fantastic creation of marble, glass, stucco, and bronze is perhaps the ultimate statement of the baroque obsession with drama and illusion.

Also under Alexander VII Bernini tackled the problem of framing the open space facing the facade of Saint Peter's, where crowds receive the papal blessing on special occasions. Employing a trick of stage design, he extended two wings from the façade to mitigate the disproportion of the façade, which was too wide for its height. Beyond the trapezoidal area he built a great oval piazza flanked by curving colonnades, each with row upon row of simple Doric columns, which have been likened to formations of papal soldiers, and the whole compared to "the arms of Mother Church gathering in her children."

Architect, painter, sculptor, engineer, and improvisor, rewarded by his patrons with handsome fees and flattering honors, Bernini stood in the great tradition of the universal man of the Renaissance. Yet, as the leading sculptor of the seventeenth century, he contributed to the precipitous decline of that medium from its Renaissance pinnacle, in the judgment of some critics. Their major evidence is his *Ecstasy of Saint Teresa,* which not only expressed her mystical experience of divine love in physical terms (as she herself had expressed it) but also prompted another of Bernini's theatrical productions. He converted a chapel in the Roman church of Santa Maria della Vittoria into a miniature theater, with sculptured boxes on the sides containing portraits of the family that had commissioned the work. On a little stage in the center he placed Teresa, voluminously gowned and swooning back onto a cloud, with a smiling angel standing by and holding the fire-tipped dart of divine love; the white marble figures are spotlighted by bright rays appearing to come from heaven but actually entering through a hidden window.

Purely as an architect, Bernini was a conservative and made only cautious departures from the classical norms of the Renaissance. His chief rival, Borromini (1599–1667), was a daring experimenter who abandoned the straight lines and right angles of classicism. In the little Roman church of San Carlo alle Quattro Fontane he ingeniously combined concave and convex surfaces to make a compact curving structure that utilized with full efficiency a small plot of land.

Although Borromini's innovations influenced fanciful late baroque buildings in Austria, Germany, and Latin America, conservatism prevailed elsewhere, most significantly in the France of Louis XIV, which replaced Rome as the trend-setter of Europe in the last third of the century. Advanced Baroque design received one setback when a major addition to the Louvre was executed in classical style, and another when the same style was chosen for the exterior of the palace at Versailles. Still, there are Baroque qualities at Versailles—the superhuman dimensions the conscious effort to be overwhelming, and the opulent interior with its allegorical paintings and the famous Hall of Mirrors, a long narrow gallery where the installation of a large mirror opposite each window creates the illusion of spaciousness. Altogether, the palace was a splendid setting for the endless ceremonies surrounding the sun king, even if it was not a comfortable residence for the thousands who inhabited it.

Beyond the palace stretches an enormous park, with statues, fountains, pavilions, and a mile-long canal that became a backdrop for fireworks displays on state occasions. Landscape architects raised their craft to a fine art in keeping the plantings close to the palace carefully manicured and leaving those more distant in their natural state. After Louis moved to Versailles, he did not neglect Paris but added to it some fine squares surrounded by the townhouses of the aristocracy with his own statue in the center (the Place Vendôme is a good surviving example). He also provided the Louvre with a majestic western approach, the broad tree-lined avenue of the Champs Elysées.

In England, baroque building was much diluted by Palladio's classicism. Under Charles II the Surveyor-General (chief architect) was Christopher Wren (1632–1723), a talented engineer and astronomer, who was deluged with commissions after the great fire destroyed much of London in 1666. He directed the rebuilding of fifty-one parish churches in addition to designing a new Saint Paul's Cathedral. Saint Paul's, in particular, strained his capacity to fuse varying styles into a harmonious whole: the walls are supported by concealed Gothic flying buttresses; the main facade and the dome are classical; and the twin towers have curving lines in the manner of Borromini. Perhaps Saint Paul's is most baroque in being so self-consciously grand, as if it were quite aware that it was and would remain *the* landmark of London and that its dome would be copied for the Pantheon in eighteenth-century Paris and the Capitol in nineteenth-century Washington.

England's purest baroque monument is Blenheim Palace in Oxfordshire, named in honor of the Duke of Marlborough's victory over the French in 1704, pre-

Europe in 1715

Legend:
- Brandenburg-Prussia
- Austrian Hapsburg Lands
- Swedish possessions
- Venetian possessions
- Ottoman Empire
- Boundary of the Holy Roman Empire
- ■ Battle sites

NORWAY

Oslo

Stockholm

North Sea

DENMARK

SCOTLAND

Edinburgh
Berwick

Copenhagen

SWEDISH POMERANIA

ULSTER

IRELAND

Boyne R.
Drogheda
Dublin
Limerick

KINGDOM OF GREAT BRITAIN

ENGLAND

London

Hamburg
Bremen

Elbe R.

Fehrbellin

BRANDENBURG

Berlin

Oder R.

SILESIA

UNITED NETHERLANDS

Ryswick
Utrecht
Nimwegen

THE

WEST-PHALIA

Dresden

SAXONY

EMPIRE

Atlantic Ocean

Dover

Tor Bay

C. La Hogue

Oudenarde
AUSTRIAN NETHERLANDS
Ramillies
Aachen

Malplaquet

Rhine R.

Metz

Verdun

LORRAINE

Toul

ALSACE

Rastadt
Strasbourg

Blenheim

Prague

BOHEMIA

MORAVIA

Seine R.

Paris

Versailles

Nantes

Blois
Orléans

Loire R.

FRANCE

FRANCHE COMTÉ

Augsburg

AUSTRIA

Vienna

BAVARIA

STYRIA

SWITZERLAND

Geneva

TYROL

CARINTHIA

Bordeaux

Rhône R.

CARNIOLA

MILAN

SAVOY

Po R.

Venice

Avignon (to the Papacy)

Genoa

VENETIAN REPUBLIC

Adriatic Sea

Marseilles

Florence

PAPAL STATES

Rag

PORTUGAL

Burgos

Ebro R.

CORSICA (to Genoa)

Rome

Lisbon

Tagus R.

Madrid

SPAIN

Barcelona

Valencia

BALEARIC IS.

MINORCA (Br.)

SARDINIA (to Austria, 1714; to Savoy, 1720)

NAPLES

Naples

Guadalquivir R.

Seville

Granada

Mediterranean Sea

Palermo

Gibraltar (Br.)

SICILY

(to Savoy, 171_ to Austria, 172_

ALGERIA

TUNIS

MALTA

Scale: 0 — 500 Miles

St. Paul's Cathedral, London, begun in 1675.

sented to him by a grateful government, and financed in part by subscriptions from a grateful public. The architect Vanbrugh (1664–1726), who was also a leading Restoration playwright, designed Blenheim less as a residence than as a vast theatrical setting. The immense courtyard was overwhelmingly impressive, but the kitchens were a quarter of a mile from the main dining-room! Voltaire observed that if the rooms had been as wide as the walls were thick Blenheim would have been more livable.

The arts of good living made substantial progress in the seventeenth century, despite the ravages of disease and famine, which are estimated to have reduced the European population by at least 15 percent between 1648 and 1713. The expansion of Europe overseas made available the new beverages of coffee, tea, and cocoa, new cotton materials, and luxuries like Chinese porcelain and lacquered ware. Exotic tropical woods made possible the technique of marquetry, that is, inlaying and veneering furniture with different kinds of wood. On the whole, furniture was becoming more specialized: dining chairs replaced dining benches; chairs were made both with arms and, to accommodate hoopskirts, without; Louis XIV had his *chaise percée* (pierced chair) to accomplish his morning duties in his bedchamber.

Chests were made more convenient for storage by the installation of drawers; and when the chest became baroque and acquired a curved front and greater space, it was termed a commode. Kneehole writing desks appeared, and, especially in England, drop-leaf gateleg tables, which could stand in a narrow space by a wall or be opened up as a dining or gaming table. For dining, table napkins came into use along with individual plates and glasses in place of communal bowls and vessels. Families of moderate means could afford these innovations as well as a teapot, a pitcher, and a few items of plain silver and thus participated in what amounted to a revolution in domestic arrangements.

Music

Baroque composers, especially in Italy, moved further along the paths laid out by their Renaissance predecessors. In Rome, Frescobaldi (1583–1644) exploited the dramatic potentialities of the pipe organ, attracting thousands to his recitals at St. Peter's. In Venice, Monteverdi (1567–1643) wrote the first important operas to back up his contention that "speech should be the master of music, not its servant." The opera, a characteristically baroque compound of music and drama proved so popular that Venice soon had sixteen opera houses, which were already focusing on the celebrity of the chief singers rather than on the overall quality of the supporting cast and the orchestra. The star system reached its height at Naples, where conservatories (originally institutions for "conserving" orphans) specialized in voice training. Many Neapolitan operas were loose collections of arias designed to show off the talents of the stars, and the effect of unreality was heightened by the custom of having the male roles sung by women and some of the female by *castrati,* male sopranos.

At its best seventeenth-century opera rose above the level of stilted artificiality. In England, Purcell (1658–1695), the organist of Westminster Abbey, produced a masterpiece for the graduation exercises of a girls' school, the beautiful and moving *Dido and Aeneas.* Louis XIV, appreciating the obvious value of opera in enhancing the resplendence of his court, imported from Italy the talented Lully (1632–1687), who was not only a musician and a dancer but also a speculator and politician who vied with Molière as "cultural director" of court life. Lully's operas on mythological themes are now for the most part forgotten, but the overtures and dances that he wrote for them were the prelude to the eighteenth-century achievements in instrumental music.

Reading Suggestions on Divine-Right Monarchy— and Revolution

Europe in General

R. S. Dunn, *The Age of Religious Wars, 1559–1689* (*Norton). Crisp, comprehensive, and up-to-date survey.

M. Ashley, *The Golden Century* (Praeger, 1969). Another valuable recent introduction to seventeenth-century Europe.

C. J. Friedrich, *The Age of the Baroque, 1610–1660;* F. L. Nussbaum, *The Triumph of Science and Reason, 1660–1685;* J. B. Wolf, *The Emergence of the Great Powers, 1685–1715* (*Torchbooks). Detailed, scholarly volumes, with very full bibliographies; in the Rise of Modern Europe series.

A. Vagts, *A History of Militarism* (*Free Press), and E. M. Earle, ed., *Makers of Modern Strategy* (*Princeton Univ.). Both are helpful on seventeenth-century warfare.

E. F. Heckscher, *Mercantilism,* rev. ed., 2 vols. (Macmillan, 1955). A famous and controversial work.

F. L. Nussbaum, *A History of Economic Institutions in Modern Europe* (Crofts, 1933). An abridgement of Sombart's *Modern Capitalism,* arguing that war is economically creative; the arguments are attacked by J. U. Nef, *War and Human Progress* (*Norton).

R. B. Merriman, *Six Contemporaneous Revolutions* (Clarendon, 1938). Lectures focused on the midcentury upheavals. The implications of this crisis are examined by the essays in T. Aston, ed., *Crisis in Europe, 1560–1660* (*Anchor).

France

G. R. R. Treasure, *Seventeenth Century France* (Rivingtons, 1966). Full and lucid survey.

J. D. Lough, *An Introduction to Seventeenth Century France* (*McKay). Designed for the student of literature and useful for anyone interested in the subject.

A. Guérard, *France in the Classical Age: The Life and Death of an Ideal,* rev. ed. (Braziller, 1956). Stimulating interpretation of early modern France.

C. J. Burckhardt, *Richelieu: His Rise to Power* and *Assertion of Power and Cold War* (Allen & Unwin, 1964 and 1970). Scholarly two-volume study of the great cardinal.

O. Ranum, *Richelieu and the Councillors of Louis XIII* (Oxford Univ., 1963). An important monograph on administration.

C. V. Wedgwood, *Richelieu and the French Monarchy* (*Collier). Sound brief evaluation.

D. Bitton, *The French Nobility in Crisis, 1560–1640* (Stanford Univ., 1969). Sound study of their declining role.

A. Lublinskaya, *French Absolutism: The Crucial Phase 1620–1629* (Cambridge Univ., 1968). From the standpoint of a Russian Communist scholar.

J. B. Wolf, *Louis XIV* (*Norton). Detailed, scholarly biography, stressing politics.

P. Goubert, *Louis XIV and Twenty Million Frenchmen* (*Vintage). The relations between the Sun King and his subjects.

W. H. Lewis *The Splendid Century* (*Morrow). Stresses the nature of society in France under Louis XIV.

W. J. Stankiewicz, *Politics and Religion in Seventeenth Century France* (Univ. of California, 1960). Illuminating study of their interrelations.

W. C. Scoville, *The Persecution of the Huguenots and French Economic Development, 1680–1720* (Univ. of California, 1960). Enlightening evaluation.

C. W. Cole, *Colbert and a Century of French Mercantilism,* 2 vols. (Columbia Univ., 1939). A solid, detailed study.

J. E. King, *Science and Rationalism in the Administration of Louis XIV* (Johns Hopkins Univ., 1949). Monograph showing the relations between intellectual and political history.

W. F. Church, ed., *The Impact of Absolutism in France* (*Wiley). Useful selections from source materials and commentaries on the era of Richelieu and Louis XIV.

England

M. Ashley, *England in the Seventeenth Century* (*Penguin), and C. Hill, *The Century of Revolution, 1603–1714* (*Norton). Two sound surveys by experts.

G. Davies, *The Early Stuarts 1603–1660,* and G. N. Clark, *The Later Stuarts, 1660–1714,* rev. eds. (Clarendon, 1949). More detailed scholarly treatments, in the Oxford History of England.

W. Notestein, *The English People on the Eve of Colonization, 1603–1630* (*Torchbooks). Admirable social history.

C. W. Bridenbaugh, *Vexed and Troubled Englishmen, 1590–1642* (Oxford Univ., 1968). A more recent study covering much of the same ground as Notestein's book.

C. V. Wedgwood, *The King's Peace, 1637–1641; The King's War, 1641–1647;* and *A Coffin for King Charles* (Macmillan, 1955–1964). Detailed study of the Great Rebellion by a ranking expert.

S. R. Gardiner, *History of England, 1603–1642,* 10 vols.; *History of the Great Civil War, 1642–1649,* 4 vols.; and *History of the Commonwealth and Protectorate, 1649–1656* (Longmans, 1904–1913). An older major work of detailed history. Gardiner's views may be sampled in his brief textbook, *The First Two Stuarts and the Puritan Revolution, 1603–1660,* first published in 1876 and recently reprinted (*Apollo).

D. H. Willson, *King James VI and I* (Holt, 1956). Sound appraisal of the first Stuart.

C. Hibbert, *Charles I* (Harper, 1968). Useful biography.

P. Zagorin, *The Court and the Country* (Routledge, 1969). Appraisal of the origins of the English Revolution.

L. Stone, *The Crisis of the Aristocracy, 1558–1641* (*Oxford Univ.) and *Social Change and Revolution in England, 1540–1640* (*Barnes and Noble). Important studies by a scholar who is an expert on the controversy over the role of the gentry. That controversy is neatly summarized in J. H. Hexter, *Reappraisals in History* (*Torchbooks).

C. V. Wedgwood, *Oliver Cromwell,* rev. ed. (Duckworth, 1973) and C. Hill, *God's Englishman* (*Torchbooks). Perhaps the soundest of recent works on Cromwell.

G. Davies, *The Restoration of Charles II, 1658–1660* (Huntington Library, 1955). An authoritative monograph.

A. Bryant, *King Charles II* (Longmans, 1931). Unusually sympathetic in tone.

F. C. Turner, *James II* (Macmillan, 1948). Balanced treatment of a ruler generally subject to partisan interpretation.

S. B. Baxter, *William III and the Defense of European Liberty* (Harcourt, 1966). Recent and sympathetic.

J. R. Tanner, *English Constitutional Conflicts of the Seventeenth Century* (*Cambridge Univ.). Full and scholarly.

C. Hill, *The World Turned Upside Down* (*Compass). Sketch of the radical ideas advanced during the English Revolution. May be supplemented by the older study of G. P. Gooch, *English Democratic Ideas in the Seventeenth Century* (*Torchbooks).

O. F. Morshead, ed., *Everybody's Pepys* (Harcourt, 1926). A useful abridgment of the famous diary kept during the 1660s; a fascinating document of social history.

The Century of Genius

P. Smith, *A History of Modern Culture,* Vol. 1 (Holt, 1930). An older work, and a mine of information on aspects of culture often neglected in intellectual histories.

C. Brinton, *The Shaping of Modern Thought* (*Spectrum). A survey of intellectual history from the Renaissance on.

H. F. Kearney, *Origins of the Scientific Revolution* (*Barnes & Noble). A many-sided introduction to this controversial topic.

H. Butterfield, *The Origins of Modern Science, 1300–1800* (*Free Press). A lively and controversial survey, minimizing the contribution of scientists before Galileo.

A. N. Whitehead, *Science and the Modern World* (*Free Press). An incisive and influential critique of what modern science really means and implies; rather difficult but well worth the effort.

A. R. Hall, *The Scientific Revolution, 1500–1800* (*Beacon). A solid account, written from the standpoint of the historian.

L. S. Feuer, *The Scientific Intellectual: The Psychological and Sociological Origins of Modern Science* (Basic Books, 1963). A stimulating interpretation from a more controversial point of view.

E. J. Dijksterhuis, *The Mechanization of the World Picture* (Clarendon, 1961). Informative study of the intellectual impact of science.

F. H. Anderson, *Francis Bacon: His Career and His Thought* (Univ. of Southern California, 1962). A good appraisal of an important pioneer.

B. Willey, *The Seventeenth Century Background* (*Anchor). Essays on Descartes, Hobbes, Milton, and other figures in the intellectual life of the century.

E. Mortimer, *Blaise Pascal* (Harper, 1959). A sympathetic and well-written study.

F. Baumer, *Religion and the Rise of Skepticism* (Harcourt, 1960). Assesses the spiritual impact of science.

S. E. Bethell, *The Cultural Revolution of the Seventeenth Century* (Roy, 1951). A literary study with fruitful suggestions for the historian of ideas.

The Baroque

J. S. Held and D. Posner, *17th and 18th Century Art* (Prentice-Hall; Harry N. Abrams, 1972). A recent systematic survey of painting, sculpture and architecture, handsomely illustrated.

G. Bazin, *The Baroque* (New York Graphic Society, 1968). Less systematic but more suggestive assessment. Bazin is also the author of a brief introduction, *Baroque and Rococo Art* (*Praeger).

A. C. Sewter, *Baroque and Rococo* (*Harcourt). Compact introduction.

V. L. Tapié, *The Age of Grandeur* (Weidenfeld & Nicolson, 1960). A review of baroque and classical art throughout Europe.

R. N. Hatton, *Europe in the Age of Louis XIV* (*Harcourt). Instructive study of the links among economic, social, and cultural developments.

F. Haskell, *Patrons and Painters* (*Harper & Row). Enlightening examination of the relationship between Italian society and art in the baroque era.

M. R. Bukofzer, *Music in the Baroque Era* (Norton, 1947). A standard introduction.

R. Wittkower, *Art and Architecture in Italy, 1600–1700,* 3rd ed. (1973) and A. Blunt, *Art and Architecture in France, 1500–1700* (1953). Two scholarly volumes in "The Pelican History of Art" (Penguin).

Historical Fiction

A. Dumas, *The Three Musketeers* (*Washington Square); *The Man in the Iron Mask* (*Airmont). Swashbuckling yarns of seventeenth-century France, based on careful research.

T. Gautier, *Captain Fracasse* (Bigelow Smith, 1910). A good picaresque tale, based on conscientious research; set in the France of Louis XIII.

A. Manzoni, *The Betrothed,* trans. A. Colquhoun (*Dutton). Milan about 1630; a famous Italian novel.

N. Hawthorne, *The Scarlet Letter* (*many editions). The best introduction to the Puritan spirit through fiction.

R. Graves, *Wife to Mr. Milton* (Creative Age, 1944). A good novel; not kind to Milton.

W. M. Thackeray, *Henry Esmond* (*several editions). Set in England about 1700.

1715 to 1815

The Old Regime and the International Balance

The Prospect in 1715

Long years of peace and quiet appeared to be in prospect for Europe in 1715. In the West, the Utrecht settlement of 1713 had ended Louis XIV's prolonged threat to the balance of power, and in the Baltic the protracted Great Northern War between Russia and Sweden was nearing a settlement. The death of Louis XIV himself in 1715 gave fresh promise of international stability, for the crown of France passed to his great-grandson, Louis XV, a boy of five. During a long regency France would probably be too preoccupied with internal matters to attempt adventures abroad. Finally, the last war of Louis XIV had not only exhausted his own state but also brought his victorious opponents to the edge of bankruptcy. War-weary Europe needed an extended period of convalescence.

The term "Old Regime" describes the institutions prevailing in Europe, and especially in France, before 1789: It was the Old Regime of the eighteenth century, in contrast to the "new regime" that was to issue from the French Revolution. On the surface, the Old Regime resembled the still older regime of the Middle Ages, though the forces that were to transform the economy, society, and politics of modern Europe were already at work beneath the surface. The economy was still largely agrarian, for most Europeans lived in farming villages and retained the parochial outlook of the peasant. Whereas in western Europe the great majority of peasants had been free of the bonds of serfdom for several centuries, in eastern Europe—notably in Germany beyond the Elbe, and in Hungary, Poland, and Russia—the majority were still serfs.

The social foundations of the Old Regime rested on the medieval division of society into the first estate of the clergy, the second estate of the nobility, and the third estate of commoners, who included the urban bourgeoisie and workingmen as well as the peasantry.

Within the third estate, only the men at the top exerted much political influence—well-to-do businessmen in England and Holland, French lawyers or merchants wealthy enough to purchase government office. Generally, bourgeois influence diminished as one moved eastward. Almost everywhere the titled nobles and the landed gentry of the second estate still exerted substantial influence and wanted to regain some of the power assumed by the "vile bourgeois," in the phrase of the disgruntled French aristocrat Saint-Simon. Every government in Europe tended to represent the interests of the few rather than the many; in this respect, it made little difference whether it was an absolute monarchy like France or Prussia, a constitutional monarchy like Britain, or a republic like the Dutch United Provinces.

Europe had long been oligarchical, agrarian, and parochial, and in 1715 it looked as though it would remain so forever. The apparent stability proved to be increasingly deceptive, however, as the eighteenth century advanced. In the next chapter we shall examine the ways in which the political and social status quo came under increasing attack from the leaders of the intellectual movement called the Enlightenment. This chapter will show how the economic foundations of the Old Regime were eroding under the pressure of revolutionary change, and how rapidly the balance of power achieved by the Utrecht settlement was undermined. The defeat and death of Louis XIV did not end the worldwide rivalry of England and France, who began another round of their long conflict in 1740. Meanwhile, further shifts in the international balance resulted from the appearance of two important newcomers. Russia was moving out of semi-isolation to take an active and sometimes aggressive role in war and diplomacy, and the German electorate of Brandenburg Prussia was emerging from its previous obscurity to become a first-class military power, intent on expansion.

II The Economic "Revolutions"

The changes that undermined the Old Regime affected commerce, agriculture, and industry and were most evident in western Europe, particularly in France, the Low Countries and, above all, Britain. They were in some respects economic revolutions, though many historians shy away from the term because it suggests a more sudden upsurge of economic energy and technological inventiveness than actually occurred. In the eighteenth century the pace of economic change was slower than it was to be in the nineteenth or twentieth, and it provided less drama than such political upheavals as the American and French revolutions. Yet in the long run the consequences of the economic revolutions were fully as revolutionary as those of 1776 and 1789.

Commerce and Finance

Many of the basic institutions of European business life had developed before 1715—banks and insurance firms in the Renaissance, for example, and chartered trading companies in the sixteenth century. Mercantilism, the loosely defined set of principles determining governmental policies toward commerce, had matured in the Spain of Philip II and the France of Louis XIV and Colbert. In the eighteenth century, the steady growth of seaborne trade, stimulated by an increasing population and a rising demand for food and goods, was the main force in quickening the pace of commerce. Many ports enjoyed a great boom—in England, London, Bristol, and Liverpool; in France, Nantes and Bordeaux on the Atlantic coast, nourished by the colonial trade, and Marseilles on the Mediterranean, nourished by the Levant trade; in Italy, Leghorn, established as an admirably run free port by the Grand Duchy of Tuscany; and in Germany, Hamburg, whose location near the mouth of the Elbe and the North Sea attested to the shift in economic focus of northern Europe from the Baltic to the Atlantic.

The burgeoning maritime trade increased the demand for insurance on ships and cargoes. In London, early in the century, marine insurance brokers gathered at Edward Lloyd's coffee house in Lombard Street to discuss business, news, and politics; they continued to meet there after Lloyd's death in 1713. Thus was born Lloyd's of London, the firm that developed the standard form of policy for marine insurance and published *Lloyd's List,* the first detailed and accurate shipping newspaper. Another great London institution to emerge from the informal atmosphere of the coffee house was the stock exchange. As the buying and selling of shares in joint-stock companies increased, traders began to gather at Jonathan's; in 1773 the name was changed from Jonathan's to the Stock Exchange Coffee House.

Marine insurance prospered in part because improved charts and the installation of lighthouses and buoys made navigation safer. At sea, captains could determine their geographical position by using two new instruments, the sextant and the chronometer. The sextant, an elaboration of the telescope, showed the altitude of the sun at noon and thus indicated the ship's latitude. The chronometer, a clock unaffected by the motion of the ship, was kept on Greenwich Mean Time (the time at the meridian running through Greenwich near London). The two new instruments made it possible to calculate the ship's longitude, which represented the difference between Greenwich Mean Time and the local time aboard ship as calculated with the sextant.

On land, improvements in communication and transport came much more slowly. Except for the good highways of France, European roads were scarcely better than paths or trails. The shipment of goods overland remained slow, unsafe, and expensive until after 1750, when the construction of turnpikes and canals gradually eased the situation. The pioneer English canal, built in 1759–1761 by the duke of Bridgewater, cut in half the cost of moving coal from the mines on his estate to the new factory town of Manchester.

Businessmen also faced the handicaps imposed by restrictive guild regulations and by the abundance of coins, weights, measures, and local tolls. Sweden, for example, minted only copper money, including a monstrosity weighing 43 pounds. Baden, one of the smaller German states, had 112 separate measures for length, 65 for dry goods, 123 for liquids, and 163 for cereals, not to mention 80 different pound weights! A German merchant who shipped timber down the Elbe from Dresden in Saxony to Hamburg had to pay so many tolls to the towns and principalities along the way that of sixty planks floated at Dresden, only six would reach Hamburg. Even in France, supposedly a model of uniformity and centralization, all sorts of local taxes and other obstacles to internal trade persisted.

The survival of local vested interests showed the limitations of the power of the mercantilist state. While mercantilism required the regulation of trade on a national basis, no eighteenth-century government possessed the staff of officials needed to make national regulation effective. Austria, Prussia, and some other German states endeavored to assimilate mercantilism into the more systematized policy called *cameralism* (from *camera*, the council or chamber dealing with expenditures and income). Though the cameralists took a broad view of government's economic responsibilities and activities, their main effort was directed toward planning state budgets, especially the increase of revenues. States outside the cameralist bloc in central Europe often relied heavily on private companies and individuals to execute economic policies.

Thus the English and Dutch East India companies exercised not only a trading monopoly in their colonial preserves but also virtual sovereign powers, including the right to maintain soldiers and conduct diplomacy. Inventors worked on their own, not in government laboratories, although the state occasionally offered prizes on matters of critical importance to the business community. When the English Parliament promised £20,000 for the invention of a reliable "seagoing" clock, the inventor of the chronometer had to wait twenty-five years to collect his prize money. On the whole, private initiative accomplished more than sluggish governments, but it could also get out of control, as demonstrated by two speculative booms early in the century—the Mississippi Bubble in France and the South Sea Bubble in England.

The Mississippi and South Sea Bubbles

In 1715, hardly a state in Europe could manage the large debts that had piled up during the recent wars. Yet all of them had to find some way of meeting at least part of the large annual interest on bonds and other obligations, or else go bankrupt. The governments of France and England chose the way of experiment. They transferred the management of state debts to joint-stock companies, which they rewarded with trading concessions. The commerce of the companies, it was hoped, would prove so lucrative that their profits would easily cover the interest charges on government bonds.

John Law (1671–1729), a Scottish mathematical wizard and an inveterate gambler, presided over the experiment in France. His studies of monetary problems and banking methods in Amsterdam, at that time the "economic school of Europe," made him a mercantilist, but with a difference. Law agreed with the mercantilist doctrine that the strength of a state depended upon the quantity of money it possessed. But, he asserted, the limited supply of silver and gold made it difficult to increase the amount of specie circulating in any country and therefore difficult to promote business. Paper money, Law concluded, was the solution—paper money backed by a nation's wealth in land and in trade. The quantity of paper money in circulation could easily be raised or lowered in accordance with the needs of business. Trading companies would prosper as never before, the whole country would prosper, and in the general prosperity, government debts would be paid off.

The death of Louis XIV gave Law the opportunity to put into practice what he called his "system." The regent for Louis XV, the duke of Orléans, who was a gambling crony of Law, permitted him to set up a central bank in Paris. Whereas the value of French money had been sinking lower and lower as the government progressively debased the coinage, Law's bank, following the practice of the Bank of Amsterdam, issued paper notes of stable value. Business activity at once increased. Next, Law set up the Mississippi Company, which received a monopoly of commerce with the Louisiana colony and soon absorbed the other French colonial trading companies.

Law's system now reached to almost every corner of the French economy, and Law himself, appointed controller general, became the economic dictator of the kingdom. His company took over the government debt and agreed to accept government bonds in partial payment for shares of Mississippi stock. Many bondholders responded enthusiastically to Law's offer, because the bonds had depreciated to 20 percent or less of their face value. Law, however, had to sell additional shares of Mississippi stock in order to obtain sufficient working capital for his company. To attract cash purchasers, he promoted a boom in Mississippi stock, painting the company's prospects in the brightest colors. Investors, large and small, caught the fever of speculation, and by the close of 1719 Mississippi stock was selling at forty times its par value.

The Mississippi Bubble soon burst, for Law's paper money could not stand the pressure. As the price of Mississippi shares rose higher and higher, cautious investors decided to cash in. They sold their shares, received payment in banknotes, then took the notes to Law's bank and demanded their redemption in specie. The bank exhausted its reserves of gold and silver and suspended specie payments in February 1720. Law was forced to relinquish the post of contrôller general in May 1720; he fled France shortly thereafter.

The explosion of the Mississippi Bubble had international repercussions, for within a few weeks of Law's resignation the South Sea Bubble burst in London. It might have been expected that management of the English government's debt would devolve upon the Bank of England. Founded in 1694 as a private institution (it was fully nationalized only after World War II), the Bank of England issued banknotes and performed other services for the government during the last wars against Louis XIV. But, in negotiations for the right to manage the debt, the bank was outbid by the new South Sea Company, which paid the government the exorbitant sum of more than seven and a half million pounds. The resources of the South Sea Company were slim, consisting largely of the right to exploit the trading concessions that Britain obtained under the Asiento agreement at the end of the War of the Spanish Succession. These privileges were limited to furnishing Spain's American colonies with 4,800 slaves annually and to sending one ship a year to Panama for general trade.

The South Sea Company, like the Mississippi Company, invited government creditors to transfer their bonds into company stock. The directors of the company bought and sold shares in secret to create a more lively market for them, encouraged purchases of stock with a down payment of only 10 percent in cash, and spread reports of forthcoming sailings by the company's ships on voyages of unparalleled promise. In short, like Law, they created a speculative boom. South Sea shares, with a par value of £100, sold for £129 in January of 1720, and for £1050 in June. Dozens of other promoters sprang into action, advertising schemes for wheels of perpetual motion, for making salt water fresh, and "for carrying on an undertaking of great advantage, but nobody to know what it is." The gullibility of the investing public was remarkable, but it was not inexhaustible. South Sea shares fell to £880 in August 1720, and to £150 in September. Parliament ordered an investigation and, to protect the company's

London during the South Sea Bubble: a Hogarth engraving. The sign above the door at the upper left says "Raffleing for Husbands with Lottery Fortunes—in Here."

creditors, seized the estates of its directors, who had meantime destroyed the company's books and fled the country.

The two bubbles produced some unfortunate results. The collapse of the Mississippi scheme ruined Law, whose talents, if used more discreetly, might have revitalized the French economy. In England, the South Sea fiasco long impeded the development of new stock companies, which were henceforth required to buy costly charters. It tarnished the reputations of many in high places. The royal mistresses and King George I himself had been "let in on the ground floor" in return for endorsing the venture enthusiastically, and more than a hundred members of Parliament had borrowed money from the company in order to buy its shares on the installment plan.

Yet the bubbles were by no means total misfortunes. They were an acute instance of the economic growing pains suffered as the states of Europe groped for solutions to baffling financial problems. Voltaire later correctly observed that Law's "imaginary system gave birth to a real commerce," and released French business from the torpor induced by the defeats of Louis XIV. The Mississippi Company, reorganized after 1720, consistently made a handsome profit. In England, the strongest institutions rode out the bursting of the South Sea Bubble; the East India Company continued to pay

an annual dividend of 5 to 10 percent, and the Bank of England, no longer having to compete with the South Sea Company for government favor, again became the financial mainstay of the realm. In the political shakeup following the collapse of the bubble, the Whig statesman Robert Walpole came to power with a program of honoring the debt as a *national* debt. This was a novel concept and a great step forward in fiscal morality in an age when most states still treated their debts as the monarch's personal obligation, to be acknowledged or repudiated as he saw fit.

Agricultural Improvements

The agricultural revolution, the second of the forces transforming the modern economy, centered on improvements that enabled fewer farmers to produce more crops. The application of technological discoveries to agriculture was as old as the irrigation ditches of ancient Mesopotamia and the improved plows and horse-collars of the Middle Ages. What was new and revolutionary in the eighteenth century was the accelerating tempo of the advance in farming techniques. The Netherlands, both Dutch and Austrian, continued in the van, producing the highest yields per acre planted and pioneering in the culture of new crops, like the potato, the turnip, and clover. Turnips furnished feed for livestock until the spring pasturing season began, thus eliminating the necessity for massive slaughtering of stock at the onset of winter. Clover, by fixing nitrogen in the soil, increased the fertility of the land and ended the necessity for having fields lie fallow every third year. In England, the new crops were taken up by "Turnip" Townshend (Viscount Townshend, 1674–1738), whose plan for four-year rotation—planting a field to turnips, barley, clover, and wheat in successive years—soon became standard on many English estates.

Townshend and other "improving landlords" in England were the great publicists of the new agriculture. Jethro Tull (1674–1741) studied French truckgardens and vineyards, where farmers obtained heavy yields from small plots by planting seeds individually and by carefully hoeing the soil around each plant and vine. Tull adapted French methods to the much larger grain fields of England. In place of the inefficient custom of scattering seed broadcast, he planted it deep in regular rows with a horse-drawn "drilling machine," and he cultivated his crops with a horse-drawn hoe. The improvements of Tull and Townshend won enthusiastic praise from Arthur Young (1741–1820), the articulate publicist of the new agriculture, who published lengthy reports on his frequent trips through the farming districts of the British Isles and on the Continent. Young won an international following that included George III, George Washington, the Marquis de Lafayette, and Catherine the Great.

Before 1789, however, the new agriculture gained the support of only the most enterprising landlords, and even in Britain it was practiced mainly by the holders of large estates. Yet uneven though it was, the agricultural revolution of the eighteenth century came close to ending actual famines in Europe, even if it did not prevent recurring shortages of food. It also marked an important stage in the long, gradual shift from the largely self-sufficient manor of the Middle Ages to the modern capitalist farm producing specialized crops. The improving landlords needed large amounts of capital, and they also needed large plots of land that were not subdivided into long, narrow strips for individual cultivators or otherwise used in common by many individuals. Since these old ways hampered the new agriculture, there was a mounting demand that common fields be fenced off as the private lands of single proprietors. Enclosures, which in Tudor England were introduced to extend sheep pastures, were now sought in order to increase cropland. The new enclosure movement reached its peak in the last decades of the eighteenth century and the first decades of the nineteenth, when Parliament passed hundreds of separate enclosure acts affecting several million acres. Rural England was assuming its modern aspect of large fields fenced by hedgerows.

Enclosures, then, created large farms well suited to the application of drill-planting, horse-hoeing, and crop rotation. They enabled Britain to feed her growing population by increasing her agricultural output. But they also created widespread social misery. In Georgian England, as in ancient Greece and Rome, the development of capitalistic estates ruined many small farmers, or yeomen, who could not get along without their rights to use common lands and who could not afford to buy tools, install fences, and become improving landlords themselves. Many of them became hired hands on big farms or sought work in the expanding towns.

The Beginnings of the Industrial Revolution

By increasing productivity and at the same time releasing part of the farm labor force for other jobs, the revolution in agriculture aided that in industry. Industry also required raw materials (supplied in part by colonies overseas), markets (also furnished in part by colonies), and capital (much of it subscribed by merchants) to finance the building and equipping of factories. Thus the prosperity of commerce also nourished the growth of industry.

In textiles, the making of yarn and cloth had long been organized under the "domestic system." Spinners and weavers worked at home on simple wheels and looms; often they did not buy their own raw materials or market their finished products but worked as wage-laborers for an entrepreneur who furnished the raw materials and sold the finished yarn and cloth. In other industries, however, production was sometimes organized not under the domestic system but in primitive factories, which assembled many laborers in a large workshop, though hand processes rather than machines were still used. These early factories were particularly common in enterprises requiring close supervision for reasons of state, like cannon foundries, or because they used expensive materials, like gold or silver threads for luxury cloth.

The Industrial Revolution made the domestic system obsolete and transformed the factory system. Machines superseded the spinning wheel, hand loom, and other simple hand tools, and water or steam replaced

Hargreaves' spinning jenny.

human muscle and animal energy as the source of power. Because power-driven machines were often big and complicated, larger factories were needed to house them. By 1789 these revolutionary changes had affected only a handful of industries, but they were of critical importance—mining, metallurgy, munitions, and textiles.

Coal mining was becoming a big business, largely because of the increased demand for coke by iron smelters, which had previously employed charcoal to make ore into iron. Although charcoal continued to be used in Sweden and other countries with abundant supplies of wood, in England, where most of the great forests had been cut down, the price of charcoal rose so high that it constituted 80 percent of the cost of producing iron. By 1750, despite the abundant native supply of ore, the output of English smelters was declining rapidly, and the country was using more and more imported iron. Ordinary coal could not replace charcoal as smelter fuel because the chemicals in coal made the iron too brittle. The Darby family of Shropshire discovered how to remove the chemical impurities from coal by an oven process that converted it into coke. In England, the Darbys and other private firms were the pioneers in metallurgy. On the Continent, governments took the lead—a significant exception to the rule about the inability of states to solve economic problems. France and Prussia met their requirements for large quantities of munitions by setting up state-financed foundries and arms factories.

The revolution in textiles was focused on the cheaper production of cotton cloth. The flying shuttle, a technical device first applied to the hand loom in England (1733), enabled a single weaver to do work that had previously required the services of two. Looms equipped with the flying shuttle used up the supply of hand-spun thread so rapidly that a private organization, the London Society for the Encouragement of Arts, Manufactures and Commerce, offered a prize for improvement of the spinning process. James Hargreaves won the prize in 1764 with his spinning jenny, a series of spinning wheels geared together to make eight threads simultaneously. Soon the jenny was adapted to water power, and its output was increased to a hundred or more threads at once. The eventual emancipation of industry from dependence on unreliable water power was foreshadowed in the 1760s when the Scotsman James Watt introduced the steam engine.

Although Britain had nearly 150 cotton mills in 1789, woolens and dozens of other basic commodities were still made by hand. Full industrial development would not take place until the canal and railroad permitted cheap transport of heavy freight and until the shortages of capital and skilled labor were overcome. A Swedish inventor of the early 1700s designed excellent machines for cutting wheels and files but could not raise the money to put them into operation. And in Britain the difficulty of making precise parts for Watt's engine delayed its production in large quantities. Although the eighteenth century had taken many of the initial steps in the Industrial Revolution, it remained for the next century to apply them on a truly revolutionary scale.

III The Established Powers
Britain

Leadership in the economic revolutions was making Britain the wealthiest nation in the world. British bankers, buttressed by the Bank of England and by careful management of the national debt, extended credit to business enterprises at the relatively low interest rate of 5 percent. The square mile comprising the City of London proper and including the financial district recovered quickly from the South Sea Bubble and challenged Amsterdam's position as the international capital of trade and finance. In the course of the eighteenth century, British merchants outdistanced their old trading rivals, the Dutch, and gradually took the lead over their new competitors, the French. Judged by the three touchstones of mercantilism—commerce, colonies, and sea power—Britain was the strongest state in Europe.

The British colonial empire, however, was not a mercantilist undertaking in the full sense. Supervision of the colonies rested with a government department, the Board of Trade, which followed an easygoing policy of "salutary neglect," in sharp contrast to the rigid controls exerted by other colonial powers over their possessions. In the long run, as the American Revolution was to show, "salutary neglect" did not satisfy the colonists, but in the short run it worked reasonably well by promoting the colonists' prosperity and self-reliance.

The Royal Navy enjoyed the assets of a superior officer corps and greater size. Future captains went to sea at the age of sixteen or even younger, and passed through long practical training before receiving commissions. The ships they commanded in the mid-century wars were inferior in design to those of France and Spain; but there were more of them. Britain had a 2 to 1 advantage over France in number of warships, a 6 to 1 lead in merchant ships, and a 10 to 1 lead in total number of experienced seamen, merchant and naval. In wartime, the fleet could draw on the merchant marine for additional sailors and auxiliary vessels. Service in the Royal Navy had its grim aspects. Food was monotonous and unhealthy, and punishments included flogging and keel-hauling, in which the victim was dragged the length of the barnacle-encrusted keel. Since these were the common afflictions of all sailors in the eighteenth century, however, they did not put the British navy at a comparative disadvantage.

The British army, by contrast, was neither large nor impressive. Its officers were reputed to be the poorest in Europe, and its soldiers were in part mercenaries from the German state of Hesse-Cassel, the Hessians of the American Revolutionary War. Neglect of the army was a deliberate policy. The British Isles were relatively safe from invasion; moreover, the English people feared a standing army as an instrument of potential absolutism, for they remembered the uses that Cromwell and James II had made of this weapon.

The Glorious Revolution, which in its preliminary stage had done so much to confirm distrust of the army, had also confirmed Britain's unique and greatest asset— the supremacy of Parliament. Parliament had approved the accession of William and Mary in place of James II. When Anne, Mary's sister and the last Stuart monarch, died in 1714, Parliament had already arranged for the succession of the House of Hanover. Under the first kings of the new house—George I (1714–1727) and George II (1727–1760)—the institution that would ultimately ensure the everyday assertion of parliamentary supremacy was beginning to mature. This was the cabinet.

In our day the British cabinet is a committee of the majority party of the House of Commons, headed by the prime minister, and it remains in office as long as it can continue to enlist the support of a majority in Commons. It is Her Majesty's Government, while the chief minority party forms Her Majesty's Opposition, a loyal opposition whose leader receives an official salary. The cabinet rules because it controls the executive branch of the government; the monarch merely reigns.

Under the first two Hanoverian kings the cabinet was only starting to accumulate this immense authority. George I and George II by no means abdicated all the old royal prerogatives. They took a direct interest in the South Sea Bubble and other financial matters, and they intervened in the conduct of war and diplomacy to a degree that would be regarded as highly improper today. George II was the last English monarch to command troops in person on the battlefield—in 1743 during the War of the Austrian Succession. The two Georges chose their cabinet ministers from the Whig party, then in control of the Commons. They did so, however, not because they were required to, but because it suited their convenience and because they thoroughly distrusted the Tories, some of whom were involved in futile Jacobite plots to restore to the throne the descendants of James II (Jacobite from *Jacobus*, Latin for James). The Whigs, on the other hand, had engineered the Glorious Revolution and had arranged the Hanoverian succession.

For two decades after the collapse of the South Sea Bubble, from 1721 to 1742, Robert Walpole, who led the Whigs in the Commons, headed the cabinet; he was in fact prime minister, although the title was still unofficial. Walpole was a master politician who maintained his majority in the Commons by skillful manipulation of the Whigs. The task was not easy, for party discipline of the modern kind did not yet exist; the terms "Whig" and "Tory" referred to informal and shifting interest groups, not to parties in our sense. In 1733, when Walpole forced the resignation of ministers opposed to his plan for radical fiscal reform, he took a major step toward establishing the principle of cabinet unanimity on a crucial issue.

Under the first two Georges the Whigs were a coalition of landed and "funded" gentry; that is, of nobles and squires from the country and of business and professional men from London and provincial towns. Thus the Whigs renewed a political alliance that had first appeared in the later Middle Ages when the knights of the shire had joined the burgesses to form the Commons. In the Whig parliaments the country gentlemen predominated by sheer numbers; in 1754, for instance, they outnumbered by 5 to 1 the merchants and lawyers sitting in the House of Commons. Family ties, common political aims, and a common reverence for property bound together the rural and urban Whigs. In order to consolidate the gains of the Glorious Revolution, the Whigs opposed Jacobite schemes and supported the unprepossessing Hanoverians. To protect property, they passed legislation making death the penalty for stealing livestock, for cutting down cherry trees, and for other relatively minor offenses.

What did terms like "gentry," "gentleman," and "squire" connote about social class in the eighteenth century? Historians are still debating the question, but it is generally agreed that they referred to a class just below the titled nobility. The ranks of the gentry included the younger sons of nobles, technically not nobles themselves since the title and a seat in the House of Lords passed only to the eldest son. They also included other owners of landed estates, all of whom were addressed verbally as "sir" and in writing as "Esquire" (originally a shieldbearer, the lieutenant of the feudal knight). Historically, the gentry lived off the revenues of landed property, but by the eighteenth century many of them also had a stake in commercial ventures. Indeed, successful businessmen sometimes bought country estates, set themselves up as gentlemen, and were accepted as such by the local gentry. The intermingling of country gentlemen with men of business and intermarriage of the two classes demonstrated that Britain enjoyed more social mobility than did the states of the Old Regime on the Continent.

Robert Walpole himself exemplified the Whig fusion of landed and funded elements. He inherited his manners and his tastes from his father, a country squire. A heavy drinker and a devotee of bawdy stories, he established the English politician's tradition of the long country weekend in order to indulge his passion for hunting. Like many Whig squires, Walpole married into the aristocracy of trade; his wife was the daughter of a timber merchant and former Lord Mayor of London. As prime minister, Walpole, the country gentleman, promoted the interests of the City by ensuring political stability through Whig cabinets and financial stability through the gradual retirement of the national debt.

In social and political structure, the Britain of Walpole was, of course, oligarchic rather than demo-

A political campaign in England: Hogarth's "Canvassing for Votes" (1757).

cratic. Only gentlemen could hope to rise in the professions, to become army and navy officers, lawyers, clergymen, and physicians. In local affairs, the landed gentry alone supplied the justices of the peace, who not only presided over courts, but also fixed wage scales, superintended the relief of the poor, provided for the maintenance of bridges and highways, and were fanatic defenders of the propertied classes. Their stringent enforcement of the laws against theft accounts for the saying "As well be hanged for a sheep as for a lamb."

In the main, only gentlemen had the right to vote for members of Parliament. The small number of voters in many constituencies encouraged corruption, particularly in the "rotten" or "pocket" boroughs, which had such a tiny electorate that control of their vote reposed in the pocket of some wealthy lord. Politicians often bribed voters outright or else promised them places on the government payroll. An immensely rich Whig, the duke of Newcastle, controlled the outcome of elections in four counties and in seven pocket boroughs.

Thus in Britain, as on the Continent, the ruling classes governed the voteless masses. And the masses were sometimes in material terms worse off than their continental counterparts, as in the case of the landless agricultural workers whose numbers mounted with the enclosure movement. London was already big enough to have incipiently, at least, all the troubles of a modern metropolis—slums, crimes of violence, even traffic jams—and an almost complete lack of police and fire protection. (Of juvenile delinquency we do not hear much, partly because it melted into the very considerable adult delinquency, and partly because in those days of widespread child labor there were not many idle children.)

Yet the British ruling classes, selfish and narrow-minded though they often were, had at their best a sense of noblesse oblige, of public spirit and civic-mindedness. Within the aristocracy of land and trade there were fewer social barriers than on the Continent, and the English gentry were on the whole more responsive than their continental counterparts to the need for changes and reform. Disraeli, the great nineteenth-century Tory, dubbed the Whig cabinets of the first two Georges a "Venetian oligarchy," by which he meant that the wealthy ran the country for their private benefit, like the merchants of Renaissance Venice. And so they did; yet the Whigs, for all their oligarchy and their corruption, provided the most enlightened government in eighteenth-century Europe.

France

Where Britain was strong, France was weak. In the France of Louis XV (1715–1774), barriers to social mobility were more difficult to surmount, though commoners who were rich or aggressive enough did overcome them. France suffered particularly from the rigidity of its colonial system, the inferiority of its navy, and the very mediocre abilities of most of its statesmen. The ministry of the navy, which ruled the overseas empire, regarded these possessions as so many warships permanently at anchor. It refused to sanction steps toward self-government and applied the same regulations to colonies as different as the sugar islands of the West Indies and the wilderness of Canada. The plethora of controls stifled the initiative of the colonists, and the French imperial system lacked the elasticity to meet the test of war. The mother country, however, prospered, as commercial activity doubled in Nantes, Bordeaux, and other ports, and refineries were set up to process the raw sugar imported from the plantations of Guadeloupe and Martinique.

The French navy needed greater resources and better leadership. Its warships, though admirably designed, were inadequate in number. Since Dutch and British vessels carried much of French commerce, the merchant marine was too small to supplement the fleet. French naval officers, though rigorously trained in the classroom, lacked the experience gained by British captains in a lifetime at sea. Moreover, in a fashion characteristic of the Old Regime at its worst, officers from the aristocracy devoted much of their energies to thwarting the rise of those from the middle class.

French rulers were almost bound to neglect the navy in favor of the army, since France was above all a land power, and its vulnerable northeastern frontier, lying across the Flemish plain, invited invasion. Except in size, however, the army of Louis XV scarcely lived up to the great traditions of Louis XIV. The troops were poorly trained, and the organization was top-heavy. There was one officer to fifteen men, compared with one to thirty-five in the more efficient Prussian army. Many aristocratic officers regarded a commission simply as a convenient way of increasing their personal wealth.

Both the navy and the army underwent important reforms later in the century after the defeats suffered by France in the Seven Years' War (1756–1763). The number of warships was increased, the army officer corps was cleared of much deadwood, and more aggressive military tactics were introduced. These improvements accounted in part for the excellent showing made by France in the American Revolutionary War and in the military campaigns resulting from her own revolution. They came too late, however, to save the vanishing prestige of the Old Regime.

The Old Regime was weakest at its head, the monarchy itself. There were no sun kings in France after the death of Louis XIV, and few ministers who approached the caliber of Richelieu or Colbert. The duke of Orléans, regent from 1715 to 1723, was a gambler, drunkard, and pervert, who popularized the word *roué* by remarking that his lecherous friends deserved to be broken on the wheel (*roue* is French for "wheel"). The regent, however, did attempt two important experiments. He allowed John Law to try out his system, as we have seen, and, in place of Louis XIV's method of ruling through individual bourgeois ministers, he set up a series of ministerial councils staffed by men from distinguished noble families. Although the first experiment produced some beneficial results, the second failed, after a three-year trial, in part because of the endless squabbles among the noble councillors, particularly between the nobles of the robe and the nobles of the sword, "between the grandnephews of lawyers and the ever-so-great-grandsons of feudal lords." The French second estate had outlived its usefulness. The regency proved that the nobles were no longer able to govern; the mid-century wars proved that they were no longer able to lead French armies to victory.

They were, however, still capable of causing trouble. The strongholds of the nobles of the robe were the important courts known as parlements, in Paris and in some provincial capitals. The parlements took advantage of the regency to extend their long-standing claim to register government edicts before they were published and enforced. A papal bull condemned the doctrines of the influential French Catholic minority of Jansenists, who had family ties with the judges of the parlements, and whose differences with the Crown were now more a matter of politics than of religion. When the Parlement of Paris refused to register the bull, the regent held a *lit de justice,* a special royal session obliging the Parlement to follow the royal command. But the judges of the parlements in Paris and elsewhere retaliated by going on strike, refusing to carry on their normal court business. The cold war between parlement and king continued for half a century. It was marked by repeated strikes on the part of the judges, by the exiling of recalcitrant judges from the capital by the king, and in the 1760s by the suppression, at the behest of the parlements, of the Jesuits, the great foe of the

Jansenists. In the last years of his reign Louis XV tried to solve the problem once and for all by suppressing the parlements and substituting new courts more under royal control. But the parlements were to return, more arrogant than ever, under his successor.

Soon after the end of Orléans' regency power passed to one of the few statesmen of prerevolutionary France, Cardinal Fleury, the tutor of Louis XV and the chief minister from 1726 until his death in 1743 in his ninetieth year. Without attempting basic reforms, the aged cardinal, in the words of Voltaire, "treated the state as a powerful and robust body which could cure itself." Fleury did not remedy the chronic and deep-seated injustice and inefficiency of French fiscal methods, but he did stabilize the coinage, and he put the farming of taxes on a more businesslike basis by restricting tax-farmers to the comparatively modest profit of $7\frac{1}{2}$ percent. To make loans more readily available, he established state pawnshops in the chief cities of France. Fleury's success impressed Lady Mary Montagu, the observant wife of an English diplomat, who wrote in 1739:

France is so much improved, it is not . . . the same country we passed through twenty years ago. Everything I see speaks in praise of Cardinal Fleury; the roads are all mended . . . and such good care taken against robbers, that you may cross the country with your purse in your hand. . . . The French are more changed than their roads; instead of pale, yellow faces, wrapped up in blankets, as we saw them, the villages are filled with fresh-coloured lusty peasants, in good cloth and clean linen. It is incredible the air of plenty and content that is over the whole country. *

The administrative stability achieved by Fleury soon vanished after Louis XV began his personal rule in 1743. Intelligent but timid, lazy, and debauched, Louis XV did not have the interest or the patience to supervise the details of government in the manner of Louis XIV. He appointed and dismissed ministers on a personal whim or at the bidding of his mistresses and favorites. In thirty years he had eighteen different foreign secretaries and fourteen different controllers general (the chief fiscal officer). Each change in personnel meant a shift in policy, and Louis aggravated the instability by conspiring against his own appointees. France had two conflicting foreign policies: that of the diplomatic corps and the King's Secret, conducted by royal agents who operated at cross purposes with the regular diplomats. Yet, while allowing the reins of government to go slack, Louis refused to give them over to firmer hands.

Nevertheless, France remained a great power. Still the most populous country in Europe, she possessed almost inexhaustible reserves of strength. Her army, though enfeebled, was the largest in the world, and her

*M. W. Montagu, *Letters,* Everyman edition (New York, 1906), pp. 271–272.

navy was the second largest. She led the world in overseas trade until Britain forged ahead of her in the last quarter of the eighteenth century. French tastes, French thought, and the French language retained the international preeminence they had won in the age of Louis XIV. The misgovernment and the other weaknesses of the Old Regime were relative rather than absolute.

The Other States of Western Europe

Spain was the only other state in western Europe with a claim to great-power status. Sweden and the Dutch Republic could no longer sustain the major international roles they had taken during the seventeenth century. During the first two decades of the new century, the Great Northern War killed off the flower of Swedish manhood and withered Sweden's Baltic empire. The Dutch, exhausted by their wars against Louis XIV, could not afford a large navy or an energetic foreign policy. There was considerable truth in Frederick the Great's gibe that Holland "was a cockboat in the tow of the English frigate." When William III of Orange (and England) died in 1702, many of the Dutch provinces permitted his quasi-monarchical office of stadholder to stand vacant, and dominance passed to the merchant oligarchy. This was a swing of the political pendulum that had occurred twice before in the history of the Dutch Republic. Dutch seaborne trade, though no longer the greatest in Europe, continued to be substantial, and the republic settled down to a life of prosperity and relative obscurity.

Spain suffered comparatively little damage from the great war over the succession to her throne that was fought in the early 1700s. The loss of Belgium and parts of Italy in the Utrecht settlement of 1713 reduced the unwieldy Spanish domains to more manageable size. The new Bourbon kings were a marked improvement over the Spanish Hapsburgs. Philip V (1700–1746), the first Bourbon monarch, infused fresh life into the country's fossilized institutions by importing French advisers schooled in the system of Louis XIV. He also enlisted the aid of two able adventurers, Alberoni and Ripperda, whose fantastic careers almost outdid John Law's. Alberoni, the son of an Italian gardener, was successively a cook, a diplomat, the chief minister of Spain, and a cardinal. Ripperda, a Dutch business expert and diplomat, ultimately lost the favor of Philip, entered the service of the sultan of Morocco, and, after a lifelong alternation between the Protestant and Catholic faiths, died a Muslim. Philip and his remarkable advisers cut down the excessive formalities and endless delays of Spanish administration. They reasserted the authority of the monarchy over the traditionally powerful nobility and clergy. They improved the tax system, encouraged industry, built up the navy, and fortified strategic points in the Spanish empire in America.

The new dispensation, however, did not strike at the root causes of Spanish decline. The greed of governors and the restrictions of mercantilism still checked the progress of the colonies. The mother country remained impoverished, burdened with reactionary noble and clerical castes, and hampered by inadequate resources. Philip V himself was neurotic, refusing, for instance, to cut his toenails, which grew so long that he limped. He was dominated by his strong-willed second wife, Elizabeth Farnese, the patroness of Alberoni. Since Philip's son by his first marriage would inherit Spain, Elizabeth was determined to find thrones for her own two sons. Her persistent attempts to secure the succession of Italian states for them repeatedly threatened the peace of Europe.

Italy and Germany

By 1715, the Italian states had lost much of the political and economic power they had enjoyed during the Renaissance. It is easy to see why. The opening of new worlds overseas and the rise of Spain, England, and the other Atlantic Powers had diminished the importance of the Mediterranean. In the Mediterranean itself, the Ottoman Turks and their satellites in North Africa long menaced Italian shipping and trade. Moreover, beginning with the French invasion of 1494, Italy had been threatened with conquest by one or another of the new national monarchies.

It was the Spanish Hapsburgs who made that conquest. For almost two centuries they ruled Milan, Naples, and Sicily directly, and dominated the rest of the peninsula. In the readjustment of the European balance in 1713, Italy exchanged one foreign master for another, as the Austrian Hapsburgs took over the Italian possessions of their Spanish cousins. On the completion of the readjustment in 1720, the political map of the peninsula showed Austria established in Lombardy, flanked by the decaying commercial republics of Venice and Genoa. In the mountainous northwest was the small but rising state of Piedmont-Savoy, technically the Kingdom of Sardinia after its acquisition of that island in 1720. Farther down the peninsula were the Grand Duchy of Tuscany (formerly the Republic of Florence), the Papal States, and the Austrian Two Sicilies. None of these states was more than a minor power.

Yet Italy could not be written off as a negligible quantity in the eighteenth century. Rome remained the capital of Catholicism, Venice still produced fine painters, and Naples was the schoolmaster of European musicians. Lombardy, Tuscany, and Naples all contributed to the economic and intellectual advances of the century. Meantime, Italy was a major stake in balance-of-power politics, a perennial source of dissension and spoils. In 1720, to counter the ambitions of the Spanish queen, Elizabeth Farnese, the Austrian Hapsburgs took over the island of Sicily, which had gone to Piedmont in the Utrecht settlement; in return, Piedmont secured

Sardinia, originally assigned to Austria. In the 1730s, a series of exchanges gave the Two Sicilies to Elizabeth's elder son, "Baby Carlos," while the Austrians gained some minor bits of territory and the succession of Tuscany. In 1768, Genoa sold the island of Corsica to France. Italy was, in the old phrase, merely "a geographical expression," not a single political entity but a series of parts manipulated by ambitious dynasts and empire-builders from outside the peninsula.

In some respects Germany deserved even more to be called a geographical expression, for it was divided into three hundred states, large, small, and minute. The Peace of Westphalia in 1648 had enhanced the sovereign rights of the particular German states and reduced virtually to zero the authority of their nominal overlord, the Holy Roman Emperor. Unlike Italy, however, Germany did include two considerable powers—one long established in the family of great powers, Austria; and one newcomer, Prussia.

Austria and the Hapsburgs

The Hapsburg rulers of Austria won a series of military and diplomatic victories in the two decades before 1715. In 1699, by the peace of Karlovitz, they recovered Hungary from the Ottoman Turks, thereby advancing their own *Drang nach Osten* (push to the East). In 1713, though they failed to keep the old Hapsburg crown of Spain from going to the Bourbon Philip V, they were compensated with Spain's Belgian and Italian territories. Yet these last acquisitions were distant from the main bloc of Hapsburg lands in central Europe.

Charles VI (1711–1740), aware that his title of Holy Roman Emperor conferred little real authority, concentrated on the Hapsburg family possessions. He spent much of his reign persuading his own noble subjects to ratify the Pragmatic Sanction, a constitutional agreement whereby, in the absence of sons, his daughter Maria Theresa would succeed him in all his lands. A good deal of scorn has been directed at Charles for devoting so much time and energy to a scrap of paper, but recent historians have noted that the Pragmatic Sanction did indeed establish the principle of linking together the scattered family territories. Much, however, remained to be done to consolidate Hapsburg rule over an assemblage of lands that represented many different nations and could never be forged into a single national monarchy. In three key national areas— German Austria, Czech Bohemia, and Magyar Hungary—the nobles still kept most of their medieval prerogatives and, by controlling local estates and diets, controlled grants of taxes and the appointment of officials. The financial and military weakness of the Hapsburg regime was underlined by the fact that when Charles VI died in 1740, the exchequer was nearly empty and the pay of the army and of the civil service was more than two years in arrears. The army was well short of its paper strength of 100,000 men as it faced

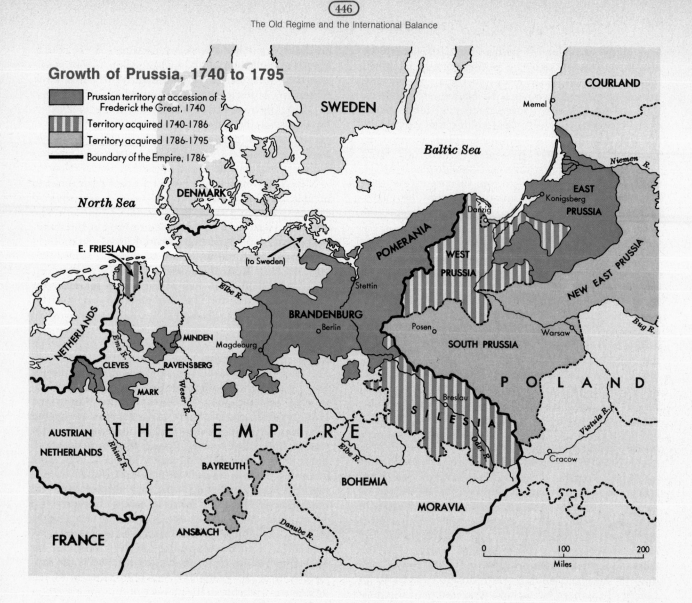

Growth of Prussia, 1740 to 1795

- ▉ Prussian territory at accession of Frederick the Great, 1740
- ▤ Territory acquired 1740-1786
- ▨ Territory acquired 1786-1795
- ▬ Boundary of the Empire, 1786

SWEDEN

COURLAND

Memel

Baltic Sea

Niemen R.

North Sea

DENMARK

EAST PRUSSIA

Konigsberg

E. FRIESLAND

Danzig

POMERANIA

WEST PRUSSIA

NEW EAST PRUSSIA

(to Sweden)

Stettin

NETHERLANDS

Elbe R.

BRANDENBURG

Berlin

Posen

SOUTH PRUSSIA

Warsaw

Bug R.

MINDEN

Magdeburg

Ems R.

CLEVES

RAVENSBERG

MARK

Weser R.

POLAND

Breslau

SILESIA

Oder R.

Vistula R.

AUSTRIAN NETHERLANDS

THE EMPIRE

Rhine R.

Elbe R.

Cracow

BAYREUTH

BOHEMIA

FRANCE

ANSBACH

Danube R.

MORAVIA

0   100   200
Miles

the great test of strength with Prussia that came in 1740.

IV The Newcomers

Prussia and the Hohenzollerns

Whereas Austria enjoyed the appearances more than the realities of great-power status, Prussia possessed few of the appearances but a great many of the realities. Its territories were scattered across north Germany from the Rhine on the west to the Vistula and beyond on the east. Consisting largely of sand and swamp, these lands had meager natural resources and supported relatively little trade. With fewer than three million inhabitants in 1715, Prussia ranked twelfth among the European states in population. Her capital city, Berlin, located on the unimportant river Spree, had few of the obvious geographical advantages enjoyed by Constantinople, Paris, London, and the other great capitals. A wise prophet in 1600 might well have foreseen that Catholic Austria would never unite a Germany in which Protestantism was so strong. But he would probably have predicted that a new Germany would be centered in Frankfurt in the heart of the Rhine country, or in Leipzig or Dresden in Saxony; he would hardly have chosen the unpromising town of Berlin and the minor house of Hohenzollern.

The Hohenzollerns had been established since the fifteenth century as electors of Brandenburg, which lay between the Elbe and Oder rivers. A Hohenzollern was the last master of the Teutonic Knights, a crusading order which in the thirteenth century had pushed the Germanic frontier beyond the Vistula to a land called Prussia at the southeast corner of the Baltic Sea. In 1618, when East Prussia fell to the Hohenzollerns, it was separated from Brandenburg by Polish West Prussia and was still nominally a fief held from the Polish king. In western Germany in the meantime (1614), the Hohenzollerns acquired Cleves, Mark, and some other parcels in the lower Rhine valley and Westphalia. Thus, when Frederick William, the Great Elector (1640–1688), succeeded to the Hohenzollern inheritance as the Thirty Years' War was drawing to a close, his lands consisted of a nucleus in Brandenburg with separate outlying regions to the east and west. With extraordinary persistence, the rulers of Brandenburg-Prussia for the next two hundred years devoted themselves to the task of making a solid block of territory out of these bits and pieces.

The Great Elector was the first in a line of able Hohenzollern rulers. In foreign policy, he won recognition from Poland as the full sovereign of Prussia, no longer subject to Polish overlordship. He also tried, with less success, to dislodge the Swedes from the Pomeranian territories between Brandenburg and the Baltic that they had acquired in 1648. Though he won military renown by defeating the Swedes at Fehrbellin in 1675, he made few practical gains because of his own tortuous diplomacy. In the wars against Louis XIV, he shifted repeatedly from the French to the anti-French side and back.

In domestic policy, his accomplishments were more substantial. He had found his domains largely ruined by war, the farms wasted, the population cut in half, the army reduced to a disorderly rabble of a few thousand men. The Great Elector repaired the damage thoroughly. To augment the population, he encouraged the immigration of Polish Jews and other refugees from religious persecution, notably twenty thousand French Huguenots to whom he gave partial exemption from taxation. He built a small but efficient standing army that enabled Prussia to command large foreign subsidies for participating in the campaigns for or against Louis XIV. In peacetime, he assigned the soldiers to the construction of public works like the canal between the Elbe and the Oder.

In administration, the Great Elector fixed the Hohenzollern pattern of militarized absolutism, a policy in which he was assisted by an educational tradition and a Lutheran state church that taught the virtues of obedience and discipline. On his accession, he found that in all three territories—Prussia, Brandenburg, and Cleves-Mark—the authority of the ruler was limited by estates, medieval assemblies representing the landed nobles and the townspeople. In all three territories he battled the estates for supremacy and won, thereby delaying for two centuries the introduction of representative government into the Hohenzollern realm. He gradually gathered into his own hands the crucial power of levying taxes. Much of the actual work of collecting taxes and performing other administrative functions was done by the war office and the army; policing, too, was done by the military. Like Louis XIV, the Great Elector reduced the independence of the aristocracy; unlike Louis, however, he relied not on bourgeois officials but on a working alliance with the landed gentry, particularly the celebrated Junkers of East Prussia. He confirmed the Junkers' absolute au-

thority over the serfs on their estates and their ascendancy over the towns, and he encouraged them to serve the state, especially as army officers. In contrast with other monarchies, the absolutism of the Hohenzollerns rested on the cooperation of the sovereign and the aristocracy, not on their mutual antagonism.

Under the Great Elector's son, Frederick I (1688–1713), Prussia played only a minor role in the last two wars against Louis XIV and made few territorial gains in the Utrecht settlement. But in 1701 Frederick made a significant gain in prestige by assuming the title "King in Prussia" and insisting on international recognition of his new status as the price for his entry into the War of the Spanish Succession. Though technically Frederick was king only in East Prussia, which lay outside the boundaries of the Holy Roman Empire, even a limited royal title conferred added dignity on the Hohenzollerns. In living up to his new eminence, however, King Frederick I nearly bankrupted his state by lavish expenditures on the trappings of monarchy. Since he thought that a suggestion of marital infidelity enhanced the majesty of a king, he maintained an official mistress with whom he took decorous afternoon promenades. Actually, he was happily married, and his talented queen enlivened the provincial Hohenzollern court by inviting intellectuals and artists to Berlin. As Frederick the Great later remarked, under Frederick I, Berlin was the "Athens of the north."

But as Frederick the Great also remarked, it became the "Sparta of the north," under the next king, Frederick William I (1713–1740). The flirtation with luxury and the finer things of life proved to be a passing exception to the usual Hohenzollern austerity. Frederick William I returned with a vengeance to the policies of the Great Elector and devoted himself entirely to economy, absolutism, and the army. As soon as he had given his father a lavish funeral, he dismissed most of the officials of the court, converted a large portion of the royal palace into offices, and reduced governmental expenses to a fraction of what they had been. He reiterated the order *Ein Plus machen* ("make a surplus"), and he bequeathed a full treasury to his son. His frugality enabled him to undertake the occasional project that he thought worthwhile, such as financing the immigration of twelve thousand South German Protestants to open up new farmlands in eastern Prussia.

To strengthen royal control over the apparatus of state, Frederick William I instituted a small board of experts, with the wonderfully Germanic title of Generaloberfinanzkriegsunddomänendirektorium (General Superior Finance, War, and Domain Directory). Individual members were charged both with administering departments of the central government and with supervising provinces. The arrangement, while cumbersome, did detach provincial administration from local interests and bring it under closer royal control. The king, who insisted on hard work and punctuality, treated the experts of the General Directory as he treated lesser officials, paying them meanly and belaboring them with his cane for slovenly performance of their duties. A late arrival at one of the daily sessions of the General Directory paid a severe fine; an unexcused absentee faced six months in jail.

Frederick William I doubled the size of the standing army and established state factories to provide it with guns and uniforms. To conserve the strength of the laboring force in his underpopulated state, he furloughed troops to work on the farms nine months a year. The army prompted his sole extravagance—a regiment of grenadiers, all six feet tall or over, who wore special caps more than a foot high to increase the impression of size. In recruiting his beloved "giants," the king threw economy to the winds, employing scores of scouts in other German states, paying exorbitant prices, and even trading royal musicians and prize stallions for especially tall specimens. Frederick William cherished his army too much to undertake an adventurous foreign policy. His only significant military campaign was against Sweden in the last phase of the Great Northern War, whereby Prussia obtained in 1720 part of Swedish Pomerania and also the important Baltic port of Stettin at the mouth of the Oder River. Thus Frederick William advanced the Great Elector's old aim of liquidating the Swedish possessions in Germany.

Eighteenth-century observers rightly called the Prussia of Frederick William an armed camp and berated its army for being a "gigantic penal institution" in which minor infractions of regulations brought the death penalty. The king himself, obsessed with military matters, neglected the education of his subjects, showed scant concern for culture, and despised everything French. He carried parsimony to the extreme of refusing pensions to soldiers' widows, and the meager fees he permitted judges and lawyers to earn encouraged the corruption and lethargy that obstructed the course of justice in Prussia. Yet his regime worked, and in terms of power, worked extremely well, despite its glaring shortcomings. The Junkers, although feudal in outlook, were intensely loyal to the Hohenzollerns and made splendid officers. The army, though smaller than those of France, Russia, and Austria, was the best drilled and disciplined in Europe. When Frederick William I died in 1740, the Prussian David was ready to fight the Austrian Goliath.

Russia and Peter the Great

Even more spectacular than the rise of Prussia was the emergence of Russia as a major power during the era of Peter the Great (1682–1725). In 1682, at the death of Czar Fëdor Romanov, Russia was still a backward country, with few diplomatic links with the West and very little knowledge of the outside world. Contemporaries, Russians as well as foreigners, report on the brutality, immorality, drunkenness, illiteracy, and filth prevalent among all classes of society. Even the clergy, most of whom could not read, set no shining example

by their mode of life. It is little wonder that those aware of conditions in Russia before the advent of Peter have saluted him as the great revolutionary who altered the face of his country. Yet the changes he made were neither so numerous nor so drastic as his admirers have often claimed. Since the foundations for most of them were already present in the society he inherited, Russia would no doubt have become a power of international importance without Peter, although it would have taken longer. Nevertheless, these dilutions of the usual estimate of his contribution do not alter the fact that Peter was an awe-inspiring—and terror-inspiring—figure.

Czar Fëdor died childless in 1682, leaving a retarded brother, Ivan, and an ugly but capable sister, Sophia, both children of Czar Alexis (1645–1676) by his first wife. The ten-year-old Peter was the halfbrother of Ivan and Sophia, the son of Alexis by his second wife, and as bright and vigorous as Ivan was debilitated. A major court feud developed between the partisans of the family of Alexis' first wife and those of the family of the second. At first the old Russian representative assembly, the Zemski Sobor, elected Peter czar. But Sophia, as leader of the opposing faction, won the support of the streltsy, or musketeers, a special branch of the military, many of whom belonged to the conservative schismatic sect of the Old Believers. Undisciplined, and angry with their officers, some of whom had been cheating them, the streltsy were a menace to orderly government. Sophia encouraged the streltsy to attack the Kremlin, and the youthful Peter saw the infuriated troops murder some of his mother's family. For good measure, they killed many nobles living in Moscow and pillaged the archives where the records of serfdom were kept. Though their movement had social implications, it was primarily a successful bid for power by Sophia, who now served as regent for both Ivan and Peter, who were hailed as joint czars.

The ungovernable streltsy continued to terrorize the capital until Sophia threatened them with the regular army. Once the streltsy were calm, she moved to punish the Old Believers and any rebellious serfs who could be captured. The first woman to govern Russia since Kievan times, Sophia was bound to face severe opposition and to be threatened by the maturing Peter, though he was out of favor and away from the court. In the end, the streltsy deserted Sophia, who was shut up in a convent in 1689; from then until Ivan's death in 1696, Peter and his half-brother ruled jointly, though only Peter counted.

The young Peter was almost seven feet tall and extremely lively. He had learned to read and write (but never to spell) from a drunken tutor. Fascinated by war and military games, he had set up a play regiment, staffed it with full-grown men, enlisted as a common soldier in its ranks (promoting himself from time to time), ordered equipment for it from the Moscow arsenals, and drilled it with unflagging vigor, himself firing off cannon or pounding on a drum with equal enjoyment. He discovered a broken-down boat in a barn and unraveled the mysteries of rigging and sail with the help of Dutch sailors living in Moscow. Maneuvers, sailing, and relaxing with his cronies resulted in Peter's neglect of his wife, whom he had married at sixteen and eventually consigned to a convent.

Peter and his cronies were a rowdy lot who smoked huge quantities of tobacco, thereby horrifying conservative Muscovites, who believed that smoking was condemned by the biblical passage which says that what cometh out of the mouth defileth a man. When drunk, they engaged in obscene parodies of church services or played highly dangerous practical jokes, roaring about Moscow in sleighs and shrieking serenades to its sleeping citizens. For parties, staid Moscow ladies, accustomed to almost haremlike seclusion, were commanded to put on low-cut evening dresses in the Western style and dance and carry on social chitchat. If a lady refused to drink with the czar and his friends, Peter simply held her nose and poured the wine down her throat. His boon companion in these escapades was Lefort, a young Swiss soldier of fortune, whom he named field marshal, grand admiral, and "chief diplomat."

The almost frantic energy Peter devoted to pleasure reflected only part of his appetite for new experience. At various times he took up carpentry, shoemaking, cooking, clockmaking, ivory-carving, etching, and—worst of all—dentistry. Once he had acquired a set of dental instruments nobody was safe, since Peter did not care whether the intended victim had a toothache or not; whenever he felt the need to practice, he practiced—and those were the days before anesthetics. Preferring to wear shabby workclothes, driving his own horses, neglecting formal obligations and paying little attention to court and church ceremony, Peter was a shock to Muscovites, and not in the least in keeping with their idea of a proper czar.

After Lefort died in 1700, Peter's favorite was Menshikov, a man of low birth who received high offices, the title of prince, and a huge fortune; like many of the public servants of the period, he was an unscrupulous grafter. Peter later took as his mistress a girl who had already passed through the hands of Menshikov and others; after she gave birth to two of his children, he finally married her in 1712. This was the empress Catherine, a hearty and affectionate woman who was able to control her difficult husband as no other human being could.

Meantime, anxious to try his hand at war, Peter led a campaign against the Turks in the area of the Black Sea. With the help of Dutch experts, he sailed a fleet of riverboats down the Don and defeated the Turks at Azov in 1696. Much curiosity was aroused abroad by this Russian contribution to the war with the Turks in which the Austrians had long been engaged. The project of forming an anti-Turkish league with the states of western Europe now gave Peter a pretext for the first trip outside Russia taken by a

Russian sovereign since the Kievan period. Though ostensibly traveling incognito, Peter was conspicuous as the only authoritarian seven-footer in the party. What fascinated him was Western technology, especially in naval matters, and he planned to go to Holland, England, and Venice, where (in his opinion) the best ships came from, to find out how they were built. He hired several hundred technicians to work in Russia, raised money by selling to an English peer the monopoly of tobacco sales in Russia, and visited every sort of factory or museum or printing press he could find.

These pictures emerge from his travels: Peter laboring as a common hand on the docks in Holland; Peter and his suite, drunk and dirty, wrecking the handsome house and garden of the English diarist John Evelyn near London ("There is a house full of people,"

Russian Expansion in Europe, 1689–1796

- Acquired by Peter the Great, 1689-1725
- Acquired between 1730-1740
- Acquired by Elizabeth, 1741-1762
- Acquired by Catherine, 1762-1796

A contemporary caricature of Peter the Great cutting the beard of a boyar as part of his campaign to modernize Russia.

wrote Evelyn's harassed servant, "and that right nasty"); Peter dancing with a German princess, mistaking her whalebone corsets for her ribs, and commenting loudly that German girls have devilish hard bones; Peter receiving an honorary degree at Oxford or deep in conversation (Dutch) with William Penn about the Quaker faith or gobbling his food without benefit of knife or fork, or asleep with a dozen followers on the floor of a tiny room in a London inn with no windows open.

Before Peter could get to Venice, the trip was interrupted by news that the streltsy had revolted again (1698); Peter rushed home and personally participated in their punishment. Though many innocent men suffered torture and death, Peter broke the streltsy as a power in Russian life. He was more determined than ever to modernize his countrymen and on the very day of his return summoned the court jester to assist him as they went about with a great pair of shears clipping off courtiers' beards. It was an action full of symbolism, for the tradition of the Orthodox Church held that God was bearded; if man was made in the image of God, man must also have a beard, and if he was deprived of it, he became a natural candidate for damnation. Peter now decreed that Russian nobles must shave, or else pay a substantial tax for the privilege of wearing their beards. Bronze beard tokens worn around the neck certified that the tax had been properly paid; without such a token a bearded man ran the risk of being clipped on sight.

Presently, Peter issued an edict commanding that all boyars, members of the gentry class, and the city population generally must abandon long robes with flowing sleeves and tall bonnets, and adopt Western-style costume. The manufacture of the traditional clothes was made illegal, and Peter took up his shears again and cut off the sleeves of people wearing them. The enactments on the beards and on dress were regarded by the victims as an assault on precious customs and a forcible introduction of hated foreign ways.

Peter's policies at home can be understood only in the light of his ever-mounting needs to support virtually incessant warfare. His plan for an international crusade against the Turks collapsed when the Austrians and the Ottoman Empire agreed to the treaty of Karlovitz in 1699. Feeling that Austria had betrayed Russia, Peter made a separate peace with the Turks in 1700. By then he was already planning a new aggression: the victim was to be Sweden, whose large Baltic empire seemed particularly vulnerable since the throne had recently passed to a youth of fifteen, Charles XII (1697–1718). Peter's allies in the enterprise were Denmark and Poland, the latter under its elected king, Augustus the Strong, who was also Elector of Saxony. The three partners might have reconsidered had they seen Charles XII strengthening his sword arm by beheading at a single stroke sheep driven down his palace corridors.

Charles won the opening campaigns of the Great Northern War (1700–1721). He knocked Denmark out of the fighting, frustrated Augustus' attempt to take the Baltic port of Riga, and completely defeated a larger but ill-prepared Russian force at Narva (1700), capturing the entire supply of cannon of which Peter was so proud. Instead of taking advantage of Peter's helplessness and marching into Russia, Charles detoured into Poland, where he spent seven years pursuing Augustus, who finally had to abandon both the Russian alliance and the Polish crown. Charles secured the election of his protégé, Stanislas Leszczyński, as king of Poland.

In the interim, Peter rebuilt his armies and conquered from the Swedes the Baltic provinces nearest to Russia, Ingria and Livonia, in the first of which he founded in 1703 the new city of St. Petersburg. In 1708, Charles swept far to the south and east into the Ukraine in an effort to join forces with the Cossacks, whose leader was his ally. Exhausted by the severe winter, the Swedish forces were defeated by the Russians in the decisive battle of Poltava (1709). Peter now reinstated Augustus as king of Poland, but he was not able to force the Turks to surrender Charles, who had taken refuge with them after Poltava.

To avenge his defeat Charles engineered a war between Turkey and Russia (1710–1711) in the course of which the Russians made their first appeal to the Balkan Christian subjects of the Turks on the basis of their common faith. Bearing banners modeled on those of Constantine, first emperor of Byzantium, Russian forces crossed the river Pruth into the Ottoman Danubian province of Moldavia (today part of Romania).

Here the Ottoman armies trapped Peter in 1711 and forced him to surrender; the Turks could have taken him captive as well but proved unexpectedly lenient, requiring only the surrender of Azov and the creation of an unfortified no man's land between Russian and Ottoman territory. Furious with the Turks for failing to take full advantage of Peter's discomfiture, Charles almost succeeded in provoking still another Russo-Turkish war before the Turks expelled their firebrand visitor in 1714.

The Great Northern War dragged on for seven more years, as Russian forces seized Finland and occupied islands only a few miles from the coast of Sweden. On the diplomatic front, Russia made a series of matrimonial and other alliances with petty German courts, involving herself in central European questions remote from her national interest. The death of Charles XII (1718) cleared the way for peace negotiations, though it took a Russian landing in Sweden proper (1719) to force a decision. At Nystadt (1721), Russia handed back Finland and agreed to pay a substantial sum for the former Swedish possessions along the eastern shore of the Baltic. The opening of this famous "window on the West" meant that seaborne traffic no longer had to sail around the northern edge of Europe to reach Russia. Next, Peter undertook a brief campaign against Persia (1722–1723). At his death in 1725, Russia had been at war for almost all of his thirty-five year reign and had risen from a little-known state somewhere behind Poland to become a major military power capable of affecting the destinies of the western European states.

Constant warfare requires constant supplies of men and money. Peter's government developed a crude form of draft system according to which a given number of households had to supply a given number of recruits. Although more of these men died of disease, hunger, and cold than at the hands of the enemy, and desertion was commonplace, the very length of the Great Northern War meant that survivors served as a tough nucleus for a regular army. Peter built a Baltic fleet at the first opportunity, but Russian naval tradition failed to strike deep roots. From 800 ships (mostly very small) in 1725, the fleet declined to fewer than 20 a decade later; there was no merchant marine whatever. The apprehensions of the English and the Dutch that Russian emergence on the Baltic would create a new maritime nation proved unfounded.

To staff the military forces and the administration, Peter rigorously enforced the rule by which all landowners owed service to the state. For those who failed to register he eventually decreed "civil death," which removed them from the protection of the law and made them subject to attack with impunity. State service became compulsory for life: At the age of fifteen, every male child of the service nobility was assigned to his future post in the army, in the civil service, or at court. Peter often forced them to do jobs they considered beneath them; he did not care whether they were interested in their work or even whether they had been trained for it. And he required that when a member of this class died he must leave his estate intact to one of his sons, not necessarily the eldest, so that it would not be divided anew in every generation.

Thus the class of service nobility—which now included the survivors of the nobility of ancient birth, the old boyars—was brought into complete dependence upon the czar. The system opened the possibility of a splendid career to men with talent, for a person without estates or rank who reached a certain level in any branch of the service (for example, major in the army) automatically received lands and a title of nobility. The nobility of ancient birth viewed this as a cheapening of their position and hated to see new recruits come into their own social order. But under Peter there was little they could do about it.

To raise cash, Peter debased the currency, taxed virtually everything—sales, rents, real estate, tanneries, baths, and beehives—and appointed special revenue-finders to think up new levies. The government held a monopoly over a bewildering variety of products, including salt and oil, coffins and caviar. However, the basic tax on each individual household was not producing enough revenue, partly because the number of households had declined as a result of war and misery, and partly because households were combining in order to evade payment. Peter's government therefore substituted a head tax on every male—the soul tax—making it useless for individuals to conceal themselves in households. This innovation required a new census, which produced a most important, and unintended, social result: The census takers now classified as serfs a large number of floaters on the edge between freedom and serfdom, who thus found themselves and their children eternally labeled as unfree. At the cost of human exploitation, Peter's government managed in its later years to balance the budget.

In the administration, new ministries (prikazy) were first set up to centralize the handling of funds received from various sources. A system of army districts adopted for reasons of military efficiency led to the creation of the first provinces, eight, then nine, then twelve, embracing all Russia. Each province had its own governor, and many of the functions previously carried on inefficiently by the central government were thus decentralized. With the czar often away from the capital, and many of the former prikazy abolished, decentralization had gone so far that Russia seemed at times to have little central government.

Ultimately, Peter copied the Swedish system of central ministries to supersede the old prikazy and created nine "colleges"—for foreign affairs, the army, justice, expenditure, and the like—each administered by an eleven-man collegium. The arrangement discouraged corruption by making any member of a collegium subject to checking by his colleagues, but caused delays in final decisions, which could only be reached after lengthy deliberations. When Peter attempted to model local government on the Swedish example, the experiment failed because of the enormous differences between the two countries in literacy, size, tradition, and attitudes toward civic responsibility. Yet, on the whole, the cumbersome machinery Peter established was superior to any previous Russian administration.

Peter also brought the Church under the collegiate system. Knowing how the clergy loathed his new regime, he began by failing to appoint a successor when the patriarch of Moscow died in 1700. Twenty-one years later he placed the Church under an agency called at first the spiritual college and then the Holy Directing Synod, headed by a procurator who was a layman. Peter's own explanation of why he made the Church a department of state is remarkably frank and also offers a revealing insight into Russian popular psychology:

> From the collegiate government of the church there is not so much danger to the country of disturbances and troubles as may be produced by one spiritual ruler. For the common people do not understand the difference between the spiritual power and that of the autocrat; but, dazzled by the splendor and glory of the highest pastor, they think that he is a second sovereign of like power with the autocrat or with even more, and that the spiritual power is that of another and better realm. If then there should be any difference of opinion between the Patriarch and the Tzar, it might easily happen that the people, perhaps misled by designing persons, should take the part of the Patriarch, in the mistaken belief that they were fighting for God's cause.*

Ever since 1703, Peter had been building a great city in the swamps he had seized from the Swedes. Thousands of men died in the effort to create a seaport and a capital worthy of its imperial resident. Remote from the rest of Russia, St. Petersburg was frightfully expensive, because food and building materials had to be transported great distances. It was also dangerous. When floods poured through the streets, Peter roared with laughter at the sight of furniture and household effects floating away. Wolves prowled the broad new boulevards and devoured a lady in front of Prince Menshikov's own house one fine day in June. Nevertheless, Peter commanded all members of the nobility to make St. Petersburg their home, although the nobles complained bitterly about abandoning their beloved Moscow for this uncomfortable and costly city.

To educate future officers and also many civil servants, Peter established naval, military, and artillery academies. Because of the inadequacy of Russian primary education, which was still controlled by the Church, foreigners had to be summoned to provide Russia with scholars. At a lower level, Peter continued the practice, begun long before him, of importing technicians and artisans to teach their skills to Russians. The czar was quite aware of the mercantilist ideas of the age and offered the inducements of protective tariffs and freedom from taxation to encourage manufac-

turing. Though sometimes employing a substantial number of laborers, industrial enterprises, chiefly in textiles and iron, remained backward. Factory owners were permitted to buy and sell serfs (otherwise a privilege restricted to the gentry), provided they were always bought or sold as a body together with the factory itself. This "possessional" industrial serfdom hardly provided much incentive for good work, and Russian produce continued inferior to comparable goods made abroad.

The records of Peter's secret police are full of the complaints his agents heard as they moved about listening for subversive remarks. Peasant husbands and fathers were snatched away to fight on distant battlefields or to labor in the swamps to build a city that nobody but Peter wanted. The number of serfs increased with the imposition of the new soul tax and the multiplication of land grants to service men. Service men found themselves in a kind of bondage of their own, condemned to work for the czar during the whole of their lives and seldom able to visit their estates. Nobles of ancient birth found themselves treated no differently from the upstarts who were flooding into their class from below. Churchmen of the conservative school were more and more convinced that Peter was the Antichrist himself, as they beheld the increase of foreigners in high places and saw the many innovations imported from the hated West.

Among the lower orders of society resistance took the form of peasant uprisings, which in turn were punished with extreme brutality. The usual allies of the peasant rebels, the Cossacks, suffered mass executions and sharp curtailment of their traditional independence. The leaders of the noble and clerical opposition focused their hopes on Peter's son by his first wife, the young heir to the throne, Alexis, who they believed would stop the expensive foreign wars and move back to Moscow and comfortable Russian conservatism. Alexis, an alcoholic, was not stable enough to lead a conspiracy against his father, but he fanned the hopes of the opposition by indicating he shared their views. Eventually, he fled abroad and sought asylum from his brother-in-law, the Austrian emperor Charles VI. Promising him fair treatment and forgiveness, Peter lured Alexis back to Russia and made him the showpiece of one of those horrible Russian investigations of nonexistent plots. Many were killed or exiled, and Alexis himself was tortured to death in his father's presence.

Among later generations of Russians both those who welcomed Peter's westernizing policies and those who condemned them as "unRussian" assumed that what he did was drastic and revolutionary. Yet in many respects Peter simply fortified already existing Russian institutions and characteristics. He made a strong autocracy even stronger, a universal service law for service men even more stringent, a serf more of a serf. His trip abroad, his fondness for foreign ways, his worship of advanced technology, his mercantilism, his wars, all had their precedents in the period of his forerunners.

*Quoted by E. Schuyler, *Peter the Great* (New York, 1884), 2:389.

The Cathedral of St. Peter and Paul within Petropavlov Fortress:
buildings from the time of Peter the Great in St. Petersburg.

The Church, which he attacked, had already been weakened by the schism of the Old Believers, itself the result of Western influences. Peter's true radicalism was in the field of everyday manners and behavior. The attack on the beards, dress, the calendar (he adopted the Western dating from the birth of Christ and abandoned the traditional dating from a hypothetical year of the Creation), his hatred of ceremony and fondness for manual labor—these things were indeed new; so too were the vigor and passion with which he acted. They were decisive in winning Peter the Great his reputation as a revolutionary.

The Polish and Ottoman Victims

By the early eighteenth century, Russia was the only great power in eastern Europe. Poland and the Ottoman Empire still bulked large on the map, but their territories included lands they were soon to lose. Both states suffered from incompetent government, from a backward economy, and from the presence of large national and religious minorities. The Orthodox in Catholic Poland and Muslim Turkey were beginning to look to Russia for protection. In addition, the evident decay of both states stimulated the aggressive appetites of their stronger neighbors. Poland was doomed to disappear as an independent power before the end of the century, the victim of partition by Russia, Austria, and Prussia. Turkey held on, but only just, and was already beginning to acquire the perilous reputation of being "the Sick Man of Europe."

The Polish government was a political curiosity shop. The monarchy was elective; each time the throne fell vacant, the Diet chose a successor, usually the candidate who had offered the biggest bribes, and sometimes even a foreigner, as with Augustus the Strong of Saxony. Once elected, the king was nearly powerless, since he was obliged to transfer the royal prerogatives to the Diet when he accepted the crown. The Diet was dominated by the nobility and was celebrated for its *liberum veto,* whereby any one of its members could block any proposal by shouting "I do not wish it!" The Diet was not a parliament in the Western sense of the term, but an assembly of aristocrats, each of whom thought of himself as a power unto himself. Unanimity was therefore almost impossible. This loosely knit Polish national state had no regular army or diplomatic corps or central bureaucracy. Unlike the English gentry or

Prussian Junkers, the dominant nobles had no concept of service to the Crown or indeed any sense of loyalty except to their own social class. They helped destroy a once-flourishing urban middle class by persecuting Jewish shopkeepers and foreign merchants. On their estates, the lot of the serfs was harsher than it was in Russia.

Compared with Poland, the Ottoman Empire was still a functioning state, yet it was falling further and further behind the major European powers, particularly in economics and technology. Not until the nineteenth century did it produce an emperor who would attempt the kind of massive assault on traditional ways that Peter the Great had mounted. In the eighteenth century, with rare exceptions, the sultans were captives of harem intrigue and could do little to discipline such powerful groups as the Janissaries, who exploited their privileges and neglected their soldierly duties. This retrograde and corrupt government did at least govern, however, and showed considerable staying power in war. The Sick Man was to linger on throughout the century, kept alive in part by Ottoman vitality, and in part by the rivalry between the two would-be heirs of the Turkish inheritance, Russia and Austria.

V War and Diplomacy, 1713–1763

From this survey of the European powers in the early eighteenth century, it is evident that the international balance was precarious. Should the strong states decide to prey upon the weak, the balance was certain to be upset. One such upset resulted from the Great Northern War, which enabled Russia to replace Sweden as the dominant power in the Baltic. The expansion of Russia continued to threaten the balance during most of the eighteenth century, and the chief victims were Poland and Turkey. A second major threat to the balance came from the expansion of Prussia at the expense of Austria, Poland, and Sweden. A third arose out of the colonial and commercial rivalry between Britain and the Bourbon monarchies of France and Spain.

These were not the only international issues of the day. The old competition between Austria and France, which dated back to the Hapsburg-Valois wars of the 1500s, remained lively. It was complicated by the ambitions of Elizabeth Farnese, second wife of Philip V of Spain, who won the support of France and threatened the Austrian hegemony in Italy. The Austrian Hapsburgs themselves were vigorous expansionists, aiming to drive the Turks from the Danube and extend their own domains southeast to the Black Sea.

While the interplay of all these rivalries led to frequent shifts in the international balance, the idea that there should be such a balance was generally maintained. Indeed, eighteenth-century war and diplomacy are often cited as the classic case history of balance-of-power politics in operation. The limited financial resources of the governments of the Old Regime allowed only limited warfare; nobody could as yet afford the enormous armies or navies required for total war. On the battlefield, generals were reluctant to risk losing soldiers who represented a costly investment in training; they favored sieges and other formal maneuvers executed according to conventions well understood by all belligerents. At the peace table, diplomats were reluctant to destroy an opponent; according to another well-understood convention, they generally sought to award him a bit of territory or a minor throne as compensation for a greater loss. Total war and unconditional surrender were not eighteenth-century concepts.

The manner in which war and diplomacy were conducted has often been likened to an elaborate game, serious and sometimes bloody, but governed by a multitude of rules that were usually observed by the players and were designed to keep any of them from being eliminated entirely from the play. The principal players—the monarchs, diplomats, generals, and admirals—were for the most part aristocrats accustomed to following a uniform code of behavior. Whatever their nationality, they usually understood and respected one another far more than they understood or respected the lower social classes in their own countries. A few of the most successful players, notably Frederick the Great of Prussia and Pitt of England, did not always act according to the rules. The custom of compensating the loser was ignored in the case of Poland, which was partitioned out of existence late in the century. Earlier in the century, however, the way the powers handled the Polish and the Turkish questions afforded instructive examples of the game of international politics in operation.

The Turkish and Polish Questions, 1716–1739

In 1716 the Ottoman Empire became embroiled in a war with Austria which resulted in the Treaty of Passarowitz (1718), by which Charles VI recovered the portion of Hungary still under Turkish rule plus some other Ottoman lands in the Danube valley. Another Austro-Turkish war, 1735–1739, modified the Passarowitz settlement and disclosed the growing infirmity of the Hapsburg army. In this second war Austria was allied with Russia, but, in a fashion foreshadowing the later struggles of the two powers for control of the Balkans, they fell to quarreling over division of the prospective spoils. In the end there was little to divide, and Charles VI had to hand back to Turkey the Danubian lands annexed in 1718. During the negotiations leading to the Austro-Turkish settlement of 1739, France gave the Ottoman Empire powerful support in order to redress the balance of power. This was one of the chief occasions when the French used their two-hundred-year-old Turkish alliance to check Hapsburg expansion.

In the early 1730s, Bourbon and Hapsburg also chose opposing sides in a crisis over the kingship of Poland. During the Great Northern War, as we have seen, Stanislas Leszczyński, the protégé of Charles XII of Sweden, had temporarily replaced Augustus the Strong as king of Poland. While Augustus recovered the Polish crown, thanks to Peter the Great, Leszczyński had by no means completed his historical role, for he gave his daughter, Marie, in marriage to Louis XV of France. When Augustus died in 1733, French diplomats engineered the election of Stanislas to succeed him. But both Austria and Russia disliked the prospect of a French puppet on the Polish throne, and Russia sent troops into Poland and convoked a rump session of the Diet that elected a rival king, Augustus III, son of Augustus the Strong. The stage was set for the War of the Polish Succession, 1733–1735—Stanislas, France, and Spain versus Augustus III, Russia, and Austria.

After French and Austrian armies had fired away at each other for a while in the Rhine Valley and in northern Italy, hundreds of miles from Poland, the diplomats worked out a compromise settlement. To the satisfaction of Austria and Russia, Augustus III secured the Polish throne. From the French standpoint, Stanislas Leszczyński was well compensated for his loss. He acquired the duchy of Lorraine, on the northeastern border of France, with the provision that when he died Lorraine would go to his daughter, Marie, and thence to the French crown. France would thus move one step closer to filling out her "natural" frontiers. The incumbent duke of Lorraine, Francis, the future husband of the Hapsburg heiress Maria Theresa, was awarded the Grand Duchy of Tuscany, where the Medici dynasty of grand dukes conveniently died out in 1737. Finally, as a byproduct of the settlement, Elizabeth Farnese of Spain capped twenty years of maternal perseverance by procuring the Kingdom of Naples for Baby Carlos, her elder and now grown-up son.

The War of the Polish Succession may well seem much ado about a kingship possessing no real power, and the postwar settlement, which affected chiefly Italy and Lorraine, may appear to be a striking case of diplomatic irrelevance. Yet the whole Polish crisis neatly illustrates the workings of dynastic politics and the balance of power. Statesmen regarded thrones as the pawns of diplomacy, to be assigned without reference to the wishes of the populations involved. No politician of the Old Regime would have contemplated canvassing Neapolitan sentiment on Carlos or holding a referendum to find whether Poles preferred Stanislas or Augustus. The complicated arrangements of the 1730s preserved the balance of power by giving something to almost everybody. Although the diplomats could not prevent a little war over Poland, they did keep it from becoming a big one.

Indeed, throughout the period from 1713 to 1739 the force of diplomacy operated to avert or at least to localize wars. Britain and France took the lead in the campaign to keep any one power from upsetting the international applecart. To frustrate Elizabeth Farnese's attempts to oust the Hapsburgs from Italy in the late 1710s, the French dispatched an army and the British deployed a fleet. The British also sent a squadron to the Baltic during the last part of the Great Northern War so that Czar Peter's gains would not be too great. To prevent the dismemberment of Ottoman territories in Europe, Britain intervened in the negotiations between Turkey and Austria at Passarowitz in 1718, and the French revived their Ottoman alliance in the 1730s.

Jenkins' Ear and the Austrian Succession, 1739–1748

The diplomatic partnership of Britain and France in the 1720s and 1730s resulted from the fact that both Walpole and Fleury sought stability abroad to promote economic recovery at home. The partnership, however, collapsed in the face of the competition between the two Atlantic powers for commerce and empire. Neither Walpole nor Fleury could prevent the worldwide war between Britain and the Bourbon monarchies that broke out in 1739 and that lasted, with many intervals of peace, until the final defeat of Napoleon in 1815. This "Second Hundred Years' War" had, in fact, already begun half a century earlier, in the days of Louis XIV. The Utrecht settlement of 1713 had not fully settled the rivalry between Britain and France (and France's Bourbon partner, Spain). Thus the war of 1739 was as much the renewal of an old struggle as the onset of a new one.

The specific issue behind the crisis of 1739 was the comparatively minor question of British chagrin at the disappointing results of the Asiento privilege. As the South Sea Company discovered, the Asiento gave Britain little more than a token share in the trade of the Spanish American colonies. What British captains could not get legitimately they got by smuggling, and Spain retaliated with a coast-guard patrol in American waters to ward off smugglers. British merchants complained of the rough treatment handed out by the Spanish guards, and in 1738 they exhibited to Parliament Captain Jenkins, who claimed that Spanish brutality had cost him an ear, which he duly produced, preserved in salt and cotton batting. Asked to state his reaction on losing the ear, he replied, "I commended my soul to God and my cause to my country." Walpole retorted that the protection of British smugglers against legitimate Spanish patrols did not constitute a very strong case. But Walpole could restrain neither the anti-Spanish fever sweeping the country to which Jenkins had commended his cause, nor the bellicose faction of Boy Patriots that had arisen among Walpole's own Whigs.

In October 1739, to the joyful pealing of church-bells, Britain began the War of Jenkins' Ear against Spain. "They are ringing their bells now," Walpole observed tartly. "They will be wringing their hands soon." As if to vindicate his prophecy, the British fleet lost the opening campaign in the Caribbean, and France showed every sign of coming to Spain's assistance. Dynastic ties had already brought the two Bour-

Maria Theresa with Francis I and their children.

advanced a flimsy family claim to Silesia, Europe generally regarded his invasion as an act of simple aggression.

In the ensuing War of the Austrian Succession, England and Austria were ranged against France, Spain, Prussia, and Bavaria. Frederick won an emphatic victory in the campaigns on the Continent. The Prussian army astounded Europe by its long night marches, sudden flank attacks, and other tactics of surprise quite different from the usual deliberate warfare of sieges. Frederick, however, antagonized his allies by repeatedly deserting them to make secret peace arrangements with Austria. And he did little to support the imperial aspirations of the Bavarian elector, who enjoyed only a brief tenure as Emperor Charles VII.

The Anglo-Austrian alliance worked no better than the Franco-Prussian one. Many Englishmen felt that George II was betraying their interests outside Europe by entangling them in the Austrian succession and other German problems, such as the defense of Hanover (from 1714 to 1837 the Kings of England were also rulers of Hanover; since the Salic law prevailed there, the succession passed to an uncle of Queen Victoria when she inherited the English crown in 1837). Nevertheless, the British preference for the Hanoverians over the Stuarts was evident when Bonnie Prince Charles, the grandson of the deposed James II, secured French backing and landed in Britain (1745). He won significant recruits only among the chronically discontented highlanders of Scotland, where he was thoroughly defeated at Culloden in 1746. Jacobitism, which had never been a very important political threat, was dead.

Outside Europe, the fighting of the 1740s was indecisive. The New England colonists took Louisburg, the French naval base on Cape Breton Island commanding the approach to the St. Lawrence. On the other side of the world, the French took the port of Madras from the English East India Company. The Treaty of Aix-la-Chapelle (1748) restored both Louisburg and Madras to their former owners, and Britain later agreed to give up the troublesome Asiento privilege. In central Europe, on the other hand, the war was a decisive step in the rise of Prussia to the first rank of powers. The new province of Silesia brought not only a large increase in the Prussian population but also an important textile industry and large deposits of coal and iron. Maria Theresa got scant compensation for the loss of Silesia. Although her husband, Francis, won recognition as Holy Roman Emperor, she had to surrender Parma and some other territorial crumbs in northern Italy to Philip, the second son of Elizabeth Farnese.

The peace made in 1748 lasted only eight years. Then another and greater conflict, the Seven Years' War of 1756–1763, broke out, caused partly by old issues left unsettled at Aix-la-Chapelle and partly by new grievances arising from the War of the Austrian Succession. The world struggle between Britain and the

bon monarchies into alliance during the Polish war; now French economic interests were at stake, for France supplied the bulk of the wares Spanish galleons carried to America, which cheaper British contraband was driving out of the Spanish colonial market.

In 1740 a chain of events linked the colonial war to the great European conflict over the Austrian succession. On the death of Charles VI in 1740, the Hapsburg dominions passed to his twenty-three-year-old daughter, Maria Theresa. Expecting to outwit Maria Theresa because of her sex and her political inexperience, the German princes ignored the Pragmatic Sanction guaranteeing her succession and looked forward to partitioning the Hapsburg inheritance. In addition, the elector of Bavaria, a cousin of the Hapsburgs, hoped to be elected Holy Roman Emperor, defeating Maria Theresa's husband, Francis of Lorraine and Tuscany. The first of the German princes to strike, however, was Frederick the Great (1740–1786), who had just inherited the Prussian throne from Frederick William I. In December 1740 Frederick suddenly invaded Silesia, a Hapsburg province located in the upper Oder valley to the southeast of Brandenburg. Though Frederick

Bourbons kept right on in the undeclared warfare waged during the years of nominal peace after 1748. In Asia, the English and French East India companies fought each other once removed, so to speak, by taking sides in the rivalries of native princes in southern India. By 1751, the energetic French administrator Dupleix had won the initial round of this indirect fight. Then the English, led by the equally energetic Clive, seized the initiative, and in 1754 Dupleix was called back home by the directors of the French company, who were unwilling to back his aggressive policy. In North America, English colonists from the Atlantic seaboard had already staked out claims to the rich wilderness between the Appalachians and the Mississippi. But the French, equally intent on appropriating the area, stole a march on them and established a string of forts in western Pennsylvania from Presqu'Isle (later Erie) south to Fort Duquesne (later Pittsburgh). In 1754, a force of Virginians under the youthful George Washington tried unsuccessfully to dislodge the French from Fort Duquesne.

Frederick the Great on the terrace of Sans Souci, his palace near Potsdam.

The Diplomatic Revolution and the Seven Years' War, 1756–1763

In Europe, the dramatic shift of alliances called the Diplomatic Revolution immediately preceded the outbreak of the Seven Years' War. In the new war the fundamental antagonisms were the same as in the old—Britain versus France, Prussia versus Austria—but the powers reversed their alliances. Britain, which had joined Austria against Prussia in the 1740s, now paired off with Frederick the Great. And, in the most revolutionary move of the Diplomatic Revolution, France, which had sided with Frederick before, not only stood against him but also joined with her hereditary enemy, Hapsburg Austria. The Diplomatic Revolution reflected the resentment of the powers at the disloyal behavior of their old partners in the War of the Austrian Succession. The French had bitter memories of Frederick's repeated desertions and secret peace arrangements. Britain deplored Austrian reluctance to defend English continental interests, which included maintaining the territorial integrity of Hanover and excluding the French from the Austrian Netherlands. Austria, in turn, regarded Hanover and Belgium as peripheral to her main concern, the recovery of Silesia.

In 1755, the British almost unwittingly touched off the Diplomatic Revolution. In order to enlist a second power in the task of defending Hanover, they concluded a treaty with Russia, which had taken a minor part in the War of the Austrian Succession as an ally of England. The Anglo-Russian treaty alarmed Frederick the Great, who feared an eventual conflict between Prussia and Russia for control of the Baltic and Poland. In January 1756 the Prussian king concluded an alliance with Britain which detached her from Russia. The alliance between England and Russia isolated France and gave the Austrian chancellor,

Kaunitz, the opportunity he had been waiting for. What Austria needed in order to avenge herself on Frederick and regain Silesia was an ally with a large army; what Austria needed was the alliance of France, not Britain. Using the Anglo-Prussian alliance as an argument, Kaunitz convinced Louis XV and his mistress, Madame de Pompadour, to drop the traditional Bourbon-Hapsburg feud in favor of a working partnership. The last act of the Diplomatic Revolution occurred when Russia joined the Franco-Austrian alliance. The Russian empress Elizabeth (1741–1762) hated Frederick the Great and feared his aggression all the more now that he had deprived her of her English ally.

The new war, like its predecessor, was really two separate wars—one continental, the other naval and colonial. In the European campaigns of the Seven Years' War, Frederick the Great faced a formidable test. Prussia confronted the forces of Austria, France, and Russia, whose combined population was more than fifteen times larger than her own. She had almost no allies except Britain, which supplied financial subsidies but little actual military assistance. The Spartan traditions of the Hohenzollerns enabled Prussia to survive. The king himself set the example; in 1757, he wrote to one of his French friends: "In these disastrous times one must fortify oneself with iron resolutions and a heart of brass. It is a time for stoicism: the disciples of Epicurus would find nothing to say. . . ." *

Frederick's "iron resolution" and "heart of brass" led him to adopt any expedient to gain his ends. To fill up the depleted ranks of his army, he violated inter-

*Quoted in G. P. Gooch, *Frederick the Great* (London, 1947), p. 41.

national law by impressing soldiers from Prussia's smaller neighbors, Mecklenburg and Saxony (Prussian press gangs had a habit of surrounding churches at the close of Sunday services). Since British subsidies covered only a fraction of his war expenses, he seized Saxon, Polish, and Russian coins and melted them down for Prussian use.

A final factor in saving Prussia, perhaps the most important one of all, was the shakiness of the apparently formidable coalition arrayed against her. Fortunately for Frederick, his enemies were never capable of exploiting their military success to deliver a knockout blow. Russia's generals were timid, and those of France and Austria were sometimes downright incompetent. Moreover, the French, the strongest of the allies, had to fight a two-front war, in Europe and overseas, but did not have the financial resources to do both. The grand alliance created by Kaunitz suffered to an unusual extent from the frictions, mistrust, and cross-purposes endemic in wartime coalitions. In fact, the coalition did not last out the war. When Elizabeth of Russia died in January 1762, she was succeeded by Czar Peter III, a passionate admirer of Frederick the Great, who at once deserted Elizabeth's allies and placed Russia's forces at Frederick's disposal. Although he occupied the Russian throne for only a few months, Peter's reign marked a decisive turning in the Seven Years' War. In 1763 Prussia won her war, and Austria agreed to the Peace of Hubertusburg confirming the Hohenzollern retention of Silesia.

Meanwhile, Frederick's British partner was gaining a smashing victory abroad. During the first year and a half of the fighting, the British suffered setbacks on almost every front. At sea, they lost the important Mediterranean base of Minorca in the Balearic Islands, a disaster to which the home government contributed by sending (too late) reinforcements (too few) under Admiral Byng (a poor choice). Unfairly saddled with the whole blame, Byng was executed—"in order to encourage the others," Voltaire observed ironically. In North America, the British lost the outpost of Oswego on Lake Ontario and fumbled an attack on Louisburg, the key to French Canada. The most dramatic of Britain's misfortunes occurred in India. In June 1756, the nawab of Bengal, an ally of the French, crowded 146 British prisoners into a small room with only two windows. The result was the atrocious Black Hole of Calcutta incident, thus described by an officer of the English East India Company:

It was the hottest season of the year, and the night uncommonly sultry. . . . The excessive pressure of their bodies against one another, and the intolerable heat which prevailed as soon as the door was shut, convinced the prisoners that it was impossible to live through the night in this horrible confinement; and violent attempts were immediately made to force the door, but without effect for it opened inward.

At two o'clock not more than fifty remained alive. But even this number were too many to partake of the saving air, the contest for which and for life continued until the morn. . . .

An officer, sent by the nawab, came . . . with an order to open the prison. The dead were so thronged, and the survivors had so little strength remaining, that they were employed near half an hour in removing the bodies which lay against the door before they could clear a passage to go out one at a time; when of one hundred and forty-six who went in no more than twenty-three came out alive. . . .*

William Pitt turned the tide in favor of Britain. This famous representative of the Whig oligarchy sat in Parliament for Old Sarum, a notorious rotten borough. The grandson of "Diamond" Pitt, a merchant prince who had made a fortune in India, he consistently supported the interests of the City. In the late 1730s he had led the Whig rebels, the Boy Patriots who forced Britain into the War of Jenkins' Ear against Walpole's pacifistic policy. Now Pitt's great war ministry (1757–1761) at last ended the shilly-shallying policies of the cabinets that had held office since Walpole's downfall in 1742. When deficits rose higher and higher, Pitt used his personal and business connections with the City to assist the successful placement of government loans. He strengthened the Anglo-Prussian alliance by sending Frederick substantial subsidies and placing English forces in Hanover under an able Prussian commander in place of the bungling duke of Cumberland, a son of George II. Everywhere Pitt replaced blundering generals and admirals and took energetic measures that transformed the naval and colonial campaigns.

After the Royal Navy defeated both the Atlantic and Mediterranean squadrons of the French (1759), Britain commanded the seas. This enabled her to continue trading abroad at a prosperous pace, while French overseas trade rapidly sank to one-sixth of the prewar rate. Cut off from supplies and reinforcements from home and faced by generally superior British forces, the French colonies fell in quick succession. In Africa, Britain's capture of the chief French slaving station ruined the slavers of Nantes in the mother country. In India, Clive and others avenged the Black Hole by punishing the nawab of Bengal and capturing the key French posts, Chandernagore near Calcutta and Pondichéry near Madras. In the West Indies, the French lost all their sugar islands, except for Santo Domingo. In North America, the 65,000 French, poorly supplied and poorly led, were helpless against the million British colonists, fully supported by their mother country. Fort Duquesne was taken at last, and renamed after Pitt, and the British went on to other triumphs in the war that the colonists called "French and Indian." In Canada, the English general Wolfe took Louisburg (1758) and in the next year, 1759, lost his life but won immortal fame in a great victory on the Plains of

*R. Orme, *A History of the Transactions of the British Nation in Indostan* (London, 1778), 2:74 ff.

Abraham outside Quebec. When the remaining French stronghold, Montreal, fell in 1760, the doom of France's American empire was sealed.

This rain of victories led the British to expect sweeping gains in the postwar settlement; their expectations were soon disappointed. Pitt had won the war, but he did not make the peace: the accession of the obstinate and ambitious George III in 1760 led to the dismissal of the prime minister the next year. In the Peace of Paris, 1763, the successors of Pitt allowed the French to recover their islands in the West Indies, then highly valued as a major source of sugar. British planters in the Caribbean were actually much relieved, for their markets had been flooded by sugar from captured French islands during the war. But to outraged patriots it seemed as though Britain had let the grand prize slip through her fingers.

France, however, lost all her possessions on the mainland of North America. Britain secured both Canada and the disputed territories between the Appalachians and the Mississippi. Moreover, Spain, which had joined France in 1762 when the war was already lost, ceded to Britain East Florida (the peninsula) and West Florida (the coast of the Gulf of Mexico as far as the Mississippi). In compensation, France gave Spain the city of New Orleans and the vast Louisiana territories west of the Mississippi. In India France recovered Pondichéry and Chandernagore but on condition that she would not fortify them or continue her old policy of manipulating the politics and rivalries of native states. For Britain, the Seven Years' War marked the beginning of a virtually complete ascendancy in India; for France it marked the virtual end of her "old Empire."

The International Balance in Review

The peace settlements of Hubertusburg and Paris ended the greatest international crisis that was to occur between the death of Louis XIV and the outbreak of the French Revolution. New crises were to arise soon after 1763, as the next chapter will show in detail: in 1768, a Russo-Turkish war (which Russia won); in 1772, the first partition of Poland; in 1775, the American War of Independence. The new crises in the East did not fundamentally alter the international balance; they accentuated shifts that had long been underway. And, although American independence cost Britain the thirteen colonies, the maritime and imperial supremacy she had gained in 1763 was not otherwise seriously affected.

The international balance established in 1763, then, remained largely unchanged until 1789. In the incessant struggle for power during the eighteenth century, the victorious states were the strongest states—Britain, Prussia, and Russia. The states that were less fit—France, Spain, Austria, Turkey—survived, though they sometimes suffered serious losses. The weakest

units, Poland and Italy—as a Spanish diplomat observed early in the century—were being "pared and sliced up like so many Dutch cheeses."

The duke of Choiseul, foreign minister for Louis XV during the Seven Years' War, remarked that the "true balance of power resides in commerce." Choiseul's remark held a large measure of truth, but not the whole truth. The world struggle between Britain and the Bourbon empires did much to justify the mercantilist view that conceived of international relations in terms of incessant competition and strife. According to the mercantilist doctrine of the fixed amount of trade, a state could enlarge its share of the existing supply only if it reduced the shares held by rival states, either through war or, in time of peace, through smuggling and retaliatory legislation. All this was borne out by the War of Jenkins' Ear and by British success, and

North America and the Caribbean, 1763

Situation after the Seven Years' War

British Territory:

- Held before 1763
- Acquired from France
- Acquired from Spain
- Proclamation Line of 1763

French failure, in maintaining overseas trade during the course of the Seven Years' War. Yet the modern concept of economic warfare was only beginning to take shape. During the War of the Austrian Succession English visitors continued to arrive in Paris, and London brokers supplied both insurance and information on naval movements to French shipowners.

Moreover, economic factors did not wholly explain all the changes in the international balance during the century. For example, efficient utilization of Prussian resources played its part in the victories of Frederick the Great. But his success depended still more on qualities that had little to do with economics—his own brilliant and ruthless leadership, and the discipline of the society that he headed. The case of Britain seemingly offers the most compelling evidence to support Choiseul's contention, as Pitt turned her formidable financial and commercial assets to practical advantage. Yet Pitt himself is not to be explained in simple economic terms. His accession as prime minister in the dark days of 1757, like that of Churchill in the dark days of 1940, was made possible by a political system that enabled the right man to come forward at the right time.

Finally, the eighteenth century, despite its wars, was an interlude of comparative calm between the age of religious strife that had preceded it and the storms of liberalism and nationalism that were to be loosed by the French Revolution. The prospect in 1715, the prospect of long years of peace and quiet, had not, after all, been wholly deceptive. The Seven Years' War of the eighteenth century, for example, did not begin to equal in destructive force the Thirty Years' War of the seventeenth. Much more was involved here than the relative shortness of the war. Few of the combatants had the feeling of fighting for a great cause, like Catholicism or Protestantism or national independence. The fighting itself was conducted in a more orderly fashion than it had been a hundred years before; soldiers were better disciplined, and armies were better supplied; troops lived off the land less often and no longer constituted such a menace to the lives and property of civilians. Even warfare reflected the order and reason characteristic of the Age of Enlightenment.

Reading Suggestions on the Old Regime and the International Balance

General Accounts

The following volumes in the series The Rise of Modern Europe (*Torchbooks) provide a detailed introduction to eighteenth-century war and politics and have elaborate bibliographies: P. Roberts, *The Quest for Security, 1715–1740;* W. L. Dorn, *Competition for Empire, 1740–1763;* and L. Gershoy, *From Despotism to Revolution, 1763–1789.*

M. S. Anderson, *Europe in the Eighteenth Century, 1713–1783* (*Holt, 1961). A very good introductory volume by a British scholar.

R. J. White, *Europe in the Eighteenth Century* (*St. Martin's). Another good introduction, also by a British scholar, at a less advanced level.

The New Cambridge Modern History (Cambridge Univ. Press). Two volumes of this ambitious but uneven publication contain materials useful for the present chapter. VI: *The Rise of Great Britain and Russia, 1688–1725* (1970); VII; *The Old Regime, 1713–1763* (1957).

Economics and Society

H. J. Habakkuk and M. Postan, eds., *The Cambridge Economic History of Europe,* Vol. 6, Parts 1 and 2 (Cambridge Univ. Press, 1965). Scholarly essays on the economic revolutions by many writers.

E. F. Heckscher, *Mercantilism,* rev. ed., 2 vols. (Macmillan, 1955). A famous and controversial work; a mine of information on eighteenth-century economic developments.

J. Carswell, *The South Sea Bubble* (Stanford Univ. Press, 1960). Excellent monograph.

T. S. Ashton, *An Economic History of England: The Eighteenth Century* (*Barnes & Noble). Lucid introduction by an expert on the subject.

P. Mantoux, *The Industrial Revolution in the Eighteenth Century* (*Torchbooks). Classic study of the factory system in England.

P. Deane, *The First Industrial Revolution* (*Cambridge Univ. Press). Up-to-date study of the British economy, 1750–1850; based on lectures to undergraduates at Cambridge University.

A. Goodwin, ed., *The European Nobility in the Eighteenth Century* (Black, 1953). Very helpful essays arranged country by country.

D. Ogg, *Europe of the Ancien Régime* (*Torchbooks). A social study, focused on Britain.

The Established Powers

W. E. H. Lecky, *A History of England in the Eighteenth Century,* 8 vols. (Longmans, 1883–1890). A celebrated detailed study.

B. Williams, *The Whig Supremacy, 1714–1760,* 2nd ed., rev. C. H. Stuart (Clarendon, 1962). A competent modern survey.

J. Plumb, *England in the Eighteenth Century* (*Penguin). A good brief account by a scholar who has also written studies of Walpole, the elder Pitt, and the first four Georges.

L. B. Namier, *The Structure of Politics at the Accession of George III,* 2nd ed. (St. Martin's, 1957) and *England in the Age of the American Revolution* (*St. Martin's). Detailed and controversial studies, revising traditional concepts of eighteenth-century English political institutions.

L. Kronenberger, *Kings and Desperate Men* (*Vintage). Lively essays on eighteenth-century English society and personalities.

A. Cobban, *A History of Modern France.* Vol. 1: *1715–1799* (*Penguin). Good general survey by a British scholar.

J. Lough, *An Introduction to Eighteenth-Century France* (*McKay). Clear and enlightening discussion of the Old Regime.

C. B. A. Behrens, *The Ancien Régime* (*Harcourt). Readable and generously illustrated study stressing French society.

A. M. Wilson, *French Foreign Policy during the Administration of*

Cardinal Fleury (Harvard Univ. Press, 1936). A sound monograph, and one of the relatively few good books in English on the France of Louis XV.

G. P. Gooch, *Louis XV* (Longmans, 1956), and Nancy Mitford, *Madame de Pompadour* (*Pyramid). Entertaining old-fashioned biographical studies.

F. Ford, *Robe and Sword* (*Torchbooks). An instructive study of the French aristocracy during the generation following the death of Louis XIV.

H. Kamen, *The War of Succession in Spain, 1700–1715* (Univ. of Indiana Press, 1969). Detailed study of the initial Bourbon impact upon Spain.

H. Holborn, *A History of Modern Germany,* Vol. 2 (Knopf, 1964). Succinct scholarly survey of the period from 1648 to 1840.

A. Wandruszka, *The House of Hapsburg* (Sidgwick and Jackson, 1964). A useful history of the famous dynasty.

The Newcomers

H. Rosenberg, *Bureaucracy, Aristocracy, Autocracy* (*Beacon). A somewhat opinionated analysis of Prussian history, 1660–1815.

S. B. Fay, *The Rise of Brandenburg-Prussia to 1786,* rev. K. Epstein (*Holt). A lucid little volume, packed with information.

F. L. Carsten, *The Origins of Prussia* (*Oxford Univ. Press). Excellent monograph that carries the story through the reign of the Great Elector.

F. Schevill, *The Great Elector* (Univ. of Chicago Press, 1947). A helpful study of the founder of the Hohenzollern despotism.

R. R. Ergang, *The Potsdam Führer* (Columbia Univ. Press, 1941). A splendid study of Frederick William I of Prussia.

G. Craig, *The Politics of the Prussian Army, 1640–1945* (*Oxford Univ. Press). Excellent scholarly study.

V. Klyuchevsky, *Peter the Great* (*Vintage). Famous account by a Russian scholar.

E. Schuyler, *Peter the Great,* 2 vols. (Scribner's, 1884). An old but excellent appraisal by an American diplomat and scholar.

B. H. Sumner, *Peter the Great and the Emergence of Russia* (*Collier). A very good introductory account.

M. Raeff, ed., *Peter the Great Changes Russia* (*Heath). Good cross section of judgments on the controversial czar.

The International Balance

A. Sorel, *Europe Under the Old Régime* (*Torchbooks). A famous little essay on the eighteenth-century balance by a French expert.

L. Dehio, *The Precarious Balance* (*Vintage). Reflections on the balance of power by a German scholar.

J. F. C. Fuller, *A Military History of the Western World,* 3 vols. (*Minerva). The second volume of this stimulating survey covers the seventeenth and eighteenth centuries.

C. T. Atkinson, *A History of Germany, 1715–1815* (Methuen, 1908). An older account, particularly full on war and diplomacy.

B. H. Sumner, *Peter the Great and the Ottoman Empire* (Blackwell, 1949). A short and meaty monograph.

H. Dodwell, *Dupleix and Clive* (Methuen, 1920). A balanced treatment of the imperial antagonists in India.

Sources

Arthur Young, *Tours in England and Wales* (London School of Economics and Political Science, 1932). A good selection from the reports of this prolific and perceptive agricultural expert.

Lady Mary W. Montagu, *Letters* (Everyman). By perhaps the best of the century's excellent letter writers; particularly valuable on the Hapsburg and Ottoman empires.

C. A. Macartney, ed., *The Hapsburg and Hohenzollern Dynasties in the Seventeenth and Eighteenth Centuries* (*Torchbooks). Helpful collection of documentary materials on Austrian and Prussian history.

R. and E. Forster, *European Society in the Eighteenth Century* (*Harper). Excellent anthology.

G. P. Gooch, *Courts and Cabinets* (Knopf, 1946). A graceful introduction to the memoirs of some of the great personages of the era.

Historical Fiction

H. Fielding, *Tom Jones* (*several editions). The greatest of social novels on eighteenth-century England.

T. Smollett, *The Adventures of Roderick Random* (*Signet). A novel that provides a good contemporary account of life in His Majesty's Navy in the reign of George II.

D. Merezhkovsky, *Peter and Alexis* (Putnam, 1905). Novel dramatizing the conflict between the great czar and his son.

The Enlightenment

Introduction

Reason, natural law, progress—these were key words in the vocabulary of the eighteenth century. It was the Age of the Enlightenment, when it was widely assumed that human reason could cure men of past ills and help them to achieve utopian governments, perpetual peace, and a perfect society. Reason would enable men to discover the natural laws regulating existence, and the progress of the human race would thereby be assured.

The intellectuals who professed this optimistic creed were known by the French name of *philosophes,* though some of them were not French and few of them were philosophers in the strict sense. The philosophes were critics, publicists, economists, political scientists, and social reformers. By no means did all of them express their views in the naïvely simple and cheerful way formulated at the end of the last paragraph. The most famous philosophe, Voltaire, in his most famous tale, *Candide,* ridiculed the optimists who thought that all was for the best in the best of all possible worlds. Many intellectuals followed Voltaire in stressing the unreasonable aspects of human behavior and the unnatural character of human institutions. Nevertheless, though many pessimistic cross-currents eddied beneath the gleaming surface of the Enlightenment, the main current of the age was optimistic. Voltaire himself, for all his skepticism, carried on a lifelong crusade against the unnatural and the unreasonable. On the whole, the Enlightenment believed men capable of correcting the errors of their ways, once they had been pointed out to them, and of moving on to a better and brighter future. A perfect instance was the American Declaration of Independence, which listed the pursuit of happiness as a fundamental human right along with life and liberty. The idea that men could pursue happiness and that they might even attain it was indeed new and revolutionary, a profound departure from the tradi-

tional Christian belief that such joy could never be expected on earth.

The philosophes of the eighteenth century derived their basic principles from the men of the preceding "century of genius." Their faith in natural law came from Newton, and their confidence in the powers of human reason in part from Descartes, who had deduced a whole philosophy from the fact that he thought at all. But it was John Locke (1632–1704) to whom the rationalists particularly turned. In his celebrated defense of England's Glorious Revolution, the *Second Treatise of Government,* Locke contended that men are "by nature all free, equal, and independent," and submit to government because they find it convenient to do so, not because they acknowledge any divine right on the part of the monarchy.

The new psychology that Locke advanced in the *Essay Concerning Human Understanding* (1690) strengthened his case against absolute monarchy. Defenders of political and religious absolutism contended that the inclination to submit to authority was present in men's minds when they were born. Locke's *Essay* denied the existence of such innate ideas. He called the newborn mind a *tabula rasa,* a blank slate:

> Let us then suppose the mind to be . . . white paper, void of all characters, without any ideas. How comes it to be furnished? . . . To this I answer, in one word, from EXPERIENCE. . . . Our observation employed either about *external sensible objects, or about the internal operations of our minds perceived and reflected on by ourselves, is that which supplies our understandings with all the materials of thinking.* These two are the fountains of knowledge, from whence all the ideas we have, or can naturally have, do spring.*

*J. Locke, *Essay Concerning Human Understanding,* Everyman ed., (London, 1947), p. 26.

In other words, the two "fountains of knowledge" were environment, rather than heredity, and reason, rather than faith. Locke's matter-of-fact outlook and his empiricism (reliance on experience) place him among the rationalists. He believed that human reason, though unable to account for everything in the universe, explains all that men need to know. "The candle that is set up in us," he wrote, "shines bright enough for all our purposes."

Locke pointed the way to a critical examination of the Old Regime. The philosophes read and admired both his political writings and the *Essay Concerning Human Understanding*. They submitted existing social and economic institutions to the judgment of common sense and discovered many to be unreasonable and unnecessarily complex. Locke's psychology suggested to them that teachers might improve human institutions by improving the thinking of the rising generation. The philosophes sought what was in effect the right kind of chalk to use on the blank slates of impressionable young minds; their search brought them to accept the view of the universe that has been aptly termed the "Newtonian world-machine."

The Enlightenment seized on Newton's discoveries as revelations of ultimate truth. Newton had disclosed the natural force, gravitation, that held the universe together; he made the universe make sense. The philosophes believed that comparable laws could be found governing and explaining all phases of human activity. They pictured themselves as the Newtons of statecraft, justice, and economics who would reduce the most intricate institutions to formulas as neat as Sir Isaac's own mathematical laws and principles. The world, they argued, resembled a giant machine, whose functioning had hitherto been impeded because men did not understand the machinery; once they grasped the basic laws that governed it, the world-machine would operate as it should.

The optimistic implications of this credo were expressed most completely in *The Progress of the Human Mind* (1794) by the philosophe Condorcet, written, ironically enough, when he was in hiding as a victim of political persecution during the French revolutionary Reign of Terror. Condorcet asked:

Houdon's bust of Voltaire, 1781.

If men can predict, with almost complete assurance, the phenomena whose laws are known to them . . . why should it be regarded as a vain enterprise to chart, with some degree of probability, the course of the future destiny of mankind by studying the results of human history? Since the only basis of belief in the natural sciences is the idea that the general laws, known or unknown, regulating the phenomena of the universe are regular and constant, why should this principle be any less true for the development of the intellectual and moral faculties of man than for the other operations of nature?*

"Nature has placed no bounds on the perfecting of the human faculties," Condorcet concluded, "and the progress of this perfectibility is limited only by the duration of the globe on which nature has placed us."* He foresaw a society enjoying a much higher standard of living, more leisure, and a greater equality among people in general and between the sexes in particular. War would be given up as irrational, and disease would be so effectively conquered by medicine that the average life span would be greatly lengthened.

A shortcut to utopia was proposed by the advocates of enlightened despotism, who believed that rulers should act as benevolent reformers on the model of the tyrants of ancient Greece or such Renaissance despots as Cosimo and Lorenzo de' Medici. Like a new Solon,

*Condorcet, *Esquisse d'un tableau historique des progrès de l'esprit humain* (Paris, n.d.), p. 203. Our translation.

*Ibid., p. 5.

Lavoisier with his wife, in his laboratory.

studied the natural laws of family relationships in biology. He proposed a system for classifying plants and animals by genus and species, thus establishing the binomial Latin nomenclature that biologists still follow.

Modern chemical analysis started with Black and Lavoisier. Joseph Black (1728–1799), a Scottish professor, exploded the old theory that air was composed of a single element by proving the existence of several discrete gases. Black's French contemporary Lavoisier (1743–1794) continued his study of gases and demonstrated that water was made up of hydrogen and oxygen (this last a name that he invented from a Greek root meaning "acid" because the element was thought to be present in all acids). Lavoisier asserted that all substances were composed of a relatively few basic chemical elements, of which he identified twenty-three. During the French Revolution Lavoisier served on the commission of experts preparing the metric system—a reform very characteristic of the Enlightenment—until he was executed because he had been one of the hated tax farmers of the Old Regime.

In the eighteenth century astronomy and physics consolidated the great advances they had made in the seventeenth. Another member of the metric commission, Laplace (1749–1827), "the Newton of France," rounded our Sir Isaac's investigation of celestial mechanics and explained the movements of the solar system in a series of mathematical formulas and theorems. In the American colonies the versatile Benjamin Franklin (1706–1790) showed that electricity and lightning were really the same thing. He obtained an electrical charge in a key attached to the string of a kite flown during a thunderstorm in Philadelphia. This experiment, which aroused a lively interest across the Atlantic, was repeated at Versailles for the French royal family.

Almost everybody who was anybody in the eighteenth century attempted experiments. Voltaire made a serious hobby of chemistry; Montesquieu studied physics; and a noble French lady reportedly kept a cadaver in her carriage so that she might employ her travels profitably in dissection and the study of anatomy. Almost every state in Europe had its philosophes and its royal society or learned society to promote the progress of knowledge. Intellectual life was by no means limited to the capitals and big cities; by the middle of the eighteenth century, for example, many provincial towns in France possessed academies, well equipped with reading rooms and lending libraries. In addition, intellectuals paid scant attention to national frontiers and, even in wartime, continued to visit enemy countries and correspond with their citizens. It was a striking example of the eighteenth century's disposition to keep warfare within strict limits and carry on business as usual.

the enlightened despot should clear away the accumulation of artificial manmade law that was choking progress and permit natural laws decreed by God to be applied freely. Many monarchs, among them Frederick the Great of Prussia, Catherine of Russia, and Joseph II of Austria, took up the program of enlightened despotism because it gave them the opportunity to pose as the champions of reason and progress while pressing their age-old fight to make royal authority more absolute. The interplay of reason and *raison d'état*, however, made their kingdoms uncertain proving grounds of the practicality of the reforms proposed by the Enlightenment. A better test of their viability would come with the American Revolution. Yet by the time the Constitution of the United States had proved itself, the century was over, Europe was preoccupied with the revolution in France, and the Enlightenment itself was under increasing attack as too rational and too simple.

II The Philosophes and Their Program of Reform

The philosophes hailed both the improvements in industry and agriculture noted in the last chapter and the continued advance of science. Biology and chemistry were now assuming a modern look. A Swedish botanist and physician, Linnaeus (1707–1778—he observed the old custom by Latinizing his name from Linné),

French Leadership

The cosmopolitan qualities of the century appeared at their best in the Enlightenment, which had its roots in

The Eighteenth Century

In the eighteenth century the grandiose extravaganzas of baroque yielded to lighter and more delicate artistic styles. In Italy, Guardi painted a series of landscapes that he termed "fantastic" with a dreamlike quality anticipating the romantic movement that would emerge at the end of the century, and Canaletto painted views of Venice with subtly colored clouds and sky, though the canals below were thronged with ordinary citizens going about their daily rounds. In France, the paintings of Watteau and Fragonard exemplified the spontaneity and intimacy of the style called *rococo* (from the popularity of motifs derived from rock for-

mations and shells, especially in interior decoration). Another development was the emergence of Britain and her former American colonies into artistic prominence thanks to a series of accomplished portraitists— Hogarth, Lawrence, Reynolds, Gainsborough, and Romney in the one, Gilbert Stuart and Copley in the other. For the most part, eighteenth-century painting reflected the aristocratic old regime at its most elegant and frivolous, but it also hinted at the more democratic subjects and the new concern with color and light that would revolutionize the arts in the century to come.

Fantastic Landscape, by Francesco Guardi.
The Metropolitan Museum of Art, gift of Julia A. Berwind, 1953.

Scene in Venice: The Piazzetta, by Canaletto.
The Metropolitan Museum of Art, Kennedy Fund, 1910.

The Wedding of Stephen Beckingham and Mary Cox, by William Hogarth.
The Metropolitan Museum of Art, Marquand Fund, 1936.

The Painter's Daughter, Mary, by Thomas Gainsborough.

The Metropolitan Museum of Art, bequest of Maria DeWitt Jesup, from the collection of her husband, Morris K. Jesup, 1915.

Mezzetin, by Jean Antoine Watteau.

Le Billet Doux, by Jean Honoré Fragonard.
The Metropolitan Museum of Art, the Jules S. Bache Collection, 1949.

Midshipman Augustus Brine, by John Singleton Copley (1738–1815).
The Metropolitan Museum of Art, bequest of Richard De Wolfe Brixey, 1943.

James Monroe, by Gilbert Stuart, 1817.
The Metropolitan Museum of Art, bequest of Seth Low, 1929.

France and Britain and extended its branches throughout Europe and across to the New World. Yet the Age of Reason also marked the high point of French cultural hegemony, when, as the American philosophe Thomas Jefferson put it, every man had two homelands, his own and France. The French language endowed the Enlightenment with its medium of communication; the salons of Paris helped to set the tone of enlightened writing; the great *Encyclopédie,* edited and published in France, provided a vehicle for enlightened thought.

By the eighteenth century, French was the accepted international language. Louis XIV had raised it to supremacy in diplomacy; the great writers of his age, like Boileau, La Rochefoucauld, Racine, and Molière, had made it preeminent in literature and on the stage. There was much justice in the claim that "a dangerous work written in French is a declaration of war on the whole of Europe." Almost everywhere, even in distant Russia, rulers, aristocrats, and intellectuals preferred French to their native tongues. In 1783, it was the Academy of Berlin that conducted a competition for the best reply to the question "What has made the French language universal?" According to the prize-

winning essay, "Precise, popular, and reasonable, it is no longer just French; it is the language of humanity."

The Parisian salons taught writers precision, reasonableness, and the popular touch. The salon was the reception room of a large private home where guests assembled for an afternoon or evening of conversation under the guidance of the hostess, usually a wealthy woman from the nobility or the upper bourgeoisie. Here is a contemporary report of the way in which one of them conducted her salon:

This circle was formed of people who were not linked together. She had taken them from here and there, but chosen so well that when they were together they harmonised like the strings of an instrument tuned by a cunning hand. . . . She played on this instrument with an art that was almost genius; she seemed to know what sound the string she was going to touch would give: I mean that so well were our characters and minds known to her, that she had only to say one word to bring them into play. Nowhere was conversation livelier, or more brilliant, or better controlled. . . . The minds she worked upon were neither shallow nor weak. . . . Her gift for throwing out an idea, and giving it to men of this type to discuss; her gift for discussing it herself, like them, with precision, and sometimes with

A salon in the time of Louis XVI. The "serious" salons were less relaxed than this one.

eloquence; her gift for bringing in new ideas and varying the conversation . . . ; these gifts, I say, are not those of an ordinary woman. It was not with fashionable trifles or self-conceit that, every day for four hours' conversation without weariness or emptiness, she knew how to make herself interesting to these brilliant minds.*

Although some salons were snobbish and superficial, most gave young philosophes the opportunity to receive a hearing—and to obtain a square meal; they welcomed and, if the need arose, protected new men and new ideas. Pressure from the salons determined the outcome of elections to the French Academy, which passed under the control of the philosophes in the 1760s.

The great organ of the philosophes was the *Encyclopédie,* which published its first volume in 1751 and, when it was completed a generation later, totaled twenty-two folio volumes of text and eleven of plates. Its roster of 160 contributors included Voltaire, Montesquieu, Rousseau, Condorcet, Quesnay, and Turgot. For years the editor-in-chief, Denis Diderot (1713–1784), put in a fourteen-hour working day to advance his crusade for reason and progress. He commissioned the drawing of superb plates showing the details of the new industrial machines and even learned to operate some of the machines himself. Diderot and his fellow encyclopedists did not intend to compile an objective compendium of information. Rather, as Diderot explained in the article on the word "encyclopedia," they aimed to assemble knowledge "in order that the labors of past centuries should not prove useless for succeeding centuries; that our descendants, by becoming better informed, will at the same time become happier and more virtuous."

The purposes of the *Encyclopédie* were subversive and didactic: to expose and thereby ultimately to destroy the superstition, the intolerance, and the gross inequalities of the Old Regime and instruct the public in the virtues of natural law and the wonders of science. It accomplished its purposes, antagonizing many defenders of the Old Regime but gaining enough subscribers to prove a profitable business venture. Louis XV tried to prevent its being printed or circulated, the Church condemned it for its materialism and for its skepticism, and the publishers, without consulting Diderot, ordered the printers to cut out many passages likely to cause offense. But to no avail. The indignation of Diderot, the ridicule leveled by the philosophes at their enemies, the loyalty of the subscribers to the *Encyclopédie,* and the help given the editors by Choiseul, the foreign minister, and Madame de Pompadour, the king's mistress and herself an enlightened spirit—all frustrated the censors. The *Encyclopédie* reached a substantial reading public; in Dijon, for example, a small provincial city and the capital of Burgundy, there were sixty sets, each of which on the average had several readers.

Memoirs of Marmontel, trans. Brigit Patmore (London, 1930), p. 270.

Laissez Faire Economics

The economic program of the philosophes was introduced in the articles written for the *Encylopédie* by the versatile François Quesnay (1694–1774), biologist, surgeon, and personal physician to Louis XV and Madame de Pompadour. Quesnay headed a group of thinkers and publicists who adopted the name Physiocrats, believers in the rule of nature. The name revealed the basic outlook of the school. The Physiocrats expected that they would, as Quesnay claimed, discover natural economic laws "susceptible of a demonstration as severe and incontestable as those of geometry and algebra." And to arrive at such laws, the "sovereign and the nation should never lose sight of the fact that land is the only source of wealth, and that agriculture increases wealth." *

This new Physiocratic concept of natural wealth clashed with the mercantilist doctrine of equating money and wealth. "The riches which men need for their livelihood do not consist of money," Quesnay argued; "they are rather the goods necessary both for life and for the annual production of these goods." Mercantilist states, in his judgment, therefore committed a whole series of errors by placing excessive emphasis on the accumulation of specie. They tried to regulate commerce, when they should have freed it from controls. They made goods more expensive by levying tariffs and other indirect taxes, whereas they should have collected only a single, direct tax on the net income from land. *Laissez faire, laissez passer,* the Physiocrats urged, in an injunction they made famous—live and let live, let nature take its course. They repudiated the controlled economy of mercantilism and enunciated the "classical" or "liberal" doctrine of the free economy. The state ought not to disturb the free play of natural economic forces. Most of all, it ought not to interfere with private property, so necessary for the production of agricultural wealth.

The classic formulation of laissez faire economics was made by the Scotsman Adam Smith (1727–1790) in his *Inquiry into the Nature and Causes of the Wealth of Nations* (1776). Smith, too, leveled a vigorous attack on mercantilism. It was wrong to restrict imports by tariffs for the protection of home industries:

> It is the maxim of every prudent master of a family never to attempt to make at home what it will cost him more to make than to buy. The tailor does not attempt to make his own shoes, but buys them of the shoemaker. The shoemaker does not attempt to make his own clothes, but employs a tailor. . . .
>
> What is prudence in the conduct of every private family, can scarce be folly in that of a great kingdom. If a foreign country can supply us with a commodity cheaper than we ourselves can make it, better buy it of them with some part of the produce of our industry. . . .†

*F. Quesnay, "Maximes Générales du Gouvernement Economique d'un Royaume Agricole," in E. Daire, ed., *Physiocrates* (Paris, 1846), 1:82. Our translation.

†A. Smith, . . . *Wealth of Nations,* Everyman ed. (London, 1910), 1:401.

Like the Physiocrats, Adam Smith attributed the wealth of nations to the production of goods; but, as befitted a resident of Britain, the leading commercial and industrial state of the day, he took a less agrarian view of the matter. For Adam Smith, production depended less on the soil (the Physiocratic view) than on the labor of farmers, craftsmen, and millhands. Again like the Physiocrats, he minimized the role of the state, claiming that men who were freely competing to seek their own wealth would be led to enrich their whole society, as if they were being guided by "an invisible hand"—that is, by nature. A government should act mainly as a passive policeman:

> According to the system of natural liberty, the sovereign has only three duties to attend to; . . . first, the duty of protecting the society from the violence and invasion of other independent societies; secondly, the duty of protecting, as far as possible, every member of the society from the injustice and oppression of every other member of it, or the duty of establishing an exact administration of justice; and thirdly, the duty of erecting and maintaining certain public works and certain public institutions, which it can never be for the interest of any individual, or small number of individuals, to erect and maintain.*

The mercantilists had raised the state over the individual and had declared a ceaseless trade warfare among nations. Adam Smith and the Physiocrats, reversing the emphasis, proclaimed both the economic liberty of the individual and free trade among nations to be natural laws. The laissez faire program of the Enlightenment marked a revolutionary change in economic thought and was later used to justify the rugged individualism of nineteenth-century industrial barons. It did not, however, revolutionize the economic policies of the great powers, who long remained stubbornly mercantilist. As the next chapter will show, Turgot, the chief practical exponent of Physiocratic doctrine, tried in vain to emancipate French agriculture and French business from traditional restrictions during his brief tenure as chief minister of Louis XVI in the 1770s. The Physiocrats neglected what so many philosophes neglected. They overlooked the difficulty of accommodating the simple and reasonable dictates of natural law to the complexity of politics and the irrationality of human nature.

Justice and Education

The disposition to let nature take its course, so evident in laissez faire economics, also characterized the outlook of the philosophes on questions of justice. They believed that manmade legislation prevented the application of the natural laws of justice. They were horrified by the cumbersome judicial procedures of the Old Regime and by its unjust and antiquated statutes. New lawgivers were needed to humanize and simplify legal codes, and

a new science was needed to make the punishment of crime both humane and effective.

The new science, which laid the foundations of modern sociology, was promoted by Cesare Beccaria (1738–1794), a north Italian philosophe and the author of *Essay on Crimes and Punishments* (1764). Beccaria formulated three natural laws of justice, which are excellent examples of the Enlightenment's confident belief that common sense would enable men to formulate nature's truths. First, punishments should aim to

> prevent the criminal from doing further injury to society, and to prevent others from committing the like offense. Such punishments, therefore, . . . ought to be chosen, as will make the strongest and most lasting impressions on the minds of others, with the least torment to the body of the criminal.

Second, justice should act speedily,

> because the smaller the interval of time between the punishment and the crime, the stronger and more lasting will be the association of the two ideas of *Crime* and *Punishment*.

And last:

> Crimes are more effectively prevented by the *certainty* than by the *severity* of the punishment. . . . The certainty of a small punishment will make a stronger impression than the fear of one more severe. . . .*

Beccaria attacked both torture and capital punishment because they deviated so sharply from these natural laws. Torture, he claimed, falsely assumed that "pain should be the test of truth, as if truth resided in the muscles and fibres of a wretch in torture." Jail sentences, not execution, should be imposed as punishments. Like many later reformers, Beccaria asserted that punishment alone was not enough. The best method of preventing crime was to "let liberty be attended with knowledge," to "perfect the system of education."

In education, too, the Old Regime failed to pass the tests of reason and natural law. The philosophes deplored the almost universal ecclesiastical control of teaching and demanded that more stress should be placed on science and less on theology, more on modern languages and less on Greek and Latin, and more on modern history and less on ancient. Most universities contributed very little to the Enlightenment; prestigious institutions like Oxford, Cambridge, and the Sorbonne were stagnating under the dead hand of clerical influence. But there were a few exceptions. Two of the liveliest institutions were recently founded German universities—Göttingen, in the electorate of Hanover, which had an outstanding library; and Halle, in Brandenburg, renowned for its tolerance of both free philo-

---

*Ibid., chap. 9.

*C. Beccaria, *Essay on Crimes and Punishments,* reprinted ed. (Stanford, Calif., 1953), pp. 47, 75, 93.

sophical inquiry and Pietist rebellion against Lutheran orthodoxy. In addition, the medical schools at Vienna, at Leiden in Holland, and at Edinburgh in Scotland brought distinction to their universities.

In primary education the most sweeping revisions were proposed by the great nonconformist of the Enlightenment, Jean-Jacques Rousseau (1712–1778). Rousseau rebelled against the strict and disciplined society of his birthplace, Calvinist Geneva. He rebelled against the intensive bookish studies he had been forced to pursue as a young boy, and against the polite conventions he later encountered in the Paris salons. The result was *Emile* (1762), half treatise and half romance, a long and fervent plea for progressive education. *Emile* had two heroes—Emile, the student, and Rousseau himself, the teacher. The training that Rousseau prescribed for his pupil departed in every particular from eighteenth-century practice: "Life is the trade I would teach him. When he leaves me, I grant you, he will be neither a magistrate, a soldier, nor a priest; he will be a man." * Rousseau followed a laissez-faire policy toward his pupil. He did not argue with Emile, or discipline him, or force him to read at an early age. Emile observed the world of nature from firsthand experience, not in books. He learned geography by finding his own way in the woods (with his tutor's help), and agriculture by working in the fields. And when in his teens he was at last taught to read, his first assignment was "the best treatise on an education according to nature," Defoe's *Robinson Crusoe.*

Rousseau's educational program had many faults. It was impractical, for it assumed that every child should have the undivided attention of a tutor twenty-four hours a day. And it fostered the permanent dependence of pupil upon teacher; when Emile married and became a father, he implored his tutor to remain at his post: "I need you more than ever now that I am taking up the duties of manhood." And yet *Emile* was a most important book, because Rousseau returned to the Renaissance concept of the universal man and the ancient Greek ideal of the sound mind in the sound body. His theoretical program was adapted to the practical requirements of the classroom by the Swiss educator Pestalozzi (1746–1827), who set an influential example by teaching geography, drawing, and other novelties in his experimental school. Still more influential was the reaction of Pestalozzi against the barracks tradition of drilling lessons into the pupil through a combination of endless repetition and bodily punishment.

The Attack on Religion

Attacks on clerical teaching formed part of a vigorous and growing body of criticism against the role of the clergy in the Old Regime. In denouncing fanaticism and superstition, the philosophes singled out the Society

*J. Rousseau, *Emile*, Everyman ed. (New York, 1911), p. 9.

of Jesus, the symbol and the instrument of militant Catholicism. Pressure for the dissolution of the Jesuits gained the support of Catholic rulers, who had long been annoyed by Jesuit intervention in politics. In the 1760s the Jesuits were expelled from several leading Catholic countries, including Portugal, France (at the instance of the parlements rather than that of the monarch), and the homeland of Loyola himself, Spain. Pope Clement XIV dissolved the Society in 1773; it was revived half a century later, when the political and intellectual climate had become less hostile.

As champions of tolerance, the philosophes showed a particular affinity for the religious attitude called deism (from the Latin *deus,* "god"). Deist doctrines arose in seventeenth-century England, the England of the civil war and Newtonian science, where the deists sought settlement of religious strife by the use of reason rather than by resort to arms. All men, they asserted, could agree on a few broad religious principles. Since the Newtonian world-machine implied the existence of a mechanic, the deists accepted God as the creator of the universe; some of them also believed that he would preside over the Last Judgment. But they limited his role to the distant past and the remote future, and they doubted that he had any concern with day-to-day human activities or would answer prayer and bestow grace. The deists particularly denounced as superstitions Christian beliefs and practices hinging on mysteries and miracles, like the Trinity, the Virgin Birth, and the Eucharist.

The chief exponent of deism in France was Voltaire (1694–1778), a veritable one-man Enlightenment who poured forth a prodigious quantity of letters, plays, tales, epics, histories, and essays. Clear, witty, and often bitingly satirical, his writings were enormously popular, not least when they were printed under an assumed name or outside France to evade the censorship. It was Voltaire who made Frenchmen aware of great Englishmen like Locke, Newton, and Shakespeare (though Shakespeare's exuberance suggested the Renaissance far more than it did the Enlightenment). And it was Voltaire who broadened the writing of history to include economics and culture as well as war and politics. He was himself a highly successful, and sometimes unscrupulous, businessman, who made a fortune out of speculations.

Voltaire coined the anticlerical watchword *Ecrasez l'infâme*—crush the infamous thing, crush bigotry, superstition, perhaps the Church itself. He had experienced political intolerance at first hand. As a young man he had spent a year as a prisoner in the gloomy Paris Bastille and three years of exile in England because he had criticized the French government and had offended a member of the privileged nobility. The religious and political freedom of Britain made an immense impression on the refugee:

If there were just one religion in England, despotism would threaten; if there were two religions, they would cut each other's throats; but there are thirty religions, and they live together peacefully and happily.*

Back home, Voltaire carried on a lifelong crusade for tolerance. In 1762, a Protestant merchant of Toulouse, Jean Calas, was accused of having murdered his son to prevent his conversion to Catholicism. Calas was executed by being broken on the wheel, the prolonged agony usually prescribed for non-nobles, only aristocrats being allowed the much swifter punishment of beheading. Voltaire discovered that the accusation against Calas was based on rumor and that the court condemning him had acted out of anti-Protestant hysteria. He campaigned for three years until the original verdict was reversed, and the name of Calas was cleared.

The existence of evil—of injustices like that suffered by Calas—confronted the Age of Reason with a major problem. Few of the philosophes accepted the traditional Christian teaching that evil arose from original sin, from the fall of Adam and Eve. If God were purely benevolent, they asked, why then had he created a world in which evil so often prevailed? Could a perfect God produce an imperfect creation? Alexander Pope, Voltaire's English contemporary, contended that this was the best of all possible worlds:

All Nature is but Art, unknown to thee;
All chance, direction which thou canst not see;
All discord, harmony not understood;
All partial evil, universal good:
And, spite of Pride, in erring Reason's spite,
One truth is clear, Whatever is, is right.

Voltaire took his stand in *Candide,* which satirized the disasters abounding in the best of all possible worlds. A real disaster had inspired the writing of *Candide*—the great earthquake, tidal wave, and fire that engulfed the city of Lisbon on November 1, 1755, and killed upwards of 10,000 people.

Deism enabled Voltaire to effect a kind of reconciliation between a perfect God and the imperfect world. Voltaire believed that God was indeed the Creator:

When I see a watch . . . , I conclude that an intelligent being arranged the springs of this mechanism so that the hand should tell the time. Similarly, when I see the springs of the human body, I conclude that an intelligent being has arranged these organs to be kept and nourished in the womb for nine months; that the eyes have been given for seeing, the hands for grasping, etc.†

But, Voltaire concluded, there was no way to determine whether or not God would attempt to perfect his creation. On one point Voltaire had no doubts: He never questioned the usefulness of religion for the masses. "Man," he stated, "has always needed a brake." He

practiced what he preached by building a church for the tenants on his country estate at Ferney on the French-Swiss frontier.

Not all philosophes were prepared to make even this concession to religion. La Mettrie (1709–1751) eliminated any need for religion by propounding a totally materialistic philosophy in a radical application of Newtonianism, *L'Homme Machine* (Man a Machine). The world and all its inhabitants, human as well as animal, he argued, are self-regulating mechanisms made out of one universal substance and behaving as their natures compel them to behave. Helvétius (1715–1771), whose wife ran a salon, carried these ideas a step further and scandalized France by claiming that "personal interest is the only and universal estimator of the merit of human actions." * Because self-interest could act as a kind of inner brake, men did not require the external brake on their actions provided by religion.

The most outspoken atheist of the Enlightenment was Holbach (1723–1789), a German baron living in Paris who presided over a salon. Like Helvétius he regarded self-interest as the mainspring of morality:

Since we must judge men's actions according to their effects on us, we approve the self-interest which motivates them whenever an advantage for mankind results from it. . . . But in this judgment we are not ourselves disinterested. Experience, reflection, habit, reason have given us a moral taste, and we find as much pleasure in being the witnesses of a great and generous act as a man of good taste experiences on seeing a beautiful painting of which he is not the owner. . . . The virtuous man is one who has been taught by correct ideas that his self-interest or happiness lies in acting in a way that others are forced to love and to approve out of their own self-interest.†

Holbach's claim that the virtuous man is "taught by correct ideas" reflects the influence of Locke's psychology; it has sometimes been viewed as forecasting the "brainwashing" of twentieth-century totalitarian regimes, though this seems rather farfetched.

Holbach denounced churches as sinister institutions thwarting the benevolent operation of reason and of natural law. He dismissed God as a "phantom of the imagination," whose existence was denied by the evils and imperfections of the world that he was alleged to have created. A wealthy man, Holbach extended the hospitality of his salon to all, even to Jesuit refugees from anticlerical persecution. His tolerance impressed his contemporaries more favorably than his atheism did; most philosophes remained midway between belief and disbelief and preferred deism.

Political Thought

"In politics as in religion toleration is a necessity," decreed Voltaire. To him, therefore, tolerant Britain

---

Lettres Philosophiques, No. 6. Our translation.
†*Le Traité de Métaphysique,* chap. 2. Our translation.

*Helvétius, *On the Mind,* as quoted in L. G. Crocker, ed., *The Age of Enlightenment* (New York, 1969), p. 149.
†D'Holbach, *Système de la Nature,* as quoted in ibid., pp. 160–161.

seemed utopia, and he paid the British constitution the most flattering compliment at the command of his age when he claimed that it "might have been invented by Locke, Newton, or Archimedes." Montesquieu (1689–1755), an aristocratic French lawyer and philosophe, set out to analyze the political virtues of Britain. In his major work, *The Spirit of the Laws* (1748), Montesquieu laid down the premise that no one system of government suited all countries. Laws, he wrote,

> should be in relation to the climate of each country, to the quality of its soil, to its situation and extent, to the principal occupation of the natives, whether husbandmen, huntsmen, or shepherds: they should have relation to the degree of liberty which the constitution will bear; to the religion of the inhabitants, to their inclinations, riches, numbers, commerce, manners, and customs.*

Montesquieu cautioned against supposing that old customs could simply be decreed out of existence, citing the telling example of Peter the Great's failure to impose Western ways on Russia.

In spelling out the influence of tradition and environment upon forms of government, Montesquieu concluded that republics were best suited to the small and barren countries, limited monarchies to the middle-sized and more prosperous, and despotisms to vast empires. Britain, being middle-sized and prosperous, was quite properly a monarchy limited by aristocracy. The hereditary nobility sat in the House of Lords; a kind of nobility of talent, the elected representatives, composed the Commons. All this was admirable in Montesquieu's view, for he pronounced the mass of people "extremely unfit" for government. If only the French monarchy had let the aristocracy retain its old political functions, he intimated, France would never have sunk to her present low state.

Montesquieu found another key to the political superiority of Britain in the famous concept of checks and balances. In Parliament, Lords and Commons checked each other; in the government as a whole, the balance was maintained by means of the separation of powers:

> When the legislative and executive powers are united in the same person, or in the same body of magistrates, there can be no liberty; because apprehensions may arise, lest the same monarch or senate should enact tyrannical laws, to execute them in a tyrannical manner.

> Again, there is no liberty, if the judiciary power be not separated from the legislative and executive. Were it joined with the legislative the life and liberty of the subject would be exposed to arbitrary control; for the judge would be then the legislator. Were it joined to the executive power, the judge might behave with violence and oppression.†

Here Montesquieu failed to take into account a devel-

opment that was by no means obvious in the mid-eighteenth century. He did not see that the British constitution was moving toward the concentration of powers in the House of Commons rather than their greater separation, since the cabinet was becoming the instrument of legislative supremacy over the executive.

Montesquieu likewise ran into trouble when he tried to derive specific corollaries from his general theorem about the influence of climate and geography on human institutions. Autocracy and Catholicism, he asserted, flourished in the Mediterranean states where the climate is warm and natural resources are abundant. Moderate government and Protestantism, conversely, are at home in the colder and harsher environment of northern Europe. The facts did not always confirm this rule about north and south. Freedom-loving Protestant Britain and Holland behaved in good northern fashion; but if Montesquieu were correct, barren, northern, Protestant Prussia should have been a citadel of liberty, not the stronghold of Hohenzollern absolutism. By jumping to conclusions from insufficient evidence, Montesquieu committed a fault common among the philosophes. But, unlike some of them, he had too firm a grasp on political realities to assume that governments either were or should be the same everywhere. Later political thinkers made good use of the comparative methods introduced by *The Spirit of the Laws* and refined Montesquieu's judgments on the interrelationship of geography, religion, and politics.

From the standpoint of American history, as we shall see, Montesquieu and Locke proved to be the most influential political thinkers of the Enlightenment. From the standpoint of European history, the most important was Jean-Jacques Rousseau, who inspired the radicals of the French Revolution. Rousseau's ideas proceeded from a sweeping generalization very typical of the Enlightenment. Whereas nature dignifies man, he contended, civilization corrupts him; man would be corrupted less if civilized institutions followed nature more closely. This theme ran through many of Rousseau's principal writings. In *Emile*, it was at the heart of his program for educational reform; earlier, it was enunciated in the *Discourse on the Moral Effects of the Arts and Sciences* (1750), which won a competition set by the Academy of Dijon. The Academy asked: Has the restoration of the arts and sciences had a purifying effect upon morals? Certainly not, the prizewinner answered; it has nearly ruined them.

In a second discourse, *On the Origin of the Inequality of Mankind* (1755), Rousseau blamed the vices of civilization on private property:

> The first man who, having enclosed a piece of ground, bethought himself of saying, "This is mine," and found people simple enough to believe him, was the real founder of civil society. From how many crimes, wars, and murders, from how many horrors and misfortunes might not any one have saved mankind, by pulling up the stakes, or filling up the ditch, and crying to his fellows: "Beware of listening to this imposter; you are undone if you once forget that the

---

The Spirit of the Laws, trans. T. Nugent (New York, 1949), book 1, chap. 3.
†Ibid., book 21, chap. 6.

fruits of the earth belong to us all, and the earth itself to nobody."

Men accepted laws and governors in order to protect their property:

They had too many disputes among themselves to do without arbitrators, and too much ambition and avarice to go long without masters. All ran headlong to their chains, in hopes of securing their liberty; for they had just wit enough to perceive the advantages of political institutions, without experience enough to enable them to foresee their danger.

Government was evil, Rousseau concluded, but a necessary evil. "What, then, is to be done? Must societies be totally abolished? . . . Must we return again to the forest to live among bears?" No, civilized men could not return to a primitive existence, could "no longer subsist on plants or acorns, or live without laws and magistrates." *

Rousseau's major political work, *The Social Contract* (1762), attempted to reconcile the liberty of the individual and the institution of government through a new and revolutionary version of the contract theory of government. Earlier theories of contract, from the Middle Ages to Hobbes and Locke, had hinged on the agreement between the people to be governed, on the one hand, and a single governor or small group of governors, on the other. Earlier theories postulated a political contract; Rousseau's contract was social in that a whole society agreed to be ruled by its general will:

Each of us puts his person and all his power in common under the supreme direction of the general will, and, in our corporate capacity, we receive each member as an indivisible part of the whole.

"Each individual," Rousseau continued "may have a particular will contrary or dissimilar to the general will which he has as a citizen." If the individual insists on putting self-interest above community interest, he should be obliged to observe the general will. "This means nothing less than that he will be forced to be free." Thus, the general will was moral as well as political in nature, for it represented what was *best* for the whole community, what the community *ought* to do.

Formulating the general will, Rousseau believed, was the business of the whole people. The power of legislation, he argued, could never be properly transferred to an elected body:

The deputies of the people . . . are not and cannot be its representatives; they are merely its stewards, and can carry through no definitive acts. Every law the people has not ratified in person is null and void—is, in fact, not a law. The people of England regards itself as free; but it is grossly mistaken; it is free only during the election of members of Parliament.†

*In *The Social Contract and Discourses,* Everyman ed. (New York, 1913), pp. 192, 205, 228.
†Ibid., pp. 13, 15, 78.

Executing the general will, however, could legitimately be the business of a smaller group. Like Montesquieu, Rousseau believed that the number of governors should vary inversely with the size and resources of the state— monarchy for the wealthy, aristocracy for the state of middling size and wealth, and democracy for the small and poor. Rousseau doubted, however, that any state was ready for the absolute form of democracy in which the people themselves actually executed the laws. "Were there a people of gods, their government would be democratic. So perfect a government is not for men."*

Rousseau was quite aware that *The Social Contract* was not a manual of practical politics. On another occasion, when he made suggestions for the reform of the Polish government, his counsels were decidedly more cautious. He admonished the Poles to renew their national spirit through education and patriotic festivals. While favoring the abolition of the *liberum veto,* he recommended that the elective monarchy be retained, that the nobles keep many of their privileges but acquire a new sense of duty, and that the serfs be liberated but only after they had been taught responsibility.

Although these suggestions were moderate enough, the influence of Rousseau has not been exerted on the side of moderation. Almost every radical political doctrine in the past two centuries has owed something to Rousseau. Socialists justify collectivism on the basis of his attacks on private property and of his insistence that "the fruits of the earth belong to us all." Patriots and nationalists hail him as an early prophet of the creed that nations do—and should—differ. Throughout his writings as well as in his advice to the Poles, he referred to "the dear love of country." *The Social Contract* concluded with a plea for the establishment of a "civil religion," which would displace the traditional faith. The moral code of early Christianity might be retained, Rousseau allowed, but the state should no longer have to compete with the church for the allegiance of citizens.

Rousseau's concept of the general will has aroused conflicting interpretations. Because it is ethical in character, it seems to represent something more than the sum of individual wills—the whole appears to be more than the sum of its parts. Many, therefore, see in Rousseau a man who exalted the welfare of the nation over that of the citizens composing it, a man who indeed worshiped the state and proposed the "civil religion" of *The Social Contract* so that everyone would have to follow suit. Dictators have justified their totalitarianism by asserting that they have a special insight into the general will; Hitler's celebrated "intuition" is an example. The police state can be justified on the grounds that it is doing its subjects a favor by "forcing them to be free."

The authoritarian interpretation indicates some of the possible consequences of Rousseau's ideas, but it overlooks both the strongly idealistic and democratic

*Ibid., p. 56.

tone of his writings and his personal hostility toward the absolutism of the Old Regime. It seems plausible that by the general will Rousseau was describing the good citizens' acceptance of democratically achieved decisions, something like consensus or what the Friends call their "sense of the meeting." In short, the general will is an attempt to understand the psychology of obedience to man-made laws, although it does not take care of the difficulties arising when there is no sense of the meeting. Rousseau's declaration—"Were there a people of gods, their government would be demo-cratic"—has stirred ardent disciples of democracy from the French Revolution on down to the present.

But what if the people are not gods? Then they must be trained in godliness, and Rousseau himself pointed the way. *Emile* showed how education could help, and *The Social Contract* at least implied that men might one day become so virtuous that they would follow the general will naturally and would no longer have to be "forced to be free."

A political prescription more practical than *The Social Contract* and more consonant with existing mon-archical institutions was enlightened despotism. The Physiocrats, the chief theorists of enlightened despot-ism, did not share the concern of Montesquieu and Rousseau with the status of the legislative power. In the Physiocratic view, God was the legislator, nature preserved the divine legislation, and the sole duty of government was to administer these natural laws. De-mocracy and autocracy alike had the fatal weakness of delegating administrative authority to individuals whose transient selfish aims clashed with the permanent welfare of the nation. By contrast, the Physiocrats ex-plained, the personal interests of a hereditary monarch coincided with the national interests through his "co-ownership" of the territories under his rule. This amounted to saying that, since the whole of a kingdom was in a sense the king's property, whatever he did would be right, so long as it was reasonable and natu-ral. This came close to being a secular restatement of divine right theory, and it is scarcely surprising that so many eighteenth-century monarchs proclaimed themselves to be enlightened despots.

III The Enlightened Despots
Frederick the Great
Of all the eighteenth-century rulers, Frederick II the Great, king of Prussia from 1740 to 1786, appeared best attuned to the Enlightenment. As a youth, he rebelled against the drill-sergeant methods of his father, Fred-erick William I. He delighted in music, and played the flute, which he took with him even on military cam-paigns. An attentive reader of the philosophes, he ex-changed letters with them and brought Voltaire to live for a time as his pensioner in his palace at Potsdam near Berlin. He wrote a pamphlet, *Anti-Machiavel*, de-nouncing the immorality of *The Prince*. And he himself

laid down the fundamental requirements for an en-lightened despot:

> Princes, sovereigns, kings are not clothed with supreme authority to plunge with impunity into debauchery and lux-ury. . . . [The prince] should often remind himself that he is a man just as the least of his subjects. If he is the first judge, the first general, the first financier, the first minister of the nation, . . . it is in order to fulfill the duties which these titles impose upon him. He is only the first servant of the state, obliged to act with fairness, wisdom, and un-selfishness, as if at every instant he would have to render an account of his administration to his citizens.*

Frederick was indeed "the first servant of the state," shunning luxury, wearing stained and shabby clothing, and toiling long and hard at his desk. But did he also act with "fairness, wisdom, and unselfish-ness"? Despite his *Anti-Machiavel*, Frederick conducted foreign and military affairs in true Machiavellian style. "The principle of aggrandizement is the fundamental law of every government,"† he wrote, and the way he managed his invasion of Silesia in 1740 would have aroused the envy of Caesar Borgia. At home, closeted in his Potsdam palace where he conducted the business of state by correspondence, he drove his subordinates like slaves. Viewed as a general, diplomat, and the master mechanic of Prussian administration, Frederick the Great was efficient and successful, but he was scarcely enlightened. His claim to be a benevolent despot must rise or fall on the record of his social and economic reforms.

No Physiocrat could have done more than Fred-erick to improve Prussian agriculture. From western Europe he imported clover, potatoes, crop rotation, and the iron plow, which turned up the soil more effectively than the old wooden share. He drained the swamps of the lower Oder Valley, opened up farms in Silesia and elsewhere, and brought in 300,000 immigrants, mainly from other areas of Germany, to settle the new lands and augment the sparse population of East Prussia. By the time he died, one family out of five in his domains came from recent immigrant stock. After the ravages of the Seven Years' War, Frederick gave the peasants tools, stock, and seed to repair their ruined farms. He nursed along the admirable German tradition of scien-tific forestry, which was then only in its infancy.

Frederick, however, was hostile to the doctrine of laissez faire and cut imports to the bone in order to save money for support of the army. His mercantilism stimulated the growth of Prussian industry, particularly the textiles and metals needed by the army. But it also placed a staggering burden of taxation on his subjects and produced several economic absurdities. For in-stance, Frederick tried to make Prussia grow its own tobacco, for which the climate was not suited. And,

*"Essai sur les Formes de Gouvernement et sur les Devoirs des Souverains," *Oeuvres Posthumes* (Berlin, 1788), 6:64, 83–84. Our translation.
†Quoted by G. Ritter, *Frederick the Great: A Historical Profile* (Berkeley, 1968), p. 7.

since the German taste for coffee required a large outlay of money abroad, he laid a heavy duty on imported coffee beans, and even established a special corps of French "coffee smellers" to trap smugglers.

The religious and social policies of Frederick the Great likewise combined the Age of Reason at its most reasonable with the Old Regime at its least enlightened. A deist, Frederick prided himself on religious tolerance. When the Jesuits were expelled from Catholic states, he invited them to seek refuge in predominantly Lutheran Prussia; he gave the minority of Catholics, particularly important in Silesia, virtually full equality, urging them to build their church steeples as high as they liked, and set the example by constructing a large new Catholic church in the center of Berlin. He even boasted that he would build a mosque in his capital if Muslims wanted to settle there. Yet the same Frederick alleged that Jews were "useless to the state," levied special heavy taxes on his Jewish subjects, and tried to exclude them from the professions and from the civil service.

Frederick rendered Prussians a great service by his judicial reforms, which freed the courts from political pressures. He ordered a reduction in the use of torture, and he put an end to the curious custom of taking appeals from the ordinary courts to university faculties, setting up a regular system of appellate courts instead. He mitigated the venal practice of bribing judges by insisting that gratuities received from litigants be placed in a common pool, from which each judge should draw only his fair share as a supplement to his meager salary.

Yet the same Frederick took a positively medieval view of the merits of social caste, in part because of his own firmly held stoical convictions about the patriotic duties required of both ruler and subjects. He did nothing to loosen the bonds of serfdom that still shackled much of the Prussian peasantry. When he gave the peasants material assistance and urged them to learn the three Rs, his aims were severely utilitarian. Peasants were to learn nothing beyond the rudiments of reading and writing; otherwise, they might become discontented with their station in life, which was, in his view, that of "beast of burden." Regarding the middle class, too, with disdain, Frederick respected only the landed nobility and gentry. At the close of the Seven Years' War he forced all bourgeois officers in the army to resign their commissions; business and professional men were to be exempt from military service but subject to heavy taxation. He opposed membership in the Academy of Berlin for the leading German writer of his age, Lessing, because his dramas defended middle-class values of social and political freedom and were written in German, not French. Even the favored Junkers did not escape Frederick's penny-pinching. Although he appointed only Junkers as army officers, he discouraged their marrying to reduce the number of potential widows to whom the state would owe a pension.

While Frederick indulged his favorite dogs and horses, giving them special house privileges, he was temperamentally incapable of getting along with people. He despised and neglected his wife. Voltaire, that great French champion of toleration, could not tolerate the strain of prolonged daily association with Frederick. When the king requested him to edit his rather feeble French verses, Voltaire made a cutting remark about washing the dirty linen of royalty; Frederick retorted by comparing his guest to an orange, to be sucked dry and thrown away. The two men eventually renewed their friendship through the less demanding medium of correspondence.

Frederick's will directed that he be buried beside his pet dogs—"Such," remarked a French observer, "is the last mark of contempt he thought proper to cast upon mankind." The verdict has been sustained by many liberal historians, who pronounce Frederick's supposed enlightenment a mere device of propaganda, an attempt to clothe the nakedness of his absolutism with the decent intellectual garments of the age. This is, however, rather too harsh and one-sided, an attempt perhaps to fix on Frederick some of the responsibility for the atrocities committed by Hitler and the Nazis almost two centuries later. It would be fairer to argue that Frederick espoused two often conflicting philosophies—the Spartan traditions of the Hohenzollerns and the humane principles of the Enlightenment. The former, with its strong Protestant convictions of man's sinfulness, kept him from sharing the latter's optimistic estimate of human nature and potentiality. Frederick was an enlightened despot only so far as he could reconcile the precepts of the Age of Reason with the imperatives of Prussian kingship. He was a Hohenzollern, first and always.

Maria Theresa, Joseph II, and Leopold II

Frederick's decisive victory in the War of the Austrian Succession laid bare the basic weaknesses of the Hapsburgs' dynastic empire. The empress Maria Theresa (1740–1780) saw the need for reform and often took as her model the institutions of her hated but successful Hohenzollern rival. She had the advice of capable ministers, some of them schooled in cameralism, the new discipline taught at Halle and other German universities, which combined the study of mercantilism, finance, and public administration. The empress and her experts increased taxes, especially on the nobility, and strengthened the central government at the expense of local aristocratic assemblies, building up the still rather sketchy departments of central administration. They obliged the non-German provinces to accept the hegemony of the German officials and German language of Vienna. Unlike Frederick the Great, Maria Theresa also took the first steps toward the eventual abolition of serfdom by placing a ceiling on the amount of taxes and of labor service that the peasants could be compelled to render. While personally very devout, she subjected the Church to heavier taxation, confis-

Batoni's painting of Joseph II with the future emperor Leopold II.

1780. Voltaire received a glowing estimate of the new emperor from Frederick the Great:

> Born in a bigoted court, he has cast off its superstition; raised in magnificence, he has assumed simple manners; nourished on incense, he is modest; burning with a thirst for glory, he sacrifices his ambition to the filial duty which he executes scrupulously; and, having had only pedantic teachers, he still has enough taste to read Voltaire and to appreciate his merits.*

Frederick exaggerated only a little. Earnest, industrious, and puritanical in temperament, Joseph promised to make "philosophy the legislator of my empire." Thwarted and restrained by Maria Theresa in her lifetime, seeking solace in work for the grief caused by the death of his young wife, the impatient emperor plunged into activity after his mother died. During his ten years as sole ruler, 1780–1790, eleven thousand laws and six thousand decrees issued from Vienna. This frenzied pace gave the misleading impression that the son's policies always ran counter to the mother's; actually, their goals were often identical, but Joseph's methods of achieving them were more abrupt and less cautious and conciliatory than Maria Theresa's.

In religious policy, Joseph did make a genuine innovation when, for the first time in the history of Catholic Austria, Calvinists, Lutherans, and Orthodox Christians gained full toleration. And, with a generosity unparalleled in Hapsburg annals, the emperor took measures to end the ghetto existence of the Jews, exempting them from special taxes and from the requirement of wearing a yellow patch as a badge of inferiority. On the other hand, Joseph continued his mother's moves to increase state control over the Church in Austrian lands, a control that now went by the name of Josephism because of the emperor's insistence that he and not the pope was the supreme arbiter of ecclesiastical matters in Hapsburg territories. He encouraged what he considered socially useful in Catholicism and dealt ruthlessly with what he judged superfluous and harmful. Thus he established hundreds of new churches and at the same time reduced the number of religious holidays. He called monks "the most dangerous and useless subjects in every state" and promised to convert "the monk of mere show into a useful citizen." He cut in half the number of monks and nuns and, of 2,100 monasteries and nunneries, he suppressed 700, chiefly those run by the contemplative orders. Houses actively engaged in educational or charitable work were generally spared. The government sold or leased the lands of the suppressed establishments, applying the revenue to the support of the hospitals that were beginning to earn Vienna its reputation as a great medical center.

Unlike Frederick the Great, Joseph really believed in popular education and social equality. His govern-

cated some monastic property, and expelled the Jesuits. The pope declared himself deeply offended by this Hapsburg counterpart of the Gallicanism long practiced by the French monarchy in asserting the subordination of church to state.

Maria Theresa employed both force and charm to get her way. The nobles of Hungary momentarily forgot their anti-German tradition when the beautiful and spirited empress, her infant son in her arms, appealed to their chivalry in the crisis of the War of the Austrian Succession. She was the first housewife of the realm as well as the first servant of the state. She was the mother of sixteen children, and she adored and respected Francis, her grasping, fickle husband. It was characteristic of her that when Francis' will provided a large bequest to his mistress, she executed its terms to the letter. Maria Theresa, however, was fundamentally out of sympathy with the Age of Reason. Lady Prayerful, as Catherine the Great called her, banned the works of Rousseau and Voltaire from her realm and even forbade the circulation of the Catholic *Index*, lest that list of forbidden books pique the curiosity of her subjects. Although many of her other policies would qualify her as an enlightened despot, history has denied her the title and awarded it instead to her eldest son, Joseph II.

Joseph, who became emperor after Francis died in 1765, ruled jointly with his mother until her death in

*"Correspondance avec les Souverains," *Oeuvres Complètes de Voltaire* (Paris, 1828), 74:37. Our translation.

ment provided the teachers and textbooks for primary schools. More than a quarter of the school-age children in Austria actually attended school—the best record of any country in late eighteenth-century Europe. Everyone in Vienna, high and low, was invited to visit the Prater, the great public park of the capital, the entrance to which bore the inscription, "A place of pleasure for all men, prepared for them by their friend." The new Austrian legal code followed the recommendations of Beccaria in abolishing capital punishment and most tortures and in prescribing equality before the law. Aristocratic offenders, like commoners, were sentenced to stand in the pillory and to sweep the streets of Vienna. Joseph's peasant policy marked the climax of his equalitarianism. He freed the serfs, abolished most of their obligations to manorial lords, and deprived the lords of their traditional right of administering justice to the peasantry. He also experimented with the collection of a single tax on land as recommended by the Physiocrats, a revolutionary innovation from the social as well as the economic point of view, because the estates of the aristocracy were to be taxed on the same basis as the farms of the peasantry.

Joseph's economic policies, however, often followed the traditions of mercantilism and cameralism, notably in the erection of high protective tariffs and in the government's close supervision of economic life. In politics, Joseph extended his mother's efforts to diminish the influence of the nobility by appointing commoners to high governmental posts. Continuing Maria Theresa's Germanizing program, he customarily spoke German, patronized German writers, and made the French playhouse in Vienna a German-language theater. He attempted to terminate the autonomous rights of his non-German possessions, notably Bohemia, Hungary, and Belgium.

Both Joseph's enlightened reforms and his Germanizing measures aroused mounting opposition. Devout peasants, almost oblivious of his well-meaning attempts to improve their social and economic status, keenly resented his meddling with old religious customs. The nobility clamored against his equalitarian legislation; in the case of the single-tax experiment their opposition was so violent that he had to revoke the decree a month after it was issued. Hungary and Belgium rose in open rebellion against his centralizing efforts and forced him to confirm their autonomous liberties.

In foreign policy, too, his ambitious projects miscarried. By supporting Russian plans for the dismemberment of Turkey, Austria gained only a narrow strip of Balkan territory. Joseph also attempted to annex lands belonging to the neighboring south German state of Bavaria, where the death of the ruler opened another of those succession quarrels so common in the eighteenth century. But Frederick the Great was determined to check any advance of Hapsburg power in Germany. In the half-hearted "Potato War" of the late 1770s, Austrian and Prussian troops spent most of their time foraging for food, and Joseph secured only a tiny fragment of the Bavarian inheritance.

Joseph II worked himself to death, as one of his friends observed, "by governing too much and reigning too little." Where his mother had often sought to flatter or charm her opponents out of their opposition, Joseph simply laid down the law. He defended his habit of interfering personally in almost every detail of government:

> What else can I do in this country devoid of mind, without soul, without zeal, without heart in the work? I am killing myself because I cannot rouse up those whom I want to make work; but I hope I shall not die until I have so wound up the machine that others cannot put it out of order, even if they try to do so.*

Joseph never managed to wind up the machine properly; he could not transplant to the Austrian bureaucracy the almost inhuman Prussian discipline that he needed to serve his purposes. He died convinced that he had pursued the proper course, yet believing that he had accomplished nothing. The judgment of posterity dissents on both counts: his course was too radical, too insensitive to the feelings of others; but he attempted more in ten years than Frederick attempted in almost half a century, and not all of his attempts failed. Though some of his major reforms, such as the abolition of serfdom, were repealed soon after his death, others survived, helping to bring the Hapsburg lands part way along the road to becoming a more modern centralized state.

The reforms that survived profited from the conciliatory policies of Joseph's successor, his younger brother Leopold II (1790–1792), who was an enlightened despot in his own right. As grand duke of Tuscany (1765–1790), he spruced up the administration of his Italian duchy, which included the busy port of Leghorn in addition to the cities of Florence and Pisa. He also introduced economic reforms along Physiocratic lines and judicial reforms in line with the recommendations of Beccaria on the abolition of torture and the death penalty. Unlike his brother, Leopold actively enlisted the participation of his subjects in affairs of state and, unlike any other enlightened despot, he contemplated establishing a representative assembly in Tuscany and studied the constitution of Virginia for guidance.

Charles III, Pombal, Gustavus III

Earlier, another Italian state had profited from the political apprenticeship of another enlightened despot. The state was Naples, where Elizabeth Farnese's Baby Carlos, King Charles IV from 1735 to 1759, carried on a successful struggle against clericalism and feudalism. In 1759 he inherited the Spanish kingship on the death

*Quoted in Prince de Ligne, *His Memoirs, Letters, and Miscellaneous Papers* (Boston, 1902), 2:132.

Charles III of Spain in hunting costume, by Goya.

cies, and Spain soon began to slip back into her old aristocratic and clerical ways, although the influence of the Enlightenment was never entirely extinguished.

In Spain's neighbor, Portugal, the representative of enlightened despotism was not the monarch but the marquis of Pombal, the first minister of King Joseph I (1750–1777). Pombal secured his reputation by the speed and good taste he demonstrated in rebuilding Lisbon after the earthquake of 1755. The Portuguese economy depended heavily on income from the colonies, on the sale of port wine to Britain, and on the purchase of manufactured goods from Britain. Pombal tried to enlarge its base by fostering local industries and encouraging the growth of grain in addition to grapes. To weaken the grip of clericalism, he ousted the Jesuits, advanced religious toleration, and modernized the curriculum of the national University of Coimbra. To weaken that of the nobles, he attacked their rights of inheritance. Pombal's methods were in every instance high-handed, and when he fell from power in 1777 the prisons released thousands of men whom he had confined years earlier for their alleged involvement in aristocratic plots.

Equally high-handed in the long run was Sweden's benevolent despot, Gustavus III (1771–1792), a nephew of Frederick the Great. Like his uncle, Gustavus admired the French and French ideas, and when he inherited the Swedish crown, he proclaimed in ringing speeches his devotion to the Age of Reason. He also resolved not to be cramped by the oligarchical noble factions that had run the country since the death of the warrior king, Charles XII, early in the century. While he distracted Swedish party leaders at the opera one evening, his soldiers staged a coup that enabled him to revive the royal authority and to dissolve the factions. In economics and religion, his enlightenment outdistanced that of his uncle in Prussia, for he removed obstacles to both domestic and foreign trade and extended toleration to Jews as well as to the non-Lutheran Christian sects. Success, however, turned the head of Gustavus III. As he became more and more arbitrary, the nobles determined to recover their old power; in 1792, he was assassinated at a masquerade in Stockholm, and oligarchy resumed its sway. Verdi's opera *The Masked Ball* is based on the incident, although the authorities in Rome (1859), alarmed at the idea of depicting the killing of a king, obliged him to shift the locale from Stockholm to colonial Boston and to make the victim the British governor.

of his half-brother, and Naples passed to his son Ferdinand I, who was married to a daughter of Maria Theresa, moving southern Italy out of the Bourbon Spanish orbit and into that of Hapsburg Austria.

As king of Spain (1759–1788), Charles III energetically advanced the progressive policies begun under his father, Philip V, and had the help of advisers he brought with him from Naples as well as that of lawyers from the lower ranks of the Spanish nobility. Though a pious Catholic, Charles objected strongly to the political activities of the Church and forced the Jesuits out of Spain. He reduced the authority of the aristocracy, extended that of the Crown, and made Spain more nearly a centralized national state. He curbed the privileges of the great sheep ranchers, whose almost unlimited grazing rights blighted Spanish agriculture. To revivify the torpid economy, he undertook irrigation projects, reclaimed waste lands, and established new roads, canals, banks, and textile mills. The results were astonishing: Spain's foreign commerce increased fivefold during the reign of Charles III. His successors, however, abandoned many of his forward-looking poli-

The Limitations of Enlightened Despotism

The sheer number of enlightened despots in Europe during the latter half of the eighteenth century was impressive, but so too were the limitations under which they labored. The whole structure of enlightened despotism was vitiated by the problem of succession. So long as monarchs came to the throne by the accident of birth, there was nothing to prevent the unenlightened or incapable mediocrity from succeeding the enlightened despot. This happened in Spain, where the well-meaning but feeble Charles IV (1788–1808) succeeded Charles III; it happened in Sweden, where the weak Gustavus IV (1792–1809) succeeded Gustavus III; and it happened in Prussia under Frederick the Great's unenlightened nephew, Frederick William II (1786–1797). And in Austria, the apparent exception to this rule, Leopold II was followed by his very conservative son, Francis II (1792–1835).

Even the least of the enlightened despots deserve the credit for having improved a few of the bad features of the Old Regime. But not even the best of them could strike a happy balance between enlightenment and despotism. Joseph II was too doctrinaire, too inflexible in his determination to apply the full reform program of the Age of Reason. Pombal and Gustavus III, in particular, were too arbitrary. Frederick the Great, obsessed with strengthening the crown, entrenched the power of the Junkers, who were hostile to the whole Enlightenment. Finally, in Russia, events during the century after the death of Peter the Great furnished another lesson in the difficulty of adjusting rational principles to political realities.

IV Russia, 1725–1825

The Fate of the Autocracy, 1725–1762

Russia had two sovereigns with at least a nominal claim to be numbered among the enlightened despots, Catherine II the Great (1762–1796) and her grandson, Alexander I (1801–1825). But for thirty-seven years between the death of Peter the Great and the accession of Catherine, the autocracy was without an effective autocrat, as the throne changed hands seven times and the succession zigzagged across the Romanov family tree. More important than the individuals who governed during these years were the social groups contending for power and the social processes at work in Russia. The guards regiments founded by Peter came to exercise a decisive influence in the series of palace overturns, and the service nobility, no longer restrained by the czar, entered into its era of dominance.

When Peter died in 1725, his immediate circle, particularly Menshikov, feared the possible succession of his nine-year-old grandson, Peter, the son of Alexis, since the young Peter would likely hold the loyalties of the old nobility who had hated his grandfather. Menshikov therefore supported the candidacy of his one-time mistress, Peter's widow, who became the empress Catherine I (1725–1727) after the guards rallied to her side. Menshikov ran Russia during her two-year reign and tried to make himself secure by appointing a small Supreme Privy Council and planning to have the young Peter marry his daughter. On Catherine's death he took the boy, now Czar Peter II (1727–1730), into his house and proceeded to make him an alcoholic as his father had been. Menshikov's arrogance, how-

ever, alienated even his supporters; he was exiled after the boyar families of Dolgoruky and Galitsyn gained supremacy. Two Dolgoruky princes put themselves on the Supreme Privy Council, and Peter II became engaged to a member of their family.

The ascendancy of boyar families marked the return to power of a group that had been losing influence ever since the days of Ivan the Terrible. Their plans were brought to the crisis point by the sudden death of Peter II on the very day scheduled for his coronation in 1730. The leading candidate for the succession was Peter the Great's niece, Anne, widow of the Duke of Courland. Summoning her from this Baltic principality, the Dolgoruky and the Galitsyn demanded that she sign a set of articles before taking the throne. By their terms the Empress Anne (1730–1740) undertook never to remarry or name an heir and not to make peace or war, levy taxes, confer ranks in the army above colonel, nor spend state funds without the specific consent of the Supreme Privy Council. The eight councillors, who now included four Dolgoruky and two Galitsyn, also claimed the right to supervise the guards regiments. The articles were the most explicit constitutional destruction of all that Peter the Great had striven for; had Anne observed their provisions, Russia would have entered an era of boyar oligarchy.

But the prospect of taking orders indefinitely from the small group of old boyars horrified the military-service nobility, who had a powerful lever in the guards regiments. What the service gentry wanted was an autocrat who would loosen the bonds forged for them by Peter the Great. And so, when one of the councillors, the capable German Ostermann, convinced Anne to tear up the articles, the guards supported him. The gentry had now gained the real power in Russia, though they permitted Anne to bestow influential state offices on a host of Germans. When Anne died, the German favorites fell out among themselves, with Ostermann the eventual winner; meantime, Anne's eight-week-old grand-nephew became Czar Ivan VI (1740–1741). Foreign intrigue produced the next shift in the imperial title. The French were anxious to oust Ostermann, who had been instrumental in allying Russia with France's traditional enemy, Austria. A French ambassador played on the patriotic disgust of the guardsmen with the behavior of the Germans at court, and in 1741 a guards' coup put on the throne a daughter of Peter the Great by Catherine.

The empress Elizabeth (1741–1762) inherited her father's lust for life but not his brains or interest in matters of state. Though owning thousands of splendid dresses, she lived rather shabbily in grubby palaces, enjoying most of all a rousing peasant banquet with plenty to drink and lots of rustic music. Kept busy by a succession of lovers, she let important state papers languish for days without bothering to read them, much less sign them, so that Russian policy drifted. Soon after her accession she named as her heir her nephew Peter, who was more German than Russian and who married a clever little German princess, the future Catherine II. Peter III, as he became on his succession in January 1762, was eccentric and not very bright but hardly the utter lunatic portrayed in the memoirs of his wife, who loathed him. He was a passionate admirer of Frederick the Great, and his efforts to introduce rigid Prussian discipline into the Russian army and his hatred for the guards cost him the friends he needed most. He could have played his war games with toy soldiers, held courts-martial on rats whom he convicted of gnawing cardboard fortresses, and swilled his favorite English beer with impunity—and he would not have been any worse than many another czar. But to drill guards regiments in the Prussian fashion was unforgivable. The military triggered a new palace revolution (July 1762), soon after which Peter was murdered by one of his wife's lovers; the extent of her own role in her husband's overthrow has never been ascertained.

Nobles and Serfs, 1730–1762

A deeply dissatisfied social group that had the power to make and unmake autocrats naturally had a program for the redress of its own grievances. Once the gentry had enabled Anne to tear up the articles in 1730, it began strenuous efforts to emancipate itself from the servitude riveted upon it by Peter. Anne repealed the law requiring the noble to leave his estate intact to one of his sons. She founded a military school for noblemen's sons, who no longer had to start their careers in the ranks, as under Peter. Anne shortened the terms of service from life to twenty-five years, and exempted one son of every family with at least two sons, so that there would be one member of each generation to look after the estate.

Simultaneously came a deepening of the authority of noble proprietors over their serfs. The former became the government's agents for collection of the poll tax; the latter could no longer obtain their freedom by enlisting in the army and could not engage in trade or purchase land without written permission from their masters. Masters could deport their serfs to Siberia and might punish them physically in any way they wished. Moreover, under Elizabeth, a series of laws restricted the right of owning serfs to those who were already nobles, so that the class that had been open to new recruits under Peter was closed by his daughter.

In 1762, finally, Peter III decreed that the nobles no longer need serve at all unless they wished to do so; no wonder that some of the nobles proposed to erect a solid gold statue of the czar! To understand the revolutionary nature of this liberation of the nobles from a duty to serve, we must remember that they had historically obtained their lands and serfs only on condition that they would serve. Now they kept their lands and serfs but had no obligations. Yet the service that had been hated when it was compulsory became fashionable now that it was optional; there was really little else for a Russian noble to do except serve the state.

In contemplating all this, a great Russian historian remarked that by the logic of history all serfs should have been liberated the day after the nobles were released from their duty to serve. But nothing could have been further from the thoughts of Peter III or of any other Russian leader.

In these middle decades of the eighteenth century, successive waves of foreign influence affected the Russian nobility. It was not only the influx of foreigners that brought in Western habits; it was also the involvement of Russia in European wars and the increased travel abroad by Russians. Under Elizabeth, when the Germans disappeared from court, the way was clear for the French to exert their influence. With the French language came the literature, and many a Russian noble bought French books by the yard for his library because it was the thing to do. The champagne business boomed (the Russians liked the sweet kind that most Frenchmen despised), French styles of dress were copied by both men and women, and some gentlemen claimed that it would be impossible to fall in love with a girl who did not speak French. Quite literally, nobles and peasants no longer spoke the same language, and this deep rift between the frenchified gentry and the Russian people was later to prove of critical importance.

Catherine the Great (1762–1796)

With the advent of Catherine II, we come to the most arresting personality to occupy the Russian throne since the death of Peter. Brought up in a petty German court, she found herself transplanted to St. Petersburg as a mere girl, living with a husband she detested, and forced to pick her way through the intrigues that flourished around the empress Elizabeth. She managed to steer clear of trouble only by using her keen wits. Catherine fancied herself as an intellectual; she wrote plays, edited a satirical journal, and steeped herself in the literature of the Enlightenment. Both before and after ascending the throne she maintained a goodly supply of lovers, several of whom had important roles in affairs of state.

Catherine had a truly twentieth-century feeling for the importance of public relations, and was particularly concerned that leading spirits in the West should think well of her and of the condition of Russia under her rule. Hence her voluminous correspondence with Westerners. She invited Diderot to edit the *Encyclopédie* in Russia (he declined); then she bought his library, but he kept his books and received a pension—very favorable publicity for the Russian empress. When Diderot visited Russia in 1773, he reported that Catherine had the soul of Brutus and the charms of Cleopatra, while she complained that in the excitement of conversation, her guest pinched her legs until they were black and blue. Voltaire judiciously stayed out of Russia but accepted Catherine's bounty, in return for which he called her "the north star" and "the benefactress of Europe."

Catherine would perhaps have liked to reform conditions in Russia; there was something of the enlightened despot about her style. But as a woman and a foreigner and a usurper, owing the throne to a conspiracy, she could not act upon her inclinations. Depending as she did upon the good will of the nobility, she could not lay a finger on the institution of serfdom. She had to reward her supporters with vast grants of state land, inhabited by hundreds of thousands of state peasants, who once could not be sold but now became privately owned serfs who could be sold. Even in theory, Catherine felt, Russia was so large that the only possible form of government was an autocracy. As an autocrat she was as arbitrary as any of her predecessors.

Once firmly established on the throne, however, Catherine decided to convoke a commission to codify the laws of Russia, a task that had not been accomplished since 1649. Catherine herself, with the help of advisers, spent three years composing the *Instruction* to the delegates, a long, rather windy document, full of abstract argument drawn from Montesquieu's *Spirit of the Laws* and Beccaria's *Crimes and Punishments* but altered to conform with the empress's own beliefs. Here one can discern no intention to meddle with the fundamental institutions of Russia, but some concern for eliminating their worst abuses. The 564 delegates to the commission were elected by organs of the central government and by every social class in Russia except the serf peasants. Each delegate—noble, townsman, crown peasant, Cossack—was charged to bring with him a collection of written documents from his neighbors presenting their grievances and demands for change.

Many of these survive and teach us a great deal about the state of public opinion in Catherine's Russia. Nobody seems to have been dissatisfied with the autocracy; at least we find no requests that it modify its power or consult its subjects. People did seek more rights and duties for local government and wanted their own obligations more clearly defined. Each class of representatives was eager to extend the rights of that class: The free peasants wanted to own serfs; the townsmen wanted to own serfs and be the only class allowed to engage in trade; the nobles wanted to engage in trade, and to have their exclusive right to own serfs confirmed. After 203 sessions lasting over a year and a half, devoted to inconclusive and sometimes heated debate, Catherine put an end to the labors of the commission in 1768. It had not codified the laws, but from Catherine's own point of view it had been a success; she knew that most of her subjects supported her as absolute autocrat. It is important to remember that the commission, with all its imperfections, was the last effort by the czardom to consult the Russian people as a whole for 138 years—until revolution summoned the first duma into existence in 1906.

Catherine turned the spadework of the legislative commission to good advantage in her later reforms, which resulted from the great rebellion of the Cossacks under the leadership of Pugachev, 1773–1775. Puga-

Portrait of Catherine the Great.

chev roused the frontiersmen to revolt against Catherine's cancellation of their special privileges. Pretending to be Czar Peter III, and promising liberty and land to the serfs who joined his forces, Pugachev swept over a wide area of southeastern Russia and finally marched toward Moscow. Like the disturbances of the seventeenth century, Pugachev's regolt revealed the existence of bitter discontent in Russia, a discontent directed not at the supreme autocrat but at the landlords and local officials.

The ramshackle provincial administration almost collapsed under the strain of Pugachev's rebellion. Orders filtered down slowly to local officials, and the soldiers defending the government moved almost as slowly. When the rebels were finally suppressed, and Pugachev was traveling northward in an iron cage before being drawn and quartered, Catherine took action. Her reorganization of local government (1775) created fifty provinces where there had been twenty before. She thus replaced a small number of unwieldly units with a larger number of small provinces, each containing roughly three hundred to four hundred thousand inhabitants. The reform of 1775 gave the nobles the lion's share of provincial offices but subjected them to the close direction of the central government.

In the charter of 1785 the nobles received exemption from military service and taxation and secured absolute mastery over the fate of their serfs and their estates. A charter to the towns in the same year disclosed Catherine's sympathy with the tiny but growing middle class, and established the principle of municipal self-government, although it remained a dead letter because of the rigorous class distinctions maintained in the urban centers of Russia. For the serfs, needless to say, there was no charter. Indeed, besides adding almost a million to their number by the gifts of state lands to private persons, Catherine increased still further the power of the proprietors, who now received the right to sell serfs without their land; serf families were sometimes broken up, and serfs were gambled away at cards, given as presents, and mortgaged for loans. All serf-owners were not cruel any more than all slaveowners in our own slave states, but both institutions tended to degrade both master and man. As in the American South, there was a distinction in Russia between field-hands and household servants. Great landowners often had hundreds of the latter, some of whom were formed into orchestras, gave dramatic performances, tutored the sons of the family, or acted as household poets and scientists.

The contrast between the climate of the Enlightenment which surrounded the court and the actual conditions in Russia was keenly felt by sensitive men. Foremost among them was a young noble, Alexander Radishchev, educated abroad and widely traveled. In his *Journey from St. Petersburg to Moscow,* Radishchev included vivid and horrifying vignettes of serfdom and the abuses of the administration. Moreover, his poetry praised Cromwell, the regicide. It is possible that he might have gotten away with this in the early days of Catherine's reign, but the year was 1790, when the French Revolution was under way, and the empress had begun to hate the French and "their abominable bonfire." Proposing to burn the dangerous books of the Enlightenment, she could hardly overlook the subversive character of Radishchev's writings, and he went to Siberia in exile. Similarly, the humanitarian Freemason Nicholas Novikov, manager of the newly active Moscow University Press, editor of newspapers and sponsor of campaigns to raise money and food for famine-stricken peasants, was also jailed on flimsy charges. Though Novikov had done nothing against the regime, it could not tolerate the continuance of any enterprise it did not dominate. Radishchev and Novikov, the first examples of thoroughly westernized individual Russians, were the victims of the gap between Catherine's professed principles and her actual conduct.

Paul, 1796–1801, and Alexander I, 1801–1825

Catherine's son Paul, who may or may not have been the son of her husband, Peter III, succeeded her in 1796 as a man of forty-two. All his life his mother had distrusted him, fearing that there might be a conspiracy to oust her and install him, ostensibly a legitimate Romanov. The best-educated Russian royal personage to date, active and eager to serve the state, Paul was given no duties, was kept in the dark about state secrets, and was even deprived of his two eldest children, Alexander and Constantine, whose education Catherine personally supervised. Consequently, when Paul finally did become czar, he appeared to be motivated chiefly by a wish to undo his mother's work. He exiled some of her favorites and released many of her prisoners, including Radishchev and Novikov. Paul tried to bring more order to the central administration by putting the colleges under single ministers in place of the former boards of directors. Paul's behavior, however, was erratic. On the one hand, he imposed a strict curfew on St. Petersburg and forbade the importation of sheet music because he feared that all of it might be as revolutionary as the *Marseillaise.* On the other hand, he issued a manifesto limiting to three the number of days per week a serf might be required to work on his master's land, but it is not clear whether this was a binding law or only a recommendation. In any case, he continued to give away state lands, and transformed some half a million state peasants into privately owned chattels.

What was probably fatal to Paul was his policy of toughness toward the nobility. A noble, he is said to have remarked, is the man I am talking to at the moment, and he ceases to be a noble when I stop talking to him. This definition could scarcely have appealed to the privileged gentry. Paul exacted compulsory service from the nobles once more and curtailed their powers in the provinces. Nobles were forced to meet the bills for public buildings and to pay new taxes on their lands; they were also subjected to corporal punishment for crimes. Like Peter III, Paul wanted to prussianize the army, and especially to inculcate in its officers a sense of responsibility for the men. The guards' regiments detested such programs, and a conspiracy of guardsmen resulted in the murder of Paul and the succession of Alexander in 1801. The precise degree to which Alexander was informed of the coup in advance is uncertain, but he knew at least that the conspirators intended to force his father's abdication.

Educated by a liberal Swiss tutor, Alexander I had absorbed so much of the new eighteenth-century teaching that he blossomed out with a red-white-and-blue ribbon, the colors of revolutionary France, on hearing of the fall of the Bastille in 1789. Yet the application of liberal principles in Russia would involve a direct challenge to the most powerful forces in society and would also require the czar to relinquish some of the power he cherished so dearly. So, although Alexander occasionally told his intimates that someday he would grant Russia a constitution and then retire to a castle on the Rhine, in fact this was little but romantic twaddle. Tall and handsome, devastating to the ladies, charming and cultivated, Alexander liked to please everybody; he vacillated, compromised, and in the end accomplished very little.

Early in his reign, Alexander gathered a small group of young men which he called "the unofficial committee." One of the members had been an active member of the Jacobin Club in Paris during the revolution; two others greatly admired the English system of government. Meeting after dinner over coffee and brandy, the committee had as its self-appointed task the preparation of a constitution for Russia, but its discussions were little more than the unsystematic talk of pleasant, well-born young men who had dined well. A decree sponsored by the committee did abolish the administrative colleges and create eight new ministries to take their place; but this in fact had largely been accomplished by Paul. When the committee stopped meeting in 1803, it had done nothing with regard to serfdom. The czar himself did sponsor a law creating a new category of free farmers, serfs who had been freed by their masters, and prescribing that if a proprietor freed an entire village of serfs he must also confer their lands upon them. This was a very mild initiative, which depended on the voluntary cooperation of the proprietors and resulted in freeing fewer than forty thousand of the many millions of serfs.

After the first major war with Napoleon, 1805–1807, Alexander had as his chief mentor a remarkable figure, Michael Speransky, son of a Russian priest, intelligent, well educated, and conscientious. Utilizing Montesquieu's principle of the separation of powers, Speransky drafted for Alexander a constitutional project that would have made Russia a limited monarchy. A series of elected assemblies, beginning at the lowest level of administrative subdivision and continuing on up through district and province, would culminate in a great national assembly, the duma. A similar pyramid of courts and a new set of executive institutions were also planned. The duma would have to approve any law promulgated by the czar and would have been a genuine Russian parliament. It is true that the franchise Speransky proposed would have enormously favored the nobility and excluded the serfs, whose emancipation was not included in his proposal. Nonetheless, the plan was decidedly advanced, and one of the most critical moments in Russian history came when Alexander balked at implementing the project he himself had commissioned.

Why did Speransky fail? He instituted a reform of the civil service, requiring examinations and a system of promotion by merit, which disturbed many of the almost illiterate and thoroughly incompetent men in high office. He even proposed that the nobility pay an income tax. Friends and intimates of the czar spread slander about Speransky, but at bottom Alexander himself was at fault and unwilling to act on his own alleged beliefs. Speransky's scheme was shelved, except for two elements that in no way diminished the power

Alexander I.

of the czar. A council of state was created to advise the czar, but since he appointed and dismissed its members and was not obliged to take its advice, the effect was simply to increase imperial efficiency, not to limit imperial authority. Further efficiency was obtained through the reorganization of the ministries, whose duties were set out clearly for the first time, eliminating overlapping.

During a second war against Napoleon (1812–1815) Alexander fell under the influence of a Baltic baroness named Madame de Krüdener, a mystic who was repenting an ill-spent youth. She convinced the czar that he was designed by destiny to overthrow Napoleon and institute a new order. At the Russian court an atmosphere of pious mysticism and conservatism replaced the earlier flashes of liberal views. Although the leading spirits of the new religiosity were all nominally Orthodox, its character was rather Protestant. It was based upon assiduous reading of the Bible, and it also included a mixture of elements from Freemasonry, Pietism, and the more eccentric Russian sects. It aimed at the union of all Christendom in one faith and thus aroused the fear and opposition of many Orthodox clerics. Its real importance lay in its impact on Alexander, who was now convinced that as the bearer of a sacred mission all he needed to do was follow the promptings of his inmost feelings.

During the last decade of Alexander's reign, 1815–1825, the most important figure at court was

Count Arakcheev, a competent but brutal officer, who once bit off the ear of one of his men as a punishment. The chief innovation of the decade, accomplished under Arakcheev's direction, was the hated system of "military colonies," the drafting of the population of whole districts to serve in the regiments quartered there. When not drilling or fighting, the soldiers were to work their farms, and their entire lives were subject to the whims of their officers. By the end of Alexander's reign, almost four hundred thousand soldiers were living in these virtual concentration camps.

Though Alexander gave Russia no important reforms, he did act as the "liberal czar" in his dominions outside Russia proper. Made king of a partially restored Poland in 1815, he gave the Poles an advanced constitution, with their own army, their own Polish officials, and the free use of their own language. After the annexation of Finland from Sweden in 1809, he allowed the Finns to preserve their own law codes and the system of local government introduced during the long Swedish rule.

Foreign Policy, 1725–1796

Between the death of Peter the Great and that of Catherine, Russian foreign policy still pursued the traditional goals of expansion against Sweden, Poland, and Turkey. But as a new member of the European power constellation, Russia found that these goals involved her increasingly with the states of central and western Europe.

In 1726 Ostermann concluded an alliance with the Hapsburg Empire that was to be a cornerstone of Russian foreign policy. Yet, especially in joint undertakings against the Turks, the Russians and Austrians found, as early as the 1730s, that they had conflicting ambitions in southeast Europe. This early conflict of interests was a cloud, still no larger than a man's hand, but destined to swell into the colossal thunderhead that exploded in the world war of 1914–1918. To the eighteenth century also belong the first regular Russian diplomatic service, the first Russian participation in international espionage and intrigue, and the first real Russian foreign ministers: Ostermann and his Russian successor under Elizabeth, Bestuzhev-Ryumin, men of enormous personal influence on the course of Russian diplomacy.

In the War of the Polish Succession (1733–1735) Russian forces were allied with those of Austria in supporting Augustus III and forcing the abdication of Stanislas Leszczyński. The Russians and Austrians then became allies in a new war against the Turks, 1735–1739. Though the Russians invaded the Crimea successfully, their territorial gains were limited to Azov. The Austrians failed to cooperate in an invasion of the Danubian principalities and made it clear that they did not relish a Russian advance toward the Hapsburg frontiers. We have already seen how the French ambassador worked to bring about the downfall of the pro-Austrian Ostermann together with the installation of Elizabeth as empress. But, since Bestuzhev-Ryumin continued Ostermann's policies, French hopes were largely disappointed. Prussian influence, which was anti-Austrian, manifested itself with the appearance of the future Peter III as heir and with the selection of the German Catherine, whose father was a Prussian general. Thus, during the War of the Austrian Succession, there was a good deal of jockeying for Russian assistance. The advance of Frederick the Great along the Baltic shore alarmed the Russians, and a Russian corps was slowly moving westward to join the fighting as the war ended.

Anti-Prussian sentiment crystallized during the interval of peace before the outbreak of the Seven Years' War. Bestuzhev labored mightily to obtain an alliance with England, which he managed in 1755, the Russians accepting a large subsidy in exchange for a promise to keep troops in readiness against the Prussians in defense of Hanover. But in the next year the Diplomatic Revolution negated this arrangement. The Russians thus remained loyal to Austria and fought the Prussians in the Seven Years' War. Russian forces invaded East Prussia and in 1760 even entered Berlin; Elizabeth's death, early in 1762, and the accession of the pro-Prussian Peter III led the Russians to change sides and join the Prussians briefly against the Austrians and the French. When Catherine, on her accession, withdrew Russian forces, Russia was excluded from the peace conferences of 1763.

In foreign policy, Catherine the Great was vigorous and unscrupulous in pursuing Russia's traditional goals. A year after she became empress the throne of Poland fell vacant, and Catherine secured the election of her former lover, a pro-Russian Pole, Stanislas Poniatowski. Frederick the Great then joined with Catherine in a campaign to win rights for the persecuted Lutheran and Orthodox minorities in Catholic Poland. One party of the Polish nobles, their national pride offended at foreign intervention, secured the aid of France and Austria, who adopted the stratagem of pressing Turkey into war with Russia to distract Catherine from Poland.

In the Russo-Turkish War (1768–1774) the Russian Baltic fleet sailed through the Straits of Gibraltar into the Mediterranean and, thanks to the expert seamanship of British naval advisers, destroyed the Turkish fleet in the Aegean (1770). The Russians then passed up the chance to storm the Dardanelles and attack Istanbul and shifted their operations to the Crimea and the Danubian principalities. While Russians and Turks were discussing peace terms, Frederick the Great had concluded that Russia's success with the Turks might lead her to seize most of Poland unless he acted quickly. He therefore arranged the first partition of Poland (1772). She lost to Russia, Prussia, and Austria almost one-third of her territory and one-half of her population. Frederick's share of the loot—the lands immediately to the west of East Prussia—was the smallest but included the strategic region that had previously sepa-

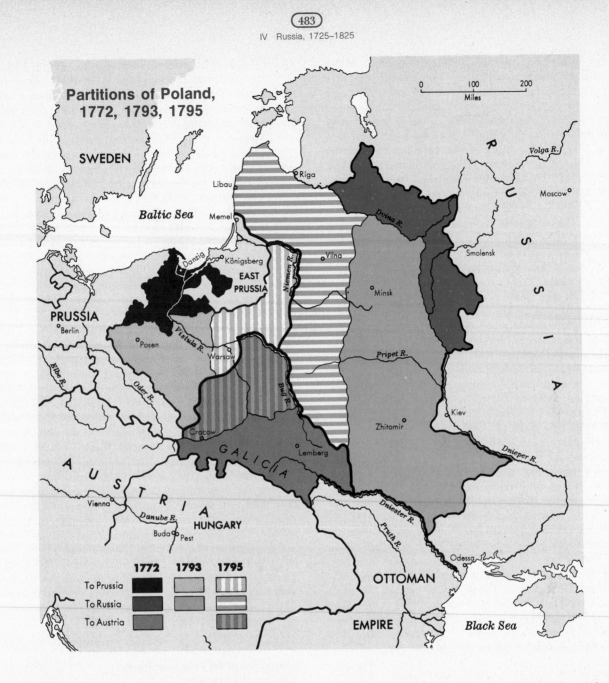

Partitions of Poland, 1772, 1793, 1795

	1772	1793	1795
To Prussia			
To Russia			
To Austria			

rated Brandenburg from East Prussia. Maria Theresa, the empress of Austria, abandoned her Turkish and Polish allies to obtain the southern Polish province of Galicia. She did seem somewhat reluctant, yet as Frederick the Great observed, "She wept, but she kept on taking." Russia received a substantial area of what is now known as Belorussia, or White Russia.

Two years later, the Russians imposed upon the Turks the humiliating treaty of Kutchuk Kainardji (1774). Catherine annexed much of the formerly Turkish stretch of Black Sea coast; the Crimea was separated from the Ottoman Empire as an independent Tatar state, which was soon (1783) annexed by Russia. She also obtained something the Russians had long coveted: freedom of navigation on the Black Sea and the right of passage through the Bosporus and the Dardanelles.

A vaguely worded clause gave her various rights to protect the Christian subjects of the sultan, thus providing a convenient excuse for Russian intervention in Turkish affairs later on.

Catherine now began to dream of expelling the Turks from Europe and reviving the Byzantine Empire under Russian protection. As part of this Greek project, she had her younger grandson christened Constantine and imported Greek-speaking nurses to train him in the language. She also proposed to set up a kingdom of Dacia (the Roman name for the area) in the Danubian principalities to be ruled by her lover and general, Potemkin. By way of preparation, in 1783, Catherine built a naval base at Sebastopol in the newly annexed Crimea. To achieve these grandiose designs, Catherine sought the consent of Austria and invited Joseph II on a boat tour of the recently acquired territories of the Russian southwest. On this tour the Austrian emperor allegedly saw the famous "Potemkin villages," mere cardboard façades facing the river to look like settlements with nothing behind them; like so many other good stories, this one is untrue. At Sebastopol, however, there were signs pointing across the Black Sea, saying "This way to Byzantium." In a second Russo-Turkish war (1787–1791), Catherine's Austrian allies again provided feeble assistance and soon became embroiled in a conflict of interests with Russia over the European lands of the sultan. In the end, Catherine abandoned her Greek project and contented herself with acquiring the remaining Turkish lands along the northern coast of the Black Sea, including the site of the important port of Odessa.

Before her death Catherine participated in two more partitions of Poland, made possible by the mounting preoccupation of the Western powers with the French Revolution. The second partition came as the result of a Polish constitutional movement, supported by the Prussians in opposition to Russian interest. Catherine intervened on the pretext of defending the established order in Poland and fighting the virus of revolution. In 1793, both the Russians and Prussians took large new slices of Polish territory; the Austrians did not participate in this second partition of Poland. An attempted Polish revolution against the reduction of their state to a wretched remnant dominated by foreigners was followed by the third and final partition of 1795, by which Poland disappeared from the map. This time Austria joined the other two powers and obtained Cracow; Prussia got Warsaw, and Russia secured Lithuania and other Baltic and east Polish lands. The spectacular successes of Catherine meant the transfer to Russia of millions of human beings—Poles, Lithuanians, Belorussians, Tatars—who loathed the Russians, and left a legacy of trouble. It also meant that Russia had destroyed useful buffers in the shape of the Polish and Tatar states, and now had common frontiers with her potential enemies, Prussia and Austria.

V   George III and American Independence

Though Catherine the Great failed to apply the ideas of the Age of Reason, her name usually appears on lists of enlightened despots. Another name might possibly be added to the list—George III, king of Great Britain (1760–1820). "Farmer George" showed very little personal enlightenment beyond taking an interest in the agrarian revolution and writing articles on turnips for Arthur Young's *Annals of Agriculture*. In politics, however, he attempted a course that may be termed a dilute form of enlightened despotism, although it may be described more exactly as a reassertion of the monarch's authority. The first of the Hanoverian monarchs born and bred in England, George III proposed to reassert some of the royal prerogatives that had lapsed under the first two Georges. He tried to wrest control of the House of Commons from the long-dominant Whig oligarchy and retain it by the Whig devices of patronage and bribery. He endeavored to beat the Whigs at their own parliamentary game.

Virtuous as a person and devoted to his family, George as a monarch was stubborn, short-sighted, and in the long run unsuccessful. It was easy for him at first to exploit the factional strife among the Whigs, maneuver Pitt out of office in 1761, and make his friend and tutor, Lord Bute, the head of the cabinet. Bute and the king, however, found it hard to justify their failure to deprive France of her sugar-rich West Indian islands in the Peace of Paris, which brought the Seven Years' War to a conclusion. The Commons ratified the treaty, but George dismissed Bute to appease the critics of British diplomacy.

The harshest criticism came from John Wilkes, a member of Commons, who dubbed the Peace of Paris "the peace of God, for it passeth all understanding." Wilkes' attack on the treaty in his paper, the *North Briton,* infuriated the king; bowing to the royal anger, the Commons ordered the offending issue of the *North Briton* to be burned. Later, Wilkes ran for Parliament three separate times, and three times the Commons, under royal pressure, threw out his election. When Wilkes finally took his seat again in 1774, he was a popular hero, and riots had occurred in defense of "Wilkes and Liberty." A wise king would have reconsidered his course, but George III did not relax his determination to manage both Parliament and cabinet. After seven years of short-lived, unstable ministries (1763–1770), George finally found a man to fill Bute's old role and do the king's bidding—Lord North, who headed the cabinet for a dozen years (1770–1782). Under North, royal intervention in politics at first stiffened, then wavered, and at length collapsed in the face of the revolt by the thirteen North American colonies.

Background of the American Revolt

The breach between colonies and mother country first became serious at the close of the Seven Years' War, when Britain began to retreat from the old policy of "salutary neglect" and to interfere more directly and more frequently in colonial matters. But by 1763 the colonies had acquired the habit of regulating their own affairs, though the acts of their assemblies remained subject to the veto of royally appointed governors or of the king himself. The vast territories in Canada and west of the Allegheny Mountains acquired in 1763 brought Britain added opportunities for profitable exploitation and added responsibilities for government and defense. When an uprising of Indians under Pontiac threatened frontier posts in the area of the Ohio Valley and the Great Lakes, colonial militias failed to take effective action, and British regulars were brought in. The continuing threat from the Indians prompted the royal proclamation of October 1763, forbidding "all our loving subjects" to settle west of a line running along the summit of the Alleghenies. To His Majesty's "loving subjects" in the seaboard colonies, however, the proclamation seemed deliberately designed to exclude them from the riches of the West.

The colonies resented still more keenly the attempt by Parliament to raise more revenue in North America. The British government had very strong arguments for increasing colonial taxes. The national debt had almost doubled during the Seven Years' War; the colonies' reluctance to recruit soldiers and raise taxes themselves had increased the cost of the war to British taxpayers; now the mother country faced continued expense in protecting the frontier. Surely the Americans would admit the reasonableness of the case for higher taxes.

That, however, was precisely what the Americans did *not* admit. The first of the new revenue measures, the Sugar Act of 1764, alarmed the merchants of the eastern seaboard because the customs officers actually undertook to collect duties on molasses, sugar, and other imports. Here was a departure from the comfortable laxity of salutary neglect. And here was a threat to the colonial economy, for the import duties had to be paid out of the colonies' meager supply of specie (metal coin). The second revenue measure, the Stamp Act of 1765, imposed levies on a wide variety of items, including legal and commercial papers, liquor licenses, playing cards, dice, newspapers, calendars, and academic degrees. These duties, too, drained the supply of specie, which sank so low that some merchants faced bankruptcy.

The revenue measures touched off a major controversy. Indignant merchants in the New World boycotted all imports rather than pay the duties, and in October 1765 delegates from nine of the thirteen colonies met in New York City as the Stamp Act Congress. The Congress complained that the new duties had "a manifest tendency to subvert the rights and liberties of the colonists."

> That His Majesty's liege subjects in these colonies are entitled to all the inherent rights and liberties of his natural born subjects within the kingdom of Great Britain.
>
> That it is inseparably essential to the freedom of a people, and the undoubted right of Englishmen, that no taxes be imposed on them but with their own consent, given personally or by their own representatives.
>
> That the people of these colonies are not, and from their local circumstances cannot be, represented in the House of Commons in Great Britain.
>
> That the only representatives of these colonies are persons chosen therein by themselves, and that no taxes ever have been, or can be constitutionally imposed on them, but by their respective legislatures.*

The Stamp Act Congress thus proclaimed the celebrated principle of no taxation without representation.

Documents of American History, ed. H. S. Commager (New York, 1940), p. 58.

Britain surrendered on the practical issue, but did not yield on the principle. The appeals of London merchants, nearly ruined by the American boycott against British goods, brought the repeal of the Stamp Act in 1765. In 1766, however, Parliament passed the Declaratory Act asserting that the king and Parliament could indeed make laws affecting the colonies.

For the next decade, Britain adhered firmly to the principles of the Declaratory Act, and colonial radicals just as firmly repeated their opposition to taxation without representation. Parliament again tried to raise revenue, this time by the Townshend duties (1767) on colonial imports of tea, paper, paint, and lead. Again the merchants of Philadelphia, New York, and Boston organized boycotts. In 1770, Lord North's cabinet withdrew the Townshend duties except for the threepenny tariff on a pound of tea, retained as a symbol of parliamentary authority over the colonies. Three years later, the English East India Company attempted the sale of surplus tea in North America, hoping to overcome American opposition to the hated duty by making the retail price of East India tea, duty included, far cheaper than that of Dutch tea smuggled by the colonists. The result was the Boston Tea Party. On December 16, 1773, to the cheers of spectators lining the waterfront, a group of Bostonians who had a large financial stake in smuggled tea disguised themselves as Indians, boarded three East India ships, and dumped into the harbor chests of tea worth thousands of pounds.

Britain answered defiance with coercion, and the colonists met coercion with resistance. The Quebec Act (1774), incorporating the lands beyond the Alleghenies into Canada, bolted the door to the westward expansion of colonial frontiers. The Intolerable Acts (1774) closed the port of Boston to trade and suspended elections in Massachusetts. At Lexington and Concord in April 1775, the "embattled farmers" of Massachusetts fired the opening shots of the War of Independence. At Philadelphia on July 4, 1776, the delegates to the Continental Congress formally declared the American colonies independent of Great Britain.

Implications of the Revolution

For the mother country, the American Revolution implied more than the secession of thirteen colonies. It involved Britain in a minor world war that jeopardized her dominance abroad and weakened the power and prestige of King George III at home. The most crucial battle in North America came early in the war—the surrender at Saratoga in 1777 of the British forces under Burgoyne, who had been marching south from Montreal with the aim of driving a wedge between New England and the other rebellious colonies. Burgoyne's surrender convinced the French that support of the American colonists would give them an excellent chance to renew their worldwide struggle with Britain and avenge the humiliation of 1763. Entering the war in 1778, France soon gained the alliance of Spain and eventually secured the help, or at least the friendly neutrality, of most other European states. French intervention prepared the way for the victory of George Washington's forces and the final British surrender at Yorktown in 1781. In the peace signed at Paris in 1783, Britain recognized the independence of her former colonies. To Spain she handed back Florida, which she had taken in 1763, and the strategic Mediterranean island of Minorca. But she kept Gibraltar, which the Spanish had also hoped to recover, and she ceded only minor territories to France.

During the early years of the war, the British public had been inclined to agree with Dr. Samuel Johnson that the Americans were "a race of convicts" and "ought to be thankful for anything we allow them short of hanging." But the temper of opinion changed as the strength of American resistance became evident, as instances of British mismanagement piled up, and as most of Europe rallied to the rebellious colonies. By 1780, George III and his policies were so unpopular that the House of Commons passed a resolution declaring that "the influence of the crown has increased, is increasing, and ought to be diminished."

The influence of the Crown *was* diminished. In 1782, Lord North, who had been imploring the king for three years to accept his resignation, finally stepped down. In the next year, the post of prime minister fell to William Pitt the Younger, son of the heroic Pitt of the Seven Years' War. Though only twenty-five years old, he was a seasoned parliamentarian who was to head the cabinet for the next eighteen years. With the advent of Pitt, control of British politics shifted away from the king and back to the professional politicians. George III briefly contemplated abdication and then gradually resigned himself to the passive role of constitutional monarch.

In the colonies, opinion was by no means unanimous in support of the revolution. Many well-to-do colonists, including southern planters and Pennsylvania Quakers, either backed the mother country or took a neutral position in the struggle; New York supplied more recruits to George III than to George Washington. Some of these "Loyalists" or "Tories" were to flee to Canada when independence became a fact. Scholars, however, now reject as too low the traditional estimate that only one-third of the colonists actively backed the Revolution. Revolutionary sentiment ran particularly high in Virginia and New England and among social groups who had the habit of questioning established authority—the pioneers living on the frontier, and the numerous Presbyterians, Congregationalists, and other strongminded Protestants.

Like adolescents everywhere, the colonists resented parental tutelage yet appealed to family precedent. They claimed that they were only following the example set by Englishmen in 1688 and defended by John Locke. The ideas of Locke and Newton were as well known and as much respected in North America as they were in Europe. They underlay the Declaration of Independence:

> When in the course of human events, it becomes necessary for one people to dissolve the political bands which have connected them with another, and to assume among the Powers of the earth, the separate and equal station to which the Laws of Nature and of Nature's God entitle them, a decent respect to the opinions of mankind requires that they should declare the causes which impel them to the separation.

The opening paragraph of the Declaration thus expressed the concept of a world-machine ruled by the Laws of Nature. The next paragraph applied to the colonies Locke's theory of contract and his justification of revolution:

> We hold these truths to be self-evident, that all men are created equal, that they are endowed by their Creator with certain unalienable Rights, that among these are Life, Liberty and the pursuit of Happiness. That to secure these rights, Governments are instituted among Men, deriving their just power from the consent of the governed. That whenever any Form of Government becomes destructive of these ends, it is the Right of the People to alter or to abolish it, and to institute new Government. . . .

Another political idea of the Enlightenment congenial to the revolutionaries was the separation of powers proposed by Locke and by Montesquieu as a guarantee against tyranny. At the heart of the draft composed by the delegates to the constitutional convention at Philadelphia in 1787 was the separation of the executive, legislative, and judicial arms of government. Each of the branches had the power to check the other two. The president, for instance, could check the Congress by applying a veto; Congress could check the executive and the judiciary through impeachment and the right of confirming appointments; and one house of Congress exercised a check on the other since the consent of both houses was required for legislation. Since these balancing devices were in part derived from Montesquieu, it may be argued that the recurrent tensions between president and Congress originated in the American adaptation of an eighteenth-century French misreading of British constitutional practice. The Founding Fathers of the American republic sought guidance not only from *The Spirit of the Laws* but also from the constitutions of the thirteen original states and from English precedents. The first ten amendments to the United States Constitution (1791), guaranteeing freedom of religion, freedom of the press, and other basic liberties, were taken mainly from the English Bill of Rights of 1689.

The Constitution abounded in compromises. It attempted a balance between states' rights and the central power of the federal government, and between the democratic principle of a directly elected House of Representatives and the aristocratic principle of an indirectly elected and conservative Senate. (Senators were chosen by state governments until 1913, when the Seventeenth Amendment provided for their direct election.) It was a compromise designed to win support from both rich and poor and from both the Tory opponents and the democratic supporters of the recent revolution. Like any compromise, it did not at first please all parties. Its democracy was watered down by the legal existence of slavery in many states and by the fact that the states themselves determined requirements for voting. A majority of them imposed significant property qualifications, which were not to be lifted until a generation or more later on.

Yet the Constitution worked well enough to make the new American republic a going concern and to arouse enthusiastic approval and envy among liberals in Europe and in the colonial societies of Latin America. The Founding Fathers of the United States had succeeded perhaps better than any other statesmen of the eighteenth century in adjusting the ideals of the philosophes to the realities of practical politics.

VI Challenges to the Enlightenment
Philosophes—and Philosophers

Elsewhere the Enlightenment seldom produced such happy political results as it did in the United States. On the whole, the philosophes expected men to see reason when it was pointed out to them, to give up the habits of centuries, and to revise their behavior in accordance with natural law. But men would not always see reason; as Joseph II discovered to his sorrow, they *would* cling perversely to irrational customs and unnatural traditions. The rationalism of the Enlightenment tended to omit from its calculations the complexities of human nature.

Responsibility for this major shortcoming lay partly with the classical spirit of the seventeenth century, inherited by the Enlightenment of the eighteenth. The writers of the Age of Louis XIV had found in their classical models not a confirmation of existing standards, but a better, simpler set of standards that the eighteenth-century philosophes easily adapted to the concept of "nature's simple plan." The great writers achieved the miracle of giving life to these abstractions. But the lesser ones created only bloodless types and encouraged in their readers the illusion that what was going on in their minds would shortly go on in reality. Like the classical spirit, the spirit of natural science went too far when it was applied uncritically to problems of human relations.

A minor philosophe, the Abbé Mably, got at this central problem when he asked: "Is society, then, a branch of physics?" Most of the philosophes and their followers believed that it was. They applied to the unpredictable activities of man the mathematical methods used in the physical sciences. The Physiocrats,

for example, tried to reduce the complexities of human economic activities to a few simple agricultural laws. Like the stars in their courses, men were assumed to fit neatly into the Newtonian world-machine.

A few outspoken critics, however, disagreed. The Italian philosopher Vico (1688–1744) published in 1725 the *Scienza Nuova* (New Science), which looked at the state not as a piece of machinery subject to natural laws but as an organism with a pattern of growth, maturity, and decay imposed by its own nature. Vico's antimechanistic and anti-Cartesian views attracted little attention until the nineteenth century, when organic interpretations came into their own.

The Scottish philosopher David Hume (1711–1776) shared the philosophes' critical attitude toward existing institutions and dramatized his opposition to mercantilism and his advocacy of free international trade by avowing that he prayed for the prosperity of other nations. Yet his profound skepticism and his corrosive common sense caused him to make short work of the philosophes' appeals to nature and reason. To Hume the laws of justice, for instance, were not unalterable but varied with circumstances and, in an emergency, might yield entirely to "stronger motives of necessity and self-preservation. Is it any crime, after a shipwreck, to seize whatever means or instrument of safety one can lay hold of, without regard to former limitations of property?"* Nor, Hume argued, could human conduct be analyzed "in the same manner that we discover by reason the truths of geometry or algebra."

It appears evident that the ultimate ends of human actions can never, in any case, be accounted for by *reason,* but recommend themselves entirely to the sentiments and affections of mankind, without any dependance on the intellectual faculties. Ask a man *why he uses exercise:* he will answer, *because he desires to keep his health,* If you then enquire, *why he desires health,* he will readily reply, *because sickness is painful.* If you push your enquiries farther, and desire a reason *why he hates pain,* it is impossible he can ever give any.†

In the generation after Hume the romantics would repeat his warnings against reason and his pleas on behalf of the "sentiments and affections of mankind." In Hume's own day, Rousseau and Kant were also troubled by rather similar problems. Rousseau was an ambiguous figure, who both exemplified the Enlightenment and foreshadowed the romantic revolt against it. No philosophe defended natural law more ardently, yet no romantic argued more powerfully on behalf of the irrational faculties of man. "Too often does reason deceive us," Rousseau wrote in *Emile.* "We have only too good a right to doubt her; but conscience never deceives us; she is the true guide of man; . . . he who obeys his

*D. Hume, *An Enquiry Concerning the Principles of Morals,* ed. L. A. Selby-Bigge (Oxford, 1902) p. 186.
†Ibid., p. 293.

conscience is following nature and he need not fear that he will go astray." *

Immanuel Kant (1724–1804), who taught philosophy at the University of Königsberg in East Prussia, raised Rousseau's argument to the level of metaphysics. While advocating many of the doctrines of the Enlightenment, Kant also believed in a higher reality reaching ultimately to God. He called the eternal verities of the higher world *noumena*, from a Greek word meaning "things thought," in contrast to the phenomena of the material world that are experienced through the senses. Knowledge of the noumenal realm, Kant believed, reached men through reason—reason, however, not as the Enlightenment used the term, not as common sense, but as intuition. The highest expression of the Kantian reason was the categorical imperative. This was the moral law within, the conscience implanted in man by God. It was the inescapable realization by the individual that, when confronted with an ethical choice, he must choose the good and avoid the evil, must follow the course that he would want to have become a universal precedent, not simply the most expedient solution to his own dilemma. Kant's redefinition of reason and his rehabilitation of conscience exemplified the philosophical reaction against the dominant rationalism of the Enlightenment. The popular reaction came in the challenge from the evangelical revival.

*J. Rousseau, *Emile,* Everyman ed. (New York, 1911), pp. 249–250.

John Wesley in 1788.

Pietists and Methodists

The evangelical revival began with the German Pietists, who were the spiritual heirs of the sixteenth-century Anabaptists and found a congenial academic base at the Prussian University of Halle. The Pietists deplored alike the growing concern of Lutherans with the external formalities of religion and the emphasis of deists upon natural law. They asserted that religion came from the heart, not the head, and that God was far more than a watchmaker, the remote creator of the world-machine. One of the chief leaders of Pietism was the German Count Zinzendorf (1700–1760), founder of the Moravian Brethren, who set up a model community based on Christian principles. Moravian emigrants to America planted a colony at Bethlehem, Pennsylvania, helping to create the reputation for thrift, hard work, and strict living enjoyed by the Pennsylvania Dutch (Dutch here meaning *Deutsch,* German).

In England, the example of Zinzendorf and other Pietists inspired John Wesley (1703–1791). Ordained in the Church of England, Wesley at first stressed the ritualistic aspects of religion and then felt his own faith evaporating after the failure of his ministry to the new colony of Georgia (1736–1737), which was settled by prisoners forcibly transported from Britain. "I went to America, to convert the Indians: but Oh! who shall convert me! Who, what is he that will deliver me from this evil heart of unbelief?" * Pietism converted Wesley and taught him that he would find faith through inner conviction. For more than fifty years, Wesley labored tirelessly to share his discovery, traveling throughout the British Isles and preaching in churches, in the fields, at the pitheads of coal mines, and even in jails. Angry crowds came to scoff but remained to pray. When Wesley died in 1791, his movement had already attracted more than a hundred thousand adherents. They were called Methodists, because of their methodical devotion to piety and to plain dress and plain living. Though Wesley always considered himself a good Anglican, the Methodists eventually set up a separate organization—their nonconformist Chapel in contrast to the established Church of England. The new sect won its following almost entirely among the lower and middle classes, among people who sought the religious excitement and consolation they did not find in deism or in the austere formalism of the Church of England.

Although the beliefs of the Methodists diverged entirely from those of the Enlightenment, they too worked to improve the condition of society. Where the philosophes advocated public reform, the Methodists favored private charity; and where the philosophes attacked the causes of social evils, the Methodists accepted these evils as part of God's plan and sought to mitigate their symptoms. They had in full measure the Puritan conscience of the nonconformists. They began agitation against drunkenness, the trade in slaves, and the barbarous treatment of prisoners, the insane, and

*J. Wesley, *Journal,* Everyman ed. (New York, 1907), 1:74.

the sick. John Wesley established schools for coalminers' children and opened dispensaries for the poor in London and Bristol. The Methodists' success derived in part from their social programs and in part from the magnetism of John Wesley and his talented associates. His brother Charles composed more than 6,500 hymns, and in America Methodist missionaries flourished under the dynamic leadership of Francis Asbury (1745–1816). The number of colleges called Wesleyan and the number of churches and streets called Asbury testify to the significance of Methodism in American social history.

Literature

The literature and art of the eighteenth century showed marked contrasts between the reasoned discipline of the classical tradition and the less inhibited expressions of the creative impulse. For example, the landmarks of architecture included both carefully proportioned Palladian buildings and more exotic and exuberant structures in the rococo or neo-Gothic styles. The literary landmarks of the century included both the classical writings of the French philosophes and the English Augustans, and new experiments in the depiction of realism and "sensibility," that is, the life of the emotions.

In England, the Augustan age of letters took its name from the claim that it boasted a group of talents comparable to those of Vergil, Horace, and Ovid, who had flourished under the emperor Augustus in Rome. While the claim was somewhat inflated, the Augustans Addison and Steele made the *Tatler* and *Spectator* vehicles for popularizing serious intellectual discussion in the early 1700s. Alexander Pope (1688–1744) chose rhymed couplets not for tragedies as Racine had, but for philosophical and satirical essays. The greatest of the Augustans was Jonathan Swift (1667–1745), a pessimistic and sometimes despondent genius, whose convictions about human depravity and folly went far beyond the moderation of the classical spirit. Recall, in *Gulliver's Travels,* the satirization of the scientific endeavors of the Royal Society in the Academy of Lagado and the startling contrast between the noble and reasonable horses, the Houyhnhnms, and the brutish and revolting human Yahoos.

Much closer to the classical temper of the other Augustans and of the Enlightenment were two works from the latter part of the eighteenth century, Gibbon's *History of the Decline and Fall of the Roman Empire* (1788) and Dr. Johnson's *Dictionary.* Edward Gibbon, who modeled his prose style on the balance and discipline of Cicero's Latin, made history the excuse for a sustained Voltairean attack on Christian fanaticism. Samuel Johnson expressed another concern of the age in the preface to his famous *Dictionary:*

When I took the first survey of my undertaking, I found our speech copious without order and energetick without rules: wherever I turned my view, there was perplexity to be dis-

Dr. Johnson and Samuel Boswell talking "till near two in the morning." Satirical etching by Thomas Rowlandson.

entangled, and confusion to be regulated; choice was to be made out of a boundless variety, without any established principle of selection; adulterations were to be detected, without a settled test of purity; and modes of expression to be rejected or received, without the suffrages of any writers of classical reputation or acknowledged authority.

Pedantry and prejudice sometimes overcame the autocratic doctor. The former is evident in his recourse to obscure Latinisms to define a cough—"a convulsion of the lungs, vellicated by some sharp serosity"; and the latter in his repeated volleys against the Scots, such as defining oats as "a grain, which in England is generally given horses, but in Scotland supports the people." In the main, however, Dr. Johnson succeeded admirably in his aim of becoming a kind of Newton of the English language.

Meantime, the rapid development of the novel as a literary form greatly increased the popularity of more down-to-earth and emotional writing. Two of the earliest examples of the new genre of fiction were by Daniel Defoe—*Robinson Crusoe* (1719) and *Moll Flanders* (1722), both purporting to be autobiographies. They were in fact novels, and both were far removed from the refinements and elevated feelings of classicism. Realism was also evident in two celebrated mid-century novels. Tobias Smollett's *Roderick Random* (1748) drew an authentic picture of life in His Majesty's Navy, with its cruelty and hardship. In the next year Henry Fielding, who gained insight into his subject matter from his work as a London magistrate, published the first truly great social novel, *Tom Jones,* with its convincing portraits of the toughs of London slums and the hard-riding, hard-drinking country squires.

Fielding also delighted in parodying the sentimental fiction of Samuel Richardson (1689–1761), a printer by trade, who turned to writing late in life and created three giant novels cast in the form of letters by the hero or heroine. We may take as an example *Clarissa Harlowe* (1748), in which 2,400 pages of small print described the misfortunes of Clarissa, whose lover was a scoundrel and whose greedy relatives were scheming to secure her considerable property. Whatever her plight, Clarissa never lost the capacity to pour out her miseries on paper. Her effusions were read aloud at family gatherings, it is said, and whenever some new disaster overwhelmed her, the family withdrew to its various rooms for solitary weeping. With all Richardson's excessive emotionalism and preachiness, his descriptions of passion and conscience carried such conviction that his novels did much to establish the tradition of moral earnestness in English fiction.

French literature was by no means monopolized by the satires and blueprints for the future issuing from the philosophes. The novel of sensibility came into its own with the very popular *Manon Lescaut* (1731) of the Abbé Prévost, a tale that still deferred to the moderation of the classical spirit in relating the vicissitudes of a young woman sent to the colony of Louisiana. Much closer to Richardson in style and tone was Rousseau's long novel about the conflict of love and duty, *La Nouvelle Héloïse* (1761), which ranked next to *Emile* as his most popular work before 1789. Because of the strict sexual morality Rousseau preached (though did not always practice), the new Héloïse, unlike her medieval namesake in the affair with Abelard, died in time to avoid adultery. On the French stage the retreat from classicism was marked by the *comédies larmoyantes* ("tearful comedies"), a popular blend of laughter, pathos, and melodrama. The way was being cleared for the romantic writers who would largely dominate French literature in the early nineteenth century.

In Germany the most important literary works were not the frenchified writings favored by Frederick the Great but the dramas of Lessing and the outpourings of the writers associated with the Sturm und Drang ("storm and stress") movement. Lessing (1729–1781) combined the sensibility of Richardson and the French *comédies larmoyantes* with an enlightened devotion to common sense and toleration. In his romantic comedy *Minna von Barnhelm,* the lively heroine pits her feminine values against a Prussian officer in a fashion hardly acceptable to the Hohenzollern tradition of military infallibility. In *Nathan the Wise* Lessing dramatizes the deistic belief that Judaism, Christianity, and Islam are all manifestations of a universal religion.

A play of a very different kind gave its name to a whole movement by young German writers in the 1770s. The hero of *Sturm und Drang,* finding himself quite incapable of settling down, flees Europe to fight in the American Revolution:

> Have been everything. Became a day-labourer to be something. Lived on the Alps, pastured goats, lay day and night under the boundless vault of the heavens, cooled by the winds, burning with an inner fire. Nowhere rest, nowhere repose. See, thus I am glutted by impulse and power, and work it out of me. I am going to take part in this campaign as a volunteer; there I can expand my soul, and if they do me the favour to shoot me down,—all the better.*

*Klinger, *Sturm und Drang,* quoted in K. Francke, *A History of German Literature as Determined by Social Forces,* 4th ed. (New York, 1931), p. 309.

Yearning, frustration, and despair characterized the most successful work of the Sturm und Drang period, *The Sorrows of Young Werther,* a lugubrious short novel by the youthful Goethe (1749–1832). Napoleon claimed to have read it seven times, weeping copiously on each occasion when the hero shoots himself because the woman he loves is already married. The themes of self-pity and self-destruction, so at odds with the Enlightenment's cheerful belief in progress, were to be prominent in the romantic movement that swept over Europe at the close of the eighteenth century.

The Arts

The classicism of the century strongly affected its art. Gibbon's history, the researches of scholars and archaeologists, and the discovery in 1748 of the ruins of Roman Pompeii, well preserved under lava from Vesuvius, raised the interest in antiquity to a high pitch. For the men of the Enlightenment, the balance and symmetry of Greek and Roman temples represented, in effect, the natural laws of building. Architects retreated somewhat from the theatricalism of the baroque style and adapted classical models with great artistry and variety. We owe to them the elegance of the London townhouse, the monumental magnificence of the buildings flanking the Place de la Concorde in Paris, and the country-manor charm of Washington's Mount Vernon. The twentieth-century vogue of the "colonial" and the "Georgian" testifies to the lasting influence of this neoclassical architecture.

In painting, neoclassicism had an eminent spokesman in Sir Joshua Reynolds (1723–1792), the president of the Royal Academy and the artistic czar of Georgian England. Beauty, Sir Joshua told the academy, rested "on the uniform, eternal, and immutable laws of nature," which could be "investigated by reason, and known by study." Sir Joshua and his contemporaries, though preaching a coldly reasoned aesthetic, gave warmth to the portraits that they painted of wealthy English aristocrats. This was the golden age of English portraiture, the age of Reynolds, Lawrence, Gainsborough, and Romney. But it was also the age of William Hogarth (1697–1764), who cast aside the academic restraints of neoclassicism to do in art what Fielding did in the novel. Instead of catering to a few wealthy patrons, Hogarth created a mass market for the engravings that he turned out in thousands of copies, graphic sermons on the vices of London—*Marriage à la Mode, The Rake's Progress, The Harlot's Progress,* and *Gin Lane.*

The realism of Hogarth was not the only exception to the prevailing neoclassicism. In France, the style called rococo prevailed during the reign of Louis XV. It was even more fantastic than the baroque, but lighter, airier, more delicate and graceful, much addicted to the use of motifs from bizarre rock formations and from shells. In painting the rococo was a return to Rubens' concern for flesh tones, combined with a light quick touch that suggested improvisation; it may be sensed in the works of Watteau (1684–1721) and of Fragonard (1732–1806).

Meanwhile, three artistic fashions that were to figure significantly in the forthcoming age of romanticism were already catching on—the taste for the oriental, for the natural, and for the Gothic. Rococo interest in the exotic created a great vogue for things Chinese—Chinese wallpaper, the "Chinese" furniture of Thomas Chippendale, and all the delicate work in porcelain or painted scrolls that goes by the name of chinoiserie. Eighteenth-century gardens were bestrewn with pagodas and minarets, and gardeners abandoned Louis XIV's geometrical landscaping for the natural English garden. Even the dominance of neoclassical architecture was challenged. At Strawberry Hill near London, Horace Walpole, the son of the great Robert, endowed his house with an abundance of Gothic "gloomth"—battlements in the medieval style, and "lean windows fattened with rich saints in painted glass."

Music

A constellation of great composers and a rapid advance in techniques made music perhaps the queen of the arts in the eighteenth century. The German choirmaster Johann Sebastian Bach (1685–1750) brought to perfection the baroque techniques of the seventeenth century. He mastered the difficult art of the fugue, an intricate version of the round in which each voice begins the theme in turn while other voices repeat it and elaborate upon it. Bach composed fugues and a wealth of other material for the organ, and for small orchestras the Brandenburg Concertos, in which successive instruments are given a chance to show off their potentialities. Bach's sacred works included many cantatas, the Mass in B minor, and the two gigantic choral settings of the Passion of Christ according to Saint Matthew and to Saint John. His religious music, dramatic and deeply felt, was a world apart from the anticlericalism of the Enlightenment.

Bach's quiet provincial life contrasted sharply with the stormy international career of his countryman Handel (1685–1759). After studying in Italy, Handel spent most of his adult years in London trying to run an opera company in the face of the intrigues, clashes of temperament, and fiscal headaches endemic in artistic enterprises. Handel wrote more than forty operas, including *Xerxes,* famous for its "Largo." He used themes from the Bible for *The Messiah* and other vigorous oratorios arranged for large choruses and directed at a mass audience. These elaborate works differed greatly from the simple earlier oratorios designed for the tiny Italian prayer chapels called oratories.

Although Bach and Handel composed many instrumental suites and concertos, it was not until the second half of the century that orchestral music really came to the fore. New instruments appeared, notably the piano, which greatly extended the limited range of the older keyboard instrument, the harpsichord. New forms of instrumental music also appeared, the sonata and the symphony, developed largely by the Austrian Haydn (1732–1809). Haydn wrote more than fifty piano pieces in the form of the sonata, in which two contrasting themes are stated in turn, developed, interwoven, repeated, and finally resolved in a *coda* (Italian for "tail"). Haydn then arranged the sonata for the orchestra, grafting it onto the Italian operatic overture to create the first movement of the symphony.

The operatic landmark of the early century was John Gay's *Beggar's Opera* (1728), a tuneful work caricaturing the London underworld. Later, the German Gluck (1714–1787) revolutionized the technique of the tragic opera. "I have striven," he said,

> to restrict music to its true office of serving poetry by means of expression and by following the situations of the story, without interrupting the action or stifling it with a useless superfluity of ornaments. . . . I did not wish to arrest an actor in the greatest heat of dialogue . . . to hold him up in the middle of a word on a vowel favorable to his voice, nor to make display of the agility of his fine voice in some long-drawn passage, nor to wait while the orchestra gives him time to recover his breath for a cadenza.*

Accordingly, Gluck's operas were well-constructed musical dramas, not just vehicles for the display of vocal pyrotechnics. He kept to the old custom of taking heroes and heroines from classical mythology, but he tried to invest shadowy figures like Orpheus, Eurydice, and Iphigenia with new vitality.

Opera, symphony, concerto, and chamber music all reached a climax in the works of the Austrian Mozart (1756–1791). As a boy, Mozart was exploited by his father, who carted him all over Europe to show off his virtuosity on the harpsichord and his amazing talent for composition. Overworked throughout his life, and in his later years overburdened with debts, Mozart died a pauper at the age of thirty-five. Yet his youthful precocity ripened steadily into mature genius, and his facility and versatility grew ever more prodigious. He tossed off the sprightly overture to *The Marriage of Figaro* in the course of an evening, and in two months during the summer of 1788, produced his three final symphonies. Mozart's concertos sometimes had solo parts for the piano or violin and sometimes, to show it could be done and done well, for bassoon or French horn. In chamber music, Mozart experimented with almost every possible combination of instruments.

Three of Mozart's great operas were in the comic Italian vein—the lighthearted *Così Fan Tutte* (Thus Do All Women); *The Marriage of Figaro* based on Beaumarchais' famous satire of the caste system of the Old Regime, in which Figaro the valet outwits and outsings his noble employers; and, though hardly comic in its implications, *Don Giovanni,* depicting the havoc wrought by Don Juan on earth before his punishment in hell. Mozart composed mournful and romantic arias for the Don's victims, elegantly seductive ballads for the Don

---

*Preface to *Alcestis,* as translated by Eric Blom and quoted in C. Sachs, *Our Musical Heritage* (New York, 1948), p. 287.

himself, and a catalog of the Don's conquests for his valet ("A thousand and three in Spain alone"). The instruments in the pit dotted the *i*'s and crossed the *t*'s of the plot—scurrying violins to accompany characters dashing about the stage, portentous trombones to announce the entrance of the Devil. For the ballroom scene of *Don Giovanni,* Mozart employed three orchestras playing simultaneously three different tunes for three different dances—a minuet for the aristocracy, a country dance for the middle class, a waltz (then considered quite plebeian) for the lower orders. In his last opera, *The Magic Flute,* Mozart tried to create a consciously German work; but only the vaguest political significance emerged from the fantastic libretto, which apparently sought to vindicate the enlightened ideas of Joseph II and to decry the conservatism of Maria Theresa.

The Magic Flute was a rare exception to the cosmopolitanism of eighteenth-century music. The great composers with the German names had very little national feeling. Almost all of them felt equally at home in Vienna, Prague, Milan, Paris, and London, and they gratefully accepted patrons in any country. The fortunate Haydn moved from the princely estate of the Hungarian Esterhazy family to score an equal success with the paying public of the London concert halls.

Italian music was never totally eclipsed; Vivaldi, the Scarlattis (father and son), and Boccherini were talented composers ranking close to the German and Austrian masters. Bach patterned his concertos on Italian models, Haydn borrowed Italian operatic overtures for his symphonies, and every operatic composer of the century profited from the labors of his Italian predecessors. The great musicians also borrowed freely from folk tunes and ballads, the popular music of their day, and were rewarded by having their themes whistled in the streets.

Of all the arts, music probably came closest to resolving the great conflict in eighteenth-century culture, the tension between reason and emotion, between the abstractions of the Enlightenment and the flesh-and-blood realities of human existence. In other realms, however, as the century drew toward its close, the lines were drawn for the vigorous prosecution of the conflict. In thought, the ideas of Kant and Hume were challenging the optimistic rationalism of the philosophes. Romantic artists and writers were beginning to defy the defenders of classicism. And in politics, as the century ended, the European powers sought to thwart the supreme effort to realize on earth the Enlightenment's dream of reason, natural law, and progress—the French Revolution.

Reading Suggestions on the Enlightenment
General

W. L. Dorn, *Competition for Empire, 1740–1763,* and L. Gershoy, *From Despotism to Revolution, 1763–1789* (*Torchbooks). These two informative volumes in the series Rise of Modern Europe have very full bibliographies.

R. R. Palmer, *The Age of the Democratic Revolution,* Vol. 1 (*Princeton Univ. Press). A thoughtful survey of political ideas and unrest in Europe and America at the close of the Old Regime.

L. Krieger, *Kings and Philosophers, 1689–1789* (*Norton). Comprehensive survey, with a succinct, up-to-date bibliography.

The Ideas of the Enlightenment

Peter Gay, *The Enlightenment,* 2 vols. (Knopf, 1966, 1969; Vol. 1 also *Vintage). Comprehensive survey by a leading expert in the field; with extensive bibliographies.

G. R. Havens, *The Age of Ideas: From Reaction to Revolution in Eighteenth-Century France* (*Free Press). Most useful biographical sketches of the philosophes.

E. Cassirer, *The Philosophy of the Enlightenment* (*Beacon, 1955). An important and lucid study of the great principles of eighteenth-century thought.

R. Anchor, *The Enlightenment Tradition* (*Harper). A stimulating interpretation.

K. Martin, *French Liberal Thought in the Eighteenth Century* (*Torchbooks). A brilliant and opinionated survey of the philosophes.

N. Hampson, *A Cultural History of the Enlightenment* (Pantheon, 1968). Concerned chiefly with ideas and their background.

C. Becker, *The Heavenly City of the Eighteenth-Century Philosophers* (*Yale Univ. Press). A delightful essay, much influenced by A. N. Whitehead. Its ideas are reassessed in R. O. Rockwood, ed., *Carl Becker's Heavenly City Revisited* (Cornell Univ. Press, 1958).

J. B. Bury, *The Idea of Progress* (*Dover, 1955). A famous old pioneering study.

L. I. Bredvold, *The Brave New World of the Enlightenment* (Univ. of Michigan Press, 1961). Controversial, basically hostile, but deserving attention.

L. G. Crocker, *An Age of Crisis* and *Nature and Culture* (Johns Hopkins Univ. Press, 1959, 1963). Penetrating criticisms of the implications of the Enlightenment.

Some Individual Thinkers

A. M. Wilson, *Diderot* (Oxford Univ. Press, 1972). The definitive scholarly biography.

N. L. Torrey, *The Spirit of Voltaire* (Columbia Univ. Press, 1938), and Peter Gay, *Voltaire's Politics* (*Vintage). Thoughtful studies.

J. Guéhenno, *Jean Jacques Rousseau,* 2 vols. (Columbia Univ. Press, 1966). A full-dress study. An excellent brief introduction is E. Cassirer, *The Question of Jean Jacques Rousseau* (*Indiana Univ. Press).

A. Cobban, *Rousseau & the Modern State* (Allen & Unwin, 1934). A good introduction to the implications of Rousseau's thought. For a highly critical appraisal see J. L. Talmon, *The Origins of Totalitarian Democracy* (*Norton).

F. Manuel, *The Prophets of Paris* (Harvard Univ. Press, 1962). Turgot and Condorcet are among those considered.

The Enlightened Despots

J. Gagliardo, *Enlightened Despotism* (*Crowell). Informative and brief.

S. Andrews, ed., *Enlightened Despotism* (*Barnes & Noble). Excerpts from writings of the despots and of modern interpreters of the age.

R. Wines, ed., *Enlightened Despotism: Reform or Reaction?* (*Heath). All sides of the question examined by various authorities.

G. Ritter, *Frederick the Great* (Univ. of California Press, 1968). Well-balanced lectures by a German scholar.

L. Reniers, *Frederick the Great* (Oswald Wolff Ltd., 1960). A critical estimate.

W. H. Bruford, *Germany in the Eighteenth Century* (*Cambridge Univ. Press). Stresses social and intellectual developments.

C. A. Macartney, *Maria Theresa and the House of Austria* (English Universities Press, 1969). Brief scholarly appraisal.

E. Crankshaw, *Maria Theresa* (Viking, 1969). A capable biographical study.

T. Blanning, *Joseph II and Enlightened Despotism* (Longmans, 1970). Good brief introduction.

P. P. Bernard, *Joseph II* (Twayne, 1968). Succinct appraisal by a scholar who has written more detailed works on Joseph's reign.

S. K. Padover, *The Revolutionary Emperor,* 2nd ed. (Shoe String, 1967). Highly favorable to Joseph II and critical of Maria Theresa.

R. Herr, *The Eighteenth-Century Revolution in Spain* (Princeton Univ. Press, 1958). Important reappraisal of the Enlightenment's effect upon Spain.

I. Andersson, *A History of Sweden* (Weidenfeld & Nicolson, 1956). Useful for Gustavus III and his background.

Catherine the Great & George the Third

G. Scott Thomson, *Catherine the Great and the Expansion of Russia* (*Collier). A sound short introduction.

M. Raeff, *Imperial Russia, 1682–1825* (*Knopf). Recently published survey from Peter the Great through Alexander I; by an able scholar.

L. J. Oliva, *Catherine the Great* (*Spectrum) and M. Raeff, ed., *Catherine the Great: A Profile* (*Hill & Wang). Instructive appraisals of the Russian empress.

P. Dukes, *Catherine the Great & the Russian Nobility* (Cambridge Univ. Press, 1968). Study of a most significant aspect of her policy.

J. S. Watson, *The Reign of George III, 1760–1815* (Clarendon, 1960). Enlightening general account in The Oxford History of England.

L. B. Namier, *England in the Age of the American Revolution* (*St. Martin's). Controversial study of British politics in the 1760s.

G. Rudé, *Wilkes and Liberty* (*Oxford Univ. Press). Analysis of the unrest in Britain during the early years of George III's reign.

American Independence

C. Becker, *The Declaration of Independence* (*Vintage). Stressing the influence of the Enlightenment upon Americans.

B. Bailyn, *Ideological Origins of the American Revolution* (*Harvard Univ. Press), and J. C. Miller, *Origins of the American Revolution* (*Stanford Univ. Press). Illuminating studies of the background.

E. S. Morgan, *The Birth of the Republic, 1763–1789* (*Phoenix); L. H. Gipson, *The Coming of the Revolution, 1763–1775;* and J. R. Alden, *The American Revolution, 1775–1783* (both *Torchbooks). Standard scholarly accounts.

The Arts

J. S. Held and D. Posner, *17th and 18th Century Art* (Prentice-Hall and Harry Abrams, 1972). A comprehensive survey discussing rococo but not neoclassicism.

G. Bazin, *Baroque and Rococo Art* (*Praeger) and A. C. Sewter, *Baroque and Rococo* (*Harcourt, Brace). Concise introductions.

A. Schönberger and H. Soehner, *The Age of Rococo* (Thames & Hudson, 1960). Handsomely illustrated survey.

T. Pignatti, *The Age of Rococo* (Paul Hamlyn, 1969). Brief, but valuable for its stress on the Italian contribution and its unusual illustrations.

J. Thuillier and A. Châtelet, *French Painting from Le Nain to Fragonard* (Skira, 1964). Handsomely illustrated survey from the mid-17th to the late 18th century.

F. Antal, *Hogarth and His Place in European Art* (Routledge, 1962). Ingenious study stressing parallels with earlier and later artists.

E. Waterhouse, *Reynolds* (Phaidon, 1973). Sympathetic assessment of Sir Joshua.

S. Faniel, ed., *French Art of the Eighteenth Century* (Simon & Schuster, 1957). Valuable for its coverage of the minor arts.

Music

M. Bukofzer, *Music in the Baroque Era* (Norton, 1947). Survey down to 1750.

C. Rosen, *The Classical Style* (*Norton). Perceptive study of Mozart, Haydn, and Beethoven.

E. M. and S. Grew, *Bach* (*McGraw-Hill); A Einstein, *Gluck* (*McGraw-Hill) and *Mozart* (*Oxford Univ. Press); E. J. Dent, *Mozart's Operas* (*Oxford Univ. Press). Enlightening works on individual composers.

Sources

R. and E. Forster, eds., *European Society in the Eighteenth Century* (*Harper). Well-selected anthology.

C. Brinton, ed., *The Portable Age of Reason Reader* (*Viking); I. Berlin, ed., *The Age of Enlightenment: The Eighteenth-Century Philosophers* (*Mentor). Two valuable anthologies.

B. R. Redman, ed., *The Portable Voltaire* (*Viking, 1949). A well-edited selection.

L. G. Crocker, ed., *The Age of Enlightenment* (Walker, 1969), and C. Macartney, ed., *The Habsburg and Hohenzollern Dynasties in the Seventeenth and Eighteenth Centuries* (Walker, 1970). Volumes in the Documentary History of Western Civilization.

M. Beloff, ed., *The Debate on the American Revolution, 1761–1783* (*Torchbooks). Handy compilation of British speeches and writings for and against the rebels.

The French Revolution and Napoleon

I Introduction

In France, as in the thirteen North American colonies, a financial crisis preceded a revolution. There was not only a parallel but also a direct connection between the revolution of 1776 and that of 1789. French participation in the War of American Independence increased an already excessive governmental debt by more than 1,500,000,000 livres,* and the example of America fired the imagination of discontented Frenchmen. To them, Benjamin Franklin, the immensely popular American envoy to France, was the very embodiment of the Enlightenment, and the new republic overseas promised to become the utopia of the philosophes. Yet it would be going too far to claim that the American Revolution actually caused the French Revolution; rather, it speeded up developments in France that had long been under way. The forces causing the upheaval of 1789 were almost fully matured in 1776. And, just as the reasons for revolution were more deeply rooted and more complicated in France than in America, so the revolution itself was to be more violent and more sweeping.

The immediate cause of the great French Revolution, then, was financial. King Louis XVI vainly tried one expedient after another to avert bankruptcy and finally summoned the Estates General, the central representative assembly that had last met 175 years earlier. Once assembled, the deputies of the nation initiated the reforms that were to destroy the Old Regime in France. The basic causes of the revolution, however, reached deep into France's society and economy and into her political and intellectual history. Behind the financial crisis of the 1780s lay many decades of fiscal misman agement; the government had been courting insolvency since the last years of Louis XIV. The nobles and clergy jealously guarding their traditional privileges, refused to pay a fair share of the taxes. Resentment agains inequitable taxation and inefficient government buil up among the unprivileged—the peasantry, the workers, and above all, the bourgeoisie.

What translated bourgeois resentment into de mands for reform and potential revolution was the program of change put forward by the philosophes Conservative apologists of the Old Regime have argued that the revolution was essentially a subversive plo hatched by a small minority of men who had beer corrupted by the destructive ideas of the Enlighten ment. Their center of operations was the network o six hundred Masonic lodges which had grown up ir France since Freemasonry was first imported from Eng land in the early eighteenth century. Modern scholar ship has demonstrated the shallowness of this conspir acy thesis. The twenty or thirty thousand Frenchmer who belonged to Masonic lodges did include many influential nobles and bourgeois, and the lodges them selves were important disseminators of enlightened ideas. But so were the provincial academies, the loca discussion groups called Sociétés de Pensée (Though Societies), the *Encyclopédie,* and all the other writings o the philosophes. In general the Masons limited their political activity to relatively innocuous statements in favor of equality and toleration, and some lodges actu ally forbade discussion of politics. It seems clear beyonc any reasonable doubt that what happened in 1789 anc subsequent years was not the result of a plot but rather the denouement of a long drama in which every ele ment of French society—king and noble, priest anc Freemason, bourgeois and peasant, craftsman and ap prentice, fishwife and laundress—played an importan

---

*It has been estimated that the prerevolutionary livre was worth somewhere between $1 and $2 in terms of the 1975 dollar. But the estimate is very rough, and it is impossible to set a value on the livre because of the enormous increase in prices in the two centuries since the Old Regime and also because of the

Marie Antoinette and her children, painted by Mme. Vigée-Lebrun.

David's sketch of the queen on her way to the guillotine.

II   The Road to Revolution

France, the home of the Enlightenment, was never ruled by an enlightened despot until the advent of Napoleon. Except for suppressing the parlements, as we shall see in a moment, Louis XV had refused to take decisive steps to remedy the abuses of the Old Regime. What Louis XV would not do, his grandson and successor, Louis XVI (1774–1792) could not do. When the new king, aged nineteen, learned that his grandfather had died of smallpox, he is said to have exclaimed: "What a burden! At my age! And I have been taught nothing!" The emperor Joseph II, his brother-in-law, later commented that Louis treated petty intrigues with the greatest attention and neglected important affairs of state. Honest, earnest, and pious, but also clumsy, irresolute, and stubborn, Louis XVI was most at home hunting, eating, or tinkering at locksmithing. He also labored under the severe handicap of a politically unfortunate marriage to a Hapsburg. Marie Antoinette, the youngest of the empress Maria Theresa's sixteen children, was badly educated, extravagant, and completely isolated in the artificial little world of Versailles. To patriotic Frenchmen she was a constant reminder of the ill-fated Franco-Austrian alliance during the Seven Years' War.

For want of a good mechanic, the machinery of centralized royal absolutism was gradually falling apart. The fact that it functioned at all could be credited to a relatively few capable administrators, notably the intendants who ran so much of provincial France. The best of the intendants, like the Physiocrat Turgot at Limoges, provided a welcome touch of enlightened despotism, but they could do little to stay the slow disintegration of the central government.

The whole legal and judicial system required reform. The law needed to be codified to eliminate obsolete medieval survivals and to end the overlapping of the two legal systems—Roman and feudal—that prevailed in France. The courts needed a thorough overhaul to make them swift, fair, and inexpensive. Many judges and lawyers purchased or inherited their offices and regarded them not as a public trust but as a means to private enrichment and elevation to the nobility of the robe. Louis XV had permitted his ministers to attack the strongholds of these vested interests, the parlements which existed in Paris and in a dozen provincial centers. One of the last acts of his reign had been their suppression and replacement by new high courts more amenable to royal control. One of the first moves taken by Louis XVI was the restoration of the parlements, a very popular measure because many Frenchmen viewed the parlements as a constitutional check on absolute monarchy. They often failed to see that the parlements were also a formidable obstacle to social and economic reform.

The Clergy and the Nobility

Like those of the monarchy itself, the social and economic foundations of the Old Regime were beginning to crumble by the middle of the eighteenth century. The first estate, the clergy, occupied a position of conspicuous importance in France. Though constituting only one-half of one percent of the population, the clergy controlled lucrative properties amounting to about 10 percent of French lands. They performed many functions normally undertaken by the state today, running schools, keeping records of vital statistics, and dispensing relief to the poor. The Gallican church, however, was a house divided. The lower clergy came almost entirely from the third estate; humble, poorly paid, and generally hardworking, the priests resented the wealth and the arrogance of their ecclesiastical superiors. The bishops and abbots maintained the outlook of the noble class into which they had been born. Although some of them took their duties seriously, others regarded clerical office as a convenient way of securing a large income. Dozens of prelates turned the administration of their bishoprics or monasteries over to subordinates, kept most of the revenue themselves, and took up residence in Paris or Versailles.

The wealth and the lax discipline of the Church aroused criticism and envy. Good Catholics deplored the dwindling number of monks and nuns and their growing tendency to stress the exploitation of their properties. Well-to-do peasants and townspeople coveted these rich ecclesiastical estates. Taxpayers hated the tithe levied by the Church, even though the full 10 percent implied by the word "tithe" was seldom demanded. They also complained about the Church's exemption from taxation and about the meager size of the "free gift" voted by the clergy to the government in lieu of taxes. The peasants on the whole remained moderately faithful Catholics and regarded the village priest, if not the bishop, with esteem and affection. The bourgeois, however, more and more accepted the anticlerical views of the philosophes. They interpreted Voltaire's plea to "crush the infamous thing" as a mandate to strip the Church of wealth and power.

Like the higher clergy, the nobles of the Old Regime, the second estate, enjoyed privilege, wealth—and unpopularity. Although forming less than 2 percent of the population, they held about 20 percent of the land. They had virtual exemption from taxation and monopolized army commissions and appointments to high ecclesiastical office. The French aristocracy, however, comprised not a single social unit but a series of differing groups. At the top were the hereditary nobles, a few of them descended from royalty or from feudal lords of the Middle Ages, but more from families ennobled within the past two or three centuries. These "nobles of the sword" tended to view most of their countrymen, including the lesser nobility, as vulgar upstarts. In spite of their failure during the regency of Orléans, they dreamed of the day when they might rule France again, as the feudal nobles had ruled in the Middle Ages. Many of them, clustered at Versailles, neglected their duties as the first landlords of the realm.

Below the nobility of the sword came the "nobility of the robe," including the justices of the parlements and other courts and a host of other officials. The nobles of the robe, or their ancestors, had originally secured aristocratic status by buying their offices. But, since these dignities were then handed down from father to son, the mercenary origins of their status had become somewhat obscured with the passage of time. By the late eighteenth century, there was often little practical distinction between the gentry of the robe and their brethren of the sword; marriages between members of the two groups were common. On the whole, the nobles of the robe were richer than the nobles of the sword, and they exerted more power and influence by virtue of their firm hold on key governmental positions. The ablest and most tenacious defenders of special privilege in the dying years of the Old Regime were the rich judges of parlement, not the elegant but ineffectual courtiers of Versailles.

Many noblemen, however, had little wealth, power, or glamor. They belonged to the lowest level of French aristocracy—the *hobereaux,* the "little falcons." Hard pinched by rising prices, they vegetated on their country estates, since they could not afford the expensive pleasures of the court. In the effort to conserve at least part of their traditional status, almost all the hobereaux insisted on the meticulous collection of the surviving feudal and manorial dues from the peasantry. Their exhumation of old documents to justify levies sometimes long forgotten earned them the abiding hatred of the peasants and prepared the way for the document-burning that occurred during the Revolution.

Not every noble was a snobbish courtier or a selfish defender of the status quo. Some hobereaux drifted down the social ladder to become simple farmers. Some nobles of the robe, attracted by the opportunities for profit, took part in business ventures—the Anzin coal mines and the Baccarat glassworks, for example. Even the loftiest noble families produced enlightened spirits, like the Marquis de Lafayette, who returned from the American War of Independence to champion reform at home, or like the young bloods who applauded the ingenious valet, Figaro, when he outwitted his social superiors in Beaumarchais' satire on aristocracy, *The Marriage of Figaro,* a great hit on the Paris stage in 1784.

The Third Estate

The first two estates included only a small fraction of the French nation; 98 percent of Frenchmen fell within the third estate in 1789. The great majority of these commoners were peasants, whose status was in some respects more favorable in France than anywhere else in Europe. Serfdom, still prevalent in central and eastern Europe, had disappeared almost entirely except in Lorraine and the Franche-Comté, both relatively recent annexations. While enclosures were gradually pushing small farmers off the land in England, small peasant holdings existed by the millions in France. Three out of every four adult peasants, it is estimated, held some land. Nevertheless, Arthur Young, the English agricultural expert, noted many signs of rural misery in his tour of France in the late 1780s. In southwestern France, for example:

> Pass Payrac, and meet many beggars, which we had not done before. All the country, girls and women, are without shoes or stockings; and the ploughmen at their work have neither sabots nor feet to their stockings. This is a poverty, that strikes at the root of national prosperity. . . . It reminded me of the misery of Ireland.*

Although the degree of agrarian distress varied greatly from province to province, the total picture was far from bright. Part of the trouble lay with such economic fundamentals as backward methods of farming, the shortage of land, and overpopulation. The efficient techniques of the agricultural revolution made little headway in France before 1789. Vast areas were not cultivated at all or lay fallow every second or third year in accordance with medieval practice. The constantly increasing rural population simply could not find steady employment or a decent livelihood. Primitive farming required large tracts of land, but the property-holding three-quarters of the French peasantry controlled less than one-third of the land. The average holding was so small that even a propertied peasant might face starvation in poor crop years. Restrictions on the free movement of grain within France, traditionally imposed to keep local flour for local consumption, promoted hoarding and speculation and increased the danger of local famines if a crop failed. Landless peasants drifted to the cities or turned to brigandage.

Inflation also hurt the peasants. The upward trend of prices in France throughout the eighteenth century brought prosperity to many urban merchants and manufacturers, but most farmers found that the prices of the products they sold rose less swiftly than those of the goods they had to buy. Moreover, the peasants owed a heavy burden of taxes and other obligations—the tithe to the Church, feudal and manorial dues to the nobility, and to the state a land tax, an income tax, a poll tax, and a variety of other duties, of which the most widely detested was the gabelle, the obligatory purchase of salt from government agents, usually at an exorbitant price.

France had a long history of agrarian unrest, going back to the jacquerie, the savage peasant uprising dur-

*A. Young, *Travels in France*, ed. Constantia Maxwell (Cambridge, England, 1929), pp. 23–24.

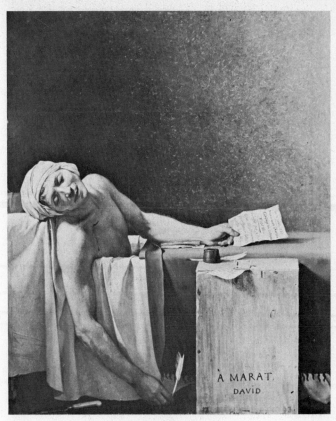

David's famous painting "The Death of Marat," 1793.

ing the Hundred Years' War. In the decades before 1789 there was no new jacquerie, but unemployment and poverty had created a revolutionary temper among the peasants. They did not want a change in the form of government; they were ignorant of the reform program of the Enlightenment. But they most emphatically wanted more land, if need be at the expense of the clergy and the nobility; they wanted an end to obsolete manorial dues; and they wanted relief from a system of taxation that bore hardest upon those who could least afford to pay.

The other members of the third estate, the urban workers and the bourgeoisie, had little reason to cherish the Old Regime. Labor, in our modern sense of a large, self-conscious body of factory workers, hardly existed in prerevolutionary France, where there were few large factories as yet. Almost every good-sized town, however, had its wage earners and apprentices employed chiefly in small businesses or workshops. These urban laborers felt with particular sharpness the pinch of rising prices. They were not, however, to take the commanding role in the Revolution itself; geographically scattered, lacking in class cohesiveness, they were ready to follow the lead of the bourgeoisie.

The bourgeoisie included Frenchmen of very divergent resources and interests—rich merchants and bankers in the cities, storekeepers and lawyers in country towns and villages, doctors and other professional men, and thousands upon thousands of craftsmen running their own little businesses. Implacable hostility to the privileged estates and warm receptiveness to the propaganda of the philosophes cemented this sprawling middle class into a political force. The bourgeoisie suffered fewer hardships than the peasants and workers did, but they resented the abuses of the Old Regime perhaps even more keenly. Though they paid a smaller proportion of their incomes in taxes, they violently denounced the inequality of assessments. While profiting by the rise in prices and able to buy up landed estates, the wealthier and more enterprising businessmen complained of guild regulations and other restrictions on free commercial activity. They found it galling to be snubbed by the nobility, treated as second-class subjects by the monarchy, and excluded from posts of power in government, Church, and army.

In sum, the men of the middle class fully realized their own growing economic importance, and they wanted social and political rights to match. Because they were wealthier, better educated, and more articulate than the peasants and wage earners, they took the leading part in formulating the grievances of the entire third estate. These grievances were compiled in statements called *cahiers* and submitted to the Estates General in 1789.

The cahier of the third estate of the Longuyon district in Lorraine may serve as a sample of bourgeois attitudes toward reform.* While it dealt in part with purely local problems, like the cutting down of forests to supply fuel for iron smelters, it also showed an awareness of the great issues of the day. The cahier pronounced the freedom of the press the "surest means of maintaining the freedom of the nation." It deplored the harshness of the criminal laws; they should conform to "the customs and the character of the French nation, the kindest people in the universe." It recommended "a social contract or act between the sovereign and his people," to safeguard "the personal freedom of all citizens" and "prevent the recurrence of those disastrous events which at present oppress the king and the nation." While insisting upon the sanctity of private property, the third estate of Longuyon advocated a large measure of equality. It proposed that "all Frenchmen should have the right and the hope of securing any state office, of whatever grade, and all military and ecclesiastical dignities." Existing taxes should be swept away, to be replaced by levies on "all property without distinction as to owners, and on all persons without distinction of order and rank."

The Financial Emergency

The chronic financial difficulties of the French monarchy strengthened the hand of the middle-class reformers. The government debt, already large at the accession

*The full text of this *cahier* is printed in B. F. Hyslop, *A Guide to the General Cahiers of 1789* (New York, 1936), pp. 318–326. The quotations that follow are in our translation.

of Louis XVI, tripled between 1774 and 1789; about half the increase resulted from French participation in the American War of Independence. In 1789, the debt stood at 4,500,000,000 livres. The budget for 1788, the only one computed for the Old Regime, made alarming reading:

	(in livres)
Estimated expenses	
For debt service	318,000,000
For the court	35,000,000
For other purposes	276,000,000
Total	629,000,000
Estimated revenues	503,000,000
Estimated deficit	126,000,000

Especially disturbing was the very high proportion of revenues consumed by interest payments on debts already contracted.

Louis XVI, in his feeble way, tried to cope with the growing emergency. On coming to the throne in 1774, he named as chief minister Turgot, who sympathized with the Physiocrats and had made a brilliant record as intendant of Limoges. Turgot temporarily reduced the deficit by imposing strict economies, particularly on the expenditures of the court. To promote the welfare of the third estate, he curtailed ancient guild monopolies, suppressed local taxes on foodstuffs, and lifted restrictions on internal shipments of grain. He replaced the corvée, the work on highways demanded of peasants, with a tax affecting nobles and commoners alike. He even contemplated restoring the Edict of Nantes to bring the Huguenots back into French life and setting up a series of representative assemblies to meet demands for liberalization of the monarchy. Dismayed, the vested interests of the Old Regime rebelled and, seconded by Marie Antoinette, secured Turgot's dismissal in 1776. The ousted minister admonished Louis XVI: "Remember, sire, that it was weakness which brought the head of Charles I to the block."

Louis ignored Turgot's warning. The government continued to raise new loans—653,000,000 livres between 1783 and 1786 alone. Then in 1786 the bankers refused to make new advances. The French government was caught between the irresistible force of the third estate's demands for tax relief and the immovable object of the other estates' refusal to yield their fiscal exemptions. The monarchy had temporized and borrowed until it could afford neither fresh delays nor new loans. Calonne, the finance minister in 1786, proposed to meet the crisis by reviving Turgot's reforms. In the hope of persuading the first two estates to consent to heavier taxation, he convoked the Assembly of Notables (1787), which included ecclesiastical dignitaries, great lords, judges of the parlements, intendants, and important provincial and municipal officials. But the Notables declined to be persuaded, whereupon the king dissolved them and dismissed Calonne.

The new chief minister, Loménie de Brienne, was an enlightened prelate who made new attempts at reform. Late in 1787 an Edict of Toleration restored the civil rights of French Protestants, thus ending the unsuccessful effort to force them into the Catholic mold begun under Louis XIV a century before. Serious trouble arose in 1788 when Loménie de Brienne persuaded the king to levy a uniform tax on all landed property without regard to the social status of the holder. The clergy replied by reducing their "free gift" for 1788 to one-sixth of the usual amount, and the Parlement of Paris declared the new tax law illegal and asserted that only the nation as a whole assembled in the Estates General could make so sweeping a change. Brienne and the king now resorted to Louis XV's expedient of shifting judicial authority from the parlements to new royal appellate courts. Again, however, there was a storm of disapproval and an outbreak of rioting led by both aristocratic and bourgeois leaders in several provincial cities (May and June 1788). The king retreated, dismissed Brienne, and announced that the Estates General would be summoned for the following spring.

The Estates General

In summoning the Estates General Louis XVI revived a half-forgotten institution that did not seem likely to initiate drastic social and economic reforms. The three estates, despite their immense variation in size, had customarily received equal representation and equal voting power, so that the two privileged orders could outvote the commoners. The Estates General of 1789, however, met under unique circumstances.

Its election and subsequent meeting took place during an economic crisis marked by a continued influx of unemployed peasants into the cities, especially Paris,

and by continued inflation, with prices rising at twice the rate of wages. In addition, there was severe unemployment in some textile centers as a result of the treaty of 1786 with England, which increased British imports of French wines and brandies in return for elimination of French barriers to importation of cheaper English textiles and hats.

A final difficulty was the weather. Hail and drought had reduced the wheat harvest in 1788, and the winter of 1788–1789 was so bitter that the Seine froze over at Paris, blocking arrivals of grain and flour by barge, in those days the usual way of shipping bulky goods. Half-starved and half-frozen, Parisians huddled around bonfires provided by the municipal government. By the spring of 1789 the price of bread had almost doubled—a very serious matter in an age when bread was the mainstay of the diet and the average workman normally spent almost half his wages on bread for his family. Now he faced the prospect of having to lay out almost all his wages for bread.

France had survived bad weather and poor harvests many times in the past without experiencing revolution. This time, however, the economic hardships were the last straw. Starving peasants begged, borrowed, and stole, poaching on the hunting preserves of the great lords and attacking their game wardens. The turbulence in Paris boiled over in a riot (April 1789) at the establishment of Réveillon, a wealthy wallpaper manufacturer. It was witnessed by Thomas Jefferson, then the American minister to France:

The Fauxbourg St. Antoine is a quarter of the city inhabited entirely by the class of day-laborers and journeymen in every line. A rumor was spread among them that a great paper manufacturer . . . had proposed . . . that their wages

Making bread—the staple food for most of the population—in an eighteenth-century French bakery. The dough is kneaded in a wooden trough (Fig. 1), weighed (Fig. 2), formed into loaves (Figs. 3 and 4), and baked in an oven (Fig. 5). The illustration is from Diderot's "Encyclopedie."

should be lowered to 15 sous a day [three-quarters of a livre]. . . . They flew to his house in vast numbers, destroyed everything in it, and in his magazines and work shops, without secreting however a pin's worth to themselves, and were continuing this work of devastation when the regular troops were called in. Admonitions being disregarded, they were of necessity fired on, and a regular action ensued, in which about 100 of them were killed, before the rest would disperse.*

The Réveillon riot, occurring only a week before the meeting of the Estates General, increased the sense of urgency pressing on the deputies.

The methods followed in electing the deputies aided the champions of reform. The suffrage was wide, especially in rural areas, where almost all males twenty-five years of age or older met the additional requirement of having their names on the tax rolls. It is probable that more Frenchmen actually voted in 1789 than in any subsequent election or referendum during the revolutionary era. In each district of France the third estate made its choice not directly by secret ballot but indirectly by choosing at a public meeting electors who later selected a deputy. Since this procedure greatly favored bourgeois orators over inarticulate farmers, middle-class lawyers and government administrators won control of the commoners' deputation. The reforming deputies of the third estate found some sympathizers in the second estate and many more in the first estate, where the discontented lower clergy had a large delegation. Moreover, in a departure from precedent, the king had agreed to "double the third," giving it as many deputies as the other two estates combined. Altogether, a majority of the deputies were prepared to make drastic changes in the Old Regime.

In all past meetings of the Estates General each estate, or order, had deliberated separately, with the consent of two estates and of the Crown required for the passage of a measure. In 1789, the king and the privileged orders favored retaining this "vote by order." The third estate, on the contrary, demanded "vote by head," with the deputies from all the orders deliberating together, each deputy having a single vote. "What is the third estate?" wrote the abbé Siéyès in an influential pamphlet of the same name. "Everything."

If votes were taken by order, five million citizens will not be able to decide anything for the general interest, because ' will not please a couple of hundred thousand privileged 'ividuals. The will of a single individual will veto and 'y the will of more than a hundred people.†

'stion of procedure became crucial soon 'es General convened on May 5, 1789, 'ès, a priest, and Mirabeau, a renegade 'them deputies of the third estate, 'r vote by head. On June 17, the

P. L. Ford (New York, 1914), pp. 133–134.
'ers Etat?, ed. E. Champion (Paris, 1888),

third estate cut the Gordian knot of procedure by accepting Siéyès' invitation to proclaim itself the National Assembly. It also invited the deputies of the other two estates to join its sessions; a majority of the clerical deputies, mainly parish priests, accepted, but the nobility refused. The king then barred the commoners from their usual meeting place, whereupon the deputies of the third estate, together with their clerical sympathizers, assembled at an indoor tennis court nearby. There, on June 20, they solemnly swore never to disband until they had given France a constitution. To the Tennis Court Oath Louis replied by a kind of *lit de justice* commanding each estate to resume its separate deliberations. The third estate and some deputies of the first disobeyed. Louis, vacillating as ever, now gave in and on June 27 directed the noble and clerical deputies to join the National Assembly. The nation, through its representatives, had successfully challenged the king and the vested interests. The Estates General was dead, and in its place sat the National Assembly, pledged to reform French society and give the nation a constitution. The Revolution had begun.

III The Dissolution of the Monarchy
Popular Uprisings, July–October 1789
The National Assembly had barely settled down to work when a new wave of rioting swept over France, undermining further the position of the king. Economic difficulties grew more severe during the summer of 1789. Unemployment increased, and bread seemed likely to remain scarce and expensive, at least until after the harvest. Meanwhile, the commoners feared that the king and the privileged orders might attempt a counterrevolution. Large concentrations of troops appeared in the Paris area early in July—to preserve order and protect the National Assembly, the king asserted. But the Parisians suspected that Louis was planning the forcible dissolution of the Assembly. Suspicion deepened into conviction after Louis dismissed Necker, the popular Swiss financier who had been serving as the chief royal adviser.

The reaction to Necker's dismissal was immediate. On July 12 and 13, the Parisian electors, the men who had been elected by the third estate in the city to choose their deputies to the Estates General, formed a new municipal government and a new militia, the National Guard, both loyal to the National Assembly. Paris was forging the weapons that made it the leader of the Revolution. Crowds were roaming the streets, demanding cheaper bread and parading busts of Necker draped in black. On July 14 they broke into government buildings in search of arms. They found one arsenal in the Invalides, the great military hospital, and they hoped to find another in the Bastille, a fortress in the eastern part of the city.

An armed group, several hundred strong, stormed the Bastille, killing part of the garrison and suffering

Early nineteenth-century engraving: the Tennis Court Oath, June 20, 1789.

many casualties themselves. The legend, cherished by defenders of the Old Regime, that participants in the assault were in the main simply "rabble" or "brigands" or a "mob" has been exploded by the facts. An official list of Vainqueurs de la Bastille (conquerors of the Bastille) carefully compiled some time after the event showed that the great majority of the accredited vainqueurs were craftsmen and tradesmen from the district of the city close to the Bastille. Of 662 names, 97 were those of joiners and cabinetmakers (woodworking was a specialty of the district); there were 41 locksmiths, 28 cobblers, 21 shopkeepers, 11 winesellers, a scattered representation of stonemasons, hatters, tailors, hairdressers, jewelers, goldsmiths, upholsterers and other skilled artisans, a dozen or so well-to-do bourgeois, and one woman (a laundress).

What the vainqueurs accomplished, though of little practical value, was of enormous symbolic significance. There were only seven prisoners to be released, all of whom had merited incarceration. Yet an aroused people had demonstrated what it could accomplish: the capture and subsequent demolition of the Bastille did much to ensure the destruction of the Old Regime. It is no wonder the Fourteenth of July became the great national holiday of Frenchmen, their counterpart of the American Fourth of July.

Rioting spread over much of France late in July

1789, as the provincial population responded to the news from Paris or acted on its own. In town after town, demonstrators attacked the local version of the Bastille. Arthur Young, who was surveying agriculture in Alsace, witnessed the scene at Strasbourg:

> The Parisian spirit of commotion spreads quickly; it is here; the troops . . . are employed to keep an eye on the people who shew signs of an intended revolt. They have broken the windows of some magistrates that are no favourites; and a great mob of them is at this moment assembled, demanding clamourously to have meat at 5 sous a pound.*

Town after town also followed the example of Paris in setting up a new and more representative municipal government.

Parts of the countryside, meantime, were experiencing the Great Fear, one of the most extraordinary attacks of mass delusion on record. From village to village word spread that "brigands" were coming, aristocratic hirelings who would destroy crops and villages and force the National Assembly to preserve the status quo. There were in fact no bands of brigands, only an occasional starving farmhand trying to steal food. But the peasants in many districts went berserk, grabbing hoes and pitchforks, anything resembling a weapon.

*Travels in France, p. 181.

When the brigands did not materialize, they attacked châteaux and broke into other buildings that might house a hoard of grain or the hated documents justifying collection of manorial dues. Some nobles voluntarily gave the peasants what they wanted; others saw their barns and archives burnt, and a few were lynched. The Great Fear, beginning as a psychological aberration, ended as an uprising of the peasantry against its traditional oppressors.

By the end of July 1789, then, four distinct sets of revolutionary events had taken place in France: (1) the constitutional revolution of June, resulting in the creation of the National Assembly; (2) the Paris revolution and the taking of the Bastille; (3) the comparable outbreaks in provincial cities and towns; and (4) the Great Fear. Each of the four drove another nail into the coffin of the Old Regime. The transformation of the Estates General into the National Assembly and the creation of new municipal governments undermined the traditional political advantages of the first two estates. The Great Fear began the destruction of their social and economic privileges. Everywhere, legally constituted officials were turned out, taxes went unpaid, and valuable records were destroyed.

The October Days, the last crisis of a momentous year, demonstrated anew the impotence of Louis XVI and the power of his aroused subjects. The harvest of 1789 had been good, but a drought crippled the operation of watermills for grinding flour from the wheat. Thus, as autumn drew on, Parisians still queued for bread and still looked suspiciously at the royal troops stationed in the neighborhood of their city. Rumors of the queen's behavior at Versailles further incensed them. Marie Antoinette made a dramatic appearance at a banquet of royal officers, clutching the dauphin (the heir to the throne) in her arms, striking the very pose that her mother, Maria Theresa, had employed so effectively to win the support of the Hungarians in the 1740s. And, on hearing that the people had no bread, she was said to have remarked callously: "Let them eat cake." This story was false, but it echoed and reechoed in the lively new Paris papers that delighted in denouncing "l'Autrichienne" ("the Austrian hussy").

The march of the women to Versailles, 1789.

The climax came on October 5, 1789, when an array of determined women—rough marketwomen and fishwives, neatly dressed milliners, even middle-class "ladies with hats"—marched the dozen miles from Paris to Versailles in the rain. They disrupted the National Assembly, extracted kisses from Louis XVI, and later penetrated the palace, where they might have lynched Marie Antoinette if she had not taken refuge with the king. Although historians have not yet discovered who planned and organized this bizarre demonstration, it had very significant political consequences. On October 6, the women marched back to Paris, escorting "the baker, the baker's wife, and the baker's boy"—in other words, the royal family—who took up residence in the Tuileries Palace. More important, the National Assembly, too, moved to Paris. The most revolutionary place in France had captured both the head of the Old Regime and the herald of the new.

Forging a New Regime

The outlines of the new regime were already starting to take shape before the October Days. The Great Fear prompted the National Assembly to abolish in law what the peasants were destroying in fact. On the evening of August 4, 1789, the Viscount de Noailles, a liberal nobleman, addressed the deputies:

> The kingdom at this moment hangs between the alternative of the destruction of society, and that of a government which will be the admiration and the exemplar of Europe.
>
> How is this government to be established? By public tranquility. . . . And to secure this necessary tranquility, I propose:
>
> (1) . . . That taxation will be paid by all the individuals of the kingdom, in proportion to their revenues;
>
> (2) That all public expenses will in the future be borne equally by all.*

The deputies voted the proposals of Noailles. In addition, the clergy gave up its tithes, and the liberal minority of the second estate surrendered the nobility's game preserves, manorial dues, and other medieval rights. The Assembly made it a clean sweep by abolishing serfdom, forbidding the sale of justice or of judicial office, and decreeing that "all citizens, without distinction of birth, can be admitted to all ecclesiastical, civil, and military posts and dignities." When the memorable session inaugurated by Noailles' speech ended at two o'clock on the morning of August 5, the Old Regime was dead. It remained dead even after the deputies had second thoughts and awarded the nobles compensation for their losses.

Three weeks later, on August 26, 1789, the National Assembly formulated the Declaration of the Rights of Man. "Men are born and remain free and equal in rights," it asserted. "These rights are liberty,

*Archives Parlementaires, Series I, VIII, 343. Our translation.

property, security and resistance to oppression." Property it called "an inviolable and sacred right," and liberty "the exercise of the natural rights of each man" within the limits "determined by law." "Law," the Declaration stated, "is the expression of the general will. All citizens have the right to take part, in person or by their representatives, in its formation." Further, "Any society in which the guarantee of rights is not assured or the separation of powers not determined has no constitution."*

The Declaration of the Rights of Man mirrored the economic and political attitudes of the middle class. It insisted on the sanctity of property, and it proclaimed that "social distinctions may be based only on usefulness," thus implying that some social distinctions were to be expected. It committed the French to the creed of constitutional liberalism already affirmed by the English in 1688–1689 and by the Americans in 1776, and it incorporated the key phrases of the philosophes: natural rights, general will, and separation of powers. The National Assembly made a resounding statement of the ideals of the Enlightenment; yet, as the subsequent history of the Revolution soon demonstrated, it found no magic formula by which to translate these ideals into practice.

The economic legislation of the National Assembly provided a case in point. Belief in the theory of the equal taxation of all Frenchmen did not solve urgent financial problems, for the new and just land tax imposed by the deputies simply could not be collected. Tax collectors had vanished in the general liquidation of the Old Regime, and naïve peasants now thought that they owed the government nothing. Once again, the French state borrowed until its credit was exhausted, and then, in desperation, the National Assembly ordered the confiscation of Church lands (November 1789). "The wealth of the clergy is at the disposition of the nation," it declared, explaining that ecclesiastical lands fell outside the bounds of "inviolable" property as defined in the Declaration of the Rights of Man because they belonged to an institution and not to private individuals.

The government thus acquired an asset worth at least two billion livres. On the basis of this collateral it issued *assignats,* paper notes used to pay the government's debts. So far, so good: The assignats had adequate security behind them and temporarily eased the financial crisis. Unfortunately, the Revolution repeated the mistake of John Law at the time of the Mississippi Bubble. It did not know when to stop. As the state sold parcels of confiscated land—that is, as it reduced the collateral securing its paper money—it should have destroyed assignats to the same amount. The temptation not to reduce the number of assignats proved too great to resist. Inflation resulted: The assignats, progressively losing their solid backing, depreciated until

in 1795 they were worth less than 5 percent of their face value.

The state sold at auction the property seized from the Church and from aristocratic émigrés. Well-to-do peasants profited by the opportunity to enlarge their holdings, and many bourgeois also bought up land, sometimes as a short-term speculation, sometimes as a long-term investment. The poor and landless peasants, however, gained nothing, since they could not afford to buy. True to the doctrine of laissez faire, the National Assembly made no move to help these marginal farmers. Following the same doctrine, it abolished the guilds and the irksome tariffs and tolls on trade within France. And deeming the few primitive organizations of labor unnatural restrictions on economic freedom, it abolished them too. In June 1791, after an outbreak of strikes, it passed the Le Chapelier Law banning both strikes and labor unions.

Reforming the Church

Since the suppression of tithes and the seizure of ecclesiastical property deprived the Church of its revenue, the National Assembly agreed to finance ecclesiastical salaries. The new arrangement made the French Church subject to constant government regulation. Few difficulties arose from the Assembly's action prohibiting the taking of monastic vows, in order to check recruiting for the regular clergy, or from the liquidation of some monasteries and convents, since many of these establishments were already far gone in decay. But an uproar arose over the legislation altering the status of the secular clergy.

The Civil Constitution of the Clergy (June 1790) redrew the ecclesiastical map of France. It reduced the number of bishoprics by more than a third, making the remaining dioceses correspond to the new civil administrative units known as departments. It transformed bishops and priests into civil officials, paid by the state and elected by the population of the diocese or parish. Since the right to vote in these elections was extended to non-Catholics as well as Catholics, the measure was a significant step in granting toleration to Protestants and Jews. A new bishop was required to take an oath of loyalty to the state, and the Civil Constitution stipulated that he might not apply to the pope for confirmation, though he might write to him as the "Visible Head of the Universal Church."

These provisions stripped the "Visible Head of the Universal Church" of effective authority over the French clergy and ran counter to the whole tradition of the Roman Church as an independent ecclesiastical monarchy. Naturally the pope denounced the Civil Constitution. The National Assembly then required that every member of the French clergy take a special oath supporting the Civil Constitution, but only Talleyrand, Loménie de Brienne, and five other bishops and fewer than half the priests complied. Thus a breach was opened between the Revolution and a large seg-

*G. Lefebvre, *The Coming of the French Revolution* (Princeton, 1947), Appendix.

ment of the population. Good Catholics, from Louis XVI down to humble peasants, rallied to the non-juring clergy, as those who refused the special oath were termed. The Civil Constitution of the Clergy, supplying an issue for rebellion, was the first great blunder of the Revolution.

The Constitution of 1791

The major undertaking of the National Assembly was the Constitution of 1791. To replace the bewildering complex of provincial units that had accumulated under the Old Regime the assembly devised a neat and orderly system of local government very much in the spirit of the Enlightenment. It divided the territory of France into eighty-three departments of approximately equal size. Each department was small enough for its chief town to be within a day's journey of the outlying towns; each bore the name of a river, a mountain range, or some other natural landmark. The departments were subdivided into *arrondissements* or districts, and the districts into communes—that is, municipalities. The commune-district-department arrangement resembled, on a reduced scale, the American hierarchy of town-county-state. In the communes and departments, elected councils and officials enjoyed considerable rights of self-government. The administration of the new France, on paper anyhow, was to be far more decentralized than that of the Old Regime.

The principle of the separation of powers guided the reconstruction of the central government. The Constitution of 1791 established an independent hierarchy of courts staffed by elected judges to replace the parlements and other tribunals of the Old Regime. It vested legislative authority in a single elected chamber. Although the king still headed the executive branch, his actions now required the approval of his ministers. The ministers, in turn, were responsible only to the king and not to the legislature, as they generally are in a parliamentary or cabinet government. Although the king received the power of veto, it was only a suspensive veto that could block legislation for a maximum of four years. Louis XVI, no longer the absolute king of France, acquired the new constitutional title "king of the French," as if to show that he was no longer the sole proprietor of the real estate called France and now had French citizens to reckon with.

The new constitution subscribed to many other principles issuing straight from the Enlightenment. It mitigated the severity of punishments, undertook to give France a new uniform code of law (an undertaking fulfilled by Napoleon), and declared marriage a civil contract, not a religious sacrament. The state took over the old ecclesiastical functions of recording vital statistics and providing charity and education. Indeed, the constitution promised a system of free public education. It also promised that the foreign policy of revolutionary France would be more virtuous than that of autocratic France: "The French nation renounces the undertaking of any war with a view of making conquests, and it will never use its forces against the liberty of any people." *

The Constitution of 1791 went a long way toward instituting popular government, but it stopped well short of full democracy. It divided Frenchmen into two classes of citizens, active and passive, and limited the right of voting to active citizens, who paid annually in taxes an amount equal to at least three days' wages for unskilled labor in the locality. The passive citizens, numbering about a third of the male population, enjoyed the full protection of the law but did not receive the franchise. Moreover, the new legislature was chosen by a process of indirect election. Active citizens did not vote for their deputies but for a series of electors, who were required to be men of substantial wealth, and who ultimately elected the deputies. It was evidently assumed that the amount of worldly goods a man possessed determined the degree of his political wisdom.

The decentralized and limited monarchy established by the Constitution of 1791 was doomed to fail. It was too radical to suit the king and most of the aristocracy, and not radical enough for the many bourgeois who were veering toward republicanism. The majority in the National Assembly supporting the constitution suffered the fate commonly experienced by the politically moderate in a revolution: they were squeezed out by the extremists. Despite their moderate intentions, they were driven to enact some drastic legislation, notably the Civil Constitution of the Clergy, which weakened their own position. And they failed to develop an effective party organization at a time when the deputies of the radical minority were consolidating their strength.

These radicals were the Jacobins, so named because they belonged to the "Society of the Friends of the Constitution," which maintained its Paris headquarters in a former Jacobin (Dominican) monastery. The Jacobins were no true friends of the Constitution of 1791. They accepted it only as a stopgap until they might end the monarchy and set up a republic based on universal suffrage. To prepare for the millennium, the Jacobins used all the techniques of a political pressure group. They planted rabble-rousing articles in the press and manipulated the crowds of noisy and volatile spectators at the sessions of the National Assembly. Their network of political clubs extended throughout the provinces, providing the only nationwide party organization in France. Almost everywhere, Jacobins captured control of the new department and commune councils. In local elections, as in the elections of the Estates General, an able and determined minority prevailed over a politically inexperienced majority.

The defenders of the Old Regime played into the hands of the Jacobins. From the summer of 1789 on, alarmed prelates and nobles, including the king's own

---

*J. H. Stewart, *A Documentary Survey of the French Revolution* (New York, 1951), p. 260.

brothers, fled France, leaving behind more rich estates to be confiscated and giving Jacobin orators and editors a splendid opportunity to denounce the rats leaving a sinking ship. Many of these émigrés gathered in the German Rhineland to intrigue for Austrian and Russian support of a counterrevolution. The king's grave misgivings about the Civil Constitution of the Clergy prompted his disastrous attempt to join the émigrés on the Franco-German frontier. In June 1791, three months before the completion of the new constitution, Louis and Marie Antoinette left the Tuileries disguised as a valet and governess. But Louis unwisely showed his face in public, and a local official along the route recognized him from his portrait on the assignats. The alarm was sent ahead, and at Varennes in northeastern France a detachment of troops forced the royal party to make a hot, dusty, dispirited journey back to Paris. After the abortive flight to Varennes, the revolutionaries viewed Louis XVI as a potential traitor and kept him closely guarded in the Tuileries. The experiment in constitutional monarchy began under most unfavorable auspices.

The Legislative Assembly

On October 1, 1791, the first and only Legislative Assembly elected under the new constitution commenced its deliberations. No one faction commanded a numerical majority in the new assembly. The seats were held as follows:*

Right (Constitutional Monarchists)	265
Center (Plain)	345
Left (Jacobins)	130

The balance of political power rested with the timid and irresolute deputies of the Center, who were neither strong defenders of the constitution nor yet convinced republicans. Since they occupied the lowest seats in the assembly hall, they received the derogatory nickname of the Plain or Marsh. The capable politicians of the Left soon captured the votes of the Plain, to demonstrate anew the power of a determined minority.

Leadership of this minority came from a loose grouping of Jacobins known as Girondins, because some of them came from Bordeaux, in the department of Gironde. Their chief spokesman was Brissot (1754–1793), an ambitious lawyer and journalist, a mediocre politician, and an inveterate champion of worthy causes, including emancipation of the blacks. Other leading Girondins were Condorcet, the distinguished philosophe and prophet of progress; Dumouriez, who later commanded the French revolutionary armies in their first victorious campaigns; and Roland, a rather obscure civil servant with a very ambitious wife who

ran a Girondin salon. The Girondins were much too loosely articulated a group to be compared to a modern political party; what held them together was largely their patriotic alarm over France's situation at home and abroad.

The Girondins specialized in fervent nationalist oratory. They pictured revolutionary France as the intended victim of a reactionary conspiracy, engineered by the émigrés, aided at home by the non-juring clergy and the royal family, and abetted abroad by a league of monarchs under Leopold II, the Austrian emperor and the brother of Marie Antoinette. But Louis XVI, despite the flight to Varennes, was no traitor, and Leopold II cautiously limited his aid to the émigrés. The sudden death of Leopold in March 1792 and the accession of his inexperienced and less cautious son, Francis II, at once increased the Austrian threat. At the same time, the mounting war fever in France convinced Louis XVI that he should name Girondin ministers, including Roland to the interior and Dumouriez to foreign affairs. On April 20, 1792, the Legislative Assembly declared war on Austria; the war was to continue, with a few brief intervals of peace, for the next twenty-three years. In the eyes of Frenchmen the war was defensive, not the campaign of conquest that the nation had forsworn in the fine phrases of its constitution.

Partly because the emigration of many nobles had depleted the corps of French officers, the war went badly for France at the outset. Prussia soon joined Austria, and morale sagged on the home front in June, when Louis XVI dismissed the Girondin ministers because they had proposed to banish non-juring priests, and appointed more conservative replacements. Spirits began to rise in July, especially with a great celebration of the third anniversary of the assault on the Bastille on the fourteenth. Paris was thronged with national guardsmen from the provinces on the way to the front, and the contingent from Marseilles introduced to the capital the patriotic hymn which became the national anthem of republican France.

It was not only the *Marseillaise* that improved morale. On July 25 the Prussian commander, the Duke of Brunswick, issued a manifesto drafted by an émigré stating the war aims of the allies:

> To put a stop to the anarchy within France, to check the attacks delivered against throne and altar, to reestablish legal authority, to restore to the king the security and freedom of which he has been deprived, and to place him in a position where he may exercise the legitimate authority which is his due.

A threat followed. "If the Tuileries is attacked, by deed or word, if the slightest outrage or violence is perpetrated against the royal family, and if immediate measures are not taken for their safety, maintenance and liberty"—then Paris would witness "a model vengeance, never to be forgotten." * The duke of Brunswick's

---

*In the practice followed by most continental European assemblies, the Right sat to the right of the presiding officer as he faced the assembly, the Left to his left, and the Center in between.

*Le Moniteur Universel, August 3, 1792. Our translation.

manifesto did not frighten the French, as it was intended to do. On the contrary, it stiffened the already firm determination of republicans to do away with the monarchy.

All through the early summer of 1792 the Jacobins of Paris had been plotting an insurrection. They won the support of a formidable following—army recruits, national guardsmen, and the rank and file of Parisians, who were angered by the depreciation of the assignats and by the high price and short supply of food and other necessities. One by one, the forty-eight *sections* or wards into which the city was divided came under the control of Jacobins, who advertised their democratic sympathies by inviting passive citizens to take part in political activity. The climax came on the night of August 9–10, when leaders of the sections ousted the regular municipal authorities from the Paris city hall and installed a new and illegal Jacobin commune.

The municipal revolution had immediate and momentous results. On the morning of August 10, the forces of the new commune, joined by national guardsmen, attacked the Tuileries and massacred the king's Swiss guards, while the royal family took refuge with the Legislative Assembly. The uprising of August 10 sealed the doom of the monarchy and made the Assembly little more than the errand boy of the new Paris commune. With most of the deputies of the Right and the Plain absent, the Assembly voted to suspend the king from office, to imprison the royal family, and to order the election of a constitutional convention. Until this new body should meet, the government was to be run by an interim ministry staffed in part by Roland and other Girondins, but in which the strongman was Danton (1759–1794), a more radical and opportunistic politician. The birth of the First Republic was at hand.

IV The First Republic

The weeks between August 10 and the meeting of the Convention on September 21 were weeks of crisis and tension. The value of the assignats depreciated by 40 percent during August alone. Jacobin propagandists, led by Marat (1743–1793), a frustrated and embittered physician turned journalist, continually excited the people of Paris, who were already deeply stirred by the economic difficulties and by the capture of the Tuileries. Excitement mounted still higher when the news arrived that Prussian troops had invaded northeastern France. In the emergency, Danton, the interim minister of justice, won immortality by urging patriots to employ *de l'audace, encore de l'audace, toujours de l'audace*—"boldness, more boldness, always boldness."

In Paris, boldness took the form of the September Massacres, lynchings of supposed traitors and enemy agents made possible by the collapse of normal police authority. For five days, beginning on September 2, bloodthirsty mobs moved from prison to prison. At each stop they held impromptu courts and summary executions. Neither the new Paris commune nor the interim national ministry could check the hysterical wave of lynchings, though Roland did try. The number of victims exceeded one thousand and included ordinary criminals and prostitutes as well as aristocrats and non-juring priests, who were often innocent of the treason charged against them. The crowning horror was the mutilation of the princesse de Lamballe, the queen's maid of honor, whose severed head was paraded on a pike before the window of the royal prison so that Marie Antoinette might see "how the people take vengeance on their tyrants." The September Massacres foreshadowed the terror to come.

Later in the month (September 20, 1792), a rather minor French victory, grandly styled "the miracle of Valmy," turned the duke of Brunswick's forces back from the road to Paris; more solid French successes in Belgium, Savoy, and the Rhineland followed during the final months of 1792. Then the tide turned again, washing away the conquests of the autumn. By the summer of 1793 half-defeated France faced a hostile coalition including almost every major power in Europe. An atmosphere of perpetual emergency surrounded the Convention.

Gironde and Mountain

In theory, the election of deputies to the National Convention in August and September 1792 marked the beginning of true political democracy in France. Both active and passive citizens were invited to the polls. Yet only 10 percent of the potential electorate of seven million actually voted; the others abstained or were turned away from the polls by the watchdogs of the Jacobin clubs, ever on the alert against "counterrevolutionaries." Politically, the Convention divided as follows:

Right (Gironde)	165
Center (Plain)	435
Left (Mountain)	150

Again, as in the Legislative Assembly, the Plain was politically irresolute, though it was now sympathetic to a republic. Many ties in common existed between the Gironde and the Mountain (so named because its deputies sat high up in the meeting hall). Deputies from both factions had Jacobin antecedents, came mainly from middle-class professions like the law, were steeped in the ideas of the philosophes, and usually regarded with some distrust the masses of people who were now acquiring the name of *sans-culottes* (literally, "without knee-breeches"). These were the workingmen, both poor day laborers and lower-middle-class artisans and craftsmen, all who proudly wore the long baggy trousers of the worker rather than the elegant breeches of the well-to-do. The term "sans-culottes," while always carrying social and economic implications, came to refer politically to any ardent supporter of the revolution, particularly a political activist in the Paris sections.

When the Convention met, Gironde and Mountain united to declare France a republic (September 21, 1792) but were soon wrangling over other questions. The Girondins favored a breathing spell in revolutionary legislation, and they also defended provincial interests against possible encroachments by Paris. As one of their deputies told the Convention (and his allusion to classical antiquity was most characteristic of the Revolution):

> I fear the despotism of Paris. . . . I do not want a Paris guided by intriguers to become to the French Empire what Rome was to the Roman Empire. Paris must be reduced to its proper one-eighty-third of influence, like the other departments.*

The Gironde, therefore, favored a large measure of "federalism," which meant decentralization in the revolutionary vocabulary, and a national government limited by many checks and balances. The details were set forth in a draft constitution completed early in 1793 by Condorcet. The executive and the legislature would be independent of each other and separately elected, the results of elections would be adjusted according to proportional representation, projected laws would be submitted to a popular referendum, and voters would have the right to recall unworthy elected officials. Condorcet's draft, though a wellspring of ideas for later political reformers, was not a practical blueprint for the emergency confronting the First Republic.

The leaders of the Mountain denounced federalism and advocated an all-powerful central government. Their chief spokesman was Maximilien Robespierre (1758–1794). This earnest young lawyer did not look like a revolutionary: He powdered his hair neatly and wore the light-blue coat and knee-breeches of the Old Regime. Yet Robespierre was a political fanatic whose speeches were lay sermons couched in the solemn language of a new faith. He put his creed most forcefully in a speech on February 5, 1794:

> What is the goal toward which we are striving? The peaceful enjoyment of liberty and equality: the rule of that eternal justice whose laws have been engraved . . . upon the hearts of men, even upon the heart of the slave who is ignorant of them and of the tyrant who denies them.
>
> We desire an order of things . . . where our country assures the welfare of each individual and where each individual enjoys with pride the prosperity and the glory of our country; where the souls of all grow through the constant expression of republican sentiments; where the arts are the ornament of the freedom which in turn ennobles them; and where commerce is the source of public wealth, not just of the monstrous opulence of a few houses.†

Apparently Robespierre truly believed that he could translate the ideas of Rousseau's *Social Contract* into a practical political program. Like Rousseau, he had faith in the natural goodness of humanity, in "the laws

engraved upon the hearts of men." He was sure that he knew the general will, and that the general will demanded a Republic of Virtue. If Frenchmen would not act in a free and virtuous fashion voluntarily, then, as Rousseau had recommended, they would be "forced to be free."

Robespierre and the Republic of Virtue triumphed. The Mountain won out over the Gironde in the competition for the votes of the relatively uncommitted deputies of the Plain in the Convention. The first step came when, after one hundred hours of continuous voting, the Convention declared "Citizen Louis Capet" guilty of treason and by a narrow margin sentenced him to the guillotine without delay. Louis XVI died bravely on January 21, 1793. Although the majority of the French population disapproved of the king's execution, the majority did not control the Convention. The Girondin deputies split their votes on the issue. Those opposed to the death penalty took a courageous stand in defense of the humanitarian principles of the Enlightenment but also exposed themselves to the charge of being counterrevolutionaries.

A combination of events at home and abroad soon destroyed the Gironde. In February 1793 the Convention rejected Condorcet's draft constitution, and in the same month it declared war on Britain, Spain, and the Netherlands. France now faced a formidable coalition of opponents, since Austria and Prussia remained at war with her. In March, the army under the Girondin Dumouriez suffered a series of defeats in the Low Countries, and in April Dumouriez deserted to the enemy. Marat now loudly denounced all associates of Dumouriez as traitors; the Girondin deputies countered by calling for the impeachment of Marat, who was brought before a special tribunal and triumphantly acquitted. In July 1793 he was assassinated in his bath by Charlotte Corday, a young woman wielding a butcher's knife and convinced that she was a new Joan of Arc called to deliver France from Jacobin radicalism.

By then, the Girondins had been completely vanquished. In the face of unemployment, high prices, and shortages of food, soap, and other necessities, they had little to prescribe except more laissez faire. The sections of Paris demanded price controls and food requisitioning; they also pressed for the expulsion of Girondins from the Jacobin clubs and the Convention. Finally, on June 2, 1793, a vast crowd of armed sans-culottes from the sections, following the precedent of August 1792, invaded the Convention and forced the arrest of twenty-nine Girondin deputies. Backed by these armed Parisians, the Mountain intimidated the Plain, and the Convention consigned the arrested Girondins to the guillotine. The Reign of Terror had begun.

The Reign of Terror
How was it that the advocates of democracy now imposed a dictatorship on France? Here is Robespierre's explanation:

---

*Lasource, September 25, 1792. *Archives Parlementaires,* Series I, LII, 130. Our translation.

† *Le Moniteur Universel,* February 7, 1794. Our translation.

French aristocrats imprisoned in the Conciergerie.

To establish and consolidate democracy, to achieve the peaceful rule of constitutional laws, we must first finish the war of liberty against tyranny. . . . We must annihilate the enemies of the republic at home and abroad, or else we shall perish.

If virtue is the mainstay of a democratic government in time of peace, then in time of revolution a democratic government must rely on *virtue* and *terror*. . . . Terror is nothing but justice, swift, severe, and inflexible; it is an emanation of virtue. . . . It has been said that terror is the mainstay of a despotic government. . . . The government of the revolution is the despotism of liberty against tyranny.*

The Convention duly voted a democratic constitution, drawn up by the Mountain, granting universal manhood suffrage and giving supreme power, unhampered by Girondin checks and balances, to a single legislative chamber. The Constitution of 1793 was approved by a large majority in a referendum attracting double the participation of the election of 1792, though still representing only a minority of potential voters. Operation of the constitution was then deferred, and it never came into force. As Robespierre explained, "To establish and consolidate democracy, we must first finish the war of liberty against tyranny."

The actual government of the Terror centered on a twelve-man Committee of Public Safety, composed of Robespierre and other stalwarts from the Mountain. Though nominally responsible to the Convention, the Committee of Public Safety exercised a large measure of independent authority and acted as a kind of war

*Ibid.

cabinet. Never under the dominance of a single individual, not even Robespierre, it really functioned as a committee—"The Twelve Who Ruled" is an appropriate description. A second committee, that of Public Security, supervised police activities and turned suspected enemies of the republic over to the new Revolutionary Tribunal. To speed the work of repression, the sixteen judges and sixty jurors of the tribunal were eventually divided into several courts.

The Mountain scrapped much of the local self-government inaugurated under the Constitution of 1791. It also whittled steadily away at the prerogatives assumed by the Paris sections, which have been likened to forty-eight independent republics or town meetings in continuous session. Local Jacobin clubs purged department and commune administrations of political unreliables, while special local courts supplemented the grim labors of the Revolutionary Tribunal. To make sure that provincial France toed the line, the Mountain sent out trusted members of the Convention as its agents, the "deputies on mission." From the standpoint of administration, the Terror marked both an anticipation of twentieth-century dictatorship and a return to the age-old French principle of centralization. The deputies on mission were the successors of the intendants of Richelieu, the enquêteurs of Saint Louis, and the missi dominici of Charlemagne. The "Twelve Who Ruled" were more effective absolutists than Louis XIV himself.

The "swift, severe, and inflexible justice" described by Robespierre took the lives of nearly twenty thousand Frenchmen. Although the Terror claimed such social outcasts as criminals and prostitutes, its main purpose was military and political—to clear France of suspected traitors, including Marie Antoinette, and to purge the Jacobins of dissidents. It fell with the greatest severity on the clergy, the aristocracy, and the Girondins, by no means always in Paris. Many of its victims came from the Vendée, a strongly Catholic and royalist area in western France which had risen in revolt. Prisoners from the Vendée were among the two thousand victims of the *noyades* (drownings) at Nantes, where the accused were manacled and set adrift on the River Loire in leaky barges. Equally grisly was the repression of an uprising of Girondin sympathizers at Lyons, where the *mitraillades* (the term refers to the simultaneous firing of multiple weapons) also claimed some two thousand victims.

The wartime hysteria that helped to account for the excesses of the Terror also inspired a very practical patriotism. On August 23, 1793, the Convention issued a decree epitomizing the democratic nationalism of the Jacobins:

> From this moment, until the time when the enemy shall have been driven from the territory of the Republic, all Frenchmen are permanently requisitioned for the service of the armies.
>
> Young men will go into combat; married men will manufacture arms and transport supplies; women will make tents and uniforms and will serve in the hospitals; children will make old linen into bandages; old men will be carried into the public squares to arouse the courage of the soldiers, excite hatred for kings, and inspire the unity of the republic.*

In an early application of universal conscription, the army drafted all bachelors and widowers between the ages of eighteen and twenty-five. Hundreds of open-air forges were installed in Paris to manufacture weapons. Since the war prevented importation of the saltpeter needed for gunpowder, the government sponsored a great campaign to scrape patches of saltpeter from cellars and stables.

By the close of 1793, the forces of the republic had driven foreign troops from French soil. Credit for this new shift in the tide of battle did not rest solely with the Jacobins. The military successes of the republic reflected in part the improvements made in the army during the dying years of the Old Regime; they resulted still more from the weaknesses of the coalition aligned against France. Yet they could scarcely have been achieved without the new democratic spirit that allowed men of the third estate to become officers and that made the French army the most determined, the most enterprising—and, perhaps, the most idealistic—in Europe.

Total mobilization demanded an equality of economic sacrifice. To exorcise the twin devils of inflation and scarcity, the Terror issued the "maximum" legislation, placing ceilings on prices and wages. In theory,

at least, wages were checked at a maximum 50 percent above the wage rate of 1790, and prices were halted at 33 percent above the price level of 1790. The government rationed meat and bread, forbidding the use of white flour, and directing all patriots to eat *pain d'égalité*—"equality bread," a loaf utilizing almost the whole of the wheat. Finally, early in 1794, the Convention passed the Laws of Ventôse, named for a month in the new revolutionary calendar. These laws authorized seizure of the remaining properties of the émigrés and other opponents of the republic and recommended their distribution to landless Frenchmen.

Socialist historians have sometimes found in the "maximum" and the Laws of Ventôse evidence that the Terror was moving from political to social democracy, that the Republic of Virtue was indeed beginning the socialist revolution. Actually the "maximum" regulations did not prove very effective. Attempts by the government to enforce wage ceilings made Parisian workingmen indignant. And, though the "maximum" on prices temporarily checked the depreciation of the assignats, many price-controlled articles were available only on the black market, which even the government had to patronize.

Moreover, the redistribution of property permitted by the Laws of Ventôse was never implemented. When the laws were proposed, a spokesman for the Committee of Public Safety explained that no general assault on property was intended:

> The revolution leads us to recognize the principle that he who has shown himself the enemy of his country cannot own property. The properties of patriots are sacred, but the goods of conspirators are there for the unfortunate.*

To the thoroughgoing socialist not even the properties of patriots are sacred. The middle-class leaders of the Terror were not genuine socialists; only the emergencies of the Revolution forced them to abandon laissez faire. They had to make food cheaper for townspeople—whence the "maximum"; and they had to promise men some hope of future well-being—whence the Laws of Ventôse.

The Terror presented its most revolutionary aspect in its drastic social and cultural reforms. The Convention abolished slavery in the colonies, though it was to be reintroduced by the Code Napoléon a decade later. At home, according to Robespierre, "we desire to substitute all the virtues and all the miracles of the Republic for all the vices and all the nonsense of monarchy." When Robespierre said all, he meant all—clothing, the arts, amusements, the calendar, religion. The Republic of Virtue could tolerate nothing that smelled of the Old Regime. Even the traditional forms of address, "Monsieur" and "Madame," gave way to "Citoyen" and "Citoyenne."

*Le Moniteur Universel, August 24, 1793. Our translation.

*Saint-Just, February 26, 1794, in Le Moniteur Universel the next day. Our translation.

Ever since 1789, revolutionists had discarded elaborate gowns and knee-breeches as symbols of idleness and privilege. With the exception of Robespierre, good citizens dressed as sans-culottes and "citizenesses" favored simple, high-waisted gowns, copied from the ancient Romans. Rome became the model for behavior—the virtuous Rome of the republic, of course, not the sordid empire. Parents named their children Brutus or Cato or Gracchus, and the theater shelved the masterpieces of Racine and Corneille for stilted dramas glorifying Roman heroes. Cabinetmakers, deserting the graceful style of Louis XV, produced sturdy neoclassical furniture decorated with Roman symbols. "The arts," said Robespierre, "are the ornament of the freedom which in turn ennobles them." Playwrights, authors, and editors who failed to ornament freedom properly experienced censorship or even the guillotine. The Jacobins reduced the lively newspapers of the early revolution to dull semiofficial organs.

They also instituted a sweeping reform of the calendar (October 1793). The first day of the republic, September 22, 1792, was designated the initial day of Year I, Roman numerals were assigned to the years, and the months received new and more "natural" names:

Fall: Vendémiaire (Grape harvest)
             Brumaire (Misty)
             Frimaire (Frosty)
Winter: Nivôse (Snowy)
             Pluviôse (Rainy)
             Ventôse (Windy)
Spring: Germinal (Sprouting)
             Floréal (Flowering)
             Prairial (Meadow)
Summer: Messidor (Wheat harvest)
             Thermidor (Heat)
             Fructidor (Ripening)

Each month had thirty days, divided into three ten-day weeks. Every tenth day was set aside for rest and for the celebration of one of the virtues so admired by Robespierre—Hatred of Tyrants and Traitors, Heroism, Frugality, Stoicism, not to mention two anticipations of Mother's Day (Filial Piety and Maternal Tenderness). The five days left over at the end of the year were dedicated to Genius, Labor, Noble Actions, Awards, and Opinion. The revolutionary calendar, for all its sanctimonious touches, was worthy of the Enlightenment. But it antagonized workmen, who disliked laboring nine days out of ten instead of six out of seven. It never really took root, and Napoleon scrapped it a decade later.

The Convention had better luck with another reform close to the spirit of the Age of Reason—the metric system. A special committee, including Condorcet, Laplace, Lavoisier, and other distinguished intellectuals, devised new weights and measures based on the uniform use of the decimal system rather than on the haphazard accumulations of custom. In August 1793 a decree made the meter the standard unit of length, and supplementary legislation in 1795 established the liter as the measure of volume and the gram as the unit of weight. Uniform prefixes from the Greek indicated larger whole numbers, as *kilo-* (1,000) and *hecto-* (100), and those from the Latin indicated fractions, as *centi-* ($\frac{1}{100}$) and *milli-* ($\frac{1}{1000}$). Although the Convention did little to implement the ambitious revolutionary ideal of universal education, it did convert establishments of the Old Regime into the nuclei of such great Parisian institutions as the Louvre Museum, the National Archives, the Museum of Natural History, and the Bibliothèque Nationale (national library).

Sometimes the forces of tradition resisted even the Terror, which tried to destroy the old religion but never succeeded in legislating a new faith. Many churches were closed and turned into barracks or administrative offices; often their medieval glass and sculpture were destroyed. Some of the Jacobins launched a "de-Christianization" campaign to make Catholics into philosophes and their churches into "temples of Reason." Robespierre, however, disliked the cult of Reason; the Republic of Virtue, he believed, should acknowledge an ultimate author of morality. The Convention therefore decreed (May 1794) that "the French people recognize the existence of the Supreme Being and the immortality of the soul." At the festival of the Supreme Being, June 8, 1794, Robespierre set fire to figures representing Vice, Folly, and Atheism, and from the embers a statue of Wisdom emerged, but smudged with smoke because of a mechanical slip-up. The audience laughed. The deistic concept of the supreme being was too remote and the mechanics of the new worship were too artificial to satisfy religious needs.

Indeed, the Republic of Virtue was too abstract in ideals, and too violent in practice, to retain popular support. Like the Geneva of Calvin, the France of Robespierre demanded superhuman devotion to duty and inhuman indifference to hardships and bloodshed. During the first half of 1794, Robespierre pressed the Terror so relentlessly that even the members of the Committees of Public Safety and General Security began to fear they would be the next victims. The Law of the 22 Prairial, Year II (June 10, 1794) enormously expanded the definition of "enemies of the people" subject to punishment by the Revolutionary Tribunal to include the following: "those who have sought to disparage the National Convention," "who have sought to impede the provisioning of Paris," "to inspire discouragement," "to mislead opinion, to deprave morals," and most significantly, "those who, charged with public office, take advantage of it in order to serve the enemies of the Revolution, to harass patriots, or to oppress the people." *

It was scarcely surprising that Robespierre began

---

*J. H. Stewart, ed., *A Documentary Survey of the French Revolution* (New York, 1951), pp. 528–529.

to lose his following both in the Convention and in the two great committees. More and more of his former supporters favored moderation and argued that the growing French success in the war argued for less, not more, terror. The crucial day was the Ninth of Thermidor (July 27, 1794) when shouts of "Down with the tyrant!" and the refusal of the presiding officer to give Robespierre the floor blocked his efforts to address the Convention. The Convention ordered his arrest, and on the next day the great fanatic went to the guillotine. The sans-culottes of Paris made no effective attempts to come to his rescue, for only a few days before the government had begun a new effort to enforce the maximum on wages. Workers greeted the news of Robespierre's death by coupling "maximum" with an obscenity.

The Thermidorean Reaction

The leaders of the Thermidorean Reaction, many of them former Jacobins, soon dismantled the machinery of the Terror. They disbanded the Revolutionary Tribunal, recalled the deputies on mission, and deprived the Committees of Public Safety and General Security of their independent authority. They closed the Paris Jacobin club and invited the surviving Girondin deputies to resume their old seats in the Convention. They took the first step toward the restoration of Catholicism by permitting priests to celebrate mass, though under state supervision and without state financial support. The press and the theater recovered their freedom, and pleasure seekers again flocked to Paris, now liberated from the somberness of the Republic of Virtue. France was resuming a normal existence.

Normality, however, exacted a price. In Paris, long-haired young bourgeois calling themselves the *jeunesse dorée* ("gilded youth") went about foppishly dressed and carrying long sticks, which they used to attack suspected Jacobins. They organized the destruction of busts of Marat and forced the removal of his remains from the Pantheon (the former church of Saint Geneviève, patroness of Paris, converted into a mausoleum for national heroes and renamed after the great Roman temple of all the gods). In southern and western France a counterrevolutionary White Terror, equaling the great Terror in fury, claimed many lives, not only of supporters of the Mountain but also of purchasers of former church and noble lands. The men of Thermidor caused an acute inflation by canceling the economic legislation of the Terror. No longer checked even slightly by the maximum, the prices of some foods rose to a hundred times the level of 1790, and the assignats sank so low in value that businessmen refused to accept them. Popular suffering was now more intense than it had ever been under the Terror. Desperate, half-starving Parisians staged several demonstrations against the Thermidoreans during 1795. Sometimes the rioters voiced their support of the discredited Mountain and its democratic Constitution of 1793, and sometimes they let themselves be used by royalist agents, but always they clamored for bread and lower prices.

The Thermidorean Reaction concluded with the passage of the Constitution of 1795, the last major act of the Convention. The men of Thermidor wanted both to retain the republic and to assure the dominance of the propertied classes. The Constitution of 1795 therefore denied the vote to the poorest quarter of the nation and required that candidates for public office possess considerable property. It established two legislative councils, the Five Hundred and the Elders (who had to be at least forty years old and either married or widowed); both councils were to be elected piecemeal after the American practice of renewing one-third of the Senate every two years. Two-thirds of the initial members of the councils were to be drawn from the deputies of the Convention, who were therefore labeled "les perpetuels." The Council of Five Hundred nominated, and the Elders chose, five directors who headed the executive Directory, which otherwise was almost totally independent of the legislative councils.

The Constitution of 1795 marked the third great effort of the Revolution to provide France with an enduring government. It followed in part a classical example, for the two councils were patterned on the Areopagus and the Five Hundred of ancient Athens; it also followed the American precedent of 1787 and the French precedent of 1791. It embodied the separation of powers and deferred to the aristocracy of wealth, though not to that of birth. By abandoning the political democracy of the stillborn Constitution of 1793 and by reverting to the restricted suffrage of 1791, it demonstrated that the most radical phase of the Revolution had passed.

The Directory

Three weeks before the new constitution was to go into operation, more trouble broke out in Paris, touched off by the widespread disgust with the constitutional provision for "perpetual" deputies and exploited by the jeunesse dorée and other conservatives in hopes of ending the First Republic and restoring the monarchy. The counterrevolutionary insurgents were put down in the massacre of Vendémiaire (October 5, 1795), dispersed in part by the "whiff of grapeshot" ordered by Napoleon Bonaparte, who commanded troops loyal to the Thermidorean Convention. The first winter of the Directory (1795–1796) brought France the most intense popular suffering of the revolutionary period as a consequence of inflation and the chronic shortage of food. Thereafter, the situation steadily improved, thanks to good harvests and to the Directory's vigorous attack on economic problems.

The new regime levied high protective tariffs, both as a measure of war against England and as a concession to French businessmen. Again responding to business pressure, it destroyed the plates used to print the assignats and in 1797 withdrew paper money from circulation. The return to hard money required stringent governmental economies. The Directory instituted these economies, made tax collection more efficient, and enjoyed considerable loot from France's victorious wars. It eased the crushing burden of the national debt by repudiating two-thirds of it and gave the veteran livre a new and lasting name, the franc.

The Directory suppressed with ease the amateurish "conspiracy of the equals" (1796–1797) sponsored by Gracchus Babeuf, who has come down in socialist legend as the first communist but who seems to have been little more than an impractical dreamer. The Directory experienced much greater difficulty steering a cautious middle course between the two extremes of restoring the monarchy and reverting to Jacobin terrorism. The Constitution of 1795 was repeatedly violated, as the directors and the legislative councils clashed, with each seeking to shift the political balance in its own favor. The councils sacked directors before their terms were finished, and directors refused to allow duly elected councillors to take their seats. Disgruntled politicians and apprehensive moderates, fearing the collapse of the regime, began to maneuver for the help of the army. The result was the coup d'état of Brumaire in 1799 and the dictatorship of Napoleon.

V Napoleon and France

Edmund Burke, the British political philosopher, foresaw very early the long process that culminated in Napoleon's dominance of France and Europe. In 1790, Burke warned the French—and his own countrymen—in his *Reflections on the Revolution in France:*

> Everything depends on the army in such a government as yours; for you have industriously destroyed all the opinions, . . . all the instincts which support government. Therefore the moment any difference arises between your National Assembly and any part of the nation, you must have recourse to force. Nothing else is left to you. . . .
>
> It is besides to be considered, whether an assembly like yours . . . is fit for promoting the discipline and obedience of an army. It is known, that armies have hitherto yielded a very precarious and uncertain obedience to any senate, or popular authority. . . . The officers must totally lose the characteristic disposition of military men, if they see with perfect submission and due admiration, the dominion of pleaders; especially when they find that they have a new court to pay to an endless succession of those pleaders. . . . In the weakness of one kind of authority, and in the fluctuation of all, the officers of an army will remain for some time mutinous and full of faction, until some popular general who understands the art of conciliating the soldiery, and who possesses the true spirit of command, shall draw the eyes of all men upon himself. Armies will obey him on his personal account. There is no other way of securing military obedience in this state of things. But the moment in which that event shall happen, the person who really commands the army is your master; the master

. . . of your king, the master of your assembly, the master of your whole republic.*

In 1790, however, few men outside France paid much heed to the French army. Liberals everywhere hailed the peaceful promise of the Revolution, and conservatives believed that the very intensity of domestic problems would make France incapable of a vigorous foreign policy. As late as 1792, Catherine the Great predicted that ten thousand soldiers would suffice to douse the "abominable bonfire" in France.

The war that broke out in the spring of 1792 soon destroyed the illusions of French military weakness and French liberal purity. It deserves to be called the World War of 1792–1795, for almost all the European powers eventually participated, and the fighting ranged far beyond Europe. By the time the war was a year old, Austria and Prussia, the charter members of the first coalition against France, had been joined by Holland, Spain, and Great Britain. The British had both ideological and strategic interests at stake. They regarded the attack on the Tuileries, the September massacres, and the execution of Louis XVI as outrages against human decency and the institution of monarchy. And the French invasion of the Austrian Netherlands in the fall of 1792 raised the unpleasant prospect that this Belgian "cockpit of Europe" would fall under French control. The early campaigns of the war were indecisive. Late in 1792, the French followed up their success at Valmy by invading Belgium, only to lose ground again in 1793 after the defeat and desertion of Dumouriez. Then in 1794 the French definitely gained the advantage, and by 1795 French troops had occupied Belgium, Holland, and Germany west of the Rhine.

One reason for French success we have already seen—the Convention's energetic mobilization of national resources, which enabled France to have the unprecedented total of a million men under arms by the spring of 1794. Another reason, equally important yet easy to overlook, was the weakness of the first coalition. The partners in the coalition lacked a first-rate commander; nor did they achieve effective coordination of their efforts. The duke of Brunswick's failure to take Paris in 1792 resulted as much from his own deficient generalship as from the "miracle" of Valmy. Moreover, the partitions of Poland in 1793 and 1795 greatly assisted the French because they kept Russia a nonbelligerent and greatly distracted Austria and Prussia. The pick of the Prussian army was diverted to occupation duty in newly annexed Polish provinces, and by 1795 mutual mistrust had reached the point where the Prussians dared not attack the French for fear of being attacked themselves by their nominal Austrian allies.

Prussia was the first member of the coalition to make peace. In the Treaty of Basel (1795), she yielded to France the scattered Hohenzollern holdings west of

---

*E. Burke, *Reflections on the Revolution in France,* Everyman ed. (New York, 1910), pp. 215–217.

the Rhine on the understanding that she might seek compensation elsewhere in Germany. Spain, which ceded to France the island of Haiti (Santo Domingo), soon deserted the coalition, as did the Netherlands. In 1795, then, France at last secured her "natural frontiers." In addition to Belgium and the Rhineland she had also annexed Savoy and Nice, thereby extending her southeastern border to the crest of the Alps. These conquests, however, belied the ideals of the Revolution. In declaring war on Austria in 1792, France had sworn to uphold the promise of the Constitution of 1791: that she would never undertake a war of conquest. This was to be "not a war of nation against nation, but the righteous defense of a free people against the unjust aggression of a king." But the conquering armies of the First Republic brought closer the day when nation would fight nation—when the European nations would invoke "the righteous defense of a free people against the unjust aggression," not of a king, but of revolutionary France.

Bonaparte's Early Career

At the close of 1795, only Britain and Austria remained officially at war with France. To lead the attack against Hapsburg forces in northern Italy, the Directory picked a youthful general who was something of a philosophe and revolutionary as well as a ruthless, ambitious adventurer. He was born Napoleone Buonaparte on Corsica in 1769, soon after the French acquisition of that Mediterranean island from Genoa. He retained throughout his life the intense family loyalty characteristic of the rather primitive society of Corsica and bestowed on the members of the Bonaparte clan all the spoils of conquest, even thrones.

As a boy of nine Napoleon began to attend military school in France and, though he now spelled his name in the French style, was snubbed as a foreigner by some of his fellow cadets. He immersed himself in his studies and in reading (Rousseau was his favorite) and dreamed of the day when he might liberate his native island from French control. Later, however, his zeal for Corsican independence faded in consequence of the rupture between the Bonapartes and the hero of Corsican nationalism, Paoli, who was an ally of Britain. When the Revolution broke out, the young artillery officer helped to overthrow the Old Regime in Corsica and then went back to France to resume his military career. He defended the Convention, but more out of expediency than from conviction, and commanded the artillery in December 1793, when the forces of the Convention recaptured the Mediterranean port of Toulon, which had fallen to the British earlier in the year. After Thermidor he fell under a cloud as a suspected "terrorist" and came close to going with a French team of experts to advise the Ottoman Empire on modernizing its army. But he settled for a desk job in Paris and was available to rescue the Thermidorean Convention in Vendémiaire with the "whiff of grape-

Napoleon in 1798: an unfinished portrait by David.

shot." He married Josephine de Beauharnais, a widow six years his senior and an intimate of the ruling clique of the Directory. The combination of Josephine's connections and Napoleon's own demonstrated talent gained him the Italian command in 1796.

In the Italian campaign, Major General Bonaparte, still in his twenties, cleared the Austrians out of their strongholds in the space of a year and made them sue for peace. He showed a remarkable ability to strike quickly and to surprise his opponents before they could consolidate their defenses. He also showed a gift for propaganda and public relations, as this proclamation from the early phases of the campaign illustrates:

Soldiers! In two weeks you have won six victories; you have made 15,000 prisoners; you have killed or wounded more than 10,000 men.

Deprived of everything, you have accomplished everything. You have won battles without cannon, negotiated rivers without bridges, made forced marches without shoes, encamped without brandy, and often without bread. Only the phalanxes of the Republic, only the soldiers of Liberty, would have been capable of suffering the things that you have suffered.

You all burn to carry the glory of the French people; to humiliate the proud kings who dared to contemplate shackling us; to go back to your villages, to say proudly: "I was of the conquering army of Italy!"

Friends, I promise you that conquest; but there is a condition you must swear to fulfill: to respect the people whom you are delivering; to repress horrible pillaging.

Peoples of Italy, the French army comes to break your chains; greet it with confidence; your property, religion and customs will be respected.*

It was characteristic of Napoleon to promise all things to all men. He encouraged the nationalism of underpaid and underfed French soldiers; yet he appealed also to the nationalism of the Italians, promising them liberation from Austria and guaranteeing the orderly conduct of the French army. He did not, of course, tell the Italians that they might be exchanging one master for another, nor did he publicize the money that he seized from Italian governments and the art treasures that he took from Italian galleries and shipped back to France.

In the Treaty of Campoformio (1797) terminating the Italian campaign, Austria acknowledged the loss of Belgium and recognized the two puppet states that Napoleon set up in northwestern Italy, the Ligurian Republic (Genoa) and the Cisalpine Republic (the former Austrian possession of Lombardy). In return, the Hapsburgs received the Italian territories of the Venetian Republic and a secret French assurance that Prussia, despite the specific promise made to her in 1795, would not be permitted to compensate for her losses in the Rhineland by taking lands elsewhere in Germany.

Only Britain remained at war with France. Napoleon decided to attack her indirectly through Egypt, then a semi-independent vassal of the Ottoman Empire. This would-be Alexander the Great, seeking new worlds to conquer, talked grandly of digging a canal at Suez, which would give French merchants the monopoly of a new short trade route to India and exact belated retribution from Britain for Clive's victory in the Seven Years' War. Since Napoleon shared the passion of the Enlightenment for science and antiquity, he invited over a hundred archeologists, geographers, and other savants to accompany his army and thus helped to found the study of Egyptology. The French discovered the Rosetta Stone, the first key to the translation of ancient Egyptian hieroglyphics; it was deciphered two decades later by Champollion, a young French scholar. Napoleon's experts established in Egypt an outpost of French cultural imperialism that lasted into the twentieth century.

From the military standpoint, however, the campaign failed. Having eluded the British Mediterranean

*Abridged from *Le Moniteur Universel,* May 17, 1796. Our translation.

fleet commanded by Nelson, Napoleon landed in Egypt in July 1798 and quickly routed the Mamluks, the ruling oligarchy. Then disaster struck. On August 1, 1798, Nelson discovered the French fleet moored at Abukir Bay along the Egyptian coast and destroyed it before its captains had time to weigh anchor. Nelson's victory deprived the French of both supplies and reinforcements. After a year of futile campaigning in the Near East, Napoleon suddenly left Egypt in August 1799 and returned to France.

Brumaire

Napoleon found the situation in France ripe for a decisive political stroke, for the Directory was shaken by a strong revival of Jacobinism. Several hundred deputies in the legislative councils belonged to the Society of the Friends of Liberty and Equality, essentially the old Jacobin club. Under their influence, the councils in 1799 decreed a forced loan from the rich and passed a Law of Hostages, designed to make the émigrés behave by threatening their relatives in France with reprisals if they engaged in activities hostile to the French Republic. Moderates feared that a new Reign of Terror would soon be unleashed.

Abroad, the Directory had established four new satellite republics with classical names—the Batavian (Holland), the Helvetian (Switzerland), the Roman, and the Parthenopean (Naples—where, according to Homer's *Odyssey,* the siren who failed to lure Ulysses was washed ashore). But this new success of French imperialism upset the European balance and provoked the formation of the second coalition, headed by Britain, Austria, and Russia. The Hapsburgs resented the extension of French influence in their former Italian preserve, and Czar Paul I (1796–1801) feared that Napoleon would damage Russia's Mediterranean interests. The eccentric czar was head of the Knights of Malta, a Catholic order dating back to the Crusades, whom Napoleon had expelled from their headquarters on the island of Malta. In the campaign of 1799, Russian troops fought in Italy and Switzerland, and the Russian general Suvorov, who defeated the French repeatedly, became the hero of western Europe. By August 1799 the French had been expelled from Italy, and their puppet republics—Cisalpine, Roman, and Parthenopean—had been dismantled.

In these circumstances, Napoleon got a rousing reception on his return from Egypt. Soon he was engaged in a plot to overthrow the Directory, with the complicity of two of the five directors, Roger-Ducos and Siéyès, the old champion of the third estate. On November 9 and 10, 1799 (18 and 19 Brumaire by the revolutionary calendar), the plot was executed. The three directors not in the plot resigned, and the two legislative councils named Napoleon military commander of Paris. He was then to persuade the councils to entrust to the two remaining directors and himself the task of drafting a new constitution. Napoleon came close to failure. In the Elders he made a poor impression by mumbling almost incoherently about "volcanoes," "tyrants," "Jacobins," "Cromwell." In the Council of Five Hundred, where there were many Jacobin deputies, he was greeted with cries of "Outlaw him," received a pummeling, scratched at his own face in his intense anxiety till he drew blood, and then fainted. His brother Lucien, the presiding officer of the Five Hundred, saved the day until a detachment of troops loyal to Napoleon expelled the hostile deputies.

The coup d'état of Brumaire ended the Directory. The Bonapartist minority in the councils vested full power in the victorious triumvirate of Roger-Ducos, Siéyès, and Napoleon, of whom only Napoleon really counted. It had all happened just as Edmund Burke had predicted:

> In the weakness of authority, . . . some popular general shall draw the eyes of all men upon himself. Armies will obey him on his personal account. . . . The person who really commands the army is your master.

Consulate and Empire

The Constitution of the Year VIII, drawn up after Brumaire, was the fourth attempt by revolutionary France to provide a written instrument of government, its predecessors being the constitutions of 1791, 1793, and 1795. Based on Siéyès' autocratic maxim, "Confidence from below, authority from above," the new document erected a very strong executive, the Consulate, named, like other bodies set up by the constitution, after institutions of republican Rome. Although three consuls shared the executive, Napoleon as first consul left the other two only nominal power. Four separate bodies had a hand in legislation: (1) the Council of State proposed laws; (2) the Tribunate debated them but did not vote; (3) the Legislative Corps voted them but did not debate; (4) the Senate had the right to veto legislation. The members of all four bodies were either appointed by the first consul or elected indirectly by a process so complex that Bonaparte had ample opportunity to manipulate candidates. The core of this system was the Council of State, staffed by Bonaparte's hand-picked choices, which served both as a cabinet and as the highest administrative court. The three remaining bodies were intended merely to go through the motions of enacting whatever the first consul decreed. Even so, they were sometimes unruly, and the Tribunate so annoyed Napoleon that he finally abolished it in 1807.

Meantime, step by step, Napoleon increased his own authority. In 1802, he persuaded the legislators to drop the original ten-year limitation on his term of office and make him first consul for life, with the power to designate his successor and amend the constitution at will. France was now a monarchy in all but name. In 1804, he took the next logical move and prompted the Senate to declare that "the government of the re-public is entrusted to an emperor." A magnificent coronation took place at Notre Dame in Paris on December 2. The pope consecrated the emperor, but following Charlemagne's example, Napoleon placed the crown on his own head.

Each time Napoleon revised the constitution in a nonrepublican direction he made the republican gesture of submitting the change to the electorate. Each time, the results of the plebiscite were overwhelmingly favorable: In 1799–1800, the vote was 3,011,107 for Napoleon and the Constitution of the Year VIII, and 1,562 against; in 1802, it was 3,568,885 for Napoleon and the life Consulate, and 8,374 against; in 1804, 3,572,329 for Napoleon and the Empire, and 2,579 against. Although the voters were exposed to considerable official pressure and the announced results were perhaps rigged a little, the majority of Frenchmen undoubtedly supported Napoleon. His military triumphs appealed to their growing nationalism, and his policy of stability at home ensured them against further revolutionary crises and changes. Confidence did indeed seem to increase from below as authority increased from above.

If by any chance confidence failed to materialize below, Napoleon had the authority to deal with the recalcitrant. He wiped out the local self-government remaining from the early days of the Revolution. In place of locally elected officials, he substituted those appointed by himself—prefects in departments, subprefects in arrondissements, mayors in communes—and all were instructed to enforce compliance with the emperor's dictates. Napoleon brought the old French tradition of centralization to a new peak of intensity.

Men of every political background staffed the imperial administration. Napoleon cared little whether his subordinates were returned émigrés or ex-Jacobins, so long as they had ability. Besides, their varied antecedents reinforced the impression that narrow factionalism was dead and that the empire rested on a broad political base. Napoleon paid officials well and offered the additional bait of high titles. With the establishment of the empire he created dukes by the dozen and counts and barons by the hundred. He rewarded outstanding generals with the rank of marshal and other officers with admission to the Legion of Honor, which paid its members a special annuity. "Aristocracy always exists," Napoleon remarked. "Destroy it in the nobility, it removes itself to the rich and powerful houses of the middle class." * The imperial aristocracy gave the leaders of the middle class the social distinction that they felt to be rightfully theirs.

Law and Justice

Napoleon revived some of the glamor of the Old Regime but not its glaring inequalities. His series of law codes, the celebrated Code Napoléon (1804–1810), de-

*Quoted in H. A. L. Fisher, *Napoleon* (New York, 1913), Appendix I.

clared all men equal before the law without regard to their rank and wealth. It extended to all the right to follow the occupation, and embrace the religion, of their choosing. It gave France the single coherent system of law that the philosophes had demanded and that the revolutionary governments had been too busy to formulate.

The Code Napoléon did not, however, embody the full judicial reform program of the Enlightenment; it incorporated from the old Roman law some practices that strengthened the absolutism of the empire. It favored the interests of the state over the rights of the individual, and it permitted some use of torture in trial procedure. Judges were no longer elected, as they had been under the Constitution of 1791, but appointed by the emperor; jurors were selected by his prefects. Though Napoleon confirmed the revolutionary legislation permitting divorce by mutual consent, the code canceled other revolutionary laws protecting wives, minors, and illegitimate children, and restored the man of the family to his old legal superiority. It also restored the institution of slavery in French colonies. At times confirming the principles of 1789, and at times betraying them, Napoleonic law and justice offered a fair summary of the fate of the Revolution under the Empire.

A similar ambiguity clouded Napoleon's attitude toward civil liberties. Although he prided himself on welcoming former political heretics into his administration, his generosity stemmed always from expediency, never from any fundamental belief in liberty. If he failed to get his way by conciliation, he used force. In the western departments, where royalist uprisings had become chronic since the revolt in the Vendée, he massacred the rebels who declined his offer of amnesty in 1800. In 1804, he kidnapped the duke of Enghien from the neutral German state of Baden because the duke was believed to be the choice of monarchist conspirators for the throne of France. Though Napoleon immediately discovered the duke's innocence, he had him executed nonetheless.

Napoleon cared little for freedom of speech. In July, 1801, for example, he directed his librarian to read all the newspapers carefully and

> make an abstract of everything they contain likely to affect the public point of view, especially with regard to religion, philosophy, and political opinion. He will send me this abstract between 5 and 6 o'clock every day.
>
> Once every ten days he will send me an analysis of all the books or pamphlets which have appeared. . . .
>
> He will take pains to procure copies of all the plays which are produced, and to analyse them for me, with observations of the same character as those above mentioned. This analysis must be made, at latest, within 48 hours of the production of the plays.*

And so on—through "bills, posters, advertisements, in-

*Quoted in J. M. Thompson, ed., *Napoleon's Letters* (London, 1954), pp. 93–94.

stitutes, literary meetings, sermons and fashionable trials"—no segment of public opinion escaped Napoleon's manipulation. He reduced by five-sixths the number of Paris newspapers and pestered theater managers with suggestions for improving the patriotic tone of plays. When he wanted to arouse French feelings, he simply started a press campaign, as in this instance from 1807:

> A great hue and cry is to be raised against the persecutions experienced by the Catholics of Ireland at the hands of the Anglican church. . . . Bishops will be approached so that prayers will be offered entreating an end to the persecutions of the Anglican church against the Irish Catholics. But the administration must move very delicately and make use of the newspapers without their realizing what the government is driving at. . . . And the term "Anglican church" must always be used in place of "Protestants," for we have Protestants in France, but no Anglican church.*

Religion and Education

Political considerations colored Napoleon's decisions on religion. "I do not see in religion the mystery of the incarnation," he said, "but the mystery of the social order. It attaches to heaven an idea of equality which prevents the rich man from being massacred by the poor."† Since French Catholics loathed the anticlericalism of the Revolution, Napoleon sought to appease them by working out a reconciliation with Rome.

The Concordat negotiated with Pope Pius VII (1800–1823) in 1801 accomplished the reconciliation. It canceled only the most obnoxious features of the Civil Constitution of the Clergy. The French state, while agreeing to pay clerical salaries, also agreed to suppress the popular election of bishops and priests. The bishops were to be nominated by the government and then consecrated by the pope; the priests were to be appointed by the bishops. At this point, Napoleon's concessions stopped. By declaring that Catholicism was the faith of the "great majority of Frenchmen," rather than the state religion, the Concordat implicitly admitted the toleration of Protestants and Jews, both of whom were expected to accept state supervision of their governing councils. Also by implication the pope accepted such important measures of the Revolution as the abolition of the tithe and the confiscation of ecclesiastical lands.

Finally, the Concordat made the activities of the Church in France subject to the "police regulations" of the state. These regulations were spelled out in the Organic Articles, which Napoleon appended to the Concordat without consulting the pope. The French government was to supervise the publication of papal bulls, the establishment of seminaries, the content of catechisms, and a host of other details. The Articles also reaffirmed the principle of the special autonomy en-

Letters Inédites de Napoléon (Paris, 1897), 1:93–94. Our translation.
† Quoted in Fisher, *Napoleon,* Appendix I.

joyed by the Gallican Church within Catholicism. Despite all this, the anticlericals opposed the Concordat, and it took all Napoleon's influence to obtain ratification of the Concordat by the legislative bodies of the Consulate.

The Concordat, then, made the Church a ward of the French state. Though it antagonized anticlericals, it did conciliate large numbers of Catholics, and it remained in force until 1905. The Concordat, however, did not bring complete peace between France and the Vatican, for Napoleon insisted that the pope should render to Caesar the things that were Caesar's. When Pius VII objected to Napoleon's making a French satellite of the Papal States, the new Caesar lectured him on the proper division of authority between the spiritual and temporal powers. Pius passed the last years of the Napoleonic regime as Bonaparte's prisoner, first in northern Italy and then in France.

The Revolution and Napoleon cost the Church its monopoly over education. The Constitution of 1791 had promised France a system of state schools. The Thermidorean Convention, while doing little to apply this principle to primary education, did set up institutions for advanced training, like the famous Ecole Polytechnique in Paris for engineers. In each department of France it also established a "central school" to provide secondary education of good quality at relatively low cost to students. Napoleon abolished these central schools in 1802 and replaced them with a smaller number of lycées open only to the relatively few pupils who could afford the high tuition or who received state scholarships. The change had a political motive, for Napoleon intended the lycées to groom capable and loyal administrators. The students wore uniforms and marched to military drums, and the curriculum, too, served the ends of patriotic indoctrination. To provide for the superintendence of all schools, lay and clerical, Napoleon founded in 1808 a body with the misleading name University. He neglected primary schooling almost completely; yet building on the revolutionary base, he did advance the construction of secular schools. The way was open for the bitter educational competition of church and state in nineteenth-century France.

Economics

Political aims likewise governed the economic program of an emperor determined to promote national unity. The French peasants wanted to be left alone to enjoy the new freedom acquired in 1789; Napoleon did not disturb them, except to raise army recruits. The middle class wanted a balanced national budget and the end of revolutionary experiments with paper currency and a controlled economy. Napoleon continued the sound money of the Directory and, unlike the Directory, balanced the budget, thanks to the immense plunder that he gained in war. He greatly improved the efficiency and probity of tax collectors and established the semi-official Bank of France (1800) to act as the govern-

ment's financial agent. He strengthend the curbs placed on strikes and labor unions by the Le Chapelier Law of 1791 and obliged every workman to carry a *livret* (booklet), in effect an identity card recording both his jobs and the general reputation he had earned. Though seaports suffered from the decline of overseas trade, rich war contracts and subsidies kept employment and profits generally high. As the war went on and on, however, Napoleon found it increasingly difficult to keep the peasantry and the bourgeoisie contented. Despite the levies on conquered countries, he had to draft more soldiers from the peasantry and increase the already unpopular taxes on salt, liquor, and tobacco.

In summary, the domestic policies of Napoleon I had something in common with the methods of all the celebrated one-man rulers. Like Caesar in Rome, Napoleon rendered lip service to the republic while subverting republican institutions; he used prefects to impose centralized authority as Louis XIV had used intendants; and, like modern dictators, he scorned free speech. Yet Napoleon was also a genuine enlightened despot. His law code and some of his educational reforms would have delighted the philosophes. He ended civil strife without sacrificing the redistribution of land and the equality before the law gained in 1789 and the years following. Abandoning some revolutionary policies, modifying others, and completing still others, Napoleon regimented the Revolution without wholly destroying it.

VI Napoleon and Europe

To many Frenchmen, Napoleon was—and still remains—the Man of Destiny, the most brilliant ruler in their long history. To most Europeans, on the other hand, Napoleon was the sinister Man on Horseback, the enemy of national independence, the foreigner who imposed French control and French reforms. As French conquests accumulated, and as nominally free countries became French puppets, Europe grew to hate the insatiable imperialism of Napoleon. Napoleonic France succeeded in building up a vast empire, but only at the cost of arousing the implacable enmity of the other European nations.

The War, 1800–1807

Napoleon had barely launched the Consulate when he took to the field again. The second coalition, which had reached the peak of its success in August 1799, was now falling to pieces. Czar Paul of Russia alarmed Britain and Austria by his interest in Italy, and Britain offended him by retaining Malta, the headquarters of his beloved Knights. The czar launched against Britain a Baltic League of Armed Neutrality linking Prussia, Sweden, and Denmark with Russia. He even contemplated joining with France to drive the British out of India; this fantastic scheme collapsed when he was

A supposed Napoleonic scheme for the invasion of England, by sea, air and cross-channel tunnel; the kites were Britain's anticipation of antiaircraft defense.

murdered in 1801 and succeeded by his son, Alexander I. The Baltic League disintegrated in the same year after Nelson violated Denmark's neutrality to bombard its fleet in port at Copenhagen. A year earlier, in the spring of 1800, Napoleon crossed the Alps with much fanfare; his public relations "releases" sounded as though no one had ever made the passage before. In Italy, he defeated the Austrians and negotiated with them the Treaty of Lunéville (1801), whereby they recognized the reconstituted French satellites in Italy and agreed that France should have a hand in redrawing the map of Germany.

After Lunéville, as after Campoformio four years before, Britain alone remained at war with France. British taxpayers, however, wanted relief from their heavy burden; British merchants longed to resume trading with continental markets partially closed to them since 1793. Though Britain had been unable to check Napoleon's expansion in Europe, she had very nearly won the colonial and naval war by 1801. She had captured former Dutch and Spanish colonies, and Nelson's fleet had expelled the French from Egypt and

Malta. The British cabinet was confident that it held a strong bargaining position and could obtain favorable terms from Napoleon. But in the Peace of Amiens (1802) the British promised to surrender part of their colonial conquests and got nothing in return. The French failed either to reopen the Continent to British exports or to relinquish Belgium, which remained, in Napoleon's phrase, "a loaded pistol aimed at the heart of Britain."

The one-sided Peace of Amiens provided only a year's truce in the worldwide struggle of France and Britain. Napoleon aroused British exporters by a more stringent tariff law (1803) and jeopardized British interests in the Caribbean by a grandiose project for a colonial empire based on the island of Haiti and on the vast Louisiana territory ceded back to France in 1800 by Spain. In Haiti, where the expectations of the black majority had been roused by the Convention's abolition of slavery, the blacks revolted against the efforts of the Consulate to reimpose slavery. Stubborn black resistance under Toussaint L'Ouverture and Jean Jacques Dessalines, an ex-slave, and an outbreak of yellow fever took a fearful toll of French troops and forced Napoleon to abandon the American project. In 1803, he sold to the United States for 80,000,000 francs (about $16,000,000) all of Louisiana, which later formed the whole or part of thirteen states.

When the Louisiana Purchase was completed, France and Britain were again at war. Napoleon interned many of the British tourists who had flocked to Paris since the Peace of Amiens, thus striking a new note of "total" war, contrasting with the eighteenth-century custom that permitted enemy citizens to circulate relatively freely even during hostilities. From 1803 through 1805, Napoleon actively prepared to invade England. He assembled more than a hundred thousand troops and a thousand landing barges on the French side of the Straits of Dover. In 1805, he sent Admiral Villeneuve and the French fleet to the West Indies to lure the British fleet away from Europe. Then Villeneuve was to slip back to Europe posthaste to escort the French invasion force across the Channel while Nelson was still combing the Caribbean in search of the French fleet.

Villeneuve failed to give Nelson the slip; back in European waters, he put in at a friendly Spanish port instead of heading directly for the Channel as Napoleon had ordered. Nelson engaged the combined French and Spanish fleets off Cape Trafalgar at the southwest corner of Spain (October 1805). He lost his own life but not before he had destroyed half of his adversaries' ships without sacrificing a single one of his own. The hapless Villeneuve, long aware of French naval inferiority, committed suicide. The Battle of Trafalgar gave the British undisputed control of the seas and blasted French hopes of a cross-Channel invasion.

By the time of Trafalgar, Austria and Russia had joined with Britain in the third coalition. Austria, in particular, had been alarmed by Napoleon's efforts to promote a major revision of the political map of Germany. In 1803 the Reichsdeputationshauptschluss (a fine German word, "chief decree of the imperial deputation") abolished more than a hundred of the Germanies, chiefly city-states and small ecclesiastical principalities. The chief beneficiaries of this readjustment were the south German states of Bavaria, Württemberg, and Baden, which Napoleon clearly intended to form into a "third" Germany, dominated by France, as opposed to the "first" and "second" Germanies of Austria and Prussia, respectively.

Bonaparte routed the continental members of the third coalition in the most dazzling campaign of his career. At Ulm, on the upper Danube (October 1805), he captured 30,000 Austrians who had moved westward without waiting for their Russian allies. He met the main Russian force and the balance of the Austrian army near the Moravian village of Austerlitz. The ensuing battle (December 2, 1805) fittingly celebrated the first anniversary of Napoleon's coronation as emperor. Bringing up reinforcements secretly and with great speed, Napoleon completely surprised his opponents;

their casualties were three times greater than his own. Within the month he forced the Hapsburg emperor, Francis II, to sign the humiliating Treaty of Pressburg, giving the Austrian Tyrol to Bavaria and Venetia to the Napoleonic puppet kingdom of Italy.

A still harsher fate awaited the Prussians, brought back into the war for the first time since 1795 by Napoleon's repeated interventions in German affairs. The fact that the inept duke of Brunswick was still the Prussian commander, thirteen years after he had lost the battle of Valmy, indicated how much the army had deteriorated since the days of Frederick the Great. In October 1806 the French pulverized the main Prussian contingents in the twin battles of Jena and Auerstädt, and occupied Berlin. Napoleon postponed a final settlement with Prussia until he had beaten his only remaining continental opponent. Russia went down at Friedland (June 1807).

Napoleon's great string of victories against the third coalition resulted partly from the blunders of his enemies. The miscalculations of Austrian, Prussian, and Russian generals contributed to French successes at Austerlitz and at Jena. Furthermore, the French army was the most seasoned force in Europe. New recruits were furnished by conscription, which raised an average of 85,000 men a year under Napoleon, and were quickly toughened by being assigned in small batches to veteran units—a process called the amalgame and developed during the Revolution to meet the emergencies of the war against the first coalition. French officers were promoted on the basis of ability rather than seniority or influence, and they were, on the whole, more concerned with maintaining the morale of their men than with imposing strict discipline. Bonaparte seldom risked an engagement unless his forces were the numerical equal of the enemy's; then he staked everything on a dramatic surprise, as at Austerlitz. Yet even his seemingly invincible French army had defects. The medical services were poor, so that a majority of deaths on campaigns were the result of disease or improperly treated wounds. Pay was low and irregular, and supplies were also irregular, since it was French policy to have men and horses live off the land as much as they could to save the expense and delays of bringing up elaborate supply trains. Though eventually serious in their impact, these shortcomings did not prevent Napoleon's widening his ascendancy over Europe in 1807.

The Tilsit Settlement

Napoleon reached the pinnacle of his career when he met Czar Alexander I on the "neutral ground" of a raft anchored in the Niemen River at Tilsit, on the frontier between East Prussia and Russia. There, in July 1807, the two emperors drew up a treaty dividing Europe between them. Alexander acknowledged France's hegemony over central and western Europe and secured in return the recognition of eastern Europe as the Russian sphere. Napoleon pledged Russia a share

Meeting of Napoleon and Czar Alexander I on a raft at Tilsit, where they drew up the peace treaty of 1807.

in the spoils if the Ottoman Empire should be dismembered. He demanded no territory from the defeated czar, only a commitment to cease trade with Britain and to join the war against her. The Tilsit settlement, however, made Alexander bitterly unpopular at home, where Russian propaganda had been denouncing Napoleon as Antichrist.

While the two emperors negotiated on the raft, Frederick William III (1797–1840), the Prussian king, nervously paced the banks of the Niemen. He had good cause to be nervous, for Tilsit cost him almost half his territory. Prussia's Polish provinces formed a new puppet state, the Grand Duchy of Warsaw, which Napoleon assigned to a French ally, the king of Saxony. Prussian territory west of the Elbe River went to Napoleon to dispose of as he wished. Napoleon also stationed occupation troops in Prussia and fixed the maximum size of its army at 42,000 men.

Under this latter-day Caesar almost all Europe could be divided into three parts. First came the French Empire, including France proper and the territories annexed since 1789. Second were the satellites, ruled in many cases by relatives of Napoleon. And third came Austria, Prussia, and Russia, forced by defeat to become the allies of France. The only powers remaining outside the Napoleonic system were Britain, Turkey, and Sweden. In 1810, Bernadotte, one of Napoleon's marshals, was invited by the Swedes to become crown prince for their childless king; he then proceeded to turn Swedish policy against France.

The Satellites

The frontiers of the French Empire at their most extensive enclosed Belgium and Holland; the sections of Germany west of the Rhine and along the North Sea; the Italian lands of Piedmont, Genoa, Tuscany, and Rome; and finally, physically detached from the rest, the Illyrian Provinces, stretching along the Dalmatian coast of the Adriatic, taken from Austria in 1809, and named after a unit of the old Roman Empire. The annexed territories were usually subdivided into departments and ruled by prefects, just like the departments of France proper.

The satellites flanked the French Empire. The Kingdom of Italy, an enlarged version of the Cisalpine Republic, included Lombardy, Venetia, and the central Italian lands not directly annexed by France. Napoleon was the king, and his stepson, Eugène de Beauharnais, was viceroy. In southern Italy, Napoleon had agreed to withdraw the French garrison from Naples in the Peace of Amiens; three years later, in 1805, he deposed the Bourbon king of Naples and gave the crown first to his brother Joseph and then, when he transferred Joseph to Madrid in 1808, to Joachim Murat, husband of his sister Caroline.

In central Europe, Napoleon energetically pursued his project of a "third" Germany. He decreed a further reduction in the number of German states, and in 1806 aided the formal dissolution of that museum piece, the Holy Roman Empire. Francis II, the reigning Hapsburg, last of the Holy Roman emperors, now styled himself emperor of Austria. To replace the vanished empire, Napoleon created the Confederation of the Rhine, which included almost every German state except Austria and Prussia. At the heart of this confederation Napoleon carved out for his brother Jerome the Kingdom of Westphalia, which incorporated the Prussian holdings west of the Elbe seized at Tilsit. Two states completed the roster of French satellites—Switzerland and the Grand Duchy of Warsaw. Europe had not seen such an empire since the heyday of imperial Rome.

Napoleon longed to give dignity and permanence to his creations. It was not enough that his brothers and his in-laws should sit on thrones; he himself must found a dynasty, must have the heir so far denied him in fifteen years of childless marriage. He divorced Josephine, therefore, and in 1810 married Marie-Louise, the daughter of the Hapsburg Francis II. In due time, Marie-Louise bore a son, called "the king of Rome," but destined never to rule in Rome or anywhere else.

Throughout the new French acquisitions and the satellites Bonaparte and his relatives played the part of enlightened despots, curbing the power of the Church, abolishing serfdom, building roads, and introducing the metric system and the new French law codes. Everywhere, however, they exacted a heavy toll of tribute and subjection. Napoleon flooded his relatives with instructions on the government of their domains and brought them abruptly to heel whenever they showed signs of putting local interests above those of France. When Louis Bonaparte in Holland dared to disobey the imperial orders, his brother delivered a crushing rebuke:

> In ascending the throne of Holland, Your Majesty has forgotten that he is French and has stretched all the springs of his reason and tormented his conscience in order to persuade himself that he is Dutch. Dutchmen inclining toward France have been ignored and persecuted; those serving England have been promoted. . . . I have experienced the sorrow of seeing the name of France exposed to shame in a Holland ruled by a prince of my blood.*

Lettres Inédites de Napoléon (Paris, 1897), 1:382–383. Our translation.

Louis' boldness cost him his throne; his Dutch kingdom was annexed to France in 1810.

The Continental System

Nowhere was Napoleon's imperialism more evident than in his Continental System. This attempt to regulate the economy of the whole Continent had a double aim: to build up the export trade of France and to cripple that of Britain. The collapse of Napoleon's cross-Channel invasion plans led him to expand the earlier tariff measures against Britain into a great campaign to bankrupt the nation of shopkeepers. The defeat of the third coalition gave him the opportunity to experiment with economic warfare on a continental scale and to carry mercantilism to extremes.

The Berlin Decree, issued by Napoleon in November 1806, forbade all trade with the British Isles and all commerce in British merchandise. It ordered the arrest of all Britons on the Continent and the confiscation of their property. Britain replied by requiring that neutral vessels wishing to trade with France put in first at a British port and pay duties. This regulation enabled Britain to share in the profits of neutral shipping to France. Napoleon retaliated with the Milan Decree (December 1807), ordering the seizure of all neutral ships that complied with the new British policy. The neutrals, in effect, were damned if they did and damned if they didn't.

Napoleon's vassals and allies had to support the Continental System or suffer the consequences. Of all the "un-French" activities countenanced by Louis Bonaparte in Holland, the worst, in Napoleon's view, was his toleration of Dutch smuggling of English contraband. The emperor likewise expected the satellites to feed French industrial prosperity. When Italians objected to the regulation of their silk exports, Napoleon lectured his viceroy, Eugène, on the facts of economic life:

> All the raw silk from the Kingdom of Italy goes to England. . . . It is therefore quite natural that I should wish to divert it from this route to the advantage of my French manufacturers: otherwise my silk factories, one of the chief supports of French commerce, would suffer substantial losses. . . . My principle is: France first. . . .
>
> It is no use for Italy to make plans that leave French prosperity out of account; she must face the fact that the interests of the two countries hang together.*

The gigantic attempt to make "France first" failed almost totally. Only a few French industries benefited from the Continental System; the cessation of sugar imports from the West Indies, for example, promoted the cultivation of native sugar beets. But the decline of overseas trade depressed Bordeaux and other French Atlantic ports, and the increasing difficulty of obtaining

*Quoted in Thompson, *Napoleon's Letters*, pp. 241–242.

The executions of May 3, 1808, in Madrid. By Goya.

such raw materials as cotton caused widespread un-employment and produced a rash of bankruptcies. Since the new French markets on the Continent did not compensate for the loss of older markets overseas, the value of French exports declined by more than a third between 1805 and 1813.

The Continental System did not ruin Britain, al-though it did confront the British with a severe eco-nomic crisis. Markets abroad for British exports were uncertain; food imports were reduced; while prices rose sharply, wages lagged behind; and specie was in such short supply that not enough coins could be minted to keep pace with the demand. Both farm workers, already pinched by the enclosure movement, and fac-tory workers suffered acutely. Yet Britain, fortified by her leadership in the economic revolutions and by the overwhelming superiority of her navy and merchant marine, rode out the storm. Every tract of land at all capable of growing food was brought under the plow. Factory owners improvised substitute payments for their workers when coins were unavailable. Exporters not only developed lucrative new markets in the Ameri-cas, the Ottoman Empire, and Asia but also smuggled goods to old customers on the Continent. Napoleon lacked the vast naval force to apprehend smugglers at sea, and he lacked the large staff of incorruptible cus-toms inspectors to control contraband in the ports.

Moreover, since the French army simply could not do without some items produced only in British factories, Napoleon violated his own decrees by authorizing secret purchases of British cloth and leather for uniforms.

The Continental System antagonized both the neutral powers and Napoleon's allies. French seizure of United States merchant vessels in European ports under the terms of the Milan Decree put a dangerous strain on Franco-American relations. But British restrictions likewise bore heavily on the Americans. British impress-ment of American seamen on the pretext that they were deserters from the Royal Navy, together with the de-signs of expansionists in the United States on Canada, produced the indecisive Anglo-American War of 1812–1814.

The Peninsular War

In Europe, the political and military consequences of the Continental System formed a decisive and dis-astrous chapter in Napoleonic history. The chapter opened in 1807 when the emperor decided to impose the system on Britain's traditional ally, Portugal. The Portuguese expedition furnished Napoleon with an ex-cuse for the military occupation of neighboring Spain. In 1808 he lured the Spanish royal family away from Madrid and made his brother Joseph king of Spain.

But every measure taken by Napoleon—the removal of the ineffectual Bourbons, the installation of a foreign monarch, the attempted enforcement of the Continental System, and, not least, the suppression of the Inquisition and the curtailment of noble and clerical privileges—violated Spanish customs and offended Spanish nationalism. The irreconcilable Spaniards began fighting Napoleon when the population of Madrid rose in revolt on May 2, 1808.

Although the rising in Madrid was soon repressed, the Peninsular War (named after the Iberian peninsula) rapidly grew from a minor irritation to a deadly cancer on the body of the Napoleonic Empire. The Spaniards employed ambushes and poisoned wells and used other guerrilla devices. The expedition that Britain sent to assist them upset all the rules about British inferiority in military, as opposed to naval, matters. It was ably commanded by Sir Arthur Wellesley (later the duke of Wellington) and generously supplied from home. Napoleon poured more than 300,000 troops into the campaign, but his opponents gained the upper hand in 1812, when he detached part of his forces for the invasion of Russia. In 1813, King Joseph left Madrid forever, and Wellington, having liberated Spain, crossed into southern France.

German National Awakening

Napoleonic imperialism also aroused a nationalistic reaction among the traditionally disunited Germans. German intellectuals launched a campaign to check the great influence that the French language and French culture had gained over their divided country. Johann Grimm and his brother Wilhelm contributed not only their very popular—and very German—*Fairy Tales* (1812) but also philological researches designed to prove the innate superiority of the German language. The philosopher Fichte delivered at Berlin the highly patriotic *Addresses to the German Nation* (1807–1808), claiming that German was the *Ursprache,* the fountainhead of language. And the Germans themselves, Fichte continued, were the *Urvolk,* the oldest and most moral of nations. All this did not constitute the dramatic mass political awakening sometimes pictured by enthusiastic German historians. The response at first came largely from the intellectual and social elite and then gradually from lower down the social scale.

The new German nationalistic awareness was evident when Austria reentered the war against France in 1809 and for the first time attempted a total mobilization comparable to that decreed by the French Convention in 1793. While the new spirit enabled the Austrians to make a better showing, they were defeated by a narrow margin at Wagram (1809) and for the fourth time in a dozen years submitted to a peace dictated by Napoleon. The Treaty of Schönbrunn (1809) stripped them of the Illyrian provinces and assigned their Polish territory of Galicia to the Grand Duchy of Warsaw. Francis II gave his daughter to Napoleon in marriage, and his defeated land became the unwilling ally of France. Leadership in the German revival passed to Prussia.

The shock of Jena and Tilsit jarred Prussia out of the lethargy that had overtaken her since the death of Frederick the Great in 1786. The new University of Berlin, founded in 1810 to compensate for the loss of Halle to Saxony by the Tilsit settlement, attracted Fichte and other prophets of German nationalism. Able generals and statesmen, most of them non-Prussian, came to power. General Scharnhorst (who came from Hanover) headed a group of officers who abolished the inhuman discipline of the army and improved its efficiency. The ceiling of 42,000 soldiers imposed by Napoleon was evaded by the simple device of assigning recruits to the reserve after a fairly brief period of intensive training and then inducting another group of recruits. By 1813, Prussia had more than 150,000 trained men available for combat duty.

The social and administrative reorganization of the Prussian state was inspired by the energetic Stein— Baron vom und zum Stein, an enlightened aristocrat from the Rhineland. Stein conciliated the middle class by granting towns and cities some self-government. To improve the status of the peasantry, he sponsored the edict of October 1807, at long last abolishing serfdom in Prussia. The edict, however, did not break up the large Junker estates or provide land for the liberated serfs, many of whom subsequently led a precarious existence as day laborers. Nor did it terminate the feudal rights of justice exercised by the Junker over his peasants. Stein and the others eliminated only the worst abuses of the Old Regime and left authority where it had traditionally rested—with the king, the army, and the Junkers. The Hohenzollern state was not so much reformed as restored to the traditions of absolutism and efficiency established by the Great Elector and Frederick the Great.

The Russian Campaign

The event that enabled a still immature German nationalism to turn its force against Napoleon was the French debacle in Russia. French actions after 1807 soon convinced Czar Alexander that Napoleon was not keeping the Tilsit bargain and was intruding on Russia's sphere in eastern Europe. When Alexander and Napoleon met again at the German town of Erfurt in 1808, they could reach no agreement, though they concealed their differences by a show of great intimacy. French acquisition of the Illyrian provinces from Austria in 1809 raised the unpleasant prospect of French domination over the Balkans, and the simultaneous transfer of Galicia from Austria to the Grand Duchy of Warsaw suggested that this Napoleonic vassal might next seek to absorb Russia's acquisitions from the partitions of Poland. Meanwhile, Napoleon's insistent efforts to make Russia enforce the Continental System increasingly incensed Alexander. French annexations in north-

UNITED KINGDOM
OF GREAT BRITAIN
AND IRELAND

SCOTLAND

North Sea

IRELAND

WALES

ENGLAND

London

Atlantic Ocean

KINGDOM OF DENMARK AND NORWAY

SWEDEN

Hamburg

Oldenburg

NETHERLANDS

K. OF
WESTPHALIA

Berlin

Antwerp

Waterloo

Amiens

CONFEDERATION

Auerstädt

Leipzig

Jena

SAXONY

Weser R.

Rhine R.

Meuse R.

Seine R.

Paris

Varennes

Longuyon

OF THE

Prague

Versailles

Valmy

LORRAINE

Luneville

ALSACE

BADEN

RHINE

Austerlitz

Elbe R.

Strasbourg

Ulm

Danube R.

Vien

Pressburg

Loire R.

FRANCE

BAVARIA

Basel

Gironde R.

SWITZERLAND

TYROL

Limoges

Lyons

Bordeaux

Payrac

PIED-
MONT

Campoformio

Rhône R.

Milan

ILLYRIAN PROVINCES

Marengo

Po R.

Venice

Nice

Genoa

KINGDOM OF ITALY

Adriatic Sea

PORTUGAL

SPAIN

Madrid

Ebro R.

TUSCANY

ELBA

Tagus R.

CORSICA

PAPAL STATES

Rome

Guadalquivir R.

SARDINIA

BALEARIC IS.

Naples

KINGDOM
OF
NAPLES

CAPE
TRAFALGAR

Palermo

SICILY

MALTA
(Br.)

Napoleonic Europe, 1812

Empire of France

States under French control

Allied with France

■ Battle sites

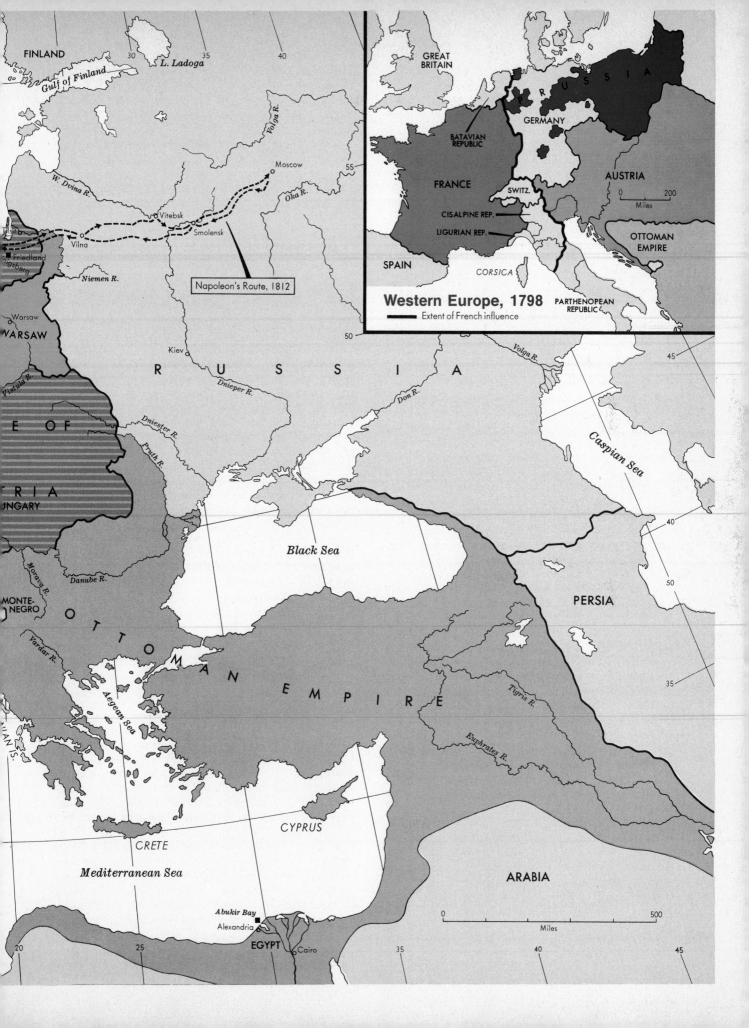

FINLAND

Gulf of Finland

L. Ladoga

W. Dvina R.

Moscow

Vitebsk

Volga R.

Oka R.

Smolensk

Vilna

Napoleon's Route, 1812

Tilsit

Friedland
gsberg

Niemen R.

Warsaw

WARSAW

Vistula R.

Kiev

Dnieper R.

R U S S I A

Don R.

Volga R.

E OF

Dniester R.

Pruth R.

RIA
NGARY

Morava R.

MONTE-
NEGRO

Danube R.

Caspian Sea

Black Sea

PERSIA

O T T O M A N   E M P I R E

Vardar R.

Tigris R.

Aegean Sea

Euphrates R.

NS.

CYPRUS

CRETE

Mediterranean Sea

ARABIA

Abukir Bay
Alexandria

EGYPT   Cairo

Western Europe, 1798

—— Extent of French influence

GREAT
BRITAIN

P R U S S I A

GERMANY

BATAVIAN
REPUBLIC

FRANCE

AUSTRIA

SWITZ.

0   200
Miles

CISALPINE REP. ——

LIGURIAN REP. ——

OTTOMAN
EMPIRE

SPAIN

CORSICA

PARTHENOPEAN
REPUBLIC

0   500
Miles

west Germany completed the discomfiture of the czar, for they wiped out the state of Oldenburg, where his uncle was the reigning duke. All these factors caused the break between the czar and the emperor, and the famous invasion of Russia by the French in 1812.

For the invasion Napoleon assembled the Grande Armée of nearly 700,000 men, a majority of whom, however, were not Frenchmen but unwilling conscripts in the service of a foreign master. The supply system broke down almost immediately, and the Russian scorched-earth policy made it very hard for the soldiers to live off the land and impossible for horses to get fodder, so that many of them had to be destroyed. As the Grand Army marched eastward, one of Napoleon's aides reported:

> There were no inhabitants to be found, no prisoners to be taken, not a single straggler to be picked up. We were in the heart of inhabited Russia and yet we were like a vessel without a compass in the midst of a vast ocean, knowing nothing of what was happening around us.*

Napoleon hoped to strike a knockout blow, but the battle of Borodino, though the first engagement in all these wars to exceed in casualties Louis XIV's Malplaquet (1709), was indecisive. He entered Moscow and remained in the burning city for five weeks (September–October 1812) in the vain hope of bringing Czar Alexander to terms. But Russian obduracy and the shortage of supplies forced him to begin a retreat that became a nightmare. Ill-fed, inadequately clothed and sheltered, without needed medical help, the retreating soldiers suffered horribly from Russian attacks on stragglers and from the onslaughts of "General Winter." Less than a quarter of the Grand Army survived the retreat from Moscow; the rest had been taken prisoner or had died of wounds, starvation, disease, or the cold.

The Russian leaders had feared that Napoleon would liberate the serfs and turn them against their masters. But the peasants, despite the treatment to which they had been subject for so long, formed guerrilla bands, harassed Napoleon's forces, and proved that their patriotic sentiments outweighed their class grievances. Kutuzov, the victorious Russian commander, now wanted to allow Russia's allies to prosecute the war. But Alexander insisted on pursuing the French, and sent Russian armies westward beyond the Russian frontiers on the track of Napoleon's forces.

The Downfall

The British had been the first to resist Napoleon successfully, at Trafalgar and on the economic battlefields of the Continental System. Then had come Spanish resistance, then Russian. Now in 1813 almost every nation in Europe joined the final coalition against the

*A. A. L. de Caulaincourt, *With Napoleon in Russia* (New York, 1935), p. 62.

French. Napoleon raised a new army, but he could not replace so readily the equipment squandered in Russia. In October 1813 he lost the "Battle of the Nations," fought at Leipzig in Germany, and by April 1814 the forces of the coalition occupied Paris. Faced also with mounting unrest at home, the emperor abdicated. After attempting suicide by poison, which turned out to have lost much of its strength since he had procured it for the Russian campaign, he went into exile as ruler of the minute island of Elba not far from the western coast of Italy.

The statesmen of the victorious coalition gathered in the Congress of Vienna to draw up the terms of peace. The Bourbons returned to France in the person of Louis XVIII, a younger brother of Louis XVI. Realizing that he could not revive the Old Regime intact, the new king issued the Charter of 1814 establishing a constitutional monarchy. The returned émigrés, however, showed no such good sense. They unleashed a new White Terror against the Revolution and all its works. Then, on March 1, 1815, Bonaparte pulled his last surprise: He landed on the Mediterranean coast of France.

For a hundred days, from March 20, 1815, when Napoleon reentered Paris, the French Empire was reborn. Once again the emperor rallied the French people, this time by promising a truly liberal regime, with a real parliament and genuine elections. He never had time, however, to show whether his promise was sincere, for on June 18, 1815, the British under Wellington and the Prussians under Blücher delivered the final blow at Waterloo, near Brussels. Again Napoleon went into exile, to the remote British island of St. Helena in the South Atlantic. There, in 1821, he died. Bonapartism, however, did not die in 1815 or 1821, any more than the Caesarism of ancient Rome had died on the Ides of March. A Napoleonic legend arose, fostered by the emperor himself on St. Helena. It glossed over the faults and failures of the emperor, depicting him as the paladin of liberalism and patriotism, and paved the way for the advent of another Napoleon in 1848.

VII The Legacy of the Revolution

The Napoleonic legend, with its hero worship and belligerent nationalism, was one element in the legacy bequeathed by revolutionary and Napoleonic France. A second, and much more powerful element, was the great revolutionary motto—*Liberté, Egalité, Fraternité*—which lived on to inspire later generations of Jacobins in France and elsewhere. Behind the motto was the fact that Frenchmen, though not yet enjoying the full democracy of the twentieth century, possessed a larger measure of liberty, equality, and fraternity in 1815 than they had ever known before 1789. True, Napoleon's censors and prefects gave new force to the old traditions of absolutism and centralization, but the middle class had won its freedom from obsolete restraints, and Protestants, Jews, and freethinkers had gained toleration both in France and in the French satellites. Although French institutions in 1815 did not measure up to the ideals of liberty expressed in the Declaration of the Rights of Man, the ideals had been stated, and the effort to embody them in a new regime was to form the main theme of French domestic history in the nineteenth century.

The revolutionary and Napoleonic regimes established the principle of equal liability to taxation. They provided a greater degree of economic opportunity for the third estate by removing obstacles to the activity of businessmen, big and little, and by breaking up the large landholdings of the clergy and nobility. These lands passed mainly to the urban bourgeois and the well-to-do peasants; the only gesture toward equality of property was the Laws of Ventôse of 1794, and they were never implemented. Marxist historians have a case for arguing that the Revolution was an important step in the ascendancy of middle-class capitalism, both urban and rural. In this sense the work of the Revolution was not truly democratic, since the sans-culottes had apparently gained so little. Yet it must be remembered that the Code Napoléon did bury beyond all hope of exhumation the worst legal and social inequalities of the Old Regime. There was a good deal of truth in Napoleon's boast:

> Whether as First Consul or as Emperor, I have been the people's king; I have governed for the nation and in its interests, without allowing myself to be turned aside by the outcries or the private interests of certain people.*

The Revolution and Napoleon promoted fraternity in the legal sense by making all Frenchmen equal in the eyes of the law. They advanced fraternity in a broader sense by encouraging nationalism, the feeling of belonging to the great corporate body of Frenchmen who were superior to all other nations. French nationalism had existed long before 1789; Joan of Arc, Henry IV, and Louis XIV had all been nationalists in their diverse ways. But it remained for the Convention to formulate a fervent new nationalistic creed in its decree of August 23, 1793, providing for total mobilization. The Napoleonic empire then demonstrated how easily nationalism on an unprecedented scale could lead to imperialism of unprecedented magnitude. More than a century ago, Alexis de Tocqueville, the great French student of democracy, wrote:

> The French Revolution was . . . a political revolution, which in its operation and its aspect resembled a religious one. It had every peculiar and characteristic feature of a religious movement; it not only spread to foreign countries, but it was carried thither by preaching and by propaganda.
>
> It roused passions such as the most violent political revolutions had never before excited. . . . This gave to it that aspect of a religious revolution which so terrified its contemporaries, or rather . . . it became a kind of new religion in itself—a religion, imperfect it is true, without a God, without a worship, without a future life, but which nevertheless, like Islam, poured forth its soldiers, its apostles, and its martyrs over the face of the earth.*

Its early adherents were fanatics—Robespierre and the Jacobins. Its later exponents—the men of Thermidor and Brumaire—modified the creed in the interests of practicality and moderation. Even in the hands of Napoleon, however, the Revolution remained a kind of religion, demanding political orthodoxy and punishing such heretics as King Louis Bonaparte of Holland by political excommunication. And after 1815, as we shall see in the next chapter, the "new religion" of the Revolution continued to pour forth "its soldiers, its apostles, and its martyrs over the face of the earth."

*Quoted in Caulaincourt, *With Napoleon in Russia,* p. 364.

*_The Old Régime and the Revolution_ (London, 1888), part I, Chap. 3.

Reading Suggestions on the French Revolution and Napoleon
Surveys Covering Other Countries in Addition to France

G. Lefebvre, *The French Revolution,* 2 vols. (*Columbia Univ. Press) and *Napoleon,* 2 vols. (Columbia Univ. Press, 1969). Comprehensive accounts by an eminent French scholar with a modified Marxian point of view.

C. Brinton, *A Decade of Revolution, 1789–1799* and G. Bruun, *Europe & the French Imperium, 1799–1814* (*Torchbooks). Comprehensive volumes in the series The Rise of Modern Europe; with full bibliographies.

R. R. Palmer, *The Age of the Democratic Revolution,* 2 vols. (*Princeton Univ. Press). Defends the thesis that the French Revolution was part of a general democratic revolution in the West; particularly useful for detailed material on smaller European states.

J. Godechot, *France and the Atlantic Revolution, 1770–1799* (Free Press, 1965). A ranking French scholar comes to conclusions similar to Palmer's. Godechot's views on Napoleon may be sampled in J. Godechot, B. Hyslop, and D. Dowd, *The Napoleonic Era in Europe* (Holt, 1971).

P. Amann, ed., *The Eighteenth-Century Revolution: French or Western?* (*Heath). Selections both hostile and sympathetic to the Palmer thesis.

N. Hampson, *The First European Revolution, 1776–1815* (*Harcourt, Brace) and G. Rudé, *Revolutionary Europe, 1783–1815* (*Torchbooks). Two recent general surveys.

Narrative Histories of the Revolution in France

J. M. Thompson, *The French Revolution* (*Galaxy). Perhaps the most informative one-volume history down to the fall of Robespierre.

J. Michelet, *History of the French Revolution* (*Phoenix). Famous old nineteenth-century account by an enthusiastic democrat.

A. Mathiez, *The French Revolution* (*Universal). Eloquent account down to 1794 by a Marxian scholar sympathetic to Robespierre.

G. Salvemini, *The French Revolution, 1788–1792* (*Norton). Colorful narrative by an Italian scholar of warm liberal convictions.

F. Furet and D. Richet, *The French Revolution* (Weidenfeld & Nicolson, 1965); M. J. Sydenham, *The French Revolution* (*Capricorn); A. Goodwin, *The French Revolution* (*Torchbooks). Three comparatively recent brief accounts.

N. Hampson, *A Social History of the French Revolution* (*Univ. of Toronto Press). Excellent synthesis of recent scholarship.

More Specialized Studies of the Revolution

P. Farmer, *France Reviews Its Revolutionary Origins* (Octagon, 1963). A history of writings about the revolution by French scholars.

W. Church, ed., *The Influence of the Enlightenment on the French Revolution* (*Heath); J. H. Shennan, *The Parlement of Paris* (Cornell Univ. Press, 1968). Appraisals of two significant factors in the background.

G. Lefebvre, *The Coming of the French Revolution* (*Princeton Univ. Press). Masterly short study of the causes of the revolution and of its course to October 1789. Lefebvre's monograph, *The Great Fear,* has recently become available in translation (*Vintage).

J. Godechot, *The Taking of the Bastille* (Faber, 1970). Definitive monograph on July 14, 1789.

G. Rudé, *The Crowd in the French Revolution* (*Oxford Univ. Press). Study of the participants in the great revolutionary ''days'' and their motives; by a capable Marxian scholar.

A. Soboul, *The Sans-Culottes* (*Anchor). Translation of part of a detailed French monograph by another capable Marxian scholar; based on police records, it examines the role of the Parisian sans-culottes in 1793 and 1794.

A. Cobban, *Aspects of the French Revolution* (*Norton) and *The Social Interpretation of the French Revolution* (*Cambridge Univ. Press). Lively critiques of the Marxian interpretation.

C. Tilly, *The Vendée* (*Wiley). Revisionist study showing that much more was involved in the Vendean revolt than peasant devotion to throne and altar.

R. C. Cobb, *The Police and the People* (*Oxford Univ. Press). Important study of French popular protest, 1789–1820, by an English scholar.

C. Brinton, *The Jacobins* (Macmillan, 1930), and M. J. Sydenham, *The Girondins* (Oxford Univ. Press, 1961). Careful studies greatly revising popular notions about the nature of revolutionary factions.

R. R. Palmer, *Twelve Who Ruled* (*Atheneum). Highly readable collective biography of the Committee of Public Safety.

J. M. Thompson, *Leaders of the French Revolution* (*Harper) and *Robespierre and the French Revolution* (*Collier); G. Bruun, *Saint-Just: Apostle of the Terror* (Houghton, 1932); L. Gottschalk, *Jean-Paul Marat* (*Phoenix). Enlightening biographies of major revolutionary figures.

J. McManners, *The French Revolution and the Church* (*Torchbooks). Definitive brief study.

J. Godechot, *The Counter-Revolution: Doctrine and Action, 1789–1804* (*Harper). Translation of an important study of the opposition to the revolution.

Napoleon

M. Hutt, *Napoleon* (*Spectrum). A capsule biography, selections from his own words, and a sampler of other views on his career.

P. Geyl, *Napoleon, For and Against* (*Yale Univ. Press). Full survey of judgments passed on Bonaparte by historians.

D. H. Pinkney, ed., *Napoleon: Historical Enigma* (*Heath). A briefer introduction to the contrasting interpretations of the man.

J. M. Thompson, *Napoleon Bonaparte: His Rise and Fall* (Oxford, 1952), and F. Markham, *Napoleon* (*Mentor). Readable biographies by careful scholars.

H. A. L. Fisher, *Napoleon* (*Oxford), and A. L. Guérard, *Napoleon I* (Knopf, 1956). Good shorter biographies.

R. B. Holtman, *The Napoleonic Revolution* (*Lippincott). Emphasizing institutional changes under Bonaparte.

E. Heckscher, *The Continental System* (Clarendon, 1922). Important monograph by a Swedish economic historian.

D. G. Chandler, *The Campaigns of Napoleon* (Macmillan, 1966). Recent scholarly account.

O. Connelly, *Napoleon's Satellite Kingdoms* (*Free Press). Informative studies of Spain, Holland, Westphalia, Italy, and Naples.

F. Markham, *Napoleon and the Awakening of Europe* (*Collier). Brief survey, arguing that European nationalisms were as yet underdeveloped.

E. Saunders, *The Hundred Days* (Norton, 1964). The next-to-last act of the Napoleonic drama.

A. L. Guérard, *Reflections on the Napoleonic Legend* (Scribner's, 1924). Why the myths about Bonaparte survived his death.

Sources

J. H. Stewart, *A Documentary Survey of the French Revolution* (Macmillan, 1951). Excellent collection of constitutional texts and other official documents.

A. Young, *Travels in France,* C. Maxwell, ed. (Cambridge Univ. Press, 1929). Lively diary by an English farm expert who journeyed throughout France, 1787–1789.

E. Burke, *Reflections on the Revolution in France* (*several editions). The celebrated indictment of the destructive character of the Revolution.

J. M. Thompson, ed., *Napoleon's Letters* (Everyman). A fascinating collection, arranged chronologically.

J. C. Herold, ed., *The Mind of Napoleon* (*Columbia Univ. Press). Another fascinating collection, arranged topically.

A. de Caulaincourt, *With Napoleon in Russia* (Morrow, 1935), and its sequel, *No Peace with Napoleon* (Morrow, 1936). Vivid and revealing memoirs by one of Bonaparte's chief aides.

Fiction

A. France, *The Gods Are Athirst* (Roy, n.d.). Portrait of a fanatical Jacobin.

C. Dickens, *A Tale of Two Cities* (*many editions). Deficient in accuracy, but unsurpassed in color.

P. Weiss, *The Persecution and Assassination of Jean-Paul Marat as Performed by the Inmates of the Asylum of Charenton under the Direction of the Marquis de Sade* (*several editions). The play depicting the intensity of the revolutionary experience.

Victor Hugo, *Ninety-Three* (Harper, 1874). The last novel by the famous French romantic catches some of the drama going on at the Convention and in the countryside in the year when the Terror began.

L. Tolstoy, *War and Peace* (*several editions, often abridged). The epic novel about the Russian campaign.

Illustrations

Index